MARTIN LUTHER, D.D.

COMMENTARY

ON

SAINT PAUL'S
Epistle to the Galatians

BY

MARTIN LUTHER

A NEW EDITION
Corrected and Revised
BY
REV. ERASMUS MIDDLETON

With Foreword by
PROF. LEANDER S. KEYSER, D.D.

Wm. B. EERDMANS PUBLISHING COMPANY
GRAND RAPIDS, MICHIGAN
1930

Copyrighted by
Wm. B. EERDMANS PUBLISHING CO.
Grand Rapids, Michigan

FOREWORD

A GOOD MANY YEARS AGO, when I was still a young minister, I read Luther's Commentary on Galatians. Well do I remember the benefit I derived from it. It furnished me material for a good many sermons, and inspiration and suggestions for a good many more. But greatest of all was its spiritual effect upon my whole life since that first perusal. Here was set forth by the great reformer, in his unique and forceful way, the Biblical and rational grounds of SOLA GRATIA—salvation by grace alone.

Of course, my experience in conversion had shown me that men are justified by faith and saved by grace alone; but, somehow, Luther's convincing way of putting it impressed it more deeply on my consciousness, and showed me just why it must be so. Since that time, pride and self-righteousness have been banished from my heart, and I have never felt that I could be saved through any merit of my own. Yes, it is a most precious doctrine and a most wholesome experience.

For the person who had had this genuinely Christian experience, one of his favorite Biblical texts will be: "By grace are ye saved through faith; and that not of yourselves: it is the gift of God; not of works, lest any man should boast" (Ephesians 2:9). If you meet any one who thinks he can be saved by his own merit, by his own "good life," or by his own "good character," just tell him to read Luther's Commentaries, especially this one on Galatians. You see, it was Luther's own experience, which came to him by the Holy Spirit through the Word of God, that cured him of all hope and desire for being saved by "the deeds of the law," or by any system or amount of "work righteousness." He had tried the way of penance and works to the very utmost. All to no purpose; no peace came to his soul. No sooner was one good work done than another had to be undertaken. It was only when the Holy Spirit came to him with the word of assurance from God's holy Book, "The just shall live by faith," that he leaped to his feet a delivered man.

It is indeed a pleasure to recommend this new edition of Erasmus Middleton's smooth, fluent and accurate translation of Luther's truly classical work on Galatians. It is a good deal more than an ordinary commentary; it is also a profound and incisive application of the fundamental principles of the gospel to human life and Christian experience. Most sincerely do I hope that this book will have a wide circulation. Besides its powerful positive and constructive presentation of the principles of "the faith once for all delivered," it is corrective of many of the errors of the present day. By eluding error from the human heart and injecting truth, especially the true doctrine of grace, it will help to revive the spiritual life of the Church, and will, by that very token, bring forth the fruitage of truly good works and effective Christian activity.

The Eerdmans Publishing Company are to be commended for their enterprise in issuing this new edition of Luther's Commentary and for their wisdom in selecting this specific work to meet the spiritual needs of the Church of today and of all time to come.

LEANDER S. KEYSER.

Hamma Divinity School,
    Springfield, Ohio.

CONTENTS

	PAGE
CHAPTER I	9
CHAPTER II	69
CHAPTER III	162
CHAPTER IV	321
CHAPTER V	417
CHAPTER VI	505

A COMMENTARY
ON
SAINT PAUL'S EPISTLE
TO
THE GALATIANS

CHAPTER I.

VERSE 1. *Paul, an apostle (not of men, neither by men, but by Jesus Christ and God the Father, who raised him from the dead.)*

NOW that we have declared the argument and sum of this epistle to the Galatians, we think it good, before we come to the matter itself, to shew what was the occasion St. Paul wrote this epistle. He had planted among the Galatians the pure doctrine of the gospel, and the righteousness of faith; but by and by, after his departure, there crept in certain false teachers, which overthrew all that he had planted and truly taught among them. For the devil cannot but furiously impugn this doctrine with all force and subtlety, neither can he rest so long as he seeth any spark thereof remaining. We also, for this only cause, that we preach the gospel, do suffer of the world, the devil, and his ministers, all the mischief that they can work against us, both on the right hand and on the left.

For the gospel is such a doctrine as teacheth a far higher matter than is the wisdom, righteousness, and religion of the world, that is to say, free remission of sins through Christ, etc. It leaveth those things in their degree, to be as they are, and commendeth them as the good creatures of God. But the world preferreth these creatures before the Creator, and moreover, by them would put away sin, be delivered from death, and deserve everlasting life. This doth the gospel condemn. Contrariwise, the world cannot suffer those things to be condemned which it most esteemeth, and best liketh of; and therefore it chargeth the gospel that it is a seditious doctrine, and full of errors; that it overthroweth commonwealths, countries, dominions, kingdoms, and empires, and therefore offendeth both against God and the Emperor; abolisheth laws, corrupteth good manners, and setteth all men at liberty to do what they list. Wherefore, with just zeal and high service to God, (as it would seem) it persecuteth this doctrine, and abhorreth the teachers and professors thereof, as the greatest plague that can be in the wholt earth.

Moreover, by he preaching of this doctrine, the devil is overthrown, his kingdom destroyed, the law, sin, and death, (wherewith, as most mighty and invincible tyrants, he hath brought all mankind in subjection under his dominion) are wrested out of his hands: briefly, his prisoners are translated out of the kingdom of darkness, into the kingdom of Light and Liberty. Should the devil suffer all this? "Should not the father of lies employ all his force and subtile poicies, to darken, to corrupt, and utterly to root out this doctrine of salvation and everlasting life? Indeed, St. Paul complaineth in this, and all other his epistles, that even in his time the devil shewed himself a cunning workman in this business."

We thought good to shew here by the way, that the gospel is such a doctrine as condemneth all manner of righteousness, and preacheth the only righteousness of Christ, and to them that embrace the same, it bringeth peace of conscience and all good things; and yet, notwithstanding, the world hatheth and persecuteth it most bitterly.

I have said before, that the occasion why St. Paul wrote this epistle, was for that by and by after his departure, false teachers had destroyed those things among the Galatians, which he with long and great travel had built. And these false apostles being of the circumcision and sect of the Pharisees, were men of great estimation and authority, who bragged among the people that they were of that holy and chosen stock of the Jews, (John viii; Rom. iv, 4, 5, 6) that they were Israelites, of the seed of Abraham, that they had the promises and the the fathers; and finally, that they were the ministers of Christ, and the apostles' scholars, with whom they had been conversant, and had seen their miracles, and perhaps had also wrought some signs or miracles themselves; for Christ witnesseth (Matth. vii, 22) that the wicked also do work miracles. Moreover, these false apostles, by all the crafty means they could devise, defaced the authority of St. Paul, saying: "Why do ye so highly esteem of Paul? Why have ye him in so great reverence? Forsooth, he was but the last of all that were converted unto Christ. But we are the disciples of the apostles, and were familiarly conversant with them. We have seen Christ working miracles, and heard him preach. Paul came after us, and is inferior unto us: and it is not possible that God should suffer us to err who are of his holy people, the ministers of Christ, and have received the Holy

Ghost. Again, we are many, and Paul is but one, and alone, who neither is conversant with the apostles, nor hath seen Christ. Yea, he persecuted the church of Christ a great while. Would God (think ye) for Paul's sake only, suffer so many churches to be deceived?"

When men having such authority come into any country or city, by and by the people have them in great admiration, and under this colour of godliness and religion, they do not only deceive the simple, but also the learned; yea, and those also which seem to be somewhat confirmed in the faith, especially when they brag (as these did) that they are the offspring of the patriarchs, the ministers of Christ, the apostles' scholars, etc. Even so the Pope at this day, when he hath no authority of the Scripture to defend himself withal, useth this one argument continually against us, "the church, the church." Thinkest thou that God is so offended, that, for a few heretics of Luther's sect, he will cast off his whole church? Thinkest thou that he would leave his church in error so many hundred years? And this he mightily maintaineth, "that the church can never be overthrown." Now, like as many are moved with this argument at this day, so, in Paul's time, these false apostles, through great bragging, and setting forth of their own praises, blinded the eyes of the Galatians, so that Paul lost his authority among them, and his doctrine was brought in suspicion.

Against this vain bragging and boasting of the false apostles, Paul with great constancy and boldness setteth his apostolic authority, highly commending his vocation, and defending his ministry. And (although elsewhere he never doth the like) he will not give place to any, no, not to the apostles themselves, much less to any of their scholars. And to abate their pharisaical pride and shameless boldness, he maketh mention of the history done at Antiochia, where he withstood Peter himself. Besides this, not regarding the offence that might arise thereof, he saith plainly in the text, that he was bold to accuse and reprove Peter himself, the chief of the apostles, who had seen Christ, and had been most familiarly conversant with him. I am an apostle (saith he) and such a one as pass not what others are: yea, I was not afraid to chide the very pillar of all the rest of the apostles. And to conclude, in the first two chapters, he doth, in a manner, nothing else but set out his vocation, his office, and his gospel, affirming, that it was not of men, and that he had not received it by man, but by the revelation of Jesus Christ. Also, that if he, yea, or an angel from Heaven, should bring any other gospel than that which he hath preached, he should be holden accursed.

The Certainty of Calling

But what meaneth Paul by this boasting? I answer: This common place serveth to this end, that every minister of God's word should be sure of his calling, that before God and man he may with a bold conscience glory therein, that he preaches the gospel as one that is called and sent: even as the ambassador of a king glorieth and vaunteth in this, that he cometh not as a private person, but as the king's ambassador; and because of this dignity, that he is the king's ambassador, he is honoured and set in the highest place; which honour should not be given unto him if he came as a private person. Wherefore, let the preacher of the gospel be certain that his calling is from God. And it is expedient, that, according to the example of Paul, he should magnify this his calling, to the end that he may win credit and authority among the people, like as the king's ambassador magnifieth his office and calling. And thus to glory is not vain, but a kind of necessary kind of glorying, because he glorieth not in himself, but in the king which hath sent him, whose authority he desireth to be honoured and magnified.

Likewise, when Paul so highly commendeth his calling, he seeketh not his own praise, but with a necessary and a holy pride he magnified his ministry; as to the Romans xi, he saith: Forasmuch as I am the apostle of the Gentiles, I will magnify mine office: that is to say, I will that men receive me, not as Paul of Tarsus, but as Paul the apostle or ambassador of Jesus Christ. And this he doth of necessity, to maintain his authority, that the people, in hearing this, might be more attent and willing to give ear unto him. For they hear not only Paul, but in Paul, Christ himself, and God the Father, sending him out in his message: Whose authority and majesty, like as men ought religiously to honour, so ought they with great reverence to receive and to hear his messengers bringing his word and message.

This is a notable place, therefore, wherein Paul so glorieth and boasteth as touching his vocation, that he despiseth all others. If any man, after the manner of the world, should despise all others in respect of himself, and attribute all unto himself alone, he should not only shew himself a very fool, but also grievously offend. But this manner of boasting is necessary, and pertaineth not to the glory of Paul, but to the glory of God, whereby is offered unto him the sacrifices of praise and thanksgiving. For by this boasting, the name, the grace, and the mercy of God, is made known unto the world. Thus, therefore, he beginneth his epistle.

EPISTLE TO THE GALATIANS

VERSE 1. *Paul, an apostle, not of men, etc.*

Here, in the very beginning, he toucheth those false teachers which boasted themselves to be the disciples of the apostles, and to be sent of them, but despised Paul, as one that was neither the apostles' scholar, nor sent of any to preach the gospel, but came in some other way, and of his own hand thrust himself into that office. Against those Paul defendeth his calling, saying, My calling seemeth base to your preachers: but whosoever they be which are come unto you, are sent either of men, or by man: that is to say, they have entered either of themselves, being not called, or else called by others. But my calling is not of men, nor by man, but it is above all manner of calling that can be made by the apostles, "for it is by Jesus Christ, and by God the Father," etc.

Where he saith of men, I mean such as call and thrust in themselves, when neither God nor man calleth or sendeth them, but they run and speak themselves; as at this day certain fantastical spirits do, which either lurk in corners, and seek places where they may pour out their poison, and come into the public congregations, or else they resort thither, where the gospel is planted already. These I call such as are sent of men. But where he saith, by man, I understand such as have a divine calling, but yet by man as by means. God calleth them two manner of ways: by means, and without means. He calleth them to the ministry of his word at this day, not immediately by himself, but by other means; that is to say, by man. But the apostles were called immediately of Christ himself, "as the prophets in the old time were called of God himself." Therefore, when Paul saith, "not of men, neither by men," he beateth down the false apostles; as though he would say, although those vipers brag never so much, what can they brag more than that they are either come from men, that is to say, of themselves without any calling, or by man, that is to say, sent of others? I pass not upon any of these things, neither ought you to regard them. As for me, I am called and sent neither of men, nor by man, but without means, that is to wit, by Jesus Christ himself, and my calling is like in all points the calling of the apostles, and I am indeed an apostle. Paul, therefore, handleth this place, of the calling of the apostles, effectually. And elsewhere, he separateth the degree of apostleship from others, as in the first to the Corinthians, chap. xii, and in the fourth to the Ephesians, where he saith, "And God hath ordained some in the church; as, first, apostles; secondly, prophets; thirdly, teachers," etc., setting apostles in the first place: so that they be properly called apostles, "which are sent immediately of God himself," without any other ordinary means.

So Matthias was called only of God (Acts i, 23-25), for when the other apostles had appointed two, they durst not choose the one nor the other, but they cast lots, and prayed that God would shew which of them he would have. For, seeing he should be an apostle, it behoved that he should be called of God. So was Paul called to be the apostle of the Gentiles (Acts ix, 15). Hereof the apostles also are called saints; for they are sure of their calling and doctrine, and have continued faithful in their office, and none of them became a cast-away saving Judas, because their calling is holy (Matt. xxvi, 15).

This is the first assault that Paul maketh against the false apostles, which ran when no man sent them. Calling, therefore, is not to be despised; for it is not enough for a man to have the word and pure doctrine, but also he must be assured of his calling; and he that entereth without this assurance, entereth to no other end but to kill and destroy. For God never prospereth the labour of those that are not called. "And although they teach some good and profitable matters, yet they edify not. So, our fantastical spirits at this day, have the words of faith in thtir mouths, but yet they yield no fruit, but their chief end and purpose is to draw men to their false and perverse opinions." They that have a certain and holy calling,—must sustain many and great conflicts, as they must do whose doctrine is pure and sound, that they may constantly abide in their lawful calling, against the infinite and continual assaults of the devil, and rage of the world. "Here, what should he do whose calling is uncertain, and doctrine corrupt?"

This is therefore our comfort which are in the ministry of the word, "that we have an office which is heavenly and holy," to the which we being lawfully called, do triumph against all the gates of hell. On the other side, it is a horrible thing when the conscience saith, "This thou hast done without any lawful calling." Here such terror "shaketh a man's mind which is not called, that he would wish he had never heard the word which he teacheth": for, by his disobedience, he maketh all his works evil, were they never so good, insomuch, "that even his greatest works and labours become his greatest sins."

We see then how good and necessary this boasting and glorifying of our ministry is. In times past, when I was but a young divine, methought Paul did unwisely in glorying so oft of his calling, in his epistles; but I did not understand his purpose; for I knew not that the ministry of God's word was so weighty a matter. I knew nothing of the doctrine of faith and a true conscience indeed, "for that there was then no certainty taught either in the schools or churches, but all was full of the sophistical subtleties of the schoolmen;" and therefore no man was able to understand the dignity and power of this holy and spiritual boasting of the true and lawful calling, which serveth first to the glory of God, and secondly to the advancing of our office, and moreover, "to the salvation of ourselves and of the people. For, by this our boasting, we seek not estimation in the world, or praise among men, or money, or pleasures, or favour, of the world; but forasmuch as we be in a divine calling, and in the work of God, and the people have great need to be assured of our calling, that they may know our words to be the word of God, therefore we proudly vaunt and boast of it." It is not then a vain, but a most holy pride against the devil and the world, and humility before God.

VERSE 1. *And by God the Father, which hath raised him from the dead.*

Paul is so inflamed here with zeal, that he cannot tarry till he come to the matter itself, but forthwith, in the very title, he bursteth out and uttereth what he hath in his heart. His intent in this epistle is, to treat of the righteousness that cometh by faith, and to defend the same: again, to beat down the law, and the righteousness that cometh by works. Of such cogitations he is full, and out of this wonderful and exceeding great abundance of the excellent wisdom and knowledge of Christ in his heart, his mouth speaketh. This flame, this great burning fire of his heart, cannot be hid, nor suffer him to hold his tongue; and therefore, he thought it not enough to say, "that he was an apostle sent by Jesus Christ," but also added, "by God the Father, which hath raised him up from the dead."

But it seemeth here, that the adding of these words, "And by God the Father," etc., is not necessary. But because (as I said) Paul speaketh out of the abundance of his heart, his mind burneth with desire to set forth, even in the very entry of his epistle, the unsearchable riches of Christ, and to preach the righteousness of God, "which is called the resurrection of the dead." Christ who liveth, and is risen again, speaketh out of him, and moveth him thus to speak; therefore, not without cause, he addeth, "that he is also an apostle, by God the Father, who hath raised up Jesus Christ from the dead." As if he should say, I have to deal with Satan, and with those vipers, the instruments of Satan, which go about to spoil me of the righteousness of Christ, who was raised up by God the Father from the dead; by the which alone we are made righteous, by the which we also shall be raised up at the last day from death to everlasting life. "But they that in such sort go about to overthrow the righteousness of Christ, do resist the Father and the Son, and the work of them both."

Thus Paul, even at the first entrance, bursteth out into the whole matter whereof he intreateth in this epistle. For (as I said) he "treateth of the resurrection of Christ," who rose again to make us righteous, and in so doing, he hath overcome the law, sin, death, hell, and all evils (Rom. iv, 24, 25). Christ's victory, then, is the overcoming of the law, of sin, our flesh, the world, the devil, death, hell, and all evils: And this his victory he hath given unto us. "Although, then, that these tyrants, and these enemies of ours, do accuse us, and make us afraid, yet can they not drive us to despair, nor condemn us;" for Christ, whom God the Father hath raised up from the dead, "is our righteousness and victory (1 Cor. xv, 57), therefore, thanks be to God, who hath given us the victory by our Lord Jesus Christ." Amen.

But mark how fitly, and to the purpose Paul here speaketh. He saith not, by God which hath made Heaven and earth, which is Lord of angels, which commanded Abraham to go out of his own country, which sent Moses to Pharaoh the king, which brought Israel out of Egypt (as the false apostles did, who boasted of the God of their fathers, the Creator, Maintainer, and Preserver of all things, working wonders among his people) but Paul had another thing in his heart, namely, "the righteousness of Christ," and therefore he speaketh words that make much for this his purpose, saying: "I am an apostle, neither of men, nor by men, but by Jesus Christ, and God the Father, who raised him up from the dead." Ye see, then, with what fervency of spirit Paul is led in this matter, which he goeth about to establish and maintain against the whole kingdom of hell, the power and wisdom of the world, and against the devil and his apostles.

VERSE 2. *And all the brethren with me.*

This maketh much for the stopping of the mouths of these false apostles; for all his arguments tend to the advancing and magnifying of his ministry, and contrariwise, to the discrediting of theirs; as if he should thus say: "Although it be enough, that I, through a divine calling, am sent as an apostle by Jesus Christ, and God the Father, which hath raised him up from the dead; yet, lest I should be alone, I add over and besides (which is more than needeth) all the brethren, which are not apostles, but fellow soldiers: they write this epistle as well as I, and bear witness with me that my doctrine is true and godly." Wherefore, we be sure that Christ is present with us, and that he teacheth and speaketh in the midst of us, and in our church. As for the false apostles, if they be any thing, they be but sent either of men, or by men; but I am sent of God the Father, and of Jesus Christ, who is our life and resurrection (John xi, 25). My other brethren are sent from God, howbeit by man, that is, to wit, by me. Therefore, lest they might say that I only set myself proudly against them, I have my brethren with me, all of one mind, as faithful witnesses, which think, write, and teach the self-same thing that I do.

VERSE 2. *Unto the churches of Galatia.*

Paul had preached the gospel throughout all Galatia, and albeit he had not wholly converted it unto Christ, yet he had many churches in it, into the which the false apostles, Satan's ministers, had crept. So likewise at this day, the fantastical anabaptists come not to those places where the adversaries of the gospel bear rule; but where Christians and good men are which love the gospel. With such they wind in themselves even in the dominions of tyrants and persecutors of the gospel: where they, creeping into houses under crafty pretence, pour out their poison to the subversion of many. But why go they not rather in the cities, countries, and dominions of the papists, and there profess and maintain their doctrine in the presence of wicked princes, bishops and doctors in the universities, as we by God's help and assistance have done? These tender martyrs will adventure no peril, but they resort thither where the gospel hath a harbour already, where they may live without danger in great peace and quietness. So the false apostles would not endanger themselves to come to Jerusalem to Caiaphas, or to Rome to the emperor, or to other places where no man had preached afore, as Paul and the other apostles did: but they came into Galatia, which was won unto Christ already by the labour and travel of Paul, and into Asia, Corinth, and such other places, where good men were, and professed the name of Christ, persecuting no man, but suffering all things quietly. There might the enemies of Christ's cross live in great security, and without any persecution.

And here we may learn that it is the lot of all godly teachers, that besides the persecution which they suffer of the wicked and unthankful world, and the great travail which they sustain in planting of churches, they are compelled to suffer that thing, which they of long time before had purely taught, to be quickly overthrown of fantastical spirits, who afterwards reign and rule over them. This grieveth godly ministers, more than any persecution of tyrants. Therefore, let him not be a minister of the gospel, which is not content to be thus despised, or is loth to bear this reproach; or if he be, let him give over his charge to another. We also at this day do find the same thing to be true by experience. We are miserably contemned and vexed outwardly by tyrants, inwardly by those whom wt have restored co liberty by the gospel, and also by false brethren. "But this is our comfort and glory, that, being called of God, we have a promise of everlasting life, and look for that reward which eye hath not seen, nor ear hath heard, nor hath entered into the heart of man" (I Cor. ii, 9). "For when the great shepherd, Christ, shall appear, we shall receive an incorruptible crown of glory; who here also in this world will not suffer us to perish for hunger" (I Peter v, 4).

Jerom moveth here a great question, "why Paul called those churches which were no churches. It is (saith he) because Paul writeth to the Galatians that were perverted and turned back from Christ, and from grace, unto Moses, and the law?" Hereunto I answer, that Paul calleth them the churches of Galatia, by putting a part for the whole, which is a common thing in the scriptures. For writing in like manner to the Corinthians, "he rejoiceth on their behalf, that the grace of God was given them in Christ, namely, that they were made rich through him in all utterance and knowledge." And yet many of them were misled by false apostles, and believed not the resurrection of the dead.

Albeit then, that the Galatians were fallen away from the doctrine of Paul, yet did baptism, the word, and the name of Christ, remain among them. There were also some good men that were not revolted, which had a right opinion of the word and sacraments, and used them well. Moreover, these things could not be defiled through them that were revolted. For baptism, the gospel, and other things, are not therefore made unholy, because many are polluted and unholy, and have an evil opinion of them: but they abide holy and the same that they were, whether they be among the godly or the ungodly: by whom they can neither be polluted, nor made holy. By our good or evil conversation, by our good or evil life and manners, they be polluted or made holy in the sight of the heathen, but not afore God. Wherefore, wheresoever the substance of the word and sacraments remaineth, there is the holy church, although Antichrist there reign, who (as the scripture witnesseth) sitteth not in a stable of fiends, or in a swine-sty, or in a company of infidels, but in the highest and holiest place of all, namely, in the temple of God. Wherefore, although spiritual tyrants reign, yet there must be a temple of God, and

EPISTLE TO THE GALATIANS

the same must be preserved under them. Therefore I answer briefly to this question, that the church is universal throughout the whole world, wheresoever the gospel of God and the sacraments be. The Jews, the Turks, and other vain spirits, are not the church, because they fight against these things and deny them. Hitherto as touching the title or inscription of this epistle. Now followeth the salutation or greeting of Paul.

VERSE 3. *Grace be with you, and peace from God the Father, and our Lord Jesus Christ.*

I hope ye are not ignorant what grace and peace meaneth, seeing that these terms are common in Paul, and now not obscure or unknown. But forasmuch as we take in hand to expound this epistle (which we do, not because it is needful, or for any hardness that is in it, but that our consciences may be confirmed against heresies yet to come) let it not be tedious unto you, if we repeat those things again, that elsewhere, and at other times, we teach, preach, sing, and set out by writing. For if we neglect the article of justification, we lose it altogether. Therefore most necessary it is, chiefly, and above all things, that we teach and repeat this article continually: like as Moses saith of his law. For it cannot be beaten into our ears enough, or too much. Yea, though we learn it and understand it well, yet is there none that taketh hold of it perfectly, or believeth it with his heart. So frail a thing is our flesh, and disobedient to the spirit.

The greeting of the apostle is strange unto the world, and was never heard of before the preaching of the gospel. And these two words, grace and peace, comprehend in them whatsoever belongeth to Christianity. Grace releaseth sin, and peace maketh the conscience quiet. The two fiends that torment us, are sin and conscience. But Christ hath vanquished these two monsters, and trodden them under foot, both in this world and the world to come. This the world doth not know, and therefore it can teach no certainty of the overcoming of sin, conscience, and death. Only Christians have this kind of doctrine, and are exercised and armed with it, to get victory against sin, despair, and everlasting death. And it is a kind of doctrine, neither proceeding of free-will, nor invented by the reason or wisdom of man, but given from above. Moreover, these two words, grace and peace, do contain in them the whole sum of Christianity. Grace containeth the remission of sins, peace, a quiet and joyful conscience. But peace of conscience can never be had, unless sin be first forgiven. But sin is not forgiven for the fulfilling of the law: for no man is able to satisfy the law. But the law doth rather shew sin, accuse and terrify the conscience, declare the wrath of God, and drive to desperation. Much less is sin taken away by the works and inventions of men, as wicked worshippings, strange religions, vows, and pilgrimages. Finally, there is no work that can take away sin: but sin is rather increased by works. For the justiciaries and merit-mongers, the more they labour and sweat to bring themselves out of sin, the deeper they are plunged therein. For there is no means to take away sin, but grace alone. Therefore Paul, in all the greetings of his epistle, setteth grace and peace against sin and an evil conscience. This thing must be diligently marked. The words are easy. But, in temptation, it is the hardest thing that can be, to be certainly persuaded in our hearts, that by *grace alone*, all other means, either in heaven or in earth, set apart, we have remission of sins, and peace with God.

The world understandeth not this doctrine; and therefore it neither will nor can abide it, but condemneth it as heretical and wicked. It braggeth of free-will, of the light of reason, of the soundness, of the powers and qualities of nature, and of good works, as means whereby it could discern and attain grace and peace; that is to say, forgiveness of sins and a quiet conscience. But it is impossible that the conscience should be quiet and joyful, unless it have peace through grace; that is to say, through the forgiveness of sins promised in Christ. Many have carefully laboured, by finding out diverse and sundry religious orders and exercises for this purpose, to attain peace and quietness of conscience: but by so doing, they have plunged themselves in more and greater miseries; for all such devices are but means to increase doubtfulness and despair. Therefore there shall be no rest to my bones or to thine, unless we hear the word of grace, and cleave unto it steadfastly and faithfully. Then shall our conscience undoubtedly find grace and peace.

The apostle doth fitly distinguish this grace and peace from all other kinds of grace and peace whatsoever. He wisheth to the Galatians grace and peace, not from the emperor or kings and princes: for these do commonly persecute the godly, and rise up against the Lord, and Christ his anointed (Psalm ii, 2), nor from the world ("for in the world," saith Christ, "ye shall have trouble:") but from God our Father, etc., which is as much as to say, he wished unto them a heavenly peace. So Christ saith: "My peace I leave unto you: my peace I give unto you; not as the world giveth it, do I give it unto you." The peace of the world granteth nothing but the peace of our goods and bodies. So the grace or favour of the world giveth us leave to enjoy our goods, and casteth us not out of our possessions. But in affliction, and in the hour of death, the grace and favour of the world cannot help us, they cannot deliver us from affliction, despair, and death. But when the grace and peace of God are in the heart, then is man strong, so that he can neither be cast down with adversity, nor puffed up with prosperity, but walketh on plainly, and keepeth the highway. For he taketh heart and courage in the victory of Christ's death; and the confidence thereof beginneth to reign in his conscience over sin and death; because, through him, he hath assured forgiveness of his sins: which after he has once obtained, his conscience is at rest, and by the word of grace is comforted. So then a man, being comforted and heartened by the grace of God (that is, by forgiveness of sin, and by this peace of conscience), is able valiantly to bear and overcome all troubles, yea even death itself. This peace of God is not given to the world, because the world never longeth after it, nor understandeth it, but to them that believe. And this cometh to pass by no other means than by the only grace of God.

A RULE TO BE OBSERVED, THAT MEN OUGHT TO ABSTAIN FROM THE CURIOUS SEARCHING OF GOD'S MAJESTY

But why doth the apostle add moreover in this salutation, "And from our Lord Jesus Christ?" Was it not enough to say, "And from God our Father?" Why then doth he couple Jesus Christ with the Father? Ye have oftentimes heard of us, how it is a rule and principle in the scriptures, diligentyl to be marked, that we must abstain from the curious searching of God's majesty, which is intolerable to man's body, and much more to his mind. "No man" (saith the Lord) "shall see me and live" (Exod. xxxiii, 20). The Pope, the Turks, the Jews, and all such as trust in their own merits, regard not this rule, and therefore removing the mediator Christ out of their sight, they speak only of God, and before him only they pray, and do all that they do.

As for example, the monk imagineth thus: "These works which I do, please God, God will regard these my vows, and for them will save me." The Turk saith, "If I keep the things that are commanded in the Alcoran, God will accept me, and give me everlasting life." The Jew thinketh thus: "If I keep those things which the law commandeth, I shall find God merciful unto me, and so shall I be saved." So also a sort of fond heads at this day, bragging of the spirit of revelations, of visions, and such other monstrous matters, I wot not what, do walk in wonders above their reaches. These new monks have invented a new cross and new works, and they dream that by doing them they please God. To be brief, as many as know not the article of justification take away Christ the mercy seat, and will needs comprehend God in his majesty by the judgment of reason, and pacify him with their own works.

But true christian divinity (as I give you often warning), setteth not God forth unto us in his majesty, as Moses and other doctrines do. It commandeth us not to search out the nature of God: but to know his will set out to us in Christ, whom he would have to take our flesh upon him, to be born and to die for our sins, and that this should be preached among all nations. "For after that, in the wisdom of God, the world by wisdom knew not God, it pleased God by the foolishness of preaching to save them that believe" (I Cor. i, 21). Wherefore, when thy conscience standeth in conflict, wrestling against the law, sin, and death, in the presence of God, there is nothing more dangerous than to wander with curious speculations in heaven, and there to search out God in his incomprehensible power, wisdom, and majesty, how he created the world, and how he governeth it. If thou seek thus to comprehend God, and wouldst pacify him without Christ the mediator, making thy works a means between him and thyself, it cannot be but that thou must fall as Lucifer did, and in horrible despair lose God and all together. For as God is in his own nature unmeasurable, incomprehensible, and infinite, so is he to man's nature intolerable.

Wherefore, if thou wouldst be in safety, and out of peril of conscience and salvation, bridle this climbing and presumptuous spirit, and so seek God as Paul teacheth thee (1 Cor. i), "We, saith he, preach Christ crucified, a stumbling block unto the Jews, and foolishness unto the Grecians; but unto them which are called, both of the Jews and Grecians, we preach Christ the power of God and the wisdom of God." Therefore begin thou there where Christ began, namely, in the womb of the virgin, in the manger, and at his mother's breasts, etc. For to this end he came down, was born, was conversant among men, suffered, was crucified, and died, that by all means he might set forth himself plainly before our eyes, and fasten the eyes of our hearts upon himself, that he thereby might keep us from climbing up into heaven, and from the curious searching of the divine majesty.

Whensoever thou hast to do therefore in the matter of justification, and disputeth with thyself how God is to be found that justifieth and accepteth sinners; where, and in what sort he is to be sought; then know thou that there is no other God besides this man, Christ Jesus. Embrace him, and cleave to him with thy whole heart, setting aside all curious speculations of the divine majesty: "For he that is a searcher of God's majesty, shall be overwhelmed of his glory." (Prov. xvii, 15; xxv, 27.) I know by experience what I say. But these vain spirits which so deal with God, that they exclude the mediator, do not believe me. Christ himself saith, "I am the way, the truth, and the life: no man cometh to the Father but by me." (John xiv, 6.) Therefore besides this way Christ, thou shalt find no way to the Father, but wandering: no verity, but hypocrisy and lying: no life, but eternal death. Wherefore mark this well in the matter of justification, that when any of us all shall have to wrestle with the law, sin, and death, and all other evils, we must look upon no other God, but only this God, incarnate and clothed with man's nature.

But out of the matter of justification, when thou must dispute with Jews, Turks, Papists, Heretics, etc., concerning the power, wisdom, and majesty of God, then employ all thy wit and industry to that end, and be as profound and as subtle a disputer as thou canst: for then thou art in another vein. But in the case of conscience, of righteousness and life (which I wish here diligently to be marked) against the law, sin, death, and the devil, or in the matter of satisfaction, of remission of sins, of reconciliation, and of everlasting life, thou must withdraw thy mind wholly from all cogitations and searching of the majesty of God, and look only upon this man Jesus Christ, who setteth himself forth unto us to be a mediator, and saith, "Come unto me, all ye that labour, and are heavy laden, and I will refresh you." (Matt. xi, 28.) Thus doing, thou shalt perceive the love, goodness, and sweetness of God: thou shalt see his wisdom, power, and majesty sweetened and tempered to thy capacity: yea, and thou shalt find it, this mirror and pleasant contemplation, all things according to that saying of Paul to the Colossians: "In Christ are hid all the treasures of wisdom and knowledge." And in chap. ii, "For in him dwelleth the fulness of the godhead bodily." (Col. ii, 3 and 9.) The world is ignorant of this, and therefore it searcheth out the will of God, setting aside the promise in Christ, to his great destruction. "For no man knoweth the Father but the Son, and he to whom the Son will reveal him." (Matt. xi, 27; John x, 15.)

And this is the cause why Paul is wont so often to couple Jesus Christ with God the Father, even to teach us what true Christian religion is, which beginneth not at the highest, as other religions do, but at the lowest. It will have us to climb up by Jacobs ladder, whereupon God himself leaneth, whose feet touch the very earth, hard by the head of Jacob. (Gen.

xxviii, 12.) Wherefore, whensoever thou art occupied in the matter of thy salvation, setting aside all curious speculations of God's unsearchable majesty, all cogitations of works, of traditions, of philosophy, yea, and of God's law too, run straight to the manger, and embrace this infant, and the Virgin's little babe in thine arms, and behold him as he was born, sucking, growing up, conversant among men, teaching, dying, rising again, ascending up above all the heavens, and having power above all things. By this means shalt thou be able to shake off all terrors and errors, like as the sun driveth away the clouds. And this sight and contemplation will keep thee in the right way, that thou mayest follow whither Christ is gone. Therefore, Paul, in wishing grace and peace not only from God the Father, but also from Jesus Christ, teacheth, first, that we should abstain from the curious searching of the divine majesty (for God no man knoweth), and to hear Christ, who is in the bosom of the Father, and uttereth to us his will, who also is appointed of the Father to be our teacher, to the end that we should all hear him. (John viii, 18.)

Christ is God by Nature

The other thing that Paul teacheth here, is a confirmation of our faith, "that Christ is very God." And such like sentences as this is, concerning the godhead of Christ, are to be gathered together and marked diligently, not only against the Arians, and other heretics, which either have been, or shall be hereafter, but also for the confirmation of our faith: for Satan will not fail to impugn in us all the articles of our faith ere we die. He is a most deadly enemy to faith, because he knoweth that it is the victory which overcometh the world (I John v, 4). Wherefore, it standeth us in hand to labour that our faith may be certain, and may increase and be strengthened by diligent and continual exercise of the word, and fervent prayer, that we may be able to withstand Satan.

Now, that Christ is the very God, it is manifestly declared, in that Paul attributeth the same things equally unto him which he doth unto the Father, namely, divine power, as the giving of grace, the forgiveness of sins, peace of conscience, life, victory over sin, death, the devil, and hell. This were by no means lawful for him to do, nay, it were sacrilege this to do, except he were very God, according to this saying, "I will not give my glory unto another" (Isa. xlii, 8). Again: "No man giveth that to others which he himself hath not. But seeing Christ giveth grace, peace, and the Holy Ghost, delivereth from the power of the devil, from sin, and death, it is certain that he hath an infinite and divine power, equal in all points to the power of the Father.

Neither doth Christ give grace and peace, as the apostle gave, and brought the same unto men by preaching of the gospel: but he giveth it as the author and Creator. The Father createth and giveth life, grace, peace, and all other good things. The self-same things also the Son createth and giveth. Now, to give grace, peace, everlasting life, to forgive sins, to make righteous, to quicken, to deliver from death and the devil, are not the works of any creature, but of the Divine Majesty alone. The angels can neither create nor give these things; therefore these works pertain only to the glory of the sovereign Majesty, the Maker of all things: and seeing Paul doth attribute the self-same power of creating, and giving all these things, unto Christ equally with the Father, it must needs follow that Christ is verily and naturally God.

Many such arguments are in John, where it is proved and concluded by the works which are attributed to the Son as well as to the Father, that the divinity of the Father, and of the Son, is all one. Therefore, the gifts which we receive of the Father, and which we receive of the Son, are all one. For else Paul would have spoken otherwise after this manner: Grace from God the Father, and peace from our Lord Jesus Christ; but, in knitting them both together, he attributeth them equally, as well to the Son as to the Father. I do therefore so diligently admonish you of this thing, because it is dangerous; lest, among so many errors, and in so great variety and confusion of sects, there might step up some Arians, Eunomians, Macedonians, and such other heretics, that might do harm to the churches with their subtilty.

Indeed, the Arians were sharp and subtle fellows. They granted that Christ hath two natures, and that he is called "very God of very God," howbeit, in name only, Christ (said they) is a most noble and perfect creature, above the angels, whereby God afterward created Heaven and earth, and all other things. So Mahomet also speaketh honourably of Christ. But all this is nothing else but goodly imaginations, and words pleasant and plausible to man's reason, whereby the fantastical spirits do deceive men, except they take good heed. But Paul speaketh otherwise of Christ. "Ye (saith he) are rooted and established in this belief, namely, that Christ is not only a perfect creature, but very God, who doth the self-same things that God the Father doth." He hath the divine works not of a creature, but of the Creator, because he giveth grace and peace: and to give them, is to condemn sin, to vanquish death, and to tread the devil under foot. These things no angel can give. But seeing they are attributed unto Christ, it must needs follow, that he is "very God by nature."

VERSE 4. *Which gave himself for our sins.*

Paul in a manner, in every word, handleth the argument of this epistle. He hath nothing in his mouth but Christ; and therefore in every word there is a fervency of spirit and life. And mark how well and to the purpose he speaketh. He saith not, which hath received our works at our hands, nor which hath received the sacrifice of Moses' law, worshipping, religions, masses, vows, and pilgrimages; but hath given—What? Not gold, nor silver, nor beasts, nor paschal lambs, nor an angel, but himself! For what? Not for a crown, nor for a kingdom, not for our holiness and righteousness, but "for our sins." These words are very thunder-claps from Heaven against all kinds of righteousness. Like as is also this sentence of John: "Behold the Lamb of God, that taketh away the sins of the world." Therefore, we must with diligent attention mark every word of Paul, and not slenderly consider them, or lightly pass them over; for they are full of consolation, and confirm fearful consciences exceedingly.

But how may we obtain remission of our sins? Paul answereth, "that the man which is called Jesus Christ, the Son of God, hath given himself for them." These are excellent and comfortable words, and are promises of the old law, that our sins are taken away by none other means than by the Son of God delivered unto death. With such gun-shot and such artillery must the papacy be destroyed, and all the religions of the heathen, all works, all merits and superstitious ceremonies. For if our sins may be taken away by our own works, merits, and satisfaction, what needed the Son of God to be given for them? But seeing he was given for them, it followeth that we cannot put them away by our own works.

Again, by this sentence, it is declared, that our sins are so great, so infinite and invincible, that it is impossible for the whole world to satisfy for one of them. And surely the greatness of the ransom (namely, Christ the Son of God, who gave himself for our sins) declareth sufficiently, that we can neither satisfy for sin, nor have dominion over it. The force and power of sin is set forth and amplified exceedingly by these words: "Which gave himself for our sins." Therefore here is to be marked the infinite greatness of the price bestowed for it, and then it will appear evidently that the power of it is so great, that by no means it could be put away, but that the Son of God must be given for it. He that considereth these things well, understandeth that this one word *sin* comprehendeth God's everlasting wrath and the whole kingdom of Satan, and that it is a thing more horrible than can be expressed; which ought to move us and make us afraid indeed. But we are careless, yea, we make light of sin, and a matter of nothing: which although it bring with it the sting and remorse of conscience, yet notwithstanding we think it not to be of such weight and force, but that, by some little work or merit, we may put it away.

This sentence therefore witnesseth, "that all men are servants and bond-slaves to sin, and (as Paul saith in another place) are sold under sin," (Rom. vii, 14). And again, "that sin is a most cruel and mighty tyrant over all men;" which cannot be vanquished by the power of any creatures, whether they be angels or men, but by the sovereign and infinite power of Jesus Christ, who hath given himself for the same.

Furthermore, this sentence setteth out to the consciences of all men which are terrified with the greatness of their sins, a singular comfort. For, albeit sin be never so invincible a tyrant, yet notwithstanding, forasmuch as Christ hath overcome it through his death, it cannot hurt them that believe in him. Moreover, if we arm ourselves with this belief, and cleave with all our hearts unto this man Christ Jesus, then is there a light opened, and a sound judgment given unto us, so as we may most certainly and freely judge of all kinds of life. For when we hear that sin is such an invincible tyrant, thus incontinent by a necessary consequence we infer; then what do the Papists, Monks, Nuns, Priests, Mahometists, Anabaptists, and all such as trust in their own works, which will abolish and overcome sin by their own traditions, works preparative, satisfactions, etc. Here forthwith we judge all those sects to be wicked and pernicious, whereby the glory of God and of Christ is not only defaced, but also utterly taken away, and our own advanced and established.

But weigh diligently every word of Paul, and specially mark well this pronoun, *our;* for the effect altogether consisteth in the well applying of the pronouns, which we find very often in the scriptures; wherein also there is ever some vehemency and power. Thou wilt easily say and believe that Christ the Son of God was given for the sins of Peter, of Paul, and of other saints, whom we account to have been worthy of this grace; but it is a very hard thing, that thou, which judgest thyself unworthy of this grace, shouldst from thy heart say and believe, that Christ was given for thine invincible, infinite, and horrible sins. Therefore, generally, and without the pronoun, it is an easy matter to magnify and amplify the benefit of Christ, namely, that Christ was given for sins, but for other men's sins, which are worthy. But when it cometh to the putting to of this pronoun *our*, there our weak nature and reason starteth back, and dare not come nigh unto God, nor promise to herself, that so great a treasure shall be freely given unto her, and therefore she will not have to do with God, except first she be pure and without sin; wherefore, although she read or hear this sentence: "which gave himself for our sins," or such like, yet doth she not apply this pronoun (our) unto herself, but unto others which are worthy and holy; and as for herself, she will tarry till she be made worthy by her own works.

This then is nothing else, but that man's reason fain would that sin were of no greater force and power than she herself dreameth it to be. Hereof it cometh, that the hypocrites, being ignorant of Christ, although they feel the remorse of sin, do think, notwithstanding, that they shall be able easily to put it away by their good works and merits, and secretly, in their hearts, they wish that these words, "which gave himself for our sins," were but as words spoken in humility, and would have their sins not to be true and very sins indeed, but light and small matters. To be short, man's reason would fain bring and present unto God a feigned and counterfeit sinner, which is nothing afraid, nor hath any feeling of sin. It would bring him that is whole, and not him that hath need of a physician; and when it feeleth no sin, then would it believe that Christ was given for our sins.

The whole world is thus affected, and especially they that would be counted more holy and righteous than others, as monks, and all justiciaries. These confess with their mouths that they are sinners, and they confess also that they commit sins daily, howbeit not so great and many, but that they are able to put them away by their own works: yea, and besides all this, they will bring their righteousness and deserts to Christ's judgment-seat, and demand the recompence of eternal life for them at the judge's hand. In the mean while, notwithstanding, (as they pretend great humility) because they will not vaunt themselves to be utterly void of sin, they feign certain sins, that, for the forgiveness thereof, they may with great devotion pray with the publican, "God be merciful unto me a sinner!" (Luke xviii, 13). Unto them, these words of St. Paul, "for our sins," seems to be but light and trifling; therefore, they neither understand them, nor in temptation, when they feel sin indeed, can they take any comfort of them, but are compelled flatly to despair.

This is then the chief knowledge and true wisdom of Christians, to count these words of Paul, "that Christ was delivered to death, not for our righteousness or holiness, but for our sins," (which are very sins indeed, great, many, yea, infinite and invincible) to be "most true, effectual, and of great importance." Therefore, think them not to be small, and such as may be done away by thine own works; neither yet despair thou for the greatness of them, if thou feel thyself oppressed therewith, either in life or death; but learn here of Paul, to believe that Christ was given, not for feigned or counterfeit sins, nor yet for small sins, but for great and huge sins; not for one or two, but for all; not for vanquished sins, (for no man, no, nor angel, is able to overcome the least sin that is) but for invincible sins. And except thou be found in the number of those that say "our sins," that is, which have this doctrine of faith, and teach, hear, learn, love, and believe the same, there is no salvation for thee.

Labour therefore diligently, that not only out of the time of temptation, but also in the time and conflict of death, when thy conscience is thoroughly afraid with the remembrance of thy sins past, and the devil assaileth thee with great violence, going about to overwhelm thee with heaps, floods, and whole seas of sins, to terrify thee, to draw thee from Christ, and to drive thee to despair, that then I say, thou mayest be able to say with sure confidence, Christ, the Son of God, was given, not for the righteous and holy, but for the unrighteous and sinners. If I were righteous, and had no sin, I should have no need of Christ to be my reconciler. Why then, O thou peevish holy Satan, wilt thou make me to be holy, and to seek righteousness in myself, when, in very deed, I have nothing in me but sins, and most grievous sins? Not feigned or trifling sins, but such as are against the first table: to wit, great infidelity, doubting, despair, contempt of God, hatred, ignorance, and blaspheming of God, unthankfulness, abusing of God's name, neglecting, loathing, and despising the word of God, and such like. And moreover, these carnal sins against the second table: as not to yield honour to my parents, not to obey the magistrates, to covet another man's goods, his wife, and such like; albeit that these be light faults in respect of those former sins. And admit that I have not committed murder, whoredom, theft, and such other sins against the second table, in fact, yet I have committed them in heart, and therefore I am a transgressor of all God's commandments; and the multitude of my sins is so great, that they cannot be numbered: "for I have sinned above the number of the sands of the sea."

Besides this, Satan is such a cunning juggler, that he can

make of my righteousness and good works, great sin. For so much, then, as my sins are so weighty, so infinite, so horrible, and invincible, and that my righteousness doth nothing further me, but rather hinder me before God; therefore "Christ, the Son of God, was given to death for them, to put them away and so save all men which believe." Herein therefore consisteth the effect of eternal salvation, namely, in taking these words to be effectual, true, and of great importance. I say not this for nought, for I have oftentimes proved by experience, and I daily find what a hard matter it is to believe (especially in the conflict of conscience) "that Christ was given," not for the holy, righteous, worthy, and such as were his friends, "but for wicked sinners, for the unworthy, and for his enemies, which have deserved God's wrath and everlasting death."

Let us therefore arm ourselves with these, and such like sentences of the holy scripture, that we may be able to answer the devil (accusing us, and saying, "thou art a sinner, and therefore thou art damned"), in this sort: Because thou sayest, I am a sinner, therefore I will be righteous and saved; Nay, (saith the devil) "thou shalt be damned." No, (say I) for I fly unto Christ, "who hath given himself for my sins;" therefore, Satan, "thou shalt not prevail against me," in that thou goest about to terrify me, in setting forth the greatness of my sins, and so to bring me into heaviness, distrust, despair, hatred, contempt, and blaspheming of God. Yea, raher, in that thou sayest, I am a sinner, thou givest me armour and weapons against thyself, that with thine own sword I may cut thy throat, and tread thee under my feet; for Christ died for sinners. Moreover, thou thyself preachest unto me the glory of God; for thou puttest me in mind of God's fatherly love towards me, wretched and damned sinner; "Who so loved the world, that he gave his only begotten Son, that whosoever believeth in him shall not perish, but have everlasting life," (John iii, 16). And as often as thou objectest that I am a sinner, so often thou callest me to remembrance of the benefit of Christ my Redeemer, upon whose shoulders, and not upon mine, lie all my sins; for the Lord hath "laid all our iniquity upon him," (Isaiah liii, 6). Again, "For the transgressions of his people was he smitten," (chap. liii, 8). Wherefore, when thou sayest I am a sinner, thou dost not terrify me, but comfortest me above measure.

Whoso knoweth this one point of cunning well, shall easily avoid all the engines and snares of the devil, who, by putting man in mind of his sins, driveth him to despair, and destroyeth him, unless he withstand him with this cunning, and with this heavenly wisdom, whereby only sin, death, and the devil, are overcome. But the man that putteth not away the remembrance of his sin, but keepeth it still and tormenteth himself with his own cogitations, thinketh either to help himself by his own strength or policy, or to tarry the time till his conscience may be quieted, falling into Satan's snares, and miserably afflicteth himself, and at length is overcome with the continuance of the temptation; for the devil will never cease to accuse his conscience.

Against this temptation we must use these words of St. Paul, in the which he giveth a very good and true definition of Christ in this manner: "Christ is the Son of God, and of the Virgin, delivered, and put to death for our sins." Here, if the devil allege any other definition of Christ, say thou, the definition, and the thing defined, are false: therefore, I will not receive this definition. I speak not this without cause: for I know what moveth me to be so earnest, that we should learn to define Christ out of the words of Paul. For indeed Christ is no cruel exactor, but a forgiver of the sins of the whole world. Wherefore, if thou be a sinner (as indeed we are all) sit not Christ down upon the rainbow, as a judge, (for so thou shalt not be terrified, and despair of his mercy) but take hold of his true definition, namely, that Christ, the Son of God, and of the Virgin, is a person, not that terrifieth, not that afflicteth, not that condemneth us of sin, not that demandeth an account of us for our life evil passed: but hath given himself for our sins, and with one oblation hath put away the "sins of the whole world," (Col. ii, 14) hath fastened them upon the cross, and put them clean out by himself.

Learn this definition diligently, and especially so exercise this pronoun *our*, that this one syllable being believed, may swallow up all thy sins: that is to say, that thou mayest know assuredly, that Christ hath taken away the sins, not of certain men only, but also of thee, yea, and of the whole world. Then let not thy sins be sins only, but even thy own sins indeed; that is, to wit, believe thou that Christ was not only given for other men's sins but also for thine. Hold this fast, and suffer not thyself by any means to be drawn away from this most sweet definition of Christ, which rejoiceth even the very angels in heaven: that is to say, that Christ, according to the proper and true definition, is no Moses, no lawgiver, no tyrant, but a mediator for sins, a free giver of grace, righteousness, and life; who gave himself, not for our merits, holiness, righteousness, and godly life, but for our sins. Indeed, Christ doth interpret the law, but that is not his proper and principal office.

These things, as touching the words, we know well enough, and can talk of them. But in practice, and in the conflict, when the devil goeth about to deface Christ, and to pluck the word of grace out of our hearts, we find that we do not yet know them well, and as we should do. He that at that time could define Christ truly, and could magnify him and behold him as his most sweet Saviour and High-priest, and not as a strait judge, this man hath overcome all evils, and were already in the kingdom of heaven. But this to do in the conflict, is of all things the most hard. I speak this by experience. For I know the devil's subtleties, who at that time not only goeth about to fear us with the terror of the law, yea, and also of a little mote maketh many beams; that is to say, of that which is no sin he maketh a very hell (for he is marvellous crafty both in aggravating sin, and in puffing up the conscience even in good works): but also is wont to fear us with the very person of the Mediator: into the which he transformeth himself; and, laying before us some place of scripture or saying of Christ, suddenly he striketh our hearts and sheweth himself unto us in such sort as if he were Christ indeed, leaving us sticking so fast in that cogitation, that our conscience would swear it were the same Christ whose saying he alleged. Moreover, such is the subtlety of the enemy, that he will not set before us Christ entirely and wholly, but a piece of Christ only, namely, that he is the Son of God, and man born of the Virgin. And by-and-by he patcheth thereto some other thing; that is to say, some saying of Christ, wherewith he terrifieth the impenitent sinners, such as that it is in the thirteenth of Luke, "Except ye repent, ye shall all likewise perish." And so, corrupting the true definition of Christ with his poison, he bringeth to pass that albeit we believe him to be Christ the true mediator, yet, in very deed, our troubled conscience feeleth and judgeth him to be a tyrant and a judge. Thus we, being deceived by Satan, do easily lose that sweet sight of our High-priest and Saviour Christ, which, being once lost, we shun him no less than the devil himself.

And this is the cause why I do so earnestly call upon you, to learn the true and proper definition of Christ out of these words of Paul, "Which gave himself for our sins." If he gave himself to death for our sins, then undoubtedly he is no tyrant or judge which will condemn us for our sins. He is no caster-down of the afflicted, but a raiser-up of those that are fallen, a merciful reliever and comforter of the heavy and broken-hearted. Else should Paul lie in saying, "which gave himself for our sins." If I define Christ thus, I define him rightly, and take hold of the true Christ, and possess him indeed. And here I let pass all curious speculations touching the divine majesty, and stay myself in the humanity of Christ, and so I learn truly to know the will of God. Here is then no fear, but altogether sweetness, joy, peace of conscience, and such like. And herewithal there is a light opened, which sheweth me the true knowledge of God, of myself, of all creatures, and of all the iniquity of the devil's kingdom. We teach no new thing, but we repeat and establish old things, which the apostles and all godly teachers have taught before us. And would to God we could so teach and establish them, that we might not only have them in our mouth, but also well-grounded in the bottom of our heart, and especially that we might be able to use them in the agony and conflict of death.

VERSE 4. *That he might deliver us from this present evil world.*

In these words also Paul handleth yet more effectually the argument of this epistle. He calleth this whole world, which hath been, is, and shall be, the present world, to put a difference between this and the everlasting world to come. Moreover, he calleth it evil, because that whatsoever is in this world, is subject to the malice of the devil reigning over the whole world. For this cause the world is the kingdom of the devil. For there is in it nothing but ignorance, contempt, blasphemy, hatred of God, and disobedience against all the words and works of God. In and under this kingdom of the world are we.

Here again you see that no man is able, by his own works or his own power, to put away sin, because this present world is evil, and (as St. John saith) "is set upon mischief." As many therefore as are in the world are the bondslaves of the devil, constrained to serve him, and do all things at his pleasure. What availeth it then, to set up so many orders of religion, for the abolishing of sin; to devise so many great and most painful works, as to wear shirts of hair, to beat the body with whips till the blood followed, to go on pilgrimage to St. James in harness, and such other like? Be it so that thou doest all these things, yet notwithstanding this is true, that thou art in this present evil world, and not in the kingdom of Christ. And if thou be not in the kingdom of Christ, it is certain that thou belongest to the kingdom of Satan, which is this evil world. Therefore all the gifts, either of the body or of the mind, which thou enjoyest, as wisdom, righteousness, holiness, eloquence, power, beauty, and riches, are but the slavish instruments of the devil, and with all these thou art compelled to serve him, and to advance his kingdom.

First, with thy wisdom thou darkenest the wisdom and knowledge of Christ, and, by thy wicked doctrine, leadest them out of the way, that they cannot come to the grace and knowledge of Christ. Thou settest out and praisest thine own righteousness and holiness; but the righteousness of Christ, by which only we are justified and quickened, thou dost hate and condemn as wicked and devilish. To be brief, by thy power thou destroyest the kingdom of Christ, and abusest the same to root out the gospel, to persecute and kill the ministers of Christ, and so many as hear them. Wherefore, if thou be without Christ, this thy wisdom is double foolishness, thy righteousness double sin and impiety, because it knoweth not the wisdom and righteousness of Christ: moreover, it darkeneth, hindereth, blasphemeth and persecuteth the same. Therefore Paul doth rightly call it the evil or wicked world: for when it is at the best, then is it worst. In the religious, wise, and learned men, the world is at the best, and yet, in very deed, in them it is double evil. I overpass those gross vices which are against the second table, as disobedience to parents, to magistrates, adulteries, whoredoms, covetousness, thefts, murders, and maliciousness, wherein the world is altogether drowned, which notwithstanding are light faults, if ye compare them with the wisdom and righteousness of the wicked, whereby they fight against the first table. This white devil, which forceth men to commit spiritual sins that they may sell them for righteousness, is far more dangerous than the black devil, which only enforceth them to commit fleshly sins, which the world acknowledgeth to be sins.

By these words then, "That he might deliver us," etc., Paul sheweth what is the argument of this epistle; to wit, that we have need of grace and of Christ, and that no other creature, neither man nor angel, can deliver man out of this present evil world. For these works are only belonging to the divine majesty, and are not in the power of any, either man or angel. That Christ hath put away sin, and hath delivered us from the tyranny and kingdom of the devil; that is to say, from this wicked world, which is an obedient servant, and a willing follower of the devil his God. Whatsoever the murderer and father of lies either doth or speaketh, that the world, as his most loyal and obedient son, diligently followeth and performeth. And therefore it is full of the ignorance of God, of hatred, lying, errors, blasphemy, and of the contempt of God. Moreover, of gross sins, as murders, adulteries, fornications, thefts, robberies, and such like, because he knoweth his father the devil, who is a liar and a murderer. And the more wise, righteous, and holy that men are without Christ, so much the more hurt they do the gospel. So we also, that were religious men, were double wicked in the papacy, before God did lighten us with the knowledge of his gospel, and ye, notwithstanding under the colour of true piety and holiness.

Let these words then of Paul remain, as they are indeed, true and effectual, not coloured or counterfeit, namely, "that this present world is evil." Let it nothing at all move thee, that, in a great number of men, there be many excellent virtues, and that there is so great a show of holiness in hypocrites. But mark thou rather what Paul saith: out of whose words thou mayest boldly and freely pronounce this sentence against the world, that the world with all his wisdom, power and righteousness, is the kingdom of the devil: out of the which God alone is able to deliver us by his only begotten Son.

Therefore let us praise God the Father, and give him hearty thanks for this his unmeasurable mercy, that hath delivered us out of the kingdom of the devil (in the which we were holden captives) by his own Son, when it was impossible to be done by our own strength. And let us acknowledge, together with Paul, "that all our works and righteousness," (with all which, we could not make the devil to stoop one hair's breadth) "are but loss and dung." Also let us cast under our feet, and utterly abhor all the power of free-will, all pharisaical wisdom and righteousness, all religious orders, all masses, ceremonies, vows, fastings, and such like, (Phil. iii, 8) as a most filthy defiled cloth, (Isa. lxiv, 6) and as the most dangerous poison of the devil. Contrariwise, let us extol and magnify the glory of Christ, who hath delivered us by his death, not from this world only, but from this evil world.

Paul then by this word, *evil*, sheweth that the kingdom of the world, or the devil's kingdom, is the kingdom of iniquity, ignorance, error, sin, death, blasphemy, desperation, and everlasting damnation. On the other side, the kingdom of Christ is the kingdom of equity, light, grace, remission of sins, peace, consolation, saving health, and everlasting life, into the which we are translated (Col. xiii) by our Lord Jesus Christ, to whom be glory, world without end. So be it.

VERSE 4. *According to the will of God, even our Father.*

Here Paul so placeth and ordereth every word, that there is not one of them but it fighteth against those false apostles for the article of justification. Christ (saith he) hath delivered us from this wicked kingdom of the devil, and the world. And this hath he done, "according to the will, good pleasure, and commandment of the Father." Wherefore we be not delivered by our own will, or cunning, nor by our own wisdom or policy, but for that God hath taken mercy upon us, and hath loved us: like as it is written also in another place, "Herein hath appeared the great love of God towards us, not that we have loved God, but that he hath loved us, and hath sent his only begotten Son to be a reconciliation for our sins," (1 John iv, 10). That we are then delivered from this present evil world, it is of mere grace, and no desert of ours. Paul is so plentiful, and so vehement in amplifying and extolling the grace of God, that he sharpeneth, and directeth every word against the false apostles.

There is also another cause why Paul here maketh mention of the Father's will, which also in many places of St. John's gospel is declared, where Christ, commending his office, calleth us back to his Father's will, that in his words and works we should not so much look upon him, as upon the Father. For Christ came into this world, and took man's nature upon him, that he might be made a sacrifice for the sins of the whole world, and so to reconcile us to God the Father; that he alone might declare unto us how that this was done through the good pleasure of his Father, that we, by fastening our eyes upon Christ, might be drawn and carried straight unto the Father.

For we must not think (as before we have warned you) that by the curious searching of the majesty of God, any thing concerning God can be known to our salvation, but by taking hold of Christ, who, according to the will of the Father, hath given himself to death for our sins. When thou shalt acknowledge this to be the will of God through Christ, then wrath ceaseth, fear and trembling vanisheth away, neither doth God appear any other than merciful, who by his determinate counsel would that his Son should die for us, that we might live through him. This knowledge maketh the heart cheerful, so that it stedfastly believeth that God is not angry, but he so loveth us poor and wretched sinners, that he gave his only begotten Son for us. It is not for nought, therefore, that Paul doth so often repeat, and beat into our minds, that Christ was given for our sins, and that by the good will of the Father. On the contrary part, the curious searching of the majesty of God, and his dreadful judgments, namely, how de destroyed the whole world with the flood, how he destroyed Sodom, and such other things, are very dangerous, for they bring men to desperation, and cast them down headlong into utter destruction, as I have shewed before.

VERSE 4. *Of God and our Father.*

This word *our*, must be referred to both, that the meaning may be this, "of our God and of our Father." Then is Christ's Father, and our Father all one. So in the twentieth of John, Christ saith to Mary Magdalen: "Go to my brethren, and say unto them, I ascend unto my Father, and your Father, to my God, and to your God." Therefore God is our Father, and our God, but through Christ. And this is an apostolic manner of speech, and even Paul's own phrase, who, indeed, speaketh not with such picked and gay words, but yet very fit and to the purpose, and full of burning zeal.

VERSE 5. *To whom be glory for ever and ever.*

The Hebrews are wont in their writings to intermingle praise and giving of thanks. This custom the Hebrews and the apostles themselves do observe. Which thing may be very often seen in Paul. For the name of the Lord ought to be had in great reverence, and never to be named without praise and thanksgiving. And thus to do, is a certain kind of worship and service to God. So in worldly matters, when we mention the names of kings or princes, we are wont to do it with some comely gesture, reverence, and bowing of the knee: much more ought we when we speak of God, to bow the knee of our heart, and to name the name of God with thankfulness and great reverence.

VERSE 6. *I marvel.*

Ye see here how Paul handleth his Galatians, which were fallen away and seduced by the false apostles. He doth not at the first set upon them with vehement and rigorous words, but after a very fatherly sort, not only patiently bearing their fall, but also in a manner excusing the same. Furthermore, he sheweth towards them a motherly affection, and speaketh them very fair, and yet in such sort, that he reproveth them notwithstanding: howbeit with very fit words, and wisely framed to the purpose. Contrariwise he is very hot and full of indignation against those false apostles their seducers, upon whom he layeth the whole fault; and therefore forthwith, even in the entrance of his epistle, he bursteth out into plain thunderings and lightnings against them. "If any man" (saith he) "preach any other gospel than that ye have received, let him be accursed." And afterwards, in the fifth chapter, he threateneth damnation unto them: "Whoso troubleth you shall bear his condemnation, whatsoever he be" (Gal. v, 10). Moreover, he curseth them with horrible words, saying: 'Would to God they were cut off trouble you." These are dreadful thunderclaps against the righteousness of the flesh or the law.

He might have handled the Galatians more uncourteously, and have inveighed against them more roughly after this manner: "Out upon this backsliding, I am ashamed of you; your unthankfulness grieveth me; I am angry with you:" or else thus tragically have cried out against them: "O ungracious world, O wicked dealings," etc. But forasmuch as his purpose is to raise up them that were fallen, and with a fatherly care to call them back again from their error to the purity of the gospel, he leaveth those rough and sharp words, especially in the first entrance, and most gently and mildly he speaketh unto them. For, seeing he went about to heal them that were wounded, it was not meet that he should now further vex their green wound, by laying to it a sharp and a fretting plaister, and so rather hurt the wounds than heal them. Therefore, of all the sweetest and mildest words, he could not have chosen any one more fit than this, "I marvel:" whereby he signifieth both that it grieved him, and also displeased him, that they had fallen away from him.

And here Paul is mindful of his own rule, which he giveth hereafter in the sixth chapter, where he saith: "Brethren, if a man be fallen by occasion into any fault, ye which are spiritual, restore such a one with the spirit of meekness, considering thyself also tempted." This example must we also follow, that we shew ourselves to bear like affection toward such as are misled, as parents bear towards their children, that they may perceive our fatherly and motherly affection towards them, and may see that we seek not their destruction, but their welfare. But as for the devil and his ministers, the authors of false doctrine and sects, against them we ought, by the example of the apostle, to be impatient, proud, sharp, and bitter, detesting and condemning their false jugglings and deceits with as much rigor and severity as may be. So parents, when their child is hurt with the biting of a dog, are wont to pursue the dog only, but the weeping child they bemoan and speak fair unto it, comforting it with the most sweet words.

The spirit therefore that is in Paul is wonderful cunning in handling the afflicted consciences of such as are fallen. Contrariwise, the Pope (because he is led with a wicked spirit) breaketh out violently like a tyrant, and rappeth out his thunder-cracks and cursings against the miserable and terrified in consciences; which things may be seen in his bulls, and especially in that bull touching the Lord's Supper. The bishops also do their duty never a whit better. They teach not the gospel, they are not careful for the saving of men's souls, but only they seek lordship and sovereignty over them, and therefore their speakings and doings are altogether to maintain and support the same. In like manner are all the vain-glorious doctors and teachers affected.

Verse 6. *That so soon.*

Ye see how Paul complaineth, that to fall in faith is an easy matter. In respect whereof, he warneth the faithful in another place, "That he which standeth, should take heed that he fall not," (1 Cor. x, 12). We also do daily prove by experience, how hardly the mind conceiveth and retaineth a sound and stedfast faith. Also with what great difficulty a perfect people is gotten to the Lord. A man may labour half a score of years ere he shall get some little church to be rightly and religiously ordered; and, when it is so ordered, there creepeth in some madbrain, yea and a very unlearned idiot, which can do nothing else but speak slanderously and spitefully against sincere preachers of the word, and he in one moment overthroweth all. Whom would not this wicked and outrageous dealing move?

We, by the grace of God, have gotten here at Wittenberg the form of a Christian church. The word among us is purely taught, the sacraments are rightly used, exhortations and prayers are made for all estates; and, to be brief, all things go forward prosperously. This most happy course of the gospel some madhead would soon stop, and, in one moment, would overturn all that we, in many years, with great labour, have builded. Even so it befell to Paul, the elect vessel of Christ. He had won the churches of Galatia with great care and travail, which the false apostles, in a short time after his departure, overthrew, as this and divers others of his epistles do witness. So great is the weakness and wretchedness of this present life; and we so walk in the midst of Satan's snares, that one fantastical head may destroy and utterly overthrow, in a short space, all that which many true ministers, labouring night and day, have builded up many years before. This we learn at this day by experience to great grief, and yet we cannot remedy this enormity.

Seeing then that the church is so soft and so tender a thing, and is so soon overthrown, men must watch cheerfully against these fantastical spirits; who, when they have heard two sermons, or have read a few leaves in the holy scriptures, by-and-by they make themselves masters and controllers of all learners and teachers, contrary to the authority of all men. Many such also thou mayest find at this day amongst handicrafts men, bold and malapert fellows, who, because they have been tried by no temptations, did never learn to fear God, nor had any taste or feeling of grace. These, for that they are void of the Holy Ghost, teach what liketh themselves best, and such things as are plausible and pleasant to the common people. Then the unskillful multitude, longing to hear news, do by-and-by join themselves unto them. Yea, and many also, which think themselves well seen in the doctrine of faith, and after a sort have been tried with temptations, are seduced by them.

Since that Paul therefore, by his own experience, may teach us that congregations, which are won by great labour, are easily and soon overthrown, we ought with singular care to watch against the devil ranging everywhere, lest he come while we sleep, and sow tares among the wheat. For though the shepherds be never so watchful and diligent, yet is the Christian flock in danger of Satan. For Paul (as I said) with singular study and diligence, had planted churches in Galatia, and yet he had scarcely set his foot (as they say) out of the door, but by-and-by the false apostles overthrew some, whose fall afterward was the cause of great ruin in the churches of Galatia. This so sudden, and so great a loss, no doubt, was more bitter unto the apostle than death itself. Therefore let us watch diligently; first, every one for himself; secondly, all teachers, not only for themselves, but also for the whole church, that we enter not into temptation.

VERSE 6. *Ye are removed away.*

Here once again he useth not a sharp, but a most gentle word. He saith not: I marvel that ye so suddenly fall away, that ye are so disobedient, light, inconstant, unthankful; but that ye are so soon removed. As if he should say, ye are altogether patients or sufferers; for ye have done no harm, but ye have suffered and received harm. To the intent therefore, that he might call back again those backsliders, he rather accuseth those that did remove, than those that were removed, and yet very modestly he blameth them also, when he complaineth that they were removed. As if he should say: Albeit I embrace you with a fatherly affection, and know that ye are deceived, not by your own default but by the default of the false apostles: yet notwithstanding I would have wished, that ye had been grown up a little more in the strength of sound doctrine. Ye took not hold enough upon the word, ye rooted not yourselves deep enough in it, and that is the cause that with so light a blast of wind, ye are carried and removed. Jerom thinketh, that Paul meant to interpret this word [Galatians] by alluding to the Hebrew word Galath, which is as much as to say, as fallen or carried away. As though he would say: ye are right Galatians, both in name and in deed; that is to say, fallen or removed away. Some think that the Germans are descended of the Galatians. Neither is this divination perhaps untrue. For the Germans are not much unlike to them in nature. And I myself also am constrained to wish to my countrymen more steadfastness and constancy; for in all things we do, at the first brunt we be very hot; but when the heat of our affections is allayed, anon we become more slack, and look, with what rashness we begin things, with the same we give them over, and utterly reject them.

At the first, when the light of the gospel, after so great darkness of men's traditions, began to appear, many were zealously turned to godliness; they heard sermons greedily, and had the ministers of God's word in reverence. But now, when religion is happily reformed with so great increase of God's word, many which before seemed to be earnest disciples, are become contemners and very enenmies thereof. Who not only cast off the study and zeal of God's word and despise the ministers thereof, but also hate all good learning, and become plain hogs, and belly-gods, worthy (doubtless) to be compared unto the foolish and inconstant Galatians.

VERSE 6. *From him that hath called you in the grace of Christ.*

This place is somewhat doubtful, and therefore it hath a double understanding. The first is: "From that Christ that hath called you in grace." The other is: "From him;" that is to say, from God which hath called you in the grace of Christ. I embrace the former. For it liketh me, that even as Paul, a little before, made Christ the Redeemer, who by his death delivereth us from this present evil world; also the giver of grace and peace equally with God the Father; so he should make him here also the caller in grace; for Paul's special purpose it, to beat into our minds the benefit of Christ, by whom we come unto the Father.

There is also in these words—from him that hath called us in grace—a great vehemency; wherein is contained without a contrary relation, as if he should say, Alas! how lightly do you suffer yourselves to be withdrawn and removed from Christ which hath called you, not as Moses did, to the law, works, sins, wrath, and damnation, but altogether to grace! So we also complain at this day with Paul, that the blindness and perverseness of men is horrible, in that none will receive the doctrine of grace and salvation. Or if there be any that receive it, yet they quickly slide back again, and fall from it; whereas, notwithstanding, it bringeth with it all good things, as well ghostly as bodily, namely, forgiveness of sins, true righteousness, peace of conscience, and everlasting life. Moreover, it bringeth light and sound judgment of all kinds of doctrine and trades of life; it approveth and establisheth civil government, household government, and all kinds of life that are ordained and appointed of God; it rooteth out all doctrines of error, sedition, confusion, and such like; and it putteth away the fear of sin and death; and to be short, it discovereth all the subtile slights and works of the devil, and openeth the benefits and love of God towards us in Christ. What (with a mischief) means the world to hate this word, this glad tidings of everlasting comfort, grace, salvation, and eternal life, so bittterly, and to persecute it with such hellish outrage?

Paul before called this present world evil and wicked, that is to say, the devil's kingdom; for else it would acknowledge the benefit and mercy of God. Forasmuch as it is under the power of the devil, therefore doth it most spitefully hate and persecute the same, loving darkness, errors, and the kingdom of the devil, more than the light, the truth and the kingdom of Christ (John iii, 19). And this it doth, not through ignorance or error, but through the malice of the devil; which thing hereby may sufficiently appear, in that Christ, the Son of God, by giving himself to death for the sins of all men, hath thereby gained nothing else of this perverse and damnable world, but that for this his inestimable benefit, it blasphemeth him, and persecuteth his most healthful word, and fain would yet still nail him to the cross if it could: therefore not only the world dwelleth in darkness, but it is darkness itself, as it is written in the first of John.

Paul therefore standeth much upon these words: "From Christ who hath called you;" as though he would say, My preaching was not of the hard laws of Moses, neither taught I that ye should be bond-slaves under the yoke; but I preached the only doctrine of grace and freedom from the law, sin, wrath, and damnation, that is to say, that Christ hath mercifully called you in grace, that ye should be freemen under Christ, and not bondmen under Moses, whose disciples ye are now become again by the means of your false apostles, who, by the law of Moses, called you not unto grace, but unto wrath, to the hating of God, to sin, and death. But Christ's calling bringeth grace and saving health; for they that be called by him, instead of the law that worketh sorrow, do gain the glad tidings of the gospel, and are translated out of God's wrath into his favour, out of sin into righteousness, and out of death into life. And will you suffer yourselves to be carried, yea, and that so soon, and so easily, another way, from such a living fountain, full of grace and life? Now, if Moses call men to God's wrath, and to sin by the law of God, whither shall the Pope call men by his own traditions? The other sense, that the Father calleth in the grace of Christ, is also good; but the former sense concerning Christ, serveth more fitly for the comforting of afflicted consciences.

VERSE 6. *Unto another gospel.*

Here we may learn to espy the crafty slights and subtleties of the devil. No heretic cometh under the title of errors and of the devil, neither doth the devil himself come as a devil in his own likeness, especially that white devil which we spake of before. Yea, even the black devil, which forceth men to manifest wickedness, maketh a cloak for them to cover that sin which they commit, or purpose to commit. The murderer, in his rage, seeth not that murder is so great and horrible a sin as it is indeed, for that he hath a cloak to cover the same. Whoremongers, thieves, covetous persons, drunkards, and such other, have wherewith to flatter themselves, and cover their sins. So the black devil also cometh out disguised and counterfeit in all his works and devices. But in spiritual matters, where Satan cometh forth not black, but white, in this likeness of an angel, or of God himself, there he passeth himself with most crafty dissimulation, and wonderful slights, and is wont to set forth to sale his most deadly poison for the doctrine of grace, for the word of God, for the gospel of Christ. For this cause, Paul calleth the doctrine of the false apostles, Satan's ministers, a gospel also, saying, "Unto another gospel;" but in derision; as though he would say, Ye Galatians have now other evangelists, and another gospel; my gospel is now despised of you; it is now no more in estimation among you.

Hereby it may be easily gathered, that these false apostles had condemned the gospel of Paul among the Galatians, saying, Paul indeed hath begun well, but to have begun well is not enough, for there remains yet many higher matters; like as they say in the fifteenth chapter of the Acts, "It is not enough for you to believe in Christ, or to be baptized, but it behoveth also that ye be circumcised; for except ye be circumcised after the law of

Moses, ye cannot be saved.' This is as much as to say, as Christ is a good workman, which hath indeed begun a building, but he hath not finished it: for this must Moses do.

So at this day, when the fantastical Anabaptists and others cannot manifestly condemn us, they say, these Lutherans have the spirit of fearfulness, they dare not frankly and freely profess the truth, and go through with it. Indeed, they have laid a foundation, that is to say, they have well taught faith in Christ, but the beginning, the middle, and the end, must be joined together. To bring this to pass, God hath not given it unto them, but hath left it unto us. So these perverse and devilish spirits extol and magnify their cursed doctrine, calling it the word of God, and so, under the colour of God's name, they deceive many. For the devil will not be ugly and black in his ministers, but fair and white; and to the end he may appear to be such a one, he setteth forth and decketh all his words and works with the colour of truth, and with the name of God. Hereof is sprung that common proverb among the Germans, "In God's name beginneth all mischief!"

Wherefore let us learn, that this is a special point of the devil's cunning, that if he cannot hurt by persecuting and destroying, he doth it under a colour of correcting and building up. So now-a-days he persecuteth us with power and sword, that when we are once taken away and dispatched, he may not only deface the gospel, but utterly overthrow it. But hitherto he hath prevailed nothing, for he hath slain many who have constantly confessed this our doctrine to be holy and heavenly, through whose blood the church is not destroyed, but watered. Forasmuch, therefore, as he could prevail nothing that way, he stirreth up wicked spirits and ungodly teachers, which, at the first, allow our doctrine, and teach the same with a common consent together with us; but afterwards they say, that it is our vocation to teach the first principles of Christian doctrine, and that the mysteries of the scriptures are revealed unto them from above, by God himself; and that they are called for this purpose, that they should open them to the world. After this manner doth the devil hinder the course of the gospel, both on the right-hand and on the left, but more on the right-hand (as I said before) by building and correcting, than on the left by persecuting and destroying; wherefore it behoveth us to pray without ceasing, to read the holy scriptures, to cleave fast unto Christ and his holy word, that we may overcome the devil's subtleties, with the which he assaileth us both on the right-hand and on the left. "For we wrestle not against flesh and blood, but against rule, against power, against the worldly governors, the princes of the darkness of this world, against the spiritual wickednesses in heavenly things."

VERSE 7. *Which is not another Gospel, but that there be some which trouble you.*

Here again he excuseth the Galatians, and most bitterly reproveth the false apostles; as though he would say, Ye Galatians are borne in hand, that the gospel, which ye have received of me, is not the true and sincere gospel, and therefore ye think ye do well to receive that new gospel, which the false apostles teach, and seemeth to be better than mine. I do not so much charge you with this fault, as those disturbers which trouble your consciences, and pull you out of my hand. Here you see again how vehement and hot he is against those deceivers, and with what rough and sharp words he painteth them out, calling them troublers of the churches, which do nothing else but seduce and deceive innumerable poor consciences, giving occasions of horrible mischiefs and calamities in the congregations. This great enormity we also at this day are constrained to see, to the great grief of our hearts, and yet are we no more able to remedy it, than Paul was at that time.

This place witnesseth, that those false apostles had reported Paul to be an unperfect apostle, and also a weak and erroneous preacher; therefore he again here calleth them the troublers of the church, and overthrowers of the gospel of Christ. Thus they condemn each other. The false apostles condemned Paul, and Paul again the false apostles. The like contending and condemning is always in the church; especially when the doctrine of the gospel flourisheth; to wit, that wicked teachers do prosecute, condemn, and oppress the godly; and on the other side, that the godly do reprove and condemn the ungodly.

The papists, and the fantastical spirits, do at this day hate us deadly, and condemn our doctrine as wicked and erroneous; yea, moreover, they lie in wait for our goods and lives; and we again do, with a perfect hatred, detest and condemn their cursed and blasphemous doctrine. In the mean time, the miserable people are at no stay, wavering hither and thither, as uncertain and doubtful to which part they may lean, or whom they may safely follow; for it is not given to every one to judge christianly of such weighty matters: but the end will shew which part teacheth truly, and justly condemn the other. Sure it is, that we persecute no man, oppress no man, put no man to death, neither doth our doctrine trouble men's consciences, but delivereth them out of innumerable errors and snares of the devil. For the truth hereof, we have the testimony of many good men who give thanks unto God, for that, by our doctrine, they have received certain and sure consolation to their consciences. Wherefore, like as Paul at that time was not to be blamed that the churches were troubled, but the false apostles, so at this day it is not our fault, but the fault of the Anabaptists, and such frantic spirits, that many and great troubles are in the church.

Mark here diligently, that every teacher of works, and of the righteousness of the law, is a troubler of the church, and of the consciences of men. And who would ever have believed that the Pope, cardinals, bishops, monks, and that whole synagogue of Satan, specially, the founders of those religious orders (of which number, nevertheless, God might save some by miracle) were troublers of men's consciences? Yea, verily, they be yet far worse than were those false apostles; for the false apostles taught, that, besides faith in Christ, the works of the law of God were also necessary to salvation; but the papists, omitting faith, have taught men's traditions and works not commanded of God, but devised by themselves without and against the word of God: and these have they not only made equal with the word of God, but also exalted them far above it. But the more holy the heretics seem to be in outward shew, so much the more mischief they do; for if the false apostles had not been endued with notable gifts, with great authority, and a shew of holiness, and had not vaunted themselves to be Christ's ministers, the apostles' disciples, and sincere preachers of the gospel, they could not so easily have defaced Paul's authority, and led the Galatians out of the way.

Now, the cause why he setteth himself so sharply against them, calling them the troublers of the churches, is for that besides faith in Christ, they taught that circumcision, and the keeping of the law, was necessary to salvation. The which thing Paul himself witnesseth in the fifth chapter following; and Luke, in the fifteenth of Acts, declareth the same thing in these words, "That certain men coming down from Judea, taught the brethren, saying, Except ye be circumcised after the custom of Moses, ye cannot be saved," (Acts xv, 1). Wherefore, the false apostles most earnestly and obstinately contended that the law ought to be observed; unto whom the stiff-necked Jews forthwith joined themselves, and so afterwards easily persuaded such as were not established in the faith, that Paul was not a sincere teacher, because he regarded not the law, but preached such a doctrine as did abolish and overthrow the law. For it seemed unto them a very strange thing, that the law of God should utterly be taken away, and the Jews, which had always until that time been counted the people of God, to whom also the promises were made, should now be rejected: yea, it seemed yet a more strange thing unto them, that the Gentiles, being wicked idolaters, should attain to this glory and dignity, to be the people of God without circumcision, and without the works of the law, by grace only, and faith in Christ.

These things had the false apostles amplified and set forth to the uttermost, that they might bring Paul into more hatred among the Galatians. And to the end that they might set them the more shaply against him, they said, that he preached unto the Gentiles freedom from the law, to bring into contempt, yea, and utterly to abolish the law of God and the kingdom of the Jews, contrary to the law of God, contrary to the custom of the Jewish nation, contrary to the example of the apostles, and to be short, contrary to his own example; whereof, he was to be shunned as an open blasphemer against God, and a rebel against the whole commonweal of the Jews, saying, that they themselves ought rather to be heard, who, besides that they preached the gospel rightly, were also the very disciples of the apostles, with whom Paul was never conversant. By this policy, they defamed and defaced Paul among the Galatians, so that by this their perverse dealing, of very necessity, Paul was compelled with all his might to set himself against these false apostles, whom he boldly reproveth and condemneth, saying, that they are the troublers of the churches, and overthrowers of Christ's gospel, as followeth.

VERSE 7. *And intend to pervert the gospel of Christ.*

That is to say, they do not only go about to trouble you, but also utterly to abolish and overthrow Christ's gospel. For these two things the devil practiseth most busily: first, he is not content to trouble and deceive many by his false apostles, but moreover, he laboureth by them utterly to overthrow the gospel, and never resteth till he hath brought it to pass. Yet such perverters of the gospel can abide nothing less than to hear that they are the apostles of the devil; nay, rather they glory above others in the name of Christ, and boast themselves to be the most sincere preachers of the gospel. But because they mingle the law with the gospel, they must needs be perverters of the gospel. For either Christ must remain, and the law perish, or the law must remain, and Christ perish; for Christ and the law can by no means agree and reign together in the conscience. —Where the righteousness of the law ruleth, there cannot the righteousness of grace rule; and again, where the righteousness of grace reigneth, there cannot the righteousness of the law reign; for one of them must needs give place unto the other. And if thou canst not believe that God will forgive thy sins for Christ's sake, whom he sent into the world to be our high priest: how then, I pray thee, wilt thou believe that he will forgive the same for the works of the law, which thou couldst never perform; or for thine own works, which (as thou must be constrained to confess) be such as it is impossible for them to countervail the judgment of God?

Wherefore, the doctrine of grace can by no means stand with the doctrine of the law. The one must simply be refused and abolished, and the other confirmed and established. For as Paul saith here, to mingle the one with the other, is to overthrow the gospel of Christ. And yet, if it come to debating, the greater part overcometh the better; for Christ, with his side is weak, and the gospel is but a foolish preaching; contrariwise, the kingdom of the world, and the devil, the prince thereof, are strong. Besides that, the wisdom and righteousness of the flesh carry a goodly shew; and by this means the righteousness of grace and faith is lost, and the other righteousness of the law and works advanced and maintained. But this is our comfort, that the devil, with all his limbs, cannot do what he would. He may trouble many, but he cannot overthrow Christ's gospel. The truth may be assailed, but vanquished it cannot be; for the word of the Lord endureth forever.

It seemeth to be a light matter to mingle the law and the gospel, faith and works, together; but it doth more mischief than a man's reason can conceive; for it doth not only blemish and darken the knowledge of grace, but it also taketh away Christ, with all his benefits, and it utterly overthroweth the gospel, as Paul saith in this place. The cause of this great evil is our flesh, which, being plunged in sins, seeth no way how to get out, but by works, and therefore it would live in the righteousness of the law, and rest in the trust and confidence of her own works. Wherefore, it is utterly ignorant of the doctrine of faith and grace, without the which, notwithstanding, it is impossible for the conscience to find rest and quietness.

It appeareth also by these words of Paul: "And intend to pervert the gospel of Christ," that the false apostles were exceeding bold and shameless, which with all their might set themselves against Paul; wherefore he again, using his spirit of zeal and fervency, and being fully persuaded of the certainty of his calling, setteth himself strongly against them, and wonderfully magnifieth his ministry, saying,

EPISTLE TO THE GALATIANS

VERSE 8. *But though that we, or an angel from heaven preach unto you otherwise than that we have preached unto you, let him be accursed.*

Here Paul casteth out very flames of fire, and his zeal is so fervent, that he beginneth also almost to curse the angels. Although, saith he, that we ourselves, even I and my brethren Timothy and Titus, and as many as teach Christ purely with me (I speak not now of those seducers of consciences;) "yea, or if an angel from heaven preach unto you," etc., notwithstanding I would rather, that I myself, my brethren, yea, and the very angels from heaven also, should be holden accursed, than that my gospel should be overthrown. This is indeed a vehement zeal, that he dare so boldly curse, not only himself, and his brethren, but also even an angel from heaven.

The Greek word *anathema*, in Hebrew *herem*, signifieth a thing accursed, execrable, and detestable, which hath nothing to do, no participation, or communion with God. So saith Joshua: "Cursed be the man before the Lord, that raiseth up and buildeth this city Jericho," (Joshua vi, 26). And in the last of Leviticus it is written: "Nothing separate from the common use, which shall be separate from man, shall be redeemed, but die the death, whether it be man or beast." So God had appointed Amaleck, and certain other cities, accursed by God's own sentence, should be utterly rased and destroyed. This is then the mind of Paul: "I had rather that myself, and other my brethren, yea, and an angel from heaven, should be accursed, than that we or others should preach any other gospel than that we have preached already." So Paul first curseth himself; for cunning artificers are wont first to find fault with themselves, that they may the more freely and sharply afterwards reprove others.

Paul therefore concludeth, that there is no other gospel besides that which he himself had preached. But he preached not a gospel which he had himself devised, but the same which God promised before by his prophets in the holy scriptures, (Romans i) therefore he pronounceth himself and others, yea, even an angel from heaven, to be undoubtedly accursed, if they teach any thing contrary to the former gospel: for the voice of the gospel once sent forth, shall not be called back again till the day of judgment.

VERSE 9. *As we said before, so say we now again, if any man preach unto you otherwise than that you have received, let him be accursed.*

He repeateth the self-same thing, only changing the persons. Before he cursed himself, his brethren, and an angel from heaven, here if there be any (saith he) besides us, which preach unto you any other gospel than that ye have received of us, let them also be accursed. Therefore, he plainly excommunicateth and curseth all teachers in general, himself, his brethren, an angel, and moreover all others whatsoever, namely, all those false teachers his adversaries. Here appeareth an exceeding great fervency of spirit in the apostle, that he dare curse all teachers throughout the whole world and in heaven, which pervert his gospel and teach any other: for all men must either believe that gospel that Paul preached, or else they must be accursed and condemned. Would to God this terrible sentence of the apostle might strike a fear into their hearts that seek to pervert the gospel of Paul; of which sort, at this day, (the more it is to be lamented) the world is full.

This changing of persons is here to be marked. For Paul speaketh otherwise in his first cursing, than he doth in the second. In the first he saith: "If we, or an angel from heaven, preach unto you any other gospel than that we have preached unto you;" in the second, "Than that ye have received." And this he doth of purpose, lest the Galatians should say, We, O Paul, do not pervert the gospel that thou hast preached unto us: we understood thee not rightly, but the teachers that came after thee have declared unto us the true meaning thereof. This (saith he) will I in no case admit. They ought to add nothing, neither to correct it; but that which ye heard of me is the sincere word of God: let this only remain. Neither do I desire myself to be another manner of teacher than I was, nor you other disciples. Wherefore, if ye hear any man bringing any other gospel than that ye have heard of me, or bragging that he will deliver better things than ye have received of me, let him and his disciples be both accursed.

The first two chapters, in a manner, contain nothing else but defences of his doctrine, and confutations of errors, so that, until he cometh to the end of the second chapter, he toucheth not the chiefest matter which he handleth in this epistle, namely, the article of justification. Notwithstanding, this sentence of Paul ought to admonish us, that so many as think the Pope to be the judge of the scripture, are accursed: which thing the popish schoolmen have wickedly taught, standing upon this ground: The church hath allowed four gospels only, therefore there are but four; for if it had allowed more, there had been more. Now, seeing the church might receive and allow such and so many gospels as it would, therefore the church is above the gospel. A goodly argument, forsooth.—I approve the scripture, *ergo*, I am above the scripture. John Baptist acknowledgeth and confesseth Christ, and pointeth to him with his finger, therefore he is above Christ! The church approveth the Christian faith and doctrine, therefore the church is above them! For the overthrowing of this their wicked and blasphemous doctrine, thou hast here a plain text like a thunderbolt, wherein Paul subjected both himself and an angel from heaven, and doctors upon earth, and all other teachers and masters whatsoever, under the authority of the scripture; for they ought not to be masters, judges, or arbiters, but only witnesses, disciples, and confessors, of the church, whether it be the Pope, Luther, Augustine, Paul, or an angel from heaven. Neither ought any doctrine to be taught or heard in the church besides the pure word of God, that is to say, the holy scripture; otherwise accursed be both the teachers and hearers together with their doctrine.

VERSE 10. *For now preach I man's doctrine, or God's?*

These words are spoken with the same vehemency of spirit that the former were; as if he would say, Am I, Paul, so unknown amongst you, which have preached so openly in your churches? Are my bitter conflicts, and so many sharp battles against the Jews, yet unknown unto you? It appeareth (I think) sufficiently unto you by my preaching and by so many and so great afflictions which I have suffered, whether I serve men or God; for all men see that by this my preaching, I have not only stirred up persecution against me in every place, but have also procured the cruel hatred both of mine own nation, and of all other men. I shew, therefore, plainly enough, that I seek not by my preaching, the favour or praise of men, but to set forth the benefit and glory of God.

Neither do we seek the favour of men by our doctrine: for we teach that all men are wicked by nature, and the children of wrath. We condemn man's free-will, his strength, wisdom, and righteousness, and all religion of man's own devising; and to be short, we say that there is nothing in us that is able to deserve grace, and the forgiveness of sins; but we preach, that we obtain this grace by the free mercy of God only, for Christ's sake: for so the heavens shew forth the glory of God, and his works, condemning all men generally with their works, (Eph. ii, 3). This is not to preach for the favour of men, and of the world; for the world can abide nothing less than to hear his wisdom, righteousness, religion, and power, condemned; and to speak against those mighty and glorious gifts of the world, is not to flatter the world, but rather to procure hatred and indignation of the world (Ps. xix, 1), for if we speak against men, or any thing else that pertaineth to their glory, it cannot be but that cruel hatred, persecutions, excommunications, murders, and condemnations, must needs follow.

If then (saith Paul) they see other matters, why see they not this also, that I teach the things that are of God, and not of men? that is to say, that I seek no man's favour by my doctrine, but I sent out God's mercy, offered unto us in Christ; for if I sought the favour of men I would not condemn their works. Now, forasmuch as I condemn men's works, that is to say, because I shew God's judgment out of his word (whereof I am a minister) against all men, how that they are sinners, unrighteous, wicked, children of wrath, bond-slaves of the devil, and damned, and that they are not made righteous by works or by circumcision, but by grace only, and faith in Christ; therefore I procure unto myself the deadly hate of men; for they can abide nothing less than to hear that they are such; nay, rather, they would be praised for wise, righteous and holy. Wherefore this witnesseth sufficiently, that I teach not man's doctrine. After the same manner Christ speaketh also in the seventh of John: "The world cannot hate you, but me it hateth, because I testify of it that the works thereof are evil," (John vii, 7). And in the third of John, "This is condemnation, that light is come into the world, and men loved darkness more than light because their works are evil," (John iii, 19).

Now, that I teach the things which are of God, saith the apostle, hereby it may sufficiently appear, that I preach the only grace, the mercy, the goodness and the glory of God. Moreover, he that speaketh, as Christ saith, those things which his Lord and Master hath commanded him, and glorifieth not himself, but him whose messenger he is, bringeth and teacheth the true word of God. But I teach those things only which are commanded me from above: neither glorify I myself, but him that sent me. Besides that, I stir up against myself the wrath and indignation of both the Jews and Gentiles: therefore my doctrine is true, sincere, certain, and of God, neither can there be any other, much less any better, than this my doctrine is. Wherefore, whatsoever doctrine else teacheth not as mine doth, that all men are sinners, and are justified by faith only in Christ, must needs be false, wicked, blasphemous, accursed and devilish; and even such also are they which either teach it or receive it.

So we with Paul do boldly pronounce all such doctrine to be accursed as agreeth not with ours. For neither do we speak by

EPISTLE TO THE GALATIANS

our preaching the praise of men, or the favour of princes or bishops, but the favour of God alone, whose only grace and mercy we preach, despising and treading under foot whatsoever is of ourselves. Whosoever he be then which shall teach any other gospel, or that which is contrary to ours, let us be bold to say, that he is sent of the devil, and hold him accursed.

VERSE 10. *Or go I about to please men?*

That is, do I serve men or God? he hath always a glance at the false apostles. These, saith he, must needs seek to please and to flatter men; for by this means they seek, that they again may glory in their flesh.—Moreover, because they will not bear the hatred and persecution of men, they teach circumcision, only to avoid the persecution of the cross, as followeth in the fifth chapter.

So at this day, ye may find many which seek to please men, and to the end they may live in peace and security of the flesh, they teach the things which are of men, that is to say, wicked things, or else they allow the blasphemies and wicked judgments of the adversaries, contrary to the word of God, against their own conscience, that they may keep still the favour of princes and bishops, and enjoy their goods. But we, because we endeavour to please God and not men, do stir up against us the malice of the devil, and hell itself; we suffer the reproaches and slanders of the world, death, and all the mischiefs that can be devised against us.

So saith Paul here: "I seek not to please men," that they may praise my doctrine, and report me to be an excellent teacher, but I desire only that my doctrine may please God: and by this means I make men my mortal enemies. Which thing I find by experience to be most true: for they requite me with infamy, slander, imprisonment, and the sword. Contrariwise the false apostles teach the things that are of men, that is to say, such things as be pleasant and plausible to man's reason, and that to the end they may live in ease, and purchase the favour, good-will, and praise of the people. And such men find that they seek for: for they are praised and magnified of men. So saith Christ also (Matt. vi), "That hypocrites do all things to be praised of men." And in the fifth of John he sharply reproveth such; "How can ye believe," saith he, "which receive honour one of another, and seek not the honour that cometh of God alone?" The things which Paul hath hitherto taught, are in a manner examples only. In the mean time, notwithstanding, he is very earnest everywhere in proving his doctrine to be sincere and sound.—Therefore he exhorteth the Galatians that they forsake it not for any other doctrine.

VERSE 10. *For if I should yet please men, I were not the servant of God.*

These things are to be referred to the whole office and ministry of Paul, to show what a contrariety there was between his conversation before in the Jewish law, and his conversation now under the gospel. As if he would say, do ye think that I go about still to please men, as I did in times past? So he speaketh afterwards in the fifth chapter: "If I yet preach circumcision, why do I suffer persecution? As though he would say, do ye not see and hear of my daily conflicts, great persecutions, and afflictions? After I was converted and called to the office of apostleship, I never taught man's doctrine, neither sought I to please men, but God alone. That is to say, I seek not by my ministry and doctrine the praise and favour of men, but of God.

Here again is to be marked, how maliciously and craftily the false apostles went about to bring Paul into hatred among the Galatians. They picked out of his preachings and writings certain contradictions (as our adversaries at this day do out of our books) and by this means they would have convinced him that he had taught contrary things. Wherefore they said, that there was no credit to be given unto him: but that circumcision and the law ought to be kept: which thing he himself also by his example had allowed, because he had circumcised Timothy according to the law, had purified himself with other four men in the temple at Jerusalem, and had shaven his head at Cenchrea (Acts xvi, 3; xviii, 18). These things they craftily surmised that Paul by the commandment and authority of the apostles was constrained to do: which nothwithstanding he had kept as indifferent, bearing with the infirmity of the weak brethren (which yet understood not the Christian liberty) lest they should be offended. To whose cavillations thus he answereth: how true it is which the false apostles forge against me for the overthrowing of my gospel, and setting up of the law and circumcision again, the matter itself sufficiently declareth. For if I would preach the law and circumcision, and commend the strength, the power, and the will of man, I should not be so odious unto them, but should please them.

VERSES 11 AND 12. *Now I certify you brethren, that the gospel which was preached of me, was not after man. For neither received I it of man, neither was I taught it but by the revelation of Jesus Christ.*

Here is the principal point of this matter: which containeth a confutation of his adversaries, and a defence of his doctrine, to the end of the second chapter. Upon this he standeth, this he urgeth and with an oath confirmeth, that he learned not his gospel of a man, but received it by the revelation of Jesus Christ. And in that he sweareth, he is constrained so to do, that the Galatians may believe him, and also, that they should give no ear to the false apostles: whom he reproveth as liars, because they had said, that he learned and received his gospel of the apostles.

Where he saith that his gospel is not after man, he meaneth not that his gospel is not earthly, for that is manifest of itself: and the false apostles bragged also that their doctrine was not earthly but heavenly: but he meaneth, that he learned not his gospel by the ministry of men, or received it by any earthly means, as we all learn it either by the ministry of men, or else receive it by some earthly means; some by hearing, some by reading, and some by writing: but he received the same only by the revelation of Jesus Christ. If any man list to make any other distinction, I am not against it. Here the apostle sheweth by the way, that Christ is not only man, but that he is both God and very man, when he saith, that he received not his gospel by man.

Now, Paul received his gospel in the way as he was going to Damascus, where Christ appeared unto him and talked with him. Afterwards also he talked with him in the temple at Jerusalem. But he received his gospel in the way, as Luke reciteth the story in the ninth of the Acts. "Arise," saith Christ, "and go into the city, and it shall be told thee what thou must do." He doth not bid him go into the city, that he might learn the gospel of Ananias: but Ananias was bid to go and baptize him, to lay his hands upon him, to commit the ministry of the word unto him, and to commend him unto the church, and not to teach him the gospel, which he had received afore, as he glorieth in the same place, by the only revelation of Jesus Christ. And this Ananias himself confesseth, saying, "Brother Saul, the Lord which appeared to thee in the way, hath sent me, that thou mightest receive thy sight." Therefore he received not his doctrine of Ananias, but being already called, lightened and taught of Christ in the way, he was sent to Ananias, that he might also have the testimony of men, that he was called of God to preach the gospel of Christ.

This Paul was constrained to recite, to put away the slander of the false apostles, who laboured to bring him into hatred with the Galatians, saying that Paul was inferior to the rest of the apostles' scholars, who had received of the apostles that which they taught and kept; whose conversation also they had seen a long time, and that Paul himself had also received the same things of them, although he did now deny it. Why, then, would they rather obey an inferior, and despise the authority of the apostles themselves, who were not only the fore-elders and teachers of the Galatians, but also of all the churches throughout the whole world?

This argument, which the same apostles grounded upon the authority of the apostles, was strong and mighty, whereby the Galatians were suddenly overthrown, especially in this matter. I would never have believed, had I not been taught by these examples of the churches of Galatia, of the Corinthians and others, that they which had received the word of God in the beginning with such joy, among whom were many notable men, could so quickly be overthrown. O good Lord, what horrible and infinite mischiefs may one only argument easily bring! which so pierceth a man's conscience, when God withdraweth his grace, that in one moment he loseth all together. By this subtilty then the false apostles did easily deceive the Galatians, being not fully established and grounded, but as yet weak in the faith.

Moreover, the matter of justification is brittle: not of itself, for of itself it is most sure and certain, but in respect of us. Whereof I myself have good experience. For I know in what hours of darkness I sometimes wrestle. I know how often I suddenly lose the beams of the gospel and grace, as being shadowed from me with thick and dark clouds. Briefly I know in what a slippery place even such also do stand, as are well exercised and seem to have sure footing in matters of faith. We have good experience of this matter: for we are able to teach it unto others, and this is a sure token that we understand it. But when in the very conflict we should use the gospel, which is the word of grace, consolation, and life, there doth the law, the word of wrath, heaviness and death prevent the gospel, and beginneth to rage, and the terrors which it raiseth up in the conscience, are no less than was that horrible shew in the mount Sinai. So that even one place of the Scripture containing some threatening of the law (Exod. xix, 18) overwhelmeth and drowneth all consolations besides, and so shaketh all our inward powers, that it maketh us to forget justification, grace, Christ, the gospel, and all together.

Therefore, in respect of us, it is a very brittle matter, because we are brittle. Again, we have against us even the one half of ourselves: that is to say, reason, and all the powers thereof. Besides all this, the flesh resisteth the spirit, which cannot believe assuredly that the promises of God are true. It fighteth therefore against the spirit, and as Paul saith, "it holdeth the spirit captive" (Gal. v, 17; Rom. vii, 23), so that it cannot believe so stedfastly as it would. Wherefore, we teach continually, that the knowledge of Christ, and of faith, is no work of man, but simply the gift of God, who as he createth faith, so doth he keep it in us. And even as he first giveth faith unto us through the word, so afterwards he exerciseth, increaseth, strengtheneth and maketh perfect the same in us by the word. Therefore the greatest service that a man can do unto God, and the very sabbath of sabbaths, is, to exercise himself in true godliness, diligently to hear and to read the word. Contrariwise, there is nothing more dangerous than to be weary of the word. He therefore that is so cold, that he thinketh himself to know enough, and beginneth by little and little to loathe the word, that man hath lost Christ and the gospel, and that which he "thinketh himself to know," he attaineth only by bare speculation: and he is like unto a man, as St. James saith, "who beholding his face in a glass, goeth his way, and by-and-by forgetteth what his countenance was," (James i, 23, 24).

Wherefore let every faithful man labour and strive with all diligence to learn and to keep this doctrine: and to that end, let him use humble and hearty prayer, with continual study and meditation of the word.—And when we have done never so much, yet shall we have enough to keep us occupied. For we have to do with no small enemies, but strong and mighty, and such as are in continual war against us, namely, our own flesh, all the dangers of the world, the law, sin, death, the wrath and judgment of God, and the devil himself, who never ceaseth to tempt us inwardly by his fiery darts, and outwardly by his false apostles, to the end that he may overthrow, if not all, yet the most part of us.

This argument therefore of the false apostles had a goodly shew, and seemed to be very strong. Which also at this day prevaileth with many, namely, that the apostles, the holy fathers and their successors have so taught: that the church so thinketh and believeth. Moreover that it is impossible that Christ should suffer his church so long a time to err. Art thou alone, say they, wiser than so many holy men? wiser than the whole church? After this manner, the devil being changed into an angel of light, setteth upon us craftily at this day, by certain pestiferous hypocrites, who say, we pass not for the Pope, we abhor the hypocrisy of monks, and such like; but we would have the authority of the holy church to remain untouched. the church hath thus believed, and taught, this long time. So have all the doctors of the primitive church, holy men, more ancient and better learned than thou. Who art thou, that darest dissent from all these, and bring unto us a contrary doctrine? When Satan reasoneth thus, conspiring with the flesh and reason, then is thy conscience terrified and utterly despaireth, unless thou constantly return to thyself again, and say, whether it be Cyprian, Ambrose, Augustine, either St. Peter, Paul, or John, yea, or an angel from heaven, that teacheth otherwise, yet this I know assuredly, that I teach not the things of men, but of God: that is to say, I attribute all things to God alone, and nothing to man.

When I first took upon me the defence of the gospel, I remember that Doctor Staupitius, a worthy man, said thus unto me: "This liketh me well, that this doctrine which thou preachest, yieldeth glory, and all things else unto God alone, and nothing unto man; for unto God there cannot be attributed too much glory, goodness, mercy," etc. This saying did then greatly comfort and confirm me. And true it is, that the doctrine of the gospel taketh from men all glory, wisdom, righteousness, etc., and giveth the same to the Creator alone, who made all things of nothing (Matt. vi, 12). We may also more safely attribute too much unto God, than unto man: for in this case I may say boldly: be it so, that the church, Augustine and other doctors, also Peter and Apollo, yea, even an angel from heaven, teach a contrary doctrine, yet my doctrine is such, that it setteth forth and preacheth the grace and glory of God alone, and in the matter of salvation, it condemneth the righteousness and wisdom of all men. In this I cannot offend, because I give both to God and man, that which properly and truly belongeth unto them both.

But thou wilt say, the church is holy, the fathers are holy. it is true, notwithstanding, albeit the church be holy, yet is it compelled to pray: "forgive us our trespasses." So, though the fathers be holy, yet are they saved through the forgiveness of sins. Therefore neither am I to be believed, nor the church, nor the fathers, nor the apostles, no, nor an angel from heaven, if we teach anything against the word of God; but let the word of God abide forever; for else this argument of the false apostles had mightily prevailed against Paul's doctrine. For indeed it was a great matter, a great matter, I say, to set before the Galatians the whole church, with all the company of the apostles, against Paul alone, but lately sprung up, and of small authority. This was therefore a strong argument, and concluded mightily. For no man saith willingly, that the church erreth, and yet it is necessary to say that it erreth, if it teach anything besides or against God's word.

Peter, the chief of the apostles, taught, both in life and doctrine, besides God's word, therefore he erred, and was deceived. Neither did Paul dissemble that error, although it seemed to be but a light fault, because he saw it would turn to the hurt of the whole church, but "withstood him even to his face, because he walked not after the truth of the gospel," (Gal. ii, 11). Therefore neither is the church, nor Peter, nor the apostles, nor angels from heaven, to be heard, unless they bring and teach the pure word of God.

This argument, even at this day, is not a little prejudicial to our cause. For if we may neither believe the Pope, nor the fathers, nor Luther, nor any other, except they teach us the pure word of God, whom shall we then believe? who, in the meanwhile, shall certify our adversaries? for they brag that they also have the pure word of God, and teach it. Again, we believe not the Papists, because they teach not the word of God, neither can they teach it. Contrariwise, they hate us most bitterly, and persecute us as most pestilent heretics and seducers of the people. What is to be done in this case? Shall it be lawful for every fantastical spirit to teach what himself listeth, seeing the world can neither hear or abide our doctrine? For although we glory with Paul, that we teach the pure gospel of Christ, yet we profit nothing, but are compelled to hear, that this our glorying is not only vain, rash, and arrogant, but also devilish and full of blasphemy. But if we abase ourselves, and give place to the rage of our adversaries, then both the Papists and Anabaptists wax proud. The Anabaptists will vaunt that they bring and teach some strange thing which the world never heard of before. The Papists will set up again, and establish their old abominations. Let every man therefore take heed, that he be more sure of his calling and doctrine, that he may boldly say with Paul: "Although we, or an angel from heaven, preach unto you otherwise than that we have preached unto you, let him be accursed" (Gal. i, 8).

> VERSE 13. *For ye have heard of my conversation in times past, in Jewish religion, how that I persecuted the church of God extremely, and wasted it; and profited in the Jewish religion, above many of my companions of mine own nation.*

This place hath in it no singular doctrine. Notwithstanding, Paul allegeth here his own example, saying, I have defended the traditions of the Pharisees, and the Jewish religion, more constantly than ye, and all your false teachers. Wherefore, if the righteousness of the law had been anything worth, I had not turned back from it: in the keeping whereof, notwithstanding, before I knew Christ, I did so exercise myself, and so profit therein, that I excelled many of my companions of mine own nation. Moreover, I was so zealous in defence of the same, that I persecuted the church of God extremely, and wasted it. For having received authority of the high priests, I put many in prison (Acts xxvi, 10), and when they should be put to death, I pronounced the sentence, and punished them throughout all the synagogues. I compelled them to blaspheme, and was so exceeding mad upon them, that I persecuted them even unto strange cities.

> VERSE 14. *And was much more zealous of the traditions of my fathers.*

He calleth not here the traditions of the fathers, pharisaical or human traditions: for in this place he treateth not of the pharisaical traditions, but of a far higher matter, and therefore he calleth even that holy law of Moses, the fathers' traditions: that is to say, received and left as an inheritance from the fathers. For these, said he, "when I was in the Jewish religion, I was very zealous." He speaketh after the same manner to the Philippians (chap. iii, 6). "As concerning the law," saith he, "I was a Pharisee, concerning zeal, I persecuted the church, and as concerning the righteousness of the law, I was unrebukeable." As though he would say: Here I may glory, and may compare with the whole nation of the Jews, yea, even with the best and holiest of all those who are of the circumcision: let them shew me, if they can, a more zealous and earnest defender of Moses' law, than I have been. This thing (O ye Galatians) ought to have persuaded you not to believe these deceivers, which magnify the righteousness of the law, as a matter of great importance: whereas, if there were any cause to glory in the righteousness of the law, I have more cause to glory than any other.

In like manner say I of myself, that before I was lightened with the knowledge of the gospel, I was as zealous for the papistical laws and traditions of the fathers, as ever any was, most earnestly maintaining and defending them as holy and necessary to salvation. Moreover, I endeavoured to observe and keep them myself, as much as was possible for me to do; punishing my poor body with fasting, watching, praying, and other exercises, more than all they which at this day do so bitterly hate and persecute me, because now I take from them the glory of justifying by works and merits. For I was so diligent and superstitious in the observation hereof, that I laid more upon my body, than, without danger of health, it was able to bear. I honoured the Pope of mere conscience, and unfeignedly, not seeking after prebends, promotions, and livings: but whatsoever I did, I did it with a single heart, of a good zeal, and for the glory of God. But those things which then were gainful unto me, now with Paul, I count to be but loss for the excellency of the knowledge of Jesus Christ my Lord. But our adversaries, as idle bellies, and tried with no temptations, believe not that I and many others have endured such things: I speak of such, as with great desire sought for peace and quietness of conscience, which notwithstanding in so great darkness it was not possible for them to find.

> VERSES 15, 16, AND 17. *But when it had pleased God, (which had separated me from my mother's womb, and called me by his grace) to reveal his Son in me, that I should preach him among the Gentiles, immediately I communicated not with flesh and blood. Neither came I again to Jerusalem, to them which were apostles before me, but I went into Arabia, and turned again unto Damascus.*

This is the first journey of Paul. And here he witnesseth, that straightway, after he was called by the grace of God, to preach Christ among the Gentiles, he went unto Arabia, without the advice of any man, to that work whereunto he was called. And this place witnesseth by whom he was taught, and by what means he came to the knowledge of the gospel, and to his apostleship. "When it had pleased God," saith he. As if he would say: I have not deserved it, because I was zealous of the law of God without judgment, nay rather, this foolish and wicked zeal stirred me up, that, God so permitting, I fell headlong into more abominable and outrageous sins; I persecuted the church of God, I was an enemy to Christ, I blasphemed his gospel, and to conclude, I was the author of shedding much innocent blood. This was my desert. In the midst of this cruel rage, I was called to such inestimable grace. What! was it because of this outrageous cruelty? No, forsooth. But the abundant grace of God, who calleth, and sheweth mercy to whom he will, pardoned and forgave me all those blasphemies: and for these my horrible sins, which then I thought to be perfect righteousness, and an acceptable service unto God, he gave unto me his grace, the knowledge of his truth, and called me to be an apostle.

We also are come at this day, to the knowledge of grace by the self-same merits. I crucified Christ daily in my monkish life, and blasphemed God through my false faith, wherein I then continually lived. Outwardly I was not as other men, extortioners, unjust, whoremongers: but I kept chastity, poverty, and obedience. Moreover, I was free from the cares of this present life. I was only given to fasting, watching, praying, saying of masses, and such like. Notwithstanding, in the mean time, I fostered under this cloaked holiness, and trust in mine own righteousness, continual mistrust, doubtfulness, fear, hatred, and blasphemy against God. And this my righteousness was nothing else but a filthy puddle, and the very kingdom of the devil. For Satan loveth such saints, and accounteth them for his dear darlings, who destroy their own bodies and souls, and deprive themselves of all the blessings of God's gifts. In the mean time, notwithstanding, wickedness, blindness, contempt of God, ignorance of the gospel, profanation of the sacraments, blaspheming and treading of Christ under foot, and the abuse of all the benefits and gifts of God, do reign in them at the full. To conclude, such saints are the bond-slaves of Satan, and therefore are driven to speak, think, and do whatsoever he will, although outwardly they seem to excel all others in good works, in holiness and strictness of life.

Such we were under the popedom: verily no less, if not more contumelious and blasphemous against Christ and his gospel, than Paul himself, and specially I: for I did so highly esteem the Pope's authority, that to dissent from him, even in the least point, I thought it a sin worthy of everlasting death. And that wicked opinion caused me to think that John Huss was a cursed heretic, yea, and I accounted it a heinous offence, but once to think of him, and I would myself, in defence of the Pope's authority, have ministered fire and sword, for the burning and destroying of that heretic, and thought it a high service unto God so to do. Wherefore if you compare publicans and harlots with these holy hypocrites, they are not evil. For they, when they offend, have remorse of conscience, and do not justify their wicked doings; but these men are so far from acknowledging their abominations, idolatries, wicked will-worshippings and ceremonies, to be sins, that they affirm the same to be righteousness, and a most acceptable sacrifice unto God, yea, they adore them as matters of singular holiness, and through them, do promise salvation unto others, and also sell them for money, as things available to salvation.

This is then our goodly righteousness, this is our high merit, which bringeth unto us the knowledge of grace; to wit, that we have so deadly and so devilishly persecuted, blasphemed, trodden under foot, and condemned God, Christ, the gospel, faith, the sacraments, all godly men, the true worship of God, and have taught and stablished quite contrary things. And the more holy we were, the more were we blinded, and the more did we worship the devil. There was not one of us, but he was a bloodsucker, if not in deed, yet in heart.

VERSE 15. *When it pleased God.*

As though he would say: It is the alone and inestimable favour of God, that not only he hath spared me, so wicked and so cursed a wretch, such a blasphemer, a persecutor, and a rebel against God, but besides that, hath also given unto me the knowledge of salvation, his Spirit, Christ his Son, the office of an apostle, and everlasting life. So God beholding us guilty in the like sins, hath not only pardoned our impieties and blasphemies of his mere mercy for Christ's sake, but hath also overwhelmed us with great benefits and spiritual gifts. But many of us are not only unthankful unto God for this his inestimable grace, and, as it is written (2 Peter i), do forget the cleansing of their old sins, but also opening again a window to the devil, they begin to loathe his word, and many also do pervert and corrupt it, and so become authors of new errors. "The ends of these men are worse than the beginnings," (Matt. xii, 45).

VERSE 15. *Which had separated me from my mother's womb.*

This is a Hebrew phrase. As if he said: which had sanctified, ordained, and prepared me. That is, God had appointed, when I was yet in my mother's womb, that I should so rage against his church, and that afterwards he would mercifully call me back again from the midst of my cruelty and blasphemy, by his mere grace into the way of truth and salvation. To be short, when I was not yet born, I was an apostle in the sight of God, and when the time was come, I was declared an apostle before the whole world.

Thus Paul cutteth off all deserts, and giveth glory to God alone, but to himself all shame and confusion. As though he would say: all the gifts both small and great, as well spiritual as corporal, which God purposed to give unto me, and all the good things which at any time in all my life I should do, God himself had before appointed when I was yet in my mother's womb, where I could neither wish, think, nor do any good thing. Therefore this gift also came unto me by the mere predestination and free mercy of God before I was yet born. Moreover, after I was born, he supported me, being loaded with innumerable and most horrible iniquities. And that he might the more manifestly declare the unspeakable and inestimable greatness of his mercy towards me, he of his mere grace forgave my abominable and infinite sins, and moreover replenished me with such plenty of his grace, that I did not only know what things are given unto us in Christ, but preached the same also unto others. Such are the deserts and merits of all men, and especially of those old dotards, who exercise themselves wholly in the stinking puddles of man's own righteousness.

VERSE 15. *And called me by his grace.*

Mark the diligence of the apostle. "He called me," saith he, How? Was it for my pharisaical religion, or for my blameless and holy life? For my prayers, fastings, and works? No. Much less then for my blasphemies, persecutions, oppressions. How then? By his mere grace alone.

VERSE 16. *To reveal his Son in me.*

You hear in this place, what manner of doctrine is given and committed to Paul: to wit, the doctrine of the gospel, which is the revelation of the Son of God. This is a doctrine quite contrary to the law, which revealeth not the Son of God, but it sheweth forth sin, it terrifieth the conscience, it revealeth death, the wrath and judgment of God, and hell. The gospel therefore is such a doctrine, as admitted no law: yea, it must be separate as far from the law, as there is distance between heaven and earth. This difference in itself is easy and plain, but unto us it is hard and full of difficulty. For it is an easy matter to say, that the gospel is nothing else but the revealing of the Son of God, or the knowledge of Jesus Christ, and not the revealing of the law. But in the agony and conflict of conscience, to hold this fast, and to practise it in deed, it is a hard matter, yea, and to them also that be most exercised therein.

Now, if the gospel be the revealing of the Son of God, as Paul defineth it in this place, then surely it accuseth not, it feareth not the consequence, it threateneth not death, it bringeth not to despair, as the law doth: but it is a doctrine concerning Christ, which is neither law nor work, but our righteousness, wisdom, sanctification, and redemption, (1 Cor. i, 30). Although this thing be more clear than the sun-light, yet notwithstanding the madness and blindness of the Papists hath been so great, that of the gospel they have made a law of charity, and of Christ a lawmaker, giving more strait and heavy commandments than Moses himself. But the gospel teacheth, that Christ came not to set forth a new law, and to give commandments as touching manners: but that he came to this end, that he might be made an oblation for the sins of the whole world, and that our sins might be forgiven, and everlasting life given unto us for his sake, and not for the works of the law, or for our own righteousness. Of this inestimable treasure freely bestowed upon us, the gospel properly preacheth unto us. Wherefore it is a kind of doctrine that is not learned or gotten by any study, diligence, or wisdom of man, nor yet by the law of God, but it is revealed by God himself, as Paul saith in this place; first by the external word; then by the working of God's spirit inwardly. The gospel therefore is a divine word that came down from heaven, and is revealed by the Holy Ghost, who was also sent for the same purpose: yet in such sort notwithstanding, that the outward word must go before. For Paul himself had no inward revelation, until he had heard the outward word from heaven, which was this, "Saul, Saul, why persecutest thou me?" (Acts ix, 4). First, therefore, he heard the outward word, then afterwards followed revelations, the knowledge of the word faith, and the gifts of the Holy Ghost.

VERSE 16. *That I should preach him among the Gentiles.*

It pleased God, said he, "to reveal himself in me." To what purpose? Not only that I myself should believe in the Son of God, but also that I should preach him among the Gentiles. And why not among the Jews? Lo, here we see that Paul is properly the apostle of the Gentiles, albeit he preached Christ among the Jews also.

Paul comprehendeth here in few words, as is his wont, his whole divinity, which is, to preach Christ among the Gentiles. As if he would say, I will not burden the Gentiles with the law, because I am the apostle and evangelist of the Gentiles, and not their lawgiver. Thus he directeth all his words against the false apostles. As though he would say: O ye Galatians, ye have not heard the righteousness of the law, or of works, to be taught by me: for this belongeth to Moses and not to me, Paul, being the apostle of the Gentiles. For my office and ministry is to bring the gospel unto you, and to shew unto you the same revelation which I myself have had. Therefore ought you to hear no teacher that teacheth the law. For among the Gentiles, the law ought not to be preached, but the gospel; not Moses, but the Son of God; not the righteousness of works, but the righteousness of faith. This is the preaching that properly belongeth to the Gentiles.

VERSE 17. *Immediately I communicated not with flesh and blood.*

Paul here making mention of flesh and blood, speaketh not of the apostles. For by-and-by he addeth: "Neither came I again to Jerusalem, to them which were apostles before me." But this is Paul's meaning, that after he had once received the revelation of the gospel from Christ, he consulted not with any man in Damascus, much less did he desire any man to teach him the gospel: again, that he went not to Jerusalem, to Peter and the other apostles, to learn the gospel of them, but that forthwith he preached Jesus Christ in Damascus, where he received baptism of Ananias, and imposition of hands: for it was necessary for him to have the outward sign and testimony of his calling. The same also writeth Luke, Acts ix.

VERSE 17. *Neither came I to Jerusalem, to them that were apostles before me, but went into Arabia, and turned again into Damascus.*

That is, I went into Arabia before I saw the apostles, or consulted with them, and forthwith I took upon me the office of preaching among the Gentiles: for thereunto I was called, and had also received a revelation from God. He did not then receive his gospel of any man, or of the apostles themselves, but was content with his heavenly calling, and with the revelation of Jesus Christ alone. Wherefore this whole place is a confutation of the false apostles' argument, which they used against Paul, saying that he was but a scholar, and a hearer of the apostles, who lived after the law: and moreover, that Paul himself also had lived according to the law, and therefore it was necessary that the Gentiles themselves should keep the law, and be circumcised. To the end therefore that he might stop the mouths of these cavillers, he rehearseth this long history: before my conversion, saith he, I learned not my gospel of the apostles, nor of any other of the brethren that believed (for I persecuted extremely, not only this doctrine, but also the church of God, and wasted it): neither after my conversion; for forthwith I preached, not Moses with his law, but Jesus Christ at Damascus, consulting with no man, neither as yet having seen any of the apostles.

VERSES 18 AND 19. *Then after three years, I came again to Jerusalem, to visit Peter, and abode with him fifteen days. And none other of the apostles saw I, save James, the Lord's brother.*

Paul granteth that he was with the apostles, but not with all the apostles. Howbeit he declareth, that he went up to Jerusa-

EPISTLE TO THE GALATIANS

lem to them, not commanded, but of his own accord, not to learn anything of them, but to see Peter. The same thing Luke also writeth in the ninth chapter of the Acts, that Barnabas led Paul to the apostles, and declared to them, how that he had seen the Lord in the way, and that he spake unto him: also that he had preached boldly at Damascus, in the name of Jesus. This witness beareth Barnabas of him. All his words are so framed, that they prove his gospel not to be of man. Indeed he granteth that he had seen Peter, and James the brother of our Lord, but none other of the apostles besides these two, and that he learned nothing of them.

He granteth therefore that he was at Jerusalem with the apostles; and this did the false apostles only report. He granteth moreover, that he had lived after the manner of the Jews, but yet only among the Jews. And this is it which he saith in the ninth chapter of his first epistle to the Corinthians: "when I was free from all men, I made myself servant to all men, that I might win the more. To the Jews I became as a Jew, that I might win the Jews, and I was made all things to all men, that I might by all means save some. He granteth therefore, that he was at Jerusalem with the apostles, but he denieth that he had learned his gospel of them. Also he denieth that he was constrained to teach the gospel as the apostles had prescribed. the whole effect then of this matter lieth in this word, "to see;" "I went," saith he, "to see Peter, and not to learn of him. Therefore neither is Peter my master, nor yet James." And as for the other apostles, he utterly denieth that he saw any of them.

But why doth Paul repeat this so often, that he learned not his gospel of men, nor of the apostles themselves? His purpose is this, to persuade the churches of Galatia, which were now led away by the false apostles, and to put them out of all doubt that his gospel was the true word of God, and for this cause he repeateth it so often. And if he had not prevailed herein, he never could have stopped the mouths of the false apostles. For thus they would have objected against him: We are as good as Paul, we are disciples of the apostles as well as he; moreover, he is but one alone, and we are many; therefore we excel him, both in authority and in number also.

Here Paul was constrained to glory, to affirm and swear, that he learned not his gospel of any man, neither received it of the apostles themselves. For his ministry was here in great danger, and all the churches likewise, which had used him as their chief pastor and teacher. The necessity therefore of his ministry, and of all the churches required, that with a holy pride he should vaunt of his vocation, and of the knowledge of the gospel revealed unto him by Christ, that their consciences might be thoroughly persuaded that his doctrine was the true word of God. Here had Paul a weighty matter in hand: namely, that all the churches in Galatia might be kept in sound doctrine: yea, the controversy was in deed, as touching life and death everlasting. For if the pure word of God be once taken away, there remaineth no consolation, no life, no salvation. The cause therefore why he reciteth these things, is to retain the churches in true and sound doctrine. His purpose is therefore to shew by this history, that he receiveth his gospel of no man. Again, that he preached for a certain time, namely, the space of three or four years, both in Damascus and Arabia, by revelation from God, before he had seen any of the apostles, even the self-same gospel that the apostles had preached.

VERSE 20. *And now the things which I write unto you, behold I witness before God I lie not.*

Wherefore addeth he an oath? Because he reporteth a history, he is constrained to swear, to the end that the churches might believe him, and also that the false apostles should not say, who knoweth whether Paul speaketh the truth or no? Here you see that Paul, the elect vessel of God, was in so great contempt among his own Galatians, to whom he had preached Christ, that it was necessary for him to swear that he spake the truth. If this happened then to the apostles, to have so mighty adversaries, that they durst despise them, and accuse them of lying, what marvel is it if the like at this day happen unto us, which in no respect are worthy to be compared with the apostles? He sweareth, therefore, in a matter (as it seemeth) of no weight, that he speaketh the truth, namely, that he tarried not with Peter to learn of him, but only to see him; but if you weigh the matter diligently, it is very weighty and of great importance, as may appear by that is said before. In like manner we swear after the example of Paul, in this wise: God knoweth that we lie not, etc.

VERSE 21. *After that, I went into the coasts of Syria and Cilicia.*

Syria and Cilicia are countries near situate together. This is it that he still goeth about to persuade, that as well before he had seen the apostles as after, he was always a teacher of the gospel, and that he received it by the revelation of Christ, and was never any disciple of the apostles.

VERSES 22, 23, AND 24. *For I was unknown by face unto the churches of Judea, which were in Christ. But they heard only some say, he which persecuted in times past, now preacheth the faith, which before he destroyed, and they glorified God.*

This he addeth for the sequel and continuance of the history, that after he had seen Peter, he went into Syria and Cilicia, and there preached, and so preached, that he won the testimony of all the churches in Judea. As though he would say, I appeal to the testimony of all the churches, yea, even of those which are in Judea; for the churches do witness, not only in Damascus, Arabia, Syria, and Cilicia, but also Judea, that I have preached the same faith which I once withstood and persecuted. And they glorified God in me; not because I taught that circumcision and the law of Moses ought to be kept, but for the preaching of faith, and for the edifying of the churches by my ministry in the gospel. Ye therefore have the testimony not only of the people of Damascus and of Arabia, but also of the whole catholic or universal churches of Judea.

CHAPTER II.

VERSE 1. *Then fourteen years after, I went up to Jerusalem.*

PAUL taught that the Gentiles were justified by faith only, without the works of the law. This doctrine when he had published abroad among the Gentiles, he cometh to Antioch, and declareth to the disciples what he had done. Then they which had been trained up in the old customs of the law, rose against Paul with great indignation, for that he preached to the Gentiles liberty from the bondage of the law. Whereupon followed great dissension, which afterwards stirred up new troubles. Paul and Barnabas stood strongly to the truth, and testified, saying, wheresoever we preached among the Gentiles, "the Holy Ghost came and fell upon those which heard the word: and this was done throughout all the churches of the Gentiles. But we preached not circumcision, neither did we require the keeping of the law, but we preached only faith in Jesus Christ, and at this preaching of faith, God gave to the hearers the Holy Ghost." The Holy Ghost, therefore, doth approve the faith of the Gentiles, without the law and circumcision; for if the preaching of the gospel, and faith of the Gentiles in Christ, had not pleased him, he had not come down in a visible shape upon the uncircumcised which heard the word. Seeing then by the only hearing of faith, he came down upon them, it is certain that the Holy Ghost by this sign hath approved the faith of the Gentiles; for it doth not appear that this was ever done before at the preaching of the law.

Then the Jews, and many of the Pharisees, which did believe, and notwithstanding bear yet a great zeal to the law, earnestly striving to maintain the glory thereof, set themselves fiercely against Paul (who affirmed that the Gentiles were justified by faith only, without the works of the law), contending, that the law ought to be kept, and that the Gentiles ought to be circumcised; for otherwise they could not be saved. And no marvel; for the very name of the law of God is holy and dreadful. The heathen man, which never knew anything of the law of God, if he hear any man say, this doctrine is the law of God, he is moved therewith: how then could it be but the Jews must needs be moved, and vehemently contend for the maintenance of the law of God, which even from their infancy had been nursled and trained up therein?

We see at this day, how obstinate the Papists be, in defending their traditions and doctrines of devils; wherefore, it was much less to be marvelled that the Jews did so vehemently and zealously strive for the maintenance of their law, which they had received from God. Custom is of such force, that whereas nature is of itself inclined to the observation of the law, by long continuance, it so confirmeth nature, that now it becometh a double nature; therefore, it was not possible for the Jews which were newly converted to Christ, suddenly to forsake the law; who, though they had received the faith of Christ, thought it necessary, notwithstanding, to observe the law. And with this their weakness God did bear for a time, until the doctrine of the gospel might be plainly discerned from the law; so he bare with the infirmity of Israel in the time of king Achab, when the people halted between two religions. He bare also with our weakness whilst we were under the blindness of the Pope. "For he is long-suffering and full of mercy." But we must not abuse this goodness and patience of the Lord, nor continue still in our weakness and error, since the truth is now revealed by the clear light of the gospel.

Moreover, they that stood against Paul, affirming, that the Gentiles ought to be circumcised, had to lay for themselves, first, the law and custom of the country, then the example of the apostles, and last of all, the example of Paul himself, who had circumcised Timothy. Wherefore, if Paul in his defence said, that he did not this of necessity, but for christian love and liberty, lest they which were weak in faith should be offended, which of them would believe him? Hereunto all the people would answer: Since it is evident that thou hast circumcised Timothy, thou mayest say what thou wilt; notwithstanding thou hast done it. For this is a matter far passing all men's capacity, and therefore they could not understand it. Moreover, no defence can serve when a man hath lost the favour of the people, and is fallen into such deadly hatred and contempt. Paul therefore seeing this contention, and these clamours daily to increase more and more, and being also warned by revelation from God, after fourteen years (besides those wherein he had preached in Damascus and Arabia) goeth up again to Jerusalem, to confer his gospel with the other apostles: yet not for his own cause, but for the people's sake.

Now, this contention touching the observation of the law, exerciseth Paul a long time after, and wrought him much trouble; but I do not think that this is the contention which Luke speaketh of in the fifteenth of the Acts, which happened, as it appeareth by-and-by, after the beginning of the gospel; but this history which Paul here mentioneth, seemeth to be done long after, when Paul had now almost eighteen years preached the gospel.

VERSE 1. *With Barnabas, and took with me Titus.*

He joineth unto himself two witnesses, Barnabas and Titus. Barnabas was Paul's companion in preaching to the Gentiles freedom from the servitude of the law. He was also a witness of all those things which Paul did, and had seen the Holy Ghost given unto the Gentiles, which were uncircumcised and free from Moses's law, by the only preaching of faith in Jesus Christ, and he only stuck to Paul in this point, that it was not necessary that the Gentiles should be burdened with the law, but that it was enough for them to believe in Christ: wherefore, by his own experience, he testifieth with Paul against the laws, that the Gentiles were made the children of God, and saved by faith alone in Jesus Christ, without the law of circumcision.

Titus was not only a Christian, but also the chief overseer in Crete; for unto him Paul had committed the charge of governing the churches there (Tit. i), and this Titus was a Gentile.

VERSE 2. *And I went up by revelation.*

For unless Paul had been admonished by revelation, he had not gone up to Jerusalem: but because God warned him by a special revelation, and commanded him to go up, therefore he went. And this he did to bridle, or at least to appease, the Jews that believed, and yet obstinately contended about the keeping of the law, to the end that the truth of the gospel might the more be advanced and confirmed.

> VERSE 2. *And I communicated with them teaching the gospel.*

You hear then, that at length, after eighteen years, he went up to Jerusalem, and conferred with the apostles touching his gospel.

> VERSE 2. *Which I preach among the Gentiles.*

For among the Jews he suffered the law and circumcision for a time, as the other apostles did: "I am made all things unto all men," saith he (I Cor. ix, 22). Yet ever holding the true doctrine of the gospel, which he preferred above the law, circumcision, the apostles, yea, and an angel from heaven. For thus he saith unto the Jews: "Through this Christ is preached unto you the forgiveness of sins." And he addeth very plainly: "and from all things, from the which ye could not be justified" (Acts xiii, 39). For this cause he teacheth and defendeth the doctrine of the gospel so diligently everywhere, and never suffereth it to come in danger. Notwithstanding, he did not suddenly break out at the first, but had regard unto the weak. And because the weak should not be offended, there is no doubt but he spake to the Jews after this manner: if that unprofitable service of Moses' law, which nothing availeth to righteousness, do so highly please you, ye may keep it still for me, so that the Gentiles which are not bound to this law, be not charged therewithal.

Paul therefore confesseth, that he conferred the gospel with the apostles, but saith he, they profited me, or taught me nothing; but I rather for the defence of the liberty of the gospel, in the presence of the apostles, did constantly resist those which would needs force the observation of the law upon the Gentiles, and so did overcome them. Wherefore your false apostles lie, in saying that I circumcised Timothy, that I shaved my head in Cenchrea, and that I went up to Jerusalem, at the commandment of the apostles. Nay, rather, I glory, that in going up to Jerusalem, by the revelation of God, and not at the commandment of the apostles, and there conferring my gospel with them, I brought to pass to the contrary, that is to say, obtained that the apostles did approve me, and not those which were against me.

Now, the question whereupon the apostles conferred together

EPISTLE TO THE GALATIANS

in this assembly, was this: whether the keeping the law were necessary to justification or no. To this Paul answereth: I have preached unto the Gentiles, according to my gospel which I received from God, faith in Christ, and not the law, and at this preaching of faith, they received the Holy Ghost; and hereof Barnabas shall bear me witness. Wherefore I conclude, that the Gentiles ought not to be burdened with the law, nor to be circumcised. Notwithstanding, I give no restraint to the Jews herein, who if they will needs keep the law and be circumcised, I am not against it, so that they do it with freedom of conscience. And thus have I taught and lived among the Jews, "being made a Jew unto the Jews;" holding ever the truth of the gospel notwithstanding.

VERSE 2. *But particularly with them that were the chiefest.*

That is to say, I did not only confer with the brethren, but with those that were the chiefest among them.

VERSE 2. *Lest by any means I should run, or had run in vain.*

Not that Paul doubted, that he ran, or had run in vain, forasmuch as he had now preached the gospel eighteen years (for it followeth incontinent in the text, that he had continued firm and constant all this while, and had prevailed), but for that many did think that Paul had therefore preached the gospel so many years in vain, because he had set the Gentiles at liberty from the observation of the law. Moreover, this opinion daily more and more increased, that the law was necessary to justification. Wherefore, in going up to Jerusalem by revelation, he meant so to remedy this evil, that by this conference all men might plainly see his gospel to be in one point contrary to the doctrine of the other apostles, to the end that by this means he might stop the mouths of the adversaries, which would else have said, that he ran, or had run in vain. Note here by the way, the virtue of man's own righteousness, or the righteousness of the law to be such, that they which teach it, do run and live in vain.

VERSE 3. *But neither yet Titus, which was with me, though he were a Grecian, was compelled to be circumcised.*

This word (was compelled) sufficiently declareth what the conference and conclusion was: to wit, that the Gentiles should not be constrained to be circumcised, but that circumcision should be permitted to them for a time: not as necessary to righteousness, but for a reverence to the fathers; and for charity's sake towards the weak, lest they should be offended, until they were grown up more strong in faith. For it might have seemed a very strange and unseemly thing, upon a sudden to forsake the law and traditions of the fathers, which had been given to this people from God with so great glory.

Paul then did not reject circumcision as a damnable thing, neither did he by word or deed enforce the Jews to forsake it. For in the seventh chapter of his first epistle to the Corinthians, he saith: "If any man be called, being circumcised, let him not add uncircumcision."—But he rejected circumcision as a thing, not necessary to righteousness, seeing the fathers themselves were not justified thereby (Rom. iv, 11), but it was unto them as a sign only, or a seal of righteousness, whereby they testified and exercised their faith. Notwithstanding the believing Jews which were yet weak, and, bare a zeal to the law, hearing that circumcision was not necessary to righteousness, could understand this no otherwise, but that it was altogether unprofitable and damnable. And this fond opinion of the weak Jews, the false apostles did increase, to the end, that the hearts of the people being stirred up against Paul, by this occasion, they might thoroughly discredit his doctrine. So we at this day do not reject fasting, and other good exercises as damnable things: but we teach, that by these exercises we do not obtain remission of sins. When the people hear this, by-and-by they judge us to speak against good works. And this opinion the Papists do confirm and increase by their preachings and writings. But they lie, and do us great wrong. For many years past, there was never any that taught more sound and godly doctrine as touching good works, than we do at this day.

Paul therefore did not so condemn circumcision, as though it were sin to receive it, or keep it: for the Jews would have been highly offended; but it was decided in this conference and council, that it was not necessary to justification, and therefore not to be forced upon the Gentiles. So this moderation was found, that for the reverence of the fathers, and charity towards the weak in faith, the Jews should keep the law and circumcision still for a time; notwithstanding they should not thereby seek to be justified. And moreover, that the Gentiles should not be burthened therewith, both because it would have been to them a very strange thing, and also a burden intolerable (Acts xv, 10). Briefly, that none should be constrained to be circumcised, or any constrained from circumcision.

Paul therefore compelled none that would be circumcised, to remain uncircumcised, so that he knew circumcision not to be necessary to justification. This constraint would Paul take away. Therefore he suffered the Jews to keep the law, so that they did it with a free conscience. For he had ever taught, as well the Jews as the Gentiles, that in conscience they ought to be free from the law and circumcision; like as all the patriarchs, and all the faithful in the Old Testament, were free in conscience, and justified by faith, and not by the law or circumcision. And indeed, Paul might have suffered Titus to be circumcised; but because he saw that they would compel him thereunto, he would not. For if they had prevailed therein, by-and-by they would have gathered that it had been necessary to justification, and so through this sufferance, they would have triumphed against Paul.

Now, as the false apostles would not leave circumcision and the observation of the law indifferent, but required the same as necessary to salvation, so at this day our adversaries do obstinately contend, that men's traditions cannot be omitted without peril of salvation; and thus of an example of charity, they make an example of faith, when notwithstanding there is but one example of faith, which is to believe in Jesus Christ. And this, as it is alone necessary to salvation, so doth it also indifferently pertain to all men. Notwithstanding the adversaries would rather worship the devil ten times instead of God, than they would suffer this. Therefore they are daily hardened more and more, and seek to establish their impieties and blasphemies against God, defending the same by force and tyranny, and will not agree, or consent unto us in any point. But what then? Let us go on boldly in the name of the Lord of Hosts, and for all this, let us not cease to set forth the glory of Jesus Christ: and let us fight valiantly against the kingdom of Antichrist, by the word, and by prayer, "that the name of God alone may be sanctified, that his kingdom may come, and that his will may be done." (Matt. vi, 9, 10.) And that this may speedily come to pass, we desire even from the bottom of our hearts, and say, Amen, Amen.

This triumph of Paul, therefore, was very glorious: namely, that Titus, who was a Gentile, although he were in the midst of the apostles, and all the faithful, where this question was so vehemently debated, was not yet constrained to be circumcised. This victory Paul carrieth away, and saith, that on this conference, it was decided, by the consent of all the apostles, the whole church also approving the same, that Titus should not be circumcised. This is a strong argument, and maketh very much against the false apostles. And with this argument: neither was Titus compelled to be circumcised, Paul was able to repress and mightily to convince all his adversaries: as if he should say, why do these counterfeit apostles so falsely report of me, saying, that I am compelled to keep circumcision by the commandment of the apostles, seeing I have the witness of all the faithful in Jerusalem, and moreover, of all the apostles themselves, that by my pursuit and travel, the contrary was there determined, and that I did not only there prevail that Titus should not be circumcised, but that the apostles also did approve and ratify the same? Your counterfeit apostles therefore do lie deadly, which slander me under the name of the apostles, and thereby deceive you; for I have the apostles, and all the faithful, not against me, but with me. And this I prove by the example of Titus.

Notwithstanding, Paul, as I have often said, did not condemn circumcision as an unprofitable thing, nor constrained any man thereunto. For it is neither sin nor righteousness to be circumcised or uncircumcised, as it is neither sin nor righteousness to eat or drink. "For whether thou eat or eat not, thou art neither better nor worse," (1 Cor. viii, 8). But if any man should add thereto either sin or righteousness, and say: if thou eat thou sinnest, if thou abstain thou art righteous, he should shew himself both foolish and wicked. Therefore to join ceremonies with sin or righteousness, is great impiety; as the Pope doth, who in his form of excommunication, threateneth to all those that do not obey the law of the bishop of Rome, God's great curse and indignation, and so maketh all his laws necessary to salvation. Wherefore the devil himself speaketh in the person of the Pope, in all the Pope's decrees.—For if salvation consisteth in keeping of the Pope's laws, what need have we of Christ to be our justifier and saviour.

> VERSES 4 AND 5. *For all the false brethren that crept in, who came in privily to espy out our liberty which we have in Christ Jesus, that they might bring us into bondage. To whom we gave not place by subjection for an hour, that the truth of the gospel might continue with you.*

Here Paul sheweth the cause why he went up to Jerusalem, and there conferred his gospel with the other apostles, and why he would not circumcise Titus; not that he might be the more certain, or confirmed in the gospel by the apostles, for he nothing doubted thereof; but that the truth of the gospel might continue in the churches of the Galatians, and in all the churches of the Gentiles. We see, then, that the business of Paul was no light matter.

Now, where he speaketh of the truth of the gospel, he

sheweth that there be two gospels, a true and a false gospel. Indeed, the gospel of itself is simple, true, and sincere; but by the malice of Satan's ministry, it is corrupt and defaced. Therefore where he saith "the truth of the gospel," he would have us to understand also the contrary. As if he would say: the false apostles do also preach a faith and a gospel, but they are both false: therefore have I set myself so constantly against them. And in that I would not give place unto them, this have I brought to pass, that the truth of the gospel continueth with you. So the Pope and Anabaptists do brag at this day, that they teach the gospel, and faith in Christ. True it is: but with such fruit as the false apostles once did, whom Paul calleth before, in the first chapter, troublers of the church, and subverters of the gospel of Christ. On the other side, he saith "that he teacheth the truth of the gospel." As if he should say: those things which the false apostles teach, brag they never so much that they teach the truth, are nothing else but stark lies. So all heretics pretend the name of God, of Christ, and of the church. Also they pretend that they will not teach errors or lies, but most certain truth and the pure gospel of Christ.

Now, the truth of the gospel is, that our righteousness cometh by faith alone, without the works of the law. The corruption, or falsehood of the gospel is, that we are justified by faith, but not without the works of the law. With the like condition the false apostles also preached the gospel. Even so do our Papists at this day. For they say, that we must believe in Christ, and that faith is the foundation of our salvation: but it justifieth not, except it be furnished with charity. This is not the truth of the gospel, but falsehood and dissimulation. But the true gospel indeed is, that the works of charity are not the ornament or perfection of faith: but that faith of itself is God's gift, and God's work in our hearts, which therefore justifieth us, because it apprehendeth Christ our Redeemer. Man's reason hath the law for his object, thus thinking with itself: this I have done, this I have not done. But faith being in her own proper office, hath no other object but Jesus Christ the Son of God, delivered to death for the sins of the whole world. It looketh not to charity; it saith not: what have I done? what have I offended? what have I deserved? but, what hath Christ done? what hath he deserved? Here the truth of the gospel answereth thee: he hath redeemed thee from thy sin, from the devil, and from eternal death.—Faith therefore acknowledgeth that in this one person, Jesus Christ, it hath forgiveness of sins and eternal life. He that turneth his eyes away from this object, hath no true faith, but a fantasy and a vain opinion, and turneth his eyes from the promise to the law, which terrifieth and driveth to desperation.

Wherefore those things which the popish schoolmen have taught concerning the justifying faith being furnished with charity, are nothing else but mere dreams. For that faith which apprehendeth Christ the Son of God, and is furnished with him, is the same faith that justifieth, and not the faith which includeth charity. For a true and steadfast faith must lay hold upon nothing else but Christ alone, and in the affections and terrors of conscience, it hath nothing else to lean unto, but this diamond, Christ Jesus. Wherefore he that apprehendeth Christ by faith, although he be never so much terrified with the law, and oppressed with the weight of his sins, yet may he be bold to glory that he is righteous. How, or by what means? Even by that precious pearl Christ Jesus, which he possesseth by faith. This our adversaries understand not, and therefore they cast away this precious pearl Christ, and in his place they set charity, which, they say, is their precious diamond. Now when they cannot tell what faith is, it is impossible that they should have faith: much less can they teach it in our opinion to others. And as for that which they will seem to have, it is nothing else but natural reason, an opinion, a very dream, and no faith.

This I say, to the end ye may perceive and note that by these words, "the truth of the gospel," Paul vehemently reproveth the contrary. For he reprehendeth the false apostles, because they had taught a false gospel, requiring circumcision, and the observation of the law as necessary to salvation. Moreover, they went about by wonderful craft and subtilty to entrap Paul; for they watched him narrowly, to see whether he would circumcise Titus or no; also, whether he durst withstand them in the presence of the apostles, and for this cause he reprehendeth them bitterly. "They went about," saith he, "to spy out our liberty which we have in Christ Jesus, that they might bring us into bondage." Wherefore the false apostles armed themselves on every side, that they might convince and confound him before the whole congregation. Besides this, they went about to abuse the authority of the apostles, in whose presence they accused him, saying, Paul hath brought Titus, being uncircumcised, into the company of all the faithful; he denieth and condemneth the law in your presence, which are apostles. If he dare be so bold to attempt this here and before you, what will not he attempt in your absence among the Gentiles?

Wherefore, when he perceived that he was so craftily assailed, he strongly withstood the false apostles, saying, We did not suffer our liberty which we have in Christ Jesus to come in danger, although the false brethren sought by all means to snare us, and put us to much trouble: but we overcame them even by the judgment of the apostles themselves, and we would not yield unto them, no, not one hour (for, no doubt, their drift was to have caused Paul to surcease from this liberty for a time), since we saw that they required the observation of the law, as necessary to salvation. But if they had alleged nothing else but charitable bearing with the brethren, no doubt but Paul would have given them place. But it was another thing that they sought: to wit, that they might bring Paul, and all that stuck to his doctrine, into bondage. Therefore he would not yield unto them, no, not the space of one moment.

In like manner do we also offer to the Papists all that is to be offered, yea, and more than we ought. Only we except the liberty of conscience which we have in Christ Jesus. For we will not suffer our consciences to be bound to any work, so that by doing this thing or that, we should be righteous, or leaving the same undone we should be damned. We are contented to eat the same meats that they eat, we will keep their feasts and fasting days, so they will suffer us to do the same with a free conscience, and leave these threatening words, wherewith they have terrified and brought under their subjection the whole world, saying, We command, we charge, we charge again, we excommunicate, etc., but this liberty we cannot obtain; like as Paul also could not in his time. Therefore we do as he did. For when he saw that he could not obtain this liberty, he would not give place to the false apostles, the space of one hour.

Wherefore, like as our adversaries will not leave this free unto us, that only faith in Christ justifieth; so on the other side, neither will we nor can we give place unto them, that faith furnished with charity justifieth. Here we will, and we ought also to be rebellious and obstinate against them, for else we should lose the truth of the gospel: we should lose our liberty, which we have, not in the emperor, not in kings and princes, not in that monster the Pope, not in the world, not in the flesh, blood, reason, etc. but which we have in Christ Jesus. We should lose faith in Christ, which, as before I have said, apprehended nothing else but that precious diamond Christ Jesus. This faith, whereby we are regenerate, justified, and engrafted into Christ, if our adversaries will leave unto us sound and uncorrupt, we offer unto them that we will do all things, so that they be not contrary to this faith. But because we cannot obtain this at their hands, we again for our part will not yield unto them one hair's breadth. For the matter which we have in hand is weighty and of great importance, even touching the death of the Son of God; who by the will and commandment of the Father was made flesh, was crucified, and died for the sins of the world. If faith here give place, then is this death and resurrection of the Son of God in vain; then is it but a fable, that Christ is the Saviour of the world; then is God found a liar, because he hath not performed that he promised. Our stoutness therefore in this matter is godly and holy. For by it we seek to preserve our liberty which we have in Christ Jesus, and thereby to retain the truth of the gospel; which if we lose, then do we also lose God, Christ, all the promises, faith, righteousness, and everlasting life.

But here will some men say, the law is divine and holy. Let the law have his glory, but yet no law, be it never so divine and holy, ought to teach me that I am justified, and shall live through it. I grant it may teach me that I ought to love God and my neighbor; also to live in chastity, soberness, patience, etc., but it ought not to shew me, how I should be delivered from sin, the devil, death, and hell. Here I must take counsel of the gospel. I must hearken to the gospel, which teacheth me, not what I ought to do (for that is the proper office of the law), but what Jesus Christ the Son of God hath done for me: to wit, that he suffered and died to deliver me from sin and death. The gospel willeth me to receive this, and to believe it. And this is the truth of the gospel. It is also the principal article of all Christian doctrine, wherein the knowledge of all godliness consisteth. Most necessary it is, therefore, that we should know this article well, teach it unto others, and beat it into their heads continually. For as it is very tender, so it is soon hurt. This Paul had well tried, and of this have all the godly also good experience.

To conclude, Paul would not circumcise Titus, and, as he saith, for no other cause, but for that certain false brethren were crept in, to espy out their liberty, and would have constrained Paul to circumcise Titus. Paul seeing this constraint and necessity, would give no place, no not for one hour, but strongly resisted them, and therefore he saith, "Neither Titus which was with me, being a Gentile, was compelled to be circumcised." (Gal. ii, 3.) If they had required this in the way of brotherly charity, doubtless he would not have denied it. But seeing they would have done it as a necessary thing, and that by compulsion, to the evil example of others, to the overthrowing of the gospel, and to bring men's consciences into bondage, therefore he set himself mightily against them, and prevailed so, that Titus was not circumcised.

It may seem but a small matter to be circumcised, or not circumcised. But when a man hath an affiance in keeping of it, or else is in fear for not keeping of it, here God is denied, Christ is rejected, the grace and all the promises of God are refused. But if the circumcision be kept without this addition, there is no danger. If the Pope would in this sort require of us the keeping of his traditions, as bare ceremonies, it should not be so grievous unto us to keep them: but to bind men's consciences to these ceremonies, and to make of them a high and acceptable service unto God, yea, and moreover to add, that life and salvation, or death and damnation, consisteth in the observation hereof, is a devilish superstition, and full of blasphemy. Whoso will not cry against this, accursed be he.

> VERSES 6 AND 7. *And of them which seemed to be great, I was not taught, (what they were in times past, it is no matter to me, etc.)*

This is a vehement and a stout confutation. For he giveth not to the true apostles themselves any glorious title: but as it were abasing their dignity, he saith: "Which seemed to be great"; that is, which were in authority, upon whom the determination of all matters depended. Notwithstanding, the authority of the apostles was indeed very great in all the churches. And Paul also did not seek any whit to diminish their authority, but he thus contemptuously answereth the false apostles, which set the authority and dignity of the apostles against Paul in all the churches, that thereby they might weaken his authority, and bring his whole ministry into contempt. This Paul might not suffer. To the end therefore, that the truth of the gospel, and liberty of conscience in Christ, might continue among the Galatians, and in all the churches of the Gentiles, he answereth stoutly to the false apostles, that he passed not how great the apostles were, or what they had been in times past; and whereas they alleged the authority of the name of the apostles against him, it touched him nothing at all. He confesseth that the apostles are indeed somewhat, and their authority is to be reverenced. Notwithstanding his gospel and ministry ought not to be overthrown for the name or title of any, whatsoever he be, an apostle, or an angel from heaven.

And this was one of the greatest arguments that the false apostles used against Paul. The apostles, said they, were familiarly conversant with Christ for the space of three years. They heard and saw all his preachings and miracles. Moreover, they themselves preached and wrought miracles while Christ was yet living in the world; whom Paul never saw in the flesh, and as touching his conversion, it was long after the glorification of Christ. Wherefore, they should now consider which of these they ought more to believe; Paul, which was but one and alone, and also but a disciple, yea, and one of the last of all; or the chiefest and most excellent apostles, which, long before Paul, were sent and confirmed by Christ himself. To this Paul answereth: What of all this? This argument concludeth nothing. Let the apostles be never so great, yea, let them be angels from heaven, it is no matter to me. The controversy is not here concerning the excellency of the apostles, but concerning the word of God, and the truth of the gospel. This ought to be kept pure and uncorrupt; this ought to be preferred above all things. Therefore how great Peter and the other apostles have been, what great miracles they have wrought, it is no matter to me. This is it that I only seek, even that the truth of the gospel may continue among you. This seemeth to be but a slender answer of Paul, when of purpose he so contemneth the authority of the apostles, which the false apostles alleged against him, and giveth no other solution to their mighty argument than this: It is no matter to me. Notwithstanding, he addeth a reason of the confutation.

VERSE 6. *God accepteth no man's person.*

This place he allegeth out of Moses, who useth the same, not once but many times: "Thou shalt not accept in judgment the person of the rich man or of the poor," (Levit. xix, 15). And this is a principle of divinity: "God is no accepter of persons," (2 Chron. xix, 7; Rom. ii, 11; Acts x, 34; Eph. vi, 9; Col. iii, 25). With the which saying he stopped the mouths of the false apostles. As though he would say: Ye set those against me which seem to be somewhat; but God careth not for such outward things. He regardeth not the office of apostleship. It is not the dignity or authority of men that he looketh upon. And in token hereof, he suffered Judas, one of the chiefest apostles, and Saul, one of the greatest kings, yea, and the first of all, to fall away and to be damned. Ishmael also and Esau he refused, being both first-born. So shall you find throughout all the whole scripture, that God oftentimes rejected those which in outward shew were very good and holy men. And in these examples God seemeth sometimes to be cruel; but it was most necessary, that such fearful examples should be shewn, and also be written. For this vice is naturally grafted in us, that we highly esteem the persons and outward appearance of men, and more regard the same than the word of God. Contrariwise, God will have us to fix our eyes, and to rest wholly upon the word itself, he will not have us to reverence and adore the apostleship in the persons of Peter and Paul, but Christ speaking in them, and the word which they bring and preach unto us.

This the natural man cannot see: but the spiritual man only discerneth the person from the word, the veil of God from God himself. Now this veil of God is every creature. Moreover, God here in this life dealeth not with us face to face, but covered and shadowed from us: that is, as Paul saith in another place, "We see now as it were through a glass, darkly; but then we shall see face to face." (I Cor. xiii, 12.) Therefore we cannot be without veils in this life. But here wisdom is required, which can discern the veil from God himself; and this wisdom the world hath not. The covetous man hearing, "that man liveth not by bread alone, but by every word that proceedeth out of the mouth of God" (Deut. viii, 3; Matt. iv, 4), eateth the bread, but he seeth not God in the bread; for he beholdeth the veil only and outward shew. So he doth with gold and other creatures, trusting to them so long as he hath them; but when they leave him, he despaireth. And thus he honoureth not the Creator, but the creatures, not God, but his own belly.

This I speak, lest any man should think that Paul utterly condemneth these outward veils or persons. For he saith not, that there ought to be no person, but that there is no respect of persons with God. There must be persons and outward veils: God hath given them, and they are his good creatures; but we must not trust in them. All the matter is in the right using of things, and not in the things themselves, as before I have said. There is no fault in circumcision or uncircumcision ("for circumcision is nothing, and uncircumcision is nothing"), but in the use thereof. To put righteousness in the one, and unrighteousness in the other, that use is damnable, and ought to be taken away: which being removed, circumcision and uncircumcision are things tolerable.

So the prince, the magistrate, the preacher, the schoolmaster, the scholar, the father, the mother, the children, the master, the servant, are persons and outward veils, which God will have us to acknowledge, love, and reverence as his creatures, which also must needs be had in this life; but he will not have us so to reverence them, or trust unto them, that we forget him. And to the end that we should not too much magnify the outward persons, or put any trust in them, God leaveth in them offences and sins, yea, great and foul sins, to teach us what difference there is between the person and God himself. David, that good king, because he should not seem to be a person upon whom men should trust, fell into horrible sins, adultery and murder. Peter, that excellent apostle, denied Christ. These, and such-like examples, whereof the scripture is full, ought to warn us, that we repose not our trust in the person and outward veil, nor think, that when we have the outward shews and shadows, we have all things; as it is in popery, where they judge all things according to the outward veil, and therefore all popery is nothing else but a mere respecting of persons and outward shews. God hath given his creatures to our use, and to do us service, and not as idols, that we should do service unto them. Let us then use bread, wine, apparel, possessions, gold, silver, and all other creatures. But let us not trust and glory in them: for we must trust and glory in God alone. He only is to be loved, he only is to be feared and honoured.

Paul calleth here the apostleship or office of the apostles (which wrought many and great miracles, taught and converted many to the faith, and were also familiar with Christ,) the person of man.

Briefly, this word, person, comprehendeth the whole outward conversation of the apostles, which was holy, and their authority, which was great. Notwithstanding, saith he, God esteemeth not these things; not that he esteemeth them not at all, but in the matter of justification he regardeth them not, be they never so great and so glorious. For we must diligently mark this distinction, that in matters of divinity we must speak far otherwise than in matters of policy. In matters of policy, as I have said, God will have us to honour and reverence these outward veils or persons as his instruments by whom he governeth and preserveth the world. But when the question is as touching religion, conscience, the fear of God, faith, and the service of God, we must not fear these outward persons, we must put no trust in them, look for no comfort from them, or hope deliverance by them, either corporally or spiritually. For this cause God will have no respect of persons in judgment; for judgment is a divine thing. Wherefore I ought neither to fear the judge, nor trust in the judge; but my fear and trust ought to be in God alone, who is the true judge. The civil judge or magistrate, I ought indeed to reverence for God's cause (Deut. i), whose minister he is: but my conscience may not stay or trust upon his justice and equity, or be feared through his unjust dealing or tyranny, whereby I might fall into any offence against God, in lying, in bearing false witness,

EPISTLE TO THE GALATIANS

in denying the truth, etc. Otherwise I will reverence and honour the magistrate with all my heart.

So I would also honour the Pope, and love his person, if he would leave my conscience free, and not compel me to sin against God. But he will so be feared and adored, as cannot be done without offence to the majesty of God. Here, since we must needs lose the one, let us lose the person, and stick to God. We could not be content to suffer the dominion of the Pope: but because he abuseth the same so tyrannously against us, and would compel us to deny and blaspheme God, and him only to acknowledge as our lord and master, clogging our consciences, and spoiling us of the fear and trust which we should have in God, therefore we are compelled, by the commandment of God, to resist the Pope; for it is written, "That we must rather obey God than men" (Acts iv, 19). Therefore, without offence of conscience, which is our singular comfort, we contemn the authority of the Pope.

There is a certain vehemency therefore to be noted in this word [God]. For in the cause of religion, and the word of God, there must be no respect of persons. But in matters of policy we must have regard to the person: for otherwise, there must needs follow a contempt of all reverence and order. In this world God will have an order, a reverence, and a difference of persons. For else the child, the servant, the subject would say, I am a Christian as well as my father, my schoolmaster, my master, my prince: why then should I reverence him? Before God, then, there is no respect of persons, neither of Grecian nor of Jew, but all are one in Christ: although not so before the world.

Thus Paul confuteth the argument of the false apostles, as touching the authority of the apostles, and saith, that it is nothing to the purpose. For the question is not here concerning the respect of persons, but there is a far weightier matter in hand, that is to say, a divine matter concerning God and his word, and whether this word ought to be preferred before the apostleship or no. Whereunto Paul answereth: So that the truth of the gospel may continue, so that the word of God, and the righteousness of faith, may be kept pure and uncorrupt, let the apostleship go, let an angel from heaven, let Peter, let Paul, altogether perish.

VERSE 6. *Nevertheless, they that seemed to be the chief did communicate nothing with me.*

As though he would say, I did not so confer with the apostles, that they taught me anything; for what should they teach me, since Christ, by his revelation, had before sufficiently taught me all things? And moreover, since I have now preached the gospel the space of eighteen years among the Gentiles, and Christ hath wrought so many miracles by me, whereby he hath confirmed my doctrine: wherefore it was but a conference, and no disputation. Wherein I learned nothing, neither did I recant, nor yet defend my cause, but only declared what things I had done, to wit, that I had preached to the Gentiles faith only in Christ, without the law, and that by this preaching of faith the Holy Ghost came down upon the Gentiles, which immediately spake with divers tongues. Which thing, when the apostles heard, they witnessed that I had taught the truth; wherefore the false apostles do me great wrong, which pervert and turn all these things clean contrary.

Now, if Paul would give no place to the false apostles, which set the authority of the true apostles against him, much less ought we to give place to our adversaries, which have nothing else to brag of but the authority of their idol the Pope. I know that the godly ought to be humble, but against the Pope I will and I ought to be proud with a holy pride, and say, Thou Pope, I will not be subject unto thee: I will not take thee for my master, for I am sure that my doctrine is true and godly. But the Pope will not hear this doctrine: nay, he would force us to obey his laws and his decrees, and if we will not, he will by-and-by excommunicate, curse, and condemn us as heretics. Such pride therefore against the Pope is most necessary. And if we should not be thus stout and proud, and in the Holy Ghost utterly condemn both him, with all his doctrine, and the devil, the father of lies, speaking in him, we should never be able to defend this article of the righteousness of faith. We do not then contemn the authority of the Pope because we would bear rule over him, neither would we go about to exalt ourselves above all sovereign power, since it is evident that we teach all men to humble and submit themselves to the higher powers, ordained of God; but this is it that we only seek, that the glory of God may be maintained, and the righteousness of faith may be kept pure and sound.

Wherefore, if the Pope will grant unto us, that God alone by his mere grace through Christ doth justify sinners, we will not only carry him in our hands, but will also kiss his feet. But since we cannot obtain this, we again in God are proud against him above measure; and will give no place, no, not one hair's breadth, to all the angels in heaven, not to Peter, not to Paul, not to a hundred emperors, nor to a thousand Popes, nor to the whole world. But be it far from us that we should here humble ourselves, since they would take from us our glory, even God himself, that hath created us, and given us all things, and Jesus Christ, who hath redeemed us with his blood. Let this be then the conclusion of all together, that we will suffer our goods to be taken away, our name, our life, and all that we have; but the gospel, our faith, Jesus Christ, we will never suffer to be wrested from us. And cursed be that humility which here abaseth and submitteth itself: nay, rather, let every Christian man here be proud and spare not, except he will deny Christ.

Wherefore, God assisting me, my forehead shall be more hard than all men's foreheads. Here I take upon me this title, according to the proverb, *cedo nulli,* I give place to none. Yea, I am glad even with all my heart, in this point to seem rebellious and obstinate. And here I confess that I am, and ever will be stout and stern, and will not one inch give place to any creature. Charity giveth place, "for it suffereth all things, believeth all things, hopeth all things, endureth all things" (I Cor. xiii, 7), but faith giveth no place, yea, it can suffer nothing, according to this ancient verse: *Non patiter ludum fama, fides, oculus;* that is, Man's good name, his faith, and his eye, will not be dallied withal. Wherefore, a Christian, as touching his faith, can never be too proud nor too stout, neither must he relent or give place, no, not the breadth of one hair; for faith maketh a man here like unto God: but God suffereth nothing, he giveth place to none, for he is immutable; so is faith immutable, and therefore may suffer nothing, give place to no man. But as touching charity, let a Christian man yield and suffer all things, for therein he is but a man.

VERSES 7 AND 8. *But contrariwise, when they*

> *saw that the gospel over uncircumcision was committed unto me, as the gospel over circumcision was unto Peter (for he that was mighty by Peter in the apostleship over the circumcision, was also mighty by me towards the Gentiles.)*

With these words Paul mightily confuteth the false apostles, for here he challengeth to himself the same authority which the false apostles attributed to the true apostles; and he useth here a figure which is called an inversion, returning their argument against themselves. The false apostles, saith he, do allege against me the authority of the great apostles, to maintain their cause; but I, contrariwise, do allege the same against them, for my defence, for the apostles are on my side. Wherefore, O my Galatians, believe not these counterfeit apostles, which brag so much of the authority of the apostles against me. For the apostles, when they saw the gospel over the uncircumcision to be committed to me, and knew of the grace that to me was given, gave to me and Barnabas the right-hand of fellowship, approving my ministry, and giving thanks unto God for the gifts which I had received. Thus he returned the argument of the false apostles upon themselves. And in these words there is an ardent vehemency, and more contained in matter, than in words is able to be expressed.

What meaneth Paul, when he saith, that the gospel over the uncircumcision was committed unto him, and over the circumcision unto Peter, when, notwithstanding, Paul, almost everywhere preached to the Jews in their synagogues, and Peter likewise to the Gentiles? There are examples and testimonies of both in the Acts. Peter converted the centurion, with his family, which was a Gentile (Acts x, 3). He wrote also to the Gentiles, as his first epistle testifieth. Paul preaching Christ among the Gentiles, entereth notwithstanding into the synagogues of the Jews, and there preacheth the gospel (Acts xiv, 1). And our Saviour Christ, in Matthew and Mark, commandeth his apostles to go throughout the whole world, and preach the gospel to every creature (Matt. xxviii, 20; Mark xvi, 15). Paul likewise saith, "the gospel preached to every creature which is under heaven" (Col. i, 23). Why then doth he call himself the apostle of the Gentiles, and Peter, with the other, the apostles of the circumcision?

Paul hath respect unto this, that the other apostles remained specially in Jerusalem, until God called them unto other places. Thus stood the matter then for the time, that while the political state of the Jews continued, the apostles still remained in Judea; but when the destruction of Jerusalem approached, they were dispersed throughout the whole world. But Paul, as it is written in the Acts (chap. xiii, 2), by a singular vocation was chosen to be the apostle of the Gentiles, and being sent out of Judea, he travelled through the countries of the Gentiles. Now were the Jews dispersed almost throughout the whole world, and dwelt here and there in cities and other places among the Gentiles. Paul coming thither, was wont to go into the synagogues of the Jews (Acts xiv, 1), and by this occasion he first brought unto them, as the children of the kingdom, this glad tidings, that the promises made unto the fathers were accomplished by Jesus Christ. When they would not hear this, he turned to the Gentiles, as Luke witnesseth, Acts xiii, where he bringeth in Paul thus boldly speaking against the Jews: It was necessary that we should first preach the word of God unto you; but seeing ye reject it, and judge yourselves unworthy of everlasting life, lo! we turn to the Gentiles. And in the Acts (chap. xxviii, 28), "Be it known, therefore, unto you, that this salvation of God is sent unto the Gentiles, and they shall hear it." Wherefore, Paul was sent specially unto the Gentiles. But because he was a debtor unto all, and became all things unto all men, therefore, occasion being offered, he went into the synagogues of the Jews, where, not only the Jews, but also the Gentiles, heard him preaching Christ. Otherwise, he preached publicly in the market-place, in houses, and by the rivers' sides. He was specially then the apostle of the Gentiles, as Peter was of the Jews; who, notwithstanding, preached Christ to the Gentiles also when occasion was offered.

And here he calleth uncircumcision the Gentiles, and circumcision the Jews, by a figure named synecdoche, which, under a part, comprehendeth the whole; which figure is commonly used in the scripture; the gospel then over uncircumcision, is that which was appointed to be sent unto the Gentiles. This gospel, saith he, was committed unto him, as the gospel over circumcision was unto Peter; for as Peter preached the gospel among the Jews, so did he among the Gentiles.

This he often repeateth, that Peter, James, and John, which seemed to be the pillars of the church, taught him nothing, nor committed unto him the office of preaching the gospel, as having authority and rule over him. But they themselves, saith he, did see that the gospel was committed unto me, but not by Peter; for as I did not receive or learn any gospel of man, so did I receive no commandment by man to preach the same; but both the knowledge and the commandment to preach it among the Gentiles, I received immediately from God; like as the charge was given of God unto Peter to preach the same among the Jews.

This place witnesseth very plainly that the apostles had like calling, like charge, and all one gospel. Peter preached no other gospel than the rest of the apostles did, neither did he appoint to others their charge and office; but there was an equality among them all, for they were all taught of God, that is, both their vocation and charge was wholly and immediately from God. There was none, therefore, greater than other, none that had any prerogative above other. And therefore, when the Pope vaunteth that Peter was the chief of the apostles, that thereby he might confirm and establish his usurped primacy, it is an impudent lie.

VERSE 8. *For he that was mighty by Peter.*

This is a confutation of another argument of the false apostles. Why do the false apostles boast, saith he, that the gospel of Peter was mighty, that he converted many, that he wrought many and great miracles, raised up the dead, and with his shadow healed the sick? (Acts v, 15.) I grant all these things to be true; but Peter received this power from Heaven. God gave a virtue to his word, so that many did believe him, and great miracles were wrought by him. The same power had I also; which I received not of Peter, but the same God and the same spirit which was mighty in Peter, was mighty to me also. I had the same grace; I taught many; I wrought many miracles, and through my shadow also I healed the sick. And this Luke testifieth in these words: "And God wrought no small miracles by the hands of Paul, so that from his body were brought napkins and handkerchiefs, and the diseases departed from them, and the evil spirits went out of them" (Acts xix, 11, 12). Read more hereof in Acts xiii, xvi, xx, xxviii.

To conclude, Paul will be counted in no point inferior to the rest of the apostles; and herein he glorieth with a godly and a holy pride. Necessity constrained him stoutly to withstand Peter, and the burning zeal he had for the glory of God, moved him so to do. Certain profane spirits, as Julianus and Porphirius, not considering this, thought it to be but a carnal pride that caused Paul thus to do; such as at this day we see in the Pope and his generation. But Paul had not here his own business in hand, but a matter of faith. Now, as concerning faith we ought to be invincible, and more hard, if it might be, than the adamant stone; but as touching charity, we ought to be soft, and more flexible than the reed or leaf that is shaken with the wind, and ready to yield to every thing; therefore, the controversy was not here touching the glory of Paul, but the glory of God, the word of God, the true worship of God, true religion, and the righteousness of faith, to the end that these things might still remain pure and uncorrupt.

> VERSE 9. *And when James, and Cephas, and John, knew of the grace that was given unto me, which are counted to be pillars, they gave to me, and to Barnabas, the right-hands of fellowship, that we should preach unto the Gentiles, and they unto the circumcision.*

That is to say, when they heard that I had received my calling and charge from God, to preach the gospel among the Gentiles, and that God had wrought so many miracles by me: moreover, that so great a number of the Gentiles were come to the knowledge of Christ through my ministry, and that the Gentiles had received the Holy Ghost, without the law and circumcision, by the only preaching of faith, they glorified God for his grace which was given unto me.

EPISTLE TO THE GALATIANS

He calleth grace here, whatsoever he had received of God; to wit, that of a persecutor and waster of the church he was made an apostle, was taught by Jesus Christ, and enriched with spiritual gifts. And here withal he sheweth, that Peter gave testimony unto him, that he was a true apostle, sent and taught not by himself, nor by the other apostles, but by God alone, and not only acknowledged the ministry and authority of Paul, and the gifts of the spirit, which were in him, as heavenly things, but also approved and confirmed the same, and yet not as a superior and ruler, but as a brother and witness. James and John did likewise the same. Wherefore he concludeth, that they which are esteemed for the chief pillars among the apostles, are wholly with him, and not against him.

Verse 9. *The right-hands of fellowship.*

As if they should have said: We, O Paul, in preaching the gospel, do agree with thee in all things; therefore, in doctrine we are companions, and have fellowship together therein; that is to say, we have all one doctrine, for we preach one gospel, one baptism, one Christ, and one faith. Wherefore we can teach or enjoin thee nothing, since there is one mutual consent betwixt us in all things. For we do not teach any other or more excellent things than thou dost; but the same gifts which we have, we see to be in thee also, saving that to thee is committed the gospel over uncircumcision, as the gospel over the circumcision is unto us. But we conclude here, that neither uncircumcision nor circumcision ought to hinder our society and fellowship, since it is but one gospel which we both preach.

Hitherto Paul hath proved by manifest witness, not only from God, but also from man, that is to say, the apostles, that he had truly and faithfully preached the gospel; therefore he sheweth, that whatsoever the false apostles said to diminish his authority, is but feigned and forged matter, and that the testimony of the apostles maketh for him, and not for the false apostles. But for that he is alone, and without witness, therefore he addeth an oath, and calleth God to record that the things which he hath spoken are true.

Verse 10. *Warning only that we should remember the poor, which thing also I was diligent to do.*

After the preaching of the gospel, the office and charge of a true and faithful pastor is, to be mindful of the poor. For where the church is, there must needs be poor; who, for the most part, are the only true disciples of the gospel, as Christ saith: "The poor receive the glad tidings of the gospel" (Isa. lxi, 1; Matt. xi, 5; Luke iv, 26), for the world and the devil do persecute the church, and bring many to poverty, who are afterwards forsaken and despised of the world. Moreover, the world not only offendeth herein, but also is careless for the preservation of the gospel, true religion, and the true service of God. There is none that will now take any care for the maintenance of the ministers of the church, and erecting of schools; but for the erecting and establishing of false worship, superstition, and idolatry, no cost was spared, but every man was ready to give most liberally and largely. And hereof came so many monasteries, so many cathedral churches, so many bishoprics in the Pope's church, where all impiety reigned, with so great revenues provided for their sustentation; whereas now a whole city thinketh much to find one or two poor ministers and preachers of the gospel, which before, while the Pope and all impiety reigned, did sustain sundry monasteries of monks, friars, nuns, and whole swarms of massing priests. To be brief, true religion is ever in need. And Christ complaineth, "that he is hungry, thirsty, harbourless, naked, and sick," (Matt. xxv, 42). Contrariwise, false religion and impiety flourisheth and aboundeth with all worldly wealth and prosperity. Wherefore a true and faithful pastor must have a care of the poor also: and this care Paul here confesseth that he had.

VERSE 11. *And when Peter was come to Antiochia, I withstood him to his face: for he was to be blamed.*

Paul goeth on still in his confutation, saying, "that he not only hath for his defence the testimony of Peter, and the other apostles which were at Jerusalem, but also that he withstood Peter, in the presence of the whole church of Antioch." He sheweth here a matter, not done in a corner, but in the face of the whole church. For, as before I have said, he hath here no trifling matter in hand, but the chiefest article of all Christian doctrine. The utility and majesty whereof whoso rightly esteemeth, to him all other things shall seem but vile and nothing worth. For what is Peter? What is Paul? What is an angel from heaven? What are all other creatures to the articles of justification? Which, if we know, then are we in clear light: but if we be ignorant thereof, then are we in most miserable darkness. Wherefore, if we see this article impugned, or defaced, fear not to resist either Peter or an angel from heaven, following the example of Paul, who seeing the majesty of this article to be in danger for the dignity of Peter, had no regard of his dignity and estimation, that he might keep the same pure and uncorrupt. For it is written: "He that

EPISTLE TO THE GALATIANS

loveth father or mother, or his own life more than me, is not worthy of me." (Matt. x, 37.)

Wherefore we are not ashamed, for the defence of the truth, to be counted and called of the hypocrites, proud and obstinate, and such as will be only wise, will hear none, will give place to none. Here we must needs be obstinate and inflexible. For the cause why we offend man, that is to say, tread down the majesty of the person or of the world, is so great, that the sins which the world judgeth to be most heinous, are counted singular virtues before God. "In that we love our parents, honour the magistrates, shew reverence to Peter and other ministers of the word, we do well." But here we have in hand the cause neither of Peter, nor parents, nor magistrates, nor of the world, nor of any other creatures, but of God himself. Here if I give no place to my parents, to the magistrate, or an angel from heaven, I do well. For what is the creature in respect of the Creator? Yea, what are all creatures, being compared unto him? Even as one drop of water in respect of the whole sea. Why then should I so highly esteem Peter, which is but a drop, and set God aside, which is the whole sea? Let the drop therefore give place to the sea, and let Peter give place unto God. This I say to the end that ye should diligently weigh and consider the matter wherefore Paul intreateth: for he intreateth of the word of God, which can never be magnified enough.

And where he saith (to his face) this clause maketh specially against the venomous vipers and apostles of Satan, which slander those that are absent, and in their presence dare not once open their mouths: as the false apostles did, whom also here he touched by the way: which durst not speak evil of him in his presence, but in his absence slandered him most spitefully. "So did not I (saith he) speak evil of Peter, but frankly and openly I withstood him, not of any colourable pretence, ambition, or other carnal affection, but because he was to be blamed and sharply reproved."

Here let other men debate whether an apostle may sin or no: this, say I, that we ought not to make Peter's fault less than it was indeed.—The prophets themselves have sometimes erred and been deceived. Nathan "of his own spirit said unto David, that he should build the house of the Lord," (2 Sam. vii, 3, 4). But this prophecy was by-and-by after corrected by a revelation from God, "that it should not be David, because he was a man of war and had shed much blood, but his son Solomon, that should build up the house of the Lord." So did the apostles err also; for they imagined that the kingdom of Christ should be carnal and worldly, as we may see in the first of the Acts, when they asked of Christ, saying, "Lord, wilt thou at this time restore the kingdom of Israel?" (Acts i, 6) and Peter, although he heard this commandment of Christ: "go into the whole world," etc. (Matt. xxviii), had not gone unto Cornelius, if he had not been admonished by a vision (Acts x, 10). And in this matter he did not only err, but also committed a great sin; and if Paul had not resisted him, all the Gentiles which did believe, had been constrained to receive circumcision, and to keep the law. The believing Jews also had been confirmed in their opinion; to wit, that the observation of these things were necessary to salvation; and by this means they had received again the law instead of the gospel, Moses instead of Christ. And of all this great enormity and horrible sin, Peter, by his dissimulation, had been the only occasion. Therefore we may not attribute to the saints such perfection, as though they could not sin.

Luke witnesseth "that there was such great dissension between Paul and Barnabas (which were put apart together for the ministry of the gospel among the Gentiles, and had travelled through many regions (Acts xv, 2, 39) and preached unto them the gospel) that the one departed from the other." Here we must needs say, that there was a fault either in Paul or Barnabas. And doubtless it could not be, but that the discord was exceeding great which separated these two, being joined together in such a holy fellowship, as the text witnesseth. Such examples are written for our consolation. For it is a great comfort unto us, when we hear, that even the saints, which have the Spirit of God, do sin. Which comfort they would take from us which say, that the saints do not sin.

Samson, David, and many other excellent men, full of the Holy Ghost, fell into great sins (Judges xvi; 2 Sam. xi, 15). Job and Jeremy curse the day of their nativity (Job iii, 1-12; Jer. xx, 14). Elias and Jonas are weary of their life, and desire death (Jonas iv). Such errors and offences of the saints, the scripture setteth forth to the comfort of those that are afflicted and oppressed with desperation, and to the terror of the proud. No man hath so grievously fallen at any time, but he may rise again. And on the other side, no man taketh so fast footing, but he may fall. If Peter fell, I may likewise fall. If he rose again, I may also rise again. And such examples as these are, the weak hearted and tender consciences ought to make much of, that they may the better understand what they pray for, when they say, "forgive us our trespasses;" and, "I believe the forgiveness of sins." We have the selfsame spirit of grace and prayer which the apostles and all the saints had, neither had they any prerogative above us. We have the same gifts which they had, the same Christ, baptism, word, forgiveness of sins; all which they had no less need of than we have, and by the same are sanctified and saved as we be.

> VERSE 12. *For before that certain came from James, he did eat with the Gentiles.*

The Gentiles which were converted to the faith did eat meats forbidden by the law, and Peter being conversant with the Gentiles which were converted, did eat with them, and drank wine also, which was forbidden, knowing that herein he did well, and therefore boldly transgressed the law with the Gentiles. Paul confesseth that he also did the like, when he saith, "that he became as a Jew to the Jews, and to them that were without law, as though he were without law:" that is to say, with the Gentiles he did eat and drink like a Gentile, and kept no law at all: with the Jews, according to the law, he abstained from all things forbidden in the law: for he laboured "to serve and please all men, that he might gain all," (1 Cor. ix, 19, 20, 21). Wherefore Peter, in eating and drinking with the Gentiles, sinned not, but did well, and knew that it was lawful for him so to do. For he shewed by this transgression that the law was not necessary to righteousness, and also delivered the Gentiles from the observation of the law. For if it were lawful for Peter in one thing to break the law, it was lawful for him to break it in all things. And Paul doth not here reprove Peter for his transgression, but for his dissimulation as followeth.

> VERSE 12. *But when they were come, he withdrew and separated himself, fearing them which were of the circumcision.*

Here, then, ye see Peter's offence, as Paul plainly setteth it forth. Paul accuseth him not of malice or ignorance, but of dissimulation and infirmity, in that he abstained from meats forbidden in the law, fearing lest the Jews which came from James should be offended thereby, and had more respect to the Jews than to the Gentiles. Hereby he gave occasion, as much as in him was, to overthrow the Christian liberty and truth of the gospel. For in that he did withdraw, and utterly separate himself, abstaining from meats forbidden in the law (which notwithstanding he had eaten of before) he ministered a scruple of conscience to the faithful, thus to gather upon his example: Peter abstained from meats forbidden in the law; therefore he that eateth meats forbidden in the law, sinneth and transgresseth the law; but he that abstaineth is righteous and keepeth the law, for else would not Peter have withdrawn himself; but because he did so, and of purpose refuseth those meats which before he did eat, it is a sure argument that such as eat against the law do sin, and such as abstain from meats which the law forbiddeth, do keep the law, and are justified thereby.

Here note, that the end of this fact of Peter, is reproved of Paul, and not the fact itself: for the fact in itself was not evil. To eat and drink, or not to eat or drink, is nothing: but the end, that is: "if thou eat thou sinnest: if thou abstain, thou art righteous," is evil. So circumcision of itself is good, but the end is evil: if thou be not circumcised after the law of Moses, thou canst not be saved. Also to eat meats prohibited in the law, is not evil; but this shrinking and dissimulation of Peter is evil. For it might be said, Peter abstaineth from meats forbidden in the law, wherefore if thou dost not likewise abstain, thou canst not be saved. This Paul might in no wise dissemble; for the truth of the gospel was here in danger. To the end therefore that this truth might continue sound and uncorrupt, he resisted Peter to his face.

And here we must make a distinction. For meats may be refused two manner of ways (1 Cor. ix), first, for Christian charity sake. And herein there is no danger; for to bear with the infirmity of my brother, it is good. So Paul himself both bid and taught. Secondly, by abstaining from them to obtain righteousness, and for not abstaining, to sin, and to be damned. Here accursed be charity, with all the service and works of charity whatsoever. For thus to refrain from meats, is to deny Christ, to tread his body under our feet, to blaspheme the Holy Ghost, and to despise all holy things. Wherefore, if we must lose the one, let us rather lose man, our friend and brother, than God our father. For if we lose God our father, man our friend and brother cannot continue.

Jerome, who neither understood this place, nor the whole epistle besides, thinketh this to be but a feigned reprehension of Paul, and therefore he excuseth Peter's fall, saying, "that it was done by ignorance." But Peter offended through dissimulation, and thereby had established the necessity of the law, had constrained both Gentiles and Jews to revolt from the truth of the gospel, had given them great occasion to forsake Christ, to despise grace, to return to the Jewish religion, and to bear all the burdens of the law, if Paul had not reproved him, and by that means revoked the Gentiles and Jews, which were offended through this example of Peter, to the liberty which is in Christ Jesus, and to the truth of the gospel. Wherefore, if a man would here set forth and amplify Peter's offence, it should appear to be very great, and yet was it not done by malice or ignorance, but by occasion and fear only. Thus we see what ruins may come by one man's fall and offence, if it be not well seen to and corrected in time. Wherefore, we may not trifle with this article of justification; neither is it without good cause, that we do so often and so diligently put you in mind thereof.

And it is much to be marvelled, that Peter being such an excellent apostle, should thus do; who before, in a council at Jerusalem, stood in a manner alone in defence of this article, and prevailed therein, namely, that salvation cometh by faith without the law (Acts xv).—He that before did so constantly defend the truth and liberty of the gospel, now by his fall in abstaining from meats forbidden in the law, is not only the cause of great offence, but also offendeth against his own decree. "Wherefore let him which thinketh he standeth, take heed lest he fall." (1 Cor. x, 12.) No man would think what danger there is in traditions and ceremonies: which notwithstanding we cannot want. What is more necessary than the law and the works thereof? and yet there is great danger, lest by the same men be brought to the denial of Christ. For of the law cometh oftentimes a trust and affiance in works, and where that is, there can be no trust in Christ. Christ therefore is soon denied and soon lost, as we may see in Peter, who knew this article of justification better than we do; and yet how easily should we have given occasion of such a horrible ruin, if Paul had not withstood him, that all the Gentiles should thereby have fallen away from the preaching of Paul, and by this means should have lost the gospel and Christ himself? And this should have been done under a holy pretence. For they might have said: Paul, hitherto thou hast taught us that we must be justified by grace without the law; thou seest now that Peter doth the contrary: for he abstaineth from meats forbidden in the law, and hereby he teacheth us that we cannot be saved, except we receive circumcision and observe the law.

VERSE 13. *And the other Jews dissembled likewise with him, insomuch that Barnabas was brought into their dissimulation also.*

Here you may plainly see that Paul chargeth Peter with dissimulation. If Peter dissembled, then did he certainly know what was the truth, and what was not. He that dissembleth, sinneth not of ignorance, but deceiveth by a colour which he knoweth himself to be false. "And others," saith he, "dissembled likewise with Peter, insomuch that Barnabas also (who was Paul's companion, and had now a long time preached among the Gentiles, faith in Christ, without the law, together with Paul), was brought into their dissimulation." Ye have here then Peter's offence plainly described to be mere dissimulation, which afterwards had been an occasion of the ruin of the gospel then newly received, if Paul had not resisted him.

And this is a wonderful matter, that God preserved the church, being yet but young, and the gospel itself, by one only person. Paul alone standeth to the truth; for he had lost Barnabas his companion, and Peter was against him. So sometimes one man is able to do more in a council than the whole council besides. Which things the Papists themselves do witness. And for example, they allege Paphnutius, who withstood the whole council of Nice (which was the best of all that were after the council of the apostles at Jerusalem), and prevailed against it.

This I say, to the end that we should diligently learn the article of justification, and make a plain difference between the law and the gospel, and that, in this matter, we should do nothing by dissimulation, or give place to any man, if we will retain the truth of the gospel, and faith sound and uncorrupt: which, as I have said, are soon hurt. Wherefore in this case, away with reason, which is an enemy to faith: which also in temptations of sin and death, leaneth not to the righteousness of faith (for thereof it is utterly ignorant) but to her own righteousness, or, at the least, to the righteousness of the law. Now, as soon as the law and reason join together, faith looseth her virginity: for nothing fighteth more strongly against faith, than the law and reason. And these two enemies cannot be conquered, but with great labour and difficulty; which we must conquer notwithstanding, if we will be saved.

Wherefore, when thy conscience is terrified with the law, and wrestleth with the judgment of God, ask counsel neither of reason nor of the law, but rest only upon grace and the word of consolation, and so stand herein, as if thou hadst never heard anything of the law, ascending up to the glass of faith, where neither the law nor reason do shine, but only the light of faith, which assureth us that we are saved by Christ alone, without any law. Thus the gospel leadeth us beyond and above the light of the law and reason, into the deep secrets of faith, where the law and reason have nothing to do. Notwithstanding we must hearken also into the law, but in place and time. Moses, while he was in the mountain where he talked with God face to face, had no law, made no law, ministered no law. But when he was come down from the mountain, he was a law-giver, and governed the people by the law. So the conscience must be free from the law, but the body must be obedient to the law.

Hereby it appeareth that Paul reproved Peter for no light matter, but for the chiefest article of all Christian doctrine, which, by Peter's dissimulation, was in great danger. For Barnabas and the other Jews dissembled together with him, which did all offend, not through ignorance or malice, but for fear of the Jews: whereby their hearts were so blinded, that they did not see their sin. And certainly it is much to be marvelled, that such excellent men as Peter, Barnabas, and others, should so suddenly and so lightly fall, especially in that thing which they knew to be well done, and had also before taught unto others. It is a perilous thing, therefore, to trust to our own strength, be we never so holy, never so well learned, and although we think ourselves never so sure of that we know: for in that whereof we think ourselves most sure, we may err and fall, and bring ourselves and others into great danger. Let us therefore diligently, and with all humility, exercise ourselves in the study of the holy scriptures, and let us heartily pray that we never lose the truth of the gospel.

Thus we see, then, that we are nothing with all our gifts, be they never so great, except God assist us. When he leaveth us to ourselves, our wisdom and knowledge is nothing. For, in the hour of temptation, it may suddenly come to pass, that, by the subtilty of the devil, all the comfortable places of the scripture shall be taken out of our sight, and such places only as contain threatenings, shall be set before our eyes, which shall oppress us and utterly confound us. Let us learn therefore, that, if God withdraw his hand, we may soon be overthrown; and let no man glory of his own righteousness, wisdom, and other gifts; but let him humble himself, and pray with the apostles, "Lord, increase our faith!" (Luke xvii, 5.)

VERSE 14. *But when I saw that they went not the right way to the truth of the gospel.*

This is a wonderful example of such excellent men and pillars of the church. There is none but Paul that hath his eyes open, and seeth the offence of Peter, of Barnabas, and the other Jews which dissembled with Peter. On the other side, they do not see their own offence: nay, they rather think that they do well in bearing with the infirmity of the weak Jews. Wherefore it was very necessary that Paul should reprove their offence, and not dissemble it, and therefore he accuseth Peter, Barnabas, and others, that they went not the right way to the truth of the gospel: that is to say, they swerved from the truth of the gospel. It is a great matter that Peter should be accused of Paul as one that was fallen from the truth of the gospel. He could not be more grievously reprehended. Yet he suffered it patiently; and, no doubt, but he gladly acknowledged his offence. I said before, that many have the gospel, but not the truth of the gospel. So Paul saith here, that Peter, Barnabas, and other of the Jews, "went not the right way to the truth of the gospel:" that is to say, they had the gospel, but they walked not uprightly according to the gospel. For albeit they preached the gospel, yet, through their dissimulation (which could not stand with the truth of the gospel), they established the law: but the establishing of the law is the abolishing of the gospel.

Whoso then can rightly judge between the law and the gospel, let him thank God, and know that he is a right divine. In the time of temptation, I confess that I myself do not know how to do it as I ought. Now the way to discern the one from the other, is to place the gospel in heaven, and the law on the earth; to call the righteousness of the gospel heavenly, and the righteousness of the law earthly, and to put as great difference between the righteousness of the gospel and of the law, as God hath made between heaven and earth, between light and darkness, between day and night. Let the one be as the light and the day, and the other as the darkness and the night. And would to God we could yet further separate the one from the other! Wherefore, if the question be concerning the matter of faith or conscience, let us utterly exclude the law, and leave it on the earth; but, if we have to do with works, then let us lighten the lantern of works and of the righteousness of the law. So let the sun and the inestimable light of the gospel and grace shine in the day, and the lantern of the law in the night. Wherefore, if thy conscience be terrified with the sense and feeling of sin, think thus with thyself: Thou art now remaining upon earth: there let the ass labour and travel; there let him serve and carry the burden that is laid upon him; that is to say, let the body with his members be subject to the law. But when thou mountest up into heaven, then leave the ass with his burden on the earth; for the conscience hath nothing to do with the law, or works, or with the earthly righteousness. So doth the ass remain in the valley, but the conscience ascendeth with Isaac into the mountain, knowing nothing at all of the law or works thereof, but only looking to the remission of sins and pure righteousness offered and freely given unto us in Christ.

Contrariwise in civil policy, obedience to the law must be severely required. There nothing must be known as concerning the gospel, conscience, grace, remission of sins, heavenly righteousness, or Christ himself, but Moses only, with the law and the works thereof. If we mark well this distinction, neither the one nor the other shall pass his bounds, but the law shall abide without heaven, that is, without the heart and conscience; and contrariwise, the liberty of the gospel shall abide without the earth; that is to say, without the body and members thereof. Now therefore, as soon as the law and sin come into heaven, (that is, into the conscience), let them by-and-by be cast out. For the conscience, being feared with the terror of the wrath and judgment of God, ought to know nothing of the law and sin, but of Christ only. And on the other side, when grace and liberty come into the earth (that is, into the body), then say: thou oughtest not to dwell in the dregs and dunghill of this corporeal life, but thou belongest unto heaven.

This distinction of the law and the gospel, Peter confoundeth through his dissimulation, and thereby persuaded the believing Jews, that they must be justified by the gospel and the law together. This might not Paul suffer, and therefore he reproved Peter, not to put him to any reproach, but to the end that he might again establish a plain difference between these two, namely, that the gospel justifieth in heaven, and the law on earth. The Pope hath not only mixed the law with the gospel, but also of the gospel hath made mere laws, yea, and such as are ceremonial only. He hath also confounded and mixed political and ecclesiastical matters together; which is a devilish and hellish confusion.

This place, touching the difference between the law and the gospel, is very necessary to be known, for it containeth the sum of all Christian doctrine. Wherefore, let all that love and fear God, diligently learn to discern the one from the other, not only in words, but in deed and in practice; that is to say, in heart and conscience. For, as touching the words, the distinction is easy: but in time of temptation, thou shalt find the gospel but as a stranger and a rare guest in thy conscience; but the law, contrariwise, thou shalt find a familiar and a continual dweller within thee: for reason hath the knowledge of the law naturally. Wherefore, when thy conscience is terrified with sin, which the law uttereth and increaseth, then say thou: there is a time to die, and a time to live; there is a time to hear the law, and a time to despise the law; there is a time to hear the gospel, and there is a time to be ignorant of the gospel. Let the law now depart, and let the gospel come: for there is now no time to hear the law, but the gospel. But thou hast done no good: nay, thou hast done wickedly, and hast grievously sinned. I grant, notwithstanding, I have remission of all my sins for Christ's sake. But out of the conflict of conscience, when external duties must be done, there is no time to hearken to the gospel: then must thou follow thy vocation, and the works thereof.

> VERSE 14. *I said unto Peter openly if thou, being a Jew, livest as the Gentiles, and not as the Jews, why constrainest thou the Gentiles to do like the Jews?*

That is, to wit, thou art a Jew, and therefore thou art bound to live like a Jew; that is, to abstain from meats forbidden in the law. Notwithstanding thou livest like a Gentile: that is to say, thou dost contrary to the law, and transgressest the law. For, as a Gentile, which is free from the law, thou eatest common and unclean meats, and therein thou dost well. But in that thou, being afraid at the presence of the brethren converted from the Jewish religion, abstainest from meats forbidden in the law, and keepest the law, thou compellest the Jews likewise to keep the law: that is, thou constrainest them, of necessity, to observe the law. For in that thou abstainest from profane meats, thou givest occasion to the Gentiles thus to think: Peter abstaineth from those meats which the Gentiles use to eat, which also he himself before did eat; therefore we ought likewise to avoid the same, and to live after the manner of the Jews; otherwise we cannot be justified or saved. We see then that Paul reproveth not ignorance in Peter (for he knew that he might freely eat with the Gentiles all manner of meats), but dissimulation, whereby he compelleth the Gentiles to live like the Jews.

Here I say again, that to live as the Jew, is not evil of itself, for it is a thing indifferent, either to eat swine's flesh, or any other meats. But so to play the Jew, that for conscience sake thou abstainest from certain meats, this is to deny Christ, and to overthrow the gospel. Therefore, when Paul saw that Peter's act tended to this end, he withstood him, and said, "Thou knowest that the keeping of the law is not necessary to righteousness, but that we are justified only through faith in Christ, and therefore thou keepest not the law, but transgressest the law, and eatest all manner of meats. Notwithstanding by thy example thou constrainest the Gentiles to forsake Christ, and to return to the law." For thou givest them occasion thus to think: faith only is not sufficient to righteousness, but the law and works are also required; and this Peter teacheth us by his example: therefore the observation of the law must needs be joined with faith in Christ, if we will be saved. Wherefore Peter, by his example, is not only prejudicial to the purity of doctrine, but also to the truth of faith and Christian righteousness. For the Gentiles received this of him, that the keeping of the law was necessary to righteousness; which error, in case it be admitted, then doth Christ profit us nothing at all.

Hereby it plainly appeareth to what end this discord between Paul and Peter tendeth. Paul doth nothing by dissimulation, but dealeth sincerely, and goeth plainly to work; Peter dissembleth, but his dissimulation Paul reproveth. The controversy was for the maintenance of pure doctrine, and the verity of the gospel: and in this quarrel Paul did not care for the offence of any. In this case, all people and nations, all kings and princes, all judges and magistrates ought to give place. Since then it is so dangerous a thing to have to do with the law, and that this fall was so sudden and so great, as it had been from heaven above, even down into hell, let every Christian diligently learn to discern between the law and the gospel. Let him suffer the law to rule over the body and the members thereof, but not over the conscience. For that queen and spouse may not be defiled with the law, but must be kept without spot for her only husband Christ, as Paul saith (2 Cor. xi, 2), "I have espoused you to one husband, etc." Let the conscience have her bridechamber, not in the low valley, but in the high mountain; in the which let Christ lie, and there rule and reign, who doth not terrify and afflict sinners, but comforteth them, pardoneth their sins, and saveth them. Wherefore let the afflicted conscience think upon nothing, know nothing, set nothing against the judgment of God, but the word of Christ, which is the word of grace, of remission of sins, of salvation and everlasting life. But this to perform indeed, is a hard matter. For man's reason and nature cannot stedfastly cleave unto Christ, but oftentimes it is carried away with the cogitations of the law and sin, and so always seeketh to be at liberty after the flesh, but according to conscience, a servant and slave.

VERSE 15. *We which are Jews by nature, and not sinners of the Gentiles*

That is to say, we are born unto the righteousness of the law, to Moses, and to circumcision, and even in our birth we bring the law with us. We have the righteousness of the law by nature, as Paul before saith of himself in the first chapter: "being zealous of the traditions" of the fathers. Wherefore, if we be compared with the Gentiles, we are no sinners; we are not without the law, and without works, like unto the Gentiles:

but we are Jews born, we are born righteous, and brought up in righteousness. Our righteousness beginneth even with our birth; for the Jewish religion is natural unto us. "For God commanded Abraham to circumcise every man-child the eighth day" (Gen. xvii, 10). This law of circumcision, received from the fathers, Moses afterwards confirmed. It is a great matter, therefore, that we are Jews by nature. Notwithstanding, although we have this prerogative, that we are righteous by nature, born to the law, and the works thereof, and are not sinners as the Gentiles, yet are we not therefore righteous before God.

Hereby it is evident that Paul speaketh not of ceremonies or of the ceremonial law, as some do affirm, but of a far weightier matter, namely, of the nativity of the Jews, whom he denieth to be righteous, although they be born holy, be circumcised, keep the law, have the adoption, the glory, the covenant, the fathers, the true worship, God, Christ, the promises, live in them and glory in the same; as they say (John viii), "we are the seed of Abraham." Also, "we have one father, which is God." And to the Romans (chap. ii, 17), "behold thou art called a Jew, and restest in the law," etc. Wherefore, although Peter and the other apostles were the children of God, righteous according to the law, the works and the righteousness thereof, circumcision, the adoption, the covenants, the promises, the apostleship, etc., yet Christian righteousness cometh not thereby: for none of all these is faith in Christ, which only (as followeth in the text) justifieth, and not the law: not that the law is evil or damnable, for the law, circumcision, and such like, are not therefore condemned because they justify not: but Paul therefore taketh from them the office of justification, because the false apostles contended that by them, without faith, and only by the work wrought, men are justified and saved. This was not to be suffered of Paul; for without faith all things are deadly. The law, circumcision, the adoption, the temple, the worship of God, the promises, yea, God and Christ himself, without faith, profiteth nothing. Paul therefore speaketh generally against all things which are contrary to faith, and not against ceremonies only.

VERSE 16. *Know that a man is not justified by the works of the law, but by the faith of Jesus Christ.*

This word [the work of the law] reacheth far, and comprehendeth much. We take the work of the law therefore generally for that which is contrary to grace. Whatsoever is not grace, is the law, whether it be judicial, ceremonial, or the ten commandments. Wherefore, if thou couldst do the works of the law according to this commandment: "Thou shalt love the Lord thy God with all thy heart," etc. (which no man yet ever did or could do), yet thou shouldst not be justified before God: for a man is not justified by the works of the law. But hereof we will speak more largely hereafter.

The work of the law, then, according to Paul, signifieth the work of the whole law, whether it be judicial, ceremonial, or moral. Now, if the work of the moral law do not justify, much less doth circumcision justify, which is a work of the ceremonial law. Wherefore, when Paul saith (as he oftentimes doth), "that a man is not justified by the law, or by the works of the law," (which are both one) he speaketh generally of the whole law, setting the righteousness of faith against the righteousness of the whole law. "For by the righteousness of the law," saith he, "a man is not pronounced righteous before God: but the righteousness of faith God imputeth freely through grace, for Christ's sake." The law, no doubt, is holy, righteous, and good, and consequently the works of the law are holy, righteous, and good: yet notwithstanding a man is not justified thereby before God.

Now, the works of the law may be done either before justification or after. There were many good men even amongst the Pagans, as Xenophon, Aristides, Fabius, Cicero, Pomponius, Atticus, and others, which before justification performed the deeds of the law, and did notable works. Cicero suffered death valiantly in a good and just cause. Pomponius was a constant man, and loved truth, for he never made a lie himself, nor could suffer the same in any other. Now, constancy and truth are noble virtues and excellent works of the law, and yet were they not justified thereby. After justification, Peter, Paul, and all other Christians have done and do the works of the law, yet are they not justified thereby. "I know not myself guilty in anything (saith Paul) and yet am I not thereby justified." (1 Cor. iv, 4.) We see then that he speaketh not of any part of the law, but of the whole law, and all the works thereof.

The Divinity of the Popish Sophisters, Commonly Called the Schoolmen

Wherefore, the wicked and pernicious opinion of the Papists is utterly to be condemned, which attributes the merit of grace and remission of sins to the work wrought. For they say, that a good work before grace, is able to obtain grace of congruence (which they call *meritum de congruo*), because it is meet that God should reward such a work. But when grace is obtained, the work following deserveth everlasting life of due debt and worthiness, which they call *meritum de condigno.* As for example: if a man being in deadly sin, without grace, do a good work of his own good natural inclination: that is, if he say or hear a mass, or give alms and such like, this man of congruence deserveth grace. When he hath thus obtained grace, he doth now a work which of worthiness deserveth everlasting life. For the first, God is no debtor: but because he is just and good, it behoveth him to approve such a good work, though it be done in deadly sin, and to give grace for such a service. But when grace is obtained, God is become a debtor, and is constrained of right and duty to give eternal life. For now it is not only a work of free will, done according to the substance, but also done in grace, which maketh a man acceptable unto God, that is to say, in charity.

This is the divinity of the Antichristian kingdom; which here I recite, to the end that the disputation of Paul may be the better understood (for two contrary things being set together, may be the better known): and moreover, that all men may see how far from the truth these blind guides, and leaders of the blind have wandered, and how by this wicked and blasphemous doctrine they have not only darkened the gospel, but have taken it clean away, and buried Christ utterly. For if I, being in deadly sin, can do any little work which is not only acceptable in God's sight of itself, and according to the substance, but also is able to deserve grace of congruence, and when I have received grace, I may do works according to grace, that is to say, according to charity, and get of right and duty eternal life; what need have I now of the grace of God, forgiveness of sins, of the promise, and of the death and victory of Christ? Christ is now to me unprofitable, and his benefit of none effect: for I have free will and power to do good works, whereby I deserve grace of congruence, and afterwards, by the worthiness of my work, eternal life.

Such monstrous and horrible blasphemies should have been set forth to the Turks and Jews, and not to the church of Christ. And hereby it plainly appeareth, that the Pope, with his bishops, doctors, priests, and all his religious rabble, had no knowledge or regard of holy matters, and that they were not careful for the health of the silly and miserable scattered flock. For if they had seen, but as it were through a cloud, what Paul calleth sin, and what he calleth grace, they would never have compelled the people to believe such abominations and execrable lies. By deadly sin they understood only the external work committed against the law, as murder, theft, and such like.

They could not see, that ignorance, hatred, and contempt of God in the heart, ingratitude, murmuring against God, and resisting the will of God, are also deadly sin, and that the flesh cannot think, speak, or do anything, but that which is devilish and altogether against God. If they had seen these mischiefs fast rooted in the nature of man, they would never have devised such impudent and execrable dreams touching the desert of congruence and worthiness.

Wherefore we must properly and plainly define what a wicked man or deadly sinner is. He is such a holy and bloody hypocrite as Paul was, when he went to Damascus, to persecute Jesus of Nazareth, to abolish the doctrine of the gospel, to murder the faithful, and utterly to overthrow the church of Christ. And who will not say, but that these were horrible sins? Yet could not Paul see them. For he was so blinded with a perverse zeal of God, that he thought these abominations to be perfect righteousness, and high service unto God: and shall we say, that such as defend these horrible sins to be perfect righteousness, to deserve grace?

Wherefore with Paul, we utterly deny the merit of congruence and worthiness, and affirm, that these speculations are nothing else but mere deceits of Satan, which were never done in deed, nor notified by any examples. For God never gave to any man grace and everlasting life for the merit of congruence or worthiness. These disputations therefore of the schoolmen, touching the merit of congruence and worthiness, are nothing else but vain toys and dreams of idle brains, to no other end and purpose but to draw men from the true worship of God. And hereupon is the whole papacy grounded. For there is no religious person, but he hath this imagination: I am able by the observation of my holy order to deserve grace of congruence, and by the work, which I do after that I have received this grace, I am able to heap up such treasure of merit, as shall not only be sufficient for me to obtain eternal life, but also to give or sell unto others. Thus have all the religious orders taught, and thus have they lived. And to defend this horrible blasphemy against Christ, the Papists do at this day attempt against us what they can. And there is not one of them all, but the more holy hypocrite and merit-monger he is, the more cruel and deadly enemy he is to the gospel of Christ.

THE TRUE WAY TO CHRISTIANITY

Now, the true way to Christianity is this, that a man do first acknowledge himself by the law, to be a sinner, and that it is impossible for him to do any good work. For the law saith, "thou art an evil tree, and therefore all that thou thinkest, speakest, or dost, is against God" (Matt. vii, 17). Thou canst not therefore deserve grace by thy works: which if thou go about to do, thou doublest thy offence: for since thou art an evil tree, thou canst not but bring forth evil fruits, that is to say, sins. "For whatsoever is not of faith, is sin" (Rom. xiv, 23). Wherefore he that would deserve grace by works going before faith, goeth about to please God with sins, which is nothing else but to heap sin upon sin, to mock God, and to provoke his wrath. When a man is thus taught and instructed by the law, then is he terrified and humbled, then he seeth indeed the greatness of his sin, and cannot find in himself one spark of the love of God: therefore he justifieth God in his word, and confesseth that he is guilty of death and eternal damnation. The first part then of Christianity is the preaching of repentance, and the knowledge of ourselves.

The second part is: if thou wilt be saved, thou mayest not seek salvation by works: "for God hath sent his only begotten Son into the world, that we might live through him. He was crucified and died for thee, and offered up thy sins in his own body." Here is no congruence or work done before grace, but wrath, sin, terror and death. Wherefore the law doth nothing else but utter sin, terrify and humble, and by this means prepareth us to justification, and driveth us to Christ. For God hath revealed unto us by his word, that he will be unto us a merciful father, and without our deserts (seeing we can deserve nothing) will freely give unto us remission of sins, righteousness, and life everlasting for Christ his Son's sake. For God giveth his gifts freely unto all men, and that is the praise and glory of his divinity. But the justiciaries and merit-mongers will not receive grace and everlasting life of him freely, but will deserve the same by their own works. For this cause they would utterly take from him the glory of his divinity. To the end therefore that he may maintain and defend the same, he is constrained to send his law before, which, as a lightning and thundering from heaven, may bruise and break those hard rocks.

This briefly is our doctrine as touching Christian righteousness, contrary to the abominations and blasphemies of the Papists, concerning the merit of congruence and worthiness, or works before grace and after grace. Which monstrous dreams were devised by such as were never exercised with any temptations, never had any true feeling of sin, or of the terror of death, and therefore they know not what they say, or what they teach. Moreover, they can shew no example of any work done either before or after grace that could justify before God. Wherefore they are nothing else but vain toys and foolish fables, whereby the Papists deceive both themselves and others. For Paul here plainly affirmeth, "that no man is justified by the works of the law either going before grace (whereof he speaketh in this place) or coming after grace." You see then that Christian righteousness is not such an essential quality engrafted in the nature of man, as the schoolmen do imagine, when the say:

(THE DIVINITY OF THE SCHOOLMEN:)

When a man doth any good work, God accepteth it, and for this work he poureth into him charity, which they call charity infused.—This charity, say they, is a quality remaining in the heart, and this they call formal righteousness (which manner of speaking it is expedient for you to know) and they can abide nothing less than to hear that this quality, forming and adorning the soul, as whiteness doth the wall, should not be counted righteousness. They can climb no higher than to this cogitation of man's reason, that man is righteous by his own formal righteousness, which is grace making him acceptable unto God, that is to say, charity. So to this quality cleaving unto the soul, that is to wit, charity (which is a work after the law, for the law saith, "thou shalt love the Lord thy God," etc.) *they* attribute formal righteousness, that is to say, true Christian righteousness, and they say that this righteousness is worthy of everlasting life, and he that hath it is formally righteous: and moreover he is effectually or actually righteous, because he now doth good works, whereunto everlasting life is due.—This is the opinion of the Popish schoolmen, yea, even of the best of them all.

Some others there be which are not so good, as Scotus and Occam, which said, "that for the obtaining of the grace of God, this charity infused or given of God, is not necessary: but that a man even by his own natural strength may procure this charity above all things." For so reasoneth Scotus: if a man may love a creature, a young man a maiden, a covetous man money, which are the less good, he may also love God, which is the greater good. If he have a love of the creature through his natural strength, much more hath he a love of the Creator. With this argument were all the sophisters convicted, and none of them all was able to refute it. Notwithstanding thus they reply:

The scripture compelleth us to confess, say they, that God, besides that natural love and charity which is engrafted in us (wherewith alone he is not contented) requireth also charity, which he himself giveth. And hereby they accuse God as a tyrant and a cruel exactor, who is not content that we keep and fulfil his law, but above the law (which we ourselves are able to fulfil) requireth also, that we should accomplish it with other circumstance and furniture, as apparel to the same. As if a mistress should not be contented that her cook had dressed her meat excellently well, but should chide her for that she did not prepare the same, being decked with precious apparel and adorned with a crown of gold. Now, what a mistress were this, who when her cook had done all that she was bound to do, and also exactly performed the same, would moreover require that she should wear such ornaments as she could not have? Even so, what a one should God be, if he should require his law to be fulfilled of us (which notwithstanding by our own natural strength we observe and fulfil) with such furniture as we cannot have?

But here, lest they should seem to avouch contrary things, they make a distinction, and say that the law is fulfilled two manner of ways: first, according to the substance of the deed, and secondly, according to the mind of the commander. According to the substance of the deed, say they, we may fulfil all things which the law commandeth, but not according to the mind of the commander, which is, that God is not contented that thou hast done all things which are commanded in the law [although he can require no more of thee] but he further requireth, that thou shouldst fulfil the law in charity: not that charity which thou hast by nature, but that which is above nature and heavenly, which he himself giveth. And what is this else but to make of God a tyrant and a tormentor, which requireth that of us which we are not able to perform? And it is in a manner as much as if they should say, that the fault is not in us if we be damned, but in God, which with this circumstance requireth his law to be accomplished of us.

These things I do the more diligently repeat, that you may see how far they have strayed from the true sense of the scripture, which have said that by our own natural strength we may love God above all things, or at least by the work wrought we may deserve grace and everlasting life. And because God is not content that we fulfil the law according to the substance of the deed, but will have us also to fulfil the same according to the mind of the commander: therefore the scripture further compelleth us to have a quality above nature poured into us from above, and that is charity, which they call formal righteousness, adorning and beautifying faith, being also the cause that faith justifieth us. So faith is the body, and the shell: charity the life, the kernel, the form and furniture. These are the monstrous dreams of the schoolmen.

But we, in the stead of this charity, do place faith, and we say, that faith apprehendeth Jesus Christ, who is the form which adorneth and furnisheth faith, as the colour adorneth and beautifieth the wall. Christian faith, therefore, is not an idle quality or empty husk in the heart, which may be in deadly sin until charity come and quicken it: but if it be true faith, is a sure trust and confidence in the heart, and a firm consent whereby Christ is apprehended: so that Christ is the object of faith, yea rather even in faith Christ himself is present. Faith therefore is a certain obscure knowledge, or rather darkness which seeth nothing; and yet Christ, apprehended by faith, sitteth in this darkness: like as God in Sinai and in the temple sat in the "midst of darkness," etc. (Exod. xix, 9; 1 Kings viii, 10). Wherefore our formal righteousness is not charity furnishing and beautifying faith, but it is faith itself, which is, as it were, a certain cloud in our hearts: that is to say, a stedfast trust and affiance in the thing which we see not, which is Christ: who although he be not seen at all, yet he is present.

Faith therefore justifieth, because it apprehendeth and possesseth this treasure, even Christ present. But this presence cannot be comprehended of us, because it is in darkness, as I have said. Wherefore, where assured trust and affiance of the heart is, there Christ is present, yea, even in the cloud and obscurity of faith. And this is the true formal righteousness, whereby a man is justified, and not by charity, as the Popish schoolmen do most wickedly affirm.

To conclude, like as the schoolmen say, that charity furnisheth and adorneth faith: so do we say, that it is Christ which furnisheth and adorneth faith, or rather, that he is the very form and perfection of faith. Wherefore Christ apprehended by faith, and dwelling in the heart, is the true Christian righteousness, for the which God counteth us righteous, and giveth us eternal life. Here is no work of the law, no charity, but a far other manner of righteousness, and a certain new world beyond and above the law. For Christ or faith is not the law, nor the work of the law. But concerning this matter, which the schoolmen neither well understood nor taught, we intend to speak more largely hereafter. Now it shall be enough that we have shewed, that Paul speaketh not here of the ceremonial law only, but of the whole law.

The True Rule of Christianity

Contrary to these vain trifles and doting dreams (as we have also noted before) we teach faith, and give a true rule of Christianity in this sort: first, that a man must be taught by the law to know himself, that so he may learn to say with the prophet: "All have sinned, and have need of the glory of God." Also, "There is not one righteous, no not one: not one that understandeth, not one that seeketh after God: all have gone astray." Also, "Against thee only have I sinned." (Rom. i, 23; Psalm xiv, 3; Psalm liii, 3; Psalm li, 4.) Thus we, by a contrary way, do drive men from the merit of congruence and worthiness. Now, when a man is humbled by the law, and brought to the knowledge of himself, then followeth true repentance (for true repentance beginneth at the fear and judgment of God), and he seeth himself to be so great a sinner, that he can find no means how he may be delivered from his sins by his own strength, works or merits. Then he perceiveth well what Paul meaneth when he saith, "that man is the servant and bond-slave of sin." Also, "that God hath shut up all under sin" (Rom. vii, 14; Rom. xi, 32; Rom. iii, 19), and that the whole world is guilty before God, etc., then he seeth that all the divinity of the schoolmen, touching the merit of congruence and worthiness, is nothing else but mere foolishness, and that by this means the whole papacy falleth.

Here now he beginneth to sigh, and saith in this wise: who then can give succor? For he being thus terrified with the law, utterly despaireth of his own strength: he looketh about, and sigheth for the help of a mediator and saviour. Here then cometh in good time the healthful word of the gospel, and saith, "Son, thy sins are forgiven thee" (Matt. ix, 2). Believe in Christ Jesus crucified for thy sins. If thou feel thy sins and the burden thereof, look not upon them in thyself, but remember that they are translated and laid upon Christ, whose stripes have made thee whole (Isa. liii, 5).

This is the beginning of health and salvation. By this means we are delivered from sin, justified and made inheritors of everlasting life; not for our own works and deserts, but for our faith, whereby we lay hold upon Christ. Wherefore we also do acknowledge a quality and a formal righteousness of the heart: not charity (as the sophisters do) but faith, and yet so notwithstanding, that the heart must behold and apprehend nothing but Christ the Saviour. And here it is necessary that you know the true definition of Christ. The schoolmen being utterly ignorant hereof, have made Christ a judge and a tormentor, devising this fond fancy concerning the merit of congruence and worthiness.

But Christ, according to his true definition, is no lawgiver, but a forgiver of sins, and a saviour. This doth faith apprehend, and undoubtedly believe, that he hath wrought works and merits of congruence and worthiness before and after grace abundantly. For he might have satisfied for all the sins of the world by one only drop of his blood; but now he hath shed it plentifully, and hath satisfied abundantly. (Heb. ix.) "By his own blood hath he entered into the holy place once for all, and obtained eternal redemption." Also Rom. iii and iv, "And we are justified freely by his grace, through the redemption that is in Christ Jesus, whom God hath set forth to be a reconciliation unto us, through faith in his blood." Wherefore it is a great matter to lay hold upon Christ, by faith, bearing the sins of the world. And this faith alone is counted for righteousness.

Here is to be noted, that these three things, faith, Christ, acceptation, or imputation, must be joined together. Faith taketh hold of Christ, and hath him present, and holdeth him inclosed, as the ring doth the precious stone. And whosoever shall be found having this confidence in Christ apprehended in the heart, him will God account for righteous. This is the mean, and this is the merit whereby we attain the remission of sins and righteuosness. "Because thou believest in me, saith the Lord, and thy faith layeth hold upon Christ, whom I have freely given unto thee, that he might be thy mediator and highpriest, therefore be thou justified and righteous." Wherefore God doth accept or account us as righteous, only for our faith in Christ.

And this acceptation, or imputation, is very necessary: first, because we are not yet perfectly righteous, "but while we remain in this life, sin dwelleth still in our flesh": and this remnant of sin God purgeth in us. Moreover, we are sometimes left of the Holy Ghost, and fall into sins, as did Peter, David, and other holy men. Notwithstanding we have always recourse to this article: "that our sins are covered, and that God will not lay them to our charge" (Psalm xxxii and Romans iv). Not that sin is not in us, (as the Papists have taught, saying, that we must be always working well until we feel that there is no guilt of sin remaining in us;) yea, sin is indeed always in us, and the godly do feel it, but it is covered, and is not imputed unto us of God, for Christ's sake: whom, because we do apprehend by faith, all our sins are now no sins. But where Christ and faith be not, there is no remission or covering of sins, but mere imputation of sins and condemnation. Thus will God glorify his Son, and will be glorified himself in us through him.

When we have thus taught faith in Christ, then do we teach also good works. Because thou hast laid hold upon Christ by faith, through whom thou art made righteousness, begin now to work well. Love God and thy neighbour, call upon God, give thanks unto him, praise him, confess him. These are good works indeed, which flow out of this faith, and this cheerfulness conceived in the heart, for that we have remission of sins freely by Christ.

Now what cross or affliction soever does afterwards ensue, is easily borne, and cheerfully suffered (Matt. xi, 30). "For the yoke that Christ layeth upon us is sweet, and his burden is easy." When sin is pardoned, and the conscience delivered from the burden and sting of sin, then may a Christian bear all things easily; because he feeleth all things within sweet and comfortable, therefore he doth and suffereth all things willingly. But when a man walketh in his own righteousness, whatsoever he doth is grievous and tedious unto him, because he doth it unwillingly.

We therefore do make this definition of a Christian: that a Christian is not he which hath no sin, but he to whom God imputeth not his sin, through faith in Christ. This doctrine bringeth great consolation to poor afflicted consciences in serious and inward terrors. It is not without good cause, therefore, that we do so often repeat and beat into your minds the forgiveness of sins, and imputation of righteousness for Christ's sake: also that a Christian hath nothing to do with the law and sin, especially in the time of temptation. For in that he is a Christian, he is above the law and sin. For he hath Christ the Lord of the law present and inclosed in his heart (as we have said), even as a ring hath a jewel or precious stone inclosed in it. Therefore when the law accuseth and sin terrifieth him, he looketh upon Christ, and when he hath apprehended him by faith, he hath present with him the conqueror of the law, sin, death, and the devil: who reigneth and ruleth over them, so that they cannot hurt him. Wherefore a Christian man, if ye define him rightly, is free from all laws, and is not subject unto any creature, either within or without: in that he is a Christian, I say, and not in that he is a man or a woman; that is to say, in that he hath his conscience adorned and beautified with this faith, with this great and inestimable treasure, or, as Paul saith, "this unspeakable gift" (2 Cor. ix, 15), which cannot be magnified and praised enough, for it maketh us the children and heirs of

God. And by this means a Christian is greater than the whole world; for he hath such a gift, such a treasure in his heart, that although it seemeth to be but little, yet notwithstanding the smallness thereof, is greater than heaven and earth, because Christ, which is this gift, is greater.

While this doctrine, pacifying and quieting the conscience, remaineth pure and uncorrupt, Christians are made judges over all kinds of doctrine, and are lords over the laws of the whole world. Then can they certainly judge that the Turk with his Alcoran is damned, because he goeth not the right way, that is, he acknowledgeth not himself to be miserable and damnable, nor apprehendeth Christ by faith, for whose sake he might be assured that his sins are pardoned. In like manner they boldly pronounce sentence against the Pope, that he is condemned with all his kingdom, because he so walketh and so teacheth, (with all his religious rabble of sophisters and schoolmen) that by the merit of congruence we must come to grace, and that afterward by the merit of worthiness we are received into heaven. Here, saith the Christian, this is not the right way to justify us, neither doth this way lead to heaven. For I cannot, saith he, by my works going before grace, deserve grace, nor by my works following grace, deserve eternal life; but to him that believeth, sin is pardoned, and righteousness imputed. This truth, and this confidence, maketh him the child of God, and heir of his kingdom; for in hope he possesseth already everlasting life, assured unto him by promise. Through faith in Christ therefore all things are given unto us, grace, peace, forgiveness of sins, salvation, and everlasting life, and not for the merit of congruence and worthiness.

Wherefore this doctrine of the schoolmen, with their ceremonies, masses, and infinite foundation of the papistical kingdom, are most abominable blasphemies against God, sacrileges and plain denials of Christ, as Peter hath foretold in these words: "There shall be," etc. (2 Peter ii, 1). As though he would say: the Lord hath redeemed and bought us with his blood, that he might justify and save us; this is the way of righteousness and salvation. But there shall come false teachers, which denying the Lord, shall blaspheme the way of truth, of righteousness, and salvation; they shall find out new ways of falsehood and destruction, and many shall follow their damnable ways. Peter, throughout this whole chapter, most lively painteth out the Papacy, which, neglecting and despising the gospel of faith in Christ, hath taught the works and traditions of men; as the merit of congruence and worthiness, the difference of days, meats, vows, invocation of saints, pilgrimages, purgatory, and such like. In these fantastical opinions the Papists are so nusled, that it is impossible for them to understand one syllable of the gospel, of faith, or of Christ.

And this the thing itself doth well declare. For they take that privilege unto themselves which belongeth unto Christ alone. He only forgiveth sins, he only giveth righteousness and everlasting life. And they most impudently and wickedly do vaunt that they are able to obtain these things by their own merits and worthiness before and after grace. This, saith Peter and the other apostles, is to bring in damnable heresies and sects of perdition. For by these means they deny Christ, tread his blood under their feet, blaspheme the Holy Ghost, and despise the grace of God. Wherefore no man can sufficiently conceive how horrible the idolatry of the Papists is. As inestimable as the gift is which is offered unto us by Christ, even so and no less abominable are these profanations of the Papists. Wherefore they ought not to be lightly esteemed or forgotten, but diligently weighed and considered. And this maketh very much also for the amplifying of the grace of God, and benefit of Christ, as by the contrary. For the more we know the profanation of the papistical mass, so much the more we abhor and detest the same, and embrace the true use of the holy communion, which the Pope hath taken way, and hath made merchandise thereof, that being bought for money, it might profit others. For he saith, that the massing priest, an apostate, denying Christ and blaspheming the Holy Ghost, standing at the altar, doth a good work, not only for himself, but also for others, both quick and dead, and for the whole church, and that only by the work wrought, and by no other means.

Wherefore even by this we may plainly see the inestimable patience of God, in that he hath not long ago destroyed the whole papacy, and consumed it with fire and brimstone, as he did Sodom and Gomorrah. But now these jolly fellows go about, not only to cover, but highly to advance their impiety and filthiness. This we may in no case dissemble. We must therefore with all diligence set forth the article of justification, that, as a most clear sun, it may bring to light the darkness of their hypocrisy, and discover their filthiness and shame. For this cause we do so often repeat, and so earnestly set forth the righteousness of faith, that the adversaries may be confounded, and this article established and confirmed in our hearts. And this is a most necessary thing; for if we once lose this sun, we fall again into our former darkness. And most horrible it is, that the Pope should ever be able to bring this to pass in the church, that Christ should be denied, trodden under foot, spit upon, blasphemed, yea, and that even by the gospel and sacraments; which he hath so darkened, and turned into such horrible abuse, that he hath made them to serve him against Christ, for the establishing and confirming of his detestable abominations. O deep darkness! O horrible wrath of God!

VERSE 16. *Even we, I say, have believed in Jesus Christ, that we might be justified.*

This is the true mean of becoming a Christian, even to be justified by faith in Jesus Christ, and not by the works of the law. Here we must stand, not upon the wicked gloss of the schoolmen, which say, that faith then justifieth, when charity and good works are joined withal. With this pestilent gloss the sophisters have darkened and corrupted this, and other like sentences in Paul, wherein he manifestly attributeth justification to faith only in Christ. But when a man heareth that he ought to believe in Christ, and yet notwithstanding faith justifieth not except it be formed and furnished with charity, by-and-by he falleth from faith and thus he thinketh: If faith without charity justifieth not, then is faith in vain and unprofitable, and charity alone justifieth; for except faith be formed with charity, it is nothing.

And to confirm this pernicious and pestilent gloss, the adversaries do allege this place (1 Cor. xiii, 1), "Though I speak with the tongues of men and angels, and have no love, I am nothing." And this place is their brazen wall. But they are men without understanding, and therefore they can see or understand nothing in Paul: and by this false interpretation, they have not only perverted the words of Paul, but have also denied Christ, and buried all his benefits. Wherefore we must avoid this gloss as a most deadly and devilish poison, and conclude with Paul, "that we are justified, not by faith furnished with charity, but by faith only, and alone."

We grant that we must teach also good works and charity, but it must be done in time and place, that is to say, when the question is concerning works, and toucheth not this article of justification. But here the question is, By what means we are justified, and attain eternal life?" To this we answer, with Paul, "that by faith only in Christ we are pronounced righteous, and not by the works of the law or charity": not because we reject good works, but for that we will not suffer ourselves to be removed from this anchor-hold of our salvation, which Satan most desireth. Wherefore, since we are now in the matter of justification, we reject and condemn all good works; for this place will admit no disputation of good works. In this matter therefore we do generally cut off all laws, and all the works of the law.

But the law is good, just, and holy. True, it is. But when we are in the matter of justification, there is no time or place to speak of the law: but the question is, what Christ is, and what benefit he hath brought unto us. Christ is not the law; he is not my work, or the work of the law; he is not my charity, my obedience, my poverty; but he is the lord of life and death, a mediator, a saviour, a redeemer of those that are under the law and sin. In him we are by faith, and he in us. The bridegroom must be alone with the bride in his secret chamber, all the servants and family being put apart. But afterwards, when the door is open, and he cometh forth, then let the servants and handmaidens return, to minister unto them: then let charity do her office, and let good works be done.

We must learn therefore to discern all laws, yea, even the the law of God, and all works, from the promise of the gospel, and from faith, that we may define Christ rightly. For Christ is no law, and therefore he is no exactor of the law and works, "but he is the Lamb of God, that taketh away the sins of the world" (John i, 29). This doth faith alone lay hold of, and not charity, which notwithstanding, as a certain thankfulness, must follow faith. Wherefore victory over sin and death, salvation and everlasting life, came not by the law, nor by the works of the law, nor yet by the power of free-will, but by the Lord Jesus Christ only and alone.

VERSE 16. *That we might be justified by faith in Christ, and not by the works of the law.*

Paul speaketh not here of the ceremonial law only, as before we have said, but of the whole law; for the ceremonial law was as well the law of God, as the moral law. As for example, circumcision, the institution of the priesthood, the service and ceremonies of the temple, were as well commanded of God, as the ten commandments. Moreover, when Abraham was commanded to offer up his son Isaac in sacrifice, it was a law. This work of Abraham pleased God no less than other works of the ceremonial law did, and yet was he not justified by this work, but by faith; for the scripture saith: "Abraham believed God, and it was counted to him for righteousness" (Gen. xv, 6; Rom. iv, 3).

But since the revealing of Christ, say they, the ceremonial law killeth and bringeth to death. Yea, so doth the law of the ten commandments also, without faith in Christ. Moreover, there may no law be suffered to reign in the conscience, but only the law of the spirit and life, whereby we are made free in Christ from the law of the letter and of death, from the works thereof, and from all sins: not because the law is evil, but for that it is not able to justify us: for it hath a plain contrary effect and working. It is a high and an excellent matter to be at peace with God, and therefore, in this case, we have need of a far other mediator than Moses or the law. Here we must be nothing at all, but only receive the treasure, which is Christ, and apprehend in our hearts by faith, although we feel ourselves to be never so full of sin. These words therefore of the apostle: "That we might be justified by faith, and not by the works of the law," are very effectual, and not in vain or unprofitable, as the schoolmen think, and therefore they pass them over so lightly.

Hitherto ye have heard the words of Paul which he spake unto Peter; wherein he hath briefly comprised the principal article of all Christian doctrine, which maketh true Christians indeed. Now he turneth to the Galatians, to whom he writeth, and thus he concludeth: Since it is so, that we are justified by faith in Christ, then by the works of the law shall no flesh be justified.

VERSE 16. *Because by the deeds of the law, no flesh shall be justified.*

Flesh, in Paul, doth not signify (as the schoolmen dream) manifest and gross sins, for those he useth to call by their proper names, as adultery, fornication, uncleanness, and such like: but by flesh, Paul meaneth here, as Christ doth in the third chapter of John, "That which is born of the flesh," saith he, "is flesh" (John iii, 6). Flesh therefore signifieth the whole nature of man, with reason and all other powers whatsoever do belong to man. This flesh, saith he, is not justified by works, no, not of the law. Flesh therefore, according to Paul, signifieth all the righteousness, wisdom, devotion, religion, understanding, and will, that is possible to be in a natural man; so that if a man be never so righteous, according to reason and the law of God, yet with all this righteousness, works, merits, devotion, and religion, he is not justified.

This the Papists do not believe, but being blind and obstinate, they defend their abominations against their own conscience, and continue still in this their blasphemy, having in their mouths these execrable words: He that doth this good work, or that, deserveth forgiveness of his sins: whosoever entereth this or that holy order, and keepeth his rule, to him we assuredly promise everlasting life. It cannot be uttered what a horrible blasphemy it is to attribute that to the doctrine of devils, to the decrees and ordinances of men, to the wicked traditions of the Pope, to the hypocritical works and merits of monks and friars, which Paul the apostle of Christ taketh from the law of God. For if no flesh be justified by the works of the law, much less shall it be justified by the rules of Benedict, Francis, or Augustine, in which there is not one jot of true faith in Christ; but this only they teach, that whosoever keepeth these things hath life everlasting.

Wherefore I have much and often marvelled, that these sects of perdition reigning so many years in so great darkness and errors, the church could endure and continue as it hath done. Some there were whom God called by the text of the gospel and by baptism. These walked in simplicity and humbleness of heart, thinking the monks and friars, and such only as were anointed of the bishops, to be religious and holy, and themselves to be profane and secular, and not worthy to be compared unto them. Wherefore they finding in themselves no good works to set against the wrath and judgment of God, did fly to the death and passion of Christ, and were saved in this simplicity.

Horrible and unspeakable is the wrath of God, in that he hath so long time punished the contempt of the gospel and Christ in the Papists, and also their ingratitude, in giving them over into the reprobate sense, insomuch that they blaspheming and denying Christ altogether as touching his office, instead of the gospel, received the execrable rules, ordinances, and traditions of men, which they devoutly adored and honoured, yea, and preferred the same far above the word of God, until at length they were forbidden to marry, and were bound to that incestuous single life; wherein they were outwardly polluted and defiled with all kinds of horrible wickedness, as adultery, whoredom, uncleanness, sodomy, and such other abominations. This was the fruit of that filthy single life.

So God punishing sin with sin, inwardly gave them over into a reprobate mind, and outwardly suffered them to fall into such horrible abominations, and that justly, because they blasphemed the only Son of God, in whom the Father would be glorified, and whom he delivered to death, that all which believe in him, might be saved by him, and not by their own execrable rules and orders. "Him that honoureth me," saith he, "I will honour" (1 Sam. ii, 30). Now, God is honoured in his Son. Whoso then believeth that the Son is our mediator and saviour, he honoureth the Father, and him again doth God honour; that is to say, adorneth him with his gifts, forgiveness of sins, righteousness, the Holy Ghost, and everlasting life. Contrariwise, "They that despise me," saith he, "shall be despised."

This is then a general conclusion: "by the deeds of the law no flesh shall be justified." The law of God is greater than the whole world, for it comprehendeth all men, and the works of the law do far excel even the most glorious will-workers of all the merit-mongers; and yet Paul saith, "that neither the law, nor the works of the law, do justify." Therefore we conclude with Paul, "that faith only justifieth." This proposition he goeth about to confirm in this manner.

> VERSE 17. *If then while we seek to be made righteous by Christ, we ourselves are found sinners, is Christ therefore the minister of sin? God forbid.*

If this be true, saith he, that we are justified by Christ, then is it impossible that we should be sinners, or should be justified by the law. On the contrary, if this be not true, but that we must be justified by the law, and the works of the law, it is then impossible that we should be justified by Christ. One of these two must needs be false. Either we are not justified by Christ, or we are not justified by the law. But the truth is, that we are justified by Christ: therefore we are not justified by the law. He reasoneth therefore after this manner: "If then while we seek to be made righteous by Christ," etc. That is, if we seek to be justified by Christ, and so being justified are yet found sinners, having need of the law to justify us, being sinners: if we have need, I say, of the observation of the law to justify us, so that they which are righteous in Christ are not righteous, but have yet need of the law to justify them: or if he that is justified by Christ, must yet further be justified by the law, then is Christ nothing else but a lawgiver, and a minister of sin. Therefore he that is justified and holy in Christ, is not justified or holy, but hath yet need of the righteousness and holiness of the law.

But we are indeed justified and made righteous in Christ; for the truth of the gospel teacheth us, that a man is not justified in the law, but in Christ. Now, if they which are justified in Christ, are yet found sinners, that is, do yet still belong to the law, and are under the law (as the false apostles teach) then are they not yet justified; for the law accuseth them, and sheweth them to be yet sinners, and requireth of them the works of the law, as necessary to their justification. Therefore they that are justified in Christ, are not justified; and so it followeth, that Christ is not a justifier, but a minister of the law.

With these words he vehemently chargeth the false apostles and all merit-mongers, that they pervert all together; for they make of the law grace, and of grace the law; of Moses Christ, and of Christ Moses. For they teach, that besides Christ, and all the righteousness of Christ, the observance of the law is necessary to justification. And thus we see, that by their intolerable perverseness, they make the law Christ; for by this means they attribute that to the law, which properly belongeth unto Christ. If thou do the works of the law, say they, thou shalt be saved; but if thou do them not, thou shalt not be justified, although thou do believe in Christ ever so much. Now, if it be so, that Christ justifieth not, but is the minister of sin (as it needs must follow by their doctrine) then is Christ the law; for we have nothing else of him, seeing he teacheth that we are sinners, than that we have by the law. So Christ being the minister of sin, sendeth us to the law and to Moses, as to our justifier.

It cannot be, therefore, but that the Papists, and all such as are ignorant of the righteousness of Christ, or have not the true knowledge thereof, must needs make of Christ Moses and the law, and of the law Christ. For thus they teach: it is true, say they, that faith in Christ justifieth, but withal we must needs keep the commandments of God. For it is written, "If thou wilt enter into life, keep the commandments" (Matt. xix, 17). Here, even at the first dash, Christ is denied, and faith abolished, because that is attributed to the commandments of God, or to the law, which belongeth to Christ alone. For Christ, according to his true definition, is a justifier and redeemer from sins. If I attribute this to the law, then is the law my justifier, delivering me from my sins, because I do the works thereof; and so now the law is Christ, and Christ utterly loseth his name, his office, and glory, and is nothing else but a minister of the law, reproving, terrifying, presenting and sending the sinner to another that may justify him; which is the proper office of the law.

But the proper office of Christ is, after the law hath pronounced a man to be guilty, to raise him up again, and to loose him from his sins, if he believe the gospel. For to all that do believe, "Christ is the end and the full finishing of the law unto righteousness: he is the Lamb of God that taketh away the sins of the world" (Romans x, 4; John i, 29). But the Papists and Anabaptists, because they understand not this doctrine, do turn all clean contrary, making of Christ Moses, and of Moses Christ.

And this is indeed (although they will say otherwise) their principal proposition: that Christ is Moses. Moreover, they deride us, because we do diligently teach, and so earnestly require faith. Ha, ha, say they, faith, faith: wait thou the time until thou come to heaven by faith. Nay, thou must strive to do greater and weightier matters. Thou must fulfil the law, according to that saying: "Do this and thou shalt live" (Luke x, 28). Faith, which ye do so highly extol, does nothing else but make men, careless, idle and negligent. Thus are they become nothing else but ministers of the law and law-workers, calling back the people from baptism, faith, the promises of Christ, to the law and works, turning grace into the law, and the law into grace.

Who would ever believe that these things could so easily be confounded and mingled together? There is no man so insensible, which doth not perceive this distinction of the law and grace to be most plain and manifest. For the very nature and signification of the words maketh this distinction and difference. For who understandeth not that these words, law and grace, do differ in name and signification? Wherefore it is a monstrous thing that, this distinction being so plain, the adversaries should be so devilish and perverse, as to mingle together the law and grace, and to transform Christ into Moses. Therefore I oftentimes say, that this doctrine of faith is very plain, and that every man may easily understand this distinction of the law and grace, as touching the words, but as touching the use and practice, is is very hard.

The Pope and his school-doctors do plainly confess, that the law and grace are diverse and distinct things, and yet, when they come to the use and practice thereof, they teach clean contrary. Faith in Christ, say they, whether it be gotten by the strength, operation and qualities of nature, or whether it be faith infused and poured into us of God, yet is it but a dead faith, if charity be not joined therewith. Where is now the distinction and difference of the law and grace? Indeed, they do distinguish them in name, but in effect they call them charity. Thus do all they which do straightly require the observation of the law, and attribute justification to the law and works. Wherefore, whosoever doth not perfectly understand the article of justification, must needs confound and mingle the law and grace together.

Let every man therefore diligently learn, above all things, to put a difference between the law and grace in deed and in practice: not in words only, as the Pope and the fantastical anabaptists do: who, as touching the words, do confess that they are two distinct things: but in very deed (as I have said) they confound and mingle them together, for they will not grant that faith justifieth without works. If this be true, then Christ profiteth me nothing. For though my faith be never so perfect, yet after their opinion, if this faith be without charity, I am not justified. And thus Christ apprehended by faith is not a justifier, grace profiteth nothing, neither can faith be true faith without charity.

With this doctrine these lying spirits and sects of perdition do darken and deface the benefit of Christ at this day: they take away from him the glory of a justifier, and make him a minister of sin. They are in all things like to the false apostles. For even as they throughout all the churches did require circumcision and the observation of the law besides faith in Christ, insomuch that, without circumcision and the keeping of the law, they denied the justification of faith ("for except ye be circumcised," said they, "after the law of Moses, ye cannot be saved"); even so at this day, these strait exactors of the law, besides the righteousness of faith, do require the keeping of the commandments of God, according to that saying: "Do this and thou shalt live." Also, "If thou wilt enter into life, keep the commandments" (Luke x, 28; Matt. xix, 17). Wherefore there is not one among them, be he never so wise, that understandeth the difference between the law and grace.

But we put a difference, and say that we do not here dispute whether we ought to do good works: whether the law be good, holy and just: whether it ought to be kept or no? For this is another manner of question. But our question is concerning justification, and whether the law do justify or no? This the adversaries will not hear; they will not answer to this question, nor make any distinction as we do; but only cry out, that good works ought to be done, that the law ought to be observed. We know that well enough. But because these are divers distinct matters, we will not suffer them to be mingled together. That good works ought to be done, we will hereafter declare them when time shall serve. But since we are now on the matter of justification, we set aside here all good works, for the which the adversaries do so earnestly strive, ascribing unto them wholly the office of justifying: which is to take from Christ his glory, and to ascribe the same unto works.

Wherefore this is a strong argument, which I have oftentimes used to my great comfort: "If then while we seek to be made righteous by Christ," etc. As though Paul should say: if we, being justified by Christ, are counted yet as not justified and righteous, but as sinners which are yet to be justified by the law, then may we not seek justification in Christ, but in the law. But if justification cometh by the law, then cometh it not by grace. Now if justification cometh not by grace, but by the law, what hath Christ done and wrought by his death, by his preaching, by his victory which he hath obtained over the law, sin, and death, and by sending the Holy Ghost? We must conclude, therefore, that either we are justified by Christ, or else that we are made sinners, culpable and guilty through him. But if the law do justify, then can it not be avoided, but needs it must follow, that we are made sinners through Christ, and so Christ is a minister of sin. The case standing thus, let us then set down this proposition; every one that believeth in the Lord Jesus Christ is a sinner, and is guilty of eternal death, and if he fly not unto the law, doing the works thereof, he shall not be saved.

The holy scripture, especially the New Testament, maketh often mention of faith in Christ, and highly advanceth the same; which saith, "that whosoever believeth in him is saved, perisheth not, is not judged, is not confounded, hath eternal life," etc. (John iii, 16; John v, 24). But contrariwise they say, he that believeth in him is condemned, etc., because he hath faith without works, which doth condemn. Thus do they pervert all things, making of Christ a destroyer and a murderer, and of Moses a saviour. And is not this a horrible blasphemy, so to teach, that by doing good works thou shalt be made worthy of eternal life; but by believing in Christ thou shalt be made culpable and guilty of eternal death! That the law being kept and accomplished saveth, and faith in Christ condemneth?

The self-same words, I grant, the adversaries do not use: but in very deed, such is their doctrine. For faith infused, say they, which properly they call faith in Christ, doth not make us free from sin, but that faith which is furnished with charity. Hereof it followeth, that faith in Christ, without the law, saveth us not. This is plainly to affirm, that Christ leaveth us in our sins, and in the wrath of God, and maketh us guilty of eternal death. On the other side, if thou keep the law, and do the works thereof, then faith justifieth thee, because it hath works, without the which faith availeth nothing. Therefore works justify, and not faith. O horrible impiety! What pernicious and cursed doctrine is this?

Paul therefore groundeth his argument upon an impossibility and a sufficient division. If we being justified in Christ, are yet found sinners, and cannot be justified but by another mean than Christ, that is to wit, by the law, then cannot Christ justify us, but he only accuseth and condemneth us; and so consequently it followeth, that Christ died in vain, and these with other like places are false. "Behold the Lamb of God, that taketh away the sins of the world." Also, "He that believeth in him hath everlasting life," (John i, 29; iii, 16). Yea, the whole scripture is false, which beareth witness that Christ is the justifier and saviour of the world. For if we be found sinners after that we be justified by Christ, it followeth of necessity, that they which fulfil the law are justified without Christ. If this be true, then are we either Turks, or Jews, or Tararians, professing the name and word of God in outward shew, but in deed and verity utterly denying Christ and his word. It is great impiety therefore to affirm that faith, except it be formed with charity, justifieth not. But if the adversaries will needs defend this doctrine, why do they not the reject faith in Christ altogether: especially seeing they make nothing else of it but a vain quality in the soul, which without charity availeth nothing? Why do they not say in plain words that works do justify and not faith? Yea, why do they not generally deny not only Paul, but also the whole gospel; as in very deed they do, which attribute righteousness to works, and not to faith alone? For if faith and works together do justify, then is the disputation of Paul altogether false, which plainly pronounced, "that a man is not justified by the deeds of the law, but by faith alone in Jesus Christ."

VERSE 17. *Is Christ therefore the minister of sin?*

This is a kind of speech used of the Hebrews, which Paul in 2 Cor. iii doth also use: where he most divinely and plainly speaketh of these two ministers: to wit, of the letter and the spirit of the law and grace, or of death and life. And he saith, "That Moses the minister of the law, hath the minister of sin," as he calleth it, "of wrath, death, and condemnation." For Paul is wont to give reproachful names unto the law, and amongst all the apostles he only useth this manner of speech: the other do not so speak. And very necessary it is, that such as are studious of the holy scripture should understand this manner of speech used of the apostle.

Now a minister of sin is nothing else but a lawgiver, or a schoolmaster of the law, which teacheth good works and charity, and that a man must suffer the cross and afflictions, and follow the example of Christ and of the saints. He that teacheth and requireth this, is a minister of the law, of sin, wrath, and of death: for by this doctrine he doth nothing else but terrify and afflict men's consciences, and shut them under sin. For it is impossible for the nature of man to accomplish the law: yea, in those that are justified and have the Holy Ghost, the law of the members fighteth against the law of the mind (Rom. vii, 23). What will it not then do in the wicked which have not the Holy Ghost? Wherefore he that teacheth that righteousness cometh by the law, doth not understand what he saith or what he affirmeth, and much less doth he keep the law, but rather he deceiveth himself and others, and layeth upon them such a burden as they are not able to bear, requiring and teaching impossible things, and at the last he bringeth himself and his disciples unto desperation.

The right use and end therefore of the law is, to accuse and condemn as guilty such as live in security, that they may see themselves to be in danger of sin, wrath, and death eternal, that so they may be terrified and brought even to the brink of desperation, trembling and quaking at the falling of a leaf; and in that they are such, they are under the law. For the law requireth perfect obedience unto God, and condemneth all those that do not accomplish the same. Now, it is certain, that there is no man living which is able to perform this obedience: which notwithstanding God straitly requireth of us. The law therefore justifieth not, but condemneth, according to that saying, "Cursed is he that abideth not in all things that are written in this book" (Deut. xxvii, 26; Gal. iii, 10). Therefore he that teacheth the law is the minister of the law.

Wherefore it is not without good cause, that Paul, in 2 Cor. iii, calleth the minister of the law, the minister of sin: for the law sheweth and uttereth sin, which without the law is dead. Now the knowledge of sin (I speak not here of that speculative knowledge of hypocrites, but of a true knowledge, by the which we see the wrath of God against sin, and feel a true taste of death) terrifieth the heart, driveth down to desperation, killeth and destroyeth (Rom. vii). Wherefore these schoolmasters of the law and works are called in the scripture oppressors and tyrants. For as the taskmasters in Egypt did oppress the children of Israel (Ex. v.) with corporal servitude, so do these lawgivers and taskmasters drive men into spiritual and most miserable bondage of soul, and at length bring them to desperation and utter destruction. These do neither know themselves nor the force of the law; neither is it possible for them to have quietness and peace of conscience in great and inward terrors, and in the agony of death, yea, though they have obseved the law, loved their neighbours, done many good works, and suffered great afflictions, for the law always terrifieth and accuseth, saying, thou never didst accomplish all that is commanded in the law; but accursed is he that hath not done all things contained therein. Wherefore these terrors remain still in the conscience, and increase more and more. And if such schoolmasters of the law be not raised up by faith and the righteousness of Christ, they are driven down headlong to desperation.

This also was notably figured when the law was given, as we may see in the 19th and 20th of Exodus. Moses brought the people out of the tents to meet with the Lord, that they might hear him speak unto them out of the dark cloud. Then the people being astonished and trembling for fear, fled back (which a little before had promised to do all that God had commanded) and standing aloof, off, said unto Moses: "Who can abide to see the fire, and to hear the thunderings and noise of the trumpet? Talk thou with us, and we will hear thee: but let not God talk with us, lest we die." So the proper office of the law is to lead us out of our tents and tabernacles, that is to say, from the quietness and security wherein we dwell, and from trusting in ourselves, and to bring us before the presence of God, to reveal his wrath unto us, and to set before us our sins. Here the conscience feeleth that it hath not satisfied the law, neither is it able to satisfy it, nor to bear the wrath of God, which the law revealeth when it bringeth us forth after this manner before the presence of God; that is to say, when it feareth us, accuseth us, and setteth before us our sins. Here it is impossible that we should be able to stand: and therefore, being thoroughly afraid, we fly, and we cry out with the children of Israel, "We shall die, we shall die: let not the Lord speak unto us, but speak thou unto us," etc.

He then which teacheth that faith in Christ justifieth not without the observation of the law, maketh Christ a minister of sin, that is to say, a schoolmaster of the law, which teacheth the self-same doctrine that Moses did. By this means Christ is no saviour, no giver of grace, but a cruel tyrant, who requireth such things (as Moses did) which no man is able to perform. See how all the merit-mongers do take Christ to be but a new law-giver, and the gospel to be nothing else but a certain book which containeth new laws concerning works, as the Turks dream of their Alcoran. But as touching laws there is enough in Moses. The gospel then is a preaching of Christ, which forgiveth sins, giveth grace, justified and saveth sinners. Now, whereas there are commandments found in the gospel, they are not the gospel, but expositions of the law, and matters depending upon the gospel.

To conclude, if the law be the ministry of sin, then it is also the ministry of wrath and of death. For as the law revealeth sin, so doth it terrify a man, it sheweth unto him his sin and the wrath of God, and striketh into him a terror of death and damnation. For this the conscience by-and-by gathereth: thou hast not kept the commandments of God, therefore is God angry with thee. If he be angry with thee, he will destroy and condemn thee for ever. And it thinketh this to be an infallible consequence: I have sinned, therefore I must die. And so it followeth, that the ministry of sin, is the ministry of wrath and condemnation. For after that sin is revealed, by-and-by ensueth the wrath of God, death, and damnation. And hereof it cometh, that many which are not able to bear the judgment and wrath of God, which the law setteth before their eyes, do kill, hang, or drown themselves.

VERSE 17. *God forbid.*

As though he would say, Christ is not the minister of sin, but the giver of righteousness and eternal life. Wherefore Paul separateth Moses far from Christ. Let Moses then tarry on the earth; let him be the schoolmaster of the letter, and exactor of the laws: let him torment and crucify sinners. But the believers, saith Paul, have another schoolmaster in their conscience: not Moses, but Christ, which hath abolished the law and sin, hath overcome the wrath of God, and destroyed death. He biddeth us that labour and are oppressed with all manner of calamities, to come unto him. Therefore when ye fly unto him, Moses with his law, vanishes away (Deut. xxxiii, 4), so that his sepulchre can no where be seen, sin and death can hurt us no more. For Christ our instructor is Lord over the law, sin, and death; so that they which believe in him, are delivered from the same. It is therefore the proper office of Christ to deliver from sin and death; and this Paul teacheth and repeateth every where.

We are condemned and killed by the law, but by Christ we are justified and restored to life. The law astonisheth us, and driveth us from God: but Christ reconcileth us to God, and maketh for us an entrance, that we may boldly come unto him. "For he is the Lamb of God, that hath taken away the sins of the world." Now, if the sin of the world be taken away, then is it taken away from me also, which do believe in him. If sin be taken away, then is the wrath of God, death, and damnation taken away also. And in the place of sin succeedeth righteousness; in the place of wrath, reconciliation and grace; in the place of death, life; and in the place of damnation, salvation.

Let us learn to practise this distinction, not in words only, but in life and lively experience, and with an inward feeling. For where Christ is, there must needs be joy of heart and peace of conscience: for Christ is our reconciliation, righteousness, peace, life, and salvation. Briefly, whatsoever the poor afflicted conscience desireth, it findeth in Christ abundantly. Now Paul goeth about to amplify this argument, and to persuade as followeth.

VERSE 18. *For if I build again the things that I have destroyed, I make myself a trespasser.*

As if he should say: I have not preached to this end, that I might build again those things which I once destroyed. For if I should so do, I should not only labour in vain, but should make myself also a transgressor, and overthrow all together, as the false apostles do; that is to say, of grace, and of Christ, I should again make the law and Moses: and contrariwise, of the law and Moses, I should make grace and Christ. Now, by the ministry of the gospel, I have abolished sin, heaviness of heart, wrath and death. For thus have I taught: Thy conscience, O man, is subject to the law, sin, and death; from which thou canst not be delivered either by men or angels. But now cometh the gospel, and preacheth unto thee remission of sin by Jesus Christ, who hath abolished the law, and hath destroyed sin and death: believe in him; so shalt thou be delivered from the curse of the law, and from the tyranny of sin and death: thou shalt become righteous, and have eternal life.

Behold how I have destroyed the law, by the preaching of the gospel, to the end that it should not reign in the conscience any more. For when the new guest Christ Jesus cometh into the new house, there to dwell alone, Moses the old inhabiter must give place unto him, and depart some whither else. Also where Christ the new guest is come to dwell, there can sin, wrath and death have no place: but there now dwelleth mere grace, righteousness, joy, life, true affiance and trust in the Father, now pacified and reconciled unto us, gracious, long-suffering, and full of mercy, for his Son Christ's sake. Should I then, driving out Christ, and destroying his kingdom, which I have planted through the preaching of the gospel, now build up again the law, and set up the kingdom of Moses? Indeed this should I do, if I should teach circumcision and the observation of the law to be necessary to salvation, as the false apostles do: and by this means, in the stead of righteousness and life, I should restore again sin and death. For the law doth nothing else but utter sin, procure God's wrath, kill and destroy.

What are the Papists (I pray you) yea, the best of them all, but destroyers of the kingdom of Christ, and builders up of the kingdom of the devil and of sin, of wrath and eternal death? Yea, they destroy the church, which is God's building, not by the law of Moses, as did the false apostles, but by men's traditions and doctrines of devils. And even so the fantastical heads which are at this day, and shall come after us, do destroy and shall destroy those things which we have built; do build, and shall build up again those things which we have destroyed.

But we by the grace of Christ holding the article of justification, do assuredly know that we are justified and reputed righteous before God by faith only in Christ. Therefore we do not mingle the law and grace, faith and works together: but we separate them far asunder. And this distinction or indifference between the law and grace, let every true Christian mark diligently, and let him suffer the same to take place, not in letters and syllables, but in practice and inward experience: so that when he heareth that good works ought to be done, and that the example of Christ is to be followed, he may be able to judge rightly, and say, Well, all these things will I gladly do. What then followeth? Thou shalt then be saved and obtain everlasting life. Nay, not so. I grant indeed, that I ought to do good works, patiently to suffer troubles and afflictions, and to shed my blood also, if need be, for Christ's cause: but yet am I not justified, neither do I obtain salvation thereby.

We must not therefore draw good works into the article of justification as the monks have done, which say, that not only good works, but also the punishment and torments which malefactors suffer for their wicked deeds do deserve everlasting life. For thus they comfort them, when they are brought to the gallows, or place of execution: thou must suffer willingly and patiently this shameful death: which if thou do, thou shalt deserve remission of thy sins and everlasting life. What a horrible thing is this, that a wretched thief, a murderer, a robber, should be so miserably seduced in that extreme anguish and distress, that even at the very point of death, when he is now ready to be hanged, or to have his head cut off, he should refuse the gospel and sweet promises in Christ, which are only able to bring comfort and salvation, and should be commanded to hope for pardon of his sins, if he willingly and patiently endure this opprobrious death which he suffereth for his mischievous deeds? What is this else but to heap upon him which is already most miserably afflicted, extreme perdition and destruction, and through a false conscience in his own death, to shew him the ready way to hell?

Hereby these hypocrites do plainly declare, that they neither teach nor understand one letter or syllable concerning grace, the gospel, or Christ. They retain only in outward shew the name of the gospel and of Christ, that they may beguile the hearts of the people. Notwithstanding they denying and rejecting Christ indeed, do attribute more to the traditions of men, than to the gospel of Christ. Which thing to be true, so many kinds of false worships, so many religious orders, so many ceremonies, and so many will-workers do plainly witness: all which things were instituted as available to deserve grace, righteousness and everlasting life. In their confessions they make no mention of faith or the merit of Christ, but they teach and set forth the satisfactions and merits of men, as it may plainly appear in this form of absolution (I speak nothing here of other matters) which the monks used among themselves, yea, and such as would be counted more devout and more religious than others: which I think good here to set down, that our posterity may see how great and how horrible the kingdom of the Pope is.

THE FORM OF A MONKISH ABSOLUTION

God forgive thee, my brother. The merit of the passion of our Lord Jesus Christ, and of blessed S. Mary, always a virgin, and of all the saints: the merit of thine order, the straitness of thy religion, the humility of thy confession, the contrition of thy heart, the good works which thou hast done and shalt do for the love of our Lord Jesus Christ, be unto thee available for the remission of thy sins, the increase of desert and grace, and the reward of everlasting life. AMEN.

Ye hear the merit of Christ mentioned in these words: but if ye weigh them well, ye shall perceive that Christ is there altogether unprofitable, and that the glory and name of a justifier and saviour is quite taken from him, and given to monkish merits. Is not this to take the name of God in vain? Is not this to confess Christ in words, and in very deed to deny his power, and blaspheme his name? I myself also was once entangled with this error: I thought Christ to be a judge (although I confessed with my mouth that he suffered and died for man's redemption) and ought to be pacified by the observation of my rule and order. Therefore, when I prayed, or when I said mass, I used to add this in the end: O Lord Jesus, I come unto thee, and I pray thee that these burdens and this straitness of my rule and religion may be a full recompence for all my sins. But now I give thanks unto God the Father of all mercies, which hath called me out of darkness unto the light of his glorious gospel, and hath given unto me plentiful knowledge of Christ Jesus my Lord: for whose sake I count all things to be but loss, yea, I esteem them but as dung, that I may gain Christ, and that I may be found in him, not having mine own righteousness out of the rule of Augustine, but that righteousness which cometh by faith in Christ: unto whom, with the Father and the Holy Ghost, be praise and glory, world without end. Amen.

We conclude therefore with Paul, "that we are justified by faith only in Christ, without the law." Now after that a man is once justified, and possesseth Christ by faith, and knoweth that he is his righteousness and life, doubtless he will not be idle, but as a good tree he will bring forth good fruits. For the believing man hath the Holy Ghost, and where the Holy Ghost dwelleth, he will not suffer a man to be idle, but stirreth him up to all exercises of piety and godliness, and of true religion, to the love of God, to the patient suffering of afflictions, to prayer, to thanksgiving, to the exercise of charity towards all men.

Hitherto we have handled the first argument, wherein Paul contendeth that either we cannot be justified by the law, or else that Christ must needs be the minister of sin. But this is impossible: wherefore we conclude, that justification cometh not by the law. Of this place we have largely intreated, as it is well worthy, and yet can it not be taught and beaten into men's heads sufficiently.

VERSE 19. *For I through the law am dead to the law, that I might live unto God.*

These are marvellous words, and unknown kinds of speech, which man's reason can in no wise understand. And although they be but few, yet are they uttered with great zeal and vehemency of spirit, and as it were in great displeasure. As if he should say, why do ye boast so much of the law? Whereof, in this case, I will be ignorant. But if ye will needs have the law, I also have the law. Wherefore, as though he were moved through indignation of the Holy Ghost, he calleth grace itself the law, giving a new name to the effect and working of grace, in contempt of the law of Moses and the false apostles, which contended that the law was necessary to justification: and so he setteth the law against the law. And this is a sweet kind of speech, and full of consolation, when in the scriptures, and specially in Paul, the law is set against the law, sin against sin, death against death, captivity against captivity, hell against hell, the altar against the altar, the lamb agains the lamb, the passover against the passover.

In the eighth to the Romans it is said, "For sin he condemned sin." Psalm lxviii. Eph. iv. "He hath led captivity captive." Hosea xiii. "O death, I will be thy death: O hell, I will be thy destruction." So he saith here, that through the law he is dead to the law. As if he said: the law of Moses accuseth and condemneth me: but against that accusing and condemning law, I have another law, which is grace and liberty (James i, 25). This law accuseth the accusing law, and condemneth the condemning law. So death killed death; but this killing death is life itself. But it is called the death of death, by a vehement indignation of spirit against death. So righteousness taketh the name of sin, because it condemneth sin, and this condemning of sin is true righteousness.

And here Paul seemeth to be a heretic; yea, of all heretics the greatest, and his heresy is strange and monstrous. For he saith, "That he being dead to the law, liveth to God." The false apostles taught this doctrine: Except thou live to the law, thou art dead to God; that is to say, unless thou live after the law, thou art dead before God. But Paul saith quite contrary: "Except thou be dead to the law, thou canst not live to God." The doctrine of our adversaries at this day, is like to the doctrine of the false apostles of that time. If thou wilt live to God, say they, live to the law, or after the law. But contrariwise we say: if thou wilt live to God, thou must be utterly dead to the law. Man's reason and wisdom understandeth not this doctrine: therefore it teacheth always the contrary: that is, if thou wilt live unto God, thou must keep the law: for it is written, "Do this and thou shalt live." And this is a special principle amongst all the popish divines: he that liveth after the law, liveth unto God. Paul saith the contrary: that is, we cannot live unto God, unless we be thoroughly dead to the law. Wherefore we must mount up to this heavenly altitude, that we may be assured, that we are far above the law, yea, that we are utterly dead unto the law. Now, if we be dead unto the law, then hath the law no power over us, like as it hath no power over Christ, who hath delivered us from the same, that we might live unto God. All these things tend to this end, to prove that we are not justified by the law, but by faith only in Jesus Christ.

And here Paul speaketh not of the ceremonial law only (as before we have declared more at large) but of the whole law, whether it be ceremonial or moral, which to a Christian is utterly abrogated, for he is dead unto it; not that the law is utterly taken away; nay, it remaineth, liveth, and reigneth still in the wicked. But a godly man is dead unto the law, like as he is dead unto sin, the devil, death, and hell; which notwithstanding do still remain, and the world with all the wicked shall still abide in them. Wherefore when the Papist understandeth that the ceremonial law only is abolished, understand thou, that Paul and every Christian is dead to the law, and yet the whole remaineth still.

As for example: Christ rising from death is free from the grave, and yet the grave remaineth still. Peter is delivered from the prison, the sick of the palsy from his bed, the young man from his coffin, the maiden from her couch, and yet the prison, the bed, the coffin, the couch do remain still. Even so the law is abolished when I am not subject unto it, the law is dead when I am dead unto it, and yet it remaineth still. But because I am dead unto it by another law, therefore it is dead also unto me; as the grave of Christ, the prison of Peter, the couch of the maiden, etc., do still remain: and yet Christ by his resurrection is dead unto the grave, Peter by his deliverance is freed from the prison, and the maiden through life is delivered from the couch.

Wherefore these words: "I am dead to the law," are very effectual. For he saith not: I am free from the law for a time, or I am lord over the law: but simply, I am dead to the law; that is to say, I have nothing to do with the law. Paul could have uttered nothing more effectual against the righteousness of the law than to say: I am dead to the law, that is, I care nothing at all for the law: therefore I am not justified by it.

Now, to die to the law, is, not to be bound to the law, but to be free from the law, and not to know it. Therefore let him that will live to God, endeavour that he may be found without the law, and let him come out of the grave with Christ. The soldiers were astonished when Christ was risen out of the grave: and they also which saw the maiden raised up from death to life, were amazed. So man's reason and wisdom is astonished, and becometh foolish, when it heareth that we are not justified, except we be dead to the law: for it is not able to reach unto this mystery. But we know that when we apprehend Christ by faith inwardly in conscience, we enter into a certain new law, which swalloweth up the old law that held us captive. As the grave in which Christ lay dead, after that he was risen again, was void and empty, and Christ vanished away: so when I believe in Christ, I rise again with him, and die to my grave, that is to say, the law, which held me captive: so that now the law is void, and I am escaped out of my prison and grave, that is to say, the law. Wherefore the law hath no right to accuse me, or to hold me any longer, for I am risen again.

It is necessary that men's consciences should be diligently instructed, that they may well understand the difference between the righteousness of the law and grace. The righteousness of grace, or the liberty of conscience, doth in no wise pertain to the flesh. For the flesh may not be at liberty, but must remain in the grave, the prison, the couch: it must be in subjection to the law, and exercised by the Egyptians. But the Christian conscience must be dead to the law, that is to say, free from the law, and must have nothing at all to do with it. It is good to know this: for it helpeth very much to the comforting of poor afflicted consciences. Wherefore, when you see a man terrified and cast down with the sense and feeling of his sin, say unto him: Brother, thou dost not rightly distinguish. Thou placest the law in thy conscience, which should be placed in the flesh. Awake, arise up, and remember that thou must believe in Christ, the conqueror of the law and sin. With this faith thou shalt mount up above and beyond the law, into that heaven of grace where is no law nor sin. And albeit the law and sin do still remain, yet they pertain nothing to thee: for thou art dead to the law and sin.

This is easily said, but blessed is he which knoweth how to lay sure hold on these things in time of distress; that is, which can say, when sin overweigheth him, and the law accuseth him: what is this to me, oh law, that thou accusest me, and sayest that I have committed many sins? Indeed I grant that I have committed many sins, yea, and yet still do commit sins daily without number. This toucheth me nothing: I am now deaf, and cannot hear; therefore thou talkest to me in vain, for I am dead unto thee. But if thou wilt needs dispute with me as touching my sins, get thee to my flesh and members, my servants; teach them, exercise and crucify them: but trouble not me, not me, Conscience, I say, which am a lady and a queen, and have nothing to do with thee; for I am dead to thee, and now I live to Christ, with whom I am under another law, to wit, the law of grace, which ruleth over sin and the law. By what means? By faith in Christ, as Paul declareth hereafter.

But this seemeth a strange and wonderful definition, that to live to the law, is to die to God: and to die to the law, is to live to God.—These two propositions are clean contrary to reason, and therefore no crafty sophister or law-worker can understand them. But learn thou the true understanding thereof. He that liveth to the law, that is, seeketh to be justified by the works of the law, is and remaineth a sinner: therefore he is dead and condemned. For the law cannot justify and save him, but accuseth, terrifieth, and kileth him. Therefore, to live unto the law, is to die unto God: and contrariwise, to die to the law, is to live unto God. Wherefore if thou wilt live unto God, thou must die to the law: but if thou wilt live to the law, thou shalt die to God. Now to live unto God, is to be justified by grace or by faith, for Christ's sake, without the law and works.

This is then the proper and true definition of a Christian: that he is the child of grace and remission of sins, because he is under no law, but is above the law, sin, death, and hell. And even as Christ is free from the grave, and Peter from the prison, so is a Christian free from the law. And such a respect there is between the justified conscience and the law, as is between Christ raised up from the grave, and the grave: and as is between Peter delivered from the prison, and the prison. And like as Christ by his death and resurrection is dead to the grave, so that it hath now no power over him, nor is able any longer to hold him, but the stone being rolled away (Matt. xxviii), the seals broken, and the keepers astonished, he riseth again, and goeth away without any let; and as Peter by his deliverance is freed from the prison, and goeth whither he will; even so the conscience by grace is delivered from the law. So is every one that is born of the spirit. But the flesh knoweth not from whence this cometh, nor whither it goeth, for it cannot judge but after the law. But on the contrary, the spirit saith: let the law accuse me, let sin and death terrify me never so much, yet I do not therefore despair: for I have the law against the law, sin against sin, and death against death.

Therefore, when I feel the remorse and sting of conscience for sin, I behold that brazen serpent Christ hanging upon the cross. There I find another sin against my sin which accuseth and devoureth me. Now, this other sin, namely in the flesh of Christ, which taketh away the sins of the world, is almighty, it condemneth and swalloweth up my sin.—So my sin is condemned by sin, that is, by Christ crucified: "who is made sin for us, that we might be made the righteousness of God through him" (2 Cor. v, 21). In like manner I find death in my flesh, which afflicteth and killeth me: but I have in me a contrary death, which is the death of death: for this death crucifieth and swalloweth up my death.

These things be not done by the law or works, but by Christ crucified: upon whose shoulders lie all the evils and miseries of mankind, the law, sin, death, the devil, and hell: and all these do die in him, for by his death he hath killed them. But we must receive the benefit of Christ with a sure faith. For like as neither the law nor any work thereof is offered unto us, but Christ alone: so nothing is required of us but faith alone, whereby we apprehend Christ, and believe that our sins and our death are condemned and abolished in the sin and death of Christ.

Thus have we always most certain and sure arguments which necessarily conclude that justification cometh by faith alone. For how should the law and works avail to justification, seeing that Paul is so earnest both against the law and works, and saith plainly, that we must be dead to the law, if we will live to God. But if we be dead to the law, and the law be dead to us, then hath it nothing to do with us. How then should it avail any thing at all to our justification? Wherefore we must needs say, that we be justified by grace alone, or by faith alone in Christ, without the law and works.

This the blind sophisters do not understand, and therefore they dream that faith justifieth not, except it do the works of charity. By this means faith which believeth in Christ, becometh unprofitable and of none effect: for the virtue of justifying is taken from it, except it be furnished with charity. But let us now set apart the law and charity until another time, and let us rest upon the principal point of this present matter: which is this, that Jesus Christ the Son of God died upon the cross, did bear in his body my sins, the law, death, the devil and hell. These invincible enemies and tyrants do oppress, vex, and trouble me, and therefore I am careful how I may be delivered out of their hands justified and saved. Here I find neither law, work, nor charity, which is able to deliver me from their tyranny. There is none but the Lord Jesus only and alone, which taketh away the law, killeth and destroyeth my death in his body, and by this means spoileth hell, judgeth and crucifieth the devil, and throweth him down into hell. To be brief, all the enemies which did before torment and oppress me, Christ Jesus hath brought to nought: "hath spoiled them, and made a shew of them openly, triumphing by himself over them" (Col. ii, 15), in such sort, that they can now rule and reign no more over me, but are constrained to obey me.

By this we may plainly see, that there is nothing here for us to do; only it belongeth unto us, to hear that these things have been wrought and done in this sort, and by faith to apprehend the same. And this is the true formed and furnished faith indeed. Now, when I have thus apprehended Christ by faith, and through him am dead to the law, justified from sin, delivered from death, the devil, and hell, then I do good works, I love God, I give thanks to him, I exercise charity towards my neighbour. But this charity or works following, do neither form nor adorn my faith, but my faith formeth and adorneth charity. This is our divinity, which seemeth strange and marvellous, or rather foolish to carnal reason: to wit, that I am not only blind and deaf to the law, yea, delivered and freed from the law, but also wholly dead unto the same.

This sentence of Paul, "Through the law I am dead to the law," is full of consolation; which if it may enter into a man in due season, and take sure hold in his heart, with good understanding, it may so work, that it will make him able to stand against all dangers of death, and all terrors of conscience and sin, although they assail him, accuse him, and would drive him to desperation never so much. True it is, that every man is tempted: if not in his life, yet at his death. There, when the law accuseth him and sheweth unto him his sins, his conscience by-and-by saith, thou hast sinned. If then thou take good hold of that which Paul here teacheth, thou wilt answer: I grant I have sinned. Then God will punish thee. Nay, he will not do so. Why, doth not the law of God so say? I have nothing to do with that law. Why so? Because I have another law which striketh this law dumb, that is to say, liberty. What liberty is that? The liberty of Christ, for by Christ I am utterly freed from the law. Therefore, that law which is and remaineth a law to the wicked, is to me liberty, and bindeth that law which would condemn me: and by this means, that law which would bind me and hold me captive, is now fast bound itself, and holden captive by grace and liberty, which is now my law: which saith to that accusing law, thou shalt not hold this man bound and captive, for he is mine, but I will hold thee captive, and bind thy hands that thou shalt not hurt him, for he liveth now unto Christ, and is dead unto thee.

This to do, is to dash out the teeth of the law, to wrest his sting, and all his weapons from him, and to spoil him of all his force. And yet the same law notwithstanding continueth and remaineth still to the wicked and unbelievers; and to us also that be weak, so far forth as we lack faith, it continueth yet still in its force; here it hath its edge and teeth. But if I do believe in Christ, although sin drive me never so much to despair, yet staying upon this liberty which I have in Christ, I confess that I have sinned; but my sin, which is a condemned sin, is in Christ which is a condemning sin. Now this condemning sin is stronger than that which is condemned; for it is justifying grace, righteousness, life and salvation. Thus when I feel the terror of death, I say, thou hast nothing to do with me, O death, for I have another death which killeth thee, my death; and that death which killeth, is stronger than that which is killed.

Thus a faithful man by faith only in Christ, may raise up himself, and conceive such sure and sound consolation, that he shall not need to fear the devil, sin, death, or any evils. And although the devil set upon him with all might and main, and go about with all the terror of the world to oppose him, yet he conceiveth good hope even in the midst thereof, and thus he saith: Sir Devil, I fear not thy threatenings and terrors, for there is one whose name is Jesus Christ, in whom I believe; he hath abolished the law, condemned sin, vanquished death, and destroyed hell: and he is thy tormentor, O Satan, for he hath bound thee and holdeth thee captive, to the end that thou shouldest no more hurt me, or any that believeth in him. This faith the devil cannot overcome, but is overcome of it. "For this is the victory (saith St. John) that overcometh the world, even our faith" (1 John v, 4). Who is it that overcometh the world, but he which believeth that Jesus is the Son of God?

Paul therefore, through a vehement zeal and indignation of spirit, calleth grace itself the law, which notwithstanding is an exceeding and inestimable liberty of grace which we have in Christ Jesus. Moreover, he giveth this opprobrious name unto the law (to let us understand for our consolation, that there is now a new name given unto it) that it is not now alive any more, but dead and condemned. And here (which is a pleasant sight to behold) he bringeth forth the law, and setteth it before us as a thief and a robber which is already condemned and adjudged to death. For he describeth it as it were a prisoner, having both hands and feet fast bound, and all his power taken away, so that it cannot exercise his tyranny, that is to say, it cannot accuse and condemn any more; and with this most pleasant sight, he maketh it odious and contemptible to the conscience; so that now he which believeth in Christ, dare boldly and with a holy pride triumph over the law after this manner: I am a sinner; if thou canst do any thing against me, O law, now do thy worst. So far off is it then, that the law is now terrible unto him which doth believe.

Since Christ is risen from death, why should he now fear the grave? Since Peter is delivered from the prison, why should he now fear it? When the maiden was at the point of death, then might she indeed fear the bed: but being now raised up, why should she fear it? In like manner, why should a Christian which enjoyeth and possesseth Christ by faith, fear the law? True it is, that he feeleth the terrors of the law, but he is not overcome of them; but staying upon the liberty which he hath in Christ, he saith: I hear thee murmuring, O law, that thou wouldst accuse me and condemn me: but this troubleth me nothing at all; thou art to me as the grave was unto Christ: for I see that thou art fast bound hand and foot, and this hath my law done. What law is that? Liberty, which is called the law, not because it bindeth me, but because it bindeth my law. The law of the ten commandments did bind me. But against that law I have another law, even the law of grace: which notwithstanding is to me no law, neither doth it bind me, but setteth me at liberty. And this is a law against that accusing and condemning law: which law it so bindeth, that it hath no power to hurt me any more. So against my death which bindeth me, I have another death, that is to say, life, which quickeneth me in Christ: and this death looseth and freeth me from the bonds of my death, and with the same bonds bindeth my death. So death which bound me, is now fast bound, which killed me, is now killed by death, that is to say, by life itself.

Thus Christ, with most sweet names, is called my law, my sin, my death, against the law, against sin, against death, whereas, in very deed, he is nothing else but mere liberty, righteousness, life and everlasting salvation. And for this cause he is made the law of the law, the sin of sin, the death of death, that he might redeem from the curse of the law, justify me and quicken me. So then, while Christ is the law, he is also liberty, while he is sin, he is righteousness, and while he is death, he is life. For in that he suffered the law to accuse him, sin to condemn him, and death to devour him, he abolished the law, he condemned sin, he destroyed death, he justified and saved me. So is Christ the poison of the law, sin, and death, and the remedy for the obtaining of liberty, righteousness, and everlasting life.

This manner of speech which Paul here useth, and is proper unto him alone, is full of consolation. Likewise, in the seventh chapter to the Romans, he setteth the law of the spirit against the law of the members. And because this is a strange and marvellous manner of speaking, therefore it entereth more easily into the mind, and sticketh faster in the memory. Moreover, when he saith: "I through the law am dead to the law," it soundeth more sweetly than if he should say, I through liberty am dead to the law. For he setteth before us, as it were, a certain picture, as if the law were fighting against the law. As though he should say, O law, if thou canst accuse me, terrify me, and bind me, I will set above and against thee another law, that is to say, another tormentor, which shall accuse thee, bind thee, and oppress thee. Indeed, thou art my tormentor: but I have another tormentor, even Christ, which shall torment thee. When thou art thus bound, tormented, and suppressed, then am I at liberty. So then grace is a law, not to me, for it bindeth me not, but to my law: which this law so bindeth, that it cannot hurt me any more.

Thus Paul goeth about to draw us wholly from the beholding of the law, sin, death, and all other evils, and to bring us unto Christ, that there we might behold this joyful conflict: to wit, the law fighting against the law, that it may be to me liberty: sin against sin, that it may be to me righteousness: death against death, that I may obtain life: Christ fighting against the devil, that I may be the child of God: and destroying hell, that I may enjoy the kingdom of heaven.

VERSE 19. *That I might live unto God.*

That is to say, that I might live before God. Ye see then that there is no life unless ye be without the law, yea, unless ye be utterly dead unto the law, I mean in conscience. Notwithstanding, in the mean season (as I have often said) so long as the body liveth, the flesh must be exercised with laws, and vexed with exactions and penalties of laws, as were the Egyptians. But the inward man, not subject to the law, but delivered and freed from it, is a lively, a just, and a holy person, not of himself, but in Christ, because he believeth in him, as followeth.

VERSE 20. *I am crucified with Christ.*

This he addeth, to declare that the law is a devourer of the law. Not only, saith he, I am dead to the law through the law, that I may live to God, but also I am crucified with Christ. But Christ is Lord over the law, because he is crucified and dead unto the law: therefore am I also Lord over the law; for I likewise am crucified and dead unto the law, forasmuch as I am crucified and dead with Christ. By what means? By grace and faith. Through this faith, because I am now crucified and dead unto the law, therefore the law loseth all its power which it had over me, even as it hath lost all its power which it had over Christ. Wherefore, even as Christ himself was crucified to the law, sin, death, and the devil, so that they have no further power over him: even so I through faith being now crucified with Christ in spirit, am crucified and dead to the law, sin, death, and the devil, so that they have no further power over me, but are now crucified and dead unto me.

Paul speaketh not here of crucifying by imitation or example, (for to follow the example of Christ, is also to be crucified with him) which crucifying belongeth to the flesh. Whereof Peter speaketh in his first epistle and second chapter, "Christ suffered for us," saith he, "leaving unto us an example that we should follow his steps." But he speaketh here of that high crucifying, whereby sin, the devil, and death are crucified in Christ, and not in me. Here Christ Jesus doth all himself alone. But I believing in Christ, am by faith crucified also with Christ, so that all these things are crucified and dead unto me.

VERSE 20. *Thus I live.*

I speak not so, saith he, of my death and crucifying, as though I now lived not: yea, I live, for I am quickened by this death and crucifying, through the which I die: that is, forasmuch as I am delivered from the law, sin, and death, I now live indeed. Wherefore that crucifying and that death whereby I am crucified and dead to the law, sin, death, and all evils, is to me resurrection and life. For Christ crucifieth the devil, he killeth death, condemneth sin, and bindeth the law; and I believing this, am delivered from the law, sin, death, and the devil. The law therefore is bound, dead, and crucified unto me, and I again am bound, dead, and crucified unto it. Wherefore, even by this death and crucifying, that is to say, by this grace or liberty, I now live.

Here (as before I have said) we must observe Paul's manner of speaking. He saith that we are dead and crucified to the law, whereas in very deed the law itself is dead and crucified unto us. But this manner of speech he useth here of purpose, that it may be the more sweet and comfortable unto us. For the law (which notwithstanding continueth, liveth and reigneth in the whole world, which also accuseth and condemneth all men) is crucified and dead unto those only which believe in Christ: therefore to them alone belongeth this glory, that they are dead to sin, hell, death, and the devil.

VERSE 20. *Yet now not I.*

That is to say, not in mine own person, nor in mine own substance. Here he plainly sheweth by what means he liveth: and he teacheth what true Christian righteousness is, namely, that righteousness whereby Christ liveth in us, and not that which is in our person. Therefore, when we speak of Christian righteousness, we must utterly reject the person. And here Christ and my conscience must become one body, so that nothing remain in my sight but Christ crucified and raised from the dead. But if I behold myself only, and set Christ aside, I am gone. For by-and-by I fall into this cogitation: Christ is in heaven, and thou art on the earth, how shalt thou now come unto him? Forsooth I will live holily, and do that which the law requireth, so shall I enter into life. Here, returning to myself, and considering what I am, and what I ought to be, and what I am bound to do, I lose sight of Christ, who is my righteousness and life. Who being lost, there is no counsel nor succor now remaining, but certain desperation and destruction must needs follow.

And this is a common evil among men. For such is our misery, that when temptation or death cometh, by-and-by setting Christ aside, we consider our own life past, and what we have done. Here, except we be raised up again by faith, we must needs perish. Wherefore we must learn in such conflicts and terrors of conscience (forgetting ourselves and setting the law, our life past, and all our works apart, which drive us to the consideration of ourselves only) to turn our eyes wholly to the brazen serpent Jesus Christ crucified, and assuredly believe that he is our righteousness and life, not fearing the threatenings and terrors of the law, sin, death, and the judgment of God. For Christ, on whom our eyes are fixed, in whom we live, who also liveth in us, is lord and conqueror of the law, sin, death, and all evils: in whom most certain and sure consolation is set forth unto us, and victory given.

VERSE 20. *Thus I live, yet not I now, but Christ liveth in me.*

Wherefore he said, "Thus I live," he speaketh it, as it were, in his own person. Therefore he by-and-by correcteth himself, saying, "Yet not I now." That is to say, I live not now in my own person, but Christ liveth in me. Indeed the person liveth, but not in himself, nor for any thing that is in him. But who is that I, of whom he saith, "Yet not I?" This I is he which hath the law, and is bound to do the works thereof: who also is a certain person separate from Christ. This person Paul rejecteth. For he is separate from Christ, he belongeth to death and hell. Therefore he saith, "Now not I, but Christ liveth in me." He is my form, my furniture and perfection, adorning and beautifying my faith, as the colour, the clear light, or the whiteness do garnish and beautify the wall. Thus are we constrained grossly to set forth this matter. For we cannot spiritually conceive that Christ is so nearly joined and united unto us, as the colour or whiteness are unto the wall. Christ therefore, saith he, thus joined and united unto me and abiding in me, liveth this life in me which now I live; yea Christ

EPISTLE TO THE GALATIANS

himself is this life which now I live. Wherefore Christ and I in this behalf are both one.

Now Christ living in me, abolisheth the law, condemneth sin, and destroyeth death; for it cannot be, but at his presence all these must needs vanish away. For Christ is everlasting peace, consolation, righteousness and life: and to these the terror of the law, heaviness of mind, sin, hell, and death, must needs give place. So Christ living and abiding in me, taketh away and swalloweth up all evils which vex and afflict me. This union or conjunction, then, is the cause that I am delivered from the terror of the law and sin, am separate from myself, and translated unto Christ and his kingdom, which is the kingdom of grace, righteousness, peace, joy, life, salvation, and eternal glory. Whilst I thus abide and dwell in him, what evil is there that can hurt me?

In the mean season the old man abideth without, and is subject to the law: but as concerning justification, Christ and I must be entirely conjoined and united together, so that he may live in me, and I in him. And this is a wonderful manner of speech. Now because Christ liveth in me, therefore look what grace, righteousness, life, peace and salvation is in me, it is his, and yet notwithstanding the same is mine also, by that inseparable union and conjunction which is through faith; by the which Christ and I are made as it were one body in spirit. Forasmuch then as Christ liveth in me, it followeth that as I must needs be with him partaker of grace, righteousness, life, and eternal salvation: so the law, sin, and death can have no place in me; yea, the law is crucified and swallowed up of the law. Sin of sin, and death of death. Thus Paul goeth about to draw us from the beholding of ourselves, the law and works, and to plan in us true faith in Christ: so that in the matter of justification we should think upon nothing else but grace, separating the same far from the law and works, which in this matter ought to have no place.

Paul hath his peculiar phrase or kind of speech, which is not after the manner of men, but divine and heavenly, nor used of the evangelist or of the rest of the apostles, saving only of John; who is also wont sometimes so to speak. And if Paul had not first used this phrase, and set forth the same unto us in plain words, the very saints themselves durst not have used it. For it seemeth a very strange and monstrous manner of speaking thus to say; I live, I live not; I am dead, I am not dead; I am a sinner, I am not a sinner; I have the law, I have not the law. Which phrase is sweet and comfortable to all those that believe in Christ. For in that they behold themselves, they have both the law and sin; but in that they look unto Christ, they are dead to the law, and have no sin. If therefore in the matter of justification thou separate the person of Christ from thy person, then art thou in the law, thou livest in the law and not in Christ, and so thou art condemned of the law, and dead before God. For thou hast that faith which (as the sophister's dream) is furnished with charity. Thus I speak for example's sake. For there was never any one found that was saved by this faith. And therefore what things soever the popish sophisters have written touching this faith, are nothing else but vain toys and mere deceits of Satan. But let us grant that such there be as have this faith: yet are they not therefore justified. For they have but an historical faith concerning Christ, which the devil also and all the wicked have.

Faith therefore must be purely taught: namely, that thou art so entirely and nearly joined unto Christ, that he and thou art made as it were one person; so that thou mayest boldly say, I am now one with Christ, that is to say, Christ's righteousness, victory and life are mine. And again, Christ may say, I am that sinner, that is, his sins and his death are mine, because he is united and joined unto me, and I unto him. For by faith we are so joined together, "that we are become one flesh and one bone" (Eph. v, 31), we are the members of the body of Christ, flesh of his flesh, and bone of his bones; so that this faith doth couple Christ and me more near together, than the husband is coupled to his wife. This faith therefore is not an idle quality, but the excellency thereof is such, that it utterly confoundeth these foolish dreams of the sophisters touching their formed faith and counterfeit charity, their merits, works, and worthiness. These things I would gladly set forth more fully, if by any means I could.

Hitherto we have declared this to be the first argument of Paul, that either Christ must needs be the minister of sin, or else the law doth not justify. When he had finished this argument, he set forth himself for an example, saying, "that he was dead unto that old law by a certain new law." Now he answereth two objections which might have been made against him. His first answer is against the cavillations of the proud, and the offence of the weak. For when remission of sins is freely preached, then do the malicious by-and-by slander this preaching, as Romans iii, 8, "Let us do evil that good may come thereof." For these fellows, as soon as they hear that we are not justified by the law, forthwith do maliciously conclude and say, why then let us reject the law. Again, if grace do there abound, say they, where sin doth abound, let us then abound in sin, that we may become righteous, and that grace may the more abound. These are the malicious and proud spirits which spitefully and wittingly slander the scriptures and sayings of the Holy Ghost, even as they slandered Paul whilst the apostles lived, to their own confusion and condemnation, as it is said, 2 Peter iii.

Moreover, the weak, which are not malicious, are offended when they hear that the law and good works are not to be done as necessary to justification. These must be holpen, and must be instructed how good works do not justify; how they ought to be done, how not to be done. These ought to be done, not as the cause, but as the fruits of righteousness; and when we are made righteous, we ought to do them, but not contrariwise, to the end that when we are unrighteous, we may be made righteous. The tree maketh the apple, but not the apple the tree.

He said before, "I am dead," etc. Here the presumptuous and malicious might soon take occasion to cavil after this manner. What sayst thou, Paul? Art thou dead? How then dost thou speak? How dost thou write? The weak also might soon be offended, and say unto him, What art thou, Paul? Do we not see that thou art living, and dost such things as pertain to this life? To this he answereth, "I live indeed, and yet now not I, but Christ liveth in me." There is then a double life. The first is mine, which is natural; the second is the life of another, that is to say, the life of Christ in me. As touching my natural life I am dead, and now I live another life, I live not now as Paul, but Paul is dead. Who is it then that liveth? The Christian. Paul therefore, as he liveth in himself, is wholly dead through the law: but as he liveth in Christ, or rather as Christ liveth in him, he liveth by another life: for Christ speaketh in him, liveth in him, and exerciseth all the operations of life in him. This cometh not now of the life of Paul, but of the life of the Christian and regenerate person. Therefore thou malicious spirit, where I say that I am dead, now slander my words no more. And thou that art weak, be not offended, but distinguish and divide this matter rightly. For, as I said, there are two lives; to wit, my natural life, and the life of another. By mine own life I live not: for if I did, the law would have dominion over me, and hold me in captivity. To the end therefore that it should not hold me in captivity and bondage, I am dead to it by another law: and this death purchaseth unto me the life of another, even the life of Christ; which life is not mine by nature, but is given unto me by Christ through faith.

Secondly, this objection might have been made against Paul: What sayest thou, Paul? Dost thou not live by thine own life, or in thine own flesh, but in Christ? We see thy flesh, but we see not Christ. Wouldst thou then delude us by thine enchantments, that we should not see thee present in flesh, living as thou dist before, and doing all things in this corporal life as others do? He answereth:

VERSE 20. *And in that I now live in the flesh, I live by faith in the Son of God.*

As if he should say, True it is that I live in the flesh, but this life, whatsoever it is, I esteem as no life; for in very deed it is no true life, but a shadow of life, under the which another liveth, that is to say, Christ, who is my true life indeed: which life thou seest not, but only hearest, and I feel. "Thou hearest the wind, but know not whence it cometh, or whither it goeth" (John iii). Even so thou seest me speaking, eating, laboring, sleeping, and doing other things, and yet thou seest not my life. For this time of life which I now live, I live indeed in the flesh, but not through the flesh, or according to the flesh, but through faith and according to faith. Paul then denieth not that he liveth in the flesh, because he doth all things that belong to a natural man. He useth also carnal things, as meat, drink, apparel, and such like, which is to live in the flesh; but he saith that this is not his life: and although he useth these things, yet he liveth not through them, as the world liveth through the flesh and after the flesh: so it neither knoweth nor hopeth for any life besides this.

Therefore saith he, "this life which I now live in the flesh," whatsoever it is, "I live in the faith of the Son of God." For this word which I now corporally speak, is the word not of flesh, but of the Holy Ghost, and of Christ. This sight which goeth in, or cometh out at mine eyes, proceedeth not of flesh, that is to say, it is not governed of the flesh, but of the Holy Ghost. So my hearing cometh not of the flesh, although it be in the flesh, but of the Holy Ghost. A Christian speaketh none other but chaste, sober, and holy things, which pertain unto Christ, to the glory of God and the profit of his neighbour. These things come not of the flesh, neither are done according to the flesh, and yet are they in the flesh. For I cannot teach, write, pray, or give thanks, but with these instruments of the flesh, which are necessary to the accomplishing of these works; and yet notwithstanding these works proceed not of the flesh, but are given by

God from above. In like manner I behold a woman but with a chaste eye not lusting after her. This beholding cometh not of the flesh, although it be in the flesh, because the eyes are the carnal instruments of this sight: but the chasteness of this sight cometh from heaven.

Thus a Christian useth the world and all creatures, so that there is no difference between him and the infidel. For in their apparel, in their feeding, hearing, seeing, speaking, gestures, countenances, and such other things, they are like, and in outward appearance they seem to be all one (as Paul speaketh of Christ; "In outward appearance he was found," saith he, "as a man," Philip ii, 8) yet notwithstanding there is great difference. For I live in the flesh, I grant, but I live not of myself: but in that I now live, I live in the faith of the Son of God. This which I now speak, springeth out of another fountain than that which thou heardest of me before. Paul, before his conversion, spake with the same voice and tongue wherewith he spake afterwards; but his voice and his tongue were then blasphemous, and therefore he could speak nothing else but blasphemies and abominations against Christ and his church. After he was converted he had the same flesh, the same voice and tongue which he had before, and nothing was changed: but his voice and his tongue then uttered no blasphemies, but spiritual and heavenly words, to wit, thanksgiving and the praise of God: which came of faith and the Holy Ghost. So then I live in the flesh, but not of the flesh or after the flesh, but in the faith of the Son of God.

Hereby we may plainly see whence this spiritual life cometh: which the natural man can in no wise perceive, for he knoweth not what manner of life this is. He heareth the wind, but whence it cometh, or whither it goeth, he knoweth not. He heareth the voice of the spiritual man, he knoweth his face, his manners, and his gestures: but he seeth not whence those words, which are not now wicked and blasphemous as before, but holy and godly, or whence those motions and actions do come. For this life is in the heart by faith, where the flesh is killed, and Christ reigneth with his Holy Spirit, who now seeth, heareth, speaketh, worketh, suffereth, and doth all other things in him, although the flesh do resist. To conclude, this is not the life of the flesh, although it be in the flesh: but of Christ the Son of God, whom the Christian possesseth by faith.

VERSE 20. *Who loved me, and gave himself for me.*

Here have ye the true manner of justification set before your eyes, and a perfect example of the assurance of faith. He that can with a firm and a constant faith say these words with Paul, "I live by faith in the Son of God, who loved me, and gave himself for me," is happy indeed. And with these words Paul taketh away the whole righteousness of the law and works, as afterwards we will declare. We must therefore diligently weigh and consider these words: "The Son of God loved me, and gave himself for me." It was not I then that first loved the Son of God, and delivered myself for him: as the sophisters dream, that they love the Son of God and deliver themselves for him. For they teach that a man, *ex puris naturalibus*, that is, of his own pure natural strength, is able to do meritorious works before grace, and love God and Christ above all things. These fellows pervert the love of God and Christ: for they do that is in them, say they, that is, they do not only fulfil the commandments, but also they observe the counsels, they do the works of supererogation, and sell their superfluous merits to laymen, and so, as they dream, they give themselves for Christ, and thereby save both themselves and others, turning the words of Paul, "which loved me," etc., clean contrary, and saying: we have loved Christ, and given ourselves for him. Thus when the wicked, being puffed up with the wisdom of the flesh, imagine that they do what in them lieth, they love God, they deliver themselves for Christ, what do they else but abolish the gospel, deride, deny, and blaspheme Christ, yea, spit upon him, and tread him under foot? They confess in words that he is a justifier and a saviour: in very deed they take from him the power both to justify and save, and give the same to their own will-works, their ceremonies and devotions. This is to live in their own righteousness and works, and not in the faith of the Son of God.

Wherefore this is not the true way to attain justification, to do that which in thee lieth: as the Popish sophisters and school-doctors do teach, which affirm, that if a man doth what in him lieth, God will undoubtedly give unto him his grace; but this saying may not be straitly urged, say they; for if we do those works which may be approved by the judgment of any good man, it is enough; for then grace shall surely follow, because God, in that he is good and just, must needs give grace as a recompence for such good works. And hereof cometh this verse: *Ultra posse viri non vult Deus ulla requiri*. That is,

> God will no more require of man,
> Than of himself perform he can.

Indeed this is a good saying if it be used rightly, and in place convenient: that is, in the government of commonweals or families. As if I being in the kingdom of reason, do execute the office of a magistrate, or govern a family, doing that in me lieth, I am excused. This kingdom hath its bound and limits: to the which also these sayings do pertain: to do what in us lieth: to do as much as we are able. But the Papists apply these sayings to the spiritual kingdom, wherein a man can do nothing else but sin: for he is "sold under sin" (Rom. vii, 14). But in external things (such I mean as pertain to civil and household government) he is not a servant, but a lord and a ruler. Wherefore they have done wickedly in applying these sentences to the church, which properly pertain to the government of commonweals and families. For the kingdom of man's reason and the spiritual kingdom must be separate far asunder.

Moreover, they say, that nature is corrupt, but the qualities of nature notwithstanding are sound and uncorrupt, which also they attribute even unto devils. Upon this ground they reason after this manner: if the natural qualities of man be sound and uncorrupt, then is his understanding and his will sound and uncorrupt, and so consequently all other qualities of nature are pure and perfect in him. To know these things, it is necessary for you, that ye may hold the sincerity of the doctrine of faith. Where they say then that the natural qualities of man are sound and uncorrupt, and therefore do infer, that a man is able of himself to fulfil the law, and to love God with all his heart, applying these qualities to the spiritual kingdom, I deny the consequence. And here I make a distinction between the natural and the spiritual qualities (which they confound and mingle together) and I say, that the spiritual qualities are not sound, but corrupt, yea, utterly quenched, through sin both in man and devil, so that there is in them nothing else but corrupt understanding, and a will continually striving against the will of God, which can think nothing else but that which is altogether against God. Notwithstanding, I grant that the natural qualities are uncorrupt. But what qualities are they? That a man drowned in sin and iniquity, and a bondslave of Satan, hath will, reason, and power, notwithstanding, to execute the office of a magistrate, to govern a family, to guide a ship, to build a house, and to do such other things as are subject unto man: for these things are not taken from him. We do not then deny but that these sentences are true in the corporal kingdom: but if ye wrest them to the spiritual kingdom, I utterly deny them; for there, as I said, we are clean overwhelmed and drowned in sin. Whatsoever is in our will is evil: whatsoever is in our understanding is error. Wherefore in spiritual matters man hath nothing but darkness, errors, ignorance, malice and perverseness both of will and understanding. How then shall he work well, fulfil the law, and love God?

Wherefore Paul saith here that Christ first began and not we. "He, even he (saith Paul) loved me, and gave himself for me." As if he said, he found in me no good will or right understanding: but this good Lord had mercy upon me. He saw me to be nothing else but wicked, going astray, contemning God, and flying from him more and more: yea, rebelling against God, taken, led, and carried away captive of the devil. Thus of his mere mercy preventing my reason, my will, and my understanding, he loved me, and so loved me, that he gave himself for me, to the end that I might be freed from the law, sin, the devil, and death.

Again, these words, "The Son of God loved me, and gave himself for me," are mighty thunderings and lightnings from heaven against the righteousness of the law and all the works thereof. So great and so horrible wickedness, error, darkness, and ignorance was in my will and understanding, that it was impossible for me to be ransomed by any other means than by such an inestimable price. Why do we then vaunt the integrity and soundness of nature, of the rule of reason, of free-will, and of doing what in us lieth? Why do I offer, to pacify the wrath of God, who, as Moses saith, "is a consuming fire," this my rotten stubble and straw, yea horrible sins, and claim of him to reward me with grace and everlasting life for them, since here I learn such wickedness to lie lurking in my nature, that the whole world and all creatures therein were not able to countervail the indignation of God, but that the very Son of God himself must needs be delivered for the same?

But let us consider well this price, and let us behold the captive, delivered, as Paul saith, for me; the Son of God, I mean, and we shall see him, without all comparison, to exceed and excel all creatures. What wilt thou do when thou hearest the apostle say, that such an inestimable price was given for thee? Wilt thou bring thy cowl, thy shaven crown, thy chastity, thy obedience, thy poverty, thy works, thy merits? What shall all these do? Yea, what shall the law of Moses avail? What shall the works of all men, and all the sufferings of the martyrs profit thee? What is the obedience of all the holy angels in comparison of the Son of God delivered, and that most shamefully, even to the death of the cross, so that there was no drop of his most precious blood, but it was shed, and that for thy sins? If thou couldst rightly consider this incomparable price, thou shouldst hold as accursed of all these ceremonies, vows, works, and merits before grace and after, and throw them all down to hell. For it is a horrible blasphemy to imagine that there is any work whereby thou shouldst presume to pacify God, since thou seest that there is nothing which is able to pacify him but this inestimable price, even the death and blood of the Son of God, one drop whereof is more precious than the whole world.

VERSE 20. *For me*.

Who is this me? Even I, wretched and damnable sinner, so dearly beloved of the Son of God, that he gave himself for me. If I then through works or merits could have loved the Son of God, and so come unto him, what needed he to deliver himself for me? Hereby it appeareth how coldly the Papists handled, yea, how they utterly neglected the holy scriptures, and the doctrine of faith. For if they had considered but only these words, that it behoved the Son of God to be given for me, it had been impossible that so many monstrous sects should have sprung up amongst them. For faith would by-and-by have answered: why dost thou choose this kind of life, this religion, this work? Dost thou this to please God, or to be justified thereby? Dost thou not hear, O thou wretch, that the Son of God shed his blood for thee? This true faith in Christ would easily have withstood all manners of sects.

Wherefore I say (as I have oftentimes said) that there is no remedy against sects, or power to resist them, but this only article of Christian righteousness. If we lose this article, it is impossible for us to withstand any errors or sects; as we may see at this day in the fantastical spirits the Anabaptists, and such like: who being fallen away from this article of justification, will never cease to fall, err, and seduce others, until they come to the fulness of all iniquity. There is no doubt but they will raise up innumerable sects, and still devise new works. But what are all these things (though they have never so goodly a shew of holiness) if ye compare them to the death and blood of the Son of God, "who gave himself for me?" Consider well, I pray you, who this Son of God is, how glorious he is, how mighty he is. What is heaven and earth in comparison of him? Let all the Papists and all the authors of sects, yea, though the whole world take their part, be thrown down into hell, with all their righteousness, works, and merits, rather than the truth of the gospel should be blemished, and the glory of Christ perish. What mean they, then, to brag so much of works and merits? If I, being a wretch and a damned sinner, could be redeemed by any other price, what needed the Son of God to be given for me? But because there was no other price either in heaven or in earth, but Christ the Son of God, therefore it was most necessary that he should be delivered for me. Moreover, this he did of inestimable love: for Paul saith, "which loved me."

Wherefore these words, "which loved me," are full of faith. And he that can utter this word "me," and apply it unto himself with a true and a constant faith, as Paul did, shall be a good disputer with Paul against the law. For he delivered neither sheep, ox, gold, nor silver, but even God himself, entirely and wholly, "for me," even for "me," I say, a miserable and wretched sinner. Now therefore, in that the Son of God was thus delivered to death for me, I take comfort and apply this unto myself. And this manner of applying is the very true force and power of faith.

These words (which are the pure preaching of grace and Christian righteousness indeed) Paul setteth against the righteousness of the law. As if he said: be it so that the law is a heavenly doctrine, and hath also his glory; yet notwithstanding it loved not me, nor gave itself for me: yea, it accuseth me, terrifieth me, and driveth me to desperation. But I have now another which hath delivered me from the terrors of the law, sin, and death, and hath brought me into liberty, the righteousness of God, and eternal life; who is called the Son of God, to whom be praise and glory forever.

Faith therefore, as I have said, embraceth and wrappeth in itself Christ Jesus the Son of God, delivered to death for us, as Paul here teacheth, who being apprehended by faith, giveth unto us righteousness and life. And here he setteth out most lively the priesthood and offices of Christ; which are, to pacify God, to make intercession for sinners, to offer up himself a sacrifice for their sins, to redeem, to instruct, and to comfort them. Let us learn therefore to give a true definition of Christ, not as the school-divines do, and such as seek righteousness by their own works, which make him a new lawgiver, who abolishing the old law hath established a new. To these Christ is nothing else but an exactor and a tyrant. But let us define him as Paul here doth: namely, that he is the Son of God, who not for our desert or any righteousness of ours, but of his own free mercy offered up himself a sacrifice for us sinners, that he might sanctify us forever.

Christ then is no Moses, no exactor, no giver of laws, but a giver of grace, a saviour, and one that is full of mercy: briefly, he is nothing else but infinite mercy and goodness, freely given and bountifully giving unto us. And thus shall you paint out Christ in his right colours. If you suffer him any otherwise to be painted out unto you, when temptation and trouble cometh, you shall soon be overthrown. Now, as it is the greatest knowledge and cunning that Christians can have, thus to define Christ; so of all things it is the hardest. For I myself, even in this great light of the gospel, wherein I have been so long exercised, have much ado to hold this definition of Christ which Paul here giveth: so deeply hath the doctrine and pestilent opinion that Christ is a lawgiver, entered even as it were oil into my bones. Ye young men therefore are in this case much more happy than we that are old. For ye are not infected with these pernicious errors, wherein I have been so nusled and so drowned even from my youth, that at the very hearing of the name of Christ my heart hath trembled and quaked for fear; for I was persuaded that he was a severe judge. Wherefore it is to me a double travail and trouble to correct and reform this evil: first to forget, to condemn, and to resist this old grounded error, that Christ is a lawgiver and a judge; for it always returneth and plucketh me back; then to plant in my heart a new and a true persuasion of Christ that he is a justifier and a saviour. Ye, I say, that are young, may learn with much less difficulty, to know Christ purely and sincerely, if ye will. Wherefore if any man feel himself oppressed with heaviness and anguish of heart, he must not impute it unto Christ, although it come under the name of Christ, but unto the devil, who oftentimes cometh under the colour of Christ, and transformeth himself into an angel of light.

Let us learn, therefore, to put a difference between Christ and a lawgiver, not only in word but also in deed and in practice: that when the devil shall come under the shadow of Christ, and shall go about to trouble us under his name, we may know him, not to be Christ, but a very fiend indeed. For Christ, when he cometh, is nothing else but joy and sweetness to a trembling and broken heart, as here Paul witnesseth, who setteth him out with this most sweet and comfortable title when he saith, "which loved me, and gave himself for me." Christ therefore, in very deed, is a lover of those which are in trouble and anguish, in sin, and death, and such a lover as gave himself for us: who is also our high priest, that is to say, a mediator between God and us miserable and wretched sinners. What could be said, I pray you, more sweet and comfortable to the poor afflicted conscience? Now, if these things be true (as they are indeed most true, or else the gospel must be nothing but a fable) then are we not justified by the righteousness of the law; but much less by our own righteousness.

Read therefore with great vehemency these words, "me,"

and "for me," and so inwardly practise with thyself, that thou, with a sure faith, mayst conceive and print this "me" in thy heart, and apply it unto thyself, not doubting but that thou art of the number of those to whom this "me" belongeth: also that Christ hath not only loved Peter and Paul, and given himself for them, but that the same grace also which is comprehended in this "me," as well pertaineth and cometh unto us, as unto them. For as we cannot deny but that we are all sinners, and are constrained to say that through the sin of Adam we are all lost, were made the enemies of God, subject to the wrath and judgment of God, and guilty of eternal death (for this do all terrified hearts feel and confess, and more indeed than they should do): so can we not deny but that Christ died for our sins, that he might make us righteous. For he died not to justify the righteous, but the unrighteous, and to make them the children of God, and inheritors of all spiritual and heavenly gifts. Therefore, when I feel and confess myself to be a sinner through Adam's transgression, why should I not say, that I am made righteous through the righteousness of Christ, especially when I hear that he loved me, and gave himself for me? This did Paul most stedfastly believe, and therefore he speaketh these words with so great vehemency and full assurance; which he grant unto us, in some part at the least, who hath loved us, and given himself for us.

VERSE 21. *I do not abrogate or reject the grace of God.*

Now he prepareth a way to the second argument of this epistle. And here ye must diligently consider, that to seek to be justified by the works of the law, is to reject the grace of God. But, I pray you, what sin can be more execrable or horrible, than to reject the grace of God, and to refuse that righteousness which cometh by Christ? It is enough and too much already that we are wicked sinners and transgressors of all the commandments of God: and yet we commit moreover the most execrable sin of all sins, in that we do most contemptuously refuse the grace of God and remission of sins offered unto us by Christ. This blasphemy is more horrible than can be expressed. There is no sin which Paul and the other apostles did so much detest, as the contempt of grace, and denial of Christ, and yet there is no sin more common. Hereof it cometh, that Paul, above the rest, doth so sharply inveigh against Antichrist, for that he despiseth the grace of God, and refuseth the benefit of Christ our high priest, who offered up himself a sacrifice for our sins. Now, thus to deny Christ, what is it else but to spit in his face, to tread him under foot, to set himself in his place, and to say, I will justify thee, and I will save thee? By what means? By masses, pilgrimages, pardons, merits, and such like. We see then how proudly Antichrist hath lift up himself against and above God, and set himself in the place of Christ, rejected the grace of God, and denied the faith. For this is his doctrine: faith availeth nothing, saith he, unless it be joined with works; and by this false and detestable doctrine he hath defaced, darkened, and utterly buried the benefit of Christ; and in the stead of the grace of Christ and his kingdom, he hath established the doctrine of works and the kingdom of ceremonies, and hath confirmed the same with mere trifles and doting dreams, and by this means he hath wrested the whole world out of Christ's hands (who alone ought to reign in the conscience), and hath thrown it down headlong into hell.

Hereby we may easily understand what it is to reject and refuse the grace of God, even to seek righteousness by the law. Now who hath ever heard that a man, by keeping of the law, rejecteth grace? Do we then sin in keeping of the law? No, forsooth. But we despise grace when we observe the law to this end, that we may be justified through it. The law is good, holy, and profitable, and yet it justifieth not. He then that keepeth the law to be justified thereby, rejecteth grace, denieth Christ, despiseth his sacrifice, and will not be saved by this inestimable price, but will satisfy for his sins through the righteousness of the law, or deserve grace by his own righteousness. And this man blasphemeth and despiseth the grace of God. Now, what a horrible thing it is to say that any man should be so devilish as to despise the grace and mercy of God? And yet notwithstanding all the world doth so: albeit it cannot abide that any man should so judge of it, but will seem to do high service and honour unto God. Now followeth the second argument.

VERSE 21. *For if righteousness come by the law, then Christ died in vain.*

These words of Paul ought diligently to be weighed and considered in this wise. Is it true that Christ suffered death or not? Again, did he suffer in vain or not? Here we are constrained to answer, except we be stark mad, that he suffered in very deed, and that he suffered not in vain, nor for himself, but for us. If then he suffered not in vain, it followeth of necessity that righteousness cometh not by the law.

Here again I admonish you, that Paul speaketh not of the ceremonial law only, as the Papists do continually dream. Take now therefore the ceremonial law, and even the moral law itself also, or the law of the ten commandments, wherein is contained the most perfect religion, and the highest service of God: that is to say, faith, the fear of God, the love of God, and the love of our neighbour, and shew me any man that hath been justified thereby, yet it is true notwithstanding that Christ died in vain. For he that is justified by this law, hath power in himself to obtain righteousness. For in that he doth what in him lieth, he deserveth grace, and the Holy Ghost is poured into him, whereby he is now able to love God and his neighbour. This being granted, it must needs follow that Christ died in vain. For what need of Christ hath he which both loveth Christ and giveth himself for him, so that he is able by the merit of congruence before grace to obtain grace, and then to do such works as by the merit of worthiness after grace, he is able to deserve eternal life? Then take away Christ with all his benefits, for he is utterly unprofitable. But why was he born? Why was he crucified? Why did he suffer? Why was he made my high priest, loving me and giving "himself" an inestimable sacrifice for me? In vain, no doubt, and to no purpose at all, if righteousness come by no other means than the Papists teach: for without grace and without Christ, I find no righteousness either in myself or in the law.

Is this horrible blasphemy to be suffered or dissembled, that the divine Majesty, not sparing his own dear son, but delivering him up to death for us all, should not do all these things seriously and in good earnest, but as it were in sport? Before I would admit this blasphemy, I would not only that the holiness of all the Papists and merit-mongers, but also of all the saints and holy angels, should be thrown into the bottom of hell, and condemned with the devil. Mine eyes shall behold nothing else but this inestimable price, my Lord and Saviour Christ. He ought to be such a treasure unto me, that all other things should be but dung in comparison of him. He ought to be such a light unto me, that when I have apprehended him by faith, I should not know whether there be any law, any sin, any righteousness, or any unrighteousness in the world. For what are all things which are in heaven and earth, in comparison of the Son of God, Christ Jesus my Lord and Saviour, "who loved me and gave himself for me?"

Wherefore, to reject the grace of God, is a horrible sin, and commonly reigning throughout the world; whereof all they are guilty which seek righteousness by their own works. For while they seek to be justified by their own works and merits, or by the law, they reject the grace of God and Christ, as I have said. And of all these abominations the Pope hath been the only author. For he hath not only defaced and trodden under his feet the gospel of Christ, but hath also replenished the world with his cursed traditions. And hereof, among other enormities, his bulls and pardons are a sufficient witness; whereby he absolveth, not such as believe, but such as are contrite, make confession to a priest, and reach out their helping hand to the maintenance of his pomp and traditions. Yet notwithstanding in this great light of the gospel, the blind and obstinate Papists do continue still in their wicked opinions and doting dreams, saying, that the qualities of nature do remain sound and uncorrupt, and that men are able to prepare themselves to grace, or to deserve grace by their own works and merits. And so far off is it that they will acknowledge their impiety and error, that they do yet still obstinately defend the same, even against their own conscience.

But we do constantly affirm with Paul (for we will not reject the grace of God) that either Christ died in vain, or else the law justifieth not. But Christ died not in vain: therefore the law justifieth not. Christ, the Son of God, of his own free grace and mercy, has justified us: therefore the law could not justify us, for if it could, then had Christ done unwisely in that he gave himself for our sins, that we thereby might be justified. We conclude therefore, that we are justified neither by our own works and merits before grace or after, neither yet by the law.

Now if my salvation was so costly and dear a price unto Christ, that he was constrained to die for my sins, then all my works, with all the righteousness of the law, are but vile and nothing worth in comparison of this inestimable price. For how can I buy that for a farthing, which cost many thousand talents of gold? Now the law (to speak nothing of other matters which are of much less value) with all the works and righteousness thereof, is but as a farthing, if ye compare it unto Christ: who by his death hath vanquished my death, and hath purchased righteousness and everlasting life. Should I then despise and reject this incomparable price, and by the law or by the works and merits of men (vile dross and dung, for so Paul calleth them, if they be compared unto Christ) seek that righteousness which Christ freely and of mere love hath given unto me already, and hath cost him so great a price, that he was constrained to give himself and even his own heart-blood for me? This, as I have said, the whole world doth, and especially such as will be counted more holy and religious than others. Whereby they plainly witness, that Christ died in vain, although with their mouths they confess the contrary never so much: which is most horrible, to blaspheme the Son of God, to spit in his face, to tread him under foot, to count the blood of the Testament as an unholy thing, and utterly to despise the spirit of grace.

Paul here disputing of righteousness, hath no civil matter in hand, that is, he speaketh not of civil righteousness; which God notwithstanding alloweth and requireth, and giveth rewards thereunto accordingly: which also reason is able in some part to perform: but he intreateth here of the righteousness that availeth before God, whereby we are delivered from the law, sin, death, and all evils, and are made partakers of grace, righteousness and everlasting life, and finally, are now become lords of heaven and earth, and of all other creatures. This righteousness neither man's law, neither the law of God is able to perform.

The law is given besides and above reason, to be a light and a help to man, and to shew him what he ought to do, and what to leave undone. Notwithstanding, man with all his strength and reason, yea, with this great light also and heavenly benefit (the law I mean), cannot be justified. Now if that which is the most excellent thing in the world (the law I say), which as a bright shining sun is joined to the dim and obscure light of man's reason to lighten and to direct it, is not able to justify, what can reason do, I pray you, without the law? What? Doubtless nothing else but that which the Pope with his dreaming sophisters and his whole synagogue hath done, who with their own traditions have darkened the light even of the first commandment. Wherefore there is not one of them that is able rightly to understand any one syllable of the law, but every man walketh in mere darkness of man's reason. And this error is much more pernicious and deadly, than that which proceedeth of the doctrine of works and the law.

These words therefore are very effectual and full of power when he saith: "If righteousness come by the law, then Christ died in vain."—He speaketh here nothing of man's strength, reason or wisdom, be it never so great (for the greater it is, the sooner it deceiveth a man) but he saith plainly without all condition: "If by the law," etc. Wherefore reason, lightened, aided and directed by the law, yea, even by the law of God, is so unable to attain righteousness, that it draweth a man from righteousness, and rejecteth Christ. Set thou therefore the death of Christ alone against all laws, and with Paul, "know nothing but Jesus Christ crucified (1 Cor. ii, 2). Receive no light either of reason, or of the law, or of any thing else, than of Christ alone. Then shalt thou be learned indeed, righteous and holy, and shalt receive the Holy Ghost, which shall preserve thee in the purity of the word and faith: but set Christ aside, and all things are but vain.

Here again we see what a goodly commendation Paul giveth to the righteousness of the law, or man's own righteousness, namely, that it is a contemning and rejecting of the grace of God, and an abolishing of the death of Christ. Paul is no great rhetorician, and yet see what matter he ministereth to him that listeth to play the rhetorician. What eloquence is able sufficiently to set forth these words: to reject the grace, the grace of God; also, that Christ died in vain. The horribleness whereof is such, that all the eloquence in the world is not able to express it. It is a small matter to say, that any man died in vain: but to say that Christ died in vain, is to take him quite away. Whoso listeth to play the rhetorician, hath here matter enough to dilate and amplify at large, what a horrible and blasphemous doctrine it is to set up the righteousness of the law and works. For what can be more blasphemous and horrible, than to make the death of Christ unprofitable? And what do they else which keep the law to this end, that they may be justified thereby? Now to make the death of Christ unprofitable, is to make the resurrection, his victory, his glory, his kingdom, heaven, earth, God himself, the majesty of God, and briefly all things else unprofitable, and of none effect.

This thundering and lightning from heaven against the righteousness of the law and man's own righteousness, should make us to abhor it.—And here with this thunderclap falleth down all the orders of monks and friars, with all such superstitious religions. For who will not detest his own vows, his cowls, his shaven crown, all men's traditions, yea, the very law of Moses also, if he hear that for these things he rejected the grace of God, and maketh the death of Christ unprofitable: the world hearing this, doth not believe that it is true. It thinketh that such horrible wickedness cannot enter into any man's heart, that he should reject the grace of God, and esteem the death of Christ as a thing of nought? And yet this sin commonly reigneth. For whosoever seeketh righteousness without Christ's, either by works, merits, satisfactions, afflictions, or by the law, rejecteth the grace of God, and despiseth the death of Christ, whatsoever he protesteth with his mouth to the contrary.

CHAPTER III.

VERSE 1. *O, foolish Galatians!*

PAUL here sheweth his apostolical care, and burning zeal which he beareth to the church: so that, in disputing and confuting, he intermingleth sometimes gentle exhortation, and sometimes he sharply reproveth, according to his own rule given to Timothy. "Preach," saith he, "the word: be instant in season and out of season: reprove, rebuke, exhort" (2 Tim. iv, 2). Here the simple reader may haply be deceived, if he be not circumspect, to think that Paul in teaching keepeth no order at all. And indeed, after the manner of the rhetoricians, he observeth none; but as concerning the spirit he useth a goodly order.

Now after that he hath sufficiently proved, and with two strong arguments confirmed this article, that Christian righteousness cometh not by keeping of the law, but by faith in Christ, and withal hath confuted the doctrine of the false apostles; in the midst of this discourse he turneth his talk to the Galatians, and reproveth them, saying, "O ye foolish Galatians," etc. As if he should say: Alas, from whence are ye fallen, O ye miserable Galatians? I have most carefully and diligently taught you the truth of the gospel, and ye also have received the same of me with fervent zeal and great diligence. How then cometh it to pass, that ye are so suddenly fallen away from it? "Who hath bewitched you?"

He reproveth the Galatians very sharply, as it seemeth, when he calleth them fools, bewitched and disobedient to the truth. Now whether he did this of zeal or compassion, I will not here contend: both may be true. A carnal man would interpret this to be a reviling, rather than a godly reprehension. Did Paul then give an evil example, or was he spiteful against the churches of Galatia, because he called them foolish and bewitched? No, not so. For with a Christian zeal it is lawful for an apostle, a pastor, or preacher, sharply to reprove the people committed to his charge: and such reprovings are both fatherly and godly. So parents, of a fatherly and motherly affection, do sharply reprove and rebuke their children; which they would not bear, if another should do it. The schoolmaster sometimes is angry with his scholar, he rebuketh him and beateth him: all which he taketh in good part, and would not bear it at the hands of his equal. The magistrate likewise is angry: he reproveth and punisheth such as are under his charge. And this discipline is not only good, but also very necessary; without the which, nothing can be well done. Wherefore, unless the magistrate, the minister, the father and mother be angry, and use to reprove or rebuke when the case requireth, he is unprofitable, and never shall discharge his office rightly.

Wherefore sharp chidings and bitter words are as necessary in every kind of life, as any other virtue else. Yet notwithstanding this anger must be so tempered, that it proceed not of any envy or malice, but only of a fatherly affection and Christian zeal: that is to say, it ought not to be childish or womanlike, seeking revenge; but only for the correcting of the fault: as the father correcteth not his child with desire to revenge, but only that the child thereby may be the better. And these kinds of anger are good, and are called in the scripture zeals or jealousies. For in chastising my brother, my child, my scholar, or subject in this sort, I seek not his destruction, but his profit and welfare.

It may be then that Paul here rebuketh the Galatians, either of a very zeal (not to destroy them, but by this means to reduce them into the way again, and to amend them) or else of pity and compassion, as it were by way of complaint, for that it grieveth him that they should be so miserably reduced. As if he should say: I am sorry and ashamed to hear of this your miserable case, your wretched doings, etc. In like manner do we also reprehend the miserable: not that we tread them down, or upbraid them with their misery, but as having compassion on them, and seeking their amendment. This I say, lest any man should cavil, that Paul railed upon the churches, contrary to the rule of the gospel.

In like manner Christ rebuketh the Pharisees, calling them serpents, the generation of vipers, the children of the devil. But these are the rebukings of the Holy Ghost. They are fatherly and motherly, and as the chidings of a faithful friend: as it is said also in the Proverbs: "better are the wounds of a friend than the kisses of an enemy" (Prov. xxvii, 6). Thus one and the self-same rebuke, if it come out of the mouth of a father, may be a great benefit: but if it proceed out of the mouth of our equal or enemy, it is a spiteful reproach. When two men do one thing, in the one it is commendable, and in the other it is reproved. But when Christ and Paul do reprove, it is done with singular virtue and commendation: but when a private man should do the like, it is in him a great vice. Therefore one and the selfsame word in the mouth of Paul is a benefit, but in the mouth of another it is a reproach.

There is a certain vehemency to be noted in this word, Galatians; for he calleth them not his brethren, as elsewhere he is wont to do: but he calleth them by the name which was proper to their country. And it seemeth that it was the natural vice of that nation to be foolish; like as it was the fault of the Cretenses to be liars. As if he should say: As ye are called, even so are ye indeed, and so ye continue: that is to say, foolish Galatians; and so you shew yourselves to be even now, in the business of the gospel (wherein notwithstanding ye ought to have been most wise), yet ye continue still in your own nature, and are no changelings. Thus Paul, by way of correction, putteth the Galatians in mind of their corrupt nature.

Moreover we are here admonished, that, according to the flesh, there are yet natural vices remaining in the churches, and in the godly. Grace maketh not such a change in the faithful, that by-and-by they become altogether new creatures, and perfect in all things: but there remain yet certain dregs of their old and natural corruption. As if a man, that is naturally inclined to anger be converted to Christ, although he be mollified by grace (the Holy Ghost so framing his heart, that he is now become more meek and gentle) yet this natural vice is not utterly quenched in his flesh. Likewise, such as are, by nature, severe and sharp, although they be converted to the faith, yet notwithstanding they cannot utterly forsake this vice. Hereof it cometh, that the holy scriptures, which do contain all one truth, of diverse spirits are diversely handled. One, in teaching, is mild and gentle: another more rough and rigorous. Thus the Spirit of God, being poured into diverse vessels, doth not quench at once the vices of nature: but by little and little, during this life, he purgeth that sin which is rooted, not only in the Galatians, but also in all men of all nations.

Albeit then that the Galatians were lightened and did believe, and had now received the Holy Ghost by the preaching of faith, notwithstanding this remnant of vice (this foolishness I mean), and the original corruption, which afterwards did easily burst out into a flame of false doctrine, remained in them still. Wherefore let no man trust so much in himself, as to think that when he hath received grace, he is thoroughly purged from his old vices. Indeed, many things are purged in us, and principally the head of the serpent; that is to say, infidelity and ignorance of God is cut off and bruised, but the slimy body and the remnants of sin remain still in us. Let not man therefore presume so much of himself, that when he hath once received faith, he can by-and-by be thoroughly changed into a new man: nay, he shall keep somewhat of his old vices still cleaving unto him (Heb. xii, 1), though he be never so good and so perfect a Christian. For we are not yet dead, but we still live in the flesh: which, because it is not yet pure, continually lusteth against the spirit. "I am carnal," saith Paul, "sold under sin. I see another law in my members rebelling against the law of my mind." (Rom. vii, 14, 23; Gal. v, 17.) Wherefore the natural vices that were in us before we received faith, do still remain in us after that we have received faith: saving that now they are subdued to the spirit, which hath the upper hand to keep them under, that they rule not; and yet not without great conflict. This glory is due to Christ alone; and this title he beareth, "that he is pure and without blemish: who did no sin, neither was there any guile found in his mouth." 1 Peter ii, 22.)

VERSE 1. *Who hath bewitched you, that you should not believe the truth.*

Here have ye another commendation of this goodly righteousness of the law, and of our own righteousness, namely, that it maketh us to contemn the truth: it bewitcheth us in such sort, that we do not believe nor obey the truth, but rebel against it.

OF THE BODILY AND SPIRITUAL WITCHCRAFT

Paul calleth the Galatians foolish and bewitched, comparing them to children, to whom witchcraft doth much harm. As though he should say: It happeneth to you as it doth to children whom witches, sorcerers, and enchanters are wont to charm by their enchantments, and by the illusions of the devil. Afterwards, in the fifth chapter, he rehearseth sorcery among the works of the flesh, which is a kind of witchcraft, whereby he plainly testifieth, that indeed such witchcraft and sorcery there is, and that it may be done. Moreover, it cannot be denied but that the devil liveth, yea, and reigneth throughout the whole world. Witchcraft and sorcery therefore are the works of the devil; whereby he doth not only hurt men, but also, by the permission of God, he sometimes destroyeth them. Furthermore, we are all subject to the devil, both in body and goods; and we be strangers in this world, whereof he is the prince and god. Therefore the bread which we eat, the drink which we drink, the garments which we wear, yea, the air, and whatsoever we live by in the flesh, is under his dominion.

But he doth not only bewitch men after this gross manner, but also after a more subtle sort, and much more dangerous; wherein he is a marvellous cunning workman. And hereof it cometh that Paul applieth the bewitching of the senses to the bewitching of the spirit. For by this spiritual witchcraft that old serpent bewitcheth not men's senses, but their minds with false and wicked opinions: which opinions, they that are so bewitched, do take to be true and godly. Briefly, so great is the malice of this sorcerer the devil, and his desire to hurt, that not only he deceiveth those secure and proud spirits with his enchantments, but even those also which are professors of true Christianity, and well affected in religion: yea, as touching myself, to say the truth, he sometimes assaileth me so mightily, and oppresseth me with such heavy cogitations, that he utterly shadoweth my Saviour Christ from me, and in a manner taketh him clean out of my sight. To be brief, there is none of us all which is not oftentimes bewitched by false persuasions: that is to say, which doth not fear, trust, or rejoice where he ought not, or doth not sometimes think otherwise of God, of Christ, of faith, of his vocation, etc., than he should do.

Let us therefore learn to know the subtle sleights of this sorcerer, lest if he find us sleeping in security he deceive us by his enchantments. True it is, that by his sorcery he can do no hurt to our ministry: yet is he with us in spirit. Day and night he rangeth about, seeking how he may devour every one of us alone, and unless he find us sober, and armed with spiritual weapons, that is to say, with the word of God and faith, he will devour us.

This is the cause that he oftentimes stirreth up new battles against us. And indeed it is very profitable for us that he thus assaileth us, and by his subtle trains exerciseth us; for by this means he confirmeth our doctrine, he stirreth up and increaseth faith in us. Indeed, we have been many times cast down, and yet still are cast down in this conflict, but we perish not: for Christ hath always triumphed, and doth triumph through us. Wherefore we hope assuredly, that we shall also hereafter by Jesus Christ obtain the victory against the devil. And this hope bringeth unto us sure consolation, so that in the midst of our temptations we take courage and say, Behold, Satan hath heretofore tempted us, and by his false illusions hath provoked us to infidelity, to the contempt of God, despair, etc., yet hath he not prevailed, nor shall he prevail hereafter. "He is greater that is in us, than he that is in the world" (1 John iv, 4). Christ is stronger, who hath and doth overcome that strong one in us, and shall overcome him for ever. Notwithstanding the devil sometimes overcometh us in the flesh, that we may have experience of the power of a stronger against that strong one, and may say, with Paul, "When I am weak, then am I strong."

Let no man think therefore that the Galatians only were bewitched of the devil: but let every man think that he himself might have been, and yet may be bewitched by him. There is none of us so strong that he is able to resist him, and specially if he attempt to do it by his own strength. "Job was an upright and a just man, fearing God, and there was none like unto him upon the earth" (Job i, 8). But what power had he against the devil, when God withdrew his hand? Did not this holy man horribly fall? Therefore this enchanter was not only mighty in the Galatians, but he goeth about continually to deceive, if not all men, yet as many as he can, with his illusions and false persuasions: "For he is a liar, and the father of lies" (John viii, 44).

VERSE 1. *Who hath bewitched you?*

Here Paul excuseth the Galatians, and layeth the fault upon the false apostles. As though he should say, I see that ye are not fallen through wilfulness or malice; but the devil hath sent the enchanting false apostles, his children, amongst you, and they do so bewitch you, in teaching you that ye are justified by the law, that now ye think otherwise of Christ than you did afore, when ye heard the gospel preached by me. But we labour, both by preaching and writing unto you, to uncharm that sorcery wherewith the false apostles have bewitched you, and to set at liberty those which are snared therewith.

So we also at this day do labour by the word of God against those fantastical opinions of the Anabaptists, that we may set at liberty those that are entangled therewith, and reduce them to the pure doctrine of faith, and there hold them. And this our labour is not altogether in vain; for we have called back many whom they have bewitched, and have delivered them out of their snares. Notwithstanding such there are, as will not suffer themselves to be taught, especially the chief sorcerers and authors of the witchery. They will hear no reason, nor admit the scripture: yea, they abuse and corrupt the scripture, and avoid such places as are alleged against them, with their false glosses and devilish dreams, clean contrary to the scripture; which is a manifest sign that they are bewitched of the devil. Wherefore they are nothing amended by our admonitions, but are much more hardened and more obstinate than they were before. And surely I could never have believed, but that I have good experience thereof at this day, that the power of the devil is so great, that he is able to make falsehood so like the truth. Moreover (which is yet much more horrible), when he goeth about to overwhelm sorrowful consciences with overmuch heaviness, he can so cunningly and so lively change himself into the likeness of Christ, that it is impossible for the poor tempted and afflicted soul to perceive it: whereby many simple and ignorant persons are deceived and driven down to desperation, and some also to destroy themselves; for they are so bewitched of the devil, that they believe this to be a most certain truth, that they are tempted and accused, not of the devil, but of Christ himself.

Such a thing of late happened to that miserable man Dr. Kraws of Halle, which said, "I have denied Christ, and therefore he standeth now before his Father and accuseth me." He, being blinded with the illusion of the devil, hath so strongly conceived in his mind this imagination, that by no exhortation, no consolation, no promises of God he could be brought from it; whereupon he despaired, and so miserably destroyed himself. This was a mere lie, a bewitching of the devil, and a fantastical definition of a strange Christ, whom the scripture knoweth not. For the scripture setteth forth Christ, not as a judge, a tempter, an accuser; but a reconciler, a mediator, a comforter, and a throne of grace.

But the poor man, deluded by the devil, could not then see this; and therefore, against all scripture, he thinketh this to be an undoubted truth: "Christ accuseth thee before his Father; he standeth not for thee, but against thee; therefore thou art damned." And this temptation is not of man, but of the devil, which that enchanter most strongly imprinteth in the heart of the tempted. But unto us which are led and taught by another spirit, it is a cursed lie, and a bewitching of the devil. But unto those that are thus bewitched, it is so certain a truth, that none can be more certain.

Seeing then that the devil is able to print in our heart so manifest a lie, that we would swear a thousand times it were an undoubted truth, we must not be proud, but walk in fear and humility, calling upon the Lord Jesus, that we be not led into temptation. Worldly and secure men, which, having heard the gospel once or twice preached, do by-and-by imagine that they have received abundance of the spirit, fall at length in like manner, because they fear not God, they are not thankful unto him, but persuade themselves that they are able, not only to hold and defend the doctrine of true religion, but also to stand against the devil in any assault or conflict, be it ever so great. Such are meet instruments for the devil to bewitch and to throw down to desperation.

On the other side, say not then: I am perfect: I cannot fall; but humble thyself, and fear, lest, if thou stand to-day, to-morrow thou be overthrown. I myself, although I be a doctor of divinity, and have now preached Christ, and fought against the devil in his false teachers a great while, by mine own experience have found how hard a matter this is. For I cannot shake off Satan as I desire: neither can I so apprehend Christ as the scripture setteth him forth: but oftentimes the devil setteth before mine eyes a false Christ. But, thanks be to God who keepeth us in the word, in faith and in prayer, that we may walk before him in humility and fear, and not presume of our own wisdom, righteousness, and strength, but trust in the power of Christ, who is strong when we are weak, and by us weak and feeble creatures continually overcometh and triumpheth; to whom be glory for ever.

This bewitching then, and this sorcery, is nothing else but a plain illusion of the devil, printing in the heart a false opinion of Christ and against Christ, and he that is deluded with this opinion, is bewitched. They therefore that have this opinion, that they are justified by the works of the law, or by the traditions of men, are bewitched; for this opinion is against faith and against Christ. Paul useth this word [bewitching] in contempt of the false apostles, which he so vehemently urged the doctrine of the law and works. As if he should say, What a devilish bewitching is this? For as the senses are perverted by bodily witchcraft, so are the minds of men also deluded by this spiritual witchcraft.

VERSE 1. *That ye should not obey the truth?*

The Galatians at the first did gladly hear and obey the truth. Therefore when he saith, "Who hath bewitched you?" he sheweth that they were bewitched by these false apostles, and were fallen away from the truth, which before they did obey. But this seemeth yet a more bitter and vehement kind of speech, when he saith that they do not believe the truth. For he signifieth by these words that they are bewitched, and that he would deliver them from this witchery, and yet they will not acknowledge nor receive this benefit. For it is certain that he did not reduce all from the errors of the false apostles unto the truth, but that many of them remained yet still bewitched. Therefore he useth these sharps and vehement words, "Who hath bewitched you?" As if he would say, Ye are so deluded and bewitched that now ye cannot obey the truth. I fear lest many of you are utterly lost, and so fallen away that ye will never return again to the truth.

And here you have again to note by the way, another goodly commendation of the law and man's own righteousness, that the doctrine and preaching thereof, be it never so fervent, if the preaching of Christ and of the gospel do not go withal, never bringeth with it true conversion and hearty repentance. Hereof manifest demonstrations we have, not only by plain words of the scripture, but also by evident experience. For as it is true which is written to the Hebrews, that the law bringeth none to perfection: so in this epistle, St. Paul, by manifest example, confirmeth the same, reasoning thus with the Galatians: Tell me, saith he, ye that would be justified by the law, received ye the Spirit of God by hearing the law, or by the gospel of faith preached? Proving by their own experience, that it is not the law nor the preaching thereof, but the gospel and preaching of faith that raiseth a man being fallen, and quickeneth him to true repentance, as more fully is to be expressed hereafter, when we come to the place. And yet neither is the preaching of the law without its effect: the use thereof only serveth to shew forth the wrath of God, and to cast down: but to raise up a man, that cometh by the ministration of the gospel and the preaching of faith only in Christ.

VERSE 1. *To whom Jesus Christ before was described in your sight.*

It was bitterly spoken where he said before, that they were so bewitched, that they could not obey the truth; but it is more bitterly said, when he addeth, that Christ was so lively described before them, that they might handle him with their hands, and yet they would not obey the truth. Thus he convinceth them even by their own experience. As though he would say: Ye are so bewitched and deluded with the devilish opinions of the false apostles, that now ye will not obey the truth. And whereas I have with great travail and diligence set forth Christ plainly before your eyes, yet doth this profit nothing at all.

In these words he hath respect to the former arguments, whereby he proved, that to those that will be justified by the law, Christ is but the minister of sin; that such do reject the grace of God, and that to them Christ died in vain. Which arguments he had before more vehemently prosecuted and more largely amplified in their presence, even as if a painter had portrayed Christ Jesus before their eyes. Now being absent, he putteth them in mind of the same things, saying: "to whom Jesus Christ was described in your sight." As if he said: There is no painter that with his colours can so lively set out Christ unto you, as I have painted him out by my preaching; and yet notwithstanding ye still remain most miserably bewitched.

VERSE 1. *And was among you crucified.*

What did I then paint out? Even Christ himself. How was that done? In this sort, that he is crucified in you or among you. He useth here very rought and sharp words. Before he said, that they sought righteousness by the law, rejected the grace of God, and that to them Christ died in vain. Now he addeth, moreover, that they crucify Christ, who before lived and reigned in them. As if he should say, Ye have now, not only rejected the grace of God, not only to you Christ died in vain, but also he is most shamefully crucified among you. After the same manner he speaketh, Heb. vi, "Crucifying to themselves again the Son of God, and making a mock of him," etc.

If a man did but hear the name of a monk, of his shaven crown, of his cowl, of his rule, it should make him afraid, (how much soever the Papists do adore these abominations, and brag that they are perfect religion and holiness, as I and others did judge of them, before God revealed his gospel unto us: for we were brought up in the traditions of men, which darkened Christ and made him utterly unprofitable unto us), when he heareth Paul say, that even they which seek to be justified by the law of God, be not only deniers and murderers of Christ, but also they do most wickedly crucify him again. Now, if they be crucifiers of Christ which seek to be justified by the righteousness of the law of God, and the works thereof, what are they, I pray you, which seek salvation and eternal life by the dregs and filthy dung of man's righteousness, and by the doctrine of devils?

But who could ever believe or think that it was so horrible and so abominable a sin to be made a religious man (for so they call them) namely to be made a massing priest, a monk, a friar, a nun? Doubtless, no man. Yea, they themselves say moreover, that monkery is a new baptism. Can there be any thing more horrible than that the kingdom of the Papists is the kingdom of such as spitefully spit in the face of Christ the Son of God, and crucify him again? For indeed they crucify him afresh (who was once crucified and rose again) both in themselves, in the church, and in the hearts of the faithful: for with their spiteful reproaches, rebukes, slanders, and injuries, they spit upon him, and with their wicked opinions they wound him, and thrust him through, that in them he may die most miserably: and in the stead of him they set up a glorious witchcraft, whereby men are so miserably charmed and deluded, that they cannot know Christ to be their justifier, their reconciler and saviour, but a minister of sin, their accuser, their judge, and their destroyer, which must be pacified no otherwise than by our works and merits.

And out of this opinion did afterwards spring the most pestilent and pernicious doctrine that is in the whole papacy, which is this: If thou wilt serve God, thou must merit forgiveness of sins and everlasting life, and must also help others that they may attain to salvation: thou must enter into a monastery, vow obedience, chastity, poverty, etc. Monks and friars, and the rest of that religious rabble, being puffed up with this opinion of their own holiness, bragged that they only were in the life and state of perfection, and that other Christians led but a common life, for they did no undue works, or more than they were bound to do, that is, they did not vow and keep chastity, poverty obedience, etc., they were but only baptized, and kept the ten commandments: but as for themselves, besides that which was common as well to them as to other Christians, they kept also the workes of supererogation, and the counsels of Christ; wherefore they hoped to have merits and a place in heaven among the principal saints, far above the common sort of Christians.

This was undoubtedly a horrible illusion of the devil, whereby he hath bewitched almost the whole world. And every man, the more holy he would seem to be, the more he is snared with that witchery, that is to say, with the pestilent persuasion of his own righteousness. And this was the cause that we could not know that Jesus Christ was our mediator and saviour, but we thought that he was a severe judge, which should be pacified by our works: which was nothing else but most horribly to blaspheme Christ, and, as Paul said before, to reject the grace of God, to make the death of Christ of none effect, and not only to kill him, but also most shamefully to crucify him again. And this is the right meaning of that which Christ allegeth out of Daniel: "That abomination standeth in the holy place" (Dan. ix, 27; Matt. xxiv, 15). Wherefore every monk and religious person, and every justiciary, seeking remission of sins and righteousness by his own works, or by his afflictions, is a crucifier of Christ now reigning and living, although not in the proper person of Christ, yet in his own heart and in the hearts of others. And whosoever do enter into monasteries, to the end that by their keeping of their rule they may be justified, do enter into the den of thieves, and are such as crucify Christ again.

Wherefore Paul useth in this place very severe and sharp words, to the end that he may fear and call back the Galatians from the doctrine of the false apostles. As if he should say: Consider well what you have done. Ye have crucified Christ again (and this I do so plainly shew and paint out before your eyes, that ye may see it, and touch it with your hands) because ye seek to be justified by the law. But if righteousness come by the law, then is Christ a minister of sin, and his death altogether in vain. If this be true, then must it needs follow that Christ is crucified again in you.

And it is not without cause that he addeth this clause, "in you or among you." For Christ is no more crucified, he dieth no more in his own person, as is said, Rom. vi, but he dieth in us when we, rejecting true doctrine, grace, faith, free remission of sins, seek to be justified by our own works, or else by the works commanded in the law. Here Christ is crucified in us again. Now this false and wicked persuasion, to seek righteousness by the law and works is nothing else (as I have before more amply declared) but the illusion of the devil, wherewith men are so bewitched, that in nowise they can acknowledge the benefit of Christ: yea, in all their life they can do nothing else, but deny the Lord who had bought them, and in whose name they were baptized, and crucify him again in themselves. Whosoever then hath any fear of God, or love unto Christ and his true religion, let him fly quickly out of this Babylon, and let him tremble at the very name of the papacy. For the impiety and abomination thereof is so horrible, that no man is able to express it with words, neither can it be otherwise seen, than with spiritual eyes only.

These two arguments Paul prosecuteth and beateth into the heads of the Galatians very diligently: first, that they are so bewitched of the devil, that they obey not the truth most clearly before their eyes; secondly, that they crucify Christ again in themselves. These seem to be simple and plain words, and without any high eloquence, but in very deed they are so mighty, that they exceed all the eloquence of man. It cannot therefore be comprehended, but only in spirit, how great an impiety it is to seek to be justified by the righteousness of the law, or by the righteousness and merits of man. For, as Paul saith here, it is nothing else but to be bewitched of the devil, to be disobedient to the truth, and to crucify Christ again. Are not these goodly commendations of the righteousness of the law and man's own righteousness?

The apostle therefore is inflamed with a vehement zeal, and with bitter words he reproveth and condemneth the presumption of man's own righteousness, rising upon the observation of the law of God, and chargeth it with this impiety, that it crucifieth again the Son of God. Seeing then it is so dangerous a thing, it cannot be beaten down enough, or condemned as it should be; for thereof ensueth such a fall as is no less than the fall of Lucifer, and such a loss can never be recovered, and therefore he useth so sharp and rigorous words against it, that he spareth not the very law of God: against the which he so bitterly inveigheth, that he seemeth utterly to reject and condemn it. And this doth he, being constrained by great necessity; for otherwise he could not withstand the false apostles, nor defend the righteousness of faith against them. Albeit then that the law be holy, just, and good, yet must it put on, as it were, the vizor of an hypocrite, seeking to be justified by works. Now he presseth them with an argument, whereof they themselves had good experience, and which they could not deny.

> VERSE 2. *This only would I learn of you: Received ye the Spirit by the works of the law, or by the hearing of faith preached?*

He speaketh these words with a certain indignation and contempt of the false apostles. If I had nothing else against you but even your own experience, saith he, yet have I enough. As if he should say, Go to, now; answer me, I pray you, which am your scholar, for ye are so suddenly become doctors, that ye are now my masters and teachers: "Received ye the Holy Ghost by the works of the law, or by the preaching of the gospel?" With this argument he so convinceth them, that they have nothing to reply again. For their own experience is altogether against them; to wit, that they had received the Holy Ghost, not by the work of the law, but by the preaching of the gospel.

Here again I warn you, that Paul speaketh not only of the ceremonial law, but of the whole law. For he groundeth his argument upon a sufficient division. If he should speak of the ceremonial law only, it were not a sufficient division. It is an argument therefore standing upon two parts, whereof the one must needs be true, and the other false; that is, either ye received the Holy Ghost by the law, or by the hearing of faith. If by the law, then not by the preaching of faith; if by the preaching of faith, then not by the law. There is no mean betwixt these two. For all that is not the Holy Ghost or the preaching of faith, is the law. Here are we in the matter of justification. But to attain to justification, there is no other way but either the voice of the gospel, or the voice of the law. Wherefore the law is here taken generally, as wholly separate from the gospel. But it is not the ceremonial law only that is separate from the gospel, but also the moral law, or the law of the ten commandments. Wherefore Paul speaketh here of the whole law.

He groundeth this argument upon a sufficient distinction, after this sort. Tell me, saith he, "Received ye the Holy Ghost by the works of the law, or by the preaching of the gospel?" Answer me to this. Ye cannot say that this was done by the law. For so long as ye were under the law, and did the works thereof, ye never received the Holy Ghost. Indeed ye taught and heard the law of Moses every Sabbath; but it hath not been heard or seen that ever the Holy Ghost was given to any, either doctor or disciple, through the preaching of the law. Moreover, ye have not only taught and heard the law, but also ye have laboured with all your power to perform the same by your works, whereby ye should most of all have received the Holy Ghost, if he had been given by the law, seeing ye were not only teachers and hearers, but also doers of the law; and yet ye cannot shew me that this was done at any time. But, as soon as the hearing of faith or the gospel came unto you, by-and-by ye received the Holy Ghost by the only hearing of faith, before ye had done any work, or shewed any fruit of the gospel. For as Luke witnesseth in the Acts, at the only preaching of Peter and Paul, "the Holy Ghost came upon those which heard the word, through whom also they received divers gifts, so that they spake with new tongues" (Acts x, 44; xi, 15; xix, 5, 6).

It is manifest therefore that by the only preaching of faith ye received the Holy Ghost before ye did any good work, or brought forth any fruits of the gospel. On the other side, the accomplishing of the law never brought the Holy Ghost: much less could the only hearing of the law do it. Therefore not only the hearing of the law, but that affection and zeal also, whereby ye go about to accomplish the law by your works, is vain and unprofitable, Wherefore although a man labour to do all things: that is to say, although he have a zeal of God, and with all his endeavour go about to be saved by the law, and exercise himself day and night in the righteousness thereof, notwithstanding he doth but labour and consume himself in vain. For they which are ignorant of the righteousness of God, and "go about to establish their own righteousness" (Rom. x, 3), (as Paul saith in another place) do not submit themselves unto the righteousness of God. Again: "Israel which followed the law of righteousness, attained not the law of righteousness," etc. (Rom. ix, 31). Now, Paul speaketh here of the manifestation of the Holy Ghost in the primitive church. For "the Holy Ghost came down in a manifest likeness upon those that did believe" (Matt. iii, 16), and by this sign did plainly witness that he was there present at the preaching of the apostles; also that they which heard the word of faith preached by the apostles, were accepted as righteous before God: for else the Holy Ghost would not have come down upon them.

The Argument of the Book Containing the Acts of the Apostles

Wherefore we must diligently weigh and consider the force of this argument, which is so often repeated in the Acts of the Apostles. Which book is written to confirm and establish this argument: for it teacheth nothing else but that the Holy Ghost is not given by the law, but by the hearing of the gospel. For when Peter preached, the Holy Ghost forthwith fell upon all those that heard him, "and, in one day, three thousand, which were present at the preaching of Peter, believed and received the Holy Ghost" (Acts ii). So Cornelius received the Holy Ghost, not by the alms which he gave, but when Peter had opened his mouth, and was yet speaking, the Holy Ghost fell upon all them which with Cornelius heard the word (Acts x, 44). These are manifest arguments, experiences, and divine works, which cannot deceive us.

Luke also writeth of Paul, in the fifteenth of the Acts, that when he had preached the gospel together with Barnabas among the Gentiles, and was returned to Jerusalem, he set himself against the Pharisees and disciples of the apostles, which urged circumcision and the keeping of the law, as necessary to salvation: whose mouths he so stopped (saith Luke) in shewing what things he and Barnabas had done amongst the Gentiles, that the whole church was amazed at the hearing thereof, especially when they heard that God had wrought so many and so great miracles and wonders by them among the Gentiles: and when they which bare a zeal to the law, did wonder how it could be that the uncircumcised Gentiles, not doing the law, nor the works thereof, nor having the righteousness of the law, should notwithstanding attain to this grace, to be justified and receive the Holy Ghost as well as the Jews that were circumcised; here Paul and Barnabas did allege nothing else but manifest experience: wherewith they were so confounded, that they had nothing to reply again. By this means Paulus Sergius, the lieutenant, and all those cities, regions, kingdoms, and countries where the apostles had preached, by the only preaching of faith did believe, without the law and the works thereof.

In the whole book therefore of the Acts, there is nothing else handled in effect, but that it behoveth as well Jews as Gentiles, as well righteous as unrighteous, to be justified by faith alone in Christ Jesus, without the law and the works thereof. The which thing doth appear as well by the preaching of Peter, of Paul, of Stephen, of Philip, and the other apostles, as also by the examples of the Gentiles and Jews. For as God gave the Holy Ghost to the Gentiles which lived without the law, by the

EPISTLE TO THE GALATIANS

preaching of the gospel, so did he give the same to the Jews: yet not by the law, nor by the ceremonies and sacrifices commanded in the law, but by the only preaching of faith. Now if the law had been able to justify, and the righteousness of the law had been necessary to salvation, then doubtless the Holy Ghost had not been given to the Gentiles which kept not the law. But experience itself doth plainly witness, that the Holy Ghost was given unto them without the law (and this did the apostles, both Peter, Paul, Barnabas, and others see) therefore the law doth not justify, but faith only in Christ, which the gospel setteth forth.

These things are diligently to be marked, because of the adversaries, which do not consider what is handled in the Acts of the Apostles. I myself, in times past, also read this book, when indeed I understood in it nothing at all. Therefore when thou hearest or readest in the Acts of the Apostles, or wheresoever it be in the scriptures, this word "Gentiles," thou must think that it is not to be understood literally of the common nature of the Gentiles, but it carrieth with it a spiritual meaning, and is to be taken, not for those which are under the law, as were the Jews (as before is said in the second chapter: "we by nature Jews," etc.)—but for those which are without the law. Wherefore, to say that the Gentiles are justified by faith, is nothing else, but that they which observe not the law nor do the works thereof, which are not circumcised, which sacrifice not, etc., are justified and receive the Holy Ghost. By what means? Not by the law and the works thereof (for they have no law) but freely, and without any other means, except only the hearing of the gospel.

So Cornelius and his friends, whom he had called to his house, do nothing, neither look they upon any works going before, and yet as many as are present receive the Holy Ghost. No man speaketh but Peter. They, sitting by, do nothing: they think not of the law, much less do they keep it: they sacrifice not: they care not for the receiving of circumcision, but only are bent to hear that which Peter speaketh. He by his preaching brought the Holy Ghost into their hearts, as it were visibly: "for they spake with tongues, and glorified God."

But some men may here cavil and say: who knoweth whether it were the Holy Ghost or no? Well, let them cavil. Sure it is that the Holy Ghost, so bearing witness, doth not lie, but hereby sheweth that he accepteth the Gentiles for righteous, and justifieth them by no other means, than by the only voice of the gospel, or hearing of faith in Christ preached. We may see also in the Acts how greatly the Jews marvelled at this new and strange thing. For the faithful which were of the circumcision, and came with Peter to Cæsarea, seeing the gift of the Holy Ghost to be poured out also upon the Gentiles in the house of Cornelius, were astonished (Acts x, 45). Also they that were at Jerusalem complained of Peter for that he went in to men uncircumcised, "and did eat with them" (Acts xi, 3). But when they heard the matter declared by Peter, in order, as it was done touching Cornelius, they marvelled and glorified God, saying: "then hath God also give salvation unto the Gentiles."

This report therefore, and this fame, that God had given salvation also to the Gentiles, was at the first not only intolerable, but also a great offence even to the believing Jews, which they could not easily shake off; for they had this prerogative above all other nations, "that they were the people of God. The adoption, the glory, the worship, etc., belonged to them, " Rom. ix. Moreover, they exercised themselves in the righteousness of the law, they laboured all the day long, they bare the burden and heat of the day. Moreover, they had the promise, as touching the observation of the law; therefore they could not but murmur against the Gentiles (Matt. xx), and say: "behold the Gentiles come but even now, and have not suffered any heat or borne any burden; notwithstanding they have the same righteousness and Holy Ghost, without labour, which we by labour and by the heat and burden of the day could not obtain." Indeed they have laboured, but that was but one hour, and by this labour they are more refreshed than wearied. Wherefore then hath God tormented us with the law, if it avail nothing to the obtaining of righteousness? He now preferreth the Gentiles before us, which have been so long burdened with the yoke of the law. For we which are the people of God, have been vexed all the day long: but they which are not the people of God, neither have any law, nor have done any good at all, are made equal with us.

And for this cause the council of the apostles, upon great necessity was assembled at Jerusalem, to satisfy and pacify the Jews, who though they believed in Christ, yet was this opinion notwithstanding deeply rooted in their hearts, that the law of Moses ought to be observed.—There Peter, upon his own experience, set himself against them, saying: "if God hath given the same grace unto the Gentiles, which he hath given unto us which have believed in the Lord Jesus Christ, who was I, that I could let God?" (Acts xi, 17.) Again: "God, who knoweth their hearts, bare them witness in giving unto them the Holy Ghost, even as he did unto us. And he put no difference be-

EPISTLE TO THE GALATIANS

tween us and them, purifying their hearts by faith. Now therefore, why tempt ye God, to lay a yoke on the disciples' necks, which neither our fathers nor we were able to bear?" etc. (Acts xv, 8, 9, 10). With these words Peter at once overthroweth the whole law. As if he should say: we will not keep the law, for we are not able to keep it; but we believe through the grace of our Lord Jesus Christ to be saved, even as they did. So Peter here standeth altogether upon this argument, that God gave unto the Gentiles the self-same grace that he gave to the Jews. As though he would say: when I preached to Cornelius, I learned, by my own experience, that the Holy Ghost was given without the law to the Gentiles, by the only hearing of faith; therefore in no case are they to be burthened with the law. To conclude, since it is certain that neither we nor our fathers were ever able to fulfil the law, it behoveth you also to reject this error, that righteousness and salvation cometh by the law. And this the believing Jews did, by little and little; but the wicked, which by this preaching were offended, at the length were altogether hardened.

The Commendation of the Book Containing the Acts of the Apostles

So in the Acts ye shall find the experience, the preachings, and also the examples of the apostles for the confirmation of this matter, against this obstinate opinion touching the righteousness of the law. And we ought therefore the more to love, and the more diligently to read this book, because it containeth most substantial testimonies, which are able to comfort and confirm us against the Papists or Jews; whose abominations and coloured hypocrisy we impugn and condemn by our doctrine, that we may set forth the benefits and glory of Christ. Who though they have no substantial matter to allege against us (whereas the Jews might have laid against the apostles, that they had received the law and all these ceremonies from God) yet notwithstanding they are no less obstinate in defending their cursed traditions and abominations, than the Jews were in maintaining their law, which they had received from God, glorying and bragging that they sit in the place of bishops, and that the authority to govern the churches is committed unto them.—Whereby they would bring us into bondage, and wrest from us this article, that we are justified, not by faith formed and adorned with charity (as they say) but by faith alone! But we set against them the book of the Acts. Let them read this book, and consider the examples contained in it, and they shall find this to be the sum and the argument thereof, that we are justified by faith only in Christ without works, and that the Holy Ghost is given by the only hearing of faith at the preaching of the gospel, and not at the preaching of the law, nor by the works of the law.

Wherefore thus teach we, O man: Although thou fast, give alms, honour thy parents, obey the magistrate, etc., yet art thou not justified thereby. This voice of the law, honour thy parents, or any other else, either heard or fulfilled, doth not justify. What then? To hear the voice of the spouse, to hear the word of faith: this word being heard, doth justify. Wherefore? Because it bringeth the Holy Ghost, which justifieth a man, and maketh him righteous before God.

Hereby we may see what is the difference between the law and the gospel. The law never bringeth the Holy Ghost, but only teacheth what we ought to do: therefore it justifieth not. But the gospel bringeth the Holy Ghost, because it teacheth what we ought to receive.—Therefore the law and the gospel are two contrary doctrines. To put righteousness therefore in the law, is nothing else but to fight against the gospel. For Moses with his law is a severe exactor, requireth of us that we should work, and that we should give: briefly, it requireth and exacteth. Contrariwise the gospel giveth freely and requireth of us nothing else, but to hold out our hands, and to take that which is offered. Now to exact and to give, to take and to offer, are clean contrary, and cannot stand together. For that which is given, I take: but that which I give, I do not take, but I offer it unto another. Therefore if the gospel be a gift, it requireth nothing. Contrariwise the law giveth nothing, but it requireth and straitly exacteth of us, yea even impossible things.

Of Cornelius, in the Tenth of Acts

Here our adversaries set against us the example of Cornelius. Cornelius, say they, was (as Luke witnesseth), "a good man, just and fearing God, which gave alms to the people, and prayed to God continually:" therefore of congruence he did merit the forgiveness of sins, and the sending of the Holy Ghost. I answer: Cornelius was a Gentile, and this cannot the adversaries deny: for the words which Peter allegeth, Acts x, 28, do plainly witness the same. "Ye know," saith he, "that it is unlawful for a man that is a Jew, to accompany with one of another nation: but God hath shewed me that I should not call any man polluted or unclean." He was therefore a Gentile, and not circumcised, not keeping the law, yea, not once thinking of it, because it pertaineth nothing unto him: and yet notwithstanding he was justified and received the Holy Ghost. And this argument, as I said, is handled throughout the whole book of the Acts: to wit, that the law availeth nothing to righteousness.

Let this suffice then for the defence of the article of justification, that Cornelius was a Gentile, not circumcised, not keeping the law: therefore he was not justified by the law, but by the hearing of faith.—God justifieth therefore without the law, and so consequently the law availeth nothing to righteousness. For otherwise God would have given the Holy Ghost to the Jews only, which had the law and kept it, and not to the Gentiles which had not the law, and much less did not accomplish it. But God wrought clean contrary; for the Holy Ghost was given to them that kept not the law; wherefore righteousness cometh not by the law. By this means the objection of the adversaries which do not understand the true manner of justification is answered.

Here again the adversaries object against us, and say, be it so that Cornelius was a Gentile, and did not receive the Holy Ghost by the law, yet notwithstanding, forasmuch as the text saith plainly, "that he was a just man fearing God, giving alms," etc., it may seem that by these works he deserved to have the Holy Ghost afterwards given unto him. I answer, that Cornelius was a just and a holy man in the Old Testament, because of his faith in Christ which was to come, as all the fathers, prophets and godly kings were righteous, and received secretly the Holy Ghost through faith to come. But these Popish sophisters put no difference between faith in Christ to come, and in Christ which is already come. Wherefore, if Cornelius had died before Christ was revealed, yet had he not been damned, because he had the faith of the fathers, which were saved by faith only in Christ to come (Acts xv, 11). He remaineth then always a Gentile, uncircumcised and without the law, and yet notwithstanding he worshipped the self-same God whom the father worshipped by faith in the Messias to come. But now, because the Messias was already come, necessary it was that it should be shewed unto him by the apostle Peter, that he was not now to be looked for, but that he was already come.

And this article concerning faith in Christ to be revealed, and in Christ now revealed (that I may touch this also by the way) is very necessary to be known. For seeing that Christ is now revealed, we cannot be saved by faith in Christ to come, but we must believe that he is already come, hath fulfilled all things, and abolished the law. Therefore, necessary it was also

that Cornelius should be brought to another belief, not that
Christ was yet to come, as he did believe before: but that he
was already come. So faith giveth place to faith: "from faith
to faith." (Rom. i, 17.)

The popish schoolmen therefore are deceived, when they say,
for the maintenance of their *opus congruum*, or merit before
grace, that Cornelius, by the natural and moral work of reason,
deserved grace and the sending of the Holy Ghost. For to be
a just man and fearing God, are the properties, not of a Gentile or of a natural man, but of a spiritual man, who hath faith
already. For unless he did believe in God, and fear God, he
could not hope to obtain anything of him by prayer. The first
commendation therefore that Luke giveth unto Cornelius, is
this, "That he is a righteous man and fearing God:" afterwards
he commendeth him for his works and alms-deeds. This
our adversaries do not consider, but lay hold upon this sentence,
"that he gave alms unto the poor:" for that seemeth to make
for the establishing of their merit of congruence or desert
going before grace. But first the person or the tree must be
commended, and then the works and the fruit. Cornelius is a
good tree, for he is righteous and feareth God: therefore he
bringeth forth good fruit, he giveth alms, he calleth upon God,
and these fruits please God, because of his faith. Wherefore
the angel commendeth Cornelius for his faith in Christ to come,
and bringeth him from that faith, to another faith in Christ
which was already come, when he saith: "Call for Simon, whose
sirname is Peter: he shall tell thee what thou oughtest to do,"
etc. (Acts x, 5, 6). Like as then Cornelius was without the
law before Christ was revealed: even so, after Christ was
revealed, he received neither the law nor circumcision. And
as he kept not the law before, so did he not keep it afterwards.
This argument therefore concludeth strongly: Cornelius was
justified without the law, therefore the law justifieth not.

Naaman the Syrian

Likewise Naaman the Syrian was, no doubt, a good and godly
man, and had a religious and reverent opinion of God. And
although he was a Gentile, and belonged not to the kingdom of
Moses, which then flourished; yet notwithstanding his flesh was
cleansed, and the God of Israel was revealed unto him, and he
received the Holy Ghost. For thus he saith: "now I know
assuredly that there is no other God in all the world but in
Israel" (2 Kings v, 15, etc.). He doth nothing at all, he keepeth not the law, he is not circumcised: but only he prayeth that
so much of that earth might be given unto him, as two mules

should be able to carry away. Moreover it appeareth that faith was not idle in him. For thus he speaketh to the prophet Heliseus: "Thy servant will henceforth neither offer burnt sacrifice, nor offering unto any other God, saving the Lord. But in this thing the Lord be merciful unto thy servant: that when my master goeth into the house of Rimmon to worship there, and leaneth on my hand, and I bow myself in the house of Rimmon; when I do bow down, I say, in the house of Rimmon, the Lord be merciful to thy servant in this point." To whom the prophet saith, "Go in peace." So was he justified. The Jew hearing this, fretteth for anger, and saith: What! Should the Gentile be justified without the keeping of the law? Should he be compared with us which are circumcised?

THE GENTILES JUSTIFIED WITHOUT THE LAW, EVEN WHEN THE LAW AND POLICY OF MOSES WAS YET IN FORCE

Therefore God, long before, when the kingdom of Moses was yet standing and flourishing, did shew that he justified men without the law, as indeed he justified many kings in Egypt and in Babylon: also Job, and many other nations of the East. Moreover, Nineveh, a great city, was justified, and received the promise of God, that it should not be destroyed. By what means? Not because it heard and fulfilled the law: but because it believed the word of God which the prophet Jonas preached. For so saith the prophet: "and the Ninevites believed God, and proclaimed a fast, and put on sackcloth;" that is to say, they repented. Our adversaries do craftily pass over this word [believed], and yet the effect of all together resteth therein. Thou readest not in Jonas: and the Ninevites received the law of Moses, were circumcised, offered sacrifice, fulfilled the works of the law: but believing the word, they repented in sackcloth and ashes.

This was done before Christ was revealed, when that faith yet reigned, which believed in Christ to come. If then the Gentiles were justified without the law, and received secretly the Holy Ghost, when the law was yet in force, why should the law be required as necessary to righteousness, which by the coming of Christ is now abolished? Wherefore this is a strong argument, grounded upon the experience of the Galatians: "Received ye the Holy Ghost by the works of the law, or by the hearing of faith preached?" (Gal. iii, 2.) For they were compelled to grant that they heard nothing of the Holy Ghost, before the preaching of Paul; but when he preached the gospel, then they received the Holy Ghost.

So we also, at this day, convicted by the testimony of our

own conscience, are constrained to confess, that the Holy Ghost is not given by the law, but by the hearing of faith. For many heretofore in the papacy have gone about with great labour and study, to keep the law, the decrees of the fathers, and the traditions of the Pope; and some, with painful and continual exercises in watching and praying, did so weary and weaken their bodies, that afterwards they were able to do nothing; whereby notwithstanding they gained nothing else, but that they miserably afflicted and tormented themselves. They could never attain to a quiet conscience, and peace in Christ, but continually doubted of the good will of God towards them. But now, since the gospel teacheth that the law and works do not justify, but faith alone in Jesus Christ, hereupon followeth a most certain knowledge and understanding, a most joyful conscience, and a true judgment of every kind of life, and of all things else whatsoever. The believing man may now easily judge that the papacy, with all the religious orders and traditions thereof, is wicked; which before he could not do. For so great blindness reigned in the world, that we thought those works which men had advised, not only without the will of God, but also contrary to his commandment, to be much better than those which the magistrate, the householder, the child, the servant did at the commandment of God.

Indeed we ought to have learned by the word of God, that the religious orders of the Papists (which only they call holy) are wicked, since there is no commandment of God, or testimony in the holy scriptures as touching the same. Contrariwise, other orders of life, which have the word and commandment of God, are holy and ordained of God. But we were then wrapped in such horrible darkness, that we could not truly judge of any thing. But now, since the clear light of the gospel doth appear, all kinds of life in the world are under our judgment. We may boldly pronounce out of the word of God, that the condition of servants, which before the world is most vile, is far more acceptable unto God, than all the religious orders of the Papists. For by this word he commendeth, approveth, and adorneth the state of servants, and so doth he not the orders of monks, friars, and such other. Therefore this argument, grounded upon experience, ought to prevail with us also. For although many men in the papacy wrought many and great works, yet could they never be certain of the will of God towards them, but they were always in doubt: they could never attain to the knowledge of God, of themselves, of their calling: they never felt the testimony of the Spirit in their hearts. But now that the truth of the gospel appeareth, they are fully instructed by the only hearing of faith, in all these things.

It is not without cause that I do so largely intreat of these things.—For it seemeth to reason but a small matter, that the Holy Ghost is received by the only hearing of faith, and that there is nothing else required of us, but that we, setting apart all our works, should give ourselves only to the hearing of the gospel. Man's heart doth not understand nor believe that so great a treasure, namely, the Holy Ghost, is given by the only hearing of faith; but reasoneth after this manner: forgiveness of sins, deliverance from death, the giving of the Holy Ghost, of righteousness, and everlasting life, are great things; therefore, if thou wilt obtain these inestimable benefits, thou must perform some other great and weighty matter. This opinion the devil doth well like and approve, and also increaseth the same in the heart. Therefore, when reason heareth this: thou canst do nothing for the obtaining of the forgiveness of sins, but must only hear the word of God, by-and-by it crieth out, and saith, Fie, thou makest too small account of the remission of sins, etc. So the inestimable greatness of the gift, is the cause that we cannot believe it: and because this incomparable treasure is freely offered, therefore it is despised.

But this we must needs learn, that forgiveness of sins, Christ, and the Holy Ghost are freely given unto us at the only hearing of faith preached, notwithstanding our horrible sins and demerits. And we must not weigh how great the thing is that is given, and how unworthy we are of it (for so should the greatness of the gift, and our unworthiness terrify us), but we must think that it pleaseth God freely to give unto us this unspeakable gift, unto us, I say, which are unworthy, as Christ in Luke saith, "fear not, little flock: for it is your father's pleasure to give it unto you: lo, to give unto you," saith he, "a kingdom" (Luke xii, 32). To whom? to you, unworthy, which are his little flock. If I then be little, and the thing great (nay, rather, of all things the greatest) which God hath given unto me, I must think that he also is great, and only great, which giveth it. If he offer it, and will give it, I consider not my own sin and unworthiness, but his fatherly good-will towards me which is the giver, and I receive the greatness of the gift with joy and gladness, and am thankful for so inestimable a gift, given freely unto me, to me, I say, unworthy, by the hearing of faith.

Here, again, foolish reason is offended, and reproveth us, saying, where ye teach men to do nothing at all for the obtaining of so great and inestimable a gift, but to hear the word of God, this seemeth to tend to the great contempt of grace, and to make men secure, idle, and dissolute, so that they slack their hands and do no good at all. Therefore it is not good to preach this doctrine, for it is not true: but men must be urged to labour and to exercise themselves unto righteousness, and then shall they obtain this gift. The self-same thing the Pelagians, in times past, objected against the Christians. But hear what Paul saith in this place: "ye have received the Holy Ghost:" not by your own labour and travel, not by the works of the law, "but by the hearing of faith." Briefly, hear what Christ himself saith, and what he answereth to Martha, being very careful, and hardly bearing that her sister Mary, sitting at the feet of Jesus, and hearing his word, should leave her to minister alone. "Martha, Martha," saith he, "thou carest, and art troubled about many things; but one thing is needful. Mary hath chosen the good part, which shall not be taken from her" (Luke x, 41, 42). A man therefore is made a Christian, not by working, but by hearing; wherefore, he that will exercise himself to righteousness, must first exercise himself in hearing the gospel. Now, when he hath heard and received the gospel, let him give thanks to God with a joyful and a glad heart, and afterwards let him exercise himself in those good works which are commanded in the law, so that the law and works may follow the hearing of faith. So may he quietly walk in the light, which is Christ, and boldly choose and do works, not hypocritical, but good works indeed, such as he knoweth to please God and to be commanded of him, and contemn all those hypocritical shadows of free-will works.

Our adversaries think that faith, whereby we receive the Holy Ghost, is but a light matter: but how high and hard a matter it is, I myself do find by experience, and so do all they which with me do earnestly embrace the same. It is soon said, that by the only hearing of faith, the Holy Ghost is received: but it is not so easily heard, laid hold on, believed and retained, as it is said. Wherefore if thou hear of me that Christ is that lamb of God, sacrificed for thy sins, see also that thou hear it effectually. Paul, very aptly, calleth it the "hearing of faith," and not the word of faith (although there be small difference), that is, such a word as thou hearing dost believe, so that the word be not only my voice, but may be heard of thee, and may enter into thy heart, and may be believed of thee: then it is truly and indeed the hearing of faith, through the which thou receivest the Holy Ghost: which, after thou hast once received, thou shalt also mortify thy flesh.

The faithful do find, by their own experience, how gladly they would hold and embrace the word when they hear it, with a full faith, and abandon this opinion of the law and of their own righteousness: but they feel in their flesh a mighty resistance against the spirit. For reason and the flesh will needs work together. This saying: "Ye must be circumcised and keep the law," cannot be utterly rooted in our minds, but it sticketh fast in the hearts of all the faithful. There is in the faithful, therefore, a continual conflict between the hearing of faith and the works of the law. For the conscience always murmureth, and thinketh, that this is too easy a way, that by the only hearing of the word, righteousness, the Holy Ghost, and life everlasting is promised unto us. But come once to an earnest trial thereof, and then tell me how easy a thing it is to hear the word of faith. Indeed he which giveth is great; moreover, he giveth great things willingly and freely, and upbraideth no man therewith: but thy capacity is hard and faith weak, still striving against thee, so that thou art not able to receive this gift. But let thy conscience murmur against thee never so much, and let this (*must*) come never so often into thy mind, yet stand fast and hold out, until thou overcome this (*must*). So as faith increaseth by little and little, that opinion of the righteousness of the law will diminish. But this cannot be done without great conflicts.

VERSE 3. *Are ye so foolish, that after ye have begun in the spirit, ye would now end in the flesh?*

This argument being concluded, how that the Holy Ghost cometh not by the works of the law, but by the preaching of faith, he beginneth here to exhort and terrify them from a double danger or incommodity. The first is: "Are ye so foolish, that after ye have begun in the spirit, ye would now end in the flesh?" The other followeth: "Have ye suffered so great things in vain?" As if he said, Ye began in the spirit: that is, your religion was excellently well begun. As also a little after, he saith: "Ye ran well," etc. But what have ye gotten thereby? Forsooth, ye will now end in the flesh.

Paul setteth here the spirit against the flesh. He calleth not the flesh (as before I have said) fleshly lust, beastly passions, or sensual appetites: for he intreateth not here of lust and such other fleshly desires; but of forgiveness of sins, of justifying the conscience, of obtaining righteousness before God, of deliverance from the law, sin, and death; and yet notwithstanding he saith here, that they, forsaking the spirit, do now end in the flesh. Flesh therefore is here taken away for the very righteousness and wisdom of the flesh, and the judgment of reason, which seeketh to be justified by the law. Whatsoever then is most excellent in man, the same here Paul calleth flesh, as the wisdom of reason, and the righteousness of the law itself.

And this place must be well considered, because of the slanderous and cavilling Papists, which wrest the same against us, saying, that we in popery began in the spirit, but now, having married wives, we end in the flesh. As though a single life, or that to have a wife, were a spiritual life; and as though it nothing hindered their spiritual life, if a man, not contented with one whore, have many. They are mad men, not understanding what the spirit, or what the flesh is. The spirit is whatsoever is done in us according to the spirit; the flesh, whatsoever is done in us according to the flesh, without the spirit. Wherefore, all the duties of a Christian man, as to love his wife, to bring up his children, to govern his family, and such like (which unto them are worldly and carnal) are the fruits of the spirit. These blind buzzards cannot discern things which are the good creatures of God, from vices.

Here is also to be noted the manner of speech which the apostle useth when he saith, *Ut corne consummamini,* speaking in the passive voice. As if he said, ye end, yea rather ye are ended in the flesh. For the righteousness of the law, which Paul here calleth the flesh, is so far off from justifying, that they which after the receiving of the Holy Ghost through the hearing of faith, fall back again unto it, are ended in it; that is to say, are utterly destroyed. Therefore, whosoever teach that the law ought to be fulfilled to this end, that men might be justified thereby, while they go about to quiet their consciences, they hurt them, and while they would justify them, they condemn them.

Paul hath always a glance at the false apostles; for they still urged the law, saying, Faith only in Christ taketh not away sin, pacifieth not the wrath of God, justifieth not; therefore, if ye will obtain these benefits, ye must not only believe in Christ, but therewith ye must also keep the law, be circumcised, keep the feasts, sacrifices, etc. Thus doing, ye shall be free from sin, from the wrath of God, from everlasting death. Yea, rather, saith Paul, by the self-same things ye establish unrighteousness, ye provoke the wrath of God, ye add sin to sin, ye quench the spirit, ye fall away from grace, and utterly reject the same, and ye, together with your disciples, do end in the flesh. This is the first danger, from the which he terrifieth the Galatians, lest, if they seek to be justified by the law, they lose their spirit, and forego their good beginnings for a wretched end.

EPISTLE TO THE GALATIANS

VERSE 4. *Have ye suffered so many things in vain?*

The other danger or incommodity is this: "Have ye suffered so many things in vain?" As though he would say, Consider, not only how well ye began, and how miserably ye have forsaken your good beginning, and your course well begun: moreover, that not only ye have lost the first fruits of the spirit, being fallen again into the ministry of sin and death, and into a doleful and a miserable bondage of the law: but consider this also, that ye have suffered much for the gospel's sake, and for the name of Christ: to wit, the spoiling of your goods, railings and reproaches, dangers both of bodies and lives, etc. All things were in a happy course and great towardness with you. Ye taught purely, ye lived holily, and ye endured many evils constantly, for the name of Christ. But now, all is lost, as well doctrine as faith, as well doing as suffering, as well the spirit as the fruits thereof.

Hereby it appeareth sufficiently, what incommodity the righteousness of the law, and man's own righteousness bringeth: to wit, that they which trust in it do lose at once unspeakable benefits. Now, what a miserable thing is it, so suddenly to lose such inestimable glory and assurance of conscience towards God? Also to endure so many great and grievous afflictions, as loss of goods, wife, children, body and life, and yet notwithstanding to sustain all these things in vain? And out of these two places, much matter may be gathered to set forth and amplify at large the goodly commendation of the law and man's own righteousness, if a man would stand upon every parcel by itself, and declare what spirit it was wherewith he began; what, how great, and how many the afflictions were which he endured for Christ's sake. But no eloquence can sufficiently set forth these matters: for they are inestimable things whereof Paul here entreateth: to wit, the glory of God, victory over the world, the flesh and the devil; righteousness and everlasting life: and on the other side, sin, desperation, eternal death, and hell. And yet, notwithstanding, in a moment we lose all these incomparable gifts, and procure unto ourselves these horrible and endless miseries, and all by false teachers, when they lead us away from the truth of the gospel unto false doctrine. And this do they, not only very easily, but also under a shew of great holiness, bring to pass.

VERSE 4. *If notwithstanding it be in vain.*

This he addeth as a correction: whereby he mitigateth the reprehension that goeth before, which was somewhat sharp. And this he doth as an apostle, lest he should terrify the

Galatians too much. Although he chide them, yet notwithstanding he always doth it in such sort, that he poureth in sweet oil withal, lest he should drive them to desperation.

He saith therefore, "If notwithstanding it be in vain." As if he would say, Yet I do not take away all hope from you. But if ye will so end in the flesh, that is to say, follow the righteousness of the law and forsake the spirit, as ye have begun, then know ye, that all your glory and affiance which ye have in God, is in vain, and all your afflictions are unprofitable. Indeed I must needs speak somewhat roughly unto you in this matter; I must be fervent in the defence thereof, and somewhat sharp in the chiding of you, especially the matter being so weighty, and constraining me thereunto, lest ye should think it to be but a trifle to reject the doctrine of Paul, and receive another. Notwithstanding, I will not utterly discourage you, so that ye repent and amend. For sickly and scabbed children may not be cast away, but must be tendered and cherished more diligently than they which are in health. So that Paul here, like a cunning physician, layeth all the fault in a manner upon the false apostles, the authors and only cause of this deadly disease. Contrariwise he handleth the Galatians very gently, that by his mildness he might heal them. We therefore, by the example of Paul, ought in like manner to reprehend the weak, and so to cure their infirmity, that in the meantime we leave not off to cherish and comfort them, lest if we handle them too sharply, they fall into desperation.

> VERSE 5. *He therefore that ministereth to you the spirit, and worketh miracles among you, doth he it through the works of the law, or by the hearing of faith preached?*

This argument, grounded upon the experience of the Galatians, doth so well like the apostle, that after he hath reproved and terrifieth them, setting before them a double danger, he now repeateth the same again, and that with a more large amplification, saying, "He which ministereth," etc. That is to say, ye have not only received the spirit by the hearing of faith, but whatsoever ye have either known or done, it came by the hearing of faith. As though he would say, It was not enough that God gave you once the spirit; but the same God hath also enriched you with the gifts of the spirit, and increased the same in you, to the end that when ye have once received the spirit, it might always grow, and be more and more effectual in you. Hereby it is plain, that the Galatians had wrought miracles, or at the least, had shewed such fruits of faith as the true disciples of the gospel are wont to bring forth. For the apostle elsewhere saith: "That the kingdom of God is not in word, but in power" (1 Cor. iv, 20). Now, this power is not only to be able to speak of the kingdom of God; but also in very deed to shew that God through his spirit is effectual in us. So before, in the second chapter, he saith of himself: "He that was effectual in Peter among the Jews, was also effectual in me; he that was mighty by Peter in the apostleship over the circumcision, was also mighty by me towards the Gentiles."

When a preacher then so preacheth, that the word is not fruitless, but effectual in the hearts of the hearers, that is to say, when faith, hope, love, and patience do follow, then God giveth his spirit, and worketh miracles in the hearers. In like manner Paul saith here, "that God hath given his spirit to the Galatians, and hath wrought miracles among them." As though he would say: God hath not only brought to pass, through my preaching, that ye should believe, but also that ye should live holily, bring forth many fruits of faith, and suffer many afflictions. Also, by the same power of the Holy Ghost, of adulterers, of wrathful, impatient, and covetous persons, and of very enemies, ye art become liberal, chaste, gentle, patient, and lovers of your neighbors. Whereupon afterwards he giveth testimony of them in the fourth chapter, that they received him as an angel of God, yea rather as Christ Jesus: and that they loved him so entirely, that they were ready to have plucked out their own eyes for him.

Now, to love thy neighbour so heartily, that thou art ready to bestow thy money, thy goods, thine eyes, and all that thou hast for his salvation, and moreover to suffer patiently all adversities and afflictions, these, no doubt, are the effects and fruits of the spirit, and these, saith he, ye received and enjoyed before these false teachers came among you. But ye received them not by the law, but of God, who so ministered unto you, and daily increased in you his Holy Spirit, that the gospel had a most happy course among you, in teaching, believing, working and suffering. Now, seeing ye know these things (being convicted even by the testimony of your own consciences), how cometh it to pass that ye shew not the same fruits that ye did before: that is, that ye teach not truly, that ye believe not faithfully, that ye live not holily, that ye work not rightly, and that ye suffer not patiently: finally, who hath so corrupted you, that you bear not so loving affection towards me, as ye did before? That ye receive not Paul now as an angel of God, nor as Jesus Christ? That ye will not pluck out your eyes to give them unto me? How cometh it to pass, I say, that this fervent zeal of yours waxeth so cold towards me, and that ye now prefer before me the false apostles, which do so miserably seduce you?

In like manner it happeneth unto us at this day. When we first preached the gospel, there were very many that favoured our doctrine, and had a good and reverend opinion of us: and after the preaching thereof, followed the fruits and effects of faith. But what ensued? A sort of light and brain-sick heads sprang up, and by-and-by destroyed all that we had in long time and with much travel planted before, and also made us so odious unto them which before loved us dearly, and thankfully received our doctrine, that now they hate nothing more than our name. But of this mischief the devil is the author, working in his members contrary works, which wholly fight against the works of the Holy Ghost. Therefore, saith the apostle, your experience (O ye Galatians) ought to teach you, that these excellent virtues proceedeth not of the works of the law; for as ye had them not before the hearing of faith preached, so ye have them not now, although the false apostles reign in the midst of you.

We likewise may say, at this day, to those which vaunt themselves to be gospellers, and to be freed from the tyranny of the Pope: have ye overcome the tyranny of the Pope, and obtained liberty in Christ through the Anabaptists, and such other fantastical spirits, or through us who have preached faith in Jesus Christ? Here, if they will confess the truth, they must needs say: no doubt, by the preaching of faith. And true it is, that at the beginning of our preaching, the doctrine of faith had a most happy course, and down fell the Pope's pardons, purgatory, vows, masses, and such like abominations, which drew with them the ruin of all popery. No man could justly condemn us: for our doctrine was pure, raising up and comforting many poor consciences, which had been long oppressed with men's traditions under the papacy, which was a plain tyranny, a racking and crucifying of consciences. Many therefore gave thanks unto God, that through the gospel (which we first, by the grace of God, then preached) they were so mightily delivered out of these snares, and this slaughter-house of consciences. But when these new-found heads sprang up (who went about by all means to work our discredit), then began our doctrine to be evil thought of: for it was commonly bruited abroad that the professors thereof disagreed among themselves. Whereat many being greatly offended, fell quite from the truth, putting the Papists in comfort, that we, together with our doctrine, should shortly come to nought, and by this means they should recover their former dignity and authority again.

Wherefore, like as the false apostles vehemently contended that the Galatians, now justified by faith in Christ, ought to be circumcised and keep the law of Moses, if they would be delivered from their sins, and from the wrath of God, and obtain the Holy Ghost, and yet notwithstanding by the selfsame means they burthened them the more with sins (for sin is not taken away by the law, neither is the Holy Ghost given through it, but only it worketh wrath, and driveth men into great terrors), so at this day these rash heads, which ought to provide for the safety of the catholic church, and at once to drive down all popery, have done no good, but much hurt to the church: they have not overthrown the papacy, but have more established it.

But if they had, as they begun, with a common consent together with us, taught and diligently urged the article of justification; that is to say, that we are justified neither by the righteousness of the law, nor by our own righteousness, but by only faith in Jesus Christ; doubtless this one article, by little and little, as it began, had overthrown the whole papacy, with all her brotherhoods, pardons, religious orders, relics, ceremonies, invocation of saints, purgatory, masses, watchings, vows, and infinite other like abominations. But they, leaving off the preachnig of faith and true Christian righteousness, have gone another way to work, to the great hindrance both of sound doctrine and of the churches.

VERSE 6. *As Abraham believed God, and it was imputed to him for righteousness.*

Hitherto Paul reasoneth upon the experience of the Galatians, and with this argument he urgeth them vehemently. Ye, saith he, have believed, and believing have done miracles, and have shewed many notable signs; and moreover ye have suffered many afflictions, all which things are the effects and operations, not of the law, but of the Holy Ghost. This the Galatians were constrained to confess; for they could not deny these things which were before their eyes, and manifest to their senses: and therefore this argument, grounded upon their own experience, is very strong.

Now he addeth the example of Abraham, and rehearseth the testimony of the scripture. The first is out of Gen. xv, 6, "Abraham believed God," etc. This place the apostle here mightily prosecuteth, as also he did in his epistle to the Romans: "If Abraham," saith he, "was justified by the works of the law, he hath righteousness and rejoicing, but not before God, but before men" (Rom. iv, 2, 3). For before God there is in him nothing but sin and wrath. Now he was justified before God, not because he did work, but because he did believe. For the scripture saith: "Abraham believed God, and it was imputed to him for righteousness." This place doth Paul there notably set forth and amplify, as it is most worthy: "Abraham," saith he, "was not weak in the faith, neither considered he his own body which was now dead, being almost a hundred years old; neither the deadness of Sarah's womb; neither did he doubt of the promise of God through unbelief, but was strengthened in the faith, and gave glory to God, being fully assured, that whatsoever God had promised, he was able to do. Now, it is not written for him only, that it was imputed to him for righteousness, but for us also," etc. (Rom. iv, 19, 20, etc.).

Paul by these words, "Abraham believed," of faith in God maketh the chiefest worship, the chiefest duty, the chiefest obedience, and the chiefest sacrifice. Let him that it a rhetorician, amplify this place, and he shall see that faith is an almighty thing, and that the power thereof is infinite and inestimable; for it giveth glory unto God, which is the highest service that can be given unto him. Now, to give glory unto God, is to believe in him, to count him true, wise, righteous, merciful, almighty; briefly, to acknowledge him to be the author and giver of all goodness. This reason doth not, but faith. That is it which maketh us divine people, and (as a man would say) it is the creator of a certain divinity, not in the substance of God, but in us. For without faith God loseth in us his glory, wisdom, righteousness, truth, and mercy. To conclude, no majesty or divinity remaineth unto God, where faith is not. And the chiefest thing that God requireth of man is, that he give unto him his glory and his divinity: that is to say, that he take him not for an idol, but for God, who regardeth him, heareth him, sheweth mercy unto him, and helpeth him. This being done, God hath his full and perfect divinity, that is, he hath whatsoever a faithful heart can attribute unto him. To be able therefore to give that glory unto God, it is the wisdom of wisdoms, the righteousness of righteousness, the religion of religions, and sacrifice of sacrifices. Hereby we may perceive, what a high and an excellent righteousness faith is, and so, by the contrary, what a horrible and grievous sin infidelity is.

Whosoever then believeth the word of God, as Abraham did, is righteous before God, because he hath faith, which giveth glory unto God: that is, he giveth to God that which is due to him. For faith saith thus, I believe thee, O God, when thou speakest. And what saith God? Impossible things, lies, foolish, weak, absurd, abominable, heretical, and devilish things, if ye believe reason. For what is more absurd, foolish, and impossible, than when God saith unto Abraham, that he should have a son of the barren and dead body of his wife Sarah?

So, if we will follow the judgment of reason, God setteth forth absurd and impossible things, when he setteth out unto us the articles of the Christian faith. Indeed, it seemeth to reason an absurd and a foolish thing, that in the Lord's Supper is offered unto us the body and blood of Christ; that baptism is the laver of the new birth, and of the renewing of the Holy Ghost; that the dead shall rise in the last day; that Christ the Son of God was conceived and carried in the womb of the Virgin Mary; that he was born; that he suffered the most reproachful death of the cross; that he was raised up again; that he now sitteth at the right hand of God the father; and that he hath all power both in heaven and earth. For this cause Paul calleth the gospel of Christ crucified, the word of the cross and foolish preaching (1 Cor. i, 18) which to the Jews was offensive, and to the Gentiles foolish doctrine. Wherefore reason doth not understand that to hear the word of God and to believe it, is the chiefest service that God requireth of us; but it thinketh that those things which it chooseth and doth of a good intent, as they call it, and of her own devotion, please God. Therefore, when God speaketh, reason judgeth his word to be heresy, and the word of the devil, for it seemeth unto it absurd and foolish.

But faith killeth reason, and slayeth that beast which the whole world and all creatures cannot kill. So Abraham killed it by faith in the word of God, whereby seed was promised to him of Sarah, who was barren and now past child-bearing. Unto this word, reason yielded not straightway in Abraham, but it fought against faith in him, judging it to be an absurd, a foolish and an impossible thing that Sarah, who was now not only ninety years old, but also was barren by nature, should bring forth a son. Thus faith wrestled with reason in Abraham; but herein faith got the victory, killed and sacrificed reason, that most cruel and pestilent enemy of God. So all the godly entering with Abraham into the darkness of faith, do kill reason, saying: reason, thou art foolish; thou dost not savour those things which belong unto God: therefore speak not against me, but hold thy peace: judge not, but hear the word of God and believe it. So the godly by faith kill such a beast as is greater than the whole world, and thereby do offer to God a most acceptable sacrifice and service.

And in comparison of this sacrifice of the faithful, all the religions of all nations, and all the works of all monks and merit-mongers are nothing at all. For by this sacrifice, first, as I said, they kill reason, a great and mighty enemy of God. For reason despiseth God, denieth his wisdom, justice, power, truth, mercy, majesty, and divinity. Moreover, by the same sacrifice they yield glory unto God: that is, they believe him to be just, good, faithful, true, etc., they believe that he can do all things, that all his words are holy, true, lively, and effectual, etc., which is a most acceptable obedience unto God. Wherefore there can be no greater or more holy religion in the world, nor more acceptable service unto God, than faith is.

Contrariwise, the justiciaries, and such as seek righteousness by their own works, lacking faith, do many things. They fast, they pray, they watch, they lay crosses upon themselves. But because they think to appease the wrath of God, and deserve grace by things, they give no glory to God, that is, they do not judge him to be merciful, true, and keeping promise, etc., but to be an angry judge, which must be pacified with works, and by this means they despise God, they make him a liar in all his promises, they deny Christ and all his benefits; to conclude, they thrust God out of his seat, and set themselves in his place. For they, rejecting and despising the word of God, do choose unto themselves such a service of God, and such works as God hath not commanded. They imagine that God hath a pleasure therein, and they hope to receive a reward of him for the same. Therefore they kill not reason, that mighty enemy of God, but quicken it; and they take from God his majesty and his divinity, and attribute the same unto their own works. Wherefore only faith giveth glory unto God, as Paul witnesseth of Abraham. "Abraham, saith he, was made strong in the faith, and gave glory to God, being fully assured, that whatsoever God had promised he was able to perform, and, therefore, it was imputed to him for righteousness." (Rom. iv, 20, 21, 22).

Christian righteousness consisteth in faith of the heart, and God's imputation. It is not without cause that he addeth this sentence out of the fifteenth chapter of Genesis: "and it was imputed to him for righteousness." For Christian righteousness consisteth in two things, that is to say, in faith of the heart, and in God's imputation. Faith is indeed a formal righteousness, and yet this righteousness is not enough; for, after faith, there remain yet certain remnants of sin in our flesh. This sacrifice of faith began in Abraham, but, at the last, it was finished in his death. Wherefore the other part of righteousness must needs be added also, to finish the same in us: that is to say, God's imputation. For faith giveth not enough to God, because it is imperfect, yea rather, our faith is but a little spark of faith, which beginneth only to render unto God his true divinity. We have received the first fruits of the spirit, but not yet the tenths. Besides this, reason is not utterly killed in this life; which may appear by our concupiscence, wrath, impatience, and other fruits of the flesh and of infidelity yet remaining in us. Yea, the holiest that live, have not yet a full and continual joy in God, but have their sundry passions, sometimes merry, as the scriptures witness of the prophets and apostles. But such faults are not laid to their charge, because of their faith in Christ, for otherwise no flesh should be saved. We conclude, therefore, upon these words: "It was imputed to him for righteousness," that righteousness indeed beginneth through faith, and by the same we have the first fruits of the Spirit; but because faith is weak, it is not made perfect without God's imputation. Wherefore faith beginneth righteousness, but imputation maketh it perfect unto the day of Christ.

The popish sophisters and schoolmen dispute also of imputation, when they speak of the good acceptation of the work: but besides and clean contrary to the scripture; for they wrest it only to works. They do not consider the uncleanness and inward poison lurking in the heart; as incredulity, doubting, contemning, and hating of God, which most pernicious and perilous beasts are the fountain and cause of all mischief. They consider no more but outward and gross faults and unrighteousness, which are little rivers proceeding and issuing out of those fountains. Therefore they attribute acceptation to works: that is to say, that God doth accept our works, not of duty, but of congruence. Contrariwise we, excluding all works, do go to the very head of this beast which is called reason, which is the fountain and headspring of all mischiefs. For reason feareth not God, it loveth not God, it trusteth not in God, but proudly contemneth him. It is not moved either with his threatenings or his promises. It is not delighted with his words or works, but it murmureth against him, it is angry with him, judgeth and hateth him: to be short, "it is an enemy to God, not giving him his glory" (Rom. viii, 7). This pestilent beast (reason, I say) being once slain, all outward and gross vices should be nothing.

Wherefore we must first and before all things go about, by faith, to kill infidelity, the contempt and hating of God, murmuring against his judgment, his wrath, and all his words and works: for then de we kill reason, which can be killed by none other means but by faith, which, in believing God, giveth unto him his glory, notwithstanding that he speaketh those things which seem both foolish, absurd, and impossible to reason: notwithstanding also, that God setteth forth himself otherwise than reason is able either to judge or conceive, that is to say, after this manner: I will account and pronounce thee as righteous, not for the keeping of the law, not for thy works and thy merits, but for thy faith in Jesus Christ, mine only begotten Son, who was born, suffered, was crucified, and died for thy sins: and that sin which remaineth in thee, I will not impute unto thee. If reason then be not killed, and all kinds of religion and service of God under heaven, that are invented by men to get righteousness before God, be not condemned, the righteousness of faith can take no place.

When reason heareth this, by-and-by it is offended: it rageth and uttereth all her malice against God, saying, "Are then my good works nothing? Have I then laboured and borne the burthen and heat of the day in vain?" (Matt. xx, 11). Hereof rise those uproars of nations, kings, and princes, against the Lord and his Christ (Psal. ii, 2). For the world neither will nor can suffer that her wisdom, righteousness, religions, and worshippings should be reproved and condemned. The Pope, with all his popish rabblement, will not seem to err, much less will he suffer himself to be condemned.

Wherefore let those which give themselves to the study of the holy scripture, learn out of this saying: "Abraham believed God, and it was counted to him for righteousness," to set forth truly and rightly this true Christian righteousness after this manner: that it is a faith and confidence in the Son of God, or rather a confidence of the heart in God through Jesus Christ: and let them add this clause as a difference: which faith and confidence is accounted righteousness for Christ's sake. For these two things (as I said before) work Christian righteousness: namely, faith in the heart, which is a gift of God, and assuredly believeth in Christ: and also that God accepteth this imperfect faith for perfect righteousness, for Christ's sake, in whom I have begun to believe. Because of this faith in Christ, God seeth not my doubting of his good-will towards me, my distrust, heaviness of spirit, and other sins which are yet in me. For as long as I live in the flesh, sin is truly in me. But because I am covered under the shadow of Christ's wings, as is the chicken under the wing of the hen, and dwell without all fear under that most ample and large heaven of the forgiveness of sins, which is spread over me, God covereth and pardoneth the remnant of sin in me: that is to say, because of that faith wherewith I began to lay hold upon Christ, he accepteth my imperfect righteousness even for perfect righteousness, and counteth my sin for no sin, which notwithstanding is sin indeed.

So we shroud ourselves under the covering of Christ's flesh, who is our "cloudy pillar for the day, and our pillar of fire for the night" (Exod. xiii, 21), lest God should see our sin. And although we see it, and for the same do feel the terrors of conscience, yet flying unto Christ our mediator and reconciler (through whom we are made perfect) we are sure and safe: for as all things are in him, so through him we have all things, who also doth supply whatsoever is wanting in us. When we believe this, God winketh at the sins and remnants of sin yet sticking in our flesh, and so covereth them, as if they were no sin. Because, saith he, thou believest in my Son, although thou have many sins, yet notwithstanding they shall be forgiven thee, until thou be clean delivered from them by death.

Let Christians learn with all diligence to understand this article of Christian righteousness. And to this end let them read Paul, and read him again, both often and with great diligence, and let them compare the first with the last; yea, let them compare Paul wholly and fully with himself: then shall they find it to be true, that Christian righteousness consisteth in these two things: namely, in faith, which giveth glory unto God, and in God's imputation. For faith is weak (as I have said) and therefore God's imputation must needs be joined withal; that is to say, that God will not lay to our charge the remnant of sin; that he will not punish it, nor condemn us for it, but will cover it and will freely forgive it, as though it were nothing at all; not for our sake, neither for our worthiness, and works, but for Jesus Christ's sake, in whom we believe.

Thus a Christian man is both righteous and a sinner, holy and profane, an enemy of God and yet a child of God. These contraries no sophisters will admit, for they know not the true manner of justification. And this was the cause why they constrained men to work well so long, until they should feel in themselves no sin at all. Whereby they gave occasion to many (which, striving with all their endeavour to be perfectly righteous, could not attain thereunto) to become stark mad: yea, an infinite number also of those which were the authors of this devilish opinion, at the hour of death were driven unto desperation: which thing had happened unto me also, if Christ had not mercifully looked upon me, and delivered me out of this error.

Contrariwise, we teach and comfort the afflicted sinner after this manner: Brother, it is not possible for thee to become so righteous in this life, that thou shouldst feel no sin at all, that thy body should be clear like the sun, without spot or blemish: but thou hast as yet wrinkles and spots, and yet art thou holy notwithstanding. But thou wilt say: How can I be holy, when I have and feel sin in me? I answer: In that thou dost feel and acknowledge thy sin, it is a good token: give thanks unto God, and despair not. It is one step of health, when the sick man doth acknowledge and confess his infirmity. But how shall I be delivered from sin? Run to Christ, the physician, which healeth them that are broken in heart, and saveth sinners. Follow not the judgment of reason, which telleth thee, that he is angry with sinners: but kill reason, and believe in Christ. If thou believe, thou art righteous, because thou givest glory unto God, that he is almighty, merciful, true, etc., thou justifiest and praiseth God. To be brief, thou yieldest unto him his divinity, and whatsoever else belongeth unto him: and the sin which remaineth in thee, is not laid to thy charge, but is pardoned for Christ's sake, in whom thou believest, who is perfectly just: whose righteousness is thy righteousness, and thy sin is his sin.

Here we see that every Christian is a high-priest: for first he offereth up and killeth his own reason, and the wisdom of the flesh: then he giveth glory unto God, that he is righteous, true, patient, pitiful, and merciful. And this is that daily sacrifice of the New Testament which must be offered evening and morning. The evening sacrifice is to kill reason: the morning sacrifice is to glorify God. Thus a Christian daily and continually is occupied in this double sacrifice and in the exercise thereof. And no man is able to set forth sufficiently the excellency and dignity of this Christian sacrifice.

This is therefore a strange and wonderful definition of Christian righteousness, that it is the imputation of God for righteousness or unto righteousness, because of our faith in Christ, or for Christ's sake. When the popish schoolmen hear this definition, they laugh at it; for they imagine that righteousness is a certain quality poured into the soul, and afterwards spread into all the parts of man. They cannot put away the vain imaginations of reason, which teacheth that a right judgment, and a good will or a good intent is true righteousness. This unspeakable gift therefore excelleth all reason, that God doth account and acknowledge him for righteous without works, which embraceth his son by faith alone, who was sent into the world, was born, suffered, and was crucified for us.

This matter, as touching the words, is easy (to wit, that righteousness is essentially in us, as the Papists reason out of Aristotle, but without us in the grace of God only and in his imputation: and that there is no essential substance of righteousness in us besides that weak faith or first fruits of faith, whereby we have begun to apprehend Christ, and yet sin in the mean time remaineth verily in us), but in very deed it is no small or light matter, but very weighty and of great importance. For Christ which was given for us, and whom we apprehend by faith, hath done no small thing for us, but (as Paul said before) "he hath loved us, and given himself in very deed for us: he was made accursed for us," etc. (Gal. ii, 20; iii, 13). And this is no vain speculation, that Christ was delivered for my sins, and was made accursed for me, that I might be delivered from everlasting death. Therefore to apprehend that Son by faith (Isa. ix, 6) and with the heart to believe in him given unto us and for us of God, causeth that God doth account that faith, although it be imperfect, for perfect righteousness.

And here we are altogether in another world, far from reason, where we dispute not what we ought to do, or with what works we may deserve grace and forgiveness of sins: but we are in a matter of most high and heavenly divinity, where we do hear this gospel or glad tidings, that Christ died for us, and that we, believing this, are counted righteous, though sins notwithstanding do remain in us, and that great sins. So our Saviour Christ also defineth the righteousness of faith.—"The Father," saith he "loveth you." Wherefore doth he love you? Not because ye were Pharisees, unreprovable in the righteousness of the law, circumcised, doing good works, fasting, etc., but because I have chosen you out of the world, and ye have done nothing, but that ye have loved me and believed that I came out from the Father. This object (I) being sent from the Father into the world, pleased you. And because you have apprehended and embraced this object, therefore the Father loveth you, and therefore ye please him. And yet notwithstanding in another place he calleth them evil, and commandeth them to ask forgiveness of their sins. These two things are quite contrary: to wit, that a Christian is righteous and beloved of God, and yet notwithstanding he is a sinner. For God cannot deny his own nature; that is, he must needs hate sin and sinners: and this he doth of necessity, for otherwise he should be unrighteous and love sin. How then can these two contradictions stand together: I am a sinner, and most worthy of God's wrath and indignation; and yet the Father loveth me? Here nothing cometh between, but only Christ the mediator.

The Father, saith he, doth not therefore love you because ye are worthy of love, but because ye have loved me, and have believed that I came out from him (John xvi, 27; John xviii, 8).

Thus a Christian man abideth in true humility, feeling sin in him effectually, and confessing himself to be worthy of wrath, the judgment of God, and everlasting death for the same, that he may be humbled in this life: and yet notwithstanding he continueth still in his holy pride, in the which he turneth unto Christ, and in him he lifteth up himself against this feeling of God's wrath and judgment, and believeth that, not only the remnants of sin are not imputed unto him, but that also he is loved of the Father, not for his own sake, but for Christ's sake, whom the Father loveth.

Hereby now we may see how faith justifieth without works, and yet notwithstanding, how imputation of righteousness is also necessary. Sins do remain in us, which God utterly hateth. Therefore it is necessary that we should have imputation of righteousness, which we obtain through Christ and for Christ's sake, who is given unto us and received of us by faith. In the mean time, as long as we live here, we are carried and nourished in the bosom of the mercy and long-sufferance of God, until the body of sin be abolished, and we raised up as new creatures in that great day. Then shall there be new heavens and a new earth, in which righteousness shall dwell. In the meanwhile, under this heaven sin and wicked men do dwell, and the godly also have sin dwelling in them. For this cause, Paul (Rom. vii) complaineth of sin which remaineth in the saints: yet notwithstanding he saith afterwards, in the eighth chapter, "that there is no damnation to them which are in Christ Jesus." Now, how shall these things, so contrary and repugnant, be reconciled together: that sin in us is no sin? that he which is damnable, shall not be condemned? that he which is rejected, shall not be rejected? that he which is worthy of the wrath of God and everlasting damnation, shall not be punished? The only reconciler hereof is the mediator between God and man, even the man Jesus Christ, as Paul saith: "there is no condemnation to them which are in Christ Jesus" (1 Tim. i, 15; Rom. viii, 1).

VERSE 7. *Know ye therefore, that they which are of faith, the same are the children of Abraham.*

This is the general argument and whole disputation of Paul against the Jews, that they which believe are the children of Abraham, and not they which are born of his flesh and his blood (Rom. ix, 7, 8). This disputation Paul vehemently prosecuteth in this place, and in the fourth and ninth chapters to the Romans. For this was the greatest confidence and glory of the Jews: "we are the seed and children of Abraham." He was circumcised and kept the law: therefore, if we will be the true children of Abraham, we must follow our father, etc. It was, no doubt, an excellent glory and dignity to be the seed of Abraham; for no man could deny but that God spake to the seed, and of the seed of Abraham. But this prerogative nothing profited the unbelieving Jews. By reason whereof Paul, especially in this place, mightily striveth against this argument, and wresteth from the Jews this strong affiance in themselves; and this could he, as the elect vessel of Christ (Acts ix, 15) do above all other. For if we at the beginning should have disputed with the Jews without Paul, peradventure we should have prevailed very little against them.

So, when Paul reasoneth against the Jews, which stood so proudly in this opinion, that they were the children of Abraham, saying: "we are the seed of Abraham." Well, what then? Abraham was circumcised and kept the law: we do the same. All this I grant: but will ye therefore look to be justified and saved? Nay, not so. But let us come to the patriarch Abraham himself, and let us see by what means he was justified and saved. Doubtless, not for his excellent virtues and holy works: not because he forsook his country, kindred, and father's house: not because he was circumcised and observed the law: not because he was about to offer up in sacrifice, at the commandment of God, his son Isaac, in whom he had the promise of posterity; but because he believed (Gen. xii, 1; xvii, 24; xxii, 1, 3). Wherefore he was not justified by any other means than by faith alone. If ye then will be justified by the law, much more ought Abraham your father to be justified by the law. But Abraham could not otherwise be justified, nor receive forgiveness of sins and the Holy Ghost, than by faith alone. Since this is true by the testimony of the scripture, why stand ye so much upon circumcision and the law, contending that ye have righteousness and salvation thereby, whereas Abraham himself, your father, your fountain and head-spring, of whom ye do so much glory, was justified and saved without these, by faith alone? What can be said against this argument?

Paul therefore concludeth with this sentence: "they which are of faith, are the children of Abraham," that corporal birth or carnal seed maketh not the children of Abraham before God. As though he would say, there is none before God accounted as the child of this Abraham (who is the servant of God, whom God hath chosen and made righteous by faith) through carnal generation: but such children must be given him before God, as he was a father. But he was a father of faith, was justified and pleased God, not because he could beget children after the flesh, not because he had circumcision and the law, but because he believed in God. He therefore that will be a child of the believing Abraham, must also himself believe, or else he is not a child of the elect, the beloved and the justified Abraham, but only of the begetting Abraham, which is nothing else but a man conceived, born, and wrapped in sin, without the forgiveness of sins, without faith, without the Holy Ghost, as another man is, and therefore condemned. Such also are the children carnally begotten of him, having nothing in them like unto their father, but flesh and blood, sin and death: therefore these are also damned. This glorious boasting then: "we are the seed of Abraham" (John viii, 33, 39), is to no purpose.

This argument Paul setteth out plainly in the ninth to the Romans, by two examples of the holy scripture. The first is of Ishmael and Isaac, which were both the seed and natural children of Abraham; and yet, notwithstanding, Ishmael (which was begotten of Abraham, as Isaac was, yea, and should also have been the first begotten, if carnal generation had had any prerogative, or could have made children to Abraham) is shut out, and yet the scripture saith, "in Isaac shall thy seed be called." The second is of Esau and Jacob, who when they were as yet in their mother's womb, and had done neither good nor evil, it was said: "the elder shall serve the younger. I have loved Jacob, and Esau have I hated." Therefore it is plain, that they which are of faith, are the children of Abraham.

But some will here object (as the Jews do, and certain cavilling spirits at this day) saying, that this word faith, in the Hebrew, signifieth truth, and therefore we do not rightly apply it; and moreover, that this place out of Gen. xv, 5, speaketh of a corporal thing, namely, of the promise of posterity, and therefore is not well applied of Paul to faith in Christ, but ought simply to be understood of the faith of Abraham, whereby he believed according to the promise of God, that he should have seed; and hereby they would prove that the arguments and allegations of Paul do conclude nothing. In like manner they may cavil also, that the place which Paul a little after allegeth out of Heb. ii, 4, speaketh of faith as touching the full accomplishing of the whole vision, and not of faith only in Christ, for the which Paul allegeth it. Likewise they may wrest all the eleventh chapter to the Hebrews, which speaketh of faith and the examples of faith. By these things such vain-glorious and arrogant spirits do hunt for praise, and seek to be counted wise and learned, where they least of all deserve it. But because of the simple and ignorant, we will briefly answer to their cavillations.

To the first I answer thus: that faith is nothing else but the truth of the heart; that is to say, a true and a right opinion of the heart as touching God. Now, faith only thinketh and judgeth rightly of God, and not reason. And then doth a man think rightly of God, when he believeth his word. But when he will measure God without the word, and believe him according to the wisdom of reason, he hath no right opinion of God in his heart, and therefore he cannot think or judge of him as he should do. As for example, when a monk imagineth that his cowl, or shaven crown, and his vows do please God, and that grace and everlasting life is given unto him for the same, he hath no true opinion of God, but false and full of impiety. Truth therefore is faith itself, which judgeth rightly of God, namely, that God regardeth not our works and righteousness, because we are unclean; but that he will have mercy upon us, look upon us, accept us, justify us, and save us, if we believe in his Son, whom he hath sent to be a sacrifice for the sins of the whole world (1 John iii, 2). This is a true opinion of God, and in very deed nothing else but faith itself. I cannot comprehend nor be fully assured by reason, that I am received into God's favour for Christ's sake: but I hear this to be pronounced by the gospel, and I lay hold upon it by faith.

To he second cavillation I answer, that Paul doth rightly allege the place out of the fifteenth of Genesis, applying it to faith in Christ. For with faith always must be joined a certain assurance of God's mercy. Now this assurance comprehendeth a faithful trust of remission of sins for Christ's sake. For it was impossible that thy conscience should look for anything at God's hand, except first it be assured that God is merciful unto thee for Christ's sake. Therefore all the promises are to be referred to that first promise concerning Christ; "the seed of the woman shall bruise the serpent's head" (Gen. iii, 15). So did all the prophets both understand it and teach it. By this we may see that the faith of our fathers in the Old Testament, and ours now in the New is all one, although they differ as touching their outward objects. Which thing Peter witnesseth in the Acts, when he saith, "which neither we nor our fathers were able to bear. But we believe through the grace of our Lord Jesus Christ, to be saved even as they did" (Acts xv, 10, 11). And Paul saith: "our fathers did all drink of that spiritual rock that followed them, which rock was Christ" (1 Cor. x, 4). And Christ himself saith: "Abraham rejoiced to see my day, and he saw it and was glad" (John viii, 56). Notwithstanding the faith of the fathers was grounded on Christ which was to come, as ours is on Christ which is now come. Abraham, in his time, was justified by faith in Christ to come, but if he lived at this day, he would be justified by faith in Christ, now revealed and present: like as I have said before of Cornelius, who at the first believed in Christ to come, but being instructed by Peter, he believed that Christ was already come (Acts x, 1, 3). Therefore the diversity of times never changeth faith, nor the Holy Ghost, nor the gifts thereof. For there hath been, is, and ever shall be, one mind, one judgment and understanding concerning Christ, as well in the ancient fathers, as in the faithful, which are at this day, and shall come hereafter. So we have as well Christ to come and believe in him, as the fathers in the Old Testament had; for we look for him to come again in the last day with glory, to judge both the quick and the dead, whom now we believe to be come already for our salvation. Therefore this allegation of Paul offendeth none but those blind and ignorant cavillers.

Paul therefore, as I have said, rightly allegeth that place out of Genesis, of faith in Christ, when he speaketh of the fatih of Abraham; for all the promises past, were contained in Christ to come. Therefore as well Abraham and the other fathers, as also we, are made righteous by faith in Christ: they by faith in him then to come, we by faith in him now present. For we entreat now of the nature and manner of justification, which is all one, both in them and in us, whether it be in Christ to be revealed, or in Christ now revealed and present. It is enough, therefore, that Paul sheweth that the law justifieth not, but only faith, whether it be in Christ to come, or in Christ already come.

At this day also Christ to some is present, to other some he is to come. To all believers he is present; to the unbelievers he is not yet come, neither doth he profit them anything at all; but if they hear the gospel, and believe that he is present unto them, he justifieth and saveth them.

VERSE 7. *Ye know therefore, that they which are of faith, the same are the children of Abraham.*

As if he would say, ye know by this example of Abraham, and by the plain testimony of the scripture, that they are the children of Abraham which are of faith, whether they be Jews or Gentiles, without any respect either unto the law, or unto works, or to the carnal generation of the fathers. For not by the law, but by the righteousness of faith, the promise was made unto Abraham, that he should be heir of the world: that

is to say, that in his seed all the nations of the earth should be
blessed, and that he should be called the father of nations. And
lest the Jews should falsely interpret this word nations, applying it unto themselves alone, the scripture preventeth this, and
saith not only, "a father of nations:" but "a father of many
nations have I made thee" (Gen. xvii, 4; Rom. iv, 17). Therefore Abraham is not only the father of the Jews, but also of
the Gentiles.

Hereby we may plainly see that the children of Abraham are
not the children of the flesh, but the children of faith, as Paul,
Rom. iv, declareth: "who is the father of us all (as it is written,
I have made thee a father of many nations), even before God,
whom he did believe." So that Paul maketh two Abrahams,
a begetting and a believing Abraham. Abraham hath children,
and is father of many nations.—Where? Before God, where
he believeth; not before the world, where he begetteth.

For, in the world, he is a child of Adam, and a sinner, or,
which is more, he is a worker of the righteousness of the law,
living after the rule of reason, that is, after the manner of
men; but this pertaineth nothing to the believing Abraham.

This example therefore of Abraham, wrappeth in it the holy
scripture itself, which saith that we are counted righteous by
faith. Wherefore this is a strong and a mighty argument two
manner of ways, both by the example of Abraham, and also by
the authority of the scripture.

> VERSE 8. *For the Scripture foreseeing that God
> would justify the Gentiles through faith.*

These things pertain to the former argument. As if he
should say, ye Jews do glory in the law above measure: ye
highly commend Moses, because God spake unto him in the
bush, etc. As the Jews do proudly brag against us (as I myself at sundry times heard) saying, ye Christians have apostles,
ye have a Pope, and ye have bishops; but we Jews have patriarchs, prophets, yea, we have God himself, who spake unto us
in the bush, in Sinai, where he gave unto us the law, and in
the temple, etc. Such a glory and such an excellent testimony
allege ye for yourselves against us, if ye can. To this answereth Paul, the apostle of the Gentiles: this your proud bragging
and boasting is to no purpose, for the scripture preventeth it,
and foresaw, long before the law, that the Gentiles should not
be justified by the law, but by the blessing of Abraham's seed,
which was promised unto him (as Paul saith afterwards) four
hundred and thirty years before the law was given. Now the
law being given so many years after, could not hinder or

abolish this promise of the blessing made unto Abraham, but it hath continued firm, and shall continue for ever. What can the Jews answer to this?

This argument, grounded upon the certainty of time, is very strong. The promise of blessing is given unto Abraham four hundred and thirty years before the people of Israel received the law. For it is said to Abraham: because thou hast believed God, and hast given glory unto him, therefore thou shalt be a "father of many nations" (Gen. xvii, 4). There Abraham, by the promise of God, is appointed a father of many nations, and the inheritance of the world for his posterity and issue after him, is given unto him before the law was published. Why do ye then brag, O ye Galatians, that ye obtain forgiveness of sins, and are become children, and do receive the inheritance through the law, which followed a long time, that is to say, four hundred and thirty years, after the promise?

Thus the false apostles did advance the law and the glory thereof.—But the promise made unto Abraham, four hundred and thirty years before the law was given, they neglected and despised, and would in nowise know that Abraham (of whom they gloried notwithstanding, as the father of their whole nation) being yet uncircumcised, and living so many ages before the law, was made righteous by no other means than by faith alone, as the scripture most plainly witnesseth: "Abraham believed God, and it was counted to him for righteousness" (Gen. xv, 6). Afterwards, when he was now accounted righteous because of his faith, the scripture maketh mention of circumcision, in the seventeenth of Genesis, where it saith: "This is my covenant which ye shall keep between me and you" (Gen. xvii, 10). With this argument Paul mightily convinceth the false apostle, and sheweth plainly that Abraham was justified by faith only, both without and before circumcision, and also four hundred and thirty years before the law. This self-same argument he handleth in the fourth chapter to the Romans; to wit, that righteousness was imputed to Abraham before circumcision, and that he was righteous being yet uncircumcised: much more then he was righteous before the law.

Therefore, saith Paul, the scripture did well provide against this your glorious bragging of the righteousness of the law and works. When? Before circumcision and before the law. For the law was given four hundred and thirty years after the promise, whereas Abraham was not only justified without the law and before the law, but was also dead and buried; and his righteousness without the law did not only flourish until the law, but also shall flourish even to the end of the world. If, then, the father of the whole Jewish nation was made righteous without the law and before the law, much more are the children made righteous by the same means that their father was. Therefore righteousness cometh by faith only, and not by the law.

VERSE 8. *Preached the Gospel before unto Abraham, saying: in thee shall all the Gentiles be blessed.*

The Jews do not only lightly pass over, but also do deride, and with their wicked glosses do corrupt these excellent and notable sentences: "Abraham believed God," etc. "I have appointed thee a father," etc., and such like, which highly commend faith, and contain promises of spiritual things. For they are blind and hard-hearted, and therefore they see not that these places do entreat of faith towards God, and of righteousness before God. With like malice also they handle this notable place of the spiritual blessing: "In thee all the nations of the earth shall be blessed" (Gen. xii, 3; Acts iii, 25). For, say they, to bless signified nothing else but to praise, to pray for prosperity, and to be glorious in the sight of the world. After this manner, the Jew, say they, which is born of the seed of Abraham, is blessed: and the proselyte or stranger which worshippeth the God of the Jews, and joineth himself unto them, is also blessed. Therefore they think that blessing is nothing else but praise and glory in this world; in that a man may glory and vaunt that he is of the stock and family of Abraham. But this is to corrupt and pervert the sentence sof the scriptures, and not to expound them. By these words, "Abraham believed," Paul defineth, and setteth before our eyes a spiritual Abraham, faithful, righteous, and having the promise of God; an Abraham, I say, which is not in error, and in the old flesh: which is not born of Adam, but of the Holy Ghost. And of this Abraham, renewed by faith and regenerate by the Holy Ghost, speaketh the scripture, and pronounceth of him, that he should be a father of many nations: also, that all the Gentiles should be given unto him for an inheritance, when it saith: "in thee shall all the nations of the earth be blessed." This Paul vehemently urgeth by the authority of the scripture which saith, "Abraham believed God," etc. Gen. xv.

The scripture then attributeth no righteousness to Abraham, but in that he believeth: and it speaketh of such an Abraham, as he is accounted before God. Such sentences therefore of the scripture do set forth unto us a new Abraham, which is separate from the carnal marriage and bed, and from the carnal generation, and make him such a one as he is before God; that is to say, believing and justified through faith: to whom now God maketh this promise because of his faith: "thou shalt be a father of many nations." Again, "in thee shall all the nations of the earth be blessed." And this is the meaning of Paul, where he sheweth how the scripture preventeth the vain presumption and proud brags of the Jews as touching the law. For the inheritance of the Gentiles was given unto Abraham, not by the law and circumcision, but long before the same, by the only righteousness of faith.

Therefore, whereas the Jews will be counted and called blessed, because they are the children and seed of Abraham, it is nothing else but a vain-glorious brag. It is, no doubt, a great prerogative and glory before the world, to be born of Abraham's seed, as Paul sheweth, Rom. ix, but not so before God. Wherefore the Jews do wickedly pervert this place concerning the blessing, in applying it only to a carnal blessing, and do great injury to the scripture, which speaketh most manifestly of the spiritual blessing before God, and neither can or ought otherwise to be understood. This is then the true meaning of this place: "In thee shall all be blessed." In which thee? In thee Abraham believing, or in thy faith, or in Christ (thy seed) to come, in whom thou believest, "all the nations of the earth (I say) shall be blessed;" that is, all the nations shall be thy blessed children, even like as thou art blessed: as it is written, "so shall thy seed be" (Gen. xv, 5).

Hereof it followeth that the blessing and faith of Abraham is the same that ours is; that Abraham's Christ is our Christ; that died as well for the sins of Abraham, as for us. Abraham which saw my day and rejoiced (John viii). Therefore all found one and the same thing. We may not suffer this world blessing to be corrupted. The Jews look but through a veil into the scripture, and therefore they understand not what or whereof the promise is, which was made to the fathers; which we notwithstanding ought to consider above all things: so shall we see that God speaketh to Abraham, the patriarch, not of the law nor of things to be done, but of things to be believed; that is to say, that God speaketh unto him of promises which are apprehended by faith. Now, what doth Abraham? He believeth those promises. And what doth God to that believing Abraham? He imputeth faith unto him for righteousness; and addeth further many more promises, as: "I am thy defender. In thee shall all nations be blessed. Thou shalt be a father of many nations. So shall thy seed be," (Gen. xv, 1; xii, 3;

xv, 5). These are invincible arguments, against the which nothing can be said, if the places of the holy scriptures be thoroughly considered.

VERSE 9. *So then they which are of faith, are blessed with faithful Abraham.*

All the weight and force hereof lieth in these words, "With faithful Abraham." For he putteth a plain difference between Abraham and Abraham; of one and the self-same person making two. As if he said: There is a working, and there is a believing Abraham. With the working Abraham we have nothing to do. For if he be justified by works, he hath to rejoice, but not with God. Let the Jews glory as much as they will of that begetting Abraham which is a worker, is circumcised, and keepeth the law; but we glory of the faithful Abraham, of whom the scripture saith, that he received the blessing of righteousness through his faith, not only for himself, but also for all those which believe as he did; and so the world was promised to Abraham, because he believed. Therefore all the world is blessed; that is to say, receiveth imputation of righteousness, if it believe as Abraham did.

Wherefore the blessing is nothing else but the promise of the gospel. And that all nations are blessed, is as much as to say, as all nations shall hear the blessing; that is, the promise of God shall be preached and published by the gospel among all nations. And out of this place the prophets have drawn many prophecies by spiritual understanding, as: "Ask of me, and I will give thee the heathen for thine inheritance, and the ends of the earth for thy possession" (Ps. ii, 8). And again, "Their voice hath gone through all the earth" (Ps. xix). Briefly, all the prophecies of the kingdom of Christ, and of the publishing of the gospel throughout all the world, have sprung out of this place: "In thee shall all the nations of the earth be blessed." Wherefore to say that the nations are blessed, is nothing else but that righteousness is freely given unto them; or that they are counted righteous before God, not by the law, but by the hearing of faith; for Abraham was not justified by any other means than by hearing the word of promise, of blessing, and of grace. Therefore like as Abraham obtained imputation of righteousness by the hearing of faith, even so did all the Gentiles obtain, and yet do obtain the same. For the same word that was first declared unto Abraham, was also afterward published to all the Gentiles.

Hereby then we see that to bless signifieth nothing else, but (as I said before) to preach and teach the word of the gospel, to confess Christ, and to spread abroad the knowledge of him among all the Gentiles. And this is the priestly office, and continual sacrifice of the church in the New Testament, which distributeth this blessing by preaching and by ministering of the sacraments, by comforting the broken-hearted, by distrubuting the word of grace which Abraham had, and which was also his blessing; which when he believed, he received the blessing. So we also believing the same are blessed. And this blessing is a great glory, not before the world, but before God. For we have heard that our sins are forgiven us, and that we are accepted of God: that God is our father, and that we are his children; with whom he will not be angry, but will deliver us from sin, from death, and all evils, and will give unto us righteousness, life, and eternal salvation. Of this blessing (as I have said) do the prophets preach in every place, which did not so coldly consider those promises made unto the fathers as the wicked Jews did, and as the popish schoolmen and sectaries do at this day, but did read them and weigh them with great diligence, and also drew out of those promises whatsoever they prophesied concerning Christ or his kingdom. So the prophecy of Hosea— "I will redeem them from the power of the grave: I will deliver them from death: O death, I will be thy death: O grave, I will by thy destruction" (Hosea xiii, 14), and such like places of the other prophets, did all spring out of these promises, in the which God promised to the fathers the bruising of the serpent's head, and the blessing of all nations. (Gen. iii, 15.)

Moreover, if the nations be blessed, that is to say, if they be accounted righteous before God, it followeth that they are free from sin and death, and are made partakers of righteousness, salvation, and everlasting life, not for their works, but for their faith in Christ. Wherefore that place of Gen. xii, 3, "In thee shall all the nations be blessed," speaketh not of the blessing of the mouth, but of such a blessing as belongeth to the imputation of righteousness, which is available before God, and redeemeth from the curse of sin, and from all those evils that do accompany sin. Now, this blessing is received only by faith; for the text saith plainly, "Abraham believed, and it was accounted unto him for righteousness." Wherefore, it is a mere spiritual blessing, and there is no blessing indeed but this: which although it be accursed in the world (as indeed it is) yet is it available before God. This place therefore is of great force, that they, which are of faith, are become partakers of this promise of the blessing made unto the believing Abraham. And by this means Paul preventeth the cavillation of the Jews, which brag of a begetting and a working Abraham, and just before men, and not of a believing Abraham.

Now, like as the Jews do glory only of a working Abraham, even so the Pope setteth out only a working Christ, or rather an example of Christ. He that will live godly (saith he) must walk as Christ hath walked, according to his own saying in John xiii, 15, "I have given you an example, that you should do even as I have done to you." We deny not but that the faithful ought to follow the example of Christ, and to work well; but we say that they are not justified thereby before God. And Paul doth not here reason what we ought to do, but by what means we are made righteous. In this matter we must set nothing else before our eyes, but Jesus Christ dying for our sins, and rising again for our righteousness; and him must we apprehend by faith, as a gift, not as an example. This, reason understandeth not; and therefore as the Jews follow a working and not a believing Abraham, even so the Papists, and all that seek righteousness by works, do behold and apprehend, not a justifying, but a working Christ: and by this means they swerve from Christ, from righteousness and salvation. And like as the Jews, which were saved, ought to follow the believing Abraham, so we also, if we will be delivered from our sins and be saved, must take hold of the justifying and saving Christ, whom Abraham himself also, by faith, did apprehend, and through him was blessed.

It was indeed a great glory that Abraham received circumcision at the commandment of God, that he was endued with excellent virtues, that he obeyed God in all things: as it is also a great praise and felicity to follow the example of Christ working, to love thy neighbour, to do good to them that hurt thee, to pray for thine enemies, patiently to bear the ingratitude of those which render evil for good; but all this availeth nothing to righteousness before God. The excellent deeds and virtues of Abraham were not the cause that he was accounted righteous before God; so likewise the imitation and following of the example of Christ doth not make us righteous before God. For, to make us righteous before God, there is a far more excellent price required, which is neither the righteousness of man, nor yet of the law. Here we must have Christ to bless us and save us, like as Abraham had him for his blesser and saviour. How? Not by works, but by faith. Wherefore, as there is great difference between the believing and the working Abraham; so there is great difference between Christ blessing and redeeming, and Christ working and giving example. Now Paul speaketh here of Christ redeeming, and Abraham believing; and not of Christ giving example, or of Abraham working. Therefore he addeth purposely, and that with great vehemency, "They which are of faith, are blessed with faithful Abraham."

Wherefore we must separate the believing and the working Abraham as far asunder as there is distance between heaven and earth. A man, believing in Christ, is altogether a divine person, the child of God, the inheritor of the world, a conqueror of sin, death, the world, and the devil: therefore he cannot be praised and magnified enough. Let us not suffer this faithful Abraham to lie hid in his grave, as he is hid from the Jews; but let us highly extol and magnify him; and let us fill both heaven and earth with his name; so that, in respect of this faithful Abraham, we see nothing at all in the working Abraham. For when we speak of this faithful Abraham, we are in heaven. But afterwards, doing those things which the working Abraham did, which were carnal and earthly, not divine and heavenly, (but inasmuch as they were given unto him of God), we are among men in earth. The believing Abraham therefore filleth both heaven and earth. So every Christian, through his faith, filleth heaven and earth; so that, besides it, he ought to behold nothing.

Now, by these words, "shall be blessed," Paul gathereth an argument of the contrary: for the scripture is full of oppositions, as when two contraries are compared together. And it is a point of cunning to mark well these oppositions in the scriptures, and by them to expound the sentences thereof. As here this word "blessing" importeth also to the contrary; that is to say, "malediction." For when the scripture saith that all nations which are of faith are blessed with faithful Abraham, it followeth necessarily that all, as well Jews as Gentiles, are accursed without faith, or without the faithful Abraham. "For the promise of blessing was given to Abraham, that in him all nations should be blessed." There is no blessing then to be looked for, but only in the promise made unto Abraham, now published by the gospel throughout the whole world. Therefore, whatsoever is without that blessing, is accursed. And this Paul sheweth plainly when he saith,

VERSE 10. *For as many as are of the works of the law, are accursed.*

Here ye see that the curse is as it were a flood; swallowing up whatsoever is without Abraham; that is to say, without faith, and the promise of the blessing of Abraham. Now if the law itself, given by Moses at the commandment of God, maketh them subject to the curse which are under it, much more shall the laws and traditions so do, which are devised by man. He therefore that will avoid the curse, must lay hold upon the promise of blessing, or upon the faith of Abraham, or else he shall remain under the curse. Upon this place therefore, "shall be blessed in thee," it followeth, that all nations, whether they were before Abraham, in his time, or after, are accursed, and shall abide under the curse for ever, unless they be blessed in the faith of Abraham, unto whom the promise of the blessing was given to be published by his seed throughout the whole world.

To know these things it is very necessary, for they help greatly to comfort troubled and afflicted consciences; and moreover, they teach us to separate the righteousness of faith from the righteousness of the flesh, or civil righteousness. For we must note that Paul is here in hand, not with a matter of policy, but with a divine and spiritual matter, lest any mad-brain should cavil, and say that he curseth and condemneth politic laws and magistrates. Here all the sophisters and popish schoolmen are dumb, and can say nothing. Wherefore the readers must be admonished that in this place there is nothing handled as touching civil laws, manners, or matters political, (which are the ordinances of God, and good things, and the scripture elsewhere approveth and commendeth the same), but of a spiritual righteousness, by the which we are justified before God, and are called the children of God in the kingdom of heaven. To be brief, there is nothing handled here concerning the bodily life, but concerning everlasting life, where no blessing is to be hoped for, or righteousness to be sought, either through the law, or traditions, or whatsoever can be named in this life, besides the promise of Abraham's blessing. Let the civil laws and ordinances abide in their place and order; let the magistrate make never so good and excellent laws; yet notwithstanding they deliver no man from the curse of God's law. The kingdom of Babylon, ordained of God, and by him committed unto kings, had excellent laws, and all nations were commanded to obey them: notwithstanding, the obedience of the laws did not save it from the curse of the law of God. In like manner we obey the laws of princes and magistrates, but we are not therefore righteous before God: for here we are in another matter.

It is not without cause that I do so diligently teach and repeat this distinction; for the knowledge thereof is very necessary. Albeit there are few that mark it or understand it indeed. Again, the confounding and mingling together of the heavenly and civil righteousness, is very easy. In the civil righteousness we must have regard to laws and works: but in the spiritual, divine, and heavenly righteousness, we must utterly reject all laws and works, and set the only promise and blessing before our eyes, which layeth before us Christ the giver of this blessing and grace, and our only Saviour. So that this spiritual righteousness, secluding the law and all works, looketh only unto the grace and blessing which is given by Christ, as it was promised to Abraham, and of him believed.

Hereby we may plainly see that this argument is invincible. For if we must hope to receive this blessing by Christ alone, then it must needs follow of the contrary, that it is not received by the law. For the blessing was given to faithful Abraham before the law and without the law. Now, like as Abraham believed in Christ which was to come, the giver of the blessing: so and by the same faith we believe in Christ which is come and present, and so are we now justified by faith, as Abraham was then justified by faith. They therefore which are under the law, are not blessed, but remain under the curse.

This the Pope and his proud prelates do not believe, nor can believe, neither can they abide this doctrine. Yet must we not hold our peace, but must confess the truth and say, that the papacy are accursed; yea, all the laws and civil ordinances of the emperor are accursed; for, according to Paul, whatsoever is without the promise and faith of Abraham, is accursed. When our adversaries hear this, by-and-by they pervert and slander our words, as though we taught that the magistrates should not be honoured, but that we raise up seditions against the emperor, that we condemn all laws, that we overthrow and destroy common-weals, etc. But they do us great wrong. For we put a difference between the corporal and the spiritual blessing, and we say that the emperor is blessed with a corporal blessing. For to have a kingdom, laws, and civil ordinances, to have a wife, children, house, and lands, is a blessing. For all these things are the good creatures and gifts of God. But we are not delivered from the everlasting curse by this corporal blessing, which is but temporal, and must have an end. Therefore we condemn not laws, neither do we stir up sedition against the emperor: but we teach that he must be obeyed, that he must be feared, reverenced, and honoured, but yet civilly. But when we speak of the blessing after the manner of divines, then we say boldly, with Paul, "that all things which are without the faith and promise of Abraham, are accursed and abide under that everlasting curse of God." For there we must look for another life after this, and another blessing after this corporal blessing.

To conclude, we say, that all corporal things are the good creatures of God. Therefore (as I have said), to have wife, children, goods, to have politic laws and ordinances, are the good blessings of God in their place; that is to say, they are temporal blessings belonging to this life. But these blessings the justiciaries and law-workers of all ages, as the Jews, Papists, sectaries, and such like, do confound and mingle together. For they put no difference between corporal and spiritual blessings. Therefore they say: "we have a law, and this law is good, holy, and righteous: therefore we are justified through it." Who denieth but that the law is good, holy, and righteous? But yet it is also the law of malediction, of sin, of wrath, and of death. Therefore we make here a distinction between the corporal and spiritual blessing, and say, that God hath a double blessing; one corporal for this life, and another spiritual for the everlasting life. Therefore, to have riches, and children, and such like, we say it is a blessing, but in its degree; that is to say, in this life present. But as touching life everlasting, it is not enough to have corporal blessings: for the very wicked do therein abound most of all. It is not sufficient that we have civil righteousness or the righteousness of the law; for therein also the wicked do specially flourish. These things God distributeth in the world freely, and bestoweth them both upon the good and bad, like as he suffereth the sun to rise both upon the good and evil, and sendeth rain upon the righteous and unrighteous: for he is liberal unto all; and to him it is a small matter to put all creatures under the feet of the wicked. "The creature is subject to vanity, not of his own will" (Rom. viii, 20). They therefore which have but only these corporal blessings, are not the children of God, blessed before God spiritually, as was Abraham: but they are under the curse, as Paul here saith, "Whosoever is under the works of the law, is under the curse."

Paul might have said, by a general proposition, whatsoever is without faith, is under the curse. He saith not so, but he taketh that which, besides faith, is the best, the greatest and most excellent among all corporal blessings of the world; to wit, the law of God. The law, saith he, indeed is holy and given of God: notwithstanding it doth nothing else but make all men subject to the curse, and keep them under the same. Now if the law of God do bring men under the curse, much more may the same be said of inferior laws and blessings. And that it may be plainly understood what Paul calleth it to be under the curse, he declareth by this testimony of the scripture, saying,

VERSE 10. *For it is written, Cursed is every man that continueth not in all things which are written in the book of the law, to do them.* (Deuteronomy xxvii, 26.)

Paul goeth about to prove, by this testimony taken out of Deuteronomy, that all men which are under the law, or under the works of the law, are accursed, or under the curse; that is to say, under sin, the wrath of God, and everlasting death. For he speaketh not (as I have said before) of a corporal, but of a spiritual curse, which must needs be the curse of everlasting death and hell. And this is a wonderful manner of proving. For Paul proveth this affirmative sentence, which he borroweth out of Moses, "Whosoever are of the works of the law, are under the curse," by this negative, "cursed is every one that abideth not in all things," etc. Now these two sentences of Paul and Moses seem clean contrary. Paul saith, whosoever shall do the works of the law, is accursed. Moses saith, whosoever shall not do the works of the law are accursed. How shall these two sayings be reconciled together? Or else (which is more) how shall the one be proved by the other? Indeed, no man can well understand this place, unless he also know and understand the article of justification.

Paul, no doubt, being among the Galatians, had before more largely entreated of this matter; for else they could not have understood it, seeing he doth here but touch it by the way. But because they had heard him declare the same unto them before, they, being now again put in mind thereof, do call it to remembrance. And these two sentences are not repugnant, but do very well agree. We also do teach in like manner: that the hearers of the law are not righteous before God, but the doers of the law shall be justified (Rom. ii). And contrariwise, they that are of the works of the law, are under the curse. For the article of justification teacheth, that whatsoever is without the faith of Abraham, is accursed. And yet, notwithstanding, the righteousness of the law must be fulfilled in us (Rom. viii). To a man that is ignorant of the doctrine of faith, these two sentences seem to be quite contrary.

First of all, therefore, we must mark well whereupon Paul entreateth in this place, whereabout he goeth, and how he looketh into Moses. He is here (as before I have often said) in a spiritual matter, separated from policy and from all laws, and he looketh into Moses with other eyes than the hypocrites and false apostles do, and expondeth the law spiritually. Wherefore the whole effect of the matter consisteth in this word (to do). Now to do the law, is not only to do it outwardly, but to do

EPISTLE TO THE GALATIANS

it truly and perfectly. There be two sorts then of doers of the law: the first are they which are of the works of the law, against whom Paul inveigheth throughout all this epistle. The other sort are they which are of faith, of whom we will speak hereafter. Now, to be of the law, or of the works of the law, and to be of faith, are quite contrary, yea, even as contrary as God and the devil, sin and righteousness, death and life. For they are of the law, which would be justified by the law. They are of faith, which do assuredly trust that they are justified through mercy alone, for Christ's sake. He which saith that righteousness is of faith, curseth and condemneth the righteousness of works. Contrariwise, he which saith that righteousness is of the law, curseth and condemneth the righteousness of faith. Therefore they are altogether contrary the one to the other.

He that considereth this, shall easily understand, that to observe the law, is not to do that which is commanded in the law in outward shew only (as the hypocrites imagine) but in spirit, that is to say, truly and perfectly. But where shall we find him that will so accomplish the law? Let us see him and we will praise him. Here our adversaries have their answer ready, saying, The doers of the law shall be justified (Rom. ii). Very well. But let us first define who be these doers of the law. They call him a doer of the law, which doth the works of the law, and so by those works going before, is made righteous. This is not to do the law according to Paul: for, as I have said, to be of the works of the law, and to be of faith, are contrary things. Therefore to seek to be justified by the works of the law, is to deny the righteousness of faith. Wherefore these justiciaries and law-workers, when they do the law, even in so doing deny the righteousness of faith, and sin against the first, the second, and third commandment, yea, even against the whole law. For God commandeth that we should worship him in faith, and in the fear of his name. On the contrary they make righteousness of works, without faith and against faith; therefore in that they do the law, they do clean contrary to the law, and sin most deadly. For they deny the righteousness of God, his mercy, and his promises; they deny Christ with all his benefits, and in their heart they establish, not the righteousness of the law, (which they understand not, and much less do it), but a mere fantasy and an idol of the law. Therefore we must needs say, that not only in doing of the law, they do it not, but also they sin, and deny the divine Majesty in all his promises. And to this end the law was not given.

Wherefore, they, not understanding the law, abuse the law,

and as Paul saith: "They being ignorant of the righteousness of God, and seeking to establish their own righteousness, have not submitted themselves to the righteousness of God" (Romans x, 3). For they are blind, and know not how to judge of faith and of the promises, and therefore without all understanding they rush into the scripture, taking hold but of one part thereof to wit, the law, and this they imagine that they are able to fulfil by works. But this is a very dream, a bewitching and illusion of the heart: and that righteousness of the law, which they think they do fulfil, is nothing else, in very deed, but idolatry and blasphemy against God. Therefore it cannot be but they must needs abide under the curse.

It is impossible therefore that we should do the law in such sort as they imagine, and much less that we should be justified thereby. This thing first the law itself testifieth, which hath a clean contrary effect; for it increaseth sin, it worketh wrath, it accuseth, it terrifieth, and condemneth. How then should it justify? Moreover, the promise also shweth the very same thing. For it was said unto Abraham: "In thee shall all the nations of the earth be blessed" (Gen. xii). There is no blessing therefore but in the promise of Abraham; and if thou be without that promise, thou art under the curse. If thou be under the curse, thou fulfillest not the law, because thou art under sin, the devil, and everlasting death; all which do assuredly follow the curse. To conclude, if righteousness should come by the law, then should the promise of God be in vain, and in vain should he pour out his blessing in so great abundance. Therefore when God saw that we could not fulfil the law, he provided for this long before the law, and promised the blessing to Abraham, saying, "In thee shall all the nations of the earth be blessed." And so hath he testified that all the nations should be blessed, not by the law, but through the promise made unto Abraham. They therefore that lay hold on the law, and seek to be justified thereby, despising the promise, are accursed.

Wherefore (to do) is, first of all to believe, and so through faith to perform the law. We must first receive the Holy Ghost, wherewith we being lightened and made new creatures, begin to do the law, that is to say, to love God and our neighbour. But the Holy Ghost is not received through the law (for they which are under the law, as Paul saith, are under the curse) but by the hearing of faith, that is to say, through the promise. We must be blessed only with Abraham in the promise made unto him, and in his faith. Therefore, before all things, we must hear and receive the promise, which setteth out Christ, and offereth him to all believers; and when they have taken hold upon him by faith, the Holy Ghost is given unto them for his sake. Then do they love God and their neighbour, then do they good works, then do they carry the cross patiently. This is to do the law indeed; otherwise the law remaineth always undone. Wherefore if thou wilt define truly and plainly what it is to do the law, it is nothing else, but to believe in Jesus Christ, and when the Holy Ghost is received through faith in Christ, to work those things which are commanded in the law; and otherwise we are not able to perform the law. For the scripture saith that there is no blessing without the promise; no, not in the law. It is impossible, therefore, to accomplish the law without the promise.

There is not one therefore to be found in all the world, unto whom this name and title, to be called a doer of the law, appertaineth, without the promise of the gospel. Wherefore this word (doer of the law) is a feigned term, which no man understandeth unless he be without and above the law in the blessing and faith of Abraham. So that the true doer of the law is he, who receiving the Holy Ghost through faith in Christ, beginneth to love God and to do good unto his neighbour. So that this word (to do the law) must comprehend faith also which maketh the tree, and when the tree is made, then follow the fruits. The tree must be first, and then the fruit. For the apples makes not the tree, but the tree maketh the apples. So faith first maketh the person which afterwards bringeth forth works. Therefore to do the law without faith, is to make the apples of wood and earth, without the tree: which is not to make apples, but mere fantasies. Contrariwise, if the tree be made, that is to say, the person or doer, which is made through faith in Christ, works will follow. For the doer must needs be before the things which are done, and not the things which are done before the doer.

The doer then is not so called of the things that are done, but of the things that are to be done. For Christians are not made righeous in doing righteous things, but being now made righteous by faith in Christ, they do righteous things. In politic matters it cometh so to pass, that the doer or worker is made of the things which are wrought, as a man in playing the carpenter becometh a carpenter; but in divine matters the workers are not made of the works going before, but the persons made and framed already by faith, which is in Christ, are now become doers and workers. Of such speaketh Paul, when he saith, "the doers of the law shall be justified" (Rom. ii, 13), that is, shall be counted righteous.

Yea, the very sophisters and schoolmen are compelled to confess, and so they teach also, that a moral work outwardly done, if it be not done with a pure heart, a good-will, and true intent, it is but hypocrisy. And hereof cometh the proverb among the Germans, such a cowl covereth many a knave. For the vilest and the wickedest knave in the world may counterfeit the same works that a godly man worketh by faith. Judas did the same works that the other apostles did. What fault was there in the works of Judas, seeing he did the self-same works that the other apostles did? Here mark what the popish sophister answereth out of his moral philosophy. Although he did the self-same works, saith he, which the other apostles did, notwithstanding, because the person was reprobate, and the judgment of reason perverse, therefore his works were hypocritical and not true, as were the works of the other apostles, how like soever they seemed to be in outward shew. Wherefore they themselves are constrained to grant, in politic and external matters, works do not justify, unless there be joined withal an upright heart, will, and judgment. How much more are they compelled to confess the same in spiritual matter, where before all things, there must be a knowledge of God, and faith which may purify the heart? They walk therefore in works and in the righteousness of the law, as Judas did in the works of the apostles; not understanding what they say or what they affirm. And although Paul saith plainly every where that the law justifieth not, but causeth wrath, uttereth sin, revealeth the indignation and judgment of God, and threateneth everlasting death; yet notwithstanding, reading these things they see them not, much less do they understand them. Therefore they deserve not to be called hypocrites, but visors and shadows of disguised hypocrites, most miserably bewitched, in that they dream that they are justified by the works of the law. Wherefore, as I have said, this word "doer of the law," as they define it, is an imagined term, a very monster, and no where to be found.

Wherefore, when Paul proveth this place, "Whosoever are of the works of the law, are under the curse" (Gal. iii), by this sentence of Moses, "cursed is every one that abideth not in all that is written in this book," he proveth not one contrary by another, as at the first sight it may appear, but he proveth it rightly and in due order. For Moses meaneth and teacheth the self-same thing that Paul doth when he saith, "cursed is every one which doth not all," etc. But no man doth them. Therefore whosoever are of the works of the law, keep not the law. If they keep it not, they are under the curse. But seeing there be two sorts of men that are doers of the law (as before I have said), that is to say, true doers and hyprocrites: the true doers must be separated from the hypocrites. The true doers of the law are they which through faith, are the good tree before the fruit, doers and workers before the works. Of these speaketh Moses also; and except they be such, they are under the curse. But the hypocrites are not of this sort; for they think to obtain righteousness by works, and by them to make the person just and acceptable. For thus they dream: we that are sinners and unrighteous, will be made righteous. How shall that be? By good works. Therefore they do even like as a foolish builder, which goeth about the roof to make the foundation, of the fruit to make the tree. For when they seek to be justified by works, of the works they would make the worker, which is directly against Moses, which maketh such a worker subject to the curse as well as Paul doth. Therefore while they go about to do the law, they not only do it, but also deny (as I have said) the first commandment, the promises of God, the promised blessing of Abraham, they renounce faith, and they go about to make themselves blessed by their own works: that is to say, to justify themselves, to deliver themselves from sin and death, to overcome the devil, and violently to lay hold upon the kingdom of heaven. And this is plainly to renounce God, and to set themselves in the place of God. For all these are the works of the divine majesty alone, and not of any creature, either in heaven or in earth.

Hereupon Paul was able easily to foreshew, out of the first commandment, the abominations that were to come, which Antichrist should bring into the church. For all they which teach that any other worship is necessary to salvation, than that which God requireth of us by the first commandment, which is the fear of God, faith and the love of God, are plain Antichrists, and set themselves in the place of God. That such should come, Christ himself foretold when he saith, Matt. xxiv, 5, "Many shall come in my name, saying, I am Christ." So we also at this day may boldly and easily pronounce, that whosoever seeketh righteousness by works without faith, denieth God, and maketh himself God. For thus he thinketh: If I do this work, I shall be righteous, I shall be a conqueror of sin, death, the devil, the wrath of God, and of hell, and shall obtain life everlasting. And what is this else, I pray you, but to challenge that work unto himself which doth belong to God alone, and to shew indeed that he himself is God? Therefore it is an easy matter for us to prophesy, and most certainly to judge of all those which are without faith, that they are not only idolaters, but very infidels, which deny God, and set themselves in the place of God. Upon the same ground Peter also prophesieth when he saith: "There shall be amongst you false teachers, which privily shall bring in damnable heresies, and shall deny the Lord, etc., and make merchandise of the people" (2 Peter ii, 1, 2).

And in the Old Testament all the prophecies against idolatry sprang out of the first commandment. For all the wicked kings and prophets, with all the unfaithful people, did nothing else but that which the pope and all hypocrites always do. They, contemning the first commandment and worship appointed of God, and despising the promise of Abraham's seed, even that seed in whom all nations should be blessed and sanctified, ordained a wicked worship clean contrary to the word of God, and said: With this worship will we serve God and set out his praise, which hath brought us out of the land of Egypt. So Jeroboam made two golden calves and said: "Behold thy gods, O Israel, which brought thee out of the land of Egypt," (1 Kings xii, 28). This he said of the true God which had redeemed Israel, and yet both he and all his people were idolaters: for they worshipped God contrary to the first commandment. They only regarded the work: which being done, they counted themselves righteous before God. And what was this else, but to deny God himself, whom they confessed with their mouth, and said, "that he had brought them out of the land of Egypt?" Paul speaketh of such idolaters when he saith: "they confess that they know God, but in their deeds they deny him" (Titus i, 16).

Wherefore all hypocrites and idolaters go about to do those works which properly pertain to the divine Majesty, and belong to Christ only and alone. Indeed they say not in plain words, I am God, I am Christ; and yet in very deed they proudly challenge unto themselves the divinity and office of Christ, and therefore it is as much in effect as if they said: I am Christ; I am a saviour, not only of myself, but also of others.—This the monks have not only taught, but also have made the whole world to believe: to wit, that they are able, not only to make themselves righteous through their hypocritical holiness, but also others unto whom they communicate the same: whereas notwithstanding it is the proper and only office of Christ to justify the sinner. The Pope, in like manner, by publishing and spreading his divinity throughout the whole world, hath denied and utterly buried the office and divinity of Christ.

It is expedient that these things should be well taught and well weighed: for thereby we may learn to judge of the whole Christian doctrine, and the life of man; also to confirm men's consciences; to understand all prophecies and all the holy scriptures, and rightly to judge of all other things. He that knoweth all these things rightly, may certainly judge that the pope is Antichrist, because he teacheth a far other manner of worship than the first table setteth out. He may perfectly know and understand what it is to deny God, to deny Christ, and what Christ meaneth when he saith, "many shall come in my name, saying, I am Christ" (Matt. xxiv, 5); what it is to be against God, and to be lifted up above all that is called God, or that is worshipped; what it signifieth that Antichrist sitteth in the temple of God, shewing himself as God; what it is to see the abomination of desolation standing in the holy place, etc. (2 Thess. ii, 4; Matt. xxiv, 15; Mark xiii, 14; Dan. ix, 27).

Now hereof spring all these mischiefs, that this cursed hypocrisy will not be made righteous by the divine blessing, nor created anew of God the Creator. It will in no wise be a patient, or suffer any thing to be wrought in her; but will needs be altogether an agent, and work those things which she should suffer God to work in her and receive of him.—Therefore she maketh herself a creator and a justifier through her own works, despising the blessing promised and given to Abraham and to his believing children: so that every hypocrite is both the matter and the worker: (although this be against philosophy, for one and the self-same thing cannot work upon itself) the matter, because he is a sinner; the worker, because he putteth on a cowl, or chuseth some other work, through the which he hopeth to deserve grace, and to save himself and others: therefore he is both the creature and the creator. No man therefore can express with words, how execrable and horrible it is to seek righteousness in the law by works without the blessing. For it is the abomination standing in the holy place, which denieth God, and setteth up the creature in the place of the creator.

The doers of the law therefore are not the hypocrites, one serving the law outwardly; but the true believers, who, receiving the Holy Ghost, do accomplish the law; that is to say, they love God and their neighbour, etc. So that the true doer of the law is to be understood, not in respect of the works which he worketh, but in respect of the person now regenerate by faith. For according to the gospel, they that are made righteous, do righteous things; but according to philosophy it is not so: but contrariwise, they that do righteous things, are made just and righteous. Therefore we, being justified by faith, do good works; through the which (as it is said, 2 Peter i) our calling and election is confirmed, and from day to day is made more sure. But because we have only the first fruits of the spirit, and have not as yet the tenths, and the remnants of sin do still remain in us, therefore we do not the law perfectly. But this imperfection is not imputed unto us which do believe in Christ, who was promised to Abraham, and hath blessed us. For we are nourished and tenderly cherished in the mean season, for Christ's sake, in the lap of God's long-sufferance. We are that wounded man which fell into the hands of thieves, whose wounds the Samaritan bound up, pouring in oil and wine, and afterwards laying him upon his beast, he brought him into the inn, and made provision for him, and, departing, commended him to the host, saying, "take care of him," etc. (Luke x, 30–35). And thus we in the mean time are cherished as it were in an inn, until the Lord put to his hand the second time, as Isaiah saith, "that he may deliver us" (Isaiah xi, 11).

Wherefore the sentence of Moses, "cursed is every one that abideth not in the things that are written in this book," is not contrary to Paul, who pronounceth all them to be accursed which are of the works of the law. For Moses requireth such a doer, as may do the law perfectly. But where shall we find him? No where. For Moses himself confesseth that he is not such a one, for he saith, That none is innocent before God (Exod. xxxiv). And David saith, "Lord, enter not into judgment with thy servant, for no flesh is righteous in thy sight" (Ps. cxliii, 2). And Paul saith, "For what I would, that do I not: but what I hate, that do I" (Rom. vii, 15). Wherefore Moses, together with Paul, doth necessarily drive us to Christ, through whom we are made doers of the law, and are not accounted guilty of any transgression. How so? First, by forgiveness of sins and imputation of righteousness, because of our faith in Christ. Secondly, by the gift of God and the Holy Ghost, which bringeth forth a new life and new motions in us, so that we may also do the law effectually. Now that which is not done is pardoned for Christ's sake: and moreover, what sin soever is left in us, is not imputed. So Moses agreeth with Paul, and meaneth the self-same thing that he doth, when he saith, "cursed is every one that abideth not," etc. For he saith that they do not the law, because they would justify themselves by works, and concludeth with Paul, that they are under the curse. Therefore Moses requireth true doers of the law, which are of faith, even as Paul condemneth those which are not true doers of the law; that is to say, which are not of faith. Herein is no repugnance, that Moses spake negatively and Paul affirmatively, so that you define rightly what is meant by this word "do." So both sentences are true, to wit, that all are accursed which abide not in all that is written in this book; and, that all they are accursed, which are of the works of the law.

An Answer to those Arguments which the Adversaries Allege Against the Doctrine and Righteousness of Faith.

Seeing this place offereth unto us an occasion, we must say something as touching the arguments which our adversaries do object against the doctrine of faith, which is, that we are justified by faith alone.—There are many places both in the Old Testament and in the New, as concerning works and rewards of works, which our adversaries do allege, and think themselves able thereby utterly to overthrow the doctrine of faith which we teach and maintain. Therefore we must be well furnished and armed, that we may be able, not only to instruct our brethren, but also to answer the objections of our adversaries.

The schoolmen, and all such as understand not the article of justification, do know no other righteousness than the civil righteousness and the righteousness of the law, which after a sort the Gentiles also do know. Therefore they borrow certain words out of the law and moral philosophy, as "to do, to work," and such like, and they apply the same unto spiritual matters: wherein they deal most perversely and wickedly. We must put a difference between philosophy and divinity. The schoolmen themselves grant and teach, that, in the order of nature, being goeth before working; for naturally the tree is before the fruit. Again, in philosophy they grant, that a work morally wrought is not good, except there be first a right judgment of reason, and a good will or a good intent. So then they will have a right judgment of reason, and a good intent to go before the work; that is to say, they make the person morally righteous before the work. Contrariwise, in divinity, and in spiritual matters, where they ought most of all so to do, such dull and senseless asses they are, that they pervert and turn all quite contrary, placing the work before right judgment of reason and good intent.

Wherefore, doing is one thing in nature, another in moral philosophy, and another in divinity. In nature the tree must be first, and then the fruit. In moral philosophy, doing requireth a good intent and a sound judgment of reason to work well, going before. And here all philosophers are at a stay, and go no farther. Therefore the divines say, that moral philosophy taketh not God for the object, and final cause. For Aristotle, or a Sadducee, or a man of any civil honesty, calleth this a right reason and a good intent, if he seek the public commodity of the commonwealth and the quietness and honesty thereof. A philosopher or law-worker ascendeth no higher. He thinketh not through a right judgment of reason and a good intent to obtain remission of sins and everlasting life, as the sophister or the monk doth. Wherefore the heathen philosopher is much better than such a hypocrite. For he abideth within his bounds, having only consideration of the honesty and tranquility of the commonwealth, not mingling heavenly and earthly things together. Contrariwise, the blind sophister imagineth that God regardeth his good intent and works. Therefore he mingleth earthly and heavenly things together, and polluteth the name of God. And this imagination he learneth out of moral philosophy, saving that he abuseth it much worse than the heathen man doth.

Wherefore we must ascend up higher in divinity with this word "doing," than in natural things and in philosophy, so that now it must have a new signification, and be made altogether new, joined with a right judgment of reason, and a good will, not morally, but divinely: which is, that I know and believe by the word of the gospel, that God hath sent his Son into the world to redeem us from sin and death. Here "doing" is a new thing, unknown to reason, to philosophers, to law-workers, and unto all men: for it is a wisdom hidden in a mystery.—Therefore in divinity the work necessarily requireth faith going before.

Therefore, when our adversaries do allege against us the sentences of the scripture touching the law and works, where mention is made of working and doing, thou must answer them, that they are terms pertaining to divinity, and not to natural or moral things. If they be applied to natural or moral things, they must be taken in their own signification. But if they be applied to matters of divinity, they must include such a right judgment, reason or good-will, as is incomprehensible to man's reason. Wherefore doing in divinity must be always understood of a faithful doing. So that this faithful doing is altogether as it were a new kingdom, separate from the natural or moral doing. Therefore, when we that are divines speak of doing, we must needs speak of that faithful doing: for in divinity we have no other right judgment of reason, no good-will or intent besides faith.

This rule is well observed in the eleventh chapter to the Hebrews.—There are recited many and sundry works of the saints, out of the holy scriptures: as of David, who killed a lion and a bear, and slew Goliath. There the sophister or schoolman, that foolish ass, looketh upon nothing else but the outward appearance of the work. But this work of David must be so looked upon, that first we must consider what manner of person David was, before he did this work: then shall we see that he was such a person, whose heart trusted in the Lord God of Israel, as the text plainly witnesseth. "The Lord that delivered me out of the paw of the lion, and out of the paw of the bear, will deliver me out of the hand of the Philistine;" moreover, "thou comest to me with a sword, and with a spear, and with a shield: but I come to thee in the name of the Lord of hosts, the God of the host of Israel, upon whom thou hast railed this day. This day shall the Lord close thee in my hand, and I shall smite thee, and take thine head from thee, etc. Because the Lord saveth not with the sword nor spear (for the battle is the Lord's) and he will give you into our hands" (1 Sam. xvii, 37, 45, 46, 47). You see then that he was a righteous man, beloved of God, strong and constant in faith, before he did this work. This doing of David therefore is not a natural or moral doing, but a faithful doing.

So it is said of Abel in the same epistle, "that through faith he offered up a better sacrifice unto God than Cain." If the schoolmen happen upon this place as it is read Gen. iv, 5 (where it is simply set out, how that both Cain and Abel offered up their gifts, and that the Lord had respect unto Abel and his offerings) by-and-by they take hold of these words: "they offered their oblations unto the Lord: the Lord had respect to the offerings of Abel," and cry out, saying, here ye see that God had respect to offerings: therefore works do justify. So that these filthy swine do think that righteousness is but a moral thing, only beholding the visor or outward shew of the work, and not the heart of him that doth the work: whereas notwithstanding, even in philosophy, they are constrained not to look upon the bare work, but the good will of the worker. But here they stand altogether upon these words: "they offered up gifts: the Lord had respect unto Abel and to his offerings," and see not that the text saith plainly in Genesis, that the Lord had respect first to the person of Abel, which pleased the Lord because of his faith, and afterwards to his offerings. Therefore in divinity we speak of faithful works, sacrifices, oblations, and gifts, that is to say, which are offered up and done in faith, as the Epistle to the Hebrews declareth, saying: "Through faith Abel offered up a better sacrifice: through faith Enoch was taken away: through faith Abraham obeyed God," etc. We have here then a rule set forth in the eleventh to the Hebrews, how we should simply answer to the arguments objected of the adversaries as touching the law and works, that is to say: this or that man did this or that work in faith: and by this means thou givest a solution to all their arguments, and so stoppest their mouths, that they can have nothing to reply again.

Hereby it appeareth manifestly that in divinity and divine matters, the work is nothing worth without faith, but thou must needs have faith before thou begin to work. "For without faith it is impossible to please God" (Heb. xi, 6). But he that will come unto God, must believe. Wherefore in the Epistle to the Hebrews it is said, that the sacrifice of Abel was better than the sacrifice of Cain, because he believed; therefore the work or the sacrifice of Abel was faithful. Contrariwise in Cain, because he was wicked and a hypocrite, there was no faith or trust of God's grace or favour, but mere presumption of his own righteousness, and therefore his work, whereby he went about to please God, was hypocritical and unfaithful. Wherefore the adversaries themselves are compelled to grant that in all the works of the saints, faith is presupposed or goeth before, for the which their works do please God, and are accepted of him. Therefore in divinity there is a new doing, clean contrary to the moral doing.

Moreover, we are also wont to distinguish faith after this manner, that faith is sometimes taken without the work, sometimes with the work. For like as an artificer speaketh diversely of the matter whereupon he worketh, and likewise a gardener of the tree being barren or fruitful: even so the Holy Ghost speaketh diversely of faith in the scriptures: sometimes of an absolute faith, sometimes of a compound, or (as a man would say) an incarnate faith. Now, an absolute faith is this, when the scripture speaketh absolutely of justification, or of the being justified, as is to be seen in the Epistles to the Romans and to the Galatians. But when the scripture speaketh of rewards and works, then it speaketh of the compound or incarnate faith. We will rehearse some examples of this faith: as, "Faith which worketh by love. Do this and thou shalt live. If thou wilt enter into life, keep the commandments. He that doeth these things shall live in them. Decline from evil, and do that which is good" (Gal. v, 6; Lev. xviii, 5; Matt. xix, 17; Rom. x, 5; Psalm xxxvii, 27). In these and such like places (as there are many in the holy scripture) where mention is made of doing, the scripture always speaketh of faithful doing. As when it saith: "Do this and thou shalt live," it meaneth thus: see first that thou be faithful, that thou have a right judgment of reason and a good will, that is to say, faith in Christ. When thou hast this faith, work on a God's blessing.

What marvel is it then if rewards be promised to this incarnate faith: that is to say, to the working faith, as was the faith of Abel, or to faithful works? And why should not the holy scripture speak thus diversely of faith, when it speaketh divers ways of Christ, as he is God and man: that is to say, sometimes of his whole person, sometimes of his two natures apart, either of his divine or of his human nature? If it speak of the natures apart, it speaketh of Christ absolutely: but if it speak of the divine nature united in one person to the human nature, then it speaketh of Christ compound and incarnate. There is a common rule among the schoolmen of the communication of the proprieties, when the proprieties belonging to the divinity of Christ are attributed to the humanity; which we may see everywhere in the scriptures. As in Luke ii, 11, the angel calleth the infant born of the Virgin Mary, the Saviour of men, and the universal Lord both of the angels and men. And in the first chapter he calleth him the Son of God (Luke i, 32). Hereupon I may truly say, that the infant which lay in the manger and in the lap of the Virgin, created heaven and earth, and is Lord of the angels. Here I speak indeed of a man; but man in this proposition is a new word, and (as the schoolmen themselves do grant) hath relation to the divinity: that is to say, this God, which was made man, hath created all things. Creation is attributed only to the divinity of Christ; for the humanity doth not create, and yet notwithstanding it is truly said, man created, because the divinity, which only createth, is incarnate with the humanity, and therefore the humanity, together with the divinity, is partaker of the same proprieties. Wherefore it is well and godly said: this man Jesus Christ brought Israel out of Egypt, struck Pharaoh, and wrought all the wonders from the beginning of the world.

Therefore when the scripture saith, "If thou wilt enter into life, keep the commandments of God: Do this and thou shalt live," etc.; first we must see of what manner of keeping and doing he speaketh: for in these and such like places (as I have said) he speaketh of a compound faith, and not of a naked and simple faith. And the meaning of this place, "Do this, and thou shalt live," is this: thou shalt live, because of this faithful doing; or, this doing shall give unto thee life, because of thy faith alone. After this manner justification is attributed to faith alone, as creation is to the divinity. And yet notwithstanding, as it is truly said, Jesus the son of Mary created all things: so also justification is attributed to the incarnate faith, or to the faithful doing. Therefore we must in no wise think, with the sophisters and hypocrites, that works do absolutely justify, or that rewards are promised to moral works, but to faithful works only.

Let us therefore suffer the Holy Ghost to speak, as he doth in the scriptures, either of naked, simple, and absolute faith, or of compound and incarnate faith. All things which are attributed to works do properly belong unto faith. For works must not be looked upon morally, but faithfully, and with a spiritual eye. Faith is the divinity of works; and is so spread throughout the works of the faithful, as is the divinity throughout the humanity of Christ. Faith therefore doth all alone in the works of the faithful. Abraham is called faithful, because faith is spread throughout the whole person of Abraham: so that, beholding him working, I see nothing of the carnal or of the working Abraham, but of the believing Abraham.

Wherefore when thou readest in the scriptures, of the fathers, prophets, and kings, how they wrought righteousness, raised up the dead, overcame kingdoms, thou must remember that these and such like sayings are to be expounded as the Epistle to the Hebrews expoundeth them: "by faith they wrought righteousness, by faith they raised up the dead, by faith they subdued kings and kingdoms," etc. (Heb. xi, 33, 34, 35). So that faith incorporateth the work, and giveth it his perfection. And this the adversaries, if they be will in their wits, cannot deny, neither have they any thing to say or object against it. Indeed they can cry out that scripture speaketh oftentimes of doing and working. And we always answer them again, that it speaketh also of faithful doing. For first, reason must be lightened by faith before it can work. Now, when it hath a true opinion and knowledge of God, then is the work incarnate and incorporate into it: so that whatsoever is attributed to faith, is afterwards attributed to works also, but yet because of faith only and alone.

Wherefore in reading of the scriptures we must learn to put a difference between the true and the hypocritical, the moral and the spiritual doing of the law. So shall we be able to declare the true meaning of all those places which seem to maintain the righteousness of works. Now, the true doing of the law is a faithful and a spiritual doing, which he hath not, that seeketh righteousness by works. Therefore every doer of the law and every holy moral worker is accursed. For he walketh in the presumption of his own righteousness against God, whilst he will be justified by man's free-will and reason, and so in doing of the law, he doth it not. And this, according to Paul, is to be under the works of the law; that is to say, that hypocrites do the law, and yet, in doing it, they do it not: for they understand this word, doing, according to the literal sense of the law, which in true Christian divinity is nothing worth. Indeed they work many things, but in the presumption of their own righteousness, and without the knowledge of God and faith, as the Pharisee did (Luke xviii) and as Paul did before his conversion: therefore they are blind and miserably err, and so remain under the curse. Wherefore, again I admonish you, that such sentences as the adversaries do allege out of the scriptures concerning works and rewards, must be spiritually expounded. As if they allege this sentence out of Dan. iv, "Redeem thy sins by alms deeds," thou must not here expound these words morally, but spiritually. So shalt thou see that this word "redeem," signifieth no moral, but a spiritual doing, that is to say, it includeth faith. For in the scriptures, the work, as I have said, requireth also a good will and right judgment of reason to go before; not moral, as they would have it, but divine and spiritual, which is faith. By this means thou shalt be able to stop the mouths of these peevish sophisters. For they themselves are compelled to grant (and so teach they also out of Aristotle) that every good work proceedeth out of man's choice or free-will. If this be true in philosophy, much more must this good will and right judgment of reason guided by faith, go before the work in divinity and divine matters. And this do all words of the imperative mood, that is, all such words as are commanding, signify in the scriptures, and all such words also as teach the law, as the Epistle to the Hebrews doth plainly declare: "By faith Abel offered," etc.

Now, admit the case that this solution is not sufficient, (although it be indeed most sure and certain), yet notwithstanding let this be the argument of all arguments, and the principal mirror of Christians to behold, against all the temptations and objections, not only of the adversaries, but also of the devil himself, namely, to apprehend and hold fast the head, which is Christ. Moreover, admit that the sophisters, being more crafty and subtle than I, should so snare and entangle me with their arguments, which they bring for the maintenance of works against faith, that I should know no way how to wind myself out (which notwithstanding it is impossible for them to do), yet will I rather give reverence and credit to Christ alone, than be persuaded with all the places they are able to allege for the establishing of the righteousness of works against the doctrine of faith.

Wherefore, they must be simply and plainly answered after this manner: Here is Christ, there are the testimonies of the scriptures touching the law and works. Now, Christ is the Lord of the scripture and of all works. He also is Lord of heaven, the earth, the sabbath, the temple, righteousness, life, wrath, sin, death, and generally of all things whatsoever. And Paul his apostle sheweth "that he was made sin and became accursed for me" (Gal. iii, 13). I hear, then, that I could by no other means be delivered from my sin, my death, and my malediction, but by his death and blood-shedding; wherefore I conclude that it properly appertained to Christ himself to overcome my sin, death, and malediction in his own body, and not to the works of the law or mine own works. And hereunto reason is constrained to yield and say, that Christ is not the work of the law, or my work: that his blood and death is not circumcision, the observation of the ceremonies of the law, and much less a monk's cowl, a shaven crown, abstinence, vows, and such like. Wherefore if he be the price of my redemption, if he be made sin and malediction that he might justify and bless me, I care not if thou bring a thousand places of scripture for the righteousness of works against the righteousness of faith, and cry out never so much, that the scripture is against me. I have the author and Lord of the scripture with me; on whose side I will rather stand, than believe all the rabblement of law-workers and merit-mongers. Albeit it is impossible that the scripture should be against this doctrine, unless it be among the senseless and obstinate hypocrites; but to the godly, and such as have understanding, it giveth witness for Jesus Christ his Lord. See therefore how thou canst reconcile the scripture, which thou sayest is against my doctrine. As for me, I will stick to the author and Lord of the scripture.

Therefore if any man thinketh himself not well able to reconcile such places of the scripture, or answer unto the same sufficiently, and yet notwithstanding is constrained to hear the objections and cavillations of the adversaries, let him answer simply and plainly after this sort: Thou settest against me the servant, that is to say, the scripture, and that not wholly, neither yet the principal part thereof, but only certain places as touching the law and works. But I come with the Lord himself, who is above the scripture, and is made unto me the merit and price of righteousness and everlasting life. On him I lay hold, him I stick to, and leave works unto thee: which notwithstanding thou never didst. This solution neither the devil nor any justiciary can ever wrest from thee or overthrow. Moreover, thou art in safety before God: for thy heart abideth fixed in the object, which is called Christ; who being nailed to the cross and accursed, not for himself, but for us, as the text saith, was "made a curse for us." Hold fast this, and lay it against all the sentences of the law and works whatsoever, and say: Dost thou hear this, Satan? Here he must needs give place, for he knoweth that Christ is his Lord and master.

> VERSE 11. *And that no man is justified by the law in the sight of God, it is evident: for the just shall live by faith.* (Hab. ii, 4; Rom. i, 17.)

This is another argument grounded upon the testimony of the prophet Habakkuk. And it is a sentence of great weight and authority, which Paul setteth against all the sentences touching the law and works. As if he should say: What need we any long disputation? Here I bring forth a most evident testimony of the prophet, against the which no man can cavil: "The just man shall live my faith." If he live by faith, then he liveth not by the law: for the law is not of faith. And here Paul excludeth works and the law, as things contrary to faith.

The sophisters (as they are always ready to corrupt the scriptures) do wrest and pervert this place after this manner: "The just man doth live by faith;" that is to say, by a working faith, or formed and made perfect with charity: but if it be not formed with charity, then doth it not justify. This gloss they themselves have forged, and by the same they do injury to the words of the prophet. If they did call this formed or furnished faith, the true faith which the scripture teacheth, this their gloss should not offend me, for then faith should not be separated from charity, but from the vain opinion of faith: as we also put a difference between a counterfeit faith and a true faith. The counterfeit faith is that which heareth of God, of Christ, and of all the mysteries of his incarnation and our redemption: which also apprehendeth and beareth away those things which it heareth, yea, and can talk goodly thereof, and yet there remaineth nothing else in the heart, but a naked opinion, and a sound of the gospel. For it neither reneweth nor changeth the heart: it maketh not a new man, but leaveth him in the vanity of his former opinion and conversation: and this is a very pernicious faith. The moral philosopher is much better than the hypocrite having such a faith.

Wherefore, if they would make a distinction between faith

formed (and take it as the scripture taketh it) and a false or counterfeit faith, their distinction should nothing offend me. But they speak of faith formed and made perfect with charity, and make a double faith, that is to say, formed and unformed. This pestilent and devilish gloss I utterly detest. Although, say they, we have faith infused, called *fides infusa*, which is the gift of the Holy Ghost, and also faith gotten by our own industry, called *fides acquisita*; yet both of them lack their form and perfection, which is charity, and are formed with charity. This is to prefer charity before faith, and to attribute righteousness, not to faith, but to charity. Wherefore, when they do not attribute righteousness to faith, but only in respect of charity, they attribute to faith nothing at all.

Moreover, these perverters of the gospel of Christ do teach, that even that faith which they call faith infused, and not received by hearing, nor gotten by any working, but created in man by the Holy Ghost, may stand with deadly sin, and that the worst men may have this faith: therefore, say they, if it be alone, it is idle utterly and unprofitable. Thus they take from faith her office, and give it unto charity; so that faith is nothing except charity, which they call the form and perfection thereof, be joined withal. This is a devilish and blasphemous kind of doctrine, which utterly defaceth and overthroweth the doctrine of faith, and carrieth a man clean from Christ the mediator, and from faith, which is the hand and only means whereby we apprehend him. For if charity be the form and perfection of faith, as they dream, then am I by-and-by constrained to say, that charity is the principal part of the Christian religion, and so I lose Christ, his blood, and all his benefits, and now I rest altogether in a moral doing, even as the Pope, and the heathen philosopher, and the Turk doth.

But the Holy Ghost, which giveth to all men both mouth and tongue, knoweth how to speak. He could have said (as the sophisters do wickedly imagine), the righteous man shall live by faith, formed and beautified, or made perfect, by charity. But this he omitted of purpose, and saith plainly: "The righteous man liveth by faith." Let these dotish sophisters go, therefore, with this their wicked and pestilent gloss; we will still hold and extol this faith, which God himself hath called faith; that is to say, a true and a certain faith, which doubteth not of God, nor of his promises, nor of the forgiveness of sins through Christ, that we may dwell sure and safe in this our object Christ, and may keep still before our eyes the passion and blood of the mediator and all his benefits. Now, faith alone, which layeth hold upon Christ, is the only means that we suffer not these benefits to be taken out of our sight. Wherefore, rejecting this pestilent gloss, we must understand this place of faith only and alone. And this Paul himself declareth, when he reasoneth against faith formed with charity after this sort.

VERSE 12. *And the law is not of faith.*

The schoolmen say: The righteous man doth live, if his faith be formed and adorned with charity. But contrariwise Paul saith: "The law is not of faith." But what is the law? Is it not also a commandment touching charity? Yea, the law commandeth nothing else but charity, as we may see by the text itself: "Thou shalt love the Lord thy God, with all thy soul," etc. Deut. vi, 5; Matt. xxii, 37). Again, "Shewing mercy unto thousands that love him and keep his commandments" (Exodus xx, 6). Also, "In these two commandments consisteth the law and the prophets" (Matt. xxii, 40). If the law then that commandeth charity, be contrary to faith, it must needs follow, that charity is not of faith. So Paul plainly confuteth the gloss which the sophisters have forged touching their formed faith, and speaketh only of faith, as it is separate from the law. Now, the law being separate and set apart, charity is also set apart, with all that belongeth to the law, and faith only is left, which justifieth and quickeneth to everlasting life.

Paul therefore reasoneth here, out of a plain testimony of the prophet, that there is none which obtaineth justification and life before God, but the believing man, who obtaineth righteousness and everlasting life without the law, and without charity, by faith alone. The reason is, because the law is not of faith: that is, the law is not of faith, or any thing belonging to faith, for it believeth not: neither are the works of the law faith, nor yet of faith: therefore faith is a thing much differing from the law, like as the promise is a thing much differing from the law. For the promise is not apprehended by working, but by believing. Yea, there is as great a difference between the promise and the law, and consequently between faith and works, as there is a distance between heaven and earth.

It is impossible therefore that faith should be of the law. For faith only resteth in the promise, it only apprehendeth and knoweth God, and standeth only in receiving good things of God. Contrariwise, the law and works consist in exacting, in doing, and in giving unto God. As Abel, offering his sacrifice, giveth unto God; but he believing, receiveth of God. Paul therefore concludeth mightily out of that place of Habakkuk, that the righteous man liveth by faith alone. For the law in no wise belongeth unto faith, because the law is not the promise. But faith resteth only upon the promise. Wherefore as there is a difference between the law and the promise, so is there also between works and faith. That gloss therefore of the schoolmen is false and wicked, which joineth the law and faith together, yea, rather quencheth faith, and setteth law in the place of faith. And here note, that Paul always speaketh of such as would do the law morally, and not according to the scripture. But whatsoever is said of such good works as the scripture requireth, the same is attributed to faith alone.

VERSE 12. *But the man that shall do those things, shall live in them.*

Paul here goeth about to shew what is the very true righteousness of the law and of the gospel. The righteousness of the law is to fulfil the law, according to that saying: "He that shall do those things, shall live in them." The righteousness of faith is to believe, according to that saying: "The righteous man doth live by faith." The law therefore requireth that we should yield somewhat unto God. But faith requireth no works of us, or that we should give anything unto God, but that we, believing the promise of God, should receive of him. Therefore the office of the law is to work, as the office of faith is to assent unto the promises. For faith is the faith of the promise, and the work is the work of the law. Paul therefore standeth upon this word, doing: and that he may plainly shew what is the confidence of the law, and what is the confidence of works, he compareth the one with the other, the promise with the law, and faith with works. He saith that of the law there cometh nothing else but only doing: but faith is a clean contrary thing, namely, that which assenteth to the promise, and layeth hold upon it.

These four things therefore must be perfectly distinguished. For as the law hath his proper office, so hath the promise. To the law pertaineth doing, and to the promise believing. Wherefore, as far as the law and the promise are separate asunder, so far also are doing and believing. By the which distinction Paul here goeth about to separate charity from faith, and to teach that charity justifieth not, because the law worketh or helpeth nothing to justification. Faith alone therefore justifieth and quickeneth: and yet it standeth not alone, that is to say, it is not idle, albeit that in her degree and office it standeth alone. Ye see the cause then why Paul here allegeth this place, namely, that he may separate faith and charity far asunder.

Fie upon the sophisters therefore, with their cursed gloss and their blind distinction of faith formed and unformed. For these new forged terms, faith formed, faith unformed, faith gotten by man's industry, and such like, are very monsters devised by the devil, to no other end but to deface and to destroy the true Christian doctrine and faith, to blaspheme and tread Christ under foot, and to establish the righteousness of works. Indeed, works must follow faith, but faith must not be works, or works faith; but the bounds and the kingdoms of the law or works, and of faith, must be rightly distinguished the one from the other.

When we believe therefore, we live only by faith in Christ, who is without sin, who is also our mercy-seat and remission of sins. Contrariwise, when we observe the law, we work indeed, but we have no righteousness nor life. For the office of the law is not to justify and give life, but to shew forth sin and to destroy. Indeed the law saith, "He that shall do those things shall live in them." But where is he which doth the law: that is, "which loveth God with all his heart, and his neighbour as himself?" Therefore no man doth the law, and although he go about to do it never so much, yet in doing it, he doth it not; therefore he abideth under the curse. But faith worketh not, but believeth in Christ the justifier. Therefore a man liveth not because of his doing, but because of his believing. But a faithful man performeth the law, and that which he doth not, is forgiven him through the remission of sins for Christ's sake, and that which is remaining is not imputed unto him.

Paul therefore in this place, and in the tenth chapter to the Romans, compareth the righteousness of the law and of faith together, where he saith, "He that shall do those things, shall live in them." As though he would say, It were indeed a goodly matter if we could accomplish the law; but because no man doth it, we must fly unto Christ, "who is the end of the law to righteousness to every one that believeth. He was made under the law, that he might redeem us that were under the law" (Rom. x, 4; Gal. iv, 4). Believing in him we receive the Holy Ghost, and we begin to do the law: and that which we do not, is not imputed unto us because of our faith in Christ. But in the life to come we shall no more have need of faith (1 Cor. xiii, 12). For then we shall not see darkly through a glass (as we now do) but we shall see face to face: that is to say, there shall be a most glorious brightness of the eternal majesty, in which we shall see God even as he is. There shall be a true and a perfect knowledge and love of God, a perfect light of reason and a good will: not such a moral and philosophical will as the popish schoolmen dream of, but a heavenly, divine, and eternal will. Here in the meantime, inspirited by faith, we look for the hope of righteousness. Contrariwise, they that seek forgiveness of sins by the law and not by Christ, do never perform the law, but abide under the curse.

Paul therefore calleth them only righteous, which are justified through the promise, or through faith in the promise without the law. Wherefore, they that are of the works of the law, and will seem to do the law, do it not. For the apostle generally concludeth, that all they which are of the works of the law, are under the curse: under the which they should not be, if they fulfilled the law. Indeed it is true, that a man doing the works of the law shall live in them, that is, shall be blessed: but such a one cannot be found. Now, seeing there is a double use of the law, the one politic, and the other spiritual, he that will understand this sentence civilly, may do it after this sort: "He that shall do these things shall live in them:" that is, if a man obey the magistrate outwardly, and in the politic government, he shall avoid punishment and death: for then the civil magistrate hath no power over him. This is the politic use of the law, which serveth to bridle those that are rude and untractable. But Paul here speaketh not of this use, but entreateth of this place like a divine: therefore there is a condition necessarily included. As if he said, if men could keep the law, they should be happy. But where are they? They are not therefore doers of the law, except they be justified before and without the law, through faith.

Wherefore, when Paul curseth and condemneth those which are of the works of the law, he speaketh not of such as are justified through faith, but of such as go about to be justified by works, without faith in Christ. This I say, lest any man should follow the fond imagination of Jerome, who being deceived by Origen, understood nothing at all in Paul, but took him as a mere civil lawyer. Hereupon he reasoneth after this manner: the holy patriarch, prophets, and kings, were circumcised and offered sacrifice; therefore they observed the law. But it were a wicked thing to say, that they are under the curse; therefore, all they that are of the works of the law are not under the curse. Thus he setteth himself against Paul without all judgment, making no difference between the true doers of the law justified by faith, and those workers which seek to be justified by the law, without faith.

But Paul speaketh here nothing against those that are justified by faith, and are true doers of the law indeed, for they are not of the works of the law; but against those which not only do not keep the law, but also sin against the same. For the law commandeth that we should fear, love, and worship God with a true faith. This they do not, but choose out new kinds of worship and works, which were never commanded of God, by the which God is not pacified, but more provoked to anger, according to that saying: "They worship me in vain with the commandments of men" (Matt. xv, 9). Therefore they are full of impiety, rebels against God, and idolaters, sinning grievously against the first commandment above all the rest. Moreover, they are full of wicked concupiscence, wrath, and other great passions. Briefly, there is no good thing in them, but that outwardly they would seem to be righteous and to accomplish the law.

So we also which are justified by faith, as were the patriarchs, prophets, and all the saints, are not of the works of the law, as concerning justification; but in that we are in the flesh, and have as yet the remnants of sin in us, we are under the law, and yet not under the curse, because the remnants of sin are not imputed unto us for Christ's sake, in whom we believe. For the flesh is an enemy unto God, and that concupiscence which yet remaineth in us, not only fulfilleth not the law, but also sinneth against the same, rebelling against us and leading us captive into bondage (Rom. vii). Now if the law be not fulfilled in the saints, but that many things are done in them contrary to the law; if evil concupiscence and the remnants of sin are yet remaining in them, which do so hinder them that they cannot fear and love God, they cannot call upon God with assured trust, they cannot praise God and reverence his word as they should do; much more is this true in a man which is not yet justified by faith, but is an enemy unto God, and with all his heart despiseth and hateth the word and work of God. Ye see then that Paul speaketh here of such as will fulfil the law, and be justified thereby, although they have not yet received faith, and not of the fathers and saints (as Jerome imagineth) which are justified by faith already.

VERSE 13. *Christ hath redeemed us from the curse of the law, when he was made a curse for us. (For it is written: Cursed is every one that hangeth on a tree,* Deut. xxi, 23).

Here again Jerome, and the popish sophisters which follow him, are much troubled, and miserably rack this most comfortable place, seeking, as they would seem, with a godly zeal, to turn away this reproach from Christ, that he should be called a curse or execration. They shift off this sentence after this manner: that Paul spake not here in good earnest; and therefore they most wickedly affirm, that the scripture in Paul agreeth not with itself. And this they prove after this manner: the sentence, say they, of Moses, which Paul here allegeth, speaketh not of Christ. Moreover, this general clause (whosoever) which Paul allegeth, is not added in Moses. Again, Paul omitteth this word (of God) which is in Moses. To conclude, it is evident enough, that Moses speaketh of a thief or a malefactor, which by his evil deeds hath deserved the gallows, as the scripture plainly witnesseth in the twenty-first chapter of Deuteronomy. Therefore they ask this question, How this sentence may be applied to Christ, that he is accursed of God, and hanged upon a tree, seeing that he is no malefactor or thief, but righteous and holy? This may peradventure move the simple and ignorant, thinking that the sophisters do speak it, not only wittily, but also very godly, and thereby do defend the honour and glory of Christ, and give warning to all Christians to beware that they think not so wickedly of Christ, that he should be made a curse, etc. Let us see therefore what the meaning and purpose of Paul is.

But here again we must make a distinction, as the words of Paul do plainly shew. For he saith not, that Christ was made a curse for himself, but for us. Therefore all the weight of the matter standeth in this word, "for us." For Christ is innocent as concerning his own person, and therefore he ought not to have been hanged upon a tree: but because, according to the law of Moses, every thief and malefactor ought to be hanged, therefore Christ also, according to the law, ought to be hanged, for he sustained the person of a sinner and of a thief, not of one, but of all sinners and thieves. For we are sinners and thieves, and therefore guilty of death and everlasting damnation. But Christ took all our sins upon him, and for them died upon the cross; therefore it behoveth that he should become a transgressor, and (as Isaiah the prophet saith, chap. liii) "to be reckoned and accounted among transgressors and trespassers."

And this, no doubt, all the prophets did foresee in spirit, that Christ should become the greatest transgressor, murderer, adulterer, thief, rebel, and blasphemer, that ever was or could be in the world. For he being made a sacrifice for the sins of the whole world, is not now an innocent person and without sins, is not now the Son of God born of the Virgin Mary; but a sinner, which hath and carrieth the sin of Paul, who was a blasphemer, an oppressor, and a persecutor; of Peter which denied Christ; of David, which was an adulterer, a murderer, and caused the Gentiles to blaspheme the name of the Lord;

and briefly, which hath and beareth all the sins of all men in his body: not that he himself committed them, but for that he received them, being committed or done of us, and laid them upon his own body, that he might make satisfaction for them with his own blood. (Isaiah liii, 5; Matt. viii, 17.) Therefore this general sentence of Moses comprehendeth him also (albeit in his own person he was innocent), because it found him amongst sinners and transgressors: like as the magistrate taketh him for a thief, and punisheth him whom he findeth among other thieves and transgressors, though he never committed anything worthy of death. Now, Christ was not only found amongst sinners, but of his own accord, and by the will of his Father, he would also be a companion of sinners, taking upon him the flesh and blood of those which were sinners, thieves, and plunged into all kinds of sin. When the law, therefore, found him among thieves, it condemned and killed him as a thief.

The popish sophisters do spoil us of this knowledge of Christ and most heavenly comfort (namely, that Christ was made a curse, that he might deliver us from the curse of the law), when they separate him from sins and sinners, and only set him out unto us as an example to be followed. By this means they make Christ not only unprofitable unto us, but also a judge and a tyrant, which is angry with our sins, and condemneth sinners. But we must as well wrap Christ, and know him to be wrapped in our sins, in our malediction, in our death, and in all our evils, as he is wrapped in our flesh and in our blood.

But some man will say, it is very absurd and slanderous to call the Son of God a cursed sinner. I answer, if thou wilt deny him to be a sinner and to be accursed, deny also that he was crucified and dead. For it is no less absurd to say, that the Son of God (as our faith confesseth and believeth) was crucified and suffered the pains of sin and death, than to say that he is a sinner and accursed. But if it be not absurd to confess and believe that Christ was crucified between two thieves, then it is not absurd to say also that he was accursed, and of all sinners the greatest. These words of Paul are not spoken in vain: "Christ was made a curse for us: God made Christ which knew no sin, to become sin for us, that we in him might be made the righteousness of God." (2 Cor. v, 21.)

After the same manner John the Baptist calleth him, "The Lamb of God, which taketh away the sins of the world" (John i, 29). He verily is innocent, because he is the unspotted and undefiled Lamb of God. But because he beareth the sins of the world, his innocency is burdened with the sins and guilt of the whole world. Whatsoever sins I, thou, and we all have done, or shall do hereafter, they are Christ's own sins, as verily as if he himself had done them. To be brief, our sin must needs become Christ's own sin, or else we shall perish forever. This true knowledge of Christ, which Paul and the prophets have most plainly delivered unto us, the wicked sophisters have darkened and defaced.

Isaiah speaketh thus of Christ: "God," saith he, "laid the iniquity of us all upon him." (Isa. liii.) We must not make these words less than they are, but leave them in their own proper signification. For God dallieth not in the words of the prophet, but speaketh earnestly, and of great love; to wit, that Christ this Lamb of God should bear the sins of us all. But what is it to bear? The sophisters answer, to be punished. Very well: But wherefore is Christ punished? Is it not because he hath sin and beareth sin? Now that Christ hath sin, the Holy Ghost witnesseth in the fortieth psalm, "My sins have taken such hold of me, that I am not able to look up, yea, they are more in number than the hairs of my head." In this psalm, and certain others, the Holy Ghost speaketh in the person of Christ, and in plain words witnesseth that he had sins. For this testimony is not the voice of an innocent, but of a suffering Christ, which took upon him to bear the person of all sinners, and therefore was made guilty of the sins of the whole world.

Wherefore Christ was not only crucified and died, but sin also (through the love of the divine Majesty) was laid upon him. When sin was laid upon him, then cometh the law and saith: "Every sinner must die." Therefore, O Christ, if thou wilt answer, become guilty, and suffer punishment for sinners, thou must also bear sin and malediction. Paul therefore doth very well allege this general sentence out of Moses as concerning Christ: "Every one that hangeth upon the tree is the accursed of God:" but Christ hath hanged upon the tree, therefore Christ is the accursed of God.

And this is a singular consolation for all Christians, so to clothe Christ with our sins, and to wrap him in my sins, thy sins, and the sins of the whole world, and so to behold him bearing all our iniquities. For the beholding of him after this manner, shall easily vanquish all the fantastical opinions of the Papists, concerning the justification of works. For they do imagine (as I have said) a certain faith formed and adorned with charity. By this (they say) sins are taken away, and men are justified before God. And what is this else (I pray you) but to unwrap Christ, and to strip him quite out of our sins, to make him innocent, and to charge and overwhelm ourselves with our own sins, and to look upon them, not in Christ, but in ourselves? yea, what is this else but to take Christ clean away, and to make him utterly unprofitable unto us, For if it be so, that we put away sin by the works of the law and charity, then Christ taketh them not away. For if he be the Lamb of God ordained from everlasting to take away the sins of the world; and moreover, if he be so wrapped in our sins that he became accursed for us, it must needs follow that we cannot be justified by works. For God hath laid our sins, not upon us, but upon his Son Christ, that he, bearing the punishment thereof, might be our peace: and that, by his stripes, we might be healed (Isa. liii, 5). Therefore they cannot be taken away by us. To this all the scripture beareth witness; and we also do confess the same in the articles of the Christian belief, when we say: "I believe in Jesus Christ, the son of God, which suffered, was crucified and died for us."

Hereby it appeareth that the doctrine of the gospel (which of all other is most sweet and full of singular consolation) speaketh nothing of our works, or of the works of the law, but of the inestimable mercy and love of God towards most wretched and miserable sinners: to wit that our most merciful Father, seeing us to be oppressed and overwhelmed with the curse of the law, and so to be holden under the same, that we could never be delivered from it by our own power, sent his only Son into the world, and laid upon him all the sins of all men, saying, be thou Peter that denier; Paul, that persecutor, blasphemer, and cruel oppressor; David, that adulterer; that sinner which did eat the apple in paradise; that thief which hanged upon the cross, and briefly, be thou the person which hath committed the sins of all men: see therefore that thou pay and satisfy for them. Here now cometh the law, and saith: I find him a sinner, and that such a one as hath taken upon him the sins of all men, and I see no sins else but in him: therefore let him die upon the cross; and so he setteth upon him, and killeth him. By this means the whole world is purged and cleansed from all sins, and so delivered from death and all evils. Now sin being vanquished and death abolished by this one man, God would see nothing else in the whole world, if it did believe, but a mere cleansing and righteousness. And if any remnants of sin should remain, yet for the great glory that is in Christ, God would wink at them, and would not see them.

Thus we must magnify the article of Christian righteousness against the righteousness of the law and works, albeit no eloquence is able sufficiently to set forth the inestimable greatness thereof. Wherefore the argument that Paul handleth in this place, of all other is most mighty against all the righteousness of the law. For it containeth this invincible opposition: that is, if the sins of the whole world be in that one man Jesus Christ, then are they not in the world; but if they be not in him, then are they yet in the world. Also, if Christ be made guilty of all the sins which we have committed, then are we delivered from all sins, but not by ourselves, nor by our own works or merits, but by him. But if he be innocent and bear not our sins, then do we bear them, and in them we shall die and be damned. "But thanks be to God who hath given us the victory by our Lord Jesus Christ. Amen." (1 Cor. xv, 57.)

But now let us see by what means these two things, so contrary and so repugnant, may be reconciled in this one person Christ. Not only my sins and thine, but also the sins of the whole world, either past, present, or to come, take hold upon him, go about to condemn him, and do indeed condemn him. But because in the self-same person, which is the highest, the greatest, and the only sinner, there is also an everlasting and invincible righteousness: therefore these two do encounter together, the highest, the greatest, and the only sin, and the highest, the greatest, and the only righteousness. Here one of them must needs be overcome and give place to the other, seeing they fight together with so great force and power. The sin therefore of the whole world cometh upon righteousness with all might and main. In this combat, what is done? Righteousness is everlasting, immortal and invincible. Sin also is a most mighty and cruel tyrant, ruling and reigning over the whole world, subduing and bringing all men into bondage. To conclude, sin is a mighty and a strong god, which devoureth all mankind, learned, unlearned, holy, mighty, and wise men. This tyrant, I say, flieth upon Christ, and will needs swallow him up, as he doth all other. But he seeth not that he is a person of invincible and everlasting righteousness. Therefore, in this combat, sin must needs be vanquished and killed, and righteousness must overcome, live, and reign. So in Christ all sin is vanquished, killed, and buried, and righteousness remaineth a conqueror and reigneth forever.

In like manner death, which is an omnipotent queen and empress of the whole world, killing kings, princes, and generally all men, doth mightily encounter with life, thinking utterly to overcome it and to swallow it up: and that which it goeth about, it bringeth to pass indeed. But because life was immortal, therefore when it was overcome, yet did it overcome and get the victory, vanquishing and killing death. Death therefore through Christ is vanquished and abolished throughout the whole world, so that now it is but a painted death, which, losing his sting, can no more hurt those that believe in Christ, who is become the death of death, as Hosea the prophet saith: "O death, I will be thy death." (Hos. xiii, 14.)

So the curse, which is the wrath of God upon the whole world, hath the like conflict with the blessing: that is to say, with grace and the eternal mercy of God in Christ. The curse therefore fighteth against the blessing, and would condemn it and bring it to nought: but it cannot do so. For the blessing is divine and everlasting, and therefore the curse must needs give place. For if the blessing in Christ could be overcome, then should God himself also be overcome. But this is impossible: therefore Christ the power of God, righteousness, blessing, grace, and life, overcometh and destroyeth these monsters, sin, death, and the curse, without war or weapons, in his own body, and in himself, as Paul delighteth to speak: "Spoiling," said he, "all principalities and powers, and triumphing over them in himself" (Col. ii, 15) so that they cannot any more hurt those that do believe.

And this circumstance, "in himself," maketh that combat much more wonderful and glorious. For it sheweth that it was necessary that these inestimable things should be accomplished in that one only person (to wit, that the curse, sin and death should be destroyed, and the blessing, righteousness and life, should succeed in their place), and that so the whole creature through this one person should be renewed. Therefore, if thou look upon this person Christ, thou shalt see sin, death, the wrath of God, hell, the devil, and all evils vanquished and mortified in him. Forasmuch then as Christ reigneth by his grace in the hearts of the faithful, there is no sin, no death, no curse: but where Christ is not known, there all these things do still remain. Therefore all they which believe not, do lack this inestimable benefit and glorious victory. "For this (as St. John saith) is our victory that overcometh the world, even our faith." (1 John v, 4.)

This is the principal article of all Christian doctrine, which the popish schoolmen have altogether darkened. And here ye see how necessary a thing it is to believe and to confess the article of the divinity of Christ, which, when Arius denied, he must needs also deny the article of our redemption. For to overcome the sin of the world, death, the curse, and the wrath of God in himself, is not the work of any creature, but of the divine power. Therefore he which in himself should overcome these, must needs be truly and naturally God. For against this mighty power of sin, death, and the curse (which of itself reigneth throughout the world, and in the whole creature), it was necessary to set a more high and mighty power. But besides the sovereign and divine power, no such power can be found. Wherefore, to abolish sin, to destroy death, to take away the curse in himself; and again, to give righteousness, to bring life to light, and to give the blessing, are the works of the divine power only and alone. Now, because the scripture doth attribute all these to Christ, therefore he in himself is life, righteousness, and blessing, which is naturally and substantially God. Wherefore they that deny the divinity of Christ, do lose all Christianity, and become altogether Gentiles and Turks. We must learn therefore diligently the article of justification (as I often admonish you.) For all the other articles of our faith are comprehended in it: and if that remain sound, then are all the rest sound. Wherefore, when we teach that men are justified by Christ, that Christ is the conqueror of sin, death, and the everlasting curse, we witness therewithal that he is naturally and substantially God.

Hereby we may plainly see how horrible the wickedness and blindness of the Papists was, which taught that these cruel and mighty tyrants, sin, death, and the curse (which swallow up all mankind) must be vanquished, not by the righteousness of the law of God (which, although it be just, good and holy, can do nothing but bring men under the curse:) but by the righteousness of man's own works, as by fasting, pilgrimages, masses, vows, and such other like paltry. But, I pray you, was there ever any found, that, being furnished with this armour, overcame sin, death, and the devil? Paul, in the sixth chapter to the Ephesians, 13, 14, etc., describeth a far other manner of armour, which we must use against these most cruel and raging beasts. Therefore, in that these blind buzzards, and leaders of the blind, have set us naked and without armour before these invincible and most mighty tyrants, they have not only delivered us unto them to be devoured, but also have made us ten times greater and more wicked sinners than either thieves, whores, or murderers. For it belongeth only to the divine power to destroy sin and to abolish death, to create righteousness and to give life. They have attributed this divine power to our own works, saying, if thou do this work or that, thou shalt overcome sin, death, and the wrath of God: and by this means they set us in God's place, making us in very deed naturally, if I may so say, God himself. And herein the Papists, under the name of Christ, have shewed themselves to be seven-fold more wicked idolaters than ever were the Gentiles. (2 Peter ii, 22.) For it happeneth to them, as it doth to the sow, which, after she is washed, walloweth herself again in the mire. And as Christ saith, "after they are fallen away from faith, an evil spirit entereth again into the house, out of the which he was driven, and taketh unto him seven worse spirits than himself, and there dwelleth: and then the latter end of that man is worse than the beginning" (Luke xi, 26).

Let us therefore receive this most sweet doctrine and full of comfort, with thanksgiving, and with an assured faith, which teacheth that Christ being made a curse for us (that is, a sinner subject to the wrath of God), did put upon him our person, and laid our sins upon his own shoulders, saying, I have committed the sins which all men have committed.—Therefore he was made a curse indeed according to the law, not for himself, but, as Paul saith, for us. For unless he had taken upon himself my sins and thine, and the sins of the whole world, the law had had no right over him, which condemneth none but sinners only, and holdeth them under the curse. Wherefore he could neither have been made a curse nor die, since the only cause of the curse and of death is sin, from the which he was free. But because he had taken upon him our sins, not by constraint, but of his own good will, it behoved him to bear the punishment and wrath of God: not for his own person (which was just and invincible, and therefore could be found in no wise guilty) but for our person.

So making a happy change with us, he took upon him our sinful person, and gave unto us his innocent and victorious person: wherewith we being now clothed, are freed from the curse of the law. For Christ was willingly made a curse for us, saying, as touching my own person, I am blessed, and need nothing. But I will abase myself, and will put upon me your person (Phil. ii, 7), that is to say, your human nature, and I will walk in the same among you, and will suffer death, to deliver you from death. Now, he thus bearing the sin of the whole world in our person, was taken, suffered, was crucified and put to death, and became a curse for us. But because he was a person divine and everlasting, it was impossible that death should hold him. Wherefore he rose again the third day from death, and now liveth forever: and there is neither sin nor death found in him any more, but mere righteousness, life, and everlasting blessedness.

This image and this mirror we must have continually before us, and behold the same with a stedfast eye of faith. He that doth so, hath this innocency and victory of Christ, although he be never so great a sinner. By faith only therefore we are made righteous, for faith layeth hold upon this innocency and this victory of Christ. Look then how much thou believest this, so much thou dost enjoy it. If thou believe sin, death, and the curse to be abolished, they are abolished. For Christ hath overcome and taken away these in himself, and will have us to believe, that like as in his own person there is now no sin nor death, even so there is none in ours, seeing he hath performed and accomplished all things for us.

Wherefore, if sin vex thee, and death terrify thee, think that it is (as it is indeed) but an imagination, and a false illusion of the devil. For in very deed there is now no sin, no curse, no death, no devil, to hurt us any more, for Christ hath vanquished and abolished all these things. Therefore, the victory of Christ is most certain, and there is no defect in the thing itself (since it is most true), but in our incredulity: for to reason it is a hard matter to believe these inestimable good things and unspeakable riches. Moreover, Satan, with his fiery darts, and his ministers, with their wicked and false doctrine, go about to wrest from us and utterly to deface this doctrine; and specially for this article, which we so diligently teach, we sustain the hatred and cruel persecution of Satan and of the world; for Satan feeleth the power and fruit of this article.

And that there is no more sin, death, or malediction, since Christ now reigneth, we daily confess also in the creed of the apostles, when we say: "I believe that there is a holy church." Which indeed is nothing else but as if we should say: I believe that there is no sin, no malediction, no death in the church of God. For they which do believe in Christ, are no sinners, are not guilty of death, but are holy and righteous, lords over sin and death, and living forever. But faith only seeth this: for we say, I believe that there is a holy church. But if thou believe reason and thine own eyes, thou wilt judge clean contrary; for thou seest many things in the godly which offend thee. Thou seest them sometimes to fall into sin, and to be weak in faith; to be subject unto wrath, envy, and such other evil affections: therefore the church is not holy. I deny the consequence. If I look upon mine own person, or the person of my brother, it shall never be holy. But if I behold Christ, who hath sanctified and cleansed his church, then is it altogether holy: for he hath taken away the sins of the whole world.

Therefore, where sins are seen and felt, then are they indeed no sins; for, according to Paul's divinity, there is no sin, no death, no malediction any more in the world, but in Christ, who is the Lamb of God that hath taken away the sins of the world:

who is made a curse, that he might deliver us from the curse. Contrariwise, according to philosophy and reason, sin, death, and the curse, are nowhere else but in the world, in the flesh, or in sinners. For a sophistical divine can speak no otherwise of sin, than doth the heathen philosopher. Like as the colour, saith he, cleaveth in the wall, even so doth sin in the world, in the flesh, or in the conscience: therefore it is to be purged by contrary operations, to wit, by charity. But the true divinity teacheth that there is no sin in the world any more: for Christ, upon whom the Father hath cast the sins of the whole world, hath vanquished and killed the same in his own body. (Isa. liii, 6.) He once dying for sin, and raised up again, dieth no more. Therefore, wheresoever is a true faith in Christ, there sin is abolished, dead and buried. But where no faith in Christ is, there sin doth still remain.—And albeit the remnants of sin be as yet in the saints, because they believe not perfectly, yet are they dead, in that they are not imputed unto them because of their faith in Christ.

This is therefore a strong and a mighty argument, which Paul here prosecuteth against the righteousness of works. It is not the law nor works that do deliver us from the everlasting curse, but Christ alone.—See therefore, good Christian reader, I beseech thee, that thou distinguish Christ from the law, and diligently mark how Paul speaketh, and what he saith. "All," saith he, "which do not fulfil the law, are necessarily under the curse. But no man fulfilleth the law: therefore all men are under the curse." He addeth moreover another proposition—"Christ hath redeemed us from the curse of the law, being made a curse for us: therefore it followeth, that the law and works do not redeem us from the curse, but bring us rather under the curse." Charity therefore (which, as the schoolmen say, giveth form and perfection unto faith) hath not only not redeemed us from the curse, but rather it wrappeth us more and more in the curse.

This text then is plain, that all men, yea, the apostles, prophets and patriarchs had remained under the curse, if Christ had not set himself against sin, death, the curse of the law, the wrath and judgment of God, and overcome them in his own body: for no power of flesh and blood could overcome these huge and hideous monsters. But now, Christ is not the law, or the work of the law, but a divine and human person, which took upon him sin, the condemnation of the law and death, not for himself, but for us: therefore all the weight and force hereof consisteth in this word, "for us."

We must not then imagine Christ to be innocent, and as a

private person (as do the schoolmen, and almost all the fathers have done) which is holy and righteous for himself only. True it is indeed that Christ is a person most pure and unspotted: but thou must not stay there: for thou hast not yet Christ, although thou know him to be God and man; but then thou hast him indeed, when thou believest that this most pure and innocent person is freely given unto thee of the Father, to be thy highpriest and Saviour, yea, rather thy servant, that he, putting off his innocency and holiness, and taking thy sinful person upon him, might bear thy sin, thy death, and thy curse, and might be made a sacrifice and a curse for thee, that by this means he might deliver thee from the curse of the law.

Ye see then with that an apostolic spirit Paul handleth this argument of the blessing of the curse, whilst he not only maketh Christ subject to the curse, but saith also that he is made a curse. So in 2 Cor. v he calleth him sin, when he saith: "he hath made him to be sin for us, which knew no sin, that we should be made the righteousness of God in him." And although these sentences may be well expounded after this manner: Christ is made a curse, that is to say, a sacrifice for the curse; and sin, that is, a sacrifice for sin: yet in my judgment it is better to keep the proper signification of the words, because there is a greater force and vehemency therein. For when a sinner cometh to the knowledge of himself indeed, he feeleth not only that he is miserable, but misery itself: not only that he is a sinner, and is accursed, but even sin and malediction itself. For it is a terrible thing to bear sin, the wrath of God, malediction and death. Wherefore that man which hath a true feeling of these things (as Christ did truly and effectually feel them for all mankind) is made even sin, death, malediction, etc.

Paul therefore handleth this place with a true apostolic spirit. There is neither sophister, nor lawyer, nor Jew, nor Anabaptist, nor any other that speaketh as he doth. For who durst allege this place out of Moses: "accursed is everyone that hangeth on a tree," and apply it unto Christ? Like as Paul then applied this sentence to Christ, even so may we apply it unto Christ, not only that whole twenty-seventh chapter of Deuteronomy, but also may gather all the curses of Moses' law together, and expound the same of Christ. For as Christ is innocent in this general law, touching his own person: so is he also in all the rest. And as he is guilty in this general law, in that he is made a curse for us, and is hanged upon the cross as a wicked man, a blasphemer, a murderer, and a traitor: even so is he also guilty in all others. For all the curses of the law are heaped together and laid upon him, and therefore he did bear and suffer them in his own body for us. He was therefore not only accursed, but also was a curse for us.

This is to interpret the scriptures truly and like an apostle. For a man is not able to speak after this manner without the Holy Ghost: that is to say, to comprehend the whole law in this one saying, "Christ is made a curse for us," and lay the same altogether upon Christ: and contrariwise to comprehend all the promises of the scripture, and say, that they are all at once fulfilled in Christ. Wherefore this is indeed an apostolic and invincible argument, not taken out of one place of the law, but out of the whole law: which Paul also useth as a sure ground.

Here we may see with what diligence Paul read the holy scriptures, and how exactly he weighed every word of this place, "in thy seed shall all the nations of the earth be blessed." First, out of this word blessing he gathereth this argument: if blessing shall be given unto all nations, then are all nations under the curse, yea, the Jews also, who have the law. And he allegeth a testimony of the scripture, whereby he proveth that all the Jews which are under the law, are under the curse; "cursed is every one that abideth not in all the things that are written in this book."

Moreover, he diligently weigheth this clause: "all nations." Out of the which he gathereth thus: that the blessing belongeth not only to the Jews, but also to all the nations of the whole world. Seeing then it belongeth to all nations, it is impossible that it should be obtained through the law of Moses, forasmuch as there was no nation that had the law, but only the Jews. And although they had the law, yet were they so far off from obtaining the blessing through it, that the more they endeavoured to accomplish it, the more they were subject to the curse of the law. Wherefore there must needs be another righteousness, which must be far more excellent than the righteousness of the law, through the which, not only the Jews, but also all nations throughout the whole world, must obtain the blessing.

Finally, these words, "in thy seed," he expoundeth after this manner: that a certain man should issue out of the seed of Abraham, that is to say, Christ, through whom the blessing should come afterwards upon all nations. Seeing therefore it was Christ that should bless all nations, it was he also that should take away the curse from them. But he could not take it away by the law, for by the law it is more and more increased. What did he then? He joined himself to the company of the accursed, taking unto him their flesh and blood, and so set himself for a mediator between God and men, saying, although I be flesh and blood, and now dwell among the accursed, yet notwithstanding I am that blessed one, through whom all men must be blessed. So in one person he joineth God and man together, and being united unto us which were accursed, he was made a curse for us, and hid his blessing in our sin, in our death, and in our curse, which condemned him and put him to death. But because he was the Son of God, he could not be holden of them, but overcame them, led them captive and triumphed over them: and whatsoever did hang upon the flesh, which for our sake he took upon him, he carried it with him. Wherefore all they that cleave unto this flesh, are blessed and delivered from the curse, that is, from sin and everlasting death.

They that understand not this benefit of Christ (whereof the gospel especially entreateth) and know not another righteousness besides the righteousness of the law, when they hear that the works of the law are not necessary to salvation, but that men do obtain the same by only hearing and believing that Christ the Son of God hath taken upon him our flesh, and joined himself to the accursed, to the end that all nations might be blessed, they, I say, are offended: for of all this they understand nothing, or else they understand it carnally. For their minds are occupied with other cogitations and fantastical imaginations: therefore these things seem unto them strange matters. Yea, even unto us which have received the first fruits of the spirit, it is impossible to understand these things perfectly; for they mightily fight against reason.

To conclude, all evils should have overwhelmed us, as they shall overwhelm the wicked forever; but Christ being made for us a transgressor of all laws, guilty of all our malediction, our sins, and all our evils, cometh between as a mediator, embracing us wicked and damnable sinners. He took upon him and bore all our evils, which should have oppressed and tormented us forever; and these cast him down for a little while, and ran over his head like water, as the prophet in the person of Christ complaineth when he saith: "thy indignation sore presseth me, and thou hast vexed me with all thy storms." Again, "thine indignations have gone over me, and thy terrors have troubled me." By this means we being delivered from these everlasting terrors and anguish through Christ, shall enjoy an everlasting and inestimable peace and felicity, so that we believe this.

These are the reverend mysteries of the scripture, which Moses also somewhat darkly in some places did foreshew: which also the prophets and apostles did know, and did deliver to their posterity. For this knowledge and benefit of Christ to come, the saints of the Old Testament rejoiced more than we now do, when he is so comfortably revealed and exhibited unto us. Indeed we do acknowledge that this knowledge of Christ and of the righteousness of faith, is an inestimable treasure; but we conceive not thereby such a full joy of spirit, as the prophets and apostles did. Hereof it cometh, that they, and especially Paul, so plentifully set forth and so diligently taught the article of justification. For this is the proper office of an apostle, to set forth the glory and benefit of Christ, and thereby to raise up and comfort troubled and afflicted consciences.

VERSE 14. *That the blessing of Abraham might come upon the Gentiles through Christ Jesus.*

Paul hath always this place before his eyes: "in thy seed, etc."—For the blessing promised unto Abraham, could not come upon the Gentiles, but only by Christ, the seed of Abraham; and that by this means, that it behoved him to be made a curse, that this promise made unto Abraham: "in thy seed shall all nations be blessed," might so be fulfilled. Therefore by no other means could this be done that here is promised, but that Jesus Christ must needs become a curse, and join himself to those that were accursed, that so he might take away the curse from them, and through his blessing might bring unto them righteousness and life. And here mark (as I have also forewarned you) that this word, blessing, is not in vain, as the Jews dream, who expound it, to be but a salutation by word of mouth or by writing. But Paul entreateth here of sin and righteousness, of death and life before God.—He speaketh therefore of inestimable and incomprehensible things, when he saith: "that the blessing of Abraham might come upon the Gentiles, through Jesus Christ."

Ye see moreover what merits we bring, and by what means we obtain this blessing. This is the merit of congruence and worthiness, these are the works preparative, whereby we obtain this righteousness, that Christ Jesus was made a curse for us. For we are ignorant of God, enemies of God, dead in sin, and accursed: and what is our desert then? what can he deserve that is accursed, ignorant of God, dead in sins, and subject to the wrath and judgment of God?—When the Pope excommunicateth a man, whatsoever he doth is accounted accursed. How much more then may we say, that he is accursed before God (as all we are before we know Christ) which doth nothing else but accursed things? Wherefore there is no other way to avoid the curse, but to believe, and with assured confidence to say, Thou Christ art my sin and my curse, or rather, I am thy sin, thy curse, thy death, thy wrath of God, thy hell; and, contrariwise, thou art my righteousness, my blessing, my life, my grace of God, and my heaven. For the text saith plainly, "Christ is made a curse for us." Therefore we are the cause that he was made a curse; nay rather, we are his curse.

This is an excellent place, and full of spiritual consolation; and albeit it satisfy not the blind and hard-hearted Jews, yet it satisfieth us that are baptized, and have received this doctrine, and concludeth most mightily, that we are blessed through the curse, the sin, and the death of Christ; that is to say, we are justified and quickened unto life. So long as sin, death, and the curse do abide in us, sin terrifieth, death killeth, and the curse condemneth us. But when these are translated and laid upon Christ's back, then are all these evils made his own, and his benefits are made ours. Let us therefore learn in all temptations to translate sin, death, the curse, and all evils which oppress us, from ourselves unto Christ: and again, from him unto ourselves, righteousness, mercy, life, and blessing. For he beareth all our evils and our miseries, "God the father cast the iniquities of us all," as Isaiah the prophet saith, "upon him; and he hath taken them upon him willingly, which was not guilty." But this he did, that he might fulfil the will of his Father, by the which we are sanctified for ever.

This is that infinite and unmeasurable mercy of God, which Paul would gladly amplify with all eloquence and plenty of words, but the slender capacity of man's heart cannot comprehend, and much less utter that unsearchable depth and burning zeal of God's love towards us. And verily the inestimable greatness of God's mercy not only engendereth in us a hardness to believe, but also incredulity itself. For I do not only hear that this Almighty God, the creator and maker of all things, is good and merciful, but also that the same high sovereign majesty was so careful for me a damnable sinner, a child of wrath and everlasting death, that he spared not his own dear Son, but delivered him to a most shameful death, that he, hanging between two thieves, might be made a curse and sin for me a cursed sinner, that I might be made blessed; that is to say, the child and heir of God. Who can sufficiently praise and magnify this exceeding great goodness of God? Not all the angels in heaven. Therefore the doctrine of the gospel speaketh of far other matters than any book of policy or philosophy, yea, or the book of Moses himself; to wit, of the unspeakable and most divine gifts of God, which far pass the capacity and understanding both of men and angels.

VERSE 14. *That we might receive the promise of the Spirit through faith.*

This is a phrase of the Hebrew: "The promise of the Spirit:" that is to say, the Spirit promised. Now, the Spirit is freedom from the law, sin, death, the curse, hell, and from the wrath and judgment of God. Here is no merit or worthiness of ours, but a free promise and a gift given through the seed of Abraham, that we may be free from all evils, and obtain all good things. And this liberty and gift of the Spirit we receive not by any other merits than by faith alone. For that only taketh hold of the promises of God, as Paul plainly saith in this place: "that we might receive the promise of the Spirit, not by works, but by faith."

This is indeed a sweet and a true apostolic doctrine, which sheweth that those things are fulfilled for us, and now given to us, which many prophets and kings desired to see and hear. And such like places as this one is, were gathered together out of divers sayings of the prophets, which foresaw long before, in spirit, that all things should be changed, repaired, and governed by this man Christ. The Jews therefore, although they had the law of God, did notwithstanding, besides that law, look for Christ. None of the prophets or governors of the people of God did make any new law, but Eli, Samuel, David, and all the other prophets did abide under the law of Moses: they did not appoint any new tables, or a new kingdom and priesthood: for that new change of the kingly priesthood of the law, and the worship, was referred and kept to him only, of whom Moses had prophesied long before: "The Lord thy God shall raise up a prophet unto thee of thine own nation and from among thy brethren: him shalt thou hear." As if he should say: thou shalt hear him only, and none besides him.

This the fathers well understood, for none could teach greater and higher points than Moses himself, who made excellent laws of high and great matters, as are the ten commandments, especially the first commandment: "I am the Lord thy God: thou shalt have none other Gods but me: thou shalt love the Lord thy God, with all thy heart," etc. (Exodus xx, 2, 3). This law concerning the love of God, comprehended the very angels also. Therefore it is the head-spring of all divine wisdom. And yet was it necessary, notwithstanding, that another teacher should come, that is to say, Christ, which should bring and teach another thing far passing the excellent laws: to wit, grace and remission of sins. This text therefore is full of power: for in this short sentence: "That we might receive the promise of the Spirit by faith:" Paul poureth out at once whatsoever he was able to say. Therefore when he can go no farther, (for he could not utter any greater or more excellent thing), he breaketh off, and here he stayeth.

> VERSE 15. *Brethren, I speak according to man: though it be but a man's covenant, when it is confirmed, yet no man doth abrogate it, or addeth any thing thereto.*

After this principal and invincible argument, Paul addeth another, grounded upon the similitude of a man's testament: which seemeth to be very weak, and such as the apostle ought not to use for the confirmation of a matter of so great importance. For in high and weighty matters, we ought to confirm earthly things by divine things, and not divine and heavenly things by earthly and worldly things. And indeed it is true, that these arguments of all other are most weak, when we go about to prove and confirm heavenly matters with earthly and corruptible things, as Scotus is wont to do. A man, saith he, is able to love God above all things, for he loveth himself above all things; therefore, much more is he able to love God above all things: for a good thing, the greater it is, the more it is to be loved. And hereof he inferreth that a man is able, *ex puris naturalibus*, that is to say, even of his own pure natural strength, easily to fulfil that high commandment: "Thou shalt love the Lord thy God with all thy heart," etc. For, saith he, a man is able to love the least good thing above all things: yea, he setteth at nought his life (of all other things most dear unto him) for a little vile money; therefore he can much more do it for God's cause.

Ye have oftentimes heard of me, that civil ordinances are of God: for God hath ordained them, and allowed them, as he doth the sun, the moon, and other creatures. Therefore an argument taken of the ordinance of the creatures of God is good, so that we use the same rightly. So the prophets have very often used similitudes and comparisons taken of creatures, calling Christ the son, the church the moon, and preachers and teachers of the word the stars. Also there are many similitudes in the prophets, of trees, thorns, flowers, and fruits of the earth. The New Testament likewise is full of such similitudes. Therefore, where

God's ordinance is in the creature, there may an argument be well borrowed and applied to divine and heavenly things.

So our Saviour Christ, in Matt. vii, arguing from earthly things to heavenly things, when he saith, "If ye then which are evil can give to your children good gifts, how much more shall your Father which is in heaven, give good things to them that ask him?" Likewise Peter: "We must obey men, therefore much more must we obey God" (Acts v, 29). Jeremiah also, in chap. xxxv, "The Rechabites obeyed their fathers; how much more ought ye to have obeyed me?" Now, these things are appointed of God, and are his ordinances, that fathers should give unto their children, and that children should obey their parents; therefore such manner of arguments are good, when they are grounded upon the ordinance of God. But if they be taken from men's corrupt affections, they are nought. Such is the argument of Scotus. I love the lesser good things, therefore I love the greater more. I deny the consequence. For my loving is not God's ordinance, but a devilish corruption. Indeed it should be so, that I, loving myself or another creature, should much more love God the Creator; but it is not so. For the love wherewith I love myself is corrupt and against God.

This I say, lest any man should cavil that an argument taken of corruptible things, and applied to divine and spiritual matters, is nothing worth. For this argument, as I have said, is strong enough, so that we ground the same upon the ordinance of God, as we see in this argument which we have in hand. For the civil law, which is an ordinance of God, saith that it is not lawful to break or to change the testament of a man. Yea, it commandeth that the last will and testament of a man be straitly kept; for it is one of the holiest and most laudable customs that are among men. Now therefore, upon this custom of man's testament, Paul argueth after this manner: How cometh it to pass that man is obeyed and not God? Politic and civil ordinances, as concerning testaments and other things, are diligently kept. There nothing is changed, nothing is added or take naway. But the testament of God is changed; that is to say, his promise concerning the spiritual blessing, that is, concerning heavenly and everlasting things, which the whole world ought not only to receive with great zeal and affection, but also ought most religiously to reverence and honour. This persuadeth vehemently, when we so argue from the examples and laws of men. Therefore he saith, I speak after the manner of men; that is to say, I bring unto you a similitude taken of the custom and manner of men. As if he should say, the testaments of men and such other corruptible things are straitly executed, and that which the law commandeth is diligently observed and kept. For when a man maketh his last will, bequeathing his lands and goods to his heirs, and thereupon dieth, this last will is confirmed and ratified by the death of the testator, so that nothing may now be either added to it, or taken from it, according to all law and equity. Now, if a man's will be kept with so great fidelity, that nothing is added to it or taken from it after his death, how much more ought the last will of God to be faithfully kept, which he promised and gave unto Abraham and his seed after him? For when Christ died, then it was confirmed in him, and after his death the writing of his last testament was opened; that is to say, "the promised blessing of Abraham was preached among all nations dispersed throughout the whole world." This was the last will and testament of God, the great testator, confirmed by the death of Christ; therefore no man ought to change it or add any thing to it, as they that teach the law and man's traditions do: for they say, unless thou be circumcised, keep the law, do many works, and suffer many things, thou canst not be saved. This is not the last will and testament of God. For he said not unto Abraham, if thou do this or that thou shalt obtain the blessing; or they that be circumcised and keep the law shall obtain the same: but he saith, "In thy seed shall all the nations of the earth be blessed." And if he should say, I of mere mercy do promise unto thee, that Christ shall come of thy seed, who shall bring the blessing upon all nations oppressed with sin and death; that is to say, which shall deliver the nations from the everlasting curse, to wit, from sin and death, receiving this promise by faith: "In thy seed," etc. Wherefore, even as the false apostles were in time past, so are all the Papists and justiciaries at this day, perverters and destroyers, not of man's testament (because they are forbidden by the law) but of God's testament, whom they fear nothing at all, although he be a consuming fire. For such is the nature of all hypocrites, that they will observe man's law exactly; but the laws of God they do despise, and most wickedly transgress. But the time shall come when they shall bear a horrible judgment, and shall feel what it is to contemn and pervert the testament of God. This argument then, grounded upon the ordinance of God, is strong enough.

VERSE 16. *Now to Abraham and his seed were the promises made. He saith not: And to the seeds, as speaking of many; but, and to thy seed, as of one, which is Christ.*

Here by a new name he calleth the promises of God made unto Abraham, concerning Christ that should bring the blessing upon all nations, a testament. And indeed the promise is nothing else but a testament, not yet revealed but sealed up. Now, a testament is not a law, but a donation or free gift. For heirs look not for laws, exactions, or any burdens to be laid upon them by a testament, but they look for the inheritance confirmed thereby.

First of all therefore he expoundeth the words. Afterwards he applieth the similitude, and standeth upon this word "seed." There were no laws given unto Abraham, saith he, but a testament was made and delivered unto him; that is to say, the promises were pronounced unto him as touching the spiritual blessing: therefore somewhat was promised and given unto him. If then the testament of a man be kept, why should not rather the testament of God be kept? whereof the testament of man is but a sign. Again, if we will keep the signs, why do we not rather keep the things which they signify?

Now, the promises are made unto him, not in all the Jews or in many seeds, but in one seed, which is Christ. The Jews will not receive this interpretation of Paul: for they say that the singular number is here put for the plural, one for many. But we gladly receive this meaning and interpretation of Paul, who oftentimes repeateth this word "seed," and expoundeth this seed to be Christ: and this he doth with an apostolic spirit. Let the Jews deny it as much as they will: we notwithstanding have arguments strong enough, which Paul hath before rehearsed, which also confirm this thing, and they cannot deny them. Hitherto, as touching the similitude of God's ordinance, that is to say, of man's testament. Now he expoundeth and amplifieth the same.

VERSE 17. *And this I say, that the law, which was four hundred and thirty years after, cannot disannul the covenant that was confirmed before of God in respect of Christ, that it should make the promise of none effect.*

Here the Jews might object, that God was not only content to give promises to Abraham, but also after four hundred and thirty years he made the law. God, therefore, mistrusting his own promises, as insufficient to justify, addeth thereto a better thing: that is to say, the law, to the end that when the same, as a better successor, was come, not the idle, but the doers of the law might be made righteous thereby. The law therefore, which followed the promise, did abrogate the promise. Such evasions and starting-holes the Jews seek out.

To this cavillation Paul answereth very well and to the purpose, and strongly confuteth the same. The law, saith he, was given four hundred and thirty years after this promise was made: "In thy seed," etc., and it could not make the promise void and unprofitable; for the promise is the testament of God, confirmed by God himself, in Christ, so many years before the law. Now, that which God once hath promised and confirmed, he calleth not back again, but it remaineth ratified and sure for ever.

Why then was the law added? Indeed it was delivered, so many ages after, to the posterity of Abraham, not to the end he might through it obtain the blessing (for it is the office of the law to bring men under the curse, and not to bless): but that there might be in the world a certain people, which might have the word and testimony of Christ, out of the which, Christ also, according to the flesh, might be born; and that men being kept and shut up under the law, might sigh and groan for their deliverance through the seed of Abraham, which is Christ, which only should and could bless, that is to say, deliver all nations from sin and everlasting death. Moreover, the ceremonies commanded in the law, did foreshadow Christ. Wherefore the promise was not abolished either by the law, or by the ceremonies of the law; but rather by the same, as by certain seals, it was for a time confirmed, until the letters themselves, or the writing of the testament (to wit, the promise) might be opened, and by the preaching of the gospel might be spread abroad among all nations.

But let us suffer the law and the promise to encounter together, and then shall we see which of them is the stronger; that is to say, whether the promise be able to abolish the law, or the law the promise. If the law abolish the promise, then it followeth, that we by our works make God a liar, and his promise of none effect. For if the law do justify us, and deliver us from sin and death, and consequently our works and our own strength accomplish the law, then the promise made unto Abraham is utterly void and unprofitable, and so consequently God is a liar and a dissembler. For when he which promiseth, will not perform his promise, but maketh it of none effect, what doth he else but shew himself to be a liar and a dissembler? But it is impossible that the law should make God a liar, or that our works should make the promise void, nay, rather it must needs be firm, and stable for ever (for God promiseth not in vain) although we are able to keep and fulfil the law. And let us admit that all men were as holy as angels, so that they should not need the promise (which notwithstanding is impossible): yet must we think that the same promise abideth most sure and certain, or else God should be found a liar, which either hath promised in vain, or else will not, or cannot perform his promises. Therefore, like as the promise was before the law, so is it far more excellent than the law.

And God did excellently well in that he gave the promise so long before the law Which he did of purpose and to this end, that it should not be said, that righteousness was given through the law, and not through the promise. For if he would that we should have been justified by the law, then would he have given the law four hundred and thirty years before the promise, or else together with the promise. But now at the first he speaketh not a word as concerning the law; but at length, after four hundred and thirty years, he giveth the law. In the mean while, all that time he speaketh only of his promises. Therefore the blessing and free gift of righteousness came before the law through the promise: the promise therefore is far more excellent than the law. And so the law doth not abolish the promise, but faith in the promise (whereby the believers even before Christ's time were saved) which is now published by the gospel throughout the whole world, destroyeth the law, so that it cannot increase sin any more, terrify sinners, or bring them in to desperation, laying hold upon the promise through faith.

And in this also lieth a certain vehemency specially to be noted, that he expressly setteth down the number of four hundred and thirty years. As if he would say, Consider with yourselves how long it was between the promise given, and the law. It is plain that Abraham received the promise a long time before the law; for the law was given to the People of Israel four hundred and thirty years after. And this is an invincible argument gathered and grounded upon a certain time. And he speaketh not here of the law in general, but only of the written law. As if he would say: God could not then have regard to the ceremonies and works of the law, and give righteousness to the observers thereof; for as yet the law was not given, which commandeth ceremonies, requireth works, and promises life to those that observe them, saying, The man that shall do these things, shall live in them And although it promise such things, yet it followeth not therefore that we obtain these promises: for it saith plainly, "The man that shall do these things," etc. Now, it is certain that no man can do them. Moreover, Paul saith that the law cannot abolish the promise; therefore that promise made unto Abraham four hundred and thirty years before the law, remaineth firm and constant. And that the matter may be better understood, I will declare the same by a similitude. If a rich man, not constrained, but of his own good will, should adopt one to be his son, whom he knoweth not, and to whom he oweth nothing, and should appoint him to be the heir of all his lands and goods, and certain years after that he hath bestowed this benefit upon him, he should lay upon him a law to do this or that: he cannot now say that he hath deserved this benefit by his own works, seeing that many years before, he asking nothing, had received the same freely and of mere favour; so God could not respect our works and deserts going before righteousness; for the promise and the gift of the Holy Ghost was four hundred and thirty years before the law.

Hereby it appeareth that Abraham obtained not righteousness before God through the law. For there was yet no law. If there were yet no law, then was their neither work nor merit. What then? Nothing else but the mere promise. This promise Abraham believed, and it was counted to him for righteousness. By the self-same means then that the father obtained this promise, the children do also obtain and retain it. So say we also at this day: Our sins were purged by the death of Christ above a thousand and five hundred years ago, when there were yet no religious orders, no canon or rule of penance, no merits of congruence and worthiness. We cannot now therefore begin to abolish the same by our own works and merits.

Thus Paul gathereth arguments of similitudes, of a certain times, and of persons, so sure and strong on every side, that no man can deny them. Let us therefore arm and fortify our consciences with such like arguments; for it helpeth us exceedingly to have them always ready in temptations. For they lead us from the law and works, to the promise and to faith; from wrath to grace; from sin to righteousness; and from death to life. Therefore these two things (as I do often repeat), to wit, the law and the promise, must be diligently distinguished. For in time, in place, and in person, and generally in all other circumstances they are separate as far asunder as heaven and earth, the beginning of the world and the latter end. Indeed they are near neighbours, for they are joined together in one man, or in one soul; but in the outward affection, and as touching their office, they ought to be separate far asunder: so that the law may have dominion over the flesh, and the promise may sweetly and comfortably reign in the conscience. When thou hast thus appointed unto them both their own proper place, then thou walkest safely between them both, in the heaven of the promise and in the earth of the law.

In spirit thou walkest in the paradise of grace and peace; in the flesh thou walkest in the earth of works and of the cross. And now the troubles which the flesh is compelled to bear shall not be hard unto thee, because of the sweetness of the promise, which comforteth and rejoiceth the heart exceedingly. But now, if thou confound and mingle these two together, and place the law in the conscience, and the promise of liberty in the flesh, then thou makest a confusion (such as was in popery): so that thou shalt not know what the law, what the promise, what sin, or what righteousness is.

Wherefore, if thou wilt rightly divide the word of truth, thou must put a great difference between the promise and the law, as touching the inward affections and whole practice of life. It is not for nought that Paul prosecuteth this argument so diligently; for he foresaw in spirit that this michief should creep into the church, that the word of God should be confounded: that is to say, that the promise should be mingled with the law, and so the promise should be utterly lost. For when the promise is mingled with the law, it is now made nothing else but the very law. Therefore accustom thyself to separate the promise and the law asunder, even in respect of time, that when the law cometh and accuseth thy conscience, thou mayest say, Lady law, thou comest not in season, for thou comest too soon; tarry ye until four hundred and thirty years be expired, and when they are past, then come and spare not. But if thou come then, yet shalt thou come too late. For then hath the promise prevented thee, four hundred and thirty years: to the which I assent, and sweetly repose myself in the same. Therefore I have nothing to do with thee: I hear thee not. For now I live with the believing Abraham, or, rather, since Christ is now revealed and given unto me, I live in him, who is my righteousness, who also hath abolished thee, O law. And thus let Christ be always before thine eyes, as a certain summary of all arguments for the defence of faith, against the righteousness of the flesh, against the law, and against all works and merits whatsoever.

Hitherto I have rehearsed almost all, but especially the principal arguments which the apostle Paul handleth in this epistle, for the confirmation of this doctrine of justification. Among which, the argument as touching the promise made unto Abraham and to the other fathers, is the weightiest, and of greatest efficacy; which Paul doth chiefly prosecute, both here and in the epistle to the Romans; the words whereof he diligently weigheth, and moreover, entreateth both of the times and persons. Also he standeth upon this word "seed," applying the same unto Christ. Finally, he declareth, by the contrary, what the law worketh: namely, that it holdeth men under the curse. And thus he fortifieth the article of christian righteousness with strong and mighty arguments. On the other side, he overthroweth the arguments of the false apostles, which they used in defence of the righteousness of the law, and turneth them upon their own heads: that is to say, whereas they contended that righteousness and life is obtained by the law, Paul sheweth that it worketh nothing but malediction and death in us. Ye contend, saith he, that the law is necessary to salvation. Have ye not read that it saith: "He that shall do these things shall live in them?" (Lev. xviii, 5). Now, who is he that performeth and accomplisheth them? No man living. Therefore, "as many as are of the works of the law are under the curse" (Gal. iii, 10). And again, in another place, "The sting of death is sin, and the strength of sin is the law" (1 Cor. xv, 56). Now followeth the conclusion of all these arguments.

VERSE 18. *For if the inheritance be of the law, it is no more by the promise, etc.*

So he saith in the fourth to the Romans: "For if they which be of the law be heirs, then is faith but vain, and the promise of none effect." And it cannot otherwise be: For this distinction is plain, that the law is a thing far differing from the promise. Yea, natural reason, although it be never so blind, is compelled to confess that it is one thing to promise, and another thing to require; one thing to give, and another thing to take. The law requireth and exacteth of us our works: the promise of the seed doth offer unto us the spiritual and everlasting benefits of God, and that freely for Christ's sake. Therefore we obtain the inheritance or blessing through the promise, and not through the law. For the promise saith, "In thy seed shall all nations of the earth be blessed." Therefore he that hath the law, hath not enough, because he hath not yet the blessing, without the which he is compelled to abide under the curse. The law therefore cannot justify, because the blessing is not joined unto it. Moreover, if the inheritance were of the law, then should God be found a liar, and the promise should be in vain. Again, if the law could obtain the blessing, why did God then make this promise, "In thy seed," etc.? Why did he not rather

EPISTLE TO THE GALATIANS

say: Do this, and thou shalt receive the blessing? Or else, by keeping of the law, thou mayest deserve everlasting life? This argument is grounded upon contraries: the inheritance is given by the promise; therefore not by the law.

VERSE 18. *But God gave it unto Abraham by promise.*

It cannot be denied but that God, before the law was, gave unto Abraham the inheritance or blessing by the promise: that is to say, remission of sins, righteousness, salvation and everlasting life, that we should be sons and heirs of God, and fellow-heirs with Christ. For it is plainly said in Genesis: "In thy seed shall all nations be blessed." There the blessing is given freely, without respect of the law or works. For God gave the inheritance before Moses was born, or before any man had yet once thought of the law. Why vaunt ye then, that righteousness cometh by the law, seeing that righteousness, life and salvation was given to your father Abraham without the law, yea, before there was any law? He that is not moved with these things is blind and obstinate. But this argument of the promise I have before handled more largely, and therefore I will but touch it by the way.

Hitherto we have heard the principal part of this epistle. Now the apostle goeth about to shew the use and office of the law, adding certain similitudes of the school-master, and of the little heir: also the allegory of the two sons of Abraham, Isaac and Ishmael, etc. Last of all he setteth forth certain precepts concerning manners.

VERSE 19. *Wherefore then serveth the law?*

When we teach that a man is justified without the law and works, then doth this question necessarily follow: If the law do not justify, why then was it given? Also, why doth God charge us and burden us with the law, if it do not justify? What is the cause that we are so hardly exercised and vexed with it, if they which work but one hour, are made equal with us that have borne the heat and burden of the day? When as that grace is once published unto us which the gospel setteth out, by-and-by ariseth this great murmuring: without which the gospel cannot be preached. The Jews had this opinion, that if they kept the law they should be justified thereby. Therefore, when they heard that the gospel was preached concerning Christ, who came into the world to save, not the righteous, but sinners, and that they should go before them into the kingdom of God (Matt. xx, 12), they were wonderfully offended, complaining that they had borne the heavy yoke of the law so many years with great labour, and toil, and that they were miserably vexed and oppressed with the tyranny of the law, without any profit, yea, rather, to their great hurt: again, that the Gentiles, who were idolaters, obtained grace without any labour or travail. So do our Papists murmur at this day, saying, What hath it profited us that we have lived in a cloister, twenty, thirty, or forty years; that we have vowed chastity, poverty, obedience; that we have said so many psalters, and so many canonical hours, and so many masses; that we have so punished our bodies with fasting, prayers, chastisements, etc., if a husband, a wife, a prince, a governor, a master, a scholar, if a hireling or a drudge bearing sacks, if a wench sweeping the house, shall not only be made equal with us, but also be acceptable as better and more worthy before God than we?

This is therefore a hard question, whereunto reason cannot answer, but is greatly offended with it. Reason, after a sort, understandeth the righteousness of the law, which also it teacheth and urgeth, and imagineth that the doers of it are righteous: but it understandeth not the office and end of the law. Therefore, when it heareth this sentence of Paul (which is strange and unknown to the world) "that the law was given for transgressions," thus it judgeth: Paul abolisheth the law, for he saith that we are not justified through it; yea, he is a blasphemer against God which gave the law, when he saith, "that the law was given for transgressions." Let us live therefore as Gentiles which have no law; "yea, let us sin, and abide in sin, that grace may abound:" also, "let us do evil that good may come thereof." This happened to the apostle Paul. And the self-same happeneth at this day unto us. For when the common people hear, out of the gospel, that righteousness cometh by the mere grace of God, through faith only, without the law, and without works, they gather by-and-by of it, as did the Jews in times past: If the law do not justify, then let us work nothing; and this do they truly perform.

What should we then do? This impiety doth indeed very much vex us, but we cannot remedy it. For when Christ preached, he must needs hear, that he was a blasphemer and a seditious person: that is to say, that through his doctrine he deceived men, and made them rebels against Cæsar. The self-same thing happened to Paul and all the rest of the apostles. And what marvel is it if the world, in like manner, accuse us at this day? Let it accuse us, let it slander us, let it persecute us and spare us not: yet must not we therefore hold our peace, but speak freely, that afflicted consciences may be delivered out of the snares of the devil. And we must not regard the foolish and ungodly people, in that they do abuse our doctrine: for, whether they have the law or no law, they cannot be reformed. But we must consider how afflicted consciences may be comforted, that they perish not with the multitude. If we should dissemble and hold our peace, miserable and afflicted consciences should have no comfort, which are so entangled and snared with men's laws and traditions, that they can wind themselves out by no means.

As Paul therefore, when he saw that some resisted his doctrine, and other some sought the liberty of the flesh, and thereby became worse, comforted himself after this sort: that he was an apostle of Jesus Christ, sent to preach the faith of God's elect; and that he must suffer all things for the elect's sake, that they also might obtain salvation; so we at this day do all things for the elect's sake, whom we know to be edified and comforted through our doctrine. But as the for the dogs and swine, (of whom the one sort persecuteth our doctrine, and the other sort treadeth under foot the liberty which we have in Christ Jesus), I am so offended with them, that in all my life, for their sakes, I would not utter so much as one word; but I would rather wish that these swine, together with our adversaries the dogs, were yet still subject to the Pope's tyranny, rather than that the holy name of God should be so blasphemed and evil spoken of through them.

Therefore, albeit not only the foolish and ignorant people, but they also which seem, in their own conceits, to be very wise, do argue after this sort: If the law do not justify, then it is in vain and of none effect; yet it is not therefore true. For like as this consequence is nothing worth: Money doth not justify, or make a man righteous, therefore it is unprofitable; the eyes do not justify, therefore they must be plucked out; the hands make not a man righteous, therefore they must be cut off: so is this naught also, The law doth not justify, therefore it is unprofitable: for we must attribute unto every thing his proper effect and use. We do not therefore destroy or condemn the law, because we say that it doth not justify; but we answer otherwise to this question, "To what end then serveth the law?" than our adversaries do, who do wickedly and perversely counterfeit an office and use of the law, which belongeth not unto it.

Against this abuse and forged office of the law we dispute, and answer with Paul, that "the law doth not justify." But, in so saying, we affirm not that the law is unprofitable, as they do by-and-by gather. If the law do not justify (say they) then it is given in vain. No, not so. For it hath its proper office and use; but not that which the adversaries do imagine, namely, to make men righteous: but it accuseth, terrifieth, and condemneth them. We say with Paul, that the law is good, if a man do rightly use it; that is to say, if he use the law as the law. If I give unto the law *his* proper definition, and keep it within the compass of *his* office and use, it is an excellent thing. But if I translate it to another use, and attribute that unto it which I should not, then do. I not only pervert the law, but also the whole scripture.

Therefore Paul fighteth here against those pestilent hypocrites who could not abide this sentence: "The law was added for transgressions;" for they think that the office of the law is to justify. And this is the general opinion of man's reason among the sophisters, and throughout the whole world, that righteousness is gotten through the works of the law; and reason will by no means suffer this pernicious opinion to be wrested from it, because it understandeth not the righteousness of faith. Hereof it cometh that the Papists both foolishly and wickedly do say: The church hath the law of God, the traditions of the fathers, the decrees of councils: if it live after them, it is holy. No man shall persuade these men, that, when they keep these things, they please not God, but provoke his wrath. To conclude, they that trust in their own righteousness, think to pacify the wrath of God by their will-worship and voluntary religion. Therefore this opinion of the righteousness of the law is the sink of all evils, and the sin of sins of the whole world. For gross sins and vices may be known and so amended, or else repressed by the punishment of the magistrate. But this sin, to wit, man's opinion concerning his own righteousness, will not only be counted no sin, but also will be esteemed for a high religion and righteousness. This pestilent sin, therefore, is the mighty power of the devil over the whole world, the very head of the serpent, and the snare whereby the devil entangleth and holdeth all men captive. For naturally all men have this opinion, that they are made righteous by keeping the law. Paul therefore, to the end he might shew the true office and use of the law, and might root out of men's hearts that false opinion concerning the righteousness thereof, answereth to this objection, Wherefore then serveth the law, if it justify not? after this sort: It was not given to make men righteous (saith he), but,

VERSE 19. *It was added because of transgressions.*

As things are divers and distinct, so the uses thereof are divers and distinct: therefore they may not be confounded. For if they be, there must needs be a confusion of the things also. A woman may not wear a man's apparel, nor a man a woman's attire. Let a man do the works that belong to a man, and the woman the works that belong to a woman. Let every man do that which his vocation and office requireth. Let pastors and preachers teach the word of God purely. Let magistrates govern their subjects, and let subjects obey their magistrates. Let every thing serve in his due place and order. Let the sun shine by day, the moon and the stars by night. Let the sea give fishes; the earth grain; the woods wild beasts and trees, etc. In like manner let not the law usurp the office and use of another, that is to say, of justification; but let it leave this only to grace, to the promise, and to faith. What is then the office of the law? Transgressions; or else (as he saith in another place), "the law entereth in that sin should abound" (Rom. v, 20). A goodly office, forsooth! "The law," saith he, "was added for transgressions;" that is to say, it was added besides and after the promise, until Christ the seed should come, unto whom it was promised.

OF THE DOUBLE USE OF THE LAW.

Here you must understand that there is a double use of the law. One is civil: for God hath ordained civil laws, yea, all laws, to punish transgressions. Every law then is given to restrain sin. If it restrain sin, then it maketh men righteous. No, nothing less. For in that I do not kill, I do not commit adultery, I do not steal, or in that I abstain from other sins, I do it not willingly, or for the love of virtue, but I fear the prison, the sword, and the hangman. These do bridle and restrain me that I sin not, as bonds and chains do restrain a lion, or a bear, that he tear and devour not every thing that he meeteth: therefore the restraining from sin is not righteousness, but rather a signification of unrighteousness. For, as a mad or a wild beast is bound, lest he should destroy every thing that he meeteth: even so the law doth bridle a mad and a furious man, that he sin not after his own lust. This restraint sheweth plainly enough that they which have need of the law (as all they have which are without Christ) are not righteous, but rather wicked and mad men, whom it is necessary, by the bonds and prison of the law, so to bridle, that they sin not. Therefore the law justifieth not.

The first use then of the law, is to bridle the wicked. For the devil reigneth throughout the whole world, and enforceth men to all kinds of horrible wickedness. Therefore God hath ordained magistrates, parents, ministers, laws, bonds, and all civil ordinances, that if they can do no more, yet, at the least, they may bind the devil's hands, that he rage not in his bond-slaves after his own lust. Like as therefore they that are possessed, in whom the devil mightily reigneth, are kept in bonds and chains, lest they should hurt others: even so, in the world, which is possessed of the devil, and carried headlong into all kinds of wickedness, the magistrate is present with his bonds and chains; that is to say, with his laws, binding his hands and feet, that he run not headlong into all mischief. And, if he suffer not himself to be bridled after this sort, then he loseth his head. This civil restraint is very necessary, and appointed of God, as well for public peace, as for the preservation of all things, but especially lest the course of the gospel should be hindered by the tumult and seditions of wicked, outrageous, and proud men. But Paul entreateth not here of this civil use and office of the law. It is indeed very necessary, but it justifieth not. For, as a possessed or a mad man is not therefore free from the snares of the devil, or well in his mind, because he hath his hands and his feet bound, and can do no hurt: even so, the world, although it be bridled by the law from outward wickedness and mischief, yet is it not therefore righteous, but still continueth wicked: yea, this restraint sheweth plainly that the world is wicked and outrageous, stirred up and enforced to all wickedness by his prince the devil; for, otherwise, it need not be bridled by laws that it should not sin.

Another use of the law is divine and spiritual, which is (as Paul saith) "to increase transgressions;" that is to say, to reveal unto a man his sin, his blindness, his misery, his impiety, ignorance, hatred, and contempt of God, death, hell, the judgment and deserved wrath of God. Of this use the apostle entreateth notably in the seventh to the Romans. This is altogether unknown to hypocrites, to the popish sophisters and school-divines, and to all that walk in the opinion of the righteousness of the law, or of their own righteousness. But to the end that God might bridle and beat down this monster, and this mad beast (I mean, the presumption of man's righteousness and religion), which naturally maketh men proud, and puffeth them up in such sort, that they think themselves thereby to please God highly; it behoved him to send some Hercules which might set upon this monster, with all force and courage, to overthrow him, and utterly to destroy him: that is to say, he was constrained to give a law in mount Sinai, with so great majesty and with so terrible a shew, that the whole multitude was astonished (Exodus xix, xx).

This, as it is the proper and the principal use of the law, so is it very profitable and also most necessary. For if any be not a murderer, an adulterer, a thief, and outwardly refrain from sin, as the Pharisee did, which is mentioned in the gospel, he would swear (because he is possessed with the devil) that he is righeous, and therefore he conceiveth an opinion of righteousness, and presumeth of his good works and merits. Such a one God cannot otherwise mollify and humble, that he may acknowledge his misery and damnation, but by the law: for that is the hammer of death, the thundering of hell, and the lightning of God's wrath, that beateth to powder the obstinate and senseless hypocrites. Wherefore this is the proper and true use of the law, by lightning, by tempest, and by the sound of the trumpet (as in mount Sinai) to terrify, and by thundering to beat down and rent in pieces that beast which is called the opinion of righteousness. Therefore, said God, by Jeremy the prophet, "my word is a hammer, breaking rocks" (Jer. xxiii, 29). For as long as the opinion of righteousness abideth in man, so long there abideth also in him incomprehensible pride, presumption, security, hatred of God, contempt of his grace and mercy, ignorance of the promises and of Christ. The preaching of free remission of sins, through Christ, cannot enter into the heart of such a one, neither can he feel any taste or savour thereof; for that mighty rock and adamant wall, to wit, the opinion of righteousness, wherewith the heart is environed, doth resist it.

As therefore the opinion of righteousness is a great and a horrible monster, a rebellious, obstinate, and stiff-necked beast, so, for the destroying and overthrowing thereof, God hath need of a mighty hammer, that is to say, the law; which then is in his proper use and office, when it accuseth and revealeth sin after this sort: Behold, thou hast transgressed all the commandments of God, etc., and so it striketh a terror into the conscience, so that it feeleth God to be offended and angry indeed, and itself to be guilty of eternal death. Here the poor afflicted sinner feeleth the intolerable burden of the law, and is beaten down even to desperation; so that now, being oppressed with great anguish and terror, he desireth death, or else seeketh to destroy himself. Wherefore the law is that hammer, that fire, that mighty strong wind, and that terrible earthquake renting the mountains, and breaking the rocks (1 Kings xix, 11, 12, 13), that is to say, the proud and obstinate hypocrites. Elijah, not being able to abide these terrors of the law, which by these things are signified, covered his face with his mantle. Notwithstanding, when the tempest ceased, of which he was a beholder, there came a soft and a gracious wind, in the which the Lord was; but it behoved that the tempest of fire, of wind, and the earthquake should pass, before the Lord should reveal himself in that gracious wind.

The terrible shew and majesty wherein God gave his law in mount Sinai, did represent the use of the law. There was in the people of Israel which came out of Egypt, a singular holiness. They gloried and said, "We are the people of God. We will do all those things which the Lord our God hath commanded." (Exod. xix, 8.) Moreover, Moses did sanctify the people, and bade them wash their garments, refrain from their wives, and prepare themselves against the third day. There was not one of them but he was full of holiness. The third day, Moses bringeth the people out of their tents to the mountain into the sight of the Lord, that they might hear his voice. What followed then? When the children of Israel did behold the horrible sight of the mount smoking and burning, the black clouds and lightnings flashing up and down in this horrible darkness, and heard the sound of the trumpet blowing long and waxing louder and louder: and moreover, when they heard the thunderings and the lightnings, they were afraid, and standing afar off, they said unto Moses: "We will do all things willingly, so that the Lord speak not unto us, lest that we die, and this great fire consume us. Teach thou us, and we will hearken unto thee." (Exod. xx, 19; Deut. v, 24; xviii, 16.) I pray you, what did their purifying, their white garments, and refraining from their wives profit then? Nothing at all. There was not one of them that could abide this presence of the Lord in his majesty and glory: but all being amazed and shaken with terror, fled back as if they had been driven by the devil. "For God is a consuming fire," in whose sight no flesh is able to stand. (Deut. iv, 24.)

The law of God, therefore, hath properly and peculiarly that office which it had then in mount Sinai, when it was first given, and was first heard of them that were washed, righteous, purified, and chaste: and yet, notwithstanding, it brought that holy people into such a knowledge of their own misery, that they were thrown down even to death and desperation. No purity nor holiness could then help them; but there was in them such a feeling of their own uncleanliness, unworthiness and sin, and of the judgment and wrath of God, that they fled from the sight of the Lord, and could not abide to hear his voice. "What flesh was there ever," say they, "that heard the voice of the living God speaking out of the midst of the fire, and yet lived? This day have we seen that God talketh with man, and yet he liveth." (Deut. v, 26.) They speak now far otherwise than they did a little before, when they said: "we are the holy people of God, whom the Lord hath chosen for his own peculiar people, before all the nations upon the earth. We will do all things which the Lord hath spoken." So it happeneth at length to all justiciaries, who being drunk with the opinion of their own righteousness, do think, when they are out of temptation, that they are beloved of God, and that God regardeth their vows, their fastings, their prayers, and their will-works, and that for the same he must give unto them a single crown in heaven. But when that thundering, lightning, fire, and that hammer which breaketh in pieces, that is to say, the law of God, cometh suddenly upon them, revealing unto them their sin, the wrath and judgment of God: then the self-same thing happeneth unto them which happened to the Jews standing at the foot of mount Sinai.

Here I admonish all such as fear God, and especially such as shall become teachers of others hereafter, that they diligently learn out of Paul to understand the true and proper use of the law: which, I fear, after our time will be trodden under foot, and utterly abolished by the enemies of the truth. For even now, while we are yet living, and employ all our diligence to set forth the office and use both of the law and the gospel, there be few, yea, even among those which will be counted Christians, and make a profession of the gospel with us, that understand these things rightly, and as they should do. What think ye then shall come to pass when we are dead and gone? I speak nothing of the Anabaptists, of the new Arians, and such other vain spirits, who are no less ignorant of these matters than are the Papists, although they talk never so much to the contrary; for they are revolted from the pure doctrine of the gospel, to laws and traditions, and therefore they teach not Christ. They brag and they swear that they seek nothing else but the glory of Christ and the salvation of their brethren, and that they teach the word of God purely: but in very deed they corrupt it and wrest it to another sense, so that they make it to sound according to their own imagination. Therefore, under the name of Christ, they teach nothing else but their own dreams; and under the name of the gospel, ceremonies and laws. They are like therefore unto themselves, and so they still continue, that is to say, monks, workers of the law, and teachers of ceremonies, saving that they devise new names, and new works.

It is no small matter, then, to understand rightly what the law is, and what is the true use and office thereof. And forasmuch as we teach these things both diligently and faithfully, we do thereby plainly testify that we reject not the law and works, as our adversaries do falsely accuse us: but we do altogether establish the law, and require the works thereof, and we say that the law is good and profitable, but in his own proper use: which is, first, to bridle civil transgressions, and then to reveal and to increase spiritual transgressions. Wherefore the law is also a light, which sheweth and revealeth, not the grace of God, not righteousness and life; but sin, death, the wrath and judgment of God. For as, in the mount Sinai, the thundering, lightning, the thick and dark cloud, the hill smoking and flaming, and all that terrible shew, did not rejoice nor quicken the children of Israel, but terrified and astonished them, and shewed how unable they were, with all their purity and holiness, to abide the majesty of God speaking to them out of the cloud: even so the law, when it is in his true use, doth nothing else but reveal sin, engender wrath, accuse and terrify men, so that it bringeth them to the very brink of desperation. This is the proper use of the law, and here it hath an end, and it ought to go no farther.

Contrariwise, the gospel is a light which lighteneth, quickeneth, comforteth, and raiseth up fearful consciences. For it sheweth that God, for Christ's sake, is merciful unto sinners, yea, and to such as are most unworthy, if they believe that by his death they are delivered from the curse, that is to say, from sin and everlasting death; and that through his victory, the blessing is freely given unto them; that is to say, grace, forgiveness of sins, righteousness, and everlasting life. Thus, putting a difference between the law and the gospel, we give to them both their own proper use and office. Of this difference between the law and the gospel, there is nothing to be found in the books of the monks, canonists, schoolmen; no, nor in the books of the ancient fathers. Augustine did somewhat understand this difference, and shewed it. Jerome and others knew it not. Briefly, there was wonderful silence many years, as touching this difference, in all schools and churches: and this brought men's consciences into great danger. For, unless the gospel be plainly discerned from the law, the true Christian doctrine cannot be kept sound and uncorrupt. Contrariwise, if this difference be well known, then is also the true manner of justification known, and then it is an easy matter to discern faith from works, Christ from Moses, and all politic works. For all things without Christ are the ministers of death for the punishing of the wicked. Therefore, Paul answereth to this question after this manner:

EPISTLE TO THE GALATIANS

VERSE 19. *The law was added, because of transgressions.*

That is to say, that transgressions might increase, and be more known and seen. And indeed so it cometh to pass. For when sin, death, the wrath and judgment of God, and hell are revealed to a man through the law, it is impossible but that he should become impatient, murmur against God, and despise his will: for he cannot bear the judgment of God, his own death and damnation; and yet, notwithstanding, he cannot escape them. Here he must needs fall into the hatred of God, and blasphemy against God. Before, when he was out of temptation, he was a very holy man; he worshipped and praised God; he bowed his knee before God, and gave him thanks as the Pharisee did (Luke xviii). But now, when sin and death is revealed unto him, he wisheth that there were no God. The law therefore, of itself, bringeth a special hatred of God. And thus sin is not only revealed and known by the law, but also is increased and stirred up by the law. Therefore Paul saith, "sin, that it might appear to be sin, wrought death in me by that which was good, that sin might be out of measure sinful by the commandment." (Rom. vii.) There he entreateth of this effect of the law very largely.

Paul answereth therefore to this question, if the law do not justify, to what end then serveth it? Although (saith he) it justify not, yet it is very profitable and necessary. For, first, it civilly restraineth such as are carnal, rebellious, and obstinate. Moreover, it is a glass that sheweth unto a man himself, that he is a sinner, guilty of death, and worthy of God's everlasting wrath and indignation. To what end serveth this humbling, this bruising and beating down by this hammer, the law, I mean? To this end, that we may have an entrance into grace. So then the law is a minister that prepareth the way unto grace. For God is the God of the humble, the miserable, the afflicted, the oppressed, and the desperate, and of those that are brought even to nothing: and his nature is to exalt the humble, to feed the hungry, to give sight to the blind, to comfort the miserable, the afflicted, the bruised and broken-hearted, to justify sinners, to quicken the dead, and to save the very desperate and damned. For he is an almighty Creator, making all things of nothing. Now that pernicious and pestilent opinion of man's own righteousness, which will not be a sinner, unclean, miserable, and damnable, but righteous and holy, suffereth not God to come to his own natural and proper work. Therefore God must needs take this maul in hand (the law, I mean) to drive down, to beat in pieces, and to bring to nothing this beast, with her vain confidence, wisdom, righteousness, and power, that she may so learn at the length, by her own misery and mischief, that she is utterly forlorn, lost, and damned. Here now, when the conscience is thus terrified with the law, then cometh the doctrine of the gospel and grace, which raiseth up and comforteth the same again, saying, Christ came into the world, not to break the bruised reed, nor to quench the smoking flax; but to preach the gospel of glad tidings to the poor, to heal the broken and contrite in heart, to preach forgiveness of sins to the captives, etc. (Isaiah xlii, 3; Matt. xii, 20.)

But here lieth all the difficulty of this matter, that when a man is terrified and cast down, he may be able to raise up himself again, and say, Now I am bruised and afflicted enough, the time of the law hath tormented and vexed me sharply enough; now is the time of grace; now is the time to hear Christ, out of whose mouth proceed the words of grace and life; now is the time to see, not the smoking and burning mount Sinai, but the mount Moria, where is the throne, the temple, the mercy-seat of God, that is to say, Christ, who is the king of righteousness and peace. There will I hearken what the Lord speaketh unto me, who speaketh nothing else but peace unto his people.

Nay, the foolishness of man's heart is so great, that, in this conflict of conscience, when the law hath done his office, and exercised his true ministry, he doth not only lay hold upon the doctrine of grace, which promiseth most assuredly the forgiveness of sins, for Christ's sake, but seeketh and procureth to himself more laws, to satisfy and quiet his conscience. If I live, saith he, I will amend my life. I will do this: I will do that. Here, except thou do quite the contrary; that is to say, except thou send Moses away, with his law, to those that are secure, proud, and obstinate, and in these terrors and in this anguish lay hold upon Christ, who was crucified and died for thy sins, look for no salvation.

So the law with his office helped by occasion to justification, in that it driveth a man to the promise of grace, and maketh the same sweet and comfortable unto him. Wherefore we do not abrogate the law, but we shew the true office of the law; to wit, that it is a true and a profitable minister, which driveth a man to Christ. Therefore, after the law hath humbled thee, terrified thee, and utterly beaten thee down, so that now thou art at the very brink of desperation, see that thou learn how to use the law rightly; for the office and use of it is not only to reveal sin and the wrath of God, but also to drive men unto Christ. This use of the law the Holy Ghost only setteth forth in the gospel, where he witnesseth that God is present unto the afflicted and broken-hearted. Wherefore, if thou be bruised with this hammer, use not this bruising perversely, so that thou load thyself with more laws, but hear Christ, saying, "Come unto me, all ye that labour and are heavy laden, and I will refresh you." (Matt. xi, 28.) When the law so oppresseth thee, that all things seem to be utterly desperate, and thereby driveth thee unto Christ, to seek help and succour at his hands, then is the law in his true use; and, through the gospel, it helpeth to justification. And this is the best and most perfect use of the law.

Wherefore Paul here beginneth afresh to entreat of the law, and defineth what it is, taking occasion of that which he said before; to wit, that the law justifieth not. For reason, hearing this, by-and-by doth thus infer: then God gave the law in vain. It was necessary, therefore, to seek how to define the law truly, and to shew what the law is, and how it ought to be understood, that it be not taken more largely or more straitly than it should be. There is no law (saith he) that is of itself necessary to justification. Therefore, when we reason as touching righteousness, life, and everlasting salvation, the law must be utterly removed out of our sight, as if it had never been, or never should be, but as though it were nothing at all. For, in the matter of justification, no man can remove the law far enough out of his sight, or behold the only promise of God sufficiently, and as he should do. Therefore I said before that the law and the promise must be separate far asunder, as touching the inward affections and the inward man; albeit, indeed, they are nearly joined together.

VERSE 19. *Until the seed came unto which the promise was made.*

Paul maketh not the law perpetual, but he saith that it was given, and added to the promises for transgressions; that is to say, to restrain them civilly, but especially to reveal and to increase them spiritually, and that not continually, but for a time. Here it is necessary to know how long the power and the tyranny of the law ought to endure, which discovereth sin, sheweth unto us what we are, and revealeth the wrath of God. They whose hearts are touched with an inward feeling of these matters, should suddenly perish, if they should not receive comfort. Therefore, if the days of the law should not be shortened, no man should be saved. A time therefore must be set, and bounds limited to the law, beyond which it may not reign. How long then ought the dominion of the law to endure? Until the seed come; to wit, that seed, of which it is written, "In thy seed shall all the nations of the earth be blessed." The tyranny of the law then must so long continue until the fulness of the time, and until that seed of the blessing come; not to the end that the law should bring this seed or give righteousness, but that it should civilly restrain the rebellious and obstinate, and shut them up, as it were, in prison; and then spiritually should reprove them of sin, humble them, and terrify them; and, when they are thus humbled and beaten down, it should constrain them to look up to that blessed seed.

We may understand the continuance of the law both according to the letter and also spiritually; according to the letter thus, that the law continueth until the time of grace. "The law and the prophets," saith Christ, "prophesied until John. From the time of John, until this day, the kingdom of heaven suffereth violence, and the violent take it by force." (Matt. xi, 12, 13.) In this time Christ was baptized, and began to preach; at what time also, after the letter, the law, and all the ceremonies of Moses ceased.

Spiritually the law may be thus understood: that it ought not to reign in the conscience any longer than to the appointed time of this blessed seed. When the law sheweth unto me my sin, terrifieth me, and revealeth the law and judgment of God, so that I begin to tremble and to despair, there hath the law his bounds, his time and his end limited, so that he now ceaseth to exercise his tyranny any more. For when he hath done his office sufficiently, he hath revealed the wrath of God, and terrified enough. Here we must say, Now leave off, law; thou hast done enough; thou hast terrified and tormented me enough. "All thy floods have run over me, and thy terrors have troubled me. Lord, turn not away thy face in thy wrath from thy servant; rebuke me not, I beseech thee, in thine anger," etc. (Ps. xlii, 7; lxix, 17; vi, 1.) When these terrors and troubles come, then is the time and the hour of the blessed seed come. Let the law then give place; which indeed is added to reveal and to increase transgressions, and yet no longer, but until that blessed seed be come. When that is come, then let the law leave off, to reveal sin and to terrify any more, and let him deliver up his kingdom to another, that is to say, to the blessed seed, which is Christ: who hath gracious lips, wherewith he accuseth and terrifieth not, but speaketh of far better things than doth the law; namely, of grace, peace, forgiveness of sins, victory over sin, death, the devil, and damnation, gotten by his death and passion, unto all believers.

Paul therefore sheweth by these words: "Until the seed

should come, unto whom the blessing was promised," how long the law should endure literally and spiritually. According to the letter, it ceased after the blessed seed came into the world, taking upon him our flesh, giving the Holy Ghost, and writing a new law in our hearts. But the spiritual time of the law doth not end at once, but continueth fast rooted in the conscience. Therefore it is a hard matter for a man which is exercised with the spiritual use of the law, to see the end of the law. For in these terrors and feeling of sin, the mind cannot conceive this hope, that God is merciful, and that he will forgive sins, for Christ's sake; but it judgeth only that God is angry with sinners, and that he accuseth and condemneth them. If faith come not here to raise up again the troubled and afflicted conscience, or else, according to that saying of Christ, "Where two or three are gathered together in my name," etc. (Matt. xviii, 20) there be some faithful brother at hand that may comfort him, by the word of God, which is so oppressed and beaten down by the law, desperation and death must needs follow. Therefore it is a perilous thing for a man to be alone. "Woe be to him that is alone," (saith the preacher) "for when he falleth, he hath none to raise him up (Eccles. iv, 10). Wherefore they that ordained that cursed monkish and solitary life, gave occasion to many thousands to despair. If a man should separate himself from the company of others for a day or two, to be occupied in prayer (as we read of Christ, that sometime he went aside alone into the mount, and by night continued in prayer), there were no danger therein. (Matt. xxvi, 39; Luke xxii, 41.) But when they constrained men continually to live a solitary life, it was a device of the devil himself. For when a man is tempted and is alone, he is not able to raise up himself, no, not in the least temptation that can be.

VERSE 19. *And it was ordained by angels in the hand of a mediator.*

This is a little digression from his purpose, which he neither declareth nor finisheth, but only toucheth it by the way, and so proceedeth. For he returneth incontinent to his purpose, when he saith, "What, is the law then contrary to the promises of God?" Now, this was the occasion of his digression. He fell into this difference between the law and the gospel: that the law, added to the promises, did differ from the gospel, not only in respect of the time, but also of the author and the efficient cause thereof. For the law was delivered by the angels (Heb. i) but the gospel by the Lord himself. Wherefore the gospel is far more excellent than the law; for the law is the voice of the servants, but the gospel is the voice of the Lord himself. Therefore, to abase and to diminish the authority of the law, and to exalt and magnify the gospel, he saith that the law was a doctrine given to continue but for a small time (for it endured but only until the fulness of the promise, that is to say, until the blessed seed came which fulfilled the promise:) but the gospel was for ever. For all the faithful have had always one and the self-same gospel from the beginning of the world, and by that they were saved. The law, therefore, is far inferior to the gospel, because it was ordained by the angels, which are but servants, and endured but for a short time, whereas the gospel was ordained by the Lord himself, to continue forever. (Heb. i.) For it was promised before all worlds. (Tit. i.)

Moreover, the word of the law was not only ordained by the angels being but servants, but also by another servant far inferior to the angels, namely, by a man; that is (as here he saith), by the hand of a mediator, that is to say, Moses. Now, Christ is not a servant, but the Lord himself. He is not a mediator between God and man, according to the law, as Moses was; but he is a mediator of a better testament. The law therefore was ordained by angels as servants. For Moses and the people heard God speaking in the mount Sinai; that is to say, they heard the angels speaking in the person of God. Therefore Stephen, in the seventh chapter of the Acts, saith, "Ye have received the law by the ministry of angels, and ye have not regarded it." Also the text in the third of Exodus sheweth plainly that the angel appeared unto Moses in a flame of fire, and spake unto him from the midst of the bush.

Paul therefore signifieth that Christ is a mediator of a far better testament than Moses. And here he alludeth to that history in Moses concerning the giving of the law, which saith that Moses led the people out of their tents to meet with God, and that he placed them at the foot of the mount Sinai. There was a heavy and a horrible sight. The whole mount was on a flame of fire. When the people saw this, they began to tremble; for they thought that they should have been suddenly destroyed in this fearful tempest. Because therefore they could not abide the law sounding so horribly out of mount Sinai (for that terrifying voice of the law would have killed the people), they said unto Moses, their mediator, "Come thou hither, and hear what the Lord saith, and speak thou unto us." And he answered, "I myself," saith he, "was a mediator, and one that stood between God and you," etc. By these places it is plain enough that Moses was appointed a mediator between the people and the law speaking.

Wherefore Paul by this history goeth about to declare, that it is impossible that righteousness should come by the law. As if he should say, How can the law justify, seeing the whole people of Israel, being purified and sanctified, yea, and Moses himself, the mediator between God and the people, were afraid, and trembled at the voice of the law? as it is said in the epistle to the Hebrews, "Here was nothing but fear and trembling." But what righteousness and holiness in this, not to be able to bear, yea, not to be able or willing to hear the law, but to fly from it, and so hate it, that it is impossible to hate and abhor anything more in the whole world? As the history most plainly testifieth that the people, when they heard the law, did hate nothing more than the law, and rather wished death, than to hear the law.

So, when sin is discovered, as it were, by certain bright beams which the law striketh into the heart, there is nothing more odious and more intolerable to man than the law is. Here he would rather chuse death, than be constrained to bear these terrors of the law, never so little a time; which is a most certain token that the law justifieth not. For if the law did justify, then, no doubt, men would love it; they would delight and take pleasure in it, and would embrace it with hearty good-will. But where is this good-will? No where; neither in Moses, nor in the whole people, for they were all astonished and fled back. And how doth a man love that which he flieth? Or how delighteth he in that which he deadly hateth?

Wherefore this flight sheweth a deadly hatred of man's heart against the law, and so consequently against God himself, the author of the law. And if there were no other argument to prove that righteousness cometh not by the law, this one history were enough, which Paul setteth out in these few words: "In the hand of a mediator." As though he would say, Do ye not remember that your fathers were so far unable to hear the law, that they had need of Moses to be their mediator? And when he was appointed to that office, they were so far from loving of the law, that they, by a fearful flight, together with their mediator, shewed themselves to hate the same, as the epistle to the Hebrews witnesseth; and if they could, they would have gone even through an iron mountain back again into Egypt. But they were enclosed round about, so that they had no way to escape. Therefore they cry unto Moses: "Speak thou unto us; for if we hear the voice of the Lord our God any more, we shall die" (Exod. xx, 19; Deut. v, 25). Now therefore, if they be not able to hear the law, how should they be able to accomplish it?

Wherefore, if the people that were under the law, were constrained by necessity to have a mediator, it followeth, by an infallible consequence, that the law justifieth them not. What did it then? Even the same thing that Paul saith: "The law is added that sin might abound." (Rom. v, 20.) The law, therefore, was a light and a sun, which struck his beams into the hearts of the children of Israel, whereby it terrified them, and struck into them such a fear of God, that they hated both the law and the author thereof, which is a horrible impiety. Would ye now say that these men were righteous? They are righteous which hear the law, and with a good-will embrace the same and delight therein. But the history of giving the law witnesseth that all men in the whole world, be they never so holy (especially seeing that they which were purified and sanctified could not hear the law), do hate and abhor the law, and wish that the law were not. Therefore it is impossible that men should be justified by the law; nay, it hath a clean contrary effect.

Although Paul (as I have said) doth but only touch this place by the way, and doth not thoroughly weigh it, nor fully finish the same, yet he that shall diligently and attentively read it, may easily understand that he speaketh very well of both mediators; that is to say, of Moses and of Christ, and compareth the one with the other, as hereafter we will declare. If he would have prosecuted this matter more largely, this only place would have ministered unto him an argument and occasion plentiful enough to write a new epistle: and that history also in the nineteenth and twentieth of Exodus, concerning the giving of the law, would minister matter enough to write a new volume, although it were read but slightly, and without affection; albeit it may seem to be very barren to those which know not the true office and use of the law, if it be compared with others holy histories.

Hereby we may see that if all the world had stood at the mount, as the people of Israel did, they would have hated the law, and would have fled from it, as they did. The whole world, therefore, is an enemy to the law, and hateth it most deadly; but the law is holy, righteous, and good, and is the perfect rule of the will of God. How then can he be righteous, which doth not only abhor and detest the law, and fly from it, but, moreover, is an enemy of God, who is the author of the law? And true it is that the flesh can do no otherwise, as Paul witnesseth, Rom. viii. "The wisdom of the flesh is enmity against God: for it is not subject to the law of God, neither indeed can it be." Therefore it is an extreme madness so to hate God and his law, that thou canst not abide to hear it;

and yet, notwithstanding, to affirm that we are made righteous thereby.

Wherefore the sophisters and school-divines are stark blind, and understand nothing at all of this doctrine. They look only upon the outward vizor of the law, thinking that it is accomplished by civil works, and that they are righteous before God, which do the same externally, not considering the true and spiritual effect thereof: which is not to justify, and to quiet and pacify afflicted consciences, but to increase sin, to terrify the conscience, and to engender wrath. They being ignorant of this, do vaunt that man hath a good will, and a right judgment of reason to do the law of God. But whether this be true or no, ask the people of the law, with their mediator, who heard the voice of the law in the mount Sinai. Ask David himself, who, as often as he complaineth in the Psalms that he was cast from the face of God, that he was even in hell, and that he was terrified and oppressed with the greatness of his sin, with the wrath and judgment of God, set not sacrifices, nor yet the law itself, against these mighty tyrants, but was raised up and comforted by the only free mercy of God. Therefore the law justifieth not.

If the law should serve mine affections, that is to say, if it should approve mine hypocrisy, mine opinion and confidence of mine own righteousness: if it should say that, without the mercy of God and faith in Christ, through the help of it alone (as all the world naturally judgeth of the law) I might be justified before God: and, moreover, if it should say that God is pacified and overcome by works, and is bound to reward the doers thereof, that so, having no need of God, I might be a God unto myself, and merit grace by my works, and setting my Saviour Christ apart, might save myself by my own merits: if, I say, the law should thus serve mine affections, then should it be sweet, delectable, and pleasant indeed; so well can reason flatter itself. Notwithstanding this should no longer continue, but until the law should come to his own use and office; then should it appear that reason cannot suffer those bright beams of the law. There some Moses must needs come between as a mediator, and yet notwithstanding without any fruit, as I will declare hereafter.

To this purpose serveth that place in the third chapter of the second epistle to the Corinthians, concerning the covered face of Moses, where Paul, out of the history of the thirty-fourth chapter of Exodus, sheweth that the children of Israel not only did not know, but also could not abide the true and spiritual use of the law; first, for that they could not look unto the end of the law (saith Paul), because of the veil which Moses put upon his face. Again, they could not look upon the face of Moses, being bare and uncovered, for the glory of his countenance. For when Moses went about to talk with them, he covered his face with a veil, without which they could not bear his talk; that is, they could not hear Moses himself, their mediator, unless he had set another mediator between, that is to say, the veil. How, then, should they hear the voice of God, or of an angel, when they could not hear the voice of Moses, being but a man, yea, and also their mediator, except his face had been covered? Therefore, except the blessed seed come to raise up and comfort him which hath heard the law, he perisheth through desperation, in detesting of the law, in hating and blaspheming of God, and daily more and more offending against God. For this fear and confusion of conscience which the law bringeth, the deeper it pierceth, and the longer it continueth, the more it increaseth hatred and blasphemy against God.

This history therefore teacheth what is the power of free-will. The people are stricken with fear, they tremble, and they fly back. Where is now free-will? Where is now that good-will, that good intent, that right judgment of reason, which the Papists do so much brag of? What availeth free-will here in these sanctified and holy men? It can say nothing. It blindeth their reason; it perverteth their will. It receiveth not, it saluteth not, it embraceth not, with joy, the Lord coming, with thundering, lightning, and fire unto the mount Sinai: It cannot hear the voice of the Lord: but contrariwise, it saith, "let not the Lord speak unto us, lest we die." We see then what the strength and power of free-will is in the children of Israel, who, though they were cleansed and sanctified, could not abide the hearing of one syllable or letter of the law. Therefore these high commendations, which the Papists give to their free-will, are nothing else but mere toys and doting dreams.

VERSE 20. *Now, a mediator is not a mediator of one.*

Here he compareth these two mediators together, and that with a marvellous brevity: yet so, notwithstanding, that he satisfieth the attentive reader, who, because this word mediator is general, by-and-by understandeth that Paul speaketh of the mediator generally, and not of Moses only. "A mediator," saith he, "is not a mediator of one only." But this word necessarily comprehendeth two, that is to say, him that is offended and him that is the offender: of whom, the one hath need of intercession, and the other needeth none. Wherefore a mediator is not of one, but of two, and of such two as be at variance between themselves. So Moses, by a general definition, is a mediator, because he doth the office of a mediator between the law and the people, which cannot abide the true and spiritual use of the law. The law therefore must have a new face, and his voice must be changed: that is to say, the voice of the law must be made spiritual, or the law must be made lively in the inward affection, and must put on a vizor or a veil, that it may now become more tolerable, so that the people may be able to hear it by the voice of Moses.

Now, the law being thus covered, speaketh no more in his majesty, but by the mouth of Moses. After this manner it doth not his office any more: that is, it terrifieth not the conscience. And this is the cause that they do neither understand nor regard it: by means whereof they become secure, negligent, and presumptuous hypocrites. And yet, notwithstanding, the one of these two must needs be done: to wit, that either the law must be without his use, and covered with a veil (but then, as I have said, it maketh hypocrites) or else it must be in his true use without the veil, and then it killeth. For man's heart cannot abide the law in his true use without the veil. It behoveth thee therefore, if thou look to the end of the law without the veil, either to lay hold on that blessed seed by faith; that is to say, thou must look beyond the end of the law unto Christ, which is the accomplishment of the law, which may say unto thee, The law hath terrified thee enough, be of good comfort, my son, thy sins are forgiven thee (whereof I will speak more anon); or else surely thou must have Moses for thy mediator, with his veil.

For this cause Paul saith, "A mediator is not a mediator of one." For it could not be that Moses should be a mediator of God alone, for God needeth no mediator. And again, he is not a mediator of the people only, but he doth the office of a mediator between God and the people, which were at variance with God. For it is the office of a mediator to pacify the party that is offended, and to reconcile unto him the party that is the offender. Notwithstanding Moses is such a mediator (as I have said) as doth nothing else but change the voice of the law, and maketh it tolerable, so that the people may abide the hearing thereof, but he giveth no power to accomplish the same. To conclude, he is a mediator of the veil, and therefore he giveth no power to perform the law, but only in the veil. Therefore his disciples, in that he is a mediator of the veil, must always be hypocrites.

But what should have come to pass, think ye, if the law had

been given without Moses, either else before or after Moses, and that there had been no mediator, and, moreover, that the people should neither have been suffered to fly, nor to have a mediator? Here the people, being beaten down with intolerable fear, should either have perished forthwith, or if they should have escaped, there must needs have come some other mediator, which should have set himself between the law and the people, to the end that both the people might be preserved, and the law remain in his force, and also an atonement might be made between the law and the people. Indeed, Moses cometh in the meantime, and is made a mediator; he putteth on a veil and covereth his face; but he cannot deliver men's consciences from the anguish and terror which the law bringeth. Therefore, when the poor sinner, at the hour of death, or in the conflict of conscience, feeleth the wrath and judgment of God for sin, which the law revealeth and increaseth, here, to keep him from desperation, setting Moses aside with his law, he must have a mediator which may say unto him, Although thou be a sinner, yet shalt thou remain; that is, thou shalt not die, although the law, with his wrath and malediction, do still remain.

This mediator is Jesus Christ, which changeth not the voice of the law, nor hideth the same with a veil, as Moses did, nor leadeth me out of the sight of the law; but he setteth himself against the wrath of the law and taketh it away, and satisfieth the law in his own body by himself. And by the gospel he saith unto me, "Indeed the law threateneth unto thee the wrath of God and eternal death; but be not afraid: fly not away, but stand fast. I supply and perform all things for thee; I satisfy the law for thee." This is the mediator which far excelleth Moses, who setteth himself between God being offended, and the offender. The intercession of Moses here profiteth nothing: he hath done his office, and he with his veil is now vanished away. Here the miserable sinner being utterly desperate, or a man now approaching unto death, and God being offended, do encounter together. Therefore there must come a far other mediator than Moses, which may satisfy the law, take away the wrath thereof, and may reconcile unto God which is angry, that poor sinner, miserable and guilty of eternal death.

Of this mediator Paul speaketh briefly when he saith, "a mediator is not a mediator of one." For this word mediator properly signifieth such a one as doth the office of a mediator between the party that is offended and the offender. We are the offenders; God, with his law, is he which is offended: And the offence is such, that God cannot pardon it, neither can we satisfy for the same. Therefore, between God (who of himself is but one) and us, there is wonderful discord. Moreover, God cannot revoke his law, but he will have it observed and kept. And we, which have transgressed the law, cannot fly from the presence of God. Christ therefore hath set himself a mediator between two which are quite contrary, and separate asunder with an infinite and everlasting separation, and hath reconciled them together. And how hath he done this? "He hath put away (as Paul saith in another place) the hand-writing which was against us, which by ordinances (that is, by the law) was contrary unto us, and he hath taken it and fastened it to the cross, and hath spoiled principalities and powers, and hath made a shew of them openly, and hath triumphed over them by himself." Therefore he is not a mediator of one, but of two, utterly disagreeing between themselves.

This is also a place full of power and efficacy to confound the righteousness of the law, and to teach us, that, in the matter of justification, it ought to be utterly removed out of our sight. Also this word [mediator] ministereth sufficient matter to prove that the law justifieth not: for else what need should we have of a mediator? Seeing then that man's nature cannot abide the hearing of the law, much less is it able to accomplish the law, or to agree with the law.

This doctrine (which I do so often repeat, and not without tediousness do still beat into your heads) is the true doctrine of the law, which every Christian ought with all diligence to learn, that he may be able truly to define what the law is, what is the true use and office, what are the limits, what is the power, the time, and the end thereof. For it hath an effect clean contrary to the judgment of all men, which have this pestilent and pernicious opinion naturally rooted in them, that the law justifieth. Therefore I fear lest this doctrine will be defaced and darkened again, when we are dead. For the world must be replenished with horrible darkness and errors, before the latter day come.

Whoso, therefore, is able to understand this, let him understand it, that the law, in true Christian divinity, and in his true and proper definition, doth not justify, but hath quite a contrary effect. For it sheweth and revealeth unto us ourselves; it setteth God before us in his anger; it revealeth God's wrath; it terrifieth us; and it doth not only reveal sin, but also mightily increaseth sin, so that where sin was before but little, now by the law, which bringeth the same to light, it becometh exceeding sinful: so that a man now beginneth to hate the law and fly from it, and with a perfect hatred to abhor God, the maker of the law. This is not to be justified by the law (and that reason itself is compelled to grant) but to commit a double sin against the law: first, not only to have a will so disagreeing from the law that thou canst not hear it, but also to do contrary to that which it commandeth: and secondly, so to hate it that thou wouldst wish it were abolished, together with God himself, who is the author thereof, and absolutely good.

Now, what greater blasphemy, what sin more horrible can be imagined than to hate God, to abhor his law, and not to suffer the hearing thereof, which notwithstanding is good and holy? For the history doth plainly witness that the people of Israel refused to hear that excellent law, those holy and most gracious words, namely, "I am the Lord thy God, which brought thee out of the land of Egypt, and out of the house of bondage. Thou shalt have none other gods, etc. Shewing mercy to thousands, etc. Honor thy father and thy mother, that it may go well with thee, and that thy days may be prolonged upon the earth," etc. (Exodus xx, 2; Deut. iv, 40) and that they had need of a mediator. They could not abide this most excellent, perfect, and divine wisdom, this most gracious, sweet, and comfortable doctrine. "Let not the Lord speak unto us," say they, "lest we die. Speak thou unto us," etc. Doubtless, it is a marvellous thing that a man cannot hear that which is his whole felicity, namely, that he hath a God, yea, and a merciful God, which will shew mercy unto him in many thousands of generations, etc. And, moreover, that he cannot abide that which is his chief safety and defence, namely, "Thou shalt not kill; thou shalt not commit adultery; thou shalt not steal." For by these words the Lord hath defended and fortified the life of man, his wife, his children, and his goods, as it were, with a wall, against the force and violence of the wicked.

The law then can do nothing, saving that by his light it lighteneth the conscience, that it may know sin, death, the judgment, and the wrath of God. Before the law come, I am secure; I feel no sin. But when the law cometh, sin, death, and hell, are revealed unto me. This is not to be made righteous, but guilty, and the enemy of God, to be condemned to death and hell-fire. The principal point therefore of the law in true Christian divinity is to make men not better, but worse; that is to say, it sheweth unto them their sin, that by the knowledge thereof, they may be humbled, terrified, bruised, and broken, and by this means may be driven to seek comfort, and so to come to that blessed seed.

EPISTLE TO THE GALATIANS

VERSE 20. *But God is one.*

God offendeth no man, and therefore needeth no mediator. But we offend God, and therefore we have need of a mediator; not Moses, but Christ, which speaketh far better things for us, etc. Hitherto he hath continued in his digression; now he returneth to his purpose.

VERSE 21. *Is the law then against the promise of God?*

Paul said before that the law justifieth not. Shall we then take away the law? No, not so. For it bringeth with it a certain commodity. What is that? It bringeth men unto the knowledge of themselves. It discovereth and increaseth sin, etc. Here now ariseth another objection: If the law do nothing else but make men worse, in shewing unto them their sin, then is it contrary to the promises of God. For it seemeth that God is but only provoked to anger and offended through the law, and therefore he regardeth not, nor performeth his promises. We Jews have thought the contrary; to wit, that we are restrained and bridled by this external discipline, to the end that God, being provoked thereby, might hasten the performing of his promise, and that by this discipline we might deserve the promise.

Paul answereth: It is nothing so. But contrariwise, if ye have regard to the law the promise is rather hindered; for natural reason offendeth God, which so faithfully promiseth, while it will not hear his good and holy law. For it saith, "Let not the Lord speak unto us," etc. How can it be, then, that God should perform his promise unto those, which not only receive not his law and his discipline, but also with a mortal hatred do shun it, and fly from it? Here, therefore, as I said, riseth this objection: "Is the law against the promise of God?" This objection Paul toucheth by the way, and briefly answereth, saying,

VERSE 21. *God forbid.*

Why so? First, for that God maketh no promise unto us because of our worthiness, our merits, our good works: but for his own goodness and mercy sake in Christ. He saith not to Abraham, All nations shall be blessed in thee, because thou hast kept the law. But when he was uncircumcised, had no law, and was yet an idolater, he said unto him: "Go out of thine own land, etc. I will be thy protector, etc.—Also: "In thy seed shall all nations be blessed" (Gen. xii, 1; xv, 1; xxii, 18). These are absolute and mere promises, which God freely giveth unto Abraham, without any condition, or respect of works, either going before, or coming after.

This maketh especially against the Jews, which think that the promises of God are hindered because of their sins. "God," (saith Paul) "doth not slack his promises because of our sins, or hasten the same for our righteousness and merits. He regardeth neither the one nor the other." Wherefore, although we become more sinful, and are brought into greater contempt and hatred of God by means of the law, yet notwithstanding, God is not moved thereby to differ his promise. For his promise doth not stand upon our weakness, but upon his only goodness and mercy. Therefore, where the Jews say, "The Messias is not yet come, because our sins do hinder his coming," it is a detestable dream. As though God should become unrighteous because of our sins, or made a liar because we are liars. He abideth always just and true: his truth therefore is the only cause that he accomplisheth and performeth his promise.

Moreover, although the law do reveal and increase sin, yet is it not against the promises of God; yea, rather, it confirmeth the promises; for as concerning his proper work and end, it humbleth and prepareth a man (so that he use it rightly) to sigh and seek for mercy. For when sin is revealed to a man, and so increased by the law, then he beginneth to perceive the wickedness and hatred of man's heart against the law, and against God himself, the author of the law. Then he feeleth, indeed, that not only he loveth not God, but also hateth and blasphemeth God, who is full of goodness and mercy, and his law which is just and holy. Then is he constrained to confess that there is no good thing in him. And thus, when he is thrown down and humbled by the law, he acknowledgeth himself to be most miserable and damnable. When the law, therefore, constraineth a man so to acknowledge his own corruption and to confess his sin from the bottom of his heart, then it hath done his office truly, and his time is accomplished and ended: and now is the time of grace, that the blessed seed may come to raise up and comfort him that is so cast down and humbled by the law.

After this manner the law is not against the promises of God. For, first, the promise hangeth not upon the law, but upon the truth and mercy of God only and alone. Secondly, when the law is in his chief end and office, it humbleth a man, and in humbling him, it maketh him to sigh and groan, and to seek the hand and aid of the mediator, and maketh his grace and his mercy exceeding sweet and comfortable (as is said, "thy mercy is sweet," Psalm cix), and his gift precious and inestimable. And by this means it prepareth us, and maketh us apt to apprehend and to receive Christ. For, as the poet saith, *Dulcia non meruit, qui non gustavit amara*: that is,

> Whoso hath not tasted the things that are bitter,
> Is not worthy to taste the things that are sweeter.

There is a common proverb, that hunger is the best cook. Like as, therefore, the dry earth coveteth the rain, even so the law maketh troubled and afflicted souls to thirst after Christ. To such, Christ savoureth sweetly: to them, he is nothing else but joy, consolation, and life And there beginneth Christ and his benefit rightly to be known.

This is, then, the principal use of the law: namely, when a man can so use it, that it may humble him and make him thirst after Christ. And, indeed, Christ requireth thirsty souls, whom he most lovingly and graciously allureth and calleth unto him, when he saith, "Come unto me, all ye that labour and are heavy laden, and I will refresh you" (Matt. xi, 28). He delighteth therefore to water these dry grounds. He poureth not his waters upon fat and rank grounds, or such as are not dry and covet no water. His benefits are inestimable, and therefore he giveth them to none but unto such as have need of them, and earnestly desire them. He preacheth glad tidings to the poor, he giveth drink to the thirsty. "If any thirst" (saith St. John), "let him come unto me," etc. "He healeth the broken hearted," etc. (John vii, 37; Psalm cxlvii, 3). That is, he comforteth those that are bruised and afflicted by the law. Therefore the law is not against the promises of God.

> VERSE 21. *For if there had been a law given which bringeth life, surely righteousness should have been by the law.*

By these words Paul signifieth, that no law of itself is able to quicken or give life, but only killeth. Therefore such works as are done, not only according to the laws and traditions of the Pope, but also according to the very law of God, do not justify a man before God, but make him a sinner: they do not pacify the wrath of God, but they kindle it: they obtain not righteousness, but they hinder it: they quicken not, but they kill and destroy. Therefore, when he saith, "If a law had been given which could have brought life," etc., he teacheth plainly that the law of itself justifieth not, but that it hath a clean contrary effect.

Although these words of Paul be plain enough, yet are they obscure and utterly unknown to the Papists. For if they did understand them indeed, they would not so magnify their free will, their own natural strength, the keeping of the counsels, the works of supererogation, etc. But, lest they should seem to be manifestly wicked, and plain infidels, in denying the words of the apostle of Christ so impudently, they have this pestilent gloss always ready (whereby they pervert the places of Paul concerning the law, which revealeth sin and engendereth wrath, that is to say, the ten commandments), that Paul speaketh only of the ceremonial, and not of the moral law. But Paul speaketh plainly when he saith, "if a law had been given," etc.; and he excepteth no law. Wherefore, this gloss of the Papists is not worth a rush; for the laws of the ceremonies were as well commanded of God, and as strictly kept, as the moral laws. The Jews also kept circumcision as precisely as they did the sabbath day; it is evident enough, therefore, that Paul speaketh of the whole law.

These words of the apostle are sung and said in the Papacy, and in all their churches; and yet, notwithstanding, they both teach and live quite contrary. Paul saith simply that no law was given to quicken and to bring life: but the Papists teach the contrary, and affirm that many and infinite laws are given to quicken and to bring life. Although they say not this in plain words, yet, in very deed, such is their opinion, as their monkish religion doth plainly witness, besides many other laws and traditions of men, their works and merits before grace and after, and innumerable wicked ceremonies and false worshippings, which they have devised of their own heads, and those only have they preached, treading the gospel under their feet, and assuredly promising grace, remission of sins, and life everlasting, to all such as should keep and accomplish the same. This, I say, cannot be denied; for their books which are yet extant, give certain testimony thereof.

But contrariwise, we affirm with Paul that there is no law, whether it be man's law or God's law, that giveth life. Therefore we put as great a difference between the law and righteousness, as is between life and death, between heaven and hell. And the cause that moveth us so to affirm, is that plain and evident place of Paul, where he saith, that the law is not given to justify, to give life, and to save, but only to kill and to destroy, contrary to the opinion of all men: for naturally they can judge no otherwise of the law, but that it is given to work righteousness, and to give life and salvation.

This difference of the offices of the law and of the gospel, keepeth all Christian doctrine in his true and proper use. Also it maketh a faithful man judge over all kinds of life, over the

EPISTLE TO THE GALATIANS

laws and decrees of all men, and over all doctrine whatsoever, and it giveth them power to try all manner of spirits. On the other side, the Papists, because they confound and mingle the law and the gospel together, can teach no certainty touching faith, works, the states and conditions of life, nor of the difference of spirits.

Now, therefore, after that Paul hath prosecuted his confutations and arguments sufficiently, and in good order, he teacheth that the law (if ye consider his true and perfect use) is nothing else but as a certain schoolmaster to lead us unto righteousness. For it humbleth men, it prepareth and maketh them apt to receive the righteousness of Christ, when it doth his own proper work and office, that is, when it maketh them guilty, terrifieth and bringeth them to the knowledge of sin, wrath, death, and hell. For when it hath done this, the opinion of man's own righteousness and holiness vanisheth away, and Christ with his benefits beginneth to wax sweet unto him. Wherefore the law is not against the promises of God, but rather confirmeth them. True it is, that it doth not accomplish the promise, nor bring righteousness: notwithstanding it humbleth us with his exercise and office, and so maketh us more thirsty, and more apt to receive the benefit of Christ. Therefore, saith he, if any law had been given which might have brought righteousness, and through righteousness life (for no man can obtain life, except first he be righteous), then, indeed, righteousness should come by the law. Moreover, if there were any state of life, any work, any religion, whereby a man might obtain remission of sins, righteousness, and life, then should these things indeed justify and give life. But this is impossible: for

VERSE 22. *The scripture hath concluded all men under sin.*

Where? First, in the promises themselves, as touching Christ, as Genesis iii, "the seed of the woman shall break the head of the serpent." And Gen. xxii, "in thy seed," etc. Wheresoever, then, is any promise in the scripture made unto the fathers concerning Christ, there the blessing is promised, that is, righteousness, salvation, and eternal life. Therefore, by the contrary it is evident that they which must receive the blessing are subject to the curse, that is to say, sin and eternal death: for else to what end was the blessing promised?

Secondly, the scripture shutteth men under sin, and under the curse, especially by the law, because it is his peculiar office to reveal sin and engender wrath, as we have declared throughout this epistle, but chiefly by this sentence of Paul: "Whosoever are of the works of the law, are under the curse" (Gal. iii, 10). Also by that place which the apostle allegeth out of the twenty-seventh chapter of Deuteronomy: "cursed is every one that abideth not in all the words of this law to do them," etc. For these sentences in plain words do shut under sin and under the curse, not only those which sin manifestly against the law, or do not outwardly accomplish the law; but also those which are under the law, and with all endeavour go about to perform the same; and such were the Jews, as before I have said. Much more, then, doth the same place of Paul shut up under sin and under the curse, all monks, friars, hermits, Carthusians, and such-like, with their professions, rules, and religions, to the which they attributed such holiness, that when a man had once made a vow of his profession, if he died by-and-by, they dreamed that he went straight to heaven. But here ye hear plainly that the scripture shutteth all under sin. Therefore, neither the vow nor the religion of the Carthusian, be it never so angelical, is righteousness before God: for the scripture hath shut all under sin, all are accursed and damned. Who pronounceth this sentence? the scripture. And where? First, by this promise, "the seed of the woman shall bruise the serpent's head;" "in thee shall be blessed," etc., and such-like places: moreover, by the whole law, whereof the principal office is to make men guilty of sin. Therefore, no monk, no Carthusian, no Celestine, bruiseth the serpent's head, but they abide bruised and broken under the head of the serpent, that is, under the power of the devil. Who will believe this?

Briefly, whatsoever is without Christ and his promise, whether it be the law of God or the law of man, the ceremonial or the moral law, without all exception, is shut under sin: for the scripture shutteth all under sin. Now, he that saith "all," excepteth nothing. Therefore we conclude, with Paul, that the policies and laws of all nations, be they never so good and necessary, with all ceremonies and religions, without faith in Christ, are and abide under sin, death, and eternal damnation, except faith in Jesus Christ go withal, or rather before, as followeth in the text. Of this matter we have spoken largely before.

Wherefore this is a true proposition: Only faith justifieth, without works (which, notwithstanding, our adversaries can by no means abide): for Paul here strongly concludeth that the law doth not quicken or give life, because it is not given to that end. If, then, the law do not justify and give life, much less do works justify. For when Paul saith that the law giveth not life, is meaning is, that works also do not give life. For it is more to say that the law quickeneth and giveth life, than to say that works do quicken and give life. If, then, the law itself, being fulfilled (although it be impossible that it should be accomplished), do not justify, much less do works justify. I conclude therefore that faith only justifieth and bringeth life, without works. Paul cannot suffer this addition: faith joined with works justifieth; but he proceedeth simply by the negative (Romans iii), as he doth also before in the second chapter: "therefore by the works of the law (saith he) shall no flesh be justified." And again in this place: "the law is not given to bring life."

VERSE 22. *That the promise by the faith of Jesus Christ should be given to them that believe.*

He said before, that the scripture hath shut all under sin. What! for ever? No; but until the promise should be given. Now, the promise is the inheritance itself, or the blessing promised to Abraham; to wit, the deliverance from the law, sin, death, and the devil, and a free giving of grace, righteousness, salvation, and eternal life. This promise, saith he, is not obtained by any merit, by any law, or by any work, but it is given. To whom? To those that believe. In whom? In Jesus Christ, who is the blessed seed, which hath redeemed all believers from the curse, that they might receive the blessing. These words be not obscure, but plain enough: notwithstanding we must mark them diligently, and weigh well the force and weight thereof. For if all be shut under sin, it followeth that all nations are accursed and are destitute of the grace of God: also that they are under the wrath of God, and the power of the devil, and that no man can be delivered from them by any other means than by faith in Jesus Christ. With these words, therefore, Paul inveigheth mightily against the fantastical opinions of the Papists and all justiciaries touching the law and works, when he saith, "that the promise by faith in Jesus Christ might be given to all believers."

Now, how we should answer to those sentences which speak of works and rewards, I have sufficiently declared before. And matter requireth not now, that we should speak any thing of works. For we have not here taken in hand to entreat of works, but of justification; to wit, that it is not obtained by the law and works, since all things are shut under sin and under the curse: but by faith in Christ. When we are out of the matter of justification, we cannot sufficiently praise and magnify those works which are commanded of God. For who can sufficiently commend and set forth the profit and fruit of only one work, which a Christian doth through faith and in faith? Indeed it is more precious than heaven or earth. The whole world, therefore, is not able to give a worthy recompence to such a good work. Yea, the world hath not the grace to magnify the holy works of the faithful as they are worthy, and much less to reward them: for it seeth them not, or if it do, it esteemeth them not as good works, but as most wicked and detestable crimes, and riddeth the world of those which are the doers thereof, as most pestilent plagues to mankind.

So Christ, the Saviour of the world, for a recompence of his incomprehensible and inestimable benefits, was put to the most ignominious death of the cross. The apostles also, bringing the word of grace and eternal life into the world, were counted the off-scouring and outcasts of the whole world. This is the goodly reward which the world giveth for so great and unspeakable benefits. But works done without faith, although they have never so goodly a shew of holiness, are under the curse. Wherefore, so far off it is, that doers thereof should deserve grace, righteousness, and eternal life, that rather they heap sin upon sin. After this manner the Pope, that child of perdition, and all that follow him, do work. So work all merit-mongers and heretics which are fallen from faith.

Verse 23. *But before faith came.*

He proceedeth in declaring the profit and necessity of the law. He said before, that the law was added for transgressions: not that it was the principal purpose of God to make a law that should bring death and damnation, as he saith, Rom. vii, "Was that which was good," saith he, "made death unto me? God forbid." For the law is a word that sheweth life, and driveth men unto it. Therefore, it is not only given as a minister of death, but the principal use and end thereof is to reveal death, that so it might be seen and known how horrible sin is. Notwithstanding it doth not so reveal death, as though it tended to no other end but to kill and to destroy; but to this end it revealeth death, that when men are terrified, cast down, and humbled, they should fear God. And this doth the twentieth chapter of Exodus declare: "Fear not," (saith Moses) "for God is come to prove you, and that his fear may be before you, that ye sin not" (Exodus xx, 20). The office, therefore, of the law is to kill, and yet so that God may revive and quicken again. The law, then, is not given only to kill: but because man is proud,

EPISTLE TO THE GALATIANS

and dreameth that he is wise, righteous, and holy: therefore it is necessary he should be humbled by the law, that so this beast, the opinion of righteousness, I say, might be slain: for otherwise no man can obtain life.

Albeit then that the law killeth, yet God useth this effect of the law, this death, I mean, to a good end: that is, to bring life. For God, seeing that this universal plague of the whole world, to wit, man's opinion of his own righteousness, his hypocrisy, and confidence in his own holiness, could not be beaten down by any other means, he would that it should be slain by the law: not for ever; but that, when it is once slain, man might be raised up again, above and beyond the law, and there might hear this voice, Fear not: I have not given the law, and killed thee by the law, that thou shouldst abide in this death; but that thou shouldst fear me and live. For the presuming of good works and righteousness standeth not with the fear of God; and where the fear of God is not, there can be no thirsting for grace or life. God must therefore have a strong hammer, or a mighty maul, to break the rocks, and a hot burning fire in the midst of heaven to overthrow the mountains; that is to say, to destroy this furious and obstinate beast (this presumption, I say); that when a man, by this bruising and breaking, is brought to nothing, he should despair of his own strength, righteousness, and holiness; and being thus thoroughly terrified, should thirst after mercy and remission of sins.

VERSE 23. *But before faith came, we were under the law, shut up unto the faith which should afterwards be revealed.*

This is to say, before the time of the gospel and grace came, the office of the law was, that we should be shut up, and kept under the same, as it were in prison. This is a goodly and a fit similitude, shewing the effect of the law, and how righteous it maketh men; therefore it is diligently to be weighed. No thief, no murderer, no adulterer, or other malefactor, loveth the chains and fetters, the dark and loathsome prison wherein he lieth fast bound; but rather, if he could, he would beat and break into powder the prison, with his irons and fetters. Indeed, while he is in prison, he refraineth from doing of evil; but not of a good will, or for righteousness' sake, but because the prison restraineth him, that he cannot do it: and now, being fast fettered, he hateth not his theft and his murder (yea, he is sorry, with all his heart, that he cannot rob and steal, cut and slay), but he hateth the prison, and, if he could cseape, he would rob and kill, as he did before.

The Law Shutteth Men Under Sin Two Ways, Civilly and Spiritually.

Such is the force of the law, and the righteousness that cometh of the law, compelling us to be outwardly good, when it threateneth death, or any other punishment, to the trangressors thereof. Here we obey the law, indeed, but for fear of punishment; that is, unwillingly, and with great indignation. But what righteousness is this, when we abstain from evil, for fear of punishment? Wherefore, this righteousness of works is indeed nothing else but to love sin and to hate righteousness, to detest God with his law, and to love and reverence that which is most horrible and abominable. For look, how heartily the thief loveth the prison and hateth his theft; so gladly do we obey the law, in accomplishing that which it commandeth, and avoiding that which it forbiddeth.

Notwithstanding, this fruit and this profit the law bringeth, although men's hearts remain never so wicked: that, first, outwardly and civilly, after a sort, it restraineth thieves, murderers, and other malefactors; for, if they did not see and understand that sin is punished in this life, by imprisonment, by the gallows, by the sword, and such-like, and after this life with eternal damnation and hell-fire, no magistrate should be able to bridle the fury and rage of men by any laws, bonds, or chains.—But the threatenings of the law strike a terror into the hearts of the wicked, whereby they are bridled after a sort, that they run not headlong, as otherwise they would do, into all kinds of wickedness. Notwithstanding, they would rather that there were no law, no punishment, no hell, and, finally, no God. If God had no hell, or did not punish the wicked, he should be loved and praised of men. But, because he punisheth the wicked, and all are wicked; therefore, inasmuch as they are shut under the law, they can do no otherwise but mortally hate and blaspheme God.

Furthermore, the law shutteth men under sin, not only civilly, but also spiritually; that is to say, the law is also a spiritual prison, and a very hell. For when it revealeth sin, threateneth death, and the eternal wrath of God, a man cannot avoid it, nor find any comfort. For it is not in the power of man to shake off these horrible terrors which the law stirreth up in the conscience, or any other anguish or bitterness of spirit. Hereof come those lamentable complaints of the saints, which are every where in the Psalms: "In hell, who shall confess thee," etc.? Psalm vi, 5. For then is a man shut up in prison; out of the which he cannot escape, nor seeth how he may be delivered out of these bonds, that is to say, these horrible terrors.

Thus the law is a prison, both civilly and spiritually. For, first, it restraineth and shutteth up the wicked, that they run not headlong, according to their own lust, into all kinds of mischief. Again, it sheweth unto us spiritually our sin, terrifieth and humbleth us, that, when we are so terrified and humbled, we may learn to know our own misery and condemnation. And this is the true and proper use of the law, so that it be not perpetual. For this shutting up and holding under the law, must endure no longer, but until faith come; and when faith cometh, then must this spiritual prison have his end.

Here again we see, that although the law and the gospel be separate far asunder, yet, as touching the inward affections, they are very nearly joined the one to the other. This Paul sheweth when he saith, "we were kept under the law, and shut up unto the faith which should be revealed unto us." Wherefore it is not enough that we are shut under the law: for if nothing else should follow, we should be driven to desperation, and die in our sins. But Paul addeth, moreover, that we are shut up, and kept under a schoolmaster (which is the law) not for ever, but to bring us unto Christ, who is the end of the law. Therefore, this terrifying, this humbling, and this shutting up must not always continue, but only until faith be revealed; that is, it shall so long continue, as shall be for our profit and our salvation: so that when we are cast down and humbled by the law, then grace, remission of sins, deliverance from the law, sin, and death, may become sweet unto us: which are not obtained by works, but are received by faith alone.

He, which in time of temptation, can join these two things together, so repugnant and contrary; that is to say, which, when he is thoroughly terrified and cast down by the law, doth know that the end of the law, and the beginning of grace, or of faith to be revealed, is now come, useth the law rightly. All the wicked are utterly ignorant of this knowledge and this cunning. Cain knew it not, when he was shut up in the prison of the law; that is, he felt no terror, although he had now killed his brother; but dissembled the matter craftily, and thought that God was ignorant thereof. "Am I my brother's keeper?" saith he: but when he heard this word: "What hast thou done? Behold, the voice of the blood of thy brother crieth unto me from the earth" (Gen. iv, 10), he began to feel this prison indeed. What did he then? He remained still shut up in prison. He joined not the gospel with the law, but said: "My punishment is greater than I can bear" (Gen. iv, 13). He only respected the prison, not considering that his sin was revealed unto him to this end, that he should fly unto God for mercy and pardon. Therefore he despaired and denied God. He believed not that he was shut up to this end, that grace and faith might be revealed unto him: but only that he should still remain in the prison of the law.

These words, "to be kept under, and to be shut up," are not vain and unprofitable, but most true, and of great importance. This keeping under, and this prison signifieth the true and spiritual terrors, whereby the conscience is so shut up, that in the wide world it can find no place where it may be in safety. Yea, as long as these terrors endure, the conscience feeleth such anguish and sorrow, that it thinketh heaven and earth, yea, if they were ten times more wide and large than they are, to be straiter and narrower than a mouse-hole. Here is a man utterly destitute of all wisdom, strength, righteousness, counsel, and succour. For the conscience is a marvellous tender thing, and therefore when it is so shut up under the prison of the law, it seeth no way how to get out; and this straitness seemeth daily so to increase, as though it would never have an end. For then doth it feel the wrath of God, which is infinite and inestimable, whose hand it cannot escape, as the 139th Psalm witnesseth: "Whither shall I fly from thy presence," etc.

Like as therefore this worldly prison or shutting up is a bodily affliction, and he that is so shut up can have no use of his body; even so the trouble and anguish of mind is a spiritual prison, and he that is shut up in this prison cannot enjoy quietness of heart and peace of conscience. And yet it is not so for ever (as reason judgeth, when it feeleth this prison), but until faith be revealed. The silly conscience, therefore, must be raised up, and comforted after this sort: Brother, thou art indeed shut up; but persuade thyself that this is not done to the end that thou shouldst remain in this prison forever. For it is written, "that we are shut up unto the faith which shall be revealed." Thou art then afflicted in this prison, not to thy destruction, but that thou mayest be refreshed by the blessed seed. Thou art killed by the law, that through Christ thou mayest be quickened again, and restored to life. Despair not, therefore, as Cain, Saul, and Judas did, who being thus shut up, looked no farther but to their dark prison, and there still remained: therefore they despaired. But thou must take another way in these terrors of conscience than they did; that is, thou must know that it is well done, and good for thee to be so shut up, confounded, and brought to nothing. Use, therefore, this shutting up rightly, and as thou shouldst do: that is, to the end that, when the law hath done his office, faith may be revealed. For God doth not therefore afflict thee, that thou shouldst still remain in this affliction. He will not kill thee, that thou shouldst abide in death. "I will not the death of a sinner," etc. (saith he, by the prophet Ezekiel, chap. xxxiii, 11). But he will afflict thee, that so thou mayest be humbled, and know that thou hast need of mercy, and the benefit of Christ.

This holding in prison, then, under the law, must not always endure, but must only continue to the coming or revealing of faith; which this sweet verse of the Psalm doth teach us: "the Lord delighteth in those that fear him" (Psalm cxlvii, 11): that is to say, which are in prison under the law. But by-and-by after he addeth, "and in those that attend upon his mercy." Therefore, we must join these two things together, which, indeed, are as contrary the one to the other as may be. For what can be more contrary than to hate and abhor the wrath of God; and, again, to trust in his goodness and mercy? The one is hell, the other is heaven, and yet they must be nearly joined together in the heart. By speculation and naked knowledge a man may easily join them together; but by experience and inward practice so to do, of all things it is the hardest; which I myself have often proved by my own experience. Of this matter the Papists and sectaries know nothing at all. Therefore, these words of Paul are to them obscure and altogether unknown: and when the law revealeth unto them their sin, accuseth and terrifieth them, they can find no counsel, no rest, no help, or succour; but fall to desperation, as Cain and Saul did.

Seeing the law therefore (as is said) is our tormentor and our prison, certain it is that we cannot love it, but hate it. He, therefore, that saith he loveth the law, is a liar, and knoweth not what he saith. A thief and a robber should shew himself to be stark mad, that would love the prison, the fetters and chains. Seeing, then, the law shutteth us up, and holdeth us in prison, it cannot be but we must needs be extreme enemies to the law. To conclude, so well we love the law and the righteousness thereof, as a murderer loveth the dark prison, the strait bonds and irons. How then should the law justify us?

VERSE 23. *And shut up under the faith which should after be revealed.*

This Paul speaketh in respect of the fulness of the time wherein Christ came. But we must apply it, not only to that time, but also to the inward man; for that which is done is a history, and according to the time wherein Christ came, abolishing the law, and bringing liberty and eternal life to light, is always done spirtually in every Christian, in whom is found continually, some while the time of the law, and some while the time of grace. For the Christian man hath a body, in whose members (as Paul saith in another place) sin dwelleth and warreth. Now, I understand sin to be, not only the deed or the work, but also the root and the tree, together with the fruits, as the scripture useth to speak of sin; which is yet not only rooted in the baptized flesh of every Christian, but also is at deadly war within it, and holdeth it captive: if not to give consent unto it, or to accomplish the work, yet doth it force him mightily thereunto. For albeit a Christian man do not fall into outward and gross sins, as murder, adultery, theft, and such-like, yet is he not free from impatiency, murmuring, hating, and blaspheming of God; which sins, to reason and the carnal man, are altogether unknown. These things constrain him, yea, sore against his will, to detest the law; they compel him to fly from the presence of God; they compel him to hate and blaspheme God. For as carnal lust is strong in a young man, in a man of full age the desire and love of glory, and in an old man covetousness; even so in a holy and a faithful man impatience, murmuring, hatred and blasphemy against God do mightily prevail. Examples hereof there are many in the Psalm, in Job, in Jeremiah, and throughout the whole scripture. Paul, therefore, describing and setting forth this spiritual warfare, useth very vehement words, and fit for the purpose, as of fighting, rebelling, holding and leading captive, etc.

Both these times, then (of the law and the gospel, I mean), are in a Christian, as touching the affections and inward man. The time of the law is when the law exerciseth me, tormenteth me with heaviness of heart, oppresseth me, bringeth me to the knowledge of sin, and increaseth the same. Here the law is in his true use and perfect work: which a Christian oftentimes feeleth as long as he liveth. So there was given unto Paul a prick in the flesh, that is, "the angel of Satan, to buffet him" (2 Cor. xii, 7). He would gladly have felt every moment the joy of conscience, the laughter of the heart, and the sweet taste of eternal life. Again, he would gladly have been delivered from all trouble and anguish of spirit, and therefore he desired that this temptation might be taken from him. Notwithstanding this was not done, but the Lord said unto him: "My grace is sufficient for thee: for my power is made perfect through weakness" (2 Cor. xii, 9). This battle doth every Christian feel. To speak of myself, there are many hours in the which I chide and contend with God, and impatiently resist him. The wrath and judgment of God displeaseth me; and again, my impatience, my murmuring, and such-like sins, do displease him. And this is the time of the law, under the which a Christian man continually liveth, as touching the flesh. "For the flesh lusteth continually against the spirit, and the spirit against the flesh" (Gal. v, 17), but in some more, and in some less.

The time of grace is, when the heart is raised up again by the promise of the free mercy of God, and saith, "Why art thou heavy, O my soul, and why dost thou trouble me" (Psalm xliii, 5). Dost thou see nothing but the law, sin, terror, heaviness, desperation, death, hell, and the devil? Is there not also grace, remission of sins, righteousness, consolation, joy, peace, life, heaven, Christ, and God? Trouble me no more, O my soul. What is the law, what is sin, what are all evils in comparison of these things? Trust in God, who hath not spared his own dear Son, but hath given him to the death of the cross for thy sins. This is then to be shut up under the law after the flesh; not for ever, but till Christ be revealed. Therefore, when thou art beaten down, tormented, and afflicted by the law, then say: Lady Law, thou art not alone, neither are thou all things; but, besides thee, there are yet other things much greater and better than thou art; namely, grace, faith, and blessing. This grace, this faith, and this blessing, do not accuse me, terrify me, condemn me; but they comfort me, they bid me trust in the Lord, and promise unto me victory and salvation in Christ. There is no cause, therefore, why I should despair.

He that is skillful in this art and this cunning, may indeed be called a right divine. The fantastical spirits and their disciples at this day, which continually brag of the spirit, do persuade themselves that they are very expert and cunning therein. But I, and such as I am, have scarcely learned the first principles thereof. It is learned, indeed; but, so long as the flesh and sin do endure, it can never be perfectly learned, and as it should be. So, then, a Christian is divided into two times. In that he is flesh, he is under the law; in that he is spirit, he is under grace. Concupiscence, covetousness, ambition, and pride, do always cleave to the flesh; also, ignorance, contempt of God, impatience, murmuring and grudging against God, because he hindereth and breaketh off our counsels, our devices, and enterprises, and because he speedily punisheth not such as are wicked, rebellious, and contemptuous persons, etc. Such manner of sins are rooted in the flesh of the faithful. Wherefore, if thou behold nothing but the flesh, thou shalt abide always under the time of the law. But these days must be shortened, or else no flesh should be saved. The law must have his time appointed, wherein it must have his end. The time of the law, therefore, is not perpetual, but hath his end, which end is Jesus Christ. But the time of grace is eternal. For "Christ being once dead, dieth no more" (Romans vi, 9). He is eternal: therefore the time of grace is also eternal.

Such notable sentences in Paul, we may not lightly pass over, as the Papists and sectaries are wont to do; for they contain words of life, which do wonderfully comfort and confirm afflicted consciences, and they which know and understand them well, can judge of faith: they can discern a true fear from a false fear; they can judge of all inward affections of the heart, and discern all spirits. The fear of God is a holy and a precious thing, but it must not always continue. Indeed it ought to be always in a Christian, because sin is always in him; but it must not be alone, for then is it the fear of Cain, Saul, and Judas, that is to say, a servile and a desperate fear. A Christian, therefore, must vanquish fear, by faith in the word of grace; he must turn away his eyes from the time of the law, and look unto Christ and unto faith which is to be revealed. Here beginneth fear to be sweet unto us, and maketh us to delight in God. For if a man do only behold the law and sin, setting faith aside, he shall never be able to put away fear, but shall at length fall to desperation..

Thus doth Paul very well distinguish the time of the law and grace. Let us also learn rightly to distinguish the time of them both, not in words, but in the inward affections: which is a very hard matter. For albeit these two things are separate far asunder, yet are they most nearly joined together in one heart. Nothing is joined more nearly together than fear and trust, than the law and the gospel, than sin and grace; for they are so united together, that the one is swallowed up of the other. Wherefore, there is no conjunction like unto this.

At this place, "Wherefore then serveth the law?" Paul beginneth to dispute of the law; also of the use and the abuse thereof; taking occasion of that which before he had affirmed, that the faithful do obtain righteousness by grace only, and by the promise, and not by the law. Upon that disputation rose this question: Wherefore then serveth the law? For reason, hearing that righteousness or the blessing is obtained by grace and by the promise, by-and-by inferreth: then the law profiteth nothing. Wherefore the doctrine of the law must be diligently considered, that we may know what and how we ought to judge thereof, lest that either we reject the same altogether, as the fantastical spirits do (which in the year 1525, stirring up the rustical people to sedition, said, that the liberty of the gospel giveth freedom to all men from all manner of laws) : or else lest we should attribute the force of justification to the law. For both sorts do offend against the law; the one on the right hand, which will be justified by the law, and the other on the left hand, which will be clean delivered from the law. We must therefore keep the highway, so that we neither reject the law, nor attribute more unto it than we ought to do.

That which I have before so often repeated, concerning both the uses of the law, namely, the civil and the spiritual use, do sufficiently declare that the law is not given for the righteous; but (as Paul saith in another place) for the unrighteous and rebellious. Now, of the unrighteous there are two sorts, that is to say, they which are to be justified, and they which are not to be justified. They which are not to be justified must be bridled by the civil use of the law; for they must be bound with the bonds of the law, as savage and untamed beasts are bound with cords and chains. This use of the law hath no end: and of this Paul here speaketh nothing. But they that are to be justified, are exercised with the spiritual use of the law for a time; for it doth not always continue, as the civil use of the law doth, but it looketh to faith which is to be revealed, and when Christ cometh it shall have its end. Hereby we may plainly see that all the sentences wherein Paul entreateth of the spiritual use of the law, must be understood of those which are to be justified, and not of those which are justified already. For they which are justified already, inasmuch as they abide in Christ, are far above all law. The law then must be laid upon those that are to be justified, that they may be shut up in the prison thereof, until the righteousness of faith come: not that they attain this righteousness through the law (for that were not to use the law rightly, but to abuse it) : but that when they are cast down and humbled by the law, they should fly unto Christ, "who is the end of the law for righteousness, to every one that beliveth" (Romans x, 4).

Now, the abusers of the law are, first of all, the justiciaries and hypocrites, which dream that men are justified by the law. For that use of the law doth not exercise and drive a man to faith which is to be revealed, but it maketh careless and arrogant hypocrites, swelling and presuming of the righteousness of the law, and hindereth the righteousness of faith. Secondly, they abuse the law, which will utterly exempt a Christian man from the law, as the brainsick Anabaptists went about to do: which was the occasion that they raised up that sedition of the rustical people. Of this sort there are very many also at this day which profess the gospel with us; who being delivered from the tyranny of the Pope by the doctrine of the gospel, do dream that the Christian liberty is a dissolute and a carnal liberty to do whatsoever they list. These (as Peter saith, 1 Peter ii, 16), have the liberty of the spirit as a cloak of maliciousness, through which the name of God and the gospel of Christ is slandered every where, and therefore they shall once suffer worthy punishment for this their ungodliness. Thirdly, such do also abuse the law, who feeling the terrors thereof, do not understand that such terrors ought no longer continue, but unto Christ, this abuse in them is the cause that they fall to desperation; as in the hypocrites it is the cause of arrogancy and presumption.

Contrariwise, the true use of the law can never be esteemed and magnified as it is worthy, namely, that when the conscience shut up under the law despaireth not, but being instructed by the wisdom of the Holy Ghost, concludeth with itself after this sort: I am indeed shut up as a prisoner under the law, but not for ever; yea, this shutting up shall turn to my great profit. How so? Because that I, being thus shut up, shall be driven to sigh and seek the hand of a helper, etc. After this manner the law is an enforcer, which by compulsion bringeth the hungry unto Christ, that he may satisfy them with his good things. Wherefore the true office of the law is to shew unto us our sins, to make us guilty, to humble us, to kill us, and to bring us down to hell, and finally, to take from us all help, all succour, all comfort; but yet altogether to this end, that we may be justified, exalted, quickened to life, carried up into heaven, and obtain all good things. Therefore it doth not only kill, but it killeth that we may live.

VERSE 24. *Wherefore the law was our schoolmaster to bring us to Christ.*

Here again he joineth the law and the gospel together (which are separate so far asunder) as touching the affections and inward man, when he saith, The law is a schoolmaster to Christ. This similitude also of the schoolmaster is worthy to be noted. Although a schoolmaster be very profitable and necessary to instruct and to bring up children, yet shew me one child or scholar which loveth his master. What love and obedience the Jews shewed unto their Moses, it appeareth in that every hour (as the history witnesseth) they would with all their hearts have stoned him to death (Ex. xvii, 4). It is not possible, therefore, that the scholar should love his master; for how can he love him which keepeth him in prison, that is to say, which suffereth him not to do that which gladly he would? And if he do any thing against his commandment, by-and-by he is rebuked and chastised, yea, and is constrained, moreover, to kiss the rod when he is beaten. Is not this (I pray you) a goodly righteousness and obedience of the scholar, that he obeyeth his master so severely threatening and so sharply correcting him, and kisseth the rod? But doth he this with a good will? As soon as his master hath turned his back, he breaketh the rod, or casteth it into the fire. And if he had any power over his master, he would not suffer himself to be beaten of him, but rather he would beat him; and yet, notwithstanding, the schoolmaster is very necessary for the child, to instruct and to chastise him: otherwise the child, without his discipline, instruction, and good education, should be utterly lost.

The schoolmaster, therefore, is appointed for the child to teach him, to bring him up, and to keep him, as it were, in prison. But to what end, or how long? Is it to the end that this strait and sharp dealing of the schoolmaster should always continue, or that the child should remain in continual bondage? Not so, but only for a time, that this obedience, this prison and correction might turn to the profit of the child, that when the time cometh he might be his father's heir; for it is not the father's will that his son should be always subject to the schoolmaster, and always beaten with rods: but that by his instruction and discipline he might be made able and meet to be his father's successor.

Even so the law (saith Paul) is nothing else but a schoolmaster: not for ever, but until it have brought us to Christ: as in other words he said also before: "The law was given for transgressions until the blessed seed should come" Also, "the scripture hath shut all under sin," etc. Again: "We were kept under, and shut up unto faith which should after be revealed." Wherefore the law is not only a schoolmaster, but it is a schoolmaster to bring us unto Christ. For what a schoolmaster were he which would always torment and beat the child, and teach him nothing at all? And yet such schoolmasters there were, in time past, when schools were nothing else but a prison and a very hell, and the schoolmasters cruel tyrants and very butchers. The children were always beaten; they learned with continual pain and travail, and yet few of them came to any proof. The law is not such a schoolmaster. For it doth not always terrify and torment (as the foolish schoolmaster beateth his scholars and teacheth them nothing); but with his rods he driveth us unto Christ, like as a good schoolmaster instructeth and exerciseth his scholars in reading writing, to the end that they may come to the knowledge of good letters and other profitable things, that afterwards they have have a delight in doing of that, which before, when they were constrained thereunto, they did against their wills.

By this goodly similitude Paul sheweth what is the true use of the law, namely, that it justifieth not hypocrites, for they remain without Christ in their presumption and security: and contrariwise, that it leaveth not in death and damnation those that are of a contrite heart (so that they use it as Paul teacheth) but driveth them unto Christ. But they which in these terrors continue still in their wickedness, and do not apprehend Christ by faith, do fall at length into desperation. Paul, therefore in this allegory of the schoolmaster, most lively expresseth the true use of the law. For like as the schoolmaster reproveth his scholars, he grieveth them, and maketh them heavy, and yet not to the end that this bondage should always continue, but that it should cease when the children are well brought up and instructed accordingly, and that afterwards, without any constraint of the schoolmaster, they should cheerfully enjoy their liberty and their father's goods: even so they which are vexed and oppressed with the law, do know that these terrors and vexations shall not always continue, but that thereby they are prepared to come unto Christ, which is to be revealed and to receive the liberty of the spirit, etc.

VERSE 24. *That we may be made righteous by faith.*

The law is not a schoolmaster to bring us unto another lawgiver which requireth good works, but unto Christ our justifier and Saviour, that by faith in him we might be justified, and not by works. But when a man feeleth the force and strength of the law, he doth not understand nor believe this; therefore he saith: I have lived wickedly, for I have transgressed all the commandments of God, and therefore I am guilty of eternal death. If God would prolong my life certain years, or at least certain months, I would amend my life and live holily hereafter. Here, of the true use of the law he maketh an abuse. Reason being overtaken in these terrors and straits, is bold to promise unto God the fulfilling of all the works of the whole law. And hereof came so many sects, and swarms of monks and religious hypocrites, so many ceremonies, and so many works, devised to deserve grace and remission of sins. And they which devised these things, thought that the law was a schoolmaster to lead them, not unto Christ, but to a new law, or unto Christ as a lawgiver, and not as one that hath abolished the law.

But the true use of the law is to teach me that I am brought to the knowledge of my sin, and humbled, that so I may come unto Christ, and may be justified by faith. But faith is neither law nor work, but an assured confidence which apprehendeth Christ, "who is the end of the law" (Romans x). And how? Not that he hath abolished the old law and given a new: or that he is a judge which must be pacified by works, as the Papists have taught; but he is the end of the law to all those that believe: that is to say, every one that believeth in him is righteous, and the law shall never accuse him. The law then is good, holy, and just, so that a man use it as he should do. Now, they that abuse the law are, first, the hypocrites which attribute unto the law a power to justify: and, secondly, they which do despair, not knowing that the law is a schoolmaster to lead men unto Christ: that is to say, that the law humbleth them, not to their destruction, but to their salvation. For God woundeth that he may heal again: he killeth that he may quicken again.

Now, Paul, as before I have said, speaketh of those which are to be justified, and not of those which are justified already. Therefore, when thou goest about to reason as concerning the law, thou must take the matter of the law, or that whereupon the law worketh, namely, the sinner and the wicked person, whom the law justifieth not, but setteth sin before his eyes, casteth him down, and bringeth him to the knowledge of himself: It sheweth unto him hell, the wrath, and the judgment of God. This is indeed the proper office of the law. Then followeth the use of this office: to wit, that the sinner may know that the law doth not reveal unto him his sin, and thus humbleth him, to the end he should despair: but that by this accusing and bruising, it may drive him unto Christ the Saviour and comforter. When this is done, he is no longer under the schoolmaster. And this use is very necessary. For seeing the whole world is overwhelmed with sin, it hath need of this ministry of the law, that sin may be revealed, otherwise no man should ever attain to righteousness, as before we have largely declared. But what worketh the law in them that are already justified by Christ? Paul answereth by these words, which are, as it were, an addition to that which goeth before:

VERSE 25. *But after that faith is come, we are no longer under a schoolmaster.*

That is to say, we are free from the law, from the prison, and from our schoolmaster; for when faith is revealed, the law terrifieth and tormenteth us no more. Paul here speaketh of faith as it were preached and published to the world by Christ in the time before appointed. For Christ, taking upon him our flesh, came once into the world: he abolished the law with all his effects, and delivered from eternal death all those which receive his benefit by faith. If, therefore, ye look unto Christ, and that which he hath done, there is now no law. For he, coming in the time appointed, took away the law. Now, since the law is gone, we are not kept under the tyranny thereof any more; but we live in joy and safety under Christ, who now sweetly reigneth in us by his spirit. Now, where the Lord reigneth, there is liberty. Wherefore, if we could perfectly apprehend Christ, which hath abolished the law by his death, and hath reconciled us unto his Father, that schoolmaster should have no power over us at all. But the law of the members, rebelling against the law of the mind, letteth us, that we cannot perfectly lay hold upon Christ. The lack, therefore, is not in Christ, but in us, which have not yet put off this flesh, to which sin continually cleaveth as long as we live. Wherefore, as touching ourselves, we are partly free from the law, and partly under the law. According to the spirit, we serve with Paul, the "law of God: but according to the flesh, the law of sin" (Romans vii).

Hereof it followeth, that, as touching the conscience, we are fully delivered from the law, and therefore that schoolmaster must not rule in it; that is, he must not afflict it with his terrors, threatenings, and captivity. And albeit it go about so to do never so much, yet is not the conscience moved therewith. For it hath Christ crucified before her eyes, who hath removed all the offices of the law out of the conscience, "putting out the handwriting of ordinances that was against us," etc. (Col. ii). Therefore, even as a virgin knoweth no man, so the conscience must not only be ignorant of the law, but also it must be utterly dead unto the law, and the law likewise unto the conscience. This is not done by any works, or by the righteousness of the law, but by faith, which apprehendeth and layeth hold upon Christ. Notwithstanding sin cleaveth still in our flesh, as touching the effect thereof, which oftentimes accuseth and troubleth the conscience. So long, then, as the flesh doth remain, so long this schoolmaster the law doth also remain, which many times terrifieth the conscience, and maketh it heavy by revealing of sin and threatening of death. Yet is it raised up again by the daily coming of Christ, who, as he came once into the world, in the time before appointed, to redeem us from the hard and sharp servitude of our schoolmaster; even so he cometh daily unto us spiritually, to the end that we may increase in faith, and in the knowledge of him; that the conscience may apprehend him more fully and perfectly from day to day; and that the law of the flesh and of sin, with the terror of death and all evils that the law bringeth with it, may be daily diminished in us more and more. As long then as we live in the flesh, which is not without sin, the law oftentimes returneth and doth his office, in one more, and in another less, as their faith is strong or weak, and yet not to their destruction, but to their salvation. For this is the exercise of the law in the saints, namely, the continual mortification of the flesh, of reason, and of our own strength, and the daily renewing of our inward man, as it is said in 2 Cor. iv.

We receive then, the first fruits of the spirit. The leaven is hid in the mass of the dough; but all the dough is not yet leavened: no, it is yet but only begun to be leavened. If I behold the leaven, I see nothing else but pure leaven; but if I behold the whole mass, I see that it is not all pure leaven. That is to say, if I behold Christ, I am altogether pure and holy, knowing nothing at all of the law; for Christ is my leaven: but if I behold my own flesh, I feel in myself covetousness, lust, anger, pride, and arrogance; also, the fear of death, heaviness, hatred, murmuring, and impatience against God. The more these sin are in me, the more is Christ absent from me; or if he be present, he is felt but a little. Here have we need of a schoolmaster, to exercise and vex this strong ass, the flesh, that by this exercise sins may be diminished, and a way prepared unto Christ. For as Christ came once corporally, at the time appointed, abolished the whole law, vanquished sin, destroyed death and hell; even so he cometh spiritually, without ceasing, and daily quencheth and killeth these sins in us.

This I say, that thou mayest be able to answer, if any shall thus object: Christ came into the world, and at once took away all our sins, and cleansed us by his blood: what need we, then, to hear the gospel, or to receive the sacraments? True it is, that inasmuch as thou beholdest Christ, the law and sin are quite abolished. But Christ is not yet come unto thee; or if he be come, yet notwithstanding there are remnants of sin in thee; thou art not yet thoroughly leavened; for where concupiscence, heaviness of spirit, and fear of death is, there is yet also the law and sin. Christ is not yet thoroughly come: but when he cometh indeed, he driveth away fear and heaviness, and bringeth peace and quietness of conscience. So far forth, then, as I do apprehend Christ by faith, so much is the law abolished unto me. But my flesh, the world, and the devil, do hinder faith in me, that it cannot be perfect. Right gladly I would that that little light of faith which is in my heart, were spread throughout all my body, and all the members thereof; but it is not done; it is not by-and-by spread, but only beginneth to be spread. In the mean season this is our consolation, that we who have the first fruits of the spirit, do now begin to be leavened; but we shall be thoroughly leavened, when this body of sin is dissolved, and we shall rise new creatures wholly, together with Christ.

Albeit then that Christ be one and the same yesterday, to-day, and shall be forever (Heb. xiii, 8), and albeit that all the faithful which were before Christ, had the gospel and faith; yet notwithstanding Christ came once in the time before determined. Faith also came once when the apostles preached and published the gospel throughout the world. Moreover, Christ cometh also spiritually every day. Faith likewise cometh daily by the word of the gospel. Now, when faith is come, the schoolmaster is constrained to give place, with his heavy and grievous office. Christ cometh also spirtually, when we still more and more do know and understand those things which by him are given unto us, and increase in grace and in the knowledge of him, 2 Peter iii.

VERSE 26. *For ye are all sons of God by faith in Christ Jesus.*

Paul, as a true and an excellent teacher of faith, hath always these words in his mouth, "by faith, in faith, of faith," which is in Christ Jesus. He saith not, ye are the children of God, because ye are circumcised, because ye have heard the law, and have done the works thereof (as the Jews do imagine, and the false apostles teach), but by faith in Jesus Christ. The law, then, maketh us not children of God, and much less men's traditions. It cannot beget us into a new nature, or a new birth, but it setteth before us the old birth, whereby we are born to the kingdom of the devil; and so it prepareth us to a new birth, which is by faith in Jesus Christ, and not by the law, as Paul plainly witnesseth: "For ye are all the sons of God by faith," etc. As if he said, Albeit ye be tormented, humbled, and killed by the law, yet hath not the law made you righteous, or made you the children of God: this is the work of faith alone. What faith? Faith in Christ. Faith, therefore, in Christ, maketh us the children of God, and not the law. The same thing witnesseth also St. John—"He gave power to as many as believed in him, to be the children of God" (John i, 12; Romans viii, 16, 17). What tongue, either of men or angels, can sufficiently extol and magnify the great mercy of God towards us, that we, which are miserable sinners, and by nature the children of wrath, should be called to his grace and glory, to be made the children and heirs of God, fellow-heirs with the Son of God, and lords over heaven and earth, and that by the only means of our faith which is in Christ Jesus.

VERSE 27. *For all ye that are baptized into Christ, have put on Christ.*

To put on Christ is taken two manner of ways: according to the law, and according to the gospel. According to the law, as it is said in the 13th chapter to the Romans: "Put ye on the Lord Jesus Christ": that is, follow the example and virtues of Christ. Do that which he did, and suffer that which he suffered. And in 1 Peter ii, "Christ hath suffered for us, leaving us an example that we should follow his steps." Now, we see in Christ a singular patience, an inestimable mildness and love, and a wonderful modesty in all things. This goodly apparel we must put on, that is to say, follow these virtues.

But the putting on of Christ, according to the gospel, consisteth not in imitation, but in a new birth and a new creation: that is to say, in putting on Christ's innocency, his righteousness, his wisdom, his power, his saving health, his life, and his spirit. We are clothed with the leather coat of Adam, which is a mortal garment, and a garment of sin; that is to say, we are all subject unto sin, all sold under sin. There is in us horrible blindness, ignorance, contempt and hatred of God: moreover, evil concupiscence, uncleanness, covetousness, etc. This garment, that is to say, this corrupt and sinful nature, we received from Adam, which Paul is wont to call "the old man." This old man must be put off, with all his works (Eph. iv; Cor. i), that of the children of Adam we may be made the children of God. This is not done by changing of a garment, or by any laws or works, but by a new birth, and by the renewing of the inward man, which is done in baptism, as Paul saith: "All ye that are baptized, have put on Christ." Also: "According to his mercy hath he saved us by the washing of the new birth, and the renewing of the Holy Ghost" (Titus iii). For, besides that they which are baptized are regenerate and renewed by the Holy Ghost to a heavenly righteousness and to eternal life, there riseth in them also a new light and a new flame; there rise in them new and holy affections, as the fear of God, true faith and assured hope, etc.; there beginneth in them also a new will. And this is to put on Christ truly, and according to the gospel.

Therefore, the righteousness of the law, or of our own works, is not given unto us in baptism; but Christ himself is our garment. Now, Christ is no law, no lawgiver, no work; but a divine and an inestimable gift, whom God hath given unto us, that he might be our justifier, our saviour, and our redeemer. Wherefore, to be apparelled with Christ according to the gospel, is not to be apparelled with the law nor with works, but with an incomparable gift; that is to say, with remission of sins, righteousness, peace, consolation, joy of spirit, salvation, life, and Christ himself.

This is diligently to be noted, because of the fond and fantastical spirits, which go about to deface the majesty of baptism, and speak wickedly of it. Paul, contrariwise, commendeth and setteth it forth with honourable titles, calling it "the washing of the new birth, and renewing of the Holy Ghost" (Titus iii). And here also he saith, that all they which are baptized, have put on Christ. As if he said, Ye are carried out of the law into a new birth, which is wrought in baptism. Therefore ye are not now any longer under the law, but ye are clothed with a new garment; to wit, with the righteousness of Christ. Wherefore baptism is a thing of great force and efficacy. Now, when we are apparelled with Christ, as with the robe of righteousness and our salvation, then we must put on Christ also as the apparel of imitation and example. These things I have handled more largely in another place, therefore I here briefly pass them over.

> VERSE 28. *There is neither Jew nor Grecian, there is neither bond nor free, there is neither male nor female; for ye are all one in Christ Jesus.*

Here might be added, moreover, many more names of persons and offices which are ordained of God, as these: there is neither magistrate nor subject, neither teacher nor hearer, neither schoolmaster nor scholar, neither master nor servant, neither mistress nor maid, etc., for in Christ Jesus all states, yea, even such as are ordained of God, are nothing. Indeed, the male, the female, the bond, the free, the Jew, the Gentile, the prince, the subject, are the good creatures of God: but in Christ, that is, in the matter of salvation, they are nothing, with all their wisdom, righteousness, religion, and power.

Wherefore, with these words, "There is neither Jew," etc., Paul mightily abolisheth the law. For here, that is, when a man is renewed by baptism, and hath put on Christ, there is neither Jew nor Grecian, etc. The apostle speaketh not here of the Jew according to his nature and substance; but he calleth him a Jew which is the disciple of Moses, is subject to the law, is circumcised, and with all his endeavour keepeth the ceremonies commanded in the law. When Christ is put on, saith he, there is neither Jew nor circumcision, nor ceremony of the law any more; for Christ hath abolished all the laws of Moses that ever were. Wherefore, the conscience believing in Christ must be so surely persuaded that the law is abolished, with all his terrors and threatenings, that it should be utterly ignorant whether there were ever any Moses, any law, or any Jew. For Christ and Moses can in no wise agree. Moses came with the law, with many works, and with many ceremonies; but Christ came without any law, without any exacting of works, giving grace and righteousness, etc. For "the law was given by Moses, but grace and truth came by Jesus Christ" (John i, 17).

Moreover, when he saith, "nor Grecian," he also rejecteth and condemneth the wisdom and righteousness of the Gentiles; for among the Gentiles there were many notable men, as Xenophon, Themistocles, Marcus Fabius, Attilius Regulus, Cicero, Pomponius, Atticus, and many others, which being endued with singular virtues, governed commonwealths excellently, and did many worthy acts for the preservation thereof: and yet all these were nothing before God, with their wisdom, their power, their notable acts, their excellent virtues, laws, religions, and ceremonies; for we must not think that the Gentiles did contemn all honesty and religion. Yea, all nations of all ages dispersed throughout the world had their laws, religions, and ceremonies, without the which it is not possible that mankind should be governed. All righteousness, therefore, concerning either the government of families, or commonwealths, or divine matters (as was the righteousness of the law), with all the obedience, execution, and holiness thereof, be it never so perfect, is nothing worth before God. What then? The garment of Christ which we put on in baptism.

So, if the servant do his duty, obey his master, serve in his vocation never so diligently and faithfully; if he that is at liberty be in authority and govern the commonwealth, or guide his own family, honestly and with praise; if the man do that pertaineth to the man in marrying a wife, in governing his family, in obeying the magistrate, in behaving himself decently towards all men; if the woman live chastely, obey her husband, see well to her household, bring up her children godly (which are indeed excellent gifts and holy works), yet are all these nothing in comparison of that righteousness which is before God. To be brief, all the laws, ceremonies, religions, righteousness, and works in the whole world, yea, of the Jews themselves, which were the first that had the kingdom and priesthood ordained and appointed of God, with their holy laws, religions, ceremonies, and worshippings, all these (I say) take not away sin, deliver not from death, nor purchase life.

Therefore your false apostles do subtilly seduce you (O, ye Galatians), when they teach you that the law is necessary to salvation; and by this means they spoil you of that excellent glory of your new birth and your adoption, and call you back to your old birth, and to the most miserable servitude of the law, making you, of the free children of God, bond-children of the law, whilst they will have a difference of persons according to the law. Indeed, there is a difference of persons in the law, and in the world, and there it ought to be; but not before God. "All have sinned, and are destitute of the glory of God" (Romans iii, 23). Let the Jews, therefore, the Gentiles, and the whole world, keep silence in the presence of God. God hath, indeed, many ordinances, laws, degrees, and kinds of life, but all these help nothing to deserve grace, and obtain eternal life. So many as are justified, therefore, are justified, not by the observation of man's law, or God's law, but by Christ alone, who hath abolished all laws. Him alone doth the gospel set forth unto us for a pacifier of God's wrath by the shedding of his own blood, and a Saviour: and without faith in him, neither shall the Jew be saved by the law, nor the monk by his order, nor the Grecian by his wisdom, nor the magistrate or master by his upright government, nor the servant by his obedience.

VERSE 28. *For ye are all one in Christ Jesus.*

These are excellent words. In the world, and according to the flesh, there is a great difference and inequality of persons, and the same must be diligently observed. For if the woman would be the man, if the son would be the father, the servant would be the master, the subject would be the magistrate, there should be nothing else but confusion of all estates and of all things. Contrariwise, in Christ there is no law, no difference of persons; there is neither Jew nor Grecian, but all are one; for there is but one body, one spirit, one hope of vocation; there is but one gospel, "one faith, one baptism, one God and Father of all, one Christ and Lord of all" (Eph. iv, 4-6). We have the same Christ, I, thou, and all the faithful, which Peter, Paul, and all the saints had. Here, therefore, the conscience knoweth nothing of the law, but hath Christ only before her eyes; therefore, Paul is always wont to add this clause, "In Christ Jesus"; who, if he be taken out of our sight, then cometh anguish and terror.

The popish school-divines do dream that faith is a quality cleaving in the heart, without Christ. This is a devilish error. But Christ should be so set forth, that thou shouldst see nothing besides him, and shouldst think that nothing can be more near unto thee, or more present within thy heart than he is. For he sitteth not idly in heaven, but is present with us, working and living in us; as he saith before, in the second chapter, "I live; yet not I, but Christ liveth in me." And here likewise: "Ye have put on Christ." Faith, therefore, is a certain, stedfast beholding, which looketh upon nothing else but Christ, the conqueror of sin and death, and the giver of righteousness, salvation, and eternal life. This is the cause that Paul nameth and setteth forth Jesus Christ so often in his epistles, yea, almost in every verse. But he setteth him forth by the word: for otherwise he cannot be comprehended than by the word.

This was notably and lively represented by the brazen serpent, which is a figure of Christ. Moses commanded the Jews which were stung of serpents in the desert, to do nothing else but stedfastly behold the brazen serpent, and not to turn away their eyes. They that did so, were healed only by that stedfast and constant beholding of the serpent (Num. xxi, 6, 7, 8). But, contrariwise, they died which obeyed not the commandment of Moses, but looked upon their wounds and not upon the serpent. So, if I would find comfort when my conscience is afflicted, or when I am at the point of death, I must do nothing but apprehend Christ by faith, and say: I believe in Jesus Christ the Son of God, who suffered, was crucified, and died for me, etc., in whose wounds and in whose death I see my sin, and in his resurrection victory over sin, death, and the devil, also righteousness and eternal life. Besides him I see nothing, I hear nothing. This is true faith concerning Christ, and in Christ, whereby "we are made members of his body, flesh of his flesh, and bone of his bones. In him, therefore, we live, we move, and we have our being" (Eph. v, 30; Acts xvii, 28). Christ and our faith must be thoroughly joined together. We must be in heaven, and Christ must live and work in us. Now, he liveth and worketh in us, not by speculation and naked knowledge, but in deed, and by a true and a substantial presence.

VERSE 29. *And if ye be Christ's, then are ye Abraham's seed, and heirs by the promise.*

That is to say, if ye believe, and be baptized into Christ; if ye believe, I say, that he is that promised seed of Abraham which brought the blessing to all the Gentiles, then are ye the children of Abraham, not by nature, but by adoption; for the scripture attributeth unto him, not only the children of the flesh, but also of adoption and of the promise, and foresheweth that they shall receive the inheritance, and the other shall be cast out of the house. So Paul, in few words, translateth the whole glory of Libanus, that is to say, of the nations of the Jews, unto the desert, that is, unto the Gentiles. And this place comprehendeth a singular consolation: to wit, that the Gentiles are the children of Abraham, and consequently the people of God. But they are the children of Abraham, not by carnal generation, but by the promise. The kingdom of heaven, then, life, and the eternal inheritance, belongeth to the Gentiles. And this the scripture signified long before, when it saith: "I have made thee a father of many nations" (Gen. xvii, 5). Again, "In thy seed shall all nations be blessed" (Gen. xxii, 18). Now, therefore, because we which are Gentiles do believe, and by faith do receive the blessing promised to Abraham, and exhibited by Christ, therefore the scripture calleth us the children and heirs of Abraham, not after the flesh, but after the promise. So that promise, "In thy seed," etc., belongeth also to all the Gentiles, and according to this promise Christ is become ours.

Indeed, the promise was made only to the Jews, and not to us that are Gentiles (Psalm cxlvii), "He sheweth his word unto Jacob, etc. He hath not dealt so with every nation," etc. Notwithstanding, that which was promised cometh unto us by faith, by the which only we apprehend the promise of God. Albeit, then, that the promise be not made unto us, yet is it made as touching us and for us: for we are named in the promise: "In thy seed shall all nations be blessed;" for the promise sheweth plainly that Abraham should be the father, not only of the Jewish nation, but of many nations, and that he should be the heir, not of one kingdom, but of all the world (Romans iv). So the glory of the whole kingdom of Christ is translated unto us. Wherefore all laws are utterly abolished in the heart and conscience of a Christian: notwithstanding they remain without, still in the flesh. And hereof we have spoken largely before.

CHAPTER IV.

VERSE 1. *This I say, That the heir, as long as he is a child, differeth nothing from a servant, though he be lord of all;*

VERSE 2. *But is under tutors and governors, until the time appointed of the father.*

Ye see with what vehement affection Paul goeth about to call back the Galatians, and what strong arguments he useth in debating the matter, gathering similitudes of experience of the example of Abraham, of the testimonies of the scripture, and of the time, so that oftentimes he seemeth to renew the whole matter again; for before, he had, in a manner, finished the disputation concerning justification, concluding that a man is justified before God by faith only and alone. But, because he calleth also to remembrance this political example of the little heir, he bringeth the same also for the confirmation of his matter; thus trying every way, he lieth in wait, with a certain holy subtlety, to take the Galatians unawares; for the ignorant people are sooner persuaded with similitudes and examples, than with deep and subtle disputations. They will rather behold an image well painted, than a book well written. Paul therefore now, after that he hath brought the similitude of a man's testament, of the person of the schoolmaster, useth also this similitude of an heir (which is familiar and well known to all men), to move and to persuade them. And, surely, it is a very profitable thing to be furnished with similitudes and examples, which not only Paul, but also the prophets, and Christ himself also did often use.

Ye see, saith he, that it is ordained by the civil laws, that an heir, albeit he be the lord of all his father's goods, differeth not from a servant. Indeed, he hath an assured hope of the inheritance: but before he come to his years, his tutors hold him in subjection, like as the schoolmaster doth his scholar. They commit not unto him the ordering of his own goods, but constrain him to serve, so that he is kept and maintained with his own goods like a servant. Therefore, as long as this bondage endureth, that is, so long as he is under tutors and governors, he differeth nothing from a servant. And this subjection and servitude is very profitable for him; for otherwise, through folly, he would soon waste all his goods. This captivity endureth not always, but hath a certain time limited and appointed by the father, wherein it must end.

VERSE 3. *So also we, as long as we were children, were in bondage under the rudiments of the world.*

In like manner, when we were little children, we were heirs, having the promise of the inheritance to come, which should be given unto us by the seed of Abraham, that is to say, by Christ, in whom all nations should be blessed. But because the fulness of time was not yet come, Moses, our tutor, governor, and schoolmaster, came, holding us in captivity, with our hands bound, so that we could bear no rule, nor possess our inheritance. In the mean time, notwithstanding, like as an heir is nourished and maintained in hope of liberty to come, even so Moses did nourish us with the hope of the promise to be revealed in the time appointed; to wit, when Christ should come, who, by his coming, should put an end to the time of the law, and begin the time of grace.

Now the time of the law endeth two manner of ways: first, (as I said) by the coming of Christ in the flesh, at the time appointed of his Father. "But when the fulness of time was come, God sent forth his Son, made of a woman, and made under the law, that he might redeem them which were under the law," etc. (Gal. iv, 4, 5.) "He entered into the holy sanctuary once through his blood, and obtained eternal redemption for us." (Heb. ix, 12.) Moreover, the same Christ, who came once in the time appointed, cometh also unto us daily and hourly in spirit. Indeed, once with his own blood he redeemed and sanctified all; but because we are not yet perfectly pure (for the remnants of sin do yet cleave to our flesh, which striveth against the spirit (Heb. x, 14; Gal. v, 17), therefore daily he cometh unto us spiritually, and continually more and more accomplisheth the appointed time of his Father, abrogating and abolishing the law.

So he came also in spirit to the fathers of the Old Testament, before he appeared in the flesh. They had Christ in spirit. They believed in Christ which should be revealed, as we believe in Christ which is now revealed, and were saved by him, as we are, according to that saying: "Jesus Christ is one, yesterday, and today, and shall be the same forever." Yesterday, before the time of his coming in the flesh; to-day, when he was revealed in the time before appointed; now and forever he is one and the same Christ. For even by him only, and alone, all the faithful which either have been, be, or shall be, are delivered from the law, justified, and saved.

"In like manner, we also," saith he, "when we were children, served under the rudiments of the world;" that is to say, the law had dominion over us, oppressed us, and kept us in a strait bondage, as servants and captives. For, first, it restrained carnal and rebellious persons, that they should not run headlong into all kinds of vice. For the law threateneth punishment to transgressors; which if they feared not, there is no mischief which they would not commit; and over those whom the law so bridleth, it ruleth and reigneth. Again, it did accuse us, terrify us, kill us, and condemn us spiritually and before God: and this was the principal dominion that the law had over us. Therefore, like as an heir is subject unto his tutors, is beaten, and is compelled to obey their laws, and diligently to execute their commandments: even so, men's consciences, before Christ come, are oppressed with the sharp servitude of the law; that is to say, they are accused, terrified, and condemned of the law. But this dominion, or rather this tyranny of the law is not continual, but must only endure until the time of grace. Wherefore the office of the law is to reprove and increase sins, not to bring righteousness; to kill, not to bring life. For "the law is a schoolmaster unto Christ." (Gal. iii, 20.) Like as therefore the tutors do handle the heir, being yet a child, straitly and hardly, rule him and command him as a servant, and he again is constrained to be subject unto them: even so the law accuseth us, humbleth us, and bringeth us into bondage, that we may be the servants of sin, death, and of the wrath of God, which is indeed a most miserable kind of bondage. But as the power of the tutors, and the subjection and bondage of the little heir is not continual, but only endureth unto the time appointed of the father, which, being ended, he needeth not to be governed by his tutors, nor remaineth under their subjection any more, but with liberty enjoyeth the inheritance: even so the law hath dominion over us, and we are constrained to be servants and captives under his government, but not forever; for this clause which followeth must be added: "Until the time appointed of the Father." For Christ, which was promised, came and redeemed us which were oppressed with the tyranny of the law.

Contrariwise, the coming of Christ profiteth not the careless hypocrites, the wicked contemners of God, nor the desperate, which think that nothing else remaineth but the terrors of the law which they feel. His coming only profiteth those which are tormented and terrified with the law for a time; that is to say, such as despair not in those great and inward terrors which the law stirreth up, but with a sure trust come unto Christ the throne of grace, which hath redeemed them from the curse of the law, being made a curse for them, and so obtain mercy and find grace. (Heb. iv, 16; Gal. iii, 13.)

There is a certain vehemency, therefore, in this word, "we did serve." As if he would say: our conscience was subject to the law, which holding us as bondslaves and captives, like as a tyrant holdeth his prisoners, whipped us, and with all his power exerciseth his tyranny upon us; that is to say, it brought unto us a terror and a heaviness of spirit, it made us to tremble and ready to despair, threatening unto us everlasting death and damnation. This spiritual bondage and slavery of the law is most sharp and bitter, and yet (as I have said) it is not continual, but endureth so long as we are children; that is, as long as Christ is absent. Whilst he is absent, we are servants, shut under the law, destitute of grace, faith, and all the gifts of the Holy Ghost.

VERSE 3. *Under the elements or rudiments of the world.*

Some have thought that Paul speaketh here of those corporal elements, the fire, the air, the water, and the earth. But Paul hath his peculiar manner of speech; and he speaketh here even of the law of God, which he calleth the elements or rudiments of the world: and his words seem to be very heretical. So is he wont in other places also to diminish and to abase the authority of the law very much, when he calleth it the letter that killeth, the ministry of death and damnation, and the power of sin. And these most odious names, which shew plainly the power and use of the law, he chuseth of purpose, to admonish us, that in the terrors of sin, wrath, and the judgment of God, we trust not to our own righteousness, or to the righteousness of the law, seeing that the law, in his principal use, can do nothing else but accuse our consciences, increase sin, threaten death and eternal damnation. Wherefore this diminishing and abasing of the law must be applied to the conflict of conscience, and not to the civil life, nor to secure and careless minds.

He calleth therefore the law, the elements of the world: that is to say, the outward laws and traditions written in a certain book. For, although the law do civilly bridle a man from evil, and constrain him to do well, yet notwithstanding being kept after this sort, it doth not deliver him from sin; it justifieth him not, it prepareth not a way for him to heaven, but leaveth him in the world. I do not obtain righteousness and everlasting life, because I kill not, I commit not adultery, I do not steal, etc. These outward virtues and honest conversations be not the kingdom of Christ, nor the heavenly righteousness, but the righteousness of the flesh and of the world; which also the Gentiles had, and not only the merit-mongers, as in the time of Christ the Pharisees, and in our time the monks and friars, etc. This righteousness some do observe, to avoid the punishments of the law; some, that they may be praised of men and esteemed righteous, constant, and patient; and therefore it is rather to be called coloured hypocrisy, than righteousness.

Moreover, the law, when it is in his principal use and office, can do nothing but accuse, terrify, condemn, and kill. But where such terror, such feeling of sin, of death, of the wrath and judgment of God is, there is no righteousness, no divine or heavenly thing, but all these are mere things of the world; which (because it is the kingdom of the devil) is nothing else but a certain puddle of sin, of death, of hell, and of all evils which the fearful, sorrowful, and heavy-hearted do feel; but the secure and careless contemners do not feel them. Wherefore the law, even in his best and most perfect use, doth nothing else but reveal and increase sin, and strike into us the terror of death; and these are but worldly things. We see, then, that the law giveth no lively, no healthful, no divine or heavenly thing, but only worldly things. Wherefore Paul doth very fitly call the law the elements or rudiments of the world.

And although Paul call the whole law the rudiments of the world (as may appear by that I have said before) yet principally he speaketh thus in contempt of the ceremonial laws, which, although they profit never so much, yet (saith he) they consist only in outward things, as meat, drink, apparel, places, times, the temple, the feasts, washings, sacrifices, etc., which be but mere worldly, and things ordained of God only for the use of this present life, but not to justify or save before God. Therefore, by this clause, "the rudiments of the world," he rejecteth and condemneth the righteousness of the law, which consisteth in these outward ceremonies, being notwithstanding ordained and commanded of God to be observed for a time, and by a contemptible name calleth it the rudiments of the world. So the emperor's laws be rudiments of the world, for they entreat of worldly matters: that is to say, of things concerning this present life, as of goods, possessions, inheritances, murders, adulteries, robberies, etc., whereof speaketh also the second table of the commandments. As for the Pope's canon laws and decretals, which forbid marriage and meats, those Paul, in another place, calleth, the doctrines of devils; which are also rudiments of the world, but that they do most wickedly bind men's consciences to the observation of outward things, contrary to the word of God and faith.

Wherefore the law of Moses giveth nothing but worldly things; that is to say, it doth but only shew, civilly and spiritually, the evils that be in the world. Notwithstanding, if it be in his true use, it driveth the conscience, by his terrors, to seek and thirst after the promise of God, and to look unto Christ. But that thou mayest so do, thou hast need of the aid and assistance of the Holy Ghost, which may say in thy heart: It is not the will of God, that after the law hath done his office in thee, thou shouldst only be terrified and killed; but that, when thou art brought by the law to the knowledge of thy misery and damnation, thou shouldst not despair, but believe in Christ, "who is the end of the law to righteousness, to every one that believeth." (Rom. x, 4.) Here is no worldly thing done; but here all worldly matters, and all laws cease, and heavenly things begin now to appear. Therefore, so long as we be under the rudiments of the world; that is to say, under the law, which giveth not only no righteousness and peace of conscience, but revealeth and increaseth sins and engendereth wrath, we be servants thrall and subject to the law, although we have the promise of the blessing to come. Indeed, the law saith, "thou shalt love the Lord thy God:" but that I may be able so to do, or to apprehend Christ, this cannot the law give.

I speak not this to the end that the law should be despised, neither doth Paul so mean, but it ought to be had in great estimation. But because Paul is here in the matter of justification, it was necessary that he should speak of the law, as of a thing very contemptible and odious; for justification is a far other manner of thing than the law is. We cannot speak basely and contemptuously enough of the law, when we are in this matter. When the conscience therefore is in this conflict, then should she think upon nothing, know nothing at all but Christ only and alone. Then should she remove the law utterly out of her sight, and embrace nothing but the promise concerning Christ. To say this, it is an easy matter; but in the time of temptation, when the conscience wrestleth in the presence of God, to do it indeed, of all things it is the hardest; to wit, that when the law accuseth thee, terrifieth thee, revealeth unto thee thy sin, threateneth the wrath of God and eternal death, that then (I say) thou shouldst have such strength of faith in Christ, as if there had never been any law or any sin, but only Christ, mere grace, and redemption; or that thou shouldst be able to say, O law, I will not hear thee, for thou hast a stammering and a slow tongue: moreover, the fulness of time is now come, and therefore I am free, and will not suffer thy tyranny any longer. Here a man may see how hard a matter it is to separate the law from grace. Again, how divine and heavenly a thing it is to hope here even against hope, and how true this proposition of Paul is, that "we are justified by faith alone."

Learn here, therefore, to speak of the law as contemptuously as thou canst, in the matter of justification, by the example of the apostle, which calleth the law, "the rudiments of the world, pernicious traditions, the strength of sin, the ministry of death," etc. For if thou suffer the law to bear rule in thy conscience, when thou standest before God, wrestling against sin and death, then is the law indeed nothing else but a sink of all evils, heresies, and blasphemies: for it doth nothing but increase sin, accuse and terrify the conscience, threaten death, and set forth God as an angry judge, which rejecteth and condemneth sinners. Here, therefore, if thou be wise, banish this stuttering and stammering Moses far from thee, with his law, and in any wise let not his terrors and threatenings move thee. Here let him be utterly suspected unto thee, as a heretic, as an excommunicated and condemned person, worse than the Pope and the Devil himself, and therefore not to be heard or obeyed in any case.

Bnt, out of the matter of justification, we ought with Paul to think reverently of the law, to commend it highly, to call it holy, righteous, good, spiritual, and divine (Rom. vii, 12). Out of the case of conscience we should make a god of it, but in the case of conscience it is a very devil. For, in the least temptation that can be, it is not able to raise up and comfort the conscience; but it doth clean contrary: it terrifieth, it oppresseth it with heaviness, and plucketh it from the assurance of righteousness, of life, and of all goodness. Hereupon Paul, a little after, calleth it "weak and beggarly rudiments." (Gal. iv, 9.) Wherefore let us not suffer the law, in any case, to bear rule in our conscience, especially seeing it cost Christ so great a price to deliver the conscience from the tyranny of the law. "For he was made a curse for us, that he might deliver us from the curse of the law." Let the godly learn, therefore, that the law and Christ are two contrary things, whereof the one cannot abide the other. For when Christ is present, the law may in no case rule, but must depart out of the conscience, and leave the bed (which is so strait that it cannot hold two, as Isaiah saith, chap. xxviii, 20), and give place only to Christ. Let him only reign in righteousness, in peace, in joy, and life, that the conscience may sleep and repose itself joyfully in Christ, without any feeling of the law, sin, and death.

Paul here of purpose useth this figurative speech, "elements of the world;" whereby (as I said) he doth much abase and diminish the glory and authority of the law, to stir up our minds. (2 Cor. iii.) For he that readeth Paul attentively, when he heareth that he calleth the law the ministry of death, the letter that killeth, etc., by-and-by he thinketh thus with himself: why doth he give such odious, and, as it appeareth to reason, blasphemous terms to the law, which is a divine doctrine revealed from heaven? To this Paul answereth, that the law is both holy, just, and good, and that it is also the ministry of sin and death, but in divers respects. Before Christ, it is holy; after Christ, it is death. Therefore, when Christ is come, we ought to know nothing at all of the law, unless it be in this respect: that it hath power and dominion over the flesh, to bridle it, and to keep it under. Here is a conflict between the law and the flesh (to whom the yoke of the law is hard and grievous) as long as we live.

Only Paul, among all the apostles, calleth the law "the rudiments of the world, weak and beggarly elements, the strength of sin, the letter that killeth," etc. (2 Cor. iii, 6.) The other apostles spake not so of the law. Whosoever, then, will be a right scholar in Christ's school, let him mark diligently this manner of speech used of the apostle. Christ calleth him an elect vessel, and therefore gave unto him an exquisite utterance, and a singular kind of speech above all the rest of the apostles, that he, as an elect vessel, might faithfully lay the foundations of the article of justification, and clearly set forth the same. (Acts ix, 15.)

> VERSE 4 *But after the fulness of time was come, God sent his Son, made of a woman, and made under the law, that he might redeemed them which were under the law.*

That is to say, after that the time of the law was fulfilled, and that Christ was revealed, and had delivered us from the law, and that the promise was published among all nations, etc.

Mark here diligently how Paul defineth Christ. Christ (saith he) is the Son of God and of a woman, which for us sinners was made under the law, to redeem us that were under the law. In these words he comprehendeth both the person of Christ and the office of Christ. His person consisteth of his divine and human nature. This he sheweth plainly, when he saith, "God sent his own Son, born of a woman." Christ, therefore, is very God and very man. His office he setteth forth in these words: "being made under the law, to redeem them that were under the law," etc.

And it seemeth that Paul here, as it were in reproach, calleth the Virgin Mary but only a woman; which thing was not well taken, even of some of the ancient doctors, who would that he should rather have called her a virgin, than a woman. But Paul entreateth in this epistle of the most high and principal matter of all; to wit, of the gospel, of faith, of Christian righteousness: also, what the person of Christ is, what is his office, what he hath taken upon him and done for our cause, and what benefits he hath brought to us wretched sinners. Wherefore the excellency of so high and so wonderful a matter was the cause that he had no regard to her virginity. It was enough for him to set forth and preach the inestimable mercy of God, which would that his Son should be born of that sex. Therefore he maketh no mention of the dignity of the sex, but of the sex only. And in that he nameth the sex, he signifieth that Christ was made true and very man of womankind. As if he said, he was not born of man and woman, but only of womankind. Therefore, when he nameth but only the womankind, saying, "made of a woman," it is as if he should have said, made of a virgin. John the evangelist, when he thus setteth forth the word, that "it was in the beginning, and was made flesh" (John i, 1), speaketh not one word of his mother.

Furthermore, this place also witnesseth that Christ, when the time of the law was accomplished, did abolish the same, and so brought liberty to those that were oppressed therewith, but made no new law after, or besides that old law of Moses. Wherefore the monks and Popish schoolmen do no less err and blaspheme Christ, in that they imagine that he hath given a new law besides the law of Moses, than do the Turks, which vaunt of their Mahomet, as of a new lawgiver after Christ, and better than Christ. Christ then came not to abolish the old law, that he might make a new, but (as Paul here saith) he was sent of his Father into the world, to redeem those which were kept in thraldom under the law. These words paint out Christ lively and truly; they do not attribute unto him the office to make any new law, but to redeem them which were under the law. And Christ himself saith, "I judge no man." And in another place: "I come not to judge the world, but that the world should be saved by me" (John viii, 15; xii, 47), that is to say, I came not to bring any law, nor to judge men according to the same, as Moses and other lawgivers; but I have a higher and a better office. The law killed you, and I again do judge, condemn and kill the law, and so I deliver you from the tyranny thereof.

We that are old men, which have been so nusled up in this pernicious doctrine of the Papists, that it hath taken deep root, even in our bones and marrow, have conceived an opinion quite contrary to that which Paul here teacheth. For, although we confessed with our mouth that Christ redeemed us from the tyranny of the law, yet in very deed in our hearts we thought him to be a lawgiver, a tyrant, and a judge, more terrible than Moses himself. And this perverse opinion we cannot yet at this day, in so great light of the truth, utterly reject; so strongly are those things rooted in our hearts which we learn in our youth. But ye which are yet young, and are not infected with this pernicious opinion, may learn Christ purely with less difficulty than we that are old can remove out of our minds these blasphemous imaginations which we have conceived of him, notwithstanding ye have not utterly escaped the deceits of the devil. For although ye be not as yet infected with this cursed opinion, that Christ is a lawgiver, yet have ye in you the root whereof it springeth; that is, ye have the flesh, reason, and the corruption of nature, which can judge no otherwise of Christ, but that he is a lawgiver. Therefore ye must endeavour, with all your power, to learn so to know and to apprehend Christ, as Paul has set him forth in this place. But if, besides this natural corruption, there come also corrupt and wicked teachers (of whom the world is full), they will increase this corruption of nature, and so shall the evil be doubled: that is to say, evil instruction will increase and confirm the pernicious error of blind reason, which naturally judgeth Christ to be a lawgiver, and printeth that error mightily in our minds, that without great travail and difficulty it can never be abolished.

Wherefore, it is very profitable for us to have always before our eyes this sweet and comfortable sentence, and such-like, which set out Christ truly and lively, that in our whole life, in all dangers, in the confession of our faith before tyrants, and in the hour of death, we may boldly and with sure confidence say, O law, thou hast no power over me, and therefore thou dost accuse and condemn me in vain. For I believe in Jesus Christ the Son of God, whom the Father sent into the world to redeem us miserable sinners oppressed with the tyranny of the law. He gave his life, and shed his blood for me. Therefore, feeling thy terrors and threatenings, O law, I plunge my conscience in the wounds, blood, death, resurrection and victory of my saviour, Christ. Besides him I will see nothing, I will hear nothing. This faith is our victory, whereby we overcome the terrors of the law, sin, death, and all evils, and yet not without great conflicts. And here do the children of God, which are daily exercised with grievous temptations, wrestle and sweat indeed. For oftentimes it cometh into their minds that Christ will accuse them, and plead against them: that he will require an account of their former life, and that he will condemn them. They cannot assure themselves that he is sent of his Father to redeem us from the tyranny and oppression of the law. And whereof cometh this? They have not yet fully put off the flesh, which rebelleth against the spirit: therefore, the terrors of the law, the fear of death, and such-like sorrowful and heavy sights, do oftentimes return, which hinder our faith, that it cannot apprehend the benefit of Christ (who hath redeemed us from the bondage of the law) with such assurance as it should do.

But how, or by what means hath Christ redeemed us? This was the manner of our redemption: "he was made under the law." Christ, when he came, found us all captives under governors and tutors, that is to say, shut up and holden in prison under the law. What doth he then? Although he be lord of the law, and therefore the law hath no authority or power over him (for he is the Son of God), yet of his own accord he maketh himself subject to the law. Here the law executeth upon him all the jurisdiction it had over us. It accuseth and terrifieth us also: it maketh us subject to sin, death, the wrath of God, and with his sentence condemneth us. And this it doth by good right: "for we are all sinners, and by nature the children of wrath." (Eph. ii, 3.) Contrariwise, Christ did no sin, neither was there any guile found in his mouth. (1 Pet. ii, 22.) Therefore he was not subject to the law. Yet notwithstanding the law was no less cruel against this innocent, righteous, and blessed lamb, than it was against us cursed and damned sinners, yea much more rigorous. For it accused him as a blasphemer, and a seditious person: it made him guilty before God of the sins of the whole world; it so terrified and oppressed him with heaviness and anguish of spirit, that he sweat blood; and, briefly, it condemned him to death, yea even to the death of the cross. (Matth. xxvi, 65; Luke xxiii, 5; xxii, 44.)

This was indeed a wonderful combat, where the law, being a creature, giveth such an assault to his creator; and, against all right and equity, practiseth his whole tyranny upon the Son of God which it exerciseth upon us the children of wrath. Now, therefore, because the law did so horribly and cursedly sin against his God, it is accused and arraigned. There Christ saith: O law, thou mighty queen, and cruel regent of all mankind, what have I done that thou hast accused me, terrified me, and condemned me, which am innocent? Here the law, which had before condemned and killed all men, when it hath nothing wherewith to defend or purge itself, is again so condemned and vanquished, that it loseth his whole right, not only over Christ, (whom it so cruelly handled and killed), but also over all them that believe in him; for to those Christ saith, "Come unto me all ye that labour under the yoke of the law." (Matt. xi, 28.)

I could have overcome the law by my absolute power, without mine own smart: for I am the Lord of the law, and therefore it hath no right over me. But I have made myself subject unto the law for your cause which were under the law, taking your flesh upon me: that is to say, of mine inestimable love I humbled and yielded myself to the same prison, tyranny, and bondage of the law, under the which ye served as captives and bond-slaves; I suffered the law to have dominion over me which was his Lord, to terrify me, to make me thrall and captive unto sin, death, and the wrath of God, which it ought not to have done. Therefore I have vanquished the law by double right and authority: first, as the Son of God, and Lord of the law; secondly, in your person; which is as much as if ye had overcome the law yourselves; for my victory is yours.

After this manner Paul speaketh everywhere of this marvellous combat between Christ and the law; and, to make the matter more delectable and more apparent, he is wont to set forth the law by a figure called *prosopopœia*, as a certain mighty person, which had condemned and killed Christ: whom Christ, again overcoming death, had conquered, condemned and killed, (Eph. ii). "Killing enmity in himself." Again, "Thou hast gone up on high, thou hast led captivity captive," etc. (Psalm lxviii.) He useth the same figure also in his epistles to the Romans, Corinthians, and Colossians. "By sin he condemned sin," etc. (Rom. viii, 3.) Christ, therefore, by this victory banished the law out of our conscience, so that now it can no more confound us in the sight of God, drive us to desperation, or condemn us. Indeed, it ceaseth not still to reveal our sin, to accuse and terrify us: but the conscience, taking hold of this word of the apostle, "Christ hath redeemed us from the law," is raised up by faith, and conceiveth great comfort. Moreover, it triumpheth over the law with a certain holy pride, saying, I care not for thy terrors and threatenings; for thou hast crucified the Son of God, and this hast thou done most unjustly; therefore, the sin that thou hast committed against him cannot be forgiven. Thou hast lost thy right and sovereignty, and now forever thou art not only overcome, condemned, and slain unto Christ, but also to me believing in him, unto whom he hath freely given this victory. So the law is dead to us forever, so that we abide in Christ. Thanks be therefore to God, which hath given us the victory, through our Lord Jesus Christ (1 Cor. xv, 57).

These things do also confirm this doctrine, that we are justified by faith only. For when this combat was fought betwixt Christ and the law, none of our works or desserts came between, but only Christ was found, who putting upon him our person, made himself subject to the law, and in perfect innocency suffered all tyranny. Therefore the law, as a thief and a cursed murderer of the Son of God, loseth all his right, and deserveth to be condemned in such sort, that wheresoever Christ is, or is once named, there it is compelled to avoid and fly away, no otherwise than the devil (as the Papists imagine) flieth from the cross. Wherefore, if we believe, we are delivered from the law through Christ, who hath triumphed over it by himself (Col. ii, 15). Therefore this glorious triumph, purchased unto us by Christ, is not gotten by any works, but only by faith: therefore faith only justifieth.

These words, then, "Christ was made under the law," etc., as they are pithy, and import a certain vehemency, so are they diligently to be weighed and considered. For they declare that the Son of God being made under the law, did not only perform one or two works of the law, that is to say, he was not only circumcised, or presented in the temple, or went up to Jerusalem with other at the times appointed, or only lived civilly under the law, but he suffered all the tyranny of the law. For the law being in his principal use, and full power, set upon Christ and so horribly assailed him, that he felt such anguish and terror, as no man upon the earth had ever felt the like. This his bloody sweat doth sufficiently witness, his comfort ministered by the angel, that mighty prayer which he made in the garden, and briefly, that lamentable complaint upon the cross: "O my God, why hast thou forsaken me?" These things he suffered, to redeem those that were under the law; that is to say, in heaviness of spirit, in anguish and terror, and ready to despair, which were oppressed with the heavy burden of their sins, as indeed we are all oppressed. For as touching the flesh we sin daily against all the commandments of God. But Paul giveth us good comfort when he saith, "God sent his Son," etc.

So Christ, a divine and human person, begotten of God without beginning, and born of the virgin in the time appointed, came not to make a law, but to feel and suffer the terrors of the law with all extremity, and to overcome the same, that so he might utterly abolish the law. He was not made a teacher of the law, but an obedient disciple to the law, that by this his obedience he might redeem them which were under the law. This is against the doctrine of the Papists, who have made Christ a lawgiver, yea, much more severe and rigorous than Moses. Paul teacheth here clean contrary; to wit, that God humbled his Son under the law, that is to say, constrained him to bear the judgment and curse of the law, sin, death, etc. For

Moses, the minister of the law, sin, wrath, and death, apprehended, bound, condemned, and killed Christ: and all this he suffered. Therefore, Christ standeth as a mere patient, and not as an agent, in respect of the law. He is not then a lawgiver, or a judge after the law; but in that he made himself subject to the law, bearing the condemnation of the law, he delivered us from the curse thereof.

Now, whereas Christ, in the gospel, giveth commandments, and teacheth the law, or rather expoundeth it, this pertaineth not to the doctrine of justification, but of good works. Moreover, it is not the proper office of Christ (for the which he came principally into the world) to teach the law, but an accidental or by-office: like as it was to heal the weak, to raise up the dead, etc. These are indeed excellent and divine works, but yet not the very proper and principal works of Christ. For the prophets also taught the law, and wrought miracles. But Christ is God and man, who, fighting against the law, suffered the utmost cruelty and tyranny thereof. And in that he suffered the tyranny of the law, he vanquished it in himself: and afterward, being raised up again from death, he condemned and utterly abolished the law, which was our deadly enemy, so that it cannot condemn and kill the faithful any more. Wherefore, the true and proper office of Christ is to wrestle with the law, with the sin and the death of the whole world, and so to wrestle that he must suffer and abide all these things; and by suffering them in himself, conquer and abolish them, and by this means deliver the faithful from the law and from all evils. Therefore, to teach the law and to work miracles, are particular benefits of Christ, for the which he came not principally into the world. For the prophets, and especially the apostles, did greater miracles than Christ did (John xiv, 12).

Seeing then that Christ ahth overcome the law in his own person, it followeth necessarily that he is naturally God. For there is none else, whether he be man or angel, which is above the law, but only God. But Christ is above the law, for he hath vanquished it: therefore he is the Son of God, and naturally God. If thou lay hold upon Christ, in such sort as Paul here painteth him out, thou canst not err nor be confounded. Moreover, thou shalt easily judge of all kinds of life, of the religions and ceremonies of the whole world. But if this true picture of Christ be defaced or in any wise darkened, then followeth a confusion of all things. For the natural man cannot judge of the law of God. Here faileth the cunning of the philosophers, of the canonists, and of all men. For the law hath power and dominion over man. Therefore the law judgeth man, and not man the law. Only the Christian hath a true and a certain judgment of the law. And how? That it doth not justify. Wherefore then is the law made, if it do not justify? Righteousness before God, which is received by faith alone, is not the final cause why the righteous do obey the law, but the peace of the world, thankfulness towards God, and good example of life, whereby others be provoked to believe the gospel. The Pope hath so confounded and mingled the ceremonial law, the moral law, and faith together, that he hath at length preferred the ceremonial law before the moral law, and the moral law before faith.

VERSE 5. *That we might receive the adoption of sons.*

Paul setteth forth and amplifieth very largely this place of Gen. xxii, "In thy seed shall all the nations of the earth be blessed." A little before he called this blessing of the seed of Abraham, righteousness, life, the promise of the spirit, deliverance from the law, the testament, etc. Here he calleth it the adoption and inheritance of everlasting life. All these this word blessing doth comprehend. For when the curse (which is sin, death, etc.) is abolished, then, in the stead thereof, succeedeth the blessing, that is, righteousness, life, and all good things.

But by what merit have we received this blessing, that is to say, this adoption and inheritance of everlasting life? By none at all. For what can men deserve that are shut under sin, subject to the curse of the law, and worthy of everlasting death? We have then received this blessing freely, and being utterly unworthy thereof, but yet not without merit. What merit is that? Not ours; but the merit of Jesus Christ the Son of God, who being made under the law, not for himself but for us (as Paul said afore, that "he was made a curse for us"), redeemed us which were under the law. Wherefore we have received this adoption by the only redemption of Jesus Christ the Son of God, which is our rich and everlasting merit, whether it be of congruence or worthiness, going before grace or coming after. And with this free adoption we have also received the Holy Ghost, which God hath sent into our hearts, crying, Abba, Father, as followeth.

VERSE 6. *And because you are sons, God hath sent forth the spirit of his Son into your hearts.*

The Holy Ghost is sent two manner of ways. In the primitive church he was sent in a manifest and visible appearance. So he came upon Christ, at Jordan, in the likeness of a dove

(Matt. iii, 16) and in the likeness of fire upon the apostles and other believers. (Acts ii, 3.) And this was the first sending of the Holy Ghost: which was necessary in the primitive church: for it was expedient that it should be established by many miracles, because of the unbelievers, as Paul witnesseth. "Strange tongues," saith he, "be for a sign and a token, not to them that believe, but to them that believe not" (1 Cor. xiv, 23). But after that the church was gathered together, and confirmed with those miracles, it was not necessary that this visible sending of the Holy Ghost should continue any longer.

Secondly, The Holy Ghost is sent by the word into the hearts of the believers, as here it is said, "God sent the spirit of his Son," etc. This sending is without any visible appearance; to wit, when, by the hearing of the external word, we receive an inward fervency and light, whereby we are changed and become new creatures; whereby also we receive a new judgment, a new feeling, and a new moving. This change, and this new judgment, is no work of reason, or of the power of man, but is the gift and operation of the Holy Ghost, which cometh with the word preached, which purifieth our hearts by faith, and bringeth forth in us spiritual motions. Therefore, there is a great difference betwixt us and those which with force and subtilty persecute the doctrine of the gospel. For we, by the grace of God, can certainly judge by the word, of the will of God towards us: also of all laws and doctrines; of our own life, and of the life of others. Contrariwise, the Papists and sectaries cannot certainly judge of anything. For they corrupt, they persecute, and blaspheme the word. Now, without the word, a man can give no certain judgment of anything.

And although it appear not before the world, that we be renewed in spirit, and have the Holy Ghost, yet notwithstanding our judgment, our speech, and our confession do declare sufficiently, that the Holy Ghost with his gifts is in us. For before we could judge rightly of nothing. We spake not as now we do. We confessed not that all our works were sin and damnable, that Christ was our only merit, both before grace and after, as now we do, in the true knowledge and light of the gospel. Wherefore let this trouble us nothing at all, that the world (whose works we testify to be evil) judgeth us to be most pernicious heretics and seditious persons, destroyers of religion, and troublers of the common peace, possessed of the devil speaking in us, and governing all our actions. Against this perverse and wicked judgment of the world, let this testimony of our conscience be sufficient, whereby we assuredly know that it is the gift of God, that we do not only believe in

Jesus Christ, but that we also preach and confess him before the world. As we believe with our heart, so do we speak with our mouth, according to that saying of the Psalmist, "I believed, and therefore have I spoken." (Psalm cxvi, 10.)

Moreover we exercise ourselves in the fear of God, and avoid sin as much as we may. If we sin, we sin not of purpose, but of ignorance, and we are sorry for it. We may slip, for the devil lieth in wait for us, both day and night. Also the remnants of sin cleave yet fast in our flesh: therefore, as touching the flesh, we are sinners, yea, after that we have received the Holy Ghost. And there is no great difference betwixt a Christian and a civil honest man. For the works of a Christian in outward shew are but base and simple. He doth his duty according to his vocation, he guideth his family, he tilleth the ground, he giveth counsel, he aideth and succoureth his neighbour. These works the carnal man doth not much esteem, but thinketh them to be common to all men, and such as the heathen may also do. For the world understandeth not the things which are of the spirit of God, and therefore it judgeth perversely of the works of the godly. But the monstrous superstition of hypocrites, and their will-works, they have in great admiration. They count them holy works, and spare no charges in maintaining the same. Contrariwise, the works of the faithful (which, although in outward appearance they seem to be but vile and nothing worth, yet are they good works indeed, and accepted of God, because they are done in faith, with a cheerful heart, and with obedience and thankfulness towards God), these works, I say, they do not only not acknowledge to be good works, but also they despise and condemn them as most wicked and abominable. The world, therefore, believeth nothing less than that we have the Holy Ghost. Notwithstanding, in the time of tribulation or of the cross, and of the confession of our faith (which is the proper and principal work of those that believe), when we must either forsake wife, children, goods, and life, or else deny Christ, then it appeareth that we make confession of our faith, that we confess Christ and his word, by the power of the Holy Ghost.

We ought not, therefore, to doubt whether the Holy Ghost dwelleth in us or not; but to be assuredly persuaded that we "are the temple of the Holy Ghost," as Paul saith (1 Cor. iii, 16). For if any man feel in himself a love towards the word of God, and willingly heareth, talketh, writeth, and thinketh of Christ, let that man know, that this is not the work of man's will or reason, but the gift of the Holy Ghost: for it is impossible that these things should be done without the Holy Ghost.

Contrariwise, where hatred and contempt of the word is, there the devil, the god of this world, reigneth, "blinding men's hearts, and holding them captive, that the light of the glorious gospel of Christ should not shine unto them." (2 Cor. iv, 4.) Which thing we see at this day in the most part of the common people, which have no love to the word, but contemn it, as though it pertained nothing at all unto them. But whosoever do feel any love or desire to the word, let them acknowledge with thankfulness, that this affection is poured unto them by the Holy Ghost. For we bring not this affection and desire with us, neither can we be taught by any laws how we may obtain it; but this change is plainly and simply the work of the right hand of the Most High. Therefore, when we willingly and gladly hear the word preached, concerning Christ the Son of God, who for us was made man, and became subject to the law, to deliver us from the malediction of the law, hell, death, and damnation; then let us assure ourselves that God, by and with this preaching, sendeth the Holy Ghost into our hearts. Wherefore it is very expedient for the godly to know that they have the Holy Ghost.

This I say, to confute that pernicious doctrine of the Papists, which taught that no man can certainly know (although his life be never so upright and blameless) whether he be in the favour of God or no. And this sentence, commonly received, was a special principle and article of faith in the whole papacy, whereby they utterly defaced the doctrine of faith, tormented men's consciences, banished Christ quite out of the church, darkened and denied all the benefits of the Holy Ghost, abolished the whole worship of God, set up idolatry, contempt of God, and blasphemy against God in men's hearts.

Augustine saith very well and godly, that "every man seeth most certainly his own faith, if he have faith." This do they deny. God forbid (say they) that I should assure myself that I am under grace, that I am holy, and that I have the Holy Ghost, yea, although I live godly, and do all good works. Ye which are young, and are not infected with this pernicious opinion (whereupon the whole kingdom of the Pope is grounded), take heed and fly from it, as from a most horrible plague. We that are old men have been trained up in this error, even from our youth, and have been so nusled therein, that it hath taken deep root in our hearts. Therefore it is to us no less labour to unlearn and forget the same, than to learn and lay hold upon true faith. But we must be assured and out of doubt that we are under grace, that we please God for Christ's sake, and that we have the Holy Ghost: "For if any man have not the spirit of Christ, the same is none of his." (Rom. viii, 9.)

Wherefore, whether thou be a minister of God's word, or a magistrate in the commonwealth, thou must assuredly think that thy office pleaseth God: but this thou canst never do, unless hou have the Holy Ghost. But thou wilt say, I doubt not but that my office pleaseth God, because it is God's ordinance; but I doubt of mine own person, whether it please God or no. Here thou must resort to the word of God, which teacheth and assureth us, that not only the office of the person, but also the person itself pleaseth God. For the person is baptized, believeth in Christ, is purged in his blood from all his sins, liveth in the communion and fellowship of his church. Moreover, he doth not only love the pure doctrine of the word, but also he is glad, and greatly rejoiceth when he seeth it advanced, and the number of the faithful increased. Contrariwise, he detesteth the Pope and all sectaries, with their wicked doctrine, according to that saying of the Psalm: "I hate them that imagine evil things, but thy law do I love." (Psalm cxix, 113.)

We ought, therefore, to be surely persuaded, that not only our office, but also our person pleaseth God; yea, whatsoever it saith, doth, or thinketh particularly, the same pleaseth God, not for our own sakes, but for Christ's sake, who was made under the law for us. Now, we are sure that Christ pleaseth God, that he is holy, etc. Forasmuch, then, as Christ pleaseth God, and we are in him, we also please God, and are holy. And although sin do still remain in our flesh, and we also daily fall and offend, yet grace is more abundant and stronger than sin. The mercy and truth of the Lord reigneth over us for ever. Wherefore sin cannot terrify us, and make us doubtful of the grace of God which is in us. For Christ, that most mighty giant, hath quite abolished the law, condemned sin, vanquished death, and all evils. So long as he is at the right hand of God, making intercession for us, we cannot doubt of the grace and favour of God towards us.

Moreover, God hath also sent the spirit of his Son into our hearts, as Paul here saith. But Christ is most certain in his spirit that he pleaseth God, etc.; therefore we also, having the same spirit of Christ, must be assured that we are under grace for his sake which is most assured. This I have said concerning the inward testimony, whereby a Christian man's heart ought to be fully persuaded that he is under grace, and hath the Holy Ghost. Now, the outward signs (as before I have said) are, gladly to hear of Christ, to preach and teach Christ, to render thanks unto him, to praise him, to confess him, yea, with the loss of goods and life: moreover, to do our duty according to our vocation as we are able: to do it (I say) in faith, joy, etc. Not to delight in, nor to thrust ourselves into another man's vocation, but to attend upon our own, to help our needy brother, to comfort the heavy hearted, etc. By these signs, as by certain effects and consequents, we are fully assured and confirmed that we are in God's favour. The wicked also do imagine that they have the same signs, but they have nothing less. Hereby we may plainly perceive that the Pope with his doctrine doth nothing else but trouble and torment men's consciences, and at length driveth them to desperation. For he not only teacheth, but also commandeth men to doubt. Therefore, as the Psalm saith, "There is no truth or certainty in his mouth" (Ps. v, 9). And in another place: "Under his tongue is iniquity and mischief" (Ps. x, 7).

Here we may see, what great infirmity is yet in the faith of the godly. For if we could be fully persuaded that we are under grace, that our sins are forgiven, that we have the spirit of Christ, that we are the children of God, then, doubtless, we should be joyful and thankful to God for this inestimable gift. But because we feel contrary motions, that is to say, fear, doubtfulness, anguish and heaviness of heart, and such-like, therefore we cannot assure ourselves hereof: yea, our conscience judgeth it a great presumption and pride to challenge this glory. Wherefore, if we will understand this thing rightly, and as we should do, we must put it in practice; for without experience and practice it can never be learned.

Wherefore, let every man so practise with himself, that his conscience may be fully assured that he is under grace, and that his person and his works do please God. And if he feel in himself any wavering or doubting, let him exercise his faith, and wrestle against this doubting, and let him labour to attain more strength and assurance of faith, so that he may be able to say, I know that I am accepted, and that I have the Holy Ghost: not for mine own worthiness, my work, my merit, but for Christ's sake, who, of his inestimable love towards us, made himself thrall and subject to the law, and took away the sins of the world. In him do I believe. If I be a sinner and err, he is righteous and cannot err. Moreover, I gladly hear, read, sing, and write of him, and I desire nothing more than that his gospel may be known to the whole world, and that many may be converted unto him.

These things do plainly witness, that the Holy Ghost is present with us and in us. For such things are not wrought in the heart by man's strength, nor gotten by man's industry or travail, but are obtained by Christ alone, who first maketh us righteous by the knowledge of himself in his holy gospel, and afterwards he created a new heart in us, bringeth forth new motions, and giveth unto us that assurance, whereby we are persuaded that we please the Father for his sake. Also he giveth us a true judgment, whereby we prove and try those things which before we knew not, or else altogether despised. It behoveth us, therefore, to wrestle against this doubting, that we may daily overcome it more and more, and attain to a full persuasion and certainty of God's favour towards us; rooting out of our hearts this cursed opinion, that a man ought to doubt of the grace and favour of God, which hath infected the whole world.

VERSE 6. *Crying, Abba, Father.*

Paul might have said, "God sent the spirit of his Son into our hearts," calling, Abba, Father. He saith not so, but crying "Abba, Father," that he might shew and set forth the temptation of a Christian, which yet is but weak, and weakly believeth. In the eighth to the Romans, he calleth this crying an unspeakable groaning. Likewise he saith: "The spirit helpeth our infirmities: for we know not how to pray as we ought, but the spirit maketh intercession for us, with unspeakable groanings," etc.

And this is a singular consolation when he saith, "that the spirit of Christ is sent unto our hearts, crying, Abba, Father:" and again, "that he helpeth our infirmities, making intercession for us with unspeakable groanings." He that could assuredly believe this, should never be overcome with any affliction, were it never so great. But there are many things that hinder this faith in us. First, our heart is born in sin: moreover, this evil is naturally grafted in us, that we doubt of the good-will of God towards us, and cannot assure ourselves that we please God, etc. Besides all this, the devil our adversary rangeth about with terrible roarings, and saith: Thou art a sinner; therefore God is angry with thee, and will destroy thee for ever. Against these horrible and intolerable roarings, we have nothing whereupon to hold and stay ourselves, but only the word, which setteth Christ before us as a conqueror over sin and death, and over all evils. But to cleave fast to the word, in this temptation and these terrors of conscience, herein standeth all the difficulty. For then Christ appeareth to no sense. We see him not; the heart feeleth not his presence or succour in temptation; but rather it seemeth that he is angry with us, and that he forsaketh us. Moreover, when a man is tempted and afflicted, he feeleth the strength of sin, and the infirmity of the flesh, he doubteth, he feeleth the fiery darts of the devil, the terrors of death, the anger and judgment of God. All these things cry out horribly against us, so that we see nothing else but desperation and eternal death. But yet, in the midst of these terrors of the law, thunderings of sin, assaults of deaths, and roarings of the devil, the Holy Ghost (saith Paul) crieth in our hearts, "Abba, Father!" And this cry surmounteth the horrible cries of the law, sin, death, the devil, etc.; it pierceth the clouds and the heavens, and ascendeth up into the ears of God.

Paul signifieth, therefore, by these words, that there is yet infirmity in the godly: As he doth also in the eighth chapter to the Romans, when he saith, "the spirit helpeth our infirmities." Forasmuch, therefore, as the sense and feeling of the contrary is strong in us; that is to say, forasmuch as we feel more the displeasure of God, than his good-will and favour towards us, therefore the Holy Ghost is sent into our hearts, which doth not only sigh and make request for us, but mightily crieth, "Abba, Father!" and prayeth for us according to the will of God, with tears and unspeakable groanings. And how is this done? When we are in terrors, and in the conflict of conscience, we take hold of Christ, and believe that he is our Saviour; but then do the law and sin terrify and torment us most of all. Moreover, the devil assaileth us with all his engines and fiery darts, and goeth about with all his power to take away Christ and all consolations from us. Here we feel ourselves almost gone, and at the point of desperation: for then are we that bruised reed and smoking flax, which Isaiah speaketh of, chap. xlii, 3. Notwithstanding, in the mean season, the Holy Ghost helpeth our infirmities, and maketh intercession for us with unspeakable groanings; (Rom. viii, 28) and certifieth our spirits that we are the children of God. Thus is the mind raised up in terrors: it looketh unto his Saviour and high bishop, Jesus Christ, it overcometh the infirmity of the flesh; it conceiveth comfort again, and saith, "Abba, Father." This groaning which then we scantly feel, Paul calleth, a crying and unspeakable groaning, which filleth both heaven and earth. Moreover, he calleth it the crying and groaning of the spirit, because the Holy Ghost stirreth up the same in our hearts when we are weak, and oppressed with temptation and terror.

Although, then, the law, sin, and the devil cry out against us never so much, with great and terrible roarings, which seem to fill heaven and earth, and far to exceed this groaning of our heart, yet can they not hurt us. For the more fiercely they assail us, accuse, and torment us with their cryings, so much the more do we groan; and in groaning lay hold upon Christ, call upon him with heart and mouth, cleave unto him, and believe that he was made under the law, that he might deliver us from the curse of the law, and destroy both sin and death. And thus, when we have taken hold of Christ by faith, we cry through him, "Abba, Father." (Gal. iv, 6.) And this our cry doth far surmount the roaring of the law, sin, the devil, etc.

But so far off is it that we think this groaning, which we make in these terrors and this our weakness, to be a cry, that scarcely we perceive it to be a groaning. For our faith, which in temptation thus groaneth unto Christ, is very weak, if we consider our own sense and feeling; and therefore we hear not the cry. "But he," saith Paul, "which searcheth the hearts, knoweth what is the meaning of the spirit," etc. (Rom. viii, 27.) To this searcher of the hearts, this small and feeble groaning (as it seemeth unto us) is a loud and a mighty cry, and an unspeakable groaning; in comparison whereof, the great and horrible roarings of the law, of sin, of death, of the devil, and of hell, are nothing; neither can they be once heard. Paul, therefore, not without cause, calleth this groaning of a godly afflicted heart, a cry and a groaning of the spirit, which cannot be expressed; for it filleth heaven, so that the angels think they hear nothing else but this cry.

But in us there is a clean contrary feeling. For it seemeth unto us that this our small groaning doth not so pierce the clouds, that there is nothing else heard in heaven of God or his angels. Nay, we think, and especially during the time of temptation, the devil horribly roareth against us, that the heavens thunder and the earth trembleth, that all will fall upon us, that all creatures threaten our destruction, that hell is open and ready to swallow us up. This feeling is in our heart: these horrible voices, and this fearful shew we hear and we see. And this is it that Paul saith, in 2 Cor. xii, 9, that "the strength of Christ is made perfect through our weakness." For then is Christ almighty indeed; then doth he truly reign and triumph in us, when we are so weak that we can scarcely groan. But Paul saith, that this groaning is, in the ears of God, a most mighty cry, which filleth both heaven and earth.

Christ also, in the eighteenth of Luke, in the parable of the wicked judge calleth this groaning of a faithful heart, a cry, yea, and such a cry as ceaseth not day and night to cry unto God, where he saith: "Hear what the unrighteous judge saith. Now, shall not God avenge his elect, which cry day and night unto him, yea though he suffer long for them? yea, I tell you, he will avenge them quickly." We at this day, in so great persecution and contradiction of the Pope, of tyrants and sectaries, which fight against us both on the right hand and on the left, can do nothing else but utter such groanings. And these were our guns and artillery, wherewith we have so many years scattered the counsels and enterprises of our adversaries; whereby, also, we have begun to overthrow the kingdom of Antichrist. They also shall provoke Christ to hasten the day of his glorious coming, wherein he shall abolish all rule, authority, and power, and shall put all his enemies under his feet. So be it.

In the fourteenth of Exodus, the Lord speaketh unto Moses at the Red Sea, saying, "Why criest thou unto me?" Yet Moses cried not, but trembled and almost despaired, for he was in great trouble. It seemed that infidelity reigned in him, and not faith. For he saw the people of Israel so compassed and enclosed with the Egyptian host and with the sea, that there was no way whereby they might escape. Here Moses durst not once open his mouth. How, then, did he cry? We must not judge, therefore, according to the feeling of our own heart, but according to the word of God, which teacheth us that the Holy Ghost is given to those that are afflicted, terrified, and ready to despair, to raise them up and to comfort them, that they be not overcome in their temptations and afflictions, but may overcome them, and yet not without great terrors and troubles.

The Papists dreamed, "that holy men had the Holy Ghost in such sort that they never had nor felt any temptation." They spake of the Holy Ghost only by speculation and naked knowledge. But Paul saith, that "the strength of Christ is made perfect through our weakness." Also, that "the spirit helpeth our infirmities, and maketh intercession for us with unspeakable groanings." Therefore we have then most need of the help and comfort of the Holy Ghost; yea, and then is he most ready to help us, when we are most weak, and nearest to desperation. If any man suffer affliction with a constant and a joyful heart, then hath the Holy Ghost done his office in him. And, indeed, he exerciseth his work specially and properly in those which have suffered great terrors and afflictions, "and have," as the Psalm saith, "approached nigh to the gates of hell." As I said of Moses, which saw present death in the waters, and on every side whithersoever he turned his face. He was therefore in extreme anguish and desperation; and (no doubt) he felt in his heart a mighty cry of the devil against him, saying, All this people shall this day perish, for they can escape no way; and of this great calamity thou only shalt be found to be the author, because thou hast led them out of Egypt? Besides all this, the people cried out against him, saying, "Were there no graves in Egypt? Thou hast brought us out, that we should die here in the wilderness. Had it not been better for us to have served the Egyptians, than here wretchedly to die in the wilderness?" (Exod. xiv, 11.) The Holy Ghost was not here in Moses by bare speculation and knowledge only, but truly and effectually, who made intercession for him with an unspeakable groaning, so that he sighed unto the Lord and said, "O Lord, at thy commandment have I led forth this people: help us, therefore." This groaning or sighing unto God, the scripture calleth a crying.

This matter I have the more largely prosecuted, that I might plainly shew what the office of the Holy Ghost is, and when he specially exerciseth the same. In temptation, therefore, we must in no wise judge thereof according to our own sense and feeling, or by the crying of the law, sin, and the devil, etc. If we then follow our own sense, and believe those cryings, we shall think ourselves to be destitute of all help and succour of the Holy Ghost, and utterly cast away from the presence of God. Nay, rather let us then remember what Paul saith, "The Spirit helpeth our infirmities," etc. Also it crieth, "Abba Father;" that is to say, it uttereth a certain feeble sighing and groaning of the heart (as it seemeth unto us), which, notwithstanding, before God is a loud cry and an unspeakable groaning. Wherefore, in the midst of thy temptation and infirmity, cleave only unto Christ, and groan unto him: he giveth the Holy Ghost, which crieth, "Abba, Father." And this feeble groaning is a mighty cry in the ears of God, and so filleth heaven and earth, that God heareth nothing else: and moreover, it stoppeth the cries of all other things whatsoever.

Thou must mark also that Paul saith, that the Spirit maketh intercession for us in our temptation; not with many words, or long prayer, but only with a groaning, which notwithstanding cannot be expressed. And that he crieth not aloud with tears, saying, "Have mercy on me, O God," etc., (Ps. li, 1) but only uttereth a little sound, and a feeble groaning, as "Ah, father." This is but a little word, and yet, notwithstanding, it comprehendeth all things. The mouth speaketh not, but the affection of the heart speaketh after this manner: Although I be oppressed with anguish and terror on every side, and seem to be forsaken and utterly cast away from thy presence, yet am I thy child, and thou art my father, for Christ's sake. I am beloved, because of the Beloved. Wherefore, this little word, "father," conceived effectually in the heart, passeth all the eloquence of Demosthenes, Cicero, and of the most eloquent rhetoricians that ever were in the world. This matter is not expressed with words, but with groanings, which groanings cannot be expressed with any words or eloquence, for no tongue can express them.

I have used many words to declare that a Christian must assure himself that he is in the favour of God, and that he hath the crying of the Holy Ghost in his heart. This have I done, that we may learn to reject and utterly to abandon that devilish opinion of the whole kingdom of the Pope, which taught that a man ought to be uncertain, and to stand in doubt of the grace and favour of God towards him. If this opinion be received, then Christ profiteth nothing; for he that doubteth of God's favour towards him, must needs doubt also of the promises of God, and so, consequently, of the will of God, and of the benefits of Christ; namely, that he was born, suffered, died, and rose again for us, etc. But there can be no greater blasphemy against God, than to deny his promises, to deny God himself, to deny Christ, etc. Wherefore, it was not only an extreme madness, but a horrible impiety that the monks did so earnestly entice the youth, both men and women, to their monasteries, and to their holy orders (as they called them), as to a most certain state of salvation; and yet, when they had thus done, they bade them doubt of the grace and favour of God towards them.

Moreover, the Pope called all the world to the obedience of the holy church of Rome, as to a holy state, in the which they might undoubtedly attain salvation; and yet, after he had brought them under the obedience of his laws, he commanded them to doubt of their salvation. So the kingdom of Antichrist braggeth and vaunteth, at the first, of the holiness of his orders, his rules, and his laws, and assuredly promiseth everlasting life to such as observe and keep them. But afterwards, when these miserable men have long afflicted their bodies with watching, fasting, and such-like exercises, according to the traditions and ordinances of men, this is all that they gain thereby, that they are uncertain whether this obedience please God or no. Thus Satan most horribly dallied in the death and destruction of souls through the Pope; and therefore is the papacy a slaughter-house of consciences, and the very kingdom of the devil.

Now, to establish and confirm this pernicious and cursed error, they alleged the saying of Solomon—"The just and the wise men are in the hands of God; and yet no man knoweth whether he be worthy of love or of hatred." (Eccles. ix, 1.) Some understand this of that hatred which is to come; and some again of that which is present; but neither of them understand Solomon, who in that place meaneth nothing less than that which they dream. Moreover, the whole scripture teacheth us, especially and above all things, that we should not doubt, but assure ourselves and undoubtedly believe that God is merciful, loving, and patient; that he is neither a dissembler nor a deceiver; but that he is faithful and true, and keepeth his promise: yea, and hath performed that he promised in delivering his only begotten Son to death for our sins, that every one that believeth in him might not perish, but have everlasting life. Here we cannot doubt but that God is pleased with us, that he loveth us indeed, that the hatred and wrath of God is taken away, seeing he suffered his Son to die for us wretched sinners. Although this matter is set out and often repeated throughout the whole gospel, yet it profited nothing at all. This one saying of Solomon, perversely understood, did more prevail (especially among the votaries and hypocrites of the straiter religion) than all the promises and consolations of the whole scripture, yea, than Christ himself. They abused the scriptures therefore, to their own destruction, and were most justly punished for despising the scriptures, and rejecting the gospel.

It is expedient for us to know these things: first, because the Papists vaunt of their holiness, as if they had never committed any evil. Therefore they must be convinced by their own abominations, wherewith they have filled the whole world, as their own books do witness, whereof there is yet an infinite number. Secondly, that we may be fully certified that we have the pure doctrine of the gospel: of which certainty the Pope cannot glory, in whose kingdom, though all things else were sound and uncorrupt, yet this monstrous doctrine, of doubting of God's grace and favour, passeth all other monsters. And although it be manifest that the enemies of Christ's gospel teach uncertain things, because they command that men's consciences should remain in doubt, yet notwithstanding they condemn and kill us as heretics, because we dissent from them, and teach those things which are certain. And this they do with such devilish rage and cruelty, as if they were most assured of their doctrine.

Let us therefore give thanks unto God, that we are delivered from this monstrous doctrine of doubting, and can now assure ourselves that the Holy Ghost crieth, and bringeth forth in our hearts unspeakable groanings; and this is our anchor-hold, and our foundation. The gospel commandeth us to behold, not our own good works, our own perfection; but God the promiser, and Christ the mediator. Contrariwise, the Pope commandeth us to look, not unto God the promiser, nor unto Christ our high bishop, but unto our works and merits. Here, on the one side, doubting and desperation must needs follow: but on the other side, assurance of God's favour and joy of the spirit. For we cleave unto God, who cannot lie. For he saith, Behold, I deliver my Son to death, that through his blood he may redeem thee from thy sins, and from eternal death. In this case I cannot doubt, unless I will utterly deny God. And this is the reason that our doctrine is most sure and certain, because it carrieth us out of ourselves, that we should not lean to our own strength, our own conscience, our own feeling, our own person, and our own works; but to that which is without us, that is to say, the promise and truth of God, which cannot deceive us. This the Pope knoweth not, and therefore he wickedly imagineth that no man knoweth, be he never so just or so wise, whether he be worthy of love or of hatred. But if he be just and wise, he knoweth assuredly that he is beloved of God, or else he is neither just nor wise.

Moreover, this sentence of Solomon speaketh nothing at all of the hatred or favour of God towards men, but it is a moral sentence, reproving the ingratitude of men. For such is the perverseness and ingratitude of the world, that the better a man deserveth, the less thanks he shall have, and oftentimes he that should be his most friend, shall be his most enemy. Contrariwise, such as least deserve, shall be most esteemed. So David, a holy man, and a good king, was cast out of his kingdom. The prophets, Christ, and his apostles were slain. To conclude, the histories of all nations witness, that many men, well deserving of their country, were cast into banishment by their own citizens, and there lived in great misery, and some also shamefully perished in prison. Wherefore Solomon in this place speaketh not of the conscience having to do with God, nor of the favour or judgment, the love or hatred of God; but of the judgments and affections of men among themselves. As though he would say, There are many just and wise men, by whom God worketh much good, and giveth peace and quietness unto men. But so far off are they from acknowledging the same, that oftentimes they requite them again most unkindly and uncourteously for their well-doings and deservings. Therefore, although a man do all things well, and never so well, yet he knoweth not whether by this his diligence and faithfulness he deserve the hatred or favour of men.

So we, at this day, when we thought we should have found favour among our own countrymen, for that we preach unto them the gospel of peace, life, and eternal salvation; instead of favour, we have found bitter and cruel hatred. Indeed, at the first, many were greatly delighted with our doctrine, and received it gladly. We thought they would have been our friends and brethren, and that with one consent, together with us, they would have planted and preached this doctrine to others. But now we find that they are false brethren and our deadly enemies, which sow and spread abroad false doctrine; and that which we teach well and godly, they wickedly pervert and overthrow, stirring up offences in the churches. Whosoever, therefore, doth his duty godly and faithfully, in what kind of life soever he be, and for his well-doing receiveth nothing again but the unkindness and hatred of men, let him not vex and torment himself therefore, but let him say with Christ, "They hated me without a cause." Again, "For that they should have loved me, they slandered me; but I did pray." (Ps. cix, 3, 4.)

The Pope, therefore, with this devilish doctrine, whereby he commanded men to doubt of the favour of God towards them, took away God and all his promises out of the church, buried all the benefits of Christ, and abolished the whole gospel. These inconveniences do necessarily follow; for men do not lean to the promises of God, but to their own works and merits. Therefore they cannot be assured of the good-will of God towards them, but must needs doubt thereof, and so at length despair. No man can understand what God's will is, and what pleaseth him, but in his good word. This word assureth us that God cast away all the anger and displeasure which he had conceived against us, when he gave his only-begotten Son for our sins, etc. Wherefore, let us utterly abandon this devilish doubting, wherewith the whole papacy was poisoned, and let us be fully assured that God is merciful unto us, that we please him, that he hath a care over us, that we have the Holy Ghost, which maketh intercession for us with such crying and groaning as cannot be expressed.

Now, this is the true crying and groaning indeed, when a man in temptation calleth upon God: not as a tyrant, not as an angry judge, not as a tormentor, but as a father, although this groaning be so soft and so secret, that it can scarcely be perceived. For in serious temptations, and in the time of trial, where the conscience wrestleth with the judgment of God, it is wont to call God, not a father, but an unjust, an angry, a cruel tyrant and judge. And this crying, which Satan stirreth up in the heart, far passeth the cry of the spirit, and is strongly felt. For then it seemeth that God hath forsaken us, and will throw us down into hell. So the faithful complain oftentimes, in the Psalms: "I am cast down from the presence of God." (Ps.

xxxi, 22.) Also, "I am become as a broken vessel," etc. This is not the groaning that crieth, "Abba, Father;" but the roaring of God's wrath, which crieth strongly, O cruel judge, O cruel tormentor, etc. Here it is now time that thou turn away thine eyes from the law, from works, and from the sense and feeling of thine own conscience, and lay hold by faith of the promise; that is to say, of the word of grace and life, which raiseth up the conscience again, so that it now beginneth to groan and say, Although the law accuse me, sin and death terrify me never so much, yet, O my God, thou promisest grace, righteousness and everlasting life through Jesus Christ. And so the promise bringeth a sighing and a groaning, which crieth Abba, Father.

VERSE 7. *Wherefore thou art no more a servant, but a son.*

This is the shutting up and the conclusion of that which he said before. As if he should say, This being true, that we have received the spirit by the Gospel, whereby we cry, Abba, Father, then is this decree pronounced in heaven, that there is now no bondage any more, but mere liberty and adoption. And who bringeth this liberty? Verily, this groaning. By what means? The Father offereth unto me, by his promise, his grace and his fatherly favour. This remaineth then, that I should receive this grace. And this is done when I again with this groaning do cry, and with a childly heart do assent unto this name, Father. Here, then, the father and son meet, and the marriage is made up without all pomp and solemnity: that is to say, nothing at all cometh between, no law nor work is here required. For what should a man do in these terrors and horrible darkness of temptations? Here is nothing else but the Father promising, and calling me his son, by Christ, who was made under the law, etc.; and I receiving and answering by this groaning, saying, "Father." Here then is no exacting; nothing is required, but only that childly groaning that apprehendeth a sure hope and trust in tribulation, and saith, Thou promisest, and callest me thy child, for Christ's sake; and I again receive thy promise, and call thee Father. This is, indeed, to be made children, simply, and without any works. But these things, without experience and practice, cannot be understood.

Paul in this place taketh this word "servant," otherwise than he did before, in the third chapter, where he saith, "There is neither bond nor free," etc. Here he calleth him a servant of the law which is subject to the law, as he did a little before:

"We were in bondage under the rudiments of the world." Wherefore to be a servant, according to Paul in this place, is to be guilty and captive under the law, under the wrath of God and death, to behold God, not as a merciful father, but as a tormentor, an enemy, and a tyrant. This is, indeed, to be kept in bondage and Babylonical captivity, and to be cruelly tormented therein. For the law delivereth not from sin and death, but revealeth and increaseth sin, and engendereth wrath. This bondage (saith Paul, Rom. iii, 20; iv, 15) continueth no longer: it oppresseth us not, nor maketh us heavy any more, etc., etc. Paul saith: "Thou shalt be no more a servant." But the sentence is more general, if we say: there shall be no bondage in Christ any more, but mere freedom and adoption. For when faith cometh, that bondage ceaseth, as he said before, in the third chapter.

Now, if we, by the spirit of Christ crying in our hearts, "Abba, Father," be no more servants, but children; then it followeth that we are not only delivered from the Pope, and all the abominations of men's traditions, but also from all the jurisdiction and power of the law of God. Wherefore we ought in no wise to suffer the law to reign in our conscience, and much less the Pope, with his vain threatenings and terrors. Indeed, he roareth mightily as a lion (Apoc. x, 3); and threateneth to all those that obey not his laws, the wrath and indignation of Almighty God and of his blessed apostles, etc. But here Paul armeth and comforteth us against these roarings, when he saith: "Thou art no more a servant, but a son." Take hold of this consolation by faith, and say, O law, thy tyranny can have no place in the throne where Christ my Lord sitteth: there I cannot hear thee (much less do I hear thee, O Antichrist), for I am free and a son, who must not be subject to any bondage, or servile law. Let not Moses, therefore, with his laws (much less the Pope) ascend up into the bridechamber, there to lie, that is to say, to reign in the conscience, which Christ hath delivered from the law, to the end that it should not be subject to any bondage. Let the servants abide with the ass in the valley: Let none but Isaac ascend up into the mountain with his father Abraham. (Gen. xxii, 5.) That is, let the law have dominion over the body, and over the old man: let him be under the law, and suffer the burden to be laid upon him: let him suffer himself to be exercised and vexed with the law: let the law limit and prescribe unto him what he ought to do, what he ought to suffer, and how he ought to live and govern himself among men. But let it not defile the bed in which Christ should rest and sleep alone: that is to say, let it not trouble the conscience. For she alone ought to live with Christ her spouse in the kingdom of liberty and adoption.

If then (saith he) by the spirit of Christ ye cry, Abba, Father, then are ye indeed no longer servants, but free men and sons. Therefore ye are without the law, without sin, without death; that is to say, ye are saved, and ye are now quite delivered from all evils. Wherefore the adoption bringeth with it the eternal kingdom, and all the heavenly inheritance. Now, how inestimable the glory of this gift is, man's heart is not able to conceive, and much less to utter. In the mean time we see this but darkly, and as it were afar off: we have this little groaning and feeble faith which only resteth upon the hearing and the sound of the voice of Christ in giving the promise. Therefore we must not measure this thing by reason, or by our own feeling, but by the promise of God. Now, because he is infinite, therefore his promise is also infinite, although it seem to be never so much inclosed in these narrow straits, these anguishes, I mean. Wherefore there is nothing that can now accuse, terrify, or bind the conscience any more. For there is no more servitude, but adoption: which not only bringeth unto us liberty from the law, sin, and death, but also the inheritance of everlasting life, as followeth.

VERSE 7. *Now, if thou be a son, thou art also the heir of God through Christ.*

For he that is a son, must be also an heir: for by his birth he is worthy to be an heir. There is no work or merit that bringeth to him the inheritance, but his birth only; and so in obtaining the inheritance he is a mere patient, and not an agent; that is to say, not to beget, not to labour, not to care: but to be born is that which maketh him an heir. So we obtain eternal gifts, namely, the forgiveness of sins, righteousness, the glory of the resurrection, and everlasting life, not as agents, but as patients; that is, not by doing, but by receiving. Nothing here cometh between, but faith alone apprehendeth the promise offered. Like as therefore a son, in the politic and household government, is made an heir by his only birth: so here, faith only maketh us sons of God, born of the word, which is the womb of God, wherein we are conceived, carried, born, and nourished up, etc. By this birth, then, we are made new creatures, formed by faith in the word: we are made Christians, children and heirs of God through Jesus Christ. Now, being heirs, we are delivered from death, sin, and the devil, and we have righteousness and eternal life.

But this far passeth all man's capacity, that he calleth us

heirs; not of some rich and mighty prince, not of the emperor, not of the world, but of God, the almighty creator of all things. This, our inheritance, then (as Paul saith in another place) is inestimable. And if a man could comprehend the great excellency of this matter, that he is the son and heir of God, and with a constant faith believe the same, this man would esteem all the power and riches of all the kingdoms of the world but as filthy dung, in comparison of his eternal inheritance. He would abhor whatsoever is high and glorious in the world; yea, the greater the pomp and glory of the world is, the more would he hate it. To conclude, whatsoever the world most highly esteemeth and magnifieth, that should be, in his eyes, most vile and abominable. For what is all the world, with all his power, riches, and glory, in comparison of God, whose son and heir he is? Furthermore, he would heartily desire with Paul (Philip. i, 23) to be loosed, and to be with Christ; and nothing could be more welcome unto him than speedy death, which he would embrace as a most joyful peace, knowing that it should be the end of all his miseries, and that through it he should attain to his inheritance, etc. Yea, a man that could perfectly believe this, should not long remain alive, but should be swallowed up incontinent with excessive joy.

But the law of the members, striving against the law of the mind, hindereth faith in us, and suffereth it not to be perfect. Therefore we have need of the help and comfort of the Holy Ghost, which in our troubles and afflictions may make intercession for us with unspeakable groanings, as before I have said. Sin yet remaineth in the flesh, which oftentimes oppresseth the conscience, and so hindereth faith, that we cannot with joy perfectly behold and desire those eternal riches which God hath given unto us through Christ. Paul himself, feeling this battle of the flesh against the spirit, crieth out: "O wretched man that I am, who shall deliver me from this body of death?" (Rom. vii, 24.) He accuseth his body, which notwithstanding it behoved him to love, calling it by an odious name, his Death. As if he would say: My body doth more afflict me, and more grievously vex me, than death itself. For it hindered in him also this joy of spirit. He had not always the sweet and joyful cogitations of the heavenly inheritance to come, but he felt oftentimes also much heaviness of spirit, great anguish, and terrors.

Hereby we may plainly see how hard a matter faith is: which is not easily and quickly apprehended, as certain full and loathing spirits dream, which swallow up at once all that is contained in the holy scriptures. The great infirmity which is in the saints, and the striving of the flesh against the spirit, do sufficiently witness how feeble faith is in them. For a perfect faith bringeth by-and-by a perfect contempt and loathing of this present life. If we could fully assure ourselves, and constantly believe that God is our father, and we his son and heirs, then should we utterly contemn this world, with all the glory, righteousness, wisdom, and power, with all the royal sceptres and crowns, and with all the riches and pleasures thereof. We should not be so careful for this life: we should not be so addicted to the world and worldly things, trusting unto them when we have them, lamenting and despairing when we lose them: but we should do all things with great love, humility, and patience. But we do the contrary: for the flesh is yet strong, but faith is feeble, and the spirit weak. Therefore Paul saith very well, that we have here, in this life, but only the first-fruits of the spirit, and that, in the world to come, we shall have the tenths also.

VERSE 7. *Through Christ.*

Paul hath Christ always in his mouth: he cannot forget him; for he did well foresee that nothing should be less known in the world (yea, among them which should profess themselves to be Christians) than Christ and his gospel. Therefore he talketh of him, and setteth him before our eyes continually. And as often as he speaketh of grace, righteousness, the promise, adoption, and inheritance, he is always wont to add, "in Christ," or "through Christ," covertly impugning the law. As if he would say: These things come unto us neither by the law nor by the works thereof; much less by our own strength, or by the works of men's traditions; but only by Christ.

> VERSES 8 AND 9. *But even then, when ye knew not God, ye did service unto them which by nature are no gods. But now, seeing ye know God, yea, rather, are known of God, how turn you again unto impotent and beggarly rudiments, whereunto, as from the beginning, ye will be in bondage again?*

This is the conclusion of Paul's disputation. From this place unto the end of the epistle he doth not much dispute, but only giveth precepts as touching manners. Notwithstanding he first reproveth the Galatians, being sore displeased that this divine and heavenly doctrine should be so suddenly and easily removed out of their hearts. As if he would say, Ye have teachers which will bring you back again into the bondage of the law. This did not I; but by my doctrine I called you out of darkness, and out of the ignorance of God, into a wonderful light

EPISTLE TO THE GALATIANS

and knowledge of him. I brought you out of bondage, and set you in the freedom of the sons of God, not by preaching unto you the works of the law, or the merits of men, but the grace and righteousness of God, and the giving of heavenly and eternal blessings through Christ. Now, seeing this is true, why do you so soon forsake the light, and return to darkness? Why do ye suffer yourselves so easliy to be brought from grace unto the law, from freedom to bondage?

Here again we see (as before I have said) that to fall in faith is an easy matter, as the example of the Galatians witnesseth. The example of the Anabaptists, libertines, and such other heretics, witnesseth the same also at this day. We, for our part, do set forth the doctrine of faith with continual travel, by preaching, by reading, and by writing; we purely and plainly distinguish the gospel from the law, and yet do we little prevail. This cometh of the devil, who goeth about by all subtle means to seduce men, and to hold them in error: he can abide nothing less than the true knowledge of grace, and faith in Christ. Therefore, to the end he may take Christ clean out of sight, he setteth before them other shows, wherewith he so deceiveth them, that by little and little he leadeth them from faith and the knowledge of grace, to the disputation of the law. When he hath brought this about, then is Christ taken away. It is not without cause, therefore, that Paul speaketh so much and so often of Christ, and that he goeth about so purely to set forth the doctrine of faith; whereunto he attributeth righteousness only and alone, and taketh it from the law, declaring that the law hath a clean contrary effect; that is, to engender wrath, to increase sin, etc. For he would gladly persuade us that we should not suffer Christ to be plucked out of our heart: that the spouse should not suffer her husband to depart out of her arms, but should always embrace him, and cleave fast unto him, who, being present, there is no danger; yea, there is the faithful groaning, fatherly good-will, adoption, and inheritance.

But why saith Paul that the Galatians turned back again to weak and beggarly rudiments or ceremonies; that is to say, to the law, whereas they never had the law; for they were Gentiles (notwithstanding he wrote these things to the Jews also, as afterwards we will declare) or why speaketh he not after this manner?—Once, when ye knew not God, ye did service unto them which by nature were no gods; but now, seeing ye know God, why turn ye back again, forsaking the true God, to worship idols? Doth Paul take it to be all one thing, to fall from the promise to the law, from faith to works, and to do service unto gods which by nature are no gods? I answer, whosoever is fallen from the article of justification, is ignorant of God, and an idolater. Therefore, it is all one thing, whether he afterwards turn again to the law, or to the worshipping of idols; it is all one whether he be called a Monk, a Turk, a Jew, or an Anabaptist. For when this article is taken away, there remaineth nothing else but error, hypocrisy, impiety, and idolatry, how much soever it seem in outward appearance to be the very truth, the true service of God, and true holiness, etc.

The reason is, because God will or can be known no otherwise than by Christ, according to that saying of John i. "The only begotten Son, which is in the bosom of the Father, he hath declared him." He is the seed promised unto Abraham, in whom God hath established all his promises. Wherefore, Christ is the only mean, and, as ye would say, the glass, by the which we see God; that is to say, we know his will. For in Christ we see that God is not a cruel exactor or a judge, but a most favourable, loving, and merciful Father, who, to the end he might bless us, that is to say, deliver us from the law, sin, death, and all evils, and might endue us with grace, righteousness, and everlasting life, "spared not his own Son, but gave him for us all," etc. (Rom. viii, 32.) This is a true knowledge of God, and a divine persuasion, which deceiveth us not, but painteth out God unto us lively.

He that is fallen from this knowledge, must needs conceive this fantasy in his heart: I will set up such a service of God; I will enter into such an order; I will choose this or that work: and so I will serve God, and I doubt not but God will accept this, and reward me with everlasting life, for the same. For he is merciful and liberal, giving all good things even to the unworthy and unthankful; much more will he give unto me grace and everlasting life, for my great and manifold good deeds and merits. This is the highest wisdom, righteousness, and religion, that reason can judge of; which is common to all nations, to the Papists, Jews, Turks, heretics, etc. They can go no higher than that Pharisee did, of whom mention is made in the gospel (Luke xviii, 11, 12). They have no knowledge of the Christian righteousness, or of the righteousness of faith; "For the natural man perceiveth not the mysteries of God" (1 Cor. ii, 14). Also, "There is none that understandeth, there is none that seeketh after God, etc. (Romans iii, 11). Therefore, there is no difference at all between a Papist, a Jew, a Turk, and an heretic. Indeed, there is a difference of the persons, the places, rites, religions, works, and worshippings; notwithstanding, there is all one and the same reason, the same heart, opinion, and cogitation, in them all. For the Turk thinketh the self-same thing that the Charter-house monk doth; namely, if I do this or that work, God will be merciful unto me; if I do it not, he will be angry. There is no mean betwixt man's working and the knowledge of Christ. If this knowledge be darkened or defaced, it is all one, whether thou be a monk, a Turk, a Jew, etc.

Wherefore, it is an extreme madness that the Papists and Turks do so strive among themselves about the religion and service of God, contending that both of them have the true religion and true worship of God. And the monks themselves agree not together: for one of them will be accounted more holy than another, for certain foolish outward ceremonies; and yet, in their hearts, the opinion of them all is so alike, that one egg is not more like to another. For this is the imagination of them all: If I do this work, God will have mercy upon me; if I do it not, he will be angry. And, therefore, every man that revolteth from the knowledge of Christ, must needs fall into idolatry, and conceive such an imagination of God, as it not agreeable to his nature. As the Charter-house monk for the observing of his rule, the Turk for the keeping of his Alcoran, hath this assurance, that he pleaseth God, and shall receive a reward of him for his labour.

Such a god as, after this sort, forgiveth sins, and justifieth sinners, can no where be found, and therefore this is but a vain imagination, a dream, and an idol of the heart. For God hath not promised that he will save and justify men for the religions, observations, ceremonies, and ordinances, devised by men; yea, God abhorreth nothing more (as the whole scripture witnesseth) that such will-works, such service, rites, and ceremonies; for the which also he overthroweth whole kingdoms and empires. Therefore, as many as trust to their own strength and righteousness, do serve a god, but such a god as they themselves have devised, and not the true God indeed. For the true God speaketh thus: No righteousness, wisdom, nor religion, pleaseth me, but that only whereby the Father is glorified through the Son. Whosoever apprehendeth this Son, and me, and my promise in him, by faith, to him I am a God, to him I am a Father, him do I accept, justify, and save. All others abide under wrath, because they worship that thing which by nature is no god.

Whosoever forsaketh this doctrine, must needs fall into the ignorance of God; he understandeth not what the true Christian righteousness, wisdom, and service of God is; he is an idolater, abiding under the law, sin, death, and the power of the devil, and all things that he doth are accursed and condemned. Therefore the Anabaptist, imagining with himself that he pleaseth God, if he be re-baptized, if he forsake his house, wife, and children; if he mortify his flesh, and suffer much adversity, and at length death itself; yet there is not one drop of the knowledge of Christ in him, but secluding Christ, he dreameth altogether of his own works, of the forsaking of his goods, of his affliction and mortification, and now differeth nothing from the Turk, Jew, or Papist, in spirit or in heart, but only in the outward appearance, works, and ceremonies, which he hath chosen to himself. The same confidence in works have all the monks and other religious orders; notwithstanding, in their apparel and other outward things, there is a difference.

There are at this day very many like unto these, which, notwithstanding, would be counted among the true professors and teachers of the gospel; and, as touching the words, they teach that men are delivered from their sins by the death of Christ. But because they teach faith in such sort, that they attribute more to charity than to faith, they highly dishonour Christ, and wickedly pervert his word. For they dream that God regardeth and accepteth us for our charities' sake, whereby, we being reconciled to God, do love God and our neighbour. If this be true, then have we no need of Christ at all. Such men serve not the true God, but an idol of their own heart, which they themselves have devised. For the true God doth not regard or accept us for our charity, virtues, or newness of life, but for Christ's sake, etc.

But they make this objection: Yet, notwithstanding, the scripture commandeth that we should love God with all our heart, etc. It is true. But it followeth not, that, because God commandeth us, therefore we do it. If we did love God with all our heart, etc., then no doubt we should be justified, and live through this obedience, as it is written: "He that shall do these things shall live in them" (Lev. xviii, 5; Rom. x, 5). But the gospel saith: Thou doest not these things, therefore thou shalt not live in them. For this sentence, "thou shalt love the Lord thy God," etc., requireth a perfect obedience, a perfect fear, trust, and love towards God. These things men neither do nor can perform, in this corrupt nature. Therefore this law, "Thou shalt love the Lord thy God," etc., justifieth not, but accuseth and condemneth all men, according to that saying, "the law causeth wrath," etc. Contrariwise, "Christ is the finishing and accomplishing of the law to righteousness, to every one that believeth" (Romans iv, 15; x, 4). Of this we have spoken largely before.

In like manner the Jew, keeping the law, with this opinion, that he by this obedience will please God, serveth not the true God; but is an idolater, worshipping a dream, and an idol of his own heart, which is no where to be found. For the God of his fathers, whom he saith he worshippeth, promised to Abraham "a seed," through the which all nations should be blessed. Therefore God is known, and the blessing is given, not by the law, but by the gospel of Christ. Although Paul speaketh these words, "Then, when ye knew not God, ye did service," etc., properly and principally to the Galatians, which were Gentiles; yet, notwithstanding, by the same words he also toucheth the Jews, who, though they had rejected their idols outwardly, yet in their hearts they worshipped them more than did the Gentiles, as it is said in Romans ii, "Thou abhorrest idols, and committest sacrilege." The Gentiles were not the people of God, they had not his word, and therefore their idolatry was gross, but the idolatrous Jews cloaked their idolatry with the name and word of God (as all justiciaries which seek righteousness by works are wont to do), and so with this outward shew of holiness they deceived many. Therefore idolatry, the more holy and spiritual it is, the more hurtful it is.

But how may these two contrary sayings which the apostle here setteth down, be reconciled together? "Ye knew not God, and ye worshipped God." I answer, all men naturally have this general knowledge, that there is a God, according to that saying, Romans i, "Forasmuch as that which may be known of God was manifest in them." For God was manifest unto them, in that the invisible things of him did appear by the creation of the world. Moreover, the ceremonies and religions which were, and always remained among all nations, sufficiently witness that all men have had a certain general knowledge of God. But whether they had it by nature, or by the tradition of their forefathers, I will not here dispute.

But here some will object again: If all men knew God, wherefore then doth Paul say, that the Galatians knew not God, before the preaching of the gospel? I answer, there is a double knowledge of God, general and particular. All men have the general knowledge, namely, that there is a God, that he created heaven and earth, that he is just, that he punisheth the wicked. But what God thinketh of us, what his will is towards us, what he will give or what he will do, to the end we may be delivered from sin and death, and be saved (which is the true knowledge of God indeed), this they know not. As it may be that I know some man by sight, whom yet, indeed, I know not thoroughly, because I understand not what affection he beareth towards me. So men know naturally that there is a God; but what his will is, or what is not his will, they do not know. For it is written, "There is none that understandeth God" (Rom. iii, 11). And in another place, "No man hath seen God" (John i, 18). That is to say, no man hath known what is the will of God. Now, what doth it avail thee, if thou know that there is a God, and yet are ignorant what is his will towards thee? Here some think one thing, and some another. The Jews imagine this to be the will of God, if they worship him according to the rule of Moses' law; the Turk, if he observe his Alcoran; the monk, if he keep his order and perform his vows. But all these are deceived, and become vain in their own cogitations, as Paul saith (Romans i), not knowing what pleaseth or displeaseth God. Therefore, instead of the true and natural God, they worship the dreams and imaginations of their own heart.

This is it that Paul meaneth, when he saith, "When ye knew not God;" that is, when ye knew not the will of God, ye served those which by nature were no gods, that is to say, ye served the dreams and imaginations of your own heart, whereby ye imagined, without the word, that God was to be worshipped with this or that work, with this or that rite or ceremony. For upon this proposition, which all men do naturally hold, namely, that there is a God, hath sprung all idolatry, which, without the knowledge of the Divinity, could never have come into the world. But, because men had this natural knowledge of God, they conceived vain and wicked imaginations of God, without and against the world, which they esteemed and maintained as the very truth itself, and so dreamed that God is such a one, as by nature he is not. So the monk imagineth him to be such a God as forgiveth sins, giveth grace and everlasting life, for the keeping of his rule. This god is no where to be found: therefore he serveth not the true God, but that which by nature is no god; to wit, the imagination and idol of his own heart: that is to say, his own false and vain opinion of God, which he dreameth to be an undoubted truth. Now, reason itself will enforce us to confess, that man's opinion is no god. Therefore, whosoever will worship God without his words, serveth not the true God (as Paul saith), but that which by nature is no god.

Therefore, whether ye call "rudiments" here the law of Moses, or else the traditions of the Gentiles (albeit he speaketh here properly and principally of the rudiments of Moses), there is no great difference. For he that falleth from grace to the law, falleth with no less danger than he that falleth from grace to idolatry. For without Christ there is nothing else but mere idolatry, an idle and false imagination of God, whether it be called Moses' law, or the Pope's ordinances, or the Turk's Alcoran, etc. Therefore he saith, with a certain admiration,

VERSE 9. *But now, seeing ye know God.*

As though he would say, This is a marvellous thing, that ye, knowing God by the preaching of faith, do so suddenly revolt from the true knowledge of his will (wherein I thought ye were so surely established, that I thought nothing less than that ye should be so easily overthrown), and do now again, by the instigation of the false apostles, return to the weak and beggarly ceremonies, which ye would serve again afresh. Ye heard before, by my preaching, that this is the will of God, to bless all nations; not by circumcision, or by the observation of the law, but by Christ promised to Abraham (Gal. iii, 7). They that believe in him, shall be blessed with faithful Abraham (Gal. iii, 9). They are the sons and heirs of God. Thus (I say) have ye known God.

VERSE 9. *Yea, rather are known of God, etc.*

He correcteth the sentence going before, "but now, seeing ye have known God;" or rather turneth it after this manner, "yea, rather ye are known of God;" for he feared lest they had lost God utterly. As if he would say: Alas! are ye come to this point, that now ye know not God, but return again from grace to the law? Yet, notwithstanding, God knoweth you. And indeed, our knowledge is rather passive than active; that is to say, it consisteth in this, that we are rather known of God, than that we know him. All our doing, that is, all our endeavour to know and to apprehend God, is to suffer God to work in us. He giveth the word, which, when we have received by faith given from above, we are new-born, and made the sons of God. This is, then, the sense and meaning: "Ye are known of God;" that is, ye are visited with the word, ye are endued with faith and the Holy Ghost, whereby ye are renewed, etc. Wherefore, even by these words, "ye are known of God," he taketh away all righteousness from the law, and denieth that we attain the knowledge of God through the worthiness of our own works. "For no man knoweth the Father, but the Son, and he to whom the Son will reveal him" (Luke x, 22). And also, "He by his knowledge shall justify many, because he shall bear their iniquities," (Isa. liii, 11). Wherefore, our knowledge concerning God consisteth in suffering, and not in doing.

He much marvelleth, therefore, that, seeing they knew God truly by the gospel, they returned so suddenly to weak and beggarly rudiments, by the persuasion of the false apostles. As I myself also should greatly marvel, if our church (which by are grace of God is godly reformed in pure doctrine and faith) should be seduced and perverted by some fond and frantic head, through the preaching of one or two sermons, that they would not acknowledge me for their pastor any more. Which thing, notwithstanding, shall one day come to pass, if not whilst we live, yet when we are dead and gone. For many shall then rise up, which will be masters and teachers, who, under a colour of true religion, shall teach false and perverse doctrine, and shall quickly overthrow all that we in so long time and with so great travail have builded. We are not better than the apostles, who, whilst they yet lived, saw (not without their great grief and sorrow) the subversion of those churches which they themselves had planted through their ministry. Therefore it is no great marvel if we be constrained to behold the like evil at this day, in those churches where sectaries do reign, who hereafter, when we are dead, shall possess those churches which we have won and planted by our ministry, and with their poison infect and subvert the same. And yet, notwithstanding, Christ shall remain and reign to the end of the world, and that marvellously, as he did under the papacy.

Paul seemeth to speak very spitefully of the law, when he calleth it the rudiments (as he did also before, in the beginning of this chapter) and not only rudiments, but weak and beggarly rudiments, and ceremonies. Is it not blasphemy to give such odious names to the law of God? The law being in his true use, ought to serve the promises, and to stand with the promises and grace. But, if it fight against them, it is no more the holy law of God, but a false and devilish doctrine, and doth nothing else but drive men to desperation, and therefore must be rejected.

Wherefore, when he calleth the law weak and beggarly rudiments, he speaketh of the law in respect of proud and presumptuous hypocrites, which would be justified by it, and not of the law being spiritually understood, which engendereth wrath, (Rom. iv, 15). For the law (as I have often said) being in his own proper use, accuseth and condemneth a man: and in this respect is is not only a strong and rich rudiment, but also most mighty and most rich, yea, rather, an invincible power and riches;

and if here the conscience be compared with the law, then is it most weak and beggarly. For it is so tender a thing, that for a small sin it is so troubled and terrified, that it utterly despaireth, unless it be raised up again. Wherefore, the law, in his proper use, hath more strength and riches than heaven and earth is able to contain; insomuch that one letter or one tittle of the law is able to kill all mankind, as the history of the law given by Moses doth witness (Exodus xix, 20). This is the true and divine use of the law, of which Paul speaketh not in this place.

Paul therefore entreateth here of hypocrites, which are fallen from grace, or which have not yet attained to grace. These, abusing the law, seek to be justified by it. They exercise and tire themselves day and night in the works thereof, as Paul witnesseth of the Jews—"For I bear them record," saith he, "that they have the zeal of God, but not according to knowledge; for they being ignorant of the righteousness of God," etc. (Rom. x). Such do hope so to be strengthened and enriched by the law, that they may be able to set their power and riches, which they have gotten by the righteousness thereof, against the wrath and judgment of God, and so to appease God, and to be saved thereby. In this respect, then, we may well say, that the law is a weak and a beggarly rudiment; that is to say, which can give neither help nor counsel.

And whoso listeth to amplify this matter, may further say, that the law is a weak and a beggarly rudiment, because it maketh men more weak and beggarly: again, because that of itself it hath no power, or riches, whereby it is able to give or to bring righteousness: and moreover, that it is not only weak and beggarly, but even weakness and beggary itself. How, then, shall it enrich or strengthen those, which were before both weak and beggarly? Therefore to seek to be justified by the law, is as much as if a man, being weak and feeble already, would seek some other greater evil, whereby he might overcome his weakness and poverty, which notwithstanding would bring him unto utter destruction. As if he which hath the falling sickness, would seek to join unto it the pestilence for a remedy; or if a leper should come to a leper, or a beggar to a beggar, the one to help and to enrich the other.

Paul therefore sheweth, that they which seek to be justified by the law, have this commodity thereby, that daily they become more and more weak and beggarly. For they be weak and beggarly of themselves; that is to say, they are by nature the children of wrath, subject to death and everlasting damnation, and yet they lay hold upon that which is nothing else but mere weakness and beggary, seeking to be strengthened and enriched thereby. Therefore, every one that falleth from the promise to the law, from faith to works, doth nothing else but lay upon himself such a burden, being weak and feeble already, as he is not able to bear (Acts xv); and in bearing thereof is made ten times more weak, so that at length he is driven to despair, unless Christ come and deliver him.

This thing the gospel also witnesseth, speaking of the woman which was grieved twelve years with a bloody issue, and suffered many things of many physicians, upon whom she had spent all her substance, and yet could not be cured: but the longer she was under their hands, the worse she was (Mark v, 25). As many, therefore, as do the works of the law, to be justified thereby, are not only not made righteous, but twice more unrighteous than they were before; that is, (as I have said) more weak and beggarly, and more unapt to do any good work. This have I proved to be true, both in myself and in many others. I have known many monks in the papacy, which with great zeal have done many great works, for the attaining of righteousness and salvation, and yet were they more impatient, more weak, more miserable, more faithless, more fearful, and more ready to despair than any other. The civil magistrates, who were ever occupied in great and weighty affairs, were not so impatient, so fearful, so faint-hearted, so superstitious, and so faithless, as these justiciaries and merit-mongers were.

Whosoever, then, seeketh righteousness by the law, what can he imagine else, but that God, being angry, must needs be pacified with works? Now, when he hath once conceived this fantasy, he beginneth to work. But he can never find so many good works as are able to quiet his conscience, but still he desireth more; yea, he findeth sin in those works he hath done already. Therefore, his conscience can never be certified, but must needs be always in doubt, and thus think with itself: Thou hast not sacrificed as thou shouldst do; thou hast not prayed aright; this thou hast left undone; this or that sin thou hast committed. Here the heart trembleth, and feeleth itself oppressed with innumerable sins, which still increase without end, so that he swerveth from righteousness more and more, until at length he fall to desperation. Hereof it cometh, that many, being at the point of death, have uttered these desperate words: O wretch that I am! I have not kept mine order. Whither shall I flee from the wrath of Christ, that angry judge? Would to God I had been made a swineherd, or the vilest wretch in the whole world.

Thus the monk, in the end of his life, is more weak, more beggarly, more faithless and fearful than he was at the beginning, when he first entered into his order. The reason is, because he would strengthen himself through weakness, and enrich himself through poverty. The law, or men's traditions, or the rule of his order, should have healed him when he was sick, and enriched him when he was poor; but he is become more feeble and more poor than the publicans and harlots. The publicans and harlots have not a heap of good works to trust unto, as the monks have: but, although they feel their sins never so much, yet they can say with the publican, "O Lord, be merciful unto me a sinner!" (Luke xviii, 13). But, contrariwise, the monk, which hath spent all his time in weak and beggarly elements, is confirmed in this opinion: if thou keep thy rule, thou shalt be saved, etc. With this false persuasion he is so deluded and bewitched, that he can not apprehend grace, no, nor once remember grace. Thus, notwithstanding all the works which either he doth, or hath done, be they never so many and so great, he thinketh that he hath never done enough, but hath still an eye to more works; and so, by heaping up of works, he goeth about to appease the wrath of God and to justify himself, until he be driven to utter desperation. Wherefore, whosoever falleth from faith, and followeth the law, is like to Æsop's dog, which foregoeth the flesh, and snatcheth at the shadow. Wherefore, it is impossible that such as seek righteousness and salvation by the law (whereunto men are naturally inclined), should ever find quietness and peace of conscience: yea, they do nothing else but heap laws upon laws, whereby they torment both themselves and others, and afflict men's consciences so miserably, that through extreme anguish of heart, many die before their time. For one law always bringeth forth ten more, and so they increase, without number and without end.

Now, who would have thought that the Galatians, which had learned so sound and so pure a doctrine, of such an excellent apostle and teacher, could be so suddenly led away from the same, and utterly perverted by the false apostles? It is not without cause that I repeat this so often, that to fall away from the truth of the gospel is an easy matter. The reason is, because men do not sufficiently consider, no, not the very faithful, what an excellent and precious treasure the true knowledge of Christ is. Therefore they do not labour so diligently and so carefully as they should do, to obtain and to retain the same. Moreover, the greater part of those that hear the word, are exercised with no cross or affliction; they wrestle not against sin, death, and the devil, but live in security, without any conflict. Such men, because they are not proved and tried with temptations, and therefore are not armed with the word of God against the subtleties of the devil, never feel the use and power of the word. Indeed, whilst they are among faithful ministers and preachers, they can follow their words, and say as they say, persuading themselves that they perfectly understand the matter of justification; but when they are gone, and wolves in sheep's clothing are come in their place, it happeneth unto them as it did to the Galatians; that is to say, they are suddenly seduced, and easily turned back to weak and beggarly rudiments.

Paul hath here his peculiar manner of speech, which the other apostles did not use. For there was none of them besides Paul, that gave such names to the law; to wit, that it is a weak and a beggarly rudiment, that is to say, utterly unprofitable to righteousness. And, surely, I durst not have given such terms unto the law, but should have thought it great blasphemy against God, if Paul had done so before. But of this I have entreated more largely before, where I shewed when the law is weak and beggarly, and when it is most strong and rich, etc. Now, if the law of God be weak and unprofitabe to justification, much more are the laws and decrees of the Pope, weak and unprofitable to justification. Therefore we give sentence against the ordinances, laws, and decrees of the Pope, with such boldness and assurance as Paul did against the law of God, that they are not only weak and beggarly rudiments, and utterly unprofitable to righteousness, but also execrable, accursed, devilish, and damnable: for they blaspheme grace, they overthrow the gospel, abolish faith, take away Christ, etc.

Forasmuch, then, as the Pope requireth that we should keep his laws as necessary to salvation, he is very Antichrist, and the vicar of Satan; and as many as cleave unto him, and confirm his abominations and blasphemies, or keep them to this end, that thereby they may merit the forgiveness of their sins, are the servants of Antichrist and of the devil. Now, such hath the doctrine of the papistical church been of a long time, that these laws ought to be kept as necessary to salvation. Thus the Pope sitteth in the temple of God, vaunting himself as God: he setteth himself against God, and exalteth himself above all that is called God, or worshipped, etc.; and men's consciences more feared and reverenced the laws and ordinances of the Pope, than the word of God and his ordinances. By this means he was made the Lord of heaven, of earth, and of hell, and bare a triple crown upon his head. The cardinals also and bishops, his creatures, were made kings and princes of the world: and therefore, if he did not burden men's consciences with his laws, he could not long maintain his terrible power, his dignity, and his riches; but his whole kingdom would quickly fall.

This place which Paul here handleth, is weighty and of great importance, and therefore the more diligently to be marked: to wit, that they which fall from grace to the law, do utterly lose the knowledge of the truth: they see not their own sins; they neither know God, nor the devil, nor themselves; and, moreover, they understand not the force and use of the law, although they brag never so much that they keep and observe the same. For without the knowledge of grace, that is to say, without the gospel of Christ, it is impossible for a man to give this definition of the law, that it is a weak and a beggarly rudiment, and unprofitable to righteousness; but he rather judgeth quite contrary of the law: to wit, that it is not only necessary to salvation, but also that it strengtheneth such as are weak, and enricheth such as are poor and beggarly: that is to say, that such as obey and observe the same, shall be able to merit righteousness and everlasting salvation. If this opinion remain, the promise of God is denied, Christ is taken away, lying, impiety, and idolatry is established. Now, the Pope, with all his bishops, his schools and whole synagogue, taught that his laws are necessary to salvation: therefore, he was a teacher of weak and beggarly elements, wherewith he made the church of Christ, throughout the whole world, most weak and beggarly; that is to say, he burdened and miserably tormented the church with his wicked laws, defacing Christ, and burying his gospel.

VERSE 9. *Whereunto ye will be in bondage again.*

This he addeth, to declare that he speaketh of proud and presumptuous hypocrites, which seek to be justified by the law, as I have shewn before. For otherwise he calleth the law holy and good. As, "we know that the law is good, if a man use it rightly" (1 Tim. i, 8), that is to say, civilly to bridle evil-doers, and spiritually to increase transgressions (Gal. iii, 19). But whosoever observeth the law, to obtain righteousness before God, maketh the law, which is good, damnable and hurtful unto himself. He reproveth the Galatians, therefore, because they would be in bondage to the law again, which doth not take away sin, but increaseth sin; for whilst a sinner, being weak and poor himself, seeketh to be justified by the law, he findeth nothing in it but weakness and poverty itself. And here two sick and feeble beggars meet together, of whom the one is not able to help and heal the other, but rather molesteth and troubleth the other.

We, as being strong in Christ, will gladly serve the law; not the weak and beggarly, but the mighty and rich law; that is to say, so far forth as it hath power and dominion over the body: for then we serve the law, but only in our body and outward members, and not in our conscience. But the Pope requireth that we should obey his laws with this opinion, that if we do this or that, we are righteous: if we do it not, we are damned. Here the law is no more than a weak and beggarly element. For whilst this bondage of the conscience continueth under the law, there can be nothing but mere weakness and poverty.— Wherefore all the weight of the matter lieth in this word "to serve." The meaning, therefore, of Paul is this: that he would not have the conscience to serve under the law as a captive, but to be free, and to have dominion over the law. For the conscience is dead to the law through Christ, and the law again unto the conscience. Whereof we have more largely entreated afore in the second chapter.

VERSE 10. *Ye observe days and months, times and years.*

By these words he plainly declareth what the false apostles taught, namely, the observation of days, months, times and years. The Jews were commanded to keep holy the sabbath day, the new moons, the first and the seventh month, the three appointed times or feasts, namely, the paschal or passover, the feast of weeks, of the tabernacles, and the year of jubilee. These ceremonies the Galatians were constrained by the false apostles to keep, as necessary to righteousness. Therefore he saith, that they, losing the grace and liberty which they had in Christ, were turned back to the serving of weak and beggarly elements. For they were persuaded by the false apostles, that these laws must needs be kept, and, by keeping of them, they should obtain righteousness; but if they kept them not, they should be damned. Contrariwise, Paul can in no wise suffer that men's consciences should be bound to the law of Moses, but always delivered them from the law. "Behold I, Paul" (saith he, a little after, in the fifth chapter), "do write unto you, that if ye be circumcised, Christ shall profit you nothing." And, "let no man judge you in meat or drink, or in a piece of a holiday, or of a new moon or sabbath day," etc (Col. ii). So saith our Saviour Christ: "the kingdom of God cometh not with observation of the law" (Luke xvii, 20). Much less, then, are men's consciences to be burthened and snared with human traditions.

EPISTLE TO THE GALATIANS 369

VERSE 11. *I am in fear of you, lest I have
bestowed on you labour in vain.*

Here Paul sheweth himself to be greatly troubled through the fall of the Galatians; whom he would more bitterly reprove, but that he feareth, lest, if he should deal with them more sharply, he should not only make them better, but more offend them, and so utterly alienate their minds from him. Therefore, in writing, he changeth and mitigateth his words: and, as though all the harm redounded unto himself, he saith, "I am in fear of you, lest I have bestowed my labour on you in vain": that is to say, it grieveth me that I have preached the gospel with so great diligence and faithfulness amongst you, and see no fruit to come thereof. Notwithstanding, although he shew a very loving and a fatherly affection towards them, yet withal he chideth them somewhat sharply, but yet covertly. For when he saith, that he had laboured in vain; that is to say, that he had preached the gospel among them without any fruit; he sheweth covertly that either they were obstinate unbelievers, or else were fallen from the doctrine of faith. Now both these, as well unbelievers as backsliders from the doctrine of faith, are sinners, wicked, unrighteous, and damned. Such, therefore, do obey the law in vain; they observe days, months, and years in vain. And in these words, "I am in fear of you, lest I have bestowed on you labour in vain," is contained a certain secret excommunication. For the apostle meaneth hereby that the Galatians were secluded and separate from Christ, unless they speedily returned to sound and sincere doctrine again: yet he pronounced no open sentence against them; for he perceived that he could do no good with over-sharp dealing; wherefore he changeth his style, and speaketh them fair, saying,

VERSE 12. *Be ye as I; for I am even as you.*

Hitherto Paul hath been occupied wholly in teaching; and being moved with this great enormity and wicked revolting of the Galatians, he was vehemently incensed against them, and chid them bitterly, calling them fools, bewitched, not believing the truth, crucifiers of Christ, etc. Now, the greater part of his epistle being finished, he beginneth to perceive that he had handled them too sharply. Therefore, being careful lest he should do more hurt than good through his severity, he sheweth that this his sharp chiding proceeded of a fatherly affection and a true apostolical heart; and so he qualifieth the matter with sweet and gentle words, to the end that, if he had offended any, (as no doubt there were many offended), by these sweet and loving words, he might win them again.

And here, by his own example, he admonisheth all pastors and ministers, that they ought to bear a fatherly and motherly affection, not towards ravening wolves, but towards the poor sheep, miserably seduced, and going astray, patiently bearing with their faults and infirmities, instructing and restoring them with the spirit of meekness: for they cannot be brought in the right way by any other means; and by over-sharp reproving and rebuking they are provoked to anger, or else to desperation, but not to repentance. And here is to be noted, by the way, that such is the nature and fruit of true and sound doctrine, that when it is well taught and well understood, it joineth men's hearts together with a singular concord: but when men reject godly and sincere doctrine, and embrace errors, this unity and concord is soon broken. Therefore, as soon as thou seest thy brethren seduced by vain and fantastical spirits, to fall from the article of justification, thou shalt perceive that by-and-by they will pursue the faithful with bitter hatred, whom before they most tenderly loved.

This we find to be true at this day, in our false brethren and other sectaries, who, at the beginning of the reformation of the gospel, were glad to hear us, and read our books with great zeal and affection; they acknowledged the grace of the Holy Ghost in us, and reverenced us for the same, as the ministers of God. Some of them also lived familiarly with us for a time, and behaved themselves very modestly and soberly; but when they were departed from us, and perverted by the wicked doctrine of the sectaries, they shewed themselves more bitter enemies to our doctrine and our name than any other. I do much and often marvel whereupon they should conceive such a deadly hatred against us, whom they before so dearly and so tenderly loved; for we offended them not in any thing, nor gave them any occasion to hate us. Yea, they are constrained to confess that we desire nothing more, than that the glory of God may be advanced, the benefit of Christ truly known, and the truth of the gospel purely taught, which God hath now again in these latter days revealed by us unto this unthankful world; which should rather provoke them to love us, than to hate us. I marvel, therefore, not without cause, whereof this change cometh. Verily, there is no other cause, but that they have gotten unto themselves new masters, and hearkened to new teachers, whose poison hath so infected them, that now of very friends they are become our mortal enemies. And I see the condition of the apostles and all other faithful ministers to be such, that their disciples and hearers being once infected with the errors of the false apostles and heretics, have and do set themselves against them, and become their enemies. There were very few amongst the Galatians which continued in the sound doctrine of the apostles. All the rest, being seduced by the false apostles, did not acknowledge Paul for their pastor and teacher any more; yea, there was nothing more odious unto them than the name and doctrine of Paul. And I fear me, that this epistle brought very few of them back again from their error.

If the like case should happen unto us; that is to say, if, in our absence, our church should be seduced by fantastical heads, and we should write hither, not one or two, but many epistles, we should prevail little or nothing at all. Our men (a few only excepted of the stronger sort) would use themselves no otherwise towards us, than they do at this day which are seduced by the sectaries; who would sooner worship the Pope, than they would obey our admonitions, or approve our doctrine. No man shall persuade them that they, rejecting Christ, do return again to weak and beggarly elements, and to those which by nature are no gods. They can abide nothing less, than to hear that their teachers, by whom they are seduced, are overthrowers of the gospel of Christ, and troublers of men's conscience. The Lutherans (say they) are not the only wise; they alone do not preach Christ, they alone have not the Holy Ghost, the gift of prophecy, and the true understanding of the scriptures; our teachers are in nothing inferior unto them; yea, in many things they excel them, because they follow the spirit, and teach spiritual things. Contrariwise, they never yet tasted what true divinity meant, but stick in the letter, and therefore they teach nothing but the catechism, faith, and charity, etc. Wherefore (as I am wont to say), like as to fall in faith is an easy matter; so is it most perilous: to wit, even from high heaven into the deep pit of hell. It is not such as properly followeth the nature of man, as murder, adultery, and such-like; but devilish, and the proper work of the devil. For they which so fall, cannot be easily recovered, but most commonly they continue perverse and obstinate in their error. Therefore the latter end of those men is worse than the beginning, as our Saviour Christ witnesseth, when he saith, "the unclean spirit being cast out of his house, when he returneth, he entereth in again, not alone, but taketh unto him seven spirits worse than himself, and there dwelleth," etc. (Matt. xii, 43, 45.)

Paul therefore perceiving, through the revelation of the Holy Ghost, that it was to be feared lest the minds of the Galatians, whom of a godly zeal he had called foolish and bewitched, etc., by this sharp chiding should rather be stirred up against him, than amended (especially since he now knew that the false apostles were among them, who would expound this sharp chiding, which proceeded from a fatherly affection, unto the worst, crying out, Now Paul, which some of you so greatly praise, sheweth what he is, and with what spirit he is led; who, when he was with you, would seem to be unto you a father, but his letters shew, in his absence, that he is a tyrant, etc.) Therefore he is so troubled, through a godly care and fatherly affection, that he cannot well tell how and what to write to them; for it is a dangerous thing for a man to defend his cause against those which are absent, and have now begun to hate him, and are persuaded by others that his cause is not good. Therefore, being in great perplexity, he saith, a little after, "I am troubled, and at my wit's end for your cause;" that is, I know not what to do, or how to deal with you.

VERSE 12. *Be ye as I am, for I am as ye are.*

These words are to be understood, not of doctrine, but of affections. Therefore the meaning is not, "Be ye as I am"; that is to say, think of doctrine as I do; but bear such an affection towards me, as I do towards you. As though he would say, Perhaps I have too sharply chidden you, but pardon this my sharpness, and judge not my heart by my words, but my words by the affection of my heart. My words seem rough, and my chastisement sharp, but my heart is loving and fatherly. Therefore, O my Galatians! take this my chiding with such a mind as I bear towards you; for the matter required that I should shew myself so sharp and severe towards you.

Even so may we also say of ourselves. Our correction is severe, and our manner of writing sharp and vehement; but, certainly, there is no bitterness in our heart, no envy, no desire of revenge against our adversaries; but there is in us a godly carefulness and sorrow of spirit. We do not so hate the Pope, and other erroneous spirits, that we wish any evil unto them, or desire their destruction; but rather we desire that they may return again to the right way, and be saved together with us. The schoolmaster chastiseth the scholar, not to hurt him, but to reform him. The rod is sharp, but correction is necessary for the child, and the heart of him that correcteth, loving and friendly. So the father chastiseth his son, not to destroy him, but to reform and amend him. Stripes are sharp and grievous to the child, but the father's heart is loving and kind; and unless he loved his child, he would not chastise him, but cast him off, despair of his welfare, and suffer him to perish. This correction, therefore, which he giveth to his child, is a token of fatherly affection, and is profitable for the child. Even so, O my Galatians! think ye likewise of my dealing towards you: then ye will not judge my chiding to be sharp and bitter, but profitable for you. "Chastisement for the present time seemeth not to be joyous, but grievous: but afterwards it bringeth the quiet fruit of righteousness unto them which are exercised thereby" (Heb. xii, 11). Let the same affection, therefore, be in you towards me, which I have towards you. I bear a loving heart towards you: the same I desire again of you.

Thus he speaketh them fair, and with this fair speech he still continueth, that he might pacify their minds which were stirred up against him by his sharp chiding. Notwithstanding he revoketh not his severe words. Indeed, he confesseth that they were sharp and bitter: but necessity (saith he) compelled me to reprehend you somewhat sharply and severely; but that which I did, proceeded of a sincere and loving heart towards you. The physician giveth a bitter potion to his patient, not to hurt him, but to cure him. If, then, the bitterness of the medicine, which is given to the sick body, is not to be imputed to the physician, but to the medicine and the malady, judge ye also in like manner of my severe and sharp reprehension.

VERSE 12. *Brethren, I beseech you: ye have not hurt me at all.*

Is this to beseech the Galatians, when he calleth them bewitched, disobedient to the truth, and crucifiers of Christ? It seemeth rather to be a great rebuke. But, contrariwise, Paul saith that it is no rebuke, but an earnest beseeching, and indeed so it is. And it is as much as if he said: I confess that I have chidden you somewhat bitterly, but take it in good part, and then shall ye find this my chiding to be no chiding, but a praying and a beseeching. If a father, likewise, do sharply correct his son, it is as much as if he said, My son, I pray thee to be a good child, etc. It seemeth indeed to be a correction; but if ye respect the father's heart, it is a gentle and earnest beseeching.

VERSE 12. *Ye have not hurt me at all.*

As if he said, Why should I be angry with you, or of a malicious mind speak evil of you, seeing ye have nothing offended me. Why, then, sayest thou that we are perverted, that we have forsaken thy doctrine, that we are foolish, bewitched, etc.? These things do witness that we have offended thee. He answereth: Ye have not offended me, but yourselves; and therefore I am thus troubled, not for mine own cause, but for the love I bear unto you. Think not, therefore, that my chiding did proceed of malice, or any evil affection; for I take God to witness, ye have done me no wrong, but, contrariwise, ye have bestowed great benefits upon me.

Thus speaking them fair, he prepareth their minds to suffer his fatherly chastisement with a child-like affection. And this is to temper wormwood or a bitter potion with honey and sugar, to make it sweet again. So parents speak their children fair when they have well beaten them, giving them apples, pears, and other like things, whereby the children know that their parents love them, and seek to do them good, how sharp soever their correction doth appear.

> VERSES 13 AND 14. *And ye know how, through the infirmity the flesh, I preached the gospel unto you at the first. And the trial of me which was in my flesh, ye despised not, neither abhorred, but ye received me as an angel of God, yea, as Christ Jesus.*

Now he declareth what pleasures he had received of the Galatians. The first benefit (saith he), which I esteem as the greatest of all, was this: When I began first to preach the gospel amongst you, and that through the infirmity of the flesh and great temptations, my cross did nothing at all offend you; but ye shewed yourselves so loving, so kind, and so friendly towards me, that not only ye were not offended with this my infirmity of the flesh, with my temptations and afflictions, wherewith I was almost overwhelmed; but also ye loved me dearly, and received me as an angel of God, yea, rather, as Christ Jesus himself. This is, indeed, a great commendation of the Galatians, that they received the gospel of a man so contemptible and afflicted on every side as Paul was. For where he preached the gospel amongst them, both the Jews and Gentiles murmured and raged against him. For all the mighty, wise, religious, and learned men, hated, persecuted, and blasphemed Paul. With all this, the Galatians were no whit offended, but, turning their eyes from the beholding of this infirmity, these temptations and dangers, they did not only hear that poor, despised, wretched, and afflicted Paul, and acknowledged themselves to be his disciples, but also they received and heard him as an angel of God, yea, as Jesus Christ himself. This is a worthy commendation, and a singular virtue of the Galatians, and indeed such a commendation as he giveth to none of all those to whom he wrote, besides these Galatians.

Jerome, and certain other of the ancient fathers, expound this infirmity of the flesh in Paul, to be some disease of the body, or some temptation of lust. These men lived when the church was outwardly in a peaceable and prosperous state, without any cross or persecution: for then the bishops began to increase in riches, estimation, and glory in the world; and many also exercised tyranny over the people which were committed to their charge, as the ecclesiastical history witnesseth. Few did their duty, and they that would seem to do it, forsaking the doctrine of the gospel, set forth their own decrees to the people. Now, when the pastors and bishops are not exercised in the word of God, but neglect the pure and sincere preaching thereof, they must needs fall into security; for they are not exercised with temptations, with the cross and persecutions, which are wont always, undoubtedly, to follow the pure preaching of the word; therefore it was impossible that they should understand Paul. But we, by the grace of God, have sound and sincere doctrine, which also we preach and teach freely, and therefore are compelled to suffer the bitter hatred, afflictions, and persecutions of the devil and the world. And if we were not exercised outwardly by tyrants and sectaries with force and subtilty, and inwardly with terrors and fiery darts of the devil, Paul should be as obscure and unknown unto us, as he was in times past to the whole world, and yet is to the Papists, the Anabaptists, and other our adversaries. Therefore, the gift of knowledge, and interpretation of the scriptures, and our study, together with our inward and outward temptations, open unto us the meaning of Paul, and the sense of the holy scriptures.

Paul, therefore, calleth the infirmity of the flesh, no disease of the body, or temptation of lust, but his suffering and affliction, which he sustained in his body; which he setteth against the virtue and power of the spirit. But, lest we should seem to wrest and pervert Paul's words, let us hear himself speaking in 2 Cor. xii. "Very gladly will I rejoice rather in mine infirmities, that the power of Christ may dwell in me. Therefore, I take pleasure in infirmities, in reproaches, in necessities, in persecutions, in anguish, for Christ's sake: For when I am weak, then am I strong." And in the eleventh chapter: "In labours more abundant, in stripes above measure, in prisons more plenteous, in death oft. Of the Jews five times received I forty stripes save one; I was thrice beaten with rods; I was once stoned; I suffered thrice shipwreck," etc. These afflictions, which he suffered in his body, he calleth the infirmity of the flesh, and not any corporeal disease. As though he would say, When I preached the gospel amongst you, I was oppressed with sundry temptations and afflictions; I was always in danger, both of the Jews, of the Gentiles, and also of false brethren. I suffered hunger, and wanted all things. I was the very filth and off-scouring of the world. He maketh mention of this his infirmity in many places, as in 1 Cor. iv, 12; 2 Cor. iv, 9, 11, 12, and in many other.

We see then that Paul calleth afflictions the infirmities of the flesh, which he suffered in the flesh, like as the other apostles, the prophets, and all godly men did: notwithstanding he was mighty in spirit. For the power of Christ was in him, which always reigned and triumphed through him. Which thing he testifieth in 2 Cor. xii in these words: "For when I am weak, then am I strong." Also, "I will gladly rejoice in my infirmities, that the power of Christ may dwell in me." And in the second chapter, "Thanks be to God, who always maketh us to triumph in Christ." As though he would say, Indeed the devil, the Jews, and the Gentiles rage cruelly against us: notwithstanding we continue constant and invincible against all their assaults, and will they, nil they, our doctrine prevaileth and triumpheth. This was the strength and power of spirit in Paul, against which he setteth here the infirmity and bondage of the flesh.

Now, this infirmity of the flesh in the godly doth wonderfully offend reason. Therefore, Paul so highly commendeth the Galatians, because they were not offended with this great infirmity, and with this vile and contemptible form of the cross which they saw in him: but received him as an angel, yea, as Christ Jesus. And Christ himself also armeth the faithful against this base and contemptible form of the cross in which he appeared, when he saith, "Blessed is he that is not offended in me" (Matt. xi, 6). And surely it is a great matter that they which believe in him, do acknowledge him to be Lord of all, and Saviour of the world; whom notwithstanding they hear to have been the most miserable of all others, the least of men, yea, a very scorn of men, and a contempt of the world (Ps. xxii, 7). Briefly, despised and hated of all men, and condemned to the death of the cross, and even of his own people, and especially of those that were esteemed the best, the wisest, and holiest of all other. This is a great matter, I say, not to be moved with these great offences, and to be able, not only to contemn them, but also to esteem this poor Christ, so spitefully scorned, spit upon, whipped and crucified, more than the riches of all the richest, the strength of all the strongest, the wisdom of all the wisest, the holiness of all the holiest men, with all the crowns and sceptres of all the kings and princes of the whole world. They therefore are worthily called blessed of Christ, which are not offended in him.

Now Paul had not only outward temptations (whereof I have spoken already), but also inward and spiritual temptations, as Christ had in the garden: such as that was whereof he complaineth in 2 Cor. xii. "That he felt the prick or sting of the flesh, and the angel of Satan which buffeted him." This I say by the way, because the Papists expound this to be a motion of fleshly lust; but it was a spiritual temptation. And herein is no repugnance, that he addeth this word flesh, saying, "A prick was given me in the flesh." Yea, he calleth it of purpose a prick (or thorn) in the flesh. For the Galatians, and others which were conversant with Paul, had seen him oftentimes in great heaviness, anguish, and terror. Wherefore the apostles had not only bodily, but also spiritual temptations; which also he confesseth in 2 Cor. vii with these words: "Fightings without, and terrors within." And Luke saith, in the last of the Acts, that Paul, when he had long striven in the tempests of the sea, even unto the heaviness of his spirit, was again refreshed, and waxed bold, when he saw the brethren that came from Rome to meet him at the market of Appius and Three Taverns. Also, in Phil. ii he confesseth, that God had mercy upon him, in that he restored Epaphroditus, so weak and near to death, unto health again, lest he should have sorrow upon sorrow. Therefore, besides outward temptations, the apostles also suffered great anguish, heaviness, and terrors.

But why saith Paul that he was not despised of the Galatians? It seemeth that they despised him, when they fell away from his gospel. Paul expoundeth himself. When I first preached to you the gospel (saith he), ye did not as other people have done, who being greatly offended through this my infirmity and temptation of the flesh, have despised and rejected me. For man's reason is soon offended with this vile and contemptible form of the cross, and judgeth those to be stark mad, which, being so afflicted, will go about to comfort, to help, and to succour others. Also, those that boast of their great riches, that is to say, of righteousness, strength, victory over sin, death, and all evils; of joy, salvation, and everlasting life, and yet, notwithstanding, are needy, weak, heavy-hearted, and despised, evil-entreated, and slain, as very noisome poisons both of commonweals and of religion; and they which kill them, think they do high service unto God (John xvi, 2). Therefore, when they promise unto others eternal treasures, and they themselves perish so wretchedly before the world, they are laughed to scorn, and compelled to hear, "Physician, cure thyself" (Luke iv, 23). And hereof come these complaints which are everywhere in the Psalms: "I am a worm, and no man," etc. Again, "Depart not from me, for tribulation is at hand, and there is none to help" (Psalm xxii, 6, 11).

This is, therefore, a great commendation of the Galatians, that they were not offended with this infirmity and temptation of Paul, but received him as an angel of God, yea, as Jesus Christ. It is, indeed, a great virtue, and worthy of great praise, to hear the apostles; but it is a greater, and a true Christian virtue, to give ear unto one so miserable, weak, and contemptible, as Paul was among the Galatians (as here he witnesseth of himself) and to receive him as an angel from heaven, and to give him such honour as if he had been Christ Jesus himself; and not to be offended with his afflictions, being so great and so many. Wherefore, by these words, he highly commendeth the virtue of the Galatians, which he saith he will keep in perpetual remembrance; and so greatly esteemeth the same, that he desireth it may be known unto all men. Notwithstanding, in setting forth so highly their benefits and praises, he sheweth covertly how entirely they loved him before the coming of the false apostles, and therewithal he moveth them to continue as they began, and to embrace him with no less love and reverence than they did before. And hereby it may also appear, that the false apostles had greater authority among the Galatians than Paul himself had; for the Galatians, being moved with their authority, preferred them far above Paul, whom before they so dearly loved, and received as an angel of God, etc.

VERSE 15. *What was then your felicity?*

As if he would say: How happy were ye counted? How much were ye then praised and commended? The like manner of speech we have in the song of the Virgin Mary—"All generations shall call me blessed." (Luke i, 48.) And these words, "What was then your felicity?" contain in them a certain vehemency. As if he should say, Ye were not only blessed, but in all things most blessed and highly commended. Thus he goeth about to qualify and mitigate his bitter potion, that is to say, his sharp chiding; fearing lest the Galatians should be offended therewith, especially seeing he knew that the false apostles would slander him, and most spitefully interpret his words; for this is the quality and nature of these vipers, that they will slander, and maliciously pervert those words which proceed from a simple and sincere heart, and wrest them clean contrary to the true sense and meaning thereof. They are mar-

EPISTLE TO THE GALATIANS

vellous cunning workmen in this matter, far passing all the wit and eloquence of all the rhetoricians in the world. For they are led with a wicked spirit, which so bewitcheth them, that they, being inflamed with a devilish rage against the faithful, can no otherwise do, but maliciously interpret, and wickedly pervert their words and writings. Therefore they are like unto the spider, that sucketh venom out of sweet and pleasant flowers; and this proceedeth not of the flowers, but of their own venemous nature, which turneth that into poison that of itself is good and wholesome. Paul, therefore, by these mild and sweet words, goeth about to prevent the false apostles, to the end they should have no occasion to slander and pervert his words after this manner: Paul handleth you very ungently; he calleth you foolish, bewitched, and disobedient to the truth, which is a sure token that he seeketh not your salvation, but accounteth you as damned and rejected of Christ.

VERSE 15. *For I bear you record, that, if it had been possible, ye would have plucked out your own eyes, and have given them to me.*

He praiseth the Galatians above measure. Ye did not only entreat me (saith he) most courteously, and with all reverence, receiving me as an angel of God, etc., but also, if necessity had required, ye would have plucked out your own eyes, and given them to me; yea, you would have bestowed your lives for me. And, indeed, the Galatians bestowed their lives for him: for in that they received and maintained Paul, (whom the world accounted most execrable and accursed,) they turned upon their own heads, as receivers and maintainers of Paul, the cruel hatred and indignation of all the Jews and Gentiles.

So also at this day the name of Luther is most odious to the world. He that praiseth me, sinneth worse than any idolater, blasphemer, perjurer, whoremonger, adulterer, murderer, or thief. It must needs be, therefore, that the Galatians were well-established in the doctrine and faith of Christ, seeing that they with so great danger of their lives received and maintained Paul, which was hated throughout all the world; for else they would never have sustained that cruel hatred of the whole world.

VERSE 16. *Am I therefore become your enemy, because I tell you the truth.*

Here he sheweth the reason why he speaketh the Galatians so fair; for he suspecteth that they take him for their enemy, because he had reproved them so sharply. I pray you (saith he) set apart these rebukes, and separate them from doctrine, and ye shall find that my purpose was not to rebuke you, but to teach you the truth. Indeed, I confess that my epistle is sharp and severe; but by this severity I go about to call you back again to the truth of the gospel, from the which ye are fallen, and to keep you in the same; therefore, apply this sharpness and this bitter potion, not to your persons, but to your disease; and judge me not to be your enemy in rebuking you so sharply, but rather think that I am your father: for unless I loved you dearly, as my children, and knew also, that I am beloved of you, I would not have reproved you so sharply.

It is the part of a friend, freely to admonish his friend, if he do amiss; and when he is so admonished, if he be wise, he is not angry with the other, which hath so friendly admonished him and told him the truth, but giveth him thanks. It is commonly seen in the world that truth bringeth hatred, and that he is accounted an enemy which speaketh the truth. But amongst friends it is not so, much less amongst Christians. Seeing, therefore, I have reprehended you of mere love, to the end ye might abide in the truth, ye ought not to be offended with me, nor lose the truth, or think me your enemy because of my friendly and fatherly reprehension. All these things are spoken of Paul, to confirm that which he said before: "Be ye as I am; ye have not hurt me," etc.

VERSE 17. *They are jealous over you amiss.*

He reproveth here the flattery of the false apostles; for Satan is wont, by his ministers, through wonderful subtilty and crafty sleights, to beguile the simple: As Paul saith, "With fair speech and flattery they deceive the hearts of the simple" (Rom. xvi). For, first of all, they make great protestations that they seek nothing else but the advancement of God's glory; and moreover, that they are moved by the spirit, (because the miserable people are neglected, or else because the truth is not purely taught of others,) to teach the infallible truth, that by this means the elect may be delivered from error, and may come to the true light and knowledge of the truth. Moreover, they promise undoubted salvation to those that receive their doctrine. If vigilant and faithful pastors do not withstand these ravening wolves, they will do great harm to the church, under this pretence of godliness, and under this sheep's clothing. For the Galatians might say, Why dost thou inveigh so bitterly against our teachers, for that they be jealous over us? for that which they do, they do of zeal and mere love; this ought not to offend thee, etc. Indeed (saith he) they are jealous over you, but their jealousy is not good.

Here note, that zeal or jealousy properly signifieth angry love, or, as ye would say, a godly envy. Elijah saith: "I have been very jealous for the Lord of Hosts" (2 Kings xix, 10). After this manner the husband is jealous towards his wife, the father towards his son, the brother towards his brother, that is to say, they love them entirely; yet so, that they hate their vices, and go about to mend them. Such a zeal the false apostles pretended to bear towards the Galatians. Paul, indeed, confesseth that they were very zealous towards the Galatians, but their zeal (saith he) was not good. Now, by this colour and subtle pretence the simple are deceived, when these seducers do make them to believe that they bear a great zeal and affection towards them, and that they are very careful for them; Paul therefore warneth us here to put a difference between a good zeal and an evil zeal. Indeed, here a good zeal is to be commended, but not an evil zeal. I am as zealous over you (saith Paul) as they: now judge ye which of our zeals is better, mine or theirs; which is good and godly; which is evil and carnal: therefore let not their zeal so easily seduce you. For,

VERSE 17. *They would exclude us, that you should altogether love them..*

As if he said: True it is, that they are very zealous towards you, but by this means they seek that ye again should be zealous towards them, and reject me. If their zeal were sincere and godly, then surely they would be content that I should be beloved of you, as well as they. But they hate our doctrine, and therefore their desire is, that it may be utterly abolished, and their own preached amongst you. Now, to the end they might bring this to pass, they go about by this jealousy to pluck your hearts from me, and to make me odious unto you; that when ye have received an hatred against me and my doctrine, and turned your affection and zeal towards them, ye should love them only, and receive no other doctrine but theirs. Thus he bringeth the false apostles into suspicion among the Galatians, shewing that by this godly pretence they go about to deceive them. So our Saviour Christ also warneth us, saying, "Take heed of false prophets, which come to you in sheep's clothing" (Matt. vii, 15).

Paul suffered the same temptation which we suffer at this day. He was marvellously troubled with this enormity, that after the preaching of his doctrine, which was divine and holy, he saw so many sects, commotions, dissipations of commonweals, changes of kingdoms, and other like things, to ensue, which were the cause of infinite evils and offences. He was accused by the Jews to be a pernicious fellow, a mover of sedition in his whole nation, and to be an author of the sect of the Nazarites (Acts xxiv, 5). As if they had said: This is a seditious and a blasphemous fellow; for he preacheth such things whereby he not only overthroweth the Jewish commonwealth, excellently well ordered and established by the laws of God, but also abolisheth even the ten commandments, the religion and service of God, and our priesthood, and publisheth throughout the world the gospel (as he calleth it); whereof are sprung infinite evils, seditions, offences, and sects. He was compelled to hear of the Gentiles also, which cried out against him in Philippi, that he was a troubler of the city, and preached ordinances which were not lawful for them to receive (Acts xvi).

Such troubles of commonweals, and other calamities, as famine, wars, dissensions, and sects, the Jews and Gentiles imputed to the doctrine of Paul, and of the other apostles; and therefore they persecuted them as common plagues, and enemies of the public peace and of religion. The apostles, notwithstanding all this, did not cease to do their office, but most constantly preached and confessed Christ; for they knew that they should rather obey God than men (Acts v, 29), and that it was better that the whole world should be troubled and in an uproar, than that Christ should not be preached, or that one soul should be neglected and perish.

In the mean time it was (no doubt) a heavy cross to the apostles to see these offences; for they were not made of iron. It was a wonderful grief unto them, that that people, for whose sakes Paul wished to be separate from Christ, should perish with all their ornaments (Rom. ix). They saw that great tumults and changes of kingdoms should follow their doctrine; and (which was more bitter unto them than death itself, but especially unto Paul), they saw that, even amongst them, there sprang up many sects. It was heavy news to Paul, when he heard that the Corinthians denied the resurrection of the dead; when he heard that the churches which were planted by his ministry were troubled; that the gospel was overthrown by the false apostles, and that all Asia was revolted from his doctrine, and certain great personages besides.

But he knew that his doctrine was not the cause of these offences and sects, and therefore he was not discouraged; he forsook not his vocation, but went forward, knowing that the gospel which he preached, was the power of God to salvation to all that believe, howsoever it seemed to the Jews and Gentiles to be a foolish and offensive doctrine (Rom. i, 16). He knew that they are blessed which are not offended by this word of the cross, whether they be teachers or hearers, as Christ himself saith: "Blessed is he which is not offended in me." Contrariwise, he knew that they were condemned, which judged this doctrine to be foolish and heretical. Therefore he saith, as Christ did of the Jews and Gentiles which were offended with his doctrine: "Let them alone, they are blind, and leaders of the blind" (Matt. xv, 14).

We also are constrained at this day to hear the same spoken of us, which was said of Paul and the other apostles; to wit, that the doctrine of the gospel, which we profess, is the cause of many and great enormities, as of seditions, wars, sects, and innumerable offences. Yea, they impute unto us all the troubles which are at this day. Surely, we teach no heresies or wicked doctrine, but we preach the glad tidings concerning Christ, that he is our high priest and our redeemer. Moreover, our adversaries are constrained (if they will confess the truth) to grant us this, that we have given no occasion through our doctrine, of seditions, wars, or tumults; but always have taught that honour and reverence must be given to the magistrates, because God hath so commanded. Neither are we the authors of offences: but in that the wicked are offended, the fault is in themselves, and not in us. God hath commanded us to preach the doctrine of the gospel, without any respect of offence. But because this doctrine condemneth the wicked doctrine and idolatry of our adversaries, they, being provoked thereby, raise offences of themselves, which the schoolmen called offences taken, which, they said, ought not to be avoided, nor can be avoided.

Christ taught the gospel, having no rgeard to the offence of the Jews. "Suffer them" (saith he), "they are blind, and leaders of the blind" (Matt. xv, 14). The more the priests forbade the apostles to preach in the name of Christ, the more the apostles gave witness that the same Jesus, whom they had crucified, is both Lord and Christ, and whosoever should call upon him should be saved, and that there is no other name given unto men under heaven, whereby they must be saved, etc. (Acts ii, 21, 36; iv, 12). Even so we preach Christ at this day, not regarding the clamours of the wicked Papists and all our adversaries, which cry out that our doctrine is seditious and full of blasphemy, that it troubleth commonweals, overthroweth religion, and teacheth heresies, and briefly, that it is the cause of all evils. When Christ and his apostles preached, the same was said likewise of them. Not long after, the Romans came, and, according to their own prophecy, destroyed both the place and the nation. Wherefore let the enemies of the gospel at this day, take heed that they be not overwhelmed with these evils, which they prophesy unto themselves.

These they make grievous and heinous offences, that monks and priests do marry wives, that we eat flesh upon the Fridays, and such-like. But this is no offence to them at all, that by their wicked doctrine they seduce and daily destroy innumerable souls; that by their evil example they offend the weak; that they blaspheme and condemn the glorious gospel of the mighty God; and that they persecute and kill those that love the sincerity of doctrine and the word of life: this (I say) is to them no offence, but an obedience, a service, and an acceptable sacrifice unto God. Let us suffer them, therefore: "For they are blind, and leaders of the blind" (Matt. xv, 14). "He that hurteth, let him hurt still; and he that is filthy, let him be more filthy" (Apoc. xxii). But we, because we believe, will speak and set forth the wonderful works of the Lord, so long as we have breath, and will endure the persecutions of our adversaries until the time that Christ, our high bishop and king, shall come from heaven, who, we hope, will come shortly, as a just judge, to take vengeance of all those that obey not his gospel. So be it.

With these offences which the wicked allege, the godly are nothing moved; for they know that the devil hateth nothing more than the pure doctrine of the gospel, and therefore he goeth about to deface it with innumerable offences, that by this means he might root it out of men's hearts for ever. Before, when nothing else was taught in the church but man's traditions, the devil did not so rage. For whilst the strong man kept the house, all that he possessed was in peace; but now, when a stronger cometh, which vanquisheth and bindeth that strong one and spoileth his house, then he beginneth to rage indeed (Luke xi, 21, 22). And this is an infallible token, that the doctrine which we profess is of God; for else (as it is said in the fortieth of Job), that "Behemoth would lie hid under the trees, in the covert of the reed and fens." But now, that he rangeth about like a roaring lion, and stirreth up such hurly-burlies, it is a manifest token that he feeleth the power of our preaching (1 Peter v, 8).

When Paul saith, "They are jealous over you, but amiss," he sheweth, by the way, who are the authors of sects; to wit, those jealous spirits which in all times overthrow the true doctrine, and trouble the public peace. For these being stirred up with a perverse zeal, imagine that they have a certain singular holiness, modesty, patience, and doctrine above others, and therefore they think that they are able to provide for the salvation of all men; that they can teach more profound and profitable things, ordain better service and ceremonies than all other teachers besides, whom they despise as nothing in comparison of themselves, and abase their authority, and corrupt those things which they have purely taught. The false apostles had such a wicked and perverse zeal, stirring up sects, not only in Galatia but also in all the places wheresoever Paul and the other apostles had preached; after the which sects followed innumerable offences and marvellous troubles. "For the devil" (as Christ saith) "is a liar and a murderer" (John viii, 44), and therefore he is wont, not only to trouble men's consciences by false doctrine, but also to stir up tumults, seditions, wars, and all mischief.

There are very many at this day which are possessed with this kind of jealousy; which pretend great religion, modesty, doctrine, and patience, and yet, in very deed, they are ravening wolves, who with their hypocrisy seek nothing else but to discredit us, that the people might esteem, love, and reverence them only, and receive no other doctrine but theirs. Now, because these men have a great opinion of themselves and despise others, it cannot be, but that there must needs follow horrible dissensions, sects, divisions, and seditions. But what should we do? We cannot remedy this matter; as Paul could not do it in his time. Notwithstanding, he gained some, which obeyed his admonitions; so I hope, also, that we have called some back from the errors of the sectaries.

> VERSE 18. *But it is a good thing to love earnestly always in a good thing, and not only when I am present with you.*

As if he should say: I commend you for this, that ye loved me so entirely when I preached the gospel amongst you in the infirmity of the flesh. Ye ought to bear the same affection towards me now, when I am absent, even as if I had never departed from you; for, although I be absent in the body, yet have ye my doctrine, which ye ought to retain and maintain, seeing ye received the Holy Ghost through it; thinking with yourselves, that Paul is always present with you, as long as ye have his doctrine. I do not, therefore, reprehend your zeal, but I praise it, and so far forth I praise it, as it is the zeal of God or of the Spirit, and not of the flesh. Now, the zeal of the Spirit is always good; for it is an earnest affection and motion of the heart to a good thing, and so is not the zeal of the flesh. He commendeth, therefore, the zeal of the Galatians, that thereby he may pacify their minds, and that they may patiently suffer his correction. As if he would say: Take my correction in good part; for it proceedeth of no displeasure, but of a sorrowful heart and careful for your salvation. This is a lively example to teach all ministers how to be careful for their sheep, and to assay every way, that by chiding, fair speaking, or entreating, they may keep them in sound doctrine, and turn them from subtle seducers and false teachers.

VERSE 19. *My little children, of whom I travail in birth again, until Christ be formed in you.*

All his words are weighty, and fitly framed to the purpose that they may move the hearts of the Galatians, and win their favour again; and these are sweet and loving words, when he calleth them his children. When he saith, "Of whom I travail in birth," it is an allegory. For the apostles are in the stead of parents, as schoolmasters also are in their place and calling. For as parents beget the bodily form, so they beget the form of the mind. Now, the form of a Christian mind is faith, or the confidence of the heart, that layeth hold upon Christ, and cleaveth to him alone, and to nothing else. The heart being furnished with this confidence or assurance, to wit, that for Christ's sake we are righteous, hath the true form of Christ. Now, this form is given by the ministry of the word, as it is said, 1 Cor. iv, "I have begotten you through the gospel," that is to say, in spirit, that ye might know Christ and believe in him. Also 2 Cor. iii, "Ye are the epistle of Christ, ministered by us and written, not with ink, but with the Spirit of the living God." For the word cometh from the mouth of the apostle or of the minister, and entereth into the heart of him that heareth it. There the Holy Ghost is present, and imprinteth the word in the heart, so that it consenteth unto it. Thus, every godly teacher is a father, which engendereth and formeth the true shape of a Christian heart, and that by the ministry of the word.

Moreover, by these words, "Of whom I travail in birth," he toucheth the false apostles. As though he would say: I did beget you rightly, through the gospel; but these corrupters have formed a new shape in your heart, not of Christ, but of Moses: so that now your affiance is not grounded any more upon Christ, but upon the works of the law. This is not the true form of Christ, but it is another form, and altogether devilish. And he saith not: of whom I travail in birth until my form be fashioned in you, but until Christ be formed in you; that is to say, I travail that ye may receive again the form and similitude of Christ, and not of Paul. In which words he again reproveth the false apostles; for they had abolished the form of Christ in the hearts of the believers, and had devised another form, that is to say, their own; as he saith in chap. vi, "They would have you circumcised, that they might rejoice in your flesh."

Of this form of Christ he speaketh also in the third to the Colossians: "Put ye on the new man, which is renewed in knowledge after the image of him that created him." Paul, therefore, goeth about to repair the form of Christ in the Galatians, that was disfigured and corrupted by the false apostles: which is, that they should think, speak, and will, as God doth, whose thought and will is, that we should obtain remission of our sins and everlasting life, by Jesus Christ his only Son, whom he sent into the world, to the end he might be the propitiation for our sins, and that we should know that through this his Son he is appeased and become our loving Father. They that believe this, are like unto God: that is to say, all their thoughts are of God, as the affection of their heart is; they have the same form in their mind which is in God, or in Christ. This is to be renewed in the spirit of our mind, and to put on the new man, which, after God, is created in righteousness and true holiness, as Paul saith (Eph. iv).

He saith then, that he travaileth again of the Galatians in birth; and yet so, notwithstanding, that the form of the children should not be the form of the apostle, so that the children should not resemble the form of Paul, or of Cephas, etc., but of another father, that is to say, of Christ. I will fashion him (saith he) in you, that the same mind may be in you, which was in Christ himself (Phil. ii, 5). To be brief: "I travail of you:" that is to say, I labour carefully to call you back to your former faith, the which ye have lost (being deceived by the craft and subtilty of the false apostles) and are returned to the law and works. Therefore, I must now again carefully travail, to bring you back from the law to the faith of Christ. This he calleth to travail in birth, etc.

VERSE 20. *And I would I were with you now, that I might change my voice, etc.*

These are the true cares of an apostle. It is a common saying, that a letter is a dead messenger; for it can give no more than it hath. And no epistle or letter is written so exactly, wherein there is not somewhat lacking. For the circumstances are divers; there is a diversity of times, places, persons, manners, and affections; all which no epistle can express: therefore it moveth the reader diversely, making him now sad, now merry, as he himself is disposed. But if any thing be spoken sharply, or out of time, the lively voice of a man may expound, mitigate, or correct the same. Therefore the apostle wisheth that he were with them, to the end he might temper and change his voice, as he should see it needful, by the qualities of their affections. As, if he should see any of them very much troubled, he might so temper his words, that they should not be oppressed thereby with more heaviness: contrariwise, if he should see others high-minded, he might sharply reprehend them, lest they should be too secure and careless, and so at length become contemners of God.

Wherefore he could not devise how he, being absent, should deal with them by letters. As if he should say: If my epistle be too sharp, I fear I shall more offend than amend some of you. Again: if it be too gentle, it will not profit those which are perverse and obstinate: for dead letters and words give no more than they have. Contrariwise, the lively voice of a man, compared to an epistle, is a queen; for it can add and diminish, it can change itself into all manner of affections, times, places, and persons. To be brief, I would gladly convert you by letters, that is to say, call you back from the law to the faith of Jesus Christ; but I fear that I shall not do so by my dead letters. But if I were with you, I could change my voice; I could reprove them bitterly that are obstinate, and comfort the weak with sweet and loving words, as occasion should require.

VERSE 20. *For I am troubled for you.*

That is to say, I am so troubled in my spirit, that I know not how by letters to behave myself towards you. Here is a lively description of the true affection of an apostle; he omitteth nothing: he chideth the Galatians, he entreateth them, he speaketh them fair, he highly commendeth their faith, labouring by all means to bring them back again to the truth of the gospel, and to deliver them out of the snares of the false apostles. These are vehement words, proceeding from a heart stirred up and inflamed with a hot burning zeal, and therefore ought diligently to be considered.

VERSE 21. *Tell me, ye that will be under the law, do ye not hear the law?*

Here would Paul have closed up his epistle: for he desired not to write any more, but rather to be present with the Galatians, and to speak unto them himself. But he, being in great perplexity, and very careful for this matter, taketh by the way this allegory, which then came into his mind; for the people are greatly delighted with allegories and similitudes, and therefore Christ himself oftentimes useth them. For they are, as it were, certain pictures, which set forth things as if they were painted before the eyes of the simple, and therefore they move and persuade very much, especially the simple and ignorant. First, therefore, he stirreth up the Galatians with words and writings. Secondly, he painteth out the matter itself before their eyes with this goodly allegory.

Now, Paul was a marvellous cunning workman in handling of allegories; for he is wont to apply them to the doctrine of faith, to grace, and to Christ, and not to the law and works thereof, as Origen and Hierome do, who are worthily reprehended for that they turned the plain sentences of the scripture, where allegories have no place, into unfit and foolish allegories. Therefore to use allegories it is oftentimes a very dangerous thing. For unless a man have the perfect knowledge of Christian doctrine, he cannot use allegories rightly and as he should do.

But why doth Paul call the book of Genesis, out of the which he allegeth the history of Ishmael and of Isaac, the law, seeing that book containeth nothing at all concerning the law; and especially that place, which he allegeth, speaketh not of any law, but only containeth a plain history of Abraham's two children? Paul is wont to call the first book of Moses the law, after the manner of the Jews; which, although it contain no law besides the law of circumcision, but principally teacheth faith, and witnesseth that the patriarchs pleased God because of their faith, yet the Jews notwithstanding, because of the law of circumcision therein contained, called the book of Genesis, with the rest of the books of Moses, the law. So did Paul, himself also being a Jew. And Christ under the name of the law comprehendeth not only the books of Moses, but also the Psalms—"But it is, that the word might be fulfilled which is written in their law: they hated me without a cause" (John xv, 25; Psalm xxxv, 19).

> VERSES 22 AND 23. *For it is written, that Abraham had two sons, one by a servant, and one by a free-woman. But he which was of the servant, was born after the flesh; and he which was of the free-woman was born after the promise.*

As if he said: Ye forsake grace, faith, and Christ, and turn back again to the law; ye will be under the law, and become wise through it; therefore I will talk with you of the law. I pray you consider the law diligently. Ye shall find that Abraham had two sons: Ishmael by Hagar, and Isaac by Sarah. They were both the true sons of Abraham. Ishmael was as well the true son of Abraham as Isaac was, for both came of one father, of one flesh, and of one seed. What was then the difference? This maketh not the difference (saith Paul) that the mother of the one was free and the other bond, (albeit it pertaineth to the allegory:) but that Ishmael, which was born of the bond-woman, was born after the flesh, that is to say, without the promise and the word of God; but Isaac was not only born of the free-woman, but also according to the promise. What then? Yet was Isaac, notwithstanding, as well born of the seed of Abraham as Ishmael was. I grant that they were both the children of one father, and yet notwithstanding there is a difference; for although Isaac was born of the flesh, yet the promise went before. None observed this difference but only Paul, which he gathered out of the text of Genesis, after this manner.

In that Hagar conceived and brought forth Ishmael, there was no word of God that foreshewed that this should come to pass; but, by the permission of Sarah, Abraham went in to his servant Hagar, whom Sarah, being barren, had given to wife to Abraham, as is said in the book of Genesis. For Sarah had heard that Abraham, by the promise of God, should have seed of his body, and she hoped that she should be the mother of this seed. But when she had waited now for the promise many years, with great anguish of spirit, and saw that the matter was so long deferred, she was out of hope. This holy woman, therefore, giveth place for the honour of her husband, and resigneth her right to another, that is to say, to her maid. Notwithstanding she suffereth not her husband to marry another wife out of his house, but she giveth unto him in marirage her servant, to the end that she might be builded by her. For so saith the history: "Now, Sarah, Abraham's wife, bare him no children; and she had a maid, an Egyptian, Hagar by name. And Sarah said unto Abraham, Behold now the Lord hath restrained me from child-bearing. I pray thee go into my maid; it may be that I shall be builded by her" (Gen. xvi). This was a great humility of Sarah, who so abased herself, and took in good part this temptation and trial of her faith. For thus she thought: God is no liar; that which he hath promised to my husband, he will surely perform. But peradventure God will not that I should be the mother of that seed. It shall not grieve me that Hagar should have this honour, unto whom let my lord enter, for I may peradventure be builded by her.

Ishmael therefore is born without the word and promise, at the only request of Sarah. For there is no word of God which commanded Abraham thus to do, or promised unto him a son, but all this is done at adventure. Which also the words of Sarah do declare—"It may be" (saith she) "that I shall be builded by her." Seeing, therefore, there was no word of God spoken to Abraham before, as there was when Sarah should bring forth Isaac, but only the word of Sarah, it is evident enough that Ishmael was the son of Abraham after the flesh only, without the word of God; therefore he was born at adventure, and unlooked-for, as another child is. This Paul observed and diligently considered.

In the ninth to the Romans he prosecuteth the same argument which here he repeateth and setteth forth in an allegory, and concludeth strongly, that all the sons of Abraham are not the sons of God. Abraham (saith he) hath two sorts of children. Some are born of his flesh and blood, but the word and promise of God goeth before, as Isaac. Other are born without the promise, as Ishmael. Therefore, the children of the flesh (saith he) are not the children of God, but the children of the promise, etc. And by this argument he mightily stoppeth the mouths of the proud Jews, which gloried that they were the seed and children of Abraham: as also Christ doth, in the third of Matthew, and in the eighth of John. As if he said: It followeth not, I am the carnal seed of Abraham, therefore I am the child of God; Esau is the natural son, therefore the heir. Nay, rather, (saith he) they that will be the children of Abraham, besides their carnal birth, must be also the sons of the promise, and must believe. And they are the true children of Abraham, and consequently, of God, who have the promise and believe.

But Ishmael, because he was not promised of God to Abraham, is a son after the flesh only, and not after the promise, and therefore he was born at adventure, as other children be. For no mother knoweth whether she shall have a child or no, or if she perceive herself to be with child, yet she cannot tell whether it shall be a son or a daughter. But Isaac was expressly named (Gen. xvii), "Sarah, thy wife" (saith the angel to Abraham) "shall bear thee a son, and thou shalt call his name Isaac." Here the son and the mother are expressly named. Thus, for this humility of Sarah, because she gave up her right, and suffered the contempt of Hagar (Gen. xvi), God requited her with this honour, that she should be the mother of the promised son, etc.

VERSE 24. *The which things are spoken by allegories.*

Allegories do not strongly persuade in divinity, but, as certain pictures, they beautify and set out the matter. For if Paul had not proved the righteousness of faith against the righteousness of works by strong and pithy arguments, he should have little prevailed by this allegory. But, because he had fortified his cause before with invincible arguments, taken of experience, of the example of Abraham, the testimonies of the scripture and similitudes; now, in the end of his disputations, he addeth an allegory, to give a beauty to all the rest. For it is a seemly thing sometimes to add an allegory, when the foundation is well laid, and the matter thoroughly proved; for as painting is an ornament to set forth and garnish a house already builded, so is an allegory the light of a matter which is already otherwise proved and confirmed.

VERSES 24 AND 25. *For these mothers are the two Testaments: the one, which is Hagar of mount Sinai, which gendereth unto bondage.* (*For Agar or Sinai is a mountain in Arabia.*)

Abraham is a figure of God, which hath two sons; that is to say, two sorts of people are represented by Ishmael and Isaac. These two are born unto him by Hagar and Sarah, the which signify the two Testaments, the Old and the New. The Old is of mount Sinai, begetting unto bondage, which is Hagar. For the Arabians in their language call Agar the same mountain which the Jews call Sinai (which seemeth to have that name of brambles and thorns), which also Ptolemæus and the Greek commentators do witness. After the same manner divers names are given to many mountains, according to the diversity of nations. So the mount which Moses calleth Hermon, of the Sidonians is called Sirion, and of the Amorites, Senir.

Now this serveth very well to the purpose, that mount Sinai, in the Arabian language signifieth as much as a handmaid; and I think the likeness of this name gave Paul light and occasion to seek out this allegory. Likewise, then, as Hagar the bond-maid brought forth to Abraham a son, and yet not an heir but a servant: so Sinai, the allegorical Agar, brought forth to God a son, that is to say, a carnal people. Again, as Ishmael was the true son of Abraham, so the people of Israel had the true God to be their Father, which gave them his law, his oracles, religion, and true service, and the temple: as it is said, in Psalm cxlvii, "He sheweth his word unto Jacob, his statutes and his judgments unto Israel." Notwithstanding this only was the difference: Ishmael was born of a bond-maid after the flesh, that is to say, without the promise, and could not therefore be the heir. So the mystical Agar, that is to say, mount Sinai, where the law was given, and the Old Testament ordained, brought forth to God, who is the great Abraham, a people, but without the promise; that is to say, a carnal and a servile people, and not the heir of God. For the promises, as touching Christ, the giver of all blessing, and as touching the deliverance from the curse of the law, from sin and death; also as touching the free remission of our sins, of righteousness and everlasting life, are not added to the law, but the law saith, "He that shall do these things shall live in them" (Lev. xviii, 5; Rom. x, 5).

Therefore, the promises of the law are conditional, promising life, not freely, but to such as fulfil the law; and therefore they leave men's consciences in doubt: for no man fulfilleth the law. But the promises of the New Testament have no such condition joined unto them, nor require any thing of us, nor depend upon any condition of our worthiness, but bring and give unto us freely, forgiveness of sins, grace, righteousness and life everlasting for Christ's sake, as I have said more largely in another place.

Therefore the law, or the Old Testament, containeth only conditional promises; for it hath always such conditions as these are, joined to it: "If ye hearken to my voice, if ye keep my statutes, if ye walk in my ways, ye shall be my people," etc. The Jews, not considering this, laid hold of those conditional promises, as if they had been absolute and without all conditions: which they supposed that God could never revoke, but must needs keep them. Hereupon, when they heard the prophets foreshadow the destruction of the city of Jerusalem, of the temple, of the kingdom and priesthood, (which could well discern betwixt the corporal promises of the law, and the spiritual promises concerning Christ and his kingdom), they persecuted and killed them, as heretics and blasphemers of God; for they saw not this condition that was annexed: "If ye keep my commandments, it shall go well with you," etc.

Therefore Hagar, the bond-maid, bringeth forth but a bond-servant. Ishmael, then, is not the heir, although he be the natural son of Abraham, but remaineth a bond-man. What is here lacking? The promise, and the blessing of the word. So the law given in mount Sinai, which the Arabians call Agar, begetteth none but servants. For the promise made, as concerning Christ, was not annexed to the law. Wherefore, O ye Galatians! if ye, forsaking the promise and faith, fall back to the law and works, ye shall always continue servants; that is, ye shall never be delivered from sin and death, but ye shall always abide under the curse of the law. For Hagar gendereth not the seed of the promise and heirs; that is to say, the law justifieth not, it bringeth not the adoption and inheritance: but rather hindereth the inheritance, and worketh wrath.

VERSE 25. *And it answereth to Jerusalem which now is, and she is in bondage with her children.*

This is a wonderful allegory. As Paul, a little before, made Hagar of Sinai, so now of Jerusalem he would gladly make Sarah, but he dareth not, neither can he so do; but is compelled to join Jerusalem with mount Sinai: for he said, "The same belongeth to Hagar, seeing mount Agar reacheth even to Jerusalem." And it is true, that there be continued mountains reaching from Arabia Petrea unto Cades Bernea of Jury. He saith, then, that this Jerusalem which now is, that is to say, this earthly and temporal Jerusalem is not Sarah, but pertaineth to Hagar, for there Hagar reigneth. For in it is the law begetting unto bondage; in it is the worship and ceremonies, the temple, the kingdom, the priesthood; and whatsoever was ordained in Sinai by the mother, which is the law, the same is done in Jerusalem. Therefore I join her with Sinai, and I comprehend both in one word, to wit, Sinai or Hagar.

I durst not have been so bold to handle this allegory after this manner, but would rather have called Jerusalem Sarah, or the New Testament, especially seeing the preaching of the gospel began in it, the Holy Ghost was there given, and the people of the New Testament were there born; and I would have thought that I had found out a very fit allergory. Wherefore it is not for every man to use allegories at his pleasure; for a goodly outward shew may soon deceive a man, and cause him to err. Who would not think it a very fit thing to call Sinai Hagar, and Jerusalem Sarah? Indeed, Paul maketh Jerusalem Sarah, but not this corporeal Jerusalem which he simply joineth unto Agar; but that spiritual and heavenly Jerusalem, in which the law reigneth not, nor the carnal people, as in that Jerusalem which is in bondage with her children, but wherein the promise reigneth, wherein is also a spiritual and a free people.

And to the end that the law should be quite abolished, and that whole kingdom which was established in Hagar, the earthly Jerusalem was horribly destroyed, with all her ornaments, the temple, the ceremonies, etc. Now, although the New Testament began in it, and so was spread throughout the whole world, yet notwithstanding it appertaineth to Agar, that is to say, it is the city of the law, of the ceremonies, and of the priesthood, instituted by Moses. Briefly, it is gendered of Hagar the bond-woman, and therefore is in bondage with her children; that is to say, it walketh in the works of the law, and never attaineth to the liberty of the spirit, but abideth continually under the law, sin, an evil conscience, the wrath and judgment of God, and under the guilt of death and hell. Indeed it hath the liberty of the flesh, it hath a corporeal kingdom, it hath magistrates, riches, and possessions, and such-like things: but we speak of the liberty of the spirit, whereby we are dead to the law, to sin, and death, and we live and reign in grace, forgiveness of sins, righteousness and everlasting life. This cannot the earthly Jerusalem perform, and therefore it abideth with Hagar.

VERSE 26. *But Jerusalem, which is above, is free: which is the mother of us all.*

That eathly Jerusalem (saith he) which is beneath, having the policy and ordinances of the law, is Hagar, and is in bondage with her children; that is to say, she is not delivered from the law, sin, and death. But Jerusalem, which is above, that is to say, the spiritual Jerusalem, is Sarah, (albeit Paul addeth not the proper name of Sarah, but giveth her another name, calling her the free-woman), that is to say, that true lady and free-woman which is the mother of us all, gendering us unto liberty, and not unto bondage, as Hagar doth. Now this heavenly Jerusalem which is above, is the church, that is to say, the faithful dispersed throughout the whole world, which have one and the same gospel, one and the same faith in Christ, the same Holy Ghost, and the same sacraments.

Therefore, understand not this word "above" of the triumphant church (as the schoolmen call it) in heaven; but of the militant church on earth. For the godly are said to have their conversation in heaven—"Our conversation is in heaven" (Phil. iii), not locally, but in that a Christian believeth, in that he layeth hold of those inestimable, those heavenly and eternal gifts, he is in heaven—"Which hath blessed us with all spiritual blessings in heavenly things in Christ" (Eph. i). We must therefore distinguish the heavenly and spiritual blessing from the earthly. For the earthly blessing is to have a good civil government, both in commonweals and families: to have children, peace, riches, fruits of the earth, and other corporeal commodities. But the heavenly blessing is to be delivered from the law, sin, and death: to be justified and quickened to life; to have peace with God; to have a faithful heart, a joyful conscience, and a spiritual consolation; to have the knowledge of Jesus Christ; to have the gift of prophecy, and the revelation of the scriptures; to have the gift of the Holy Ghost, and to rejoice in God. These are the heavenly blessings which Christ giveth to the church.

Wherefore Jerusalem which is above, that is to say, the heavenly Jerusalem, is the church which is now in the world, and not the city of the life to come, or the church triumphant, as the idle and unlearned monks and the school-doctors dreamed, which taught that the scripture hath four senses: the literal sense, the figurative sense, the allegorical sense, and the moral sense; and according to these senses they have foolishly interpreted almost all the words of the scriptures. As this word Jerusalem literally signified that city which was so named; figuratively, a pure conscience; allegorically, the church militant; morally, the celestial city, or the church triumphant. With these trifling and foolish fables they rent the scriptures into so many and divers senses, that poor silly consciences could receive no certain doctrine of any thing. But Paul saith here that the old and earthly Jerusalem belongeth unto Hagar, and that it is in bondage with her children, and is utterly abolished. But the new and heavenly Jerusalem, which is a queen and a free-woman, is appointed of God in earth and not in heaven, to be the mother of us all, of whom we have been gendered, and yet daily are gendered. Therefore, it is necessary that this our mother should be in earth among men, as also her generation is. Notwithstanding she gendereth by the Holy Ghost, by the ministry of the word and sacraments, and not in the flesh.

This I say to the end that in this matter we should not be carried away with our cogitations into heaven, but that we should know that Paul setteth the Jerusalem which is above, against the earthly Jerusalem, not locally but spiritually. For there is a distinction between those things which are spiritual, and those which are corporeal or earthly. The spiritual things are above, the earthly are beneath; so Jerusalem which is above, is distinguished from the carnal and temporal Jerusalem which is beneath, not locally (as I have said) but spiritually. For this spiritual Jerusalem, which took her beginning in the corporeal Jerusalem, hath not any certain place as hath the other in Judea; but it is dispersed throughout the whole world, and may be in Babylon, in Turkey, in Tartary, in Scythia, in Judea, in Italy, in Germany, in the isles of the Sea, in the mountains and valleys, and in all places of the world where men dwell which have the gospel and believe in Jesus Christ.

Wherefore Sarah, or Jerusalem, our free mother, is the church itself, the spouse of Christ, of whom we all are gendered. This mother gendereth free children without ceasing, to the end of the world, as long as she preacheth and publisheth the gospel, for this is truly to gender. Now, she teacheth the gospel after this manner: to wit, that we are delivered from the curse of the law, from sin, death, and all other evils, by Jesus Christ, and not by the law, neither by works. Therefore, Jerusalem which is above, that is to say, the church, is not subject to the law and works, but she is free and a mother without the law, sin, and death. Now, such a mother as she is, such children she gendereth.

This allegory teacheth very aptly that the church should do nothing else but preach and teach the gospel truly and sincerely, and by this means should gender children. So, we are all fathers and children, one to another; for we are begotten one of another. I, being begotten by other through the gospel, do now beget other, which shall also beget other hereafter, and so this begetting shall endure to the end of the world. Now, I speak of the generation, not of Hagar, the bond-maid, which gendereth her bond-servants by the law; but of Sarah, the freewoman, who gendereth heirs without the law, and without man's works or endeavours. For in that Isaac is heir, and not Ishmael, (albeit notwithstanding that both of them were the natural sons of Abraham,) Isaac had the inheritance by the word of promise, namely, "Sarah thy wife shall bring thee a son, and thou shalt call his name Isaac" (Gen. xvii, 19). This did Sarah well understand, and therefore she saith, "Cast out the bond-woman and her son:" and Paul also allegeth these words afterwards. Wherefore, as Isaac hath the inheritance of his father only by the promise and by his birth, without the law and without works: even so we are born through the gospel of that free-woman Sarah, that is to say, the church, true heirs of the promise. She instructeth us, nourisheth us, and carrieth us in her womb, in her lap, and in her arms: she formeth and fashioneth us to the image of Christ, until we grow up to a perfect man, etc. So all things are done by the ministry of the word. Wherefore the office of the free-woman is to gender children to God her husband without ceasing and without end; that is to say, such children as know that they are justified by faith, and not by the law.

VERSE 27. *For it is written, Rejoice thou barren that bearest no children; break forth and cry thou that travailest not; for the desolate hath many more children than she which hath an husband,* (Isaiah liv, 1).

Paul allegeth this place out of Isaiah the prophet, which is altogether allegorical. It is written (saith he) that the mother of many children, and she which hath a husband, must be sick and die; and contrariwise, that the barren, and she which hath no children, must have abundance of children. After the same manner Hannah singeth in her song, out of the which Isaiah the prophet took his prophecy (1 Sam. ii), "The bow and the mighty men are broken, and the weak have girded themselves with strength. They that were full are hired forth for bread, and the hungry are no more hired; so that the barren hath born seven, and she that had many children is feeble." A marvellous matter (saith he): she that was fruitful shall be made barren, and she that was barren, fruitful. Moreover, such as before were strong, full, rich, glorious, righteous, and blessed, shall become feeble, hungry, poor, ignominious sinners, subject to death and damnation; and contrariwise, the feeble and hungry, etc., shall be strong and satisfied, etc.

The apostle sheweth, by this allegory of the prophet Isaiah, the difference which is between Hagar and Sarah; that is to say, between the synagogue and the church, or between the law and the gospel. The law being the husband of the fruitful woman, that is to say, of the synagogue, begetteth very many children. For men of all ages, not only idiots, but also the wisest and best (that is to say, all mankind, except the children of the free-woman), do neither see nor know any other righteousness than the righteousness of the law, much less do they know any which is more excellent; wherefore they think themselves righteous if they follow the law, and outwardly perform the works thereof.

Now, although these be fruitful, have many disciples, and shine in the righteousness and glorious works of the law, yet notwithstanding they are not free, but bond-servants; for they are the children of Hagar, which gendereth to bondage. Now, if they be servants, they cannot be partakers of the inheritance, but shall be cast out of the house; for servants remain not in the house for ever (John viii, 35). Yea, they are already cast out of the kingdom of grace and liberty: "for he that believeth not, is condemned already" (John iii, 18). They remain, therefore, under the malediction of the law, under sin and death, under the power of the devil, and under the wrath and judgment of God.

Now, if the moral law itself, or the commandments of God, can do nothing else but gender servants, that is to say, cannot justify, but only terrify, accuse, condemn, and drive men's consciences to desperation; how then, I pray you, shall the laws of men, or the laws of the Pope justify, which are the doctrines of devils? They, therefore, that teach and set forth either the traditions of men, or the law of God, as necessary to obtain righteousness before God, do nothing else but gender servants. Notwithstanding, such teachers are counted the best men; they obtain the favour of the world, and are most fruitful mothers, for they have an infinite number of disciples. For man's reason understandeth not what faith and true godliness is, and therefore it neglecteth and despiseth it, and is naturally addicted to superstition and hypocrisy; that is to say, the righteousness of works. Now, because this righteousness shineth and flourisheth everywhere, therefore it is a mighty empress of the whole world. They, therefore, which teach righteousness of works by the law, beget many children, which outwardly seem to be free, and have a glorious shew of excellent virtues, but in conscience they are servants and bond-slaves of sin; therefore they are to be cast out of the house, and condemned.

Contrariwise, Sarah the free-woman, that is to say, the true church, seemeth to be barren. For the gospel, which is the word of the cross and affliction, which the church preacheth, shineth not so brightly as the doctrine of the law and works, and therefore she hath not so many disciples to cleave unto her; moreover, she beareth this title, that she forbiddeth good works, maketh men secure, idle, and negligent, raiseth up heresies and seditions, and is the cause of all mischief; and therefore she seemeth to bring no success or prosperity, but all things seem to be full of barrenness, desolation, and desperation. Therefore the wicked are certainly persuaded, that the church with her doctrine cannot long endure. The Jews assured themselves that the church which was planted by the apostles should be overthrown; the which, by an odious name, they called a sect. For thus they speak to Paul, in the 28th chapter of the Acts: "As concerning this sect, we know that everywhere it is spoken against." In like manner, how often (I pray you) have our adversaries been deceived, which some-whiles appointed one time, and some-whiles another, when we should be certainly destroyed? Christ and his apostles were oppressed: but after their death the doctrine of the gospel was farther spread abroad than it was during their life. In like manner our adversaries may oppress us at this day, but the word of God shall abide for ever. How much soever, then, the church seemeth to be barren and forsaken, weak and despised, and outwardly to suffer persecution, and moreover be compelled to hear this reproach, that her doctrine is heretical and seditious, notwithstanding she alone is fruitful before God; she gendereth, by the ministry of the word, an infinite number of children, heirs of righteousness and everlasting life; and although outwardly they suffer persecution, yet in spirit they are most free: who not only are judges over all doctrines and works, but also are most victorious conquerors against the gates of hell.

The prophet therefore confesseth that the church is in heaviness; for else he would not exhort her to rejoice. He granteth that she is barren before the world: for else he would not call her barren and forsaken, having no children: but before God, saith he, she is fruitful, and therefore he biddeth her to rejoice. As though he would say: Thou art, indeed, forsaken and barren, and hast not the law for thy husband, and therefore thou hast no children; but rejoice: for although thou hast not the law for thy husband, but art forsaken as a virgin that is ready to marry (for he will not call her widow), which should have a husband if she were not forsaken of him, or if he were not slain, thou (I say) which art solitary and forsaken of thy husband the law, and not subject to the marriage of the law, shalt be a mother of innumerable children. Wherefore the people, or the church of the New Testament is altogether without the law as touching the conscience, and therefore she seemeth to be forsaken in the sight of the world. But although she seem to be never so barren, without the law and without works, yet notwithstanding she is most fruitful before God, and bringeth forth an infinite number of children, not in bondage but in freedom. By what means? Not by the law, but by the word and spirit of Christ, which is given by the gospel, through the which she conceiveth, bringeth forth, and nourisheth her children.

Paul, therefore, plainly sheweth by this allegory the difference between the law and the gospel. First, when he calleth Hagar the Old Testament, and Sarah the New; again, when he calleth the one a bond-maid, the other a free-woman; moreover, when he saith that the married and fruitful is become barren and cast out of the house with her children; contrariwise, when the barren and forsaken is become fruitful, and bringeth forth an infinite number of children, and those also inheritors. By these differences are resembled the two sorts of people; of faith, and of the law, I mean. The people of faith have not the law for their husband, they serve not in bondage, they are not born of that mother Jerusalem which now is; but they have the promise, they are free, and are born of free Sarah.

He separateth, therefore, the spiritual people of the New Testament, from the other people of the law, when he saith that the spiritual people are not the children of Hagar the bondmaid, but of Sarah the free-woman, which knoweth nothing of the law; and by this means he placeth the people of faith far above and without the law. Now, then, if they be above and without the law, then are they justified by the spiritual birth only, which is nothing else but faith; and not by the law, or by the works thereof. Now, as the people of grace neither have nor can have the law; so the people of the law neither have nor can have grace; for it is impossible that the law and grace should stand together. Therefore, we must be justified by faith, and lose the righteousness of the law; or else be justified by the law, and lose the righteousness of faith. But this is a foul and a lamentable loss, to lose grace, and to return to the law. Contrariwise, it is a happy and a blessed loss, to lose the law, and lay hold of grace.

We, therefore, (following the example and diligence of Paul) do endeavour, as much as is possible, to set forth plainly the difference between the law and the gospel; which is very easy as touching the words. For who seeth not that Hagar is not Sarah, and that Sarah is not Hagar? Also, that Ishmael is not Isaac, and that he hath not that which Isaac hath? A man may easily discern these things. But, in great terrors, and in the agony of death, when the conscience wrestleth with the judgment of God, it is the hardest thing of all others to say, with a sure and stedfast hope: I am not the son of Hagar, but of Sarah; that is to say, the law belongeth nothing unto me: for Sarah is my mother, who bringeth forth free children and heirs, and not servants.

Paul, then, by this testimony of Isaiah hath proved that Sarah, that is to say, the church, is the true mother, which bringeth forth free children and heirs. Contrariwise, that Hagar, that is to say, the synagogue, gendereth many children indeed, but they are servants, and must be cast out. Moreover, because this place speaketh also of the abolishing of the law and of Christian liberty, it ought to be diligently considered. For as it is the most principal and special article of Christian doctrine, to know that we are justified and saved by Christ, so is it also very necessary to know and understand well the doctrine concerning the abolishment of the law; for it helpeth very much to confirm our doctrine, as touching faith, and to attain sound and certain consolation of conscience, when we are assured that the law is abolished, and specially in great terrors and serious conflicts.

I have often said before, and now I say again, (for it cannot be too often repeated) that a Christian, laying hold of the benefit of Christ through faith, hath no law, but all the law is to him abolished, with all his terrors and torments. This place of Isaiah teacheth the same thing, and therefore it is very notable and full of comfort, stirring up the barren and forsaken to rejoice, which was counted worthy to be mocked or pitied according to the law. For such as were barren, were accursed according to the law. But the Holy Ghost turneth this sentence, and pronounceth the barren worthy of praise and blessing; and contrariwise, the fruitful, and such as bring forth children, accursed; when he saith, "Rejoice, thou barren which bearest not: break forth into joy, and rejoice thou that travailest not: for the desolate hath many more children than the married wife" (Isa. liv, 1). Howsoever, then, Sarah, that is to say, the church, seemeth to be forsaken and barren before the world, not having the righteousness and works of the law; yet notwithstanding, she is a most fruitful mother, having an infinite number of children before God, as the prophet witnesseth. Contrariwise, although Hagar seem never so fruitful, and to bring forth never so many children, yet notwithstanding she hath no issue remaining; for the children of the bond-woman are cast out of the house together with their mother, and receive not the inheritance with the children of the free-woman: as Paul said afterwards.

Because, therefore, we are the children of the free-woman, the law our old husband is abolished (Rom. vii); who, as long as he had dominion over us, it was impossible for us to bring forth children free in spirit, or knowing grace: but we remained with the other in bondage. True it is, that, as long as the law reigneth, men are not idle, but they labour sore, they bear the burthen and the heat of the day (Matt. xx, 12); they bring forth and gender many children; but as well the fathers as the children are bastards, and do not belong to the free-mother, therefore they are at length cast out of the house and inheritance with Ishmael; they die, and are damned. It is impossible, therefore, that men should attain to the inheritance, that is to say, that they should be justified and saved by the law, although they travail never so much, and be never so fruitful therein. Accursed, therefore, be that doctrine, life, and religion, which endeavoureth to get righteousness before God, by the law or the works thereof. But let us prosecute our purpose, as touching the abolishment of the law.

The school-doctors, speaking of the abolishment of the law, say, that the judicial and the ceremonial laws are pernicious and deadly, since the coming of Christ; and, therefore, they are abolished, but not the moral law. These blind doctors knew not what they said. But, if thou wilt speak of the abolishment of the law, talk of it as it is, in his own proper use and office, and as it is spiritually taken, and comprehend withal the whole law, making no distinction at all between the judicial, ceremonial, and moral law. For when Paul saith, that we are delivered from the curse of the law by Christ, he speaketh of the whole law, and principally of the moral law, which only accuseth, curseth, and condemneth the conscience, which the other two do not. Wherefore we say that the moral law, or the law of the ten commandments, hath no power to accuse and terrify the conscience, in which Jesus Christ reigneth by his grace: for he hath abolished the power thereof.

Not that the conscience doth not at all feel the terrors of the law (for indeed it feeleth them), but that they cannot condemn it, nor bring it to desperation. "For there is no condemnation to them that are in Christ Jesus" (Rom. viii). Also, "if the Son shall make you free, ye shall be free indeed" (John viii). Howsoever, then, a Christian man be terrified through the law shewing unto him his sin, notwithstanding he despaireth not; for he believeth in Jesus Christ, and being baptized in him and cleansed by his blood, he hath remission of all his sins. Now, when our sin is pardoned through Christ, who is the Lord of the law (and yet so pardoned that he gave himself for it), the law, being a servant, hath no more power to accuse and condemn us for sin, seeing it is forgiven us, and we are now made free, forasmuch as the Son hath delivered us from bondage. Wherefore the law is wholly abolished to them that believe in Christ.

But thou wilt say: I do nothing. True it is that thou canst do nothing, whereby thou mayest be delivered from the tyranny of the law. But hear this joyful tidings which the Holy Ghost bringeth unto thee out of the words of the prophet: "rejoice, thou that art barren," etc. As if he would say, Why art thou so heavy, why dost thou so mourn, since there is no cause why thou shouldst so do? But I am barren and forsaken. Well: although thou be never so barren and forsaken, not having the righteousness of the law, notwithstanding Christ is thy righteousness; he was made a curse for thee, to deliver thee from the curse of the law. If thou believe in him, the law is dead unto thee. And so much as Christ is greater than the law, so much hast thou a more excellent righteousness than the righteousness of the law. Moreover, thou art fruitful and not barren; for thou hast many more children than she which hath a husband.

There is also another abolishment of the law, which is outward: to wit, that the politic laws of Moses do nothing belong unto us. Wherefore we ought not to call them back again, nor superstitiously bind ourselves unto them, as some went about to do, in times past, being ignorant of this liberty. Now, although the gospel make us not subject to the judicial laws of Moses, yet notwithstanding it doth not exempt us from the obedience of all politic laws, but maketh us subject, in this corporeal life, to the laws of that government wherein we live; that is to say, it commandeth every one to obey his magistrate and laws, "not only because of wrath, but also for conscience sake" (1 Pet. ii; Rom. xiii). And the emperor, or any other prince, should not offend, if he used some of the judicial laws of Moses; yea, he might use them freely, and without offence. Therefore the popish schoolmen are deceived, which dream that the judicial laws of Moses are pernicious and deadly since the coming of Christ.

Likewise we are not bound to the ceremonies of Moses, much less to the ceremonies of the Pope. But, because this bodily life cannot be altogether without ceremonies (for there must needs be some introduction) therefore the gospel suffereth ordinances to be made in the church, as touching days, times, places, etc., that the people may know upon what day, in what hour, and in what place to assemble together to hear the word of God. It permitteth, also, that lessons and readings should be appointed, as in the schools, especially for the instruction of children and such as are ignorant. These things it permitteth, to the end that all may be done comely and orderly in the church (1 Cor. xiv). Not that they which keep such ordinances do thereby merit remission of sins. Moreover, they may be changed or omitted without sin, so that it be done without offence of the weak.

Now, Paul speaketh here especially of the abolishment of the moral law, which is diligently to be considered. For he speaketh against the rgihteousness of the law, that he might establish the righteousness of faith, concluding thus: If only grace or faith in Christ justify, then is the whole law abolished, without any exception. And this he confirmeth by the testimony of Isaiah, whereby he exhorteth the barren and forsaken to rejoice; for it seemeth that she hath no child, nor hope ever to have any; that is to say, she hath no disciples, no favour nor countenance of the world, because she preacheth the word of the cross of Christ crucified, against all the wisdom of the flesh. But thou that art barren (saith the prophet) let not this any whit trouble thee: yea, rather lift up thy voice and rejoice, for she that is forsaken hath more children than she that hath a husband: that is to say, she that is married and hath a great number of children shall be made weak, and she that is forsaken shall have many children.

He calleth the church barren, because her children are not begotten by the law, by works, by any industry or endeavour of man, but by the word of faith in the spirit of God. Here is nothing else but birth; no working at all. Contrariwise, they that are fruitful, labour and exercise themselves with great travail in bearing and bringing forth. Here is altogether working, and no birth. But, because they endeavour to get the right of children and heirs by the righteousness of the law, or by their own righteousness, they are servants, and never receive the inheritance, no, though they tire themselves to death with continual travail. For they go about to obtain that by their own works against the will of God, which God of his mere grace will give to all believers for Christ's sake. The faithful work well also; but they are not thereby made sons and heirs (for this their birth bringeth unto them); but this they do, to the end that they, being now made children and heirs, might glorify God by their good works, and help their neighbours.

VERSE 28. *Therefore, brethren, we are, after the manner of Isaac, children of the promise.*

That is to say, we are not children of the flesh, as Ishmael, or as all the fleshly Israel, which gloried that they were the seed of Abraham and the people of God. But Christ answered them, John viii. "If ye were the sons of Abraham, ye would not seek to kill me, which speak the truth unto you." Also, "If God were your father, then would ye love me, and receive my word." As if he would say: Brethren born and brought up together in one house, know one another's voice: "but ye be of your father the devil," etc. We are not such children (saith he) as they are, which remain servants, and at length shall be cast out of the house; but we are children of the promise, as Isaac was; that is to say, of grace and of faith, born only of the promise. Concerning this I have spoken sufficiently before in the third chapter, in treating upon this place: "In thy seed shall all the nations of the earth be blessed." Therefore we are pronounced righteous; not by the law, by works, or our own righteousness, but by the mere mercy and grace of

God. Paul repeateth very often, and diligently setteth forth the promise which is received by faith alone; for he knew that it was very necessary so to do.

Hitherto, as touching the allegory out of Genesis, to the which Paul annexeth the place of Isaiah as an interpretation. Now he applieth the history of Ishmael and Isaac, for our example and consolation.

> VERSE 29. *But as then he that was born after the flesh, persecuted him that was born after the spirit, even so is it now.*

This place containeth a singular consolation. Whosoever are born and live in Christ, and rejoice in this birth and inheritance of God, have Ishmael for their enemy and their persecutor. This we learn at this day by experience; for we see that all the world is full of tumults, persecutions, sects, and offences. Wherefore, if we did not arm ourselves with this consolation of Paul and such-like, and well understand this article of justification, we should never be able to withstand the violence and subtle sleights of Satan. For who should not be troubled with these cruel persecutions of our adversaries, and with these sects and infinite offences, which a sort of busy and fantastical spirits stir up at this day? Verily, it is no small grief unto us, when we are constrained to hear that all things were in peace and tranquility before the gospel came abroad; but since the preaching and publishing thereof, all things are unquiet, and the whole world is in an uproar, so that every one armeth himself against another. When a man that is not endued with the spirit of God heareth this, by-and-by he is offended, and judgeth that the disobediences of subjects against their magistrates, that seditions, wars, plagues, and famine, that the overthrowing of commonweals, kingdoms, and countries, that sects, offences, and such other infinite evils do proceed altogether of the doctrine of the gospel.

Against this great offence we must comfort and arm ourselves with this sweet consolation, that the faithful must bear this name and this title in the world, that they are seditious and schismatics, and the authors of innumerable evils. And hereof it cometh, that our adversaries think they have a just cause against us, yea that they do God high service when they hate, persecute, and kill us (John xvi, 2). It cannot be, then, but that Ishmael must persecute Isaac: but Isaac again persecuteth not Ishmael. Whoso will not suffer the persecution of Ishmael, let him not profess himself to be a Christian.

But let our adversaries (which so mightily amplify these evils at this day) tell us what good things ensued the preaching of the gospel of Christ and his apostles. Did not the destruction of the kingdom of the Jews follow? Was not the Roman empire overthrown? Was not the whole world in an uproar? And yet the gospel was not the cause hereof, which Christ and his apostles preached for the profit and salvation of men, and not for their destruction. But these things followed through the iniquity of the people, the nations, the kings and princes, who, being possessed of the devil, would not hearken to the word of grace, life, and eternal salvation; but detested and condemned it as a doctrine most pernicious and hurtful to religion and commonweals. And that this should so come to pass, the Holy Ghost foretold by David, when he saith, Psalm ii, "Why do the heathen rage, and the people murmur in vain?" etc.

Such tumults and hurly-burlies we hear and see at this day. The adversaries lay the fault in our doctrine. But the doctrine of grace and peace stirreth not up these troubles: but the people, nations, kings, and princes of the earth (as the Psalmist saith) rage and murumur, conspire and take counsel, not against us (as they think) nor aganist our doctrine, which they blaspheme as false and seditious, but against the Lord and his anointed. Therefore, all their counsels and practices are and shall be disappointed and brought to nought. "He that dwelleth in the heavens shall laugh: the Lord shall have them in derision" (Psalm ii, 4). Let them cry out, therefore, as long as they list, that we raise up these tumults and seditions: notwithstanding this Psalm comforteth us, and saith that they themselves are the authors of these troubles. They cannot believe this, and much less can they believe that it is they which murmur, rise up, and take counsel against the Lord and his anointed; nay, rather they think that they maintain the Lord's cause, that they defend his glory, and do him acceptable service in persecuting us; but the Psalm lieth not, and that shall the end declare. Here we do nothing, but we only suffer, as our conscience beareth us witness in the Holy Ghost. Moreover, the doctrine for the which they raise up such tumults and offences, is not ours, but it is the doctrine of Christ. This doctrine we cannot deny, nor forsake the defence thereof, seeing Christ saith, "Whosoever shall be ashamed of me and of my words, in this adulterous and sinful nation, of him shall the Son of man be ashamed, when he shall come in his glory, and in the glory of the Father and of the holy angels" (Luke ix, 26).

He, therefore, that will preach Christ truly, and confess him to be our righteousness, must be content to hear that he is a pernicious fellow, and that he troubleth all things. "They which have troubled the world, (said the Jews, of Paul and Silas) are also come unto us, and have done contrary to the decrees of Cæsar" (Acts xvii). And in the 24th of the Acts, "We have found this pestilent fellow stirring up sedition among all the Jews throughout the whole world, and an author of the sect of the Nazarites," etc. In like manner also the Gentiles complain, in the 16th of Acts, "These men trouble our city." So at this day they accuse Luther to be a troubler of the papacy and of the Roman empire. If I would keep silence, then all things should be in peace which the strong man possesseth (Luke xi, 21, 22) and the Pope would not persecute me any more. But by this means the gospel of Jesus Christ should be blemished and defaced. If I speak, the Pope is troubled, and cruelly rageth. Either we must lose the Pope, an earthly and mortal man, or else the immortal God, Christ Jesus, life, and eternal salvation. Let the Pope perish, then, and let God be exalted; let Christ reign and triumph forever.

Christ himself, when he foresaw in spirit the great troubles which should follow his preaching, comforted himself after this manner: "I come (saith he) to send fire upon the earth, and what will I but that it be kindled?" (Luke xii, 49). In like manner we see, at this day, that great troubles follow the preaching of the gospel, through the persecution and blasphemy of our adversaries, and the ingratitude of the world. This matter so grieveth us, that oftentimes, after the flesh and after the judgment of reason, we think it had been better that the doctrine of the gospel had not been published, than that, after the preaching thereof, the public peace should be so troubled. But, according to the spirit, we say boldly with Christ, "I come to send fire upon the earth, and what will I but that it should now be kindled?" Now, after that this fire is kindled, there follow forthwith great commotions. For it is not a king or an emperor that is thus provoked; but the God of this world, which is a most mighty spirit, and the Lord of the whole world. This weak word, "preaching Christ crucified," setteth upon this mighty and terrible adversary. Behemoth, feeling the divine power of this word, stirreth up all his members, shaketh his tail, and maketh the depth of the sea to boil like a pot (Job xli). Hereof come all these tumults, all these furious and cruel rages of the world.

Wherefore let it not trouble us that our adversaries are offended and cry out, that there cometh no good by the preaching of the gospel; they are infidels, they are blind and obstinate, and therefore it is impossible that they should see any fruit of the gospel. But contrariwise, we, which believe, do see the inestimable profits and fruits thereof; although outwardly, for a time, we be oppressed with infinite evils, despised, spoiled, accused, condemned as the outcasts and filthy dung of the whole world, and put to death, and inwardly afflicted with the feeling of our sin, and vexed with devils. For we live in Christ, in whom and by whom we are made kings and lords over sin, death, the flesh, the world, hell, and all evils; in whom and by whom, also, we tread under our feet that dragon and basilisk, which is the king of sin and death. How is this done? In faith. For the blessedness, which we hope for, is not yet revealed, which in the meantime we wait for in patience; and yet, notwithstanding, do now assuredly possess the same by faith.

We ought, therefore, diligently to learn the article of justification; for that only is able to support us against these infinite slanders and offences, and to comfort us in all our temptations and persecutions. For we see that it cannot otherwise be, but that the world will be offended with the pure doctrine of the gospel, and continually cry out that no good cometh of it. For "the natural man understandeth not those things which are of the spirit of God; for they are foolishness to him" (1 Cor. ii, 14). He only beholdeth the outward evils, troubles, rebellions, murders, sects, and other such-like things; with these sights he is offended and blinded, and finally falleth into the contempt and blaspheming of God and his word.

On the contrary part, we ought to stay and comfort ourselves in this, that our adversaries do not accuse and condemn us for any manifest wickedness which we have committed, as adultery, murder, theft, and such-like, but for our doctrine. And what do we teach? That Christ, the Son of God, by the death of the cross, hath redeemed us from our sins, and from everlasting death. Therefore they do not impugn our life, but our doctrine; yea, the doctrine of Christ, and not ours. Therefore, if there be any offence, it is Christ's offence and not ours; and so the fault wherefore they persecute us, Christ has committed, and not we. Now, whether they will condemn Christ, and pluck him out of Heaven, as a heretic and seditious person, for this fault, that he is our only justifier and saviour, let them look to that. As for us, we, commending this his own cause unto himself, are quiet beholders whether of them shall have the victory, Christ or they. Indeed, after the flesh, it grieveth us that these Ishmaelites hate and persecute us so furiously; notwithstanding, according to the spirit, we glory in these afflictions, both because we know that we suffer them not for our sins, but for Christ's cause, whose benefit and whose glory we set forth, and also because Paul giveth us warning afore-hand, that Ishmael must mock Isaac and persecute him.

The Jews expound this place, which Paul allegeth out of the 21st of Genesis, of Ishmael mocking and persecuting Isaac after this manner, that Ishmael constrained Isaac to commit idolatry. If he did so, yet I believe not that it was any such gross idolatry as the Jews dream of: to wit, that Ishmael made images of clay, after the manner of the Gentiles, which he compelled Isaac to worship; for this, Abraham would in no wise have suffered. But I think that Ishmael was, in outward shew, a holy man, as Cain was, who also persecuted his brother, and at length killed him; not for any corporeal thing, but because he saw that God esteemed him above the other. In like manner, Ishmael was outwardly a lover of religion; he sacrificed and exercised himself in well-doing. Therefore he mocked his brother Isaac, and would be esteemed a better man than him, for two causes: first, for his religion and service of God; secondly, for his civil government and inheritance. And these two things he seemed justly to challenge to himself; for he thought that the kingdom and priesthood pertained to him by the right of God's law, as the first-born, and therefore he persecuted Isaac spiritually because of religion, and corporeally because of his inheritance.

This persecution always remaineth in the church, especially when the doctrine of the gospel flourisheth: to wit, that the children of the flesh mock the children of the promise, and persecute them. The Papists persecute us at this day, and for none other cause, but for that we teach that righteousness cometh by the promise; for it vexeth the Papists that we will not worship their idols, that is to say, that we set not forth their righteousness, their works and worshippings, devised and ordained by men, as available to obtain grace and forgiveness of sins. And for this cause they go about to cast us out of the house; that is to say, they vaunt that they are the church, the children and people of God, and that the inheritance belongeth to them, etc. Contrariwise, they excommunicate and banish us, as heretics and seditious persons; and, if they can, they kill us also: and in so doing they think they do God good service. So, as much as in them lieth, they cast us out of this life, and of the life to come. The Anabaptists, and such other, do hate us deadly, because we impugn and detest their errors and heresies, which they spread abroad and daily renew in the church; and for this cause they judge us to be far worse than the Papists, and therefore they have conceived a more cruel hatred against us, than against the Papists.

As soon, therefore, as the word of God is brought to light, the devil is angry, and useth all his force and subtle sleights, to persecute it, and utterly to abolish it. Therefore he can no otherwise do, but raise up infinite sects, horrible offences, cruel persecutions, and abominable murders; for he is the father of lying and a murderer. He spreadeth his lies throughout the world by false teachers, and he killeth men by tyrants. By these means he possesseth both the spiritual and the corporeal kingdom: the spiritual kingdom by the lying of false teachers, (stirring up also, without ceasing, every man, particularly by his fiery darts, to heresies and wicked opinions:) the corporeal kingdom, by the sword of tyrants. Thus this father of lying and of murder, stirreth up persecution on every side, both spiritual and corporeal, against the children of the free-woman. The spiritual persecution which we are at this day constrained to suffer of heretics, is to us most grievous and intolerable, because of the infinite offences and slanders wherewith the devil goeth about to deface our doctrine; for we are enforced to hear, that the heresies and errors of the Anabaptists and other heretics, and all other enormities, do proceed from our doctrine. The coporeal persecution by which tyrants lie in wait for our goods and lives, is more tolerable; for they persecute us not for our sins, but for the testimony of the word of God. Let us learn, therefore, even by the title which Christ giveth to the devil, to wit, that he is the father of lying and murder (John viii) that when the gospel flourisheth, and Christ reigneth, then sects of perdition must needs spring up; and murderers, persecuting the gospel, must rage every where. And Paul saith, "That there must be heresies" (1 Cor. xi, 19). He that is ignorant of this, is soon offended; and, falling away from the true God and true faith, he returneth to his old god and old false faith.

Paul, therefore, in this place armeth the godly before-hand, that they should not be offended with those persecutions, sects, and offences, saying, "But as then he that was born after the flesh," etc. As if he would say, If we be the children of the promise, and born after the spirit, we must surely look to be persecuted of our brother, which is born after the flesh; that is to say, to say, not only our enemies, which are manifestly wicked, shall persecute us, but also such as at the first were our dear friends, with whom we were familiarly conversant in one house, which received from us the true doctrine of the gospel, shall become our deadly enemies, and persecute us extremely. For they are brethren after the flesh, and must persecute the brethren which are born after the spirit. So Christ (in Ps. xli) complaineth of Judas, "The man of my peace, whom I trusted, which did eat of my bread, hath lifted up the heel against me." But this is our consolation, that we have not given any occasion to our Ishmaelites to persecute us. The Papists persecute us, because we teach the pure and sincere doctrine of the gospel; which, if we would forsake, they would persecute us no more. Moreover, if we would approve the pernicious heresies of the sectaries, they would praise us. But, because we detest and abhor the impiety both of the one and the other, therefore do they so spitefully hate and so cruelly persecute us.

But not only Paul (as I have said) armeth us against such persecutions and offences, but Christ himself also most sweetly comforteth us, in the fifteenth chapter of John, saying, "If ye were of the world, the world would love you; but because ye are not of the world, but I have chosen you out of the world, therefore the world hateth you." As if he would say, I am the cause of all these persecutions which ye endure; and if ye be killed, it is I for whose sake ye are killed. For if ye did not preach my words and confess me, the world would not persecute you. But it goeth well with you: For "the servant is not greater than his master. If they have persecuted me, they will also persecute you, for my name's sake" (John xv, 20).

By these words Christ layeth all the fault upon himself, and delivereth us from all fear. As if he would say, Ye are not the cause why the world hateth and persecuteth you, but my name, which ye preach and confess, is the cause thereof. "But be of good comfort: I have overcome the world." This comfort upholdeth us, so that we doubt nothing but that Christ is strong enough, not only to bear, but also to vanquish all the cruelty of tyrants, and the subtle sleights of heretics. And this he hath declared, in shewing forth his power against the Jews and the Romans, whose tyranny and persecutions he suffered for a time. He also suffered the subtleties and crafty practices of heretics, but in time and place he overthrew them all, and remained king and conqueror. Let the Papists, then, rage as much as they will; let the sectaries slander and corrupt the gospel of Christ as much as they can: notwithstanding, Christ shall reign eternally, and his word shall stand for ever, when all his enemies shall be brought to nought. Moreover, this is a singular consolation, that the persecution of Ishmael against Isaac shall not always continue, but shall endure for a little while, and when that is ended, the sentence shall be pronounced as followeth:

VERSE 30. *But what saith the scripture? Cast out the servant and her son: for the son of the servant shall not be heir with the son of the freewoman.* (Genesis xxi, 10.)

This word of Sarah was very grievous to Abraham; and, no doubt, when he heard this sentence, his fatherly bowels were moved with compassion towards his son Ishmael; for he was born of his flesh. And this the scripture plainly witnesseth, when it saith, "And this thing was very grievous in Abraham's sight, because of his son." But God confirmed the sentence which Sarah pronounced, saying to Abraham: "Let it not be grievous in thy sight for the child and for thy bond-woman; in all that Sarah shall say unto thee, hear her voice; for in Isaac shall thy seed be called."

The Ismaelites hear, in this place, the sentence pronounced against them, which overthroweth the Jews, Grecians, Romans, and all others which persecute the church of Christ. The selfsame sentence also shall overthrow the Papists, and as many as trust in their own works, which at this day boast themselves to be the people of God, and the church; which also trust that they shall surely receive the inheritance, and judge us, which rest upon the promise of God, not only to be barren and forsaken, but also heretics cast out of the church, and that it is impossible that we should be sons and heirs. But God overthroweth their judgment, and pronounceth this sentence against them: that, because they are children of the bond-woman, and persecute the children of the free-woman, therefore they shall be cast out of the house, and shall have no inheritance with the children of the promise; to whom only the inheritance belongeth, because they are the children of the free-woman. This sentence is ratified, and can never be revoked; wherefore it shall assuredly come to pass, that our Ismaelites shall not only lose the ecclesiastical and politic government which now they have, but also everlasting life. For the scripture hath foretold that the children of the bond-woman shall be cast out of the house, that is to say, out of the kingdom of grace; for they cannot be heirs together with the children of the free-woman.

Now, here is to be noted that the Holy Ghost calleth the people of the law and works, as it were in contempt, the children of the bond-woman. As if he said, Why do ye vaunt of the righteousness of the law and works, and why do ye glory that ye are people and children of God for the same? If ye know not of whom ye are born, I will tell you: ye are bondservants of a bond-woman. And what servants? The bondservants of the law, and consequently of sin, of death, and of everlasting damnation. Now, a servant is no inheritor, but is cast out of the house; wherefore the Pope, with all his kingdom, and all other justiciaries (what outward appearance of holiness soever they have), which hope to obtain grace and salvation by the law, are servants of that bond-woman, and have no inheritance with the children of the free-woman. I speak now, not of the Popes, cardinals, bishops, and monks, that were manifestly wicked, who have made their bellies their God, and have committed such horrible sins as I will not willingly name; but of the best of them, such I mean as lived holily, and went about, through great labour and travail, by keeping of their monkish order, to pacify the wrath of God, and to merit remission of their sins and everlasting life. These hear their sentence here pronounced, that the sons of the bond-woman must be cast out of the house, with their mother the bond-woman.

Such sentences diligently considered, make us certain of our doctrine and confirm us in the righteousness of faith, against the doctrine and righteousness of works, which the world embraceth and magnifieth, condemning and despising the other. And this troubleth and offendeth weak consciences; which, albeit they plainly see the impiety, the execrable wickedness, and horrible abominations of the Papists, yet, not withstanding, they are not easily persuaded that all the multitude which beareth the name and title of the church do err, and that there are but few of them which have a sound and a right opinion of the doctrine of faith. And if the papacy had the same holiness and austerity of life, which it had in the time of the ancient fathers, Hierome, Ambrose, Augustine, and others, when the clergy had not yet so evil a fame for their simony, excess, abundance of riches, dissolute living, voluptuousness, whoredom, sodomitry, and such other infinite abominations, but lived after the rules and decrees of the fathers, religiously and holily in outward shew, and unmarried, what could we do now against the papacy?

The single life which the clergy kept very straitly in the time of the fathers, was a goodly thing, and made of men very angels in the sight of the world; and therefore Paul, in the second chapter to the Colossians, calleth it the religion of angels. And the Papists sing thus of their virgins: they led an angelical life, whilst they lived in the flesh, and yet lived contrary to the flesh. Moreover, the life which they call the contemplative life (whereunto the clergymen were then very much given, utterly neglecting all civil and household government) had a goodly shew of holiness. Wherefore, if that outward shew and appearance of the old papacy remained at this day, we should peradventure do but little against it by our doctrine of faith, seeing we do now so little prevail, when (that old shew of outward holiness and severe discipline being utterly abolished) there is nothing to be seen but a very sink and puddle of all vices and abominations.

But, admit the case that the old discipline and religion of the papacy were yet remaining: notwithstanding, we ought, by the example of Paul (who vehemently pursued the false apostles, which outwardly appeared to be very godly and holy men) to fight against the merit-mongers of the papistical kingdom, and to say: Although ye live a single life, tiring and consuming your bodies with continual travail, and walking in the humility and religion of angels, yet are ye servants of the law, of sin, and of the devil, and must be cast out of the house; for ye seek righteousness and salvation by your works, and not by Christ.

Wherefore we ought not so much to consider the wicked life of the Papists, as their abominable doctrine and hypocrisy, against the which we specially fight. Let us suppose, then, that the religion and discipline of the old papacy doth yet still flourish, and that it is now observed with as much severity and straitness as ever it was, yet must we say, notwithstanding: If ye have nothing but this holiness and chastity of life to set against the wrath and judgment of God, ye are, in very deed, the sons of the bond-woman, which must be cast out of the kingdom of heaven, and be damned.

And now they themselves do not defend their wicked life; nay, rather, they which are the best and the soundest of them all, do detest it; but they fight for the maintenance and defence of the doctrine of devils, for hypocrisy, and for the righteousness of works. Here they allege the authority of councils and the examples of holy fathers, whom they affirm to have been the authors of their holy orders and statutes. Therefore, we fight not against the manifest wickedness and abominations of the papacy, but against the greatest holiness and holiest saints thereof, which think they lead an angelical life, whilst they dream that they keep not only the commandments of God, but also the counsels of Christ, and do works of supererogation, and such as they are not bound to do. This, we say, is to labour in vain, except they take hold of that only and alone, which Christ saith is only necessary, and choose the good part with Mary, which shall not be taken from them.

This did Bernard, a man so godly, so holy, and so chaste, that he is to be commended and preferred above them all. He being once grievously sick, and having no hope of life, put not his trust in his single life, wherein he had lived most chastely;

not in his good works and deeds of charity, whereof he had done many; but removed them far out of his sight, and, receiving the benefit of Christ by faith, he said: "I have lived wickedly. But thou, Lord Jesus Christ, by double right dost possess the kingdom of heaven: first, because thou art the Son of God; secondly, because thou hast purchased it by thy death and passion. The first thou keepest for thyself, by thy birthright. The second thou givest to me, not by the right of my works, but by the right of grace." He set not against the wrath of God his monkery, nor his angelical life; but he took hold of that one thing which was necessary, and so was saved. I think that Hierome, Gregory, and many other of the fathers, were saved after the same sort. And it is not to be doubted but that also, in the Old Testament, many kings of Israel and other idolaters were saved in like manner, who, at the hour of death, casting away their vain trust which they had in idols, took hold of the promise of God, which was made unto the seed of Abraham, that is to say, Christ, in whom all nations should be blessed. And if there be any of the papists which shall be saved, they must simply lean not to their own good deeds and deserts, but to the mercy of God offered unto us in Christ, and say with Paul: "I have not mine own righteousness which is of the law, but that which is by faith in Christ" (Phil. iii, 9).

VERSE 31. *Then, brethren, we are not children of the servant, but of the free-woman.*

Paul here concludeth his allegory of the barren church, and of the fruitful people of the law. We are not (saith he) the children of the bond-woman; that is to say, we are not under the law, which begetteth unto bondage; that is, which terrifieth, accuseth, and bringeth to desperation; but we are delivered from it by Christ: therefore it cannot terrify nor condemn us. Of this we have spoken enough before. Moreover, although the sons of the bond-woman do persecute us never so much for a time, yet this is our comfort, that they shall be compelled to leave the inheritance unto us, which belongeth unto us that are the sons of the free-woman, and shall at length be cast into utter darkness, (Matt. xxv, 30).

Paul, therefore, by these words [bond-woman and free-woman] took occasion (as we have heard) to reject the righteousness of the law, and to confirm the doctrine of justification. And of purpose he taketh hold of this word [free-woman] vehemently urging and amplfying the same, especially in the beginning of the chapter following. Whereupon he taketh occasion to reason of Christian liberty, the knowledge whereof is very necessary; for the Pope hath in a manner quite overthrown it, and made the church subject to man's traditions and ceremonies, and to a most miserable and filthy bondage. That liberty which is purchased by Christ, is unto us at this day a most strong fort, whereby we defend ourselves against the tyranny of the Pope. Wherefore we must diligently consider this doctrine of Christian liberty, as well to confirm the doctrine of justification, as also to raise up and comfort weak consciences against so many troubles and offences, which our adversaries do impute unto the gospel. Now, Christian liberty is a very spiritual things, which the carnal man doth not understand, (Rom. ix, 32). Yea, they which have the first fruits of the spirit, and can talk well thereof, do very hardly retain it in their heart. It seemeth to reason that it is a matter of small importance; therefore, if the Holy Ghost do not magnify it, that it may be esteemed accordingly, it is condemned.

CHAPTER V.

Paul now drawing towards the end of his epistle, disputeth very vehemently in defence of the doctrine of faith and Christian liberty, against the false apostles, the enemies and destroyers of the same; against whom he casteth out very thundering words to beat them down, and utterly to vanquish them. And therewithal he exhorteth the Galatians to fly their pernicious doctrine as a dangerous poison. In this exhortation he intermingleth threatenings and promises, trying every way that he may keep them in that liberty which Christ hath purchased for them, saying,

> VERSE 1. *Stand fast, therefore, in that liberty wherein Christ hath made us free.*

That is to say, Be ye steadfast. So Peter saith, (1 Peter v, 8, 9), "Be sober, and watch; for your adversary, the devil, as a roaring lion, walketh about, seeking whom he may devour; whom resist, being steadfast in the faith." Be ye not careless, (saith he), but steadfast and constant. Lie not down and sleep, but stand up. As if he would say: It standeth you in hand to be watchful and constant, that ye may keep and hold fast that liberty wherein Christ hath made you free. They that are secure and negligent, cannot keep this liberty; for Satan most deadly hateth the light of the gospel, that is to say, the doctrine of grace, liberty, consolation, and life. Therefore, when he seeth that it beginneth once to appear, forthwith he fighteth against it with all might and main, stirring up storms and tempests to hinder the course thereof, and utterly to overthrow it. Wherefore Paul warneth the faithful not to sleep, not to be negligent; but constantly and valiantly to resist Satan, that he spoil them not of that liberty which Christ hath purchased for them.

Every word hath here a certain vehemency. "Stand," (saith he): as if he should say, Here have ye need of great diligence and vigilance. "In that liberty." In what liberty? Not in that wherewith the emperor hath made us free, but in that wherewith Christ hath made us free.

The emperor hath given, or rather was compelled to give to the bishop of Rome a free city, and other lands; also immunities, privileges and prerogatives, etc. This is also a liberty; but it is a civil liberty, whereby the Pope, with all his clergy, is exempt from all public charges. Moreover, there is a fleshly, or rather a devilish liberty, whereby the devil chiefly reigneth throughout the whole world; for they that enjoy this liberty, obey neither God nor laws, but do what they list. This liberty the people seek and embrace at this day: and so do the sectaries, which will be at liberty in their opinions and in all their doings, to the end they may teach and do whatsoever they dream to be good and sound, without apprehension. These stand in that liberty wherein the devil hath made them free. But we speak not here of this liberty, albeit the whole world seeketh no other liberty; neither do we speak of the civil liberty, but of a far other manner of liberty, which the devil hateth and resisteth with all his power.

This is that liberty whereby Christ hath made us free, not from an earthly bondage, from the Babylonical captivity, or from the tyranny of the Turks, but from God's everlasting wrath. And where is this done? In the conscience. There resteth our liberty, and goeth no farther. For Christ hath made us free, not civilly, nor carnally, but divinely; that is to say, we are made free in such sort, that our conscience is free and quiet, not fearing the wrath of God to come. This is that true and inestimable liberty, to the excellency and majesty whereof if we compare the other, they are but as one drop of water in respect of the whole sea. For who is able to express what a thing it is, when a man is assured in his heart that God neither is, nor will be angry with him, but will be for ever a merciful and a loving Father unto him, for Christ's sake? This is indeed a marvellous and incomprehensible liberty, to have the most high and sovereign majesty so favourable unto us, that he doth not only defend, maintain, and succour us in this life, buth also as touching our bodies, will so deliver us, that our bodies, which are sown in corruption, in dishonour and infirmity, shall rise again in incorruption, in glory, and power (1 Cor. xv, 42-44). Wherefore, this is an inestimable liberty, that we are made free from the wrath of God for ever; and is greater than heaven and earth, and all other creatures.

Of this liberty there followeth another, whereby, through Christ, we are made free from the law, sin, death, the power of the devil, hell, etc. For, as the wrath of God cannot terrify us, for that Christ hath delivered us from the same, so the law, sin, and death, cannot accuse and condemn us. And although the law accuse us, and sin terrify us, yet they cannot drive us to desperation; for faith, which overcometh the world, by-and-by saith: These things belong not unto me; for Christ hath made me free, and delivered me from them all. Likewise death, which is the most mighty and most dreadful thing in all the world, is utterly vanquished in the conscience by the liberty of the spirit. Wherefore the majesty of this Christian liberty is highly to be esteemed, and diligently considered. It is an easy matter for a man to speak these words, "Freedom from the wrath of God, sin, and death;" but in the time of temptation, experience, and practice, to apply them to himself, and to feel the excellency of this liberty and the fruit thereof, it is a harder matter than can be expressed.

Therefore our conscience must be instructed and prepared beforehand, that when we feel the accusation of the law, the terrors of sin, the horror of death, and the wrath of God, we may remove these heavy sights and fearful fantasies out of our minds, and set in the place thereof the freedom purchased by Christ, the forgiveness of sins, righteousness, life, and the everlasting mercy of God. And albeit the feeling of the contrary be very strong, yet let us assure ourselves that it shall not long endure, according to that saying of the prophet, "For a moment, in mine anger, I hid my face from thee for a little season, but with everlasting mercy I have compassion on thee," (Isa. liv, 8). But this is very hard to do. Wherefore, that liberty which Christ hath purchased for us, is not so soon believed as it is named. If it could be apprehended with a sure and a steadfast faith, then no rage or terror of the world, of the law, sin, death, or the devil, could be so great, but by-and-by it should be swallowed up, as a little drop of water is swallowed of the main sea. And, certainly, this Christian liberty swalloweth up at once, and taketh quite away the whole heap of evils, the law, sin, death, God's wrath, and briefly, the serpent himself, with his head and whole power, and, in the stead thereof, it placeth righteousness, peace, and everlasting life, etc. (Luke xi, 28). But blessed is he that understandeth and believeth.

Let us learn, therefore, to magnify this our liberty, purchased by Jesus Christ, the Son of God; by whom all things were created, both in heaven and earth. Which liberty he hath purchased with no other price than with his own blood, to deliver us, not from any bodily or temporal servitude, but from a spiritual and everlasting bondage under mighty and invincible tyrants, to wit, the law, sin, death, and the devil, and so to reconcile us unto God his Father. Now, since these enemies are overcome, and we reconciled unto God by the death of his Son, it is certain that we are righteous before God, and that whatsoever we do, pleaseth him. And although there be certain remnants of sin yet still in us, they are not laid to our charge, but pardoned for Christ's sake.

Paul useth words of great force and vehemency. "Stand (saith he) in that liberty wherein Christ hath made you free." This liberty, then, is not given unto us by the law, or for our righteousness, but freely for Christ's sake, which thing Paul here witnesseth, and plainly declareth throughout his whole epistle. Christ also, in the eighth of John, saith, "If the Son shall make you free, ye shall be free indeed." He only is set betwixt us and the evils which trouble and afflict us: he hath overcome them, and taken them away, so that they can no more oppress us, nor condemn us. In the stead of sin and death, he giveth unto us righteousness and everlasting life; and by this means he changeth the bondage and terrors of the law into the liberty of conscience and consolation of the gospel, which saith, "Be of good comfort, my son, thy sins are forgiven thee" (Matt. ix, 2). Whosoever, then, believeth in Christ the Son of God, he hath this liberty.

Reason cannot perceive the excellency of this matter; which, when a man considereth in spirit, he shall see that it is inestimable. For who is able to conceive in his mind how great and unspeakable a gift it is to have the forgiveness of sins, righteousness, and everlasting life, in the stead of the law, sin, death, and the wrath of God, and to have God himself favourable and merciful for ever? The Papists, and the hypocrites that seek the righteousness of the law, or their own righteousness, do glory that they likewise have remission of sins, righteousness, life and the grace of God. For they vaunt that they also have this liberty, and they promise the same unto others; but, in very deed, they are the servants of corruption, and in the time of temptation all their confidence vanisheth away, even in a moment. For they trust unto the works and satisfactions of men, and not to the word of God, nor unto Christ. Wherefore it is impossible for the justiciaries, which seek to win heaven, life, and salvation by works and merits, to know what the liberty and deliverance from sin is.

Contrariwise, our liberty hath for her foundation Christ himself, who is our everlasting high bishop, sitting at the right hand of God, and making intercession for us. Wherefore the forgiveness of sins, righteousness, life, and liberty, which we have through him, is sure, certain, and perpetual, so that we believe the same. Wherefore, if we cleave unto Christ with a steadfast faith, and stand fast in that liberty wherein he hath made us free, we shall obtain those inestimable gifts; but if we be careless and negligent, we shall lose them. It is not without cause that Paul biddeth us watch and stand fast; for he knew that the devil seeketh nothing more than to spoil us of this liberty, which cost Christ so great a price, and to entangle us again by his ministers in the yoke of bondage, as followeth.

VERSE 1. *And be not entangled again with the yoke of bondage.*

Paul hath spoken most effectually and profoundly as concerning grace and Christian liberty, and with high and mighty words hath exhorted the Galatians to continue in the same, for it is easily lost; therefore he biddeth them stand fast, lest that, through negligence or security, they fall back again from grace and faith, to the law and works. Now, because reason judgeth that there can be no danger in preferring the righteousness of the law before the righteousness of faith; therefore, with a certain indignation, he inveigheth against the law, and with great contempt he calleth it a yoke, yea, a yoke of bondage. So Peter calleth it also, "Why tempt ye God, to lay a yoke on the disciples' necks, which neither our fathers nor we are able to bear?" (Acts xv). And thus he turneth all things to the contrary. For the false apostles did abase the promise, and magnified the law and the works thereof in this wise: "If ye will be made free" (say they) "from sin and death, and obtain righteousness and life, fufil the law, be circumcised, observe days, months, times, and years, offer sacrifices, and do such other like things; then shall this obedience of the law justify and save you." But Paul saith the contrary. They (saith he) that teach the law after this sort, do not set men's consciences at liberty, but snare and entangle them with a yoke, yea, and that with a yoke of bondage.

He speaketh, therefore, of the law very basely and contemptuously, and calleth it a hard bondage, and a servile yoke; and this he doth not without great cause. For this pernicious opinion of the law, that it justifieth and maketh men righteous before God, is deeply rooted in man's reason, and all mankind is so wrapped in it, that it can hardly get out. And Paul seemeth here to compare those that seek righteousness by the law, unto oxen that be tied to the yoke, to the end he might take from it the glory of justifying and of righteousness. For, like as oxen that draw in the yoke with great toil, receive nothing thereby but forage and pasture, and when they be able to draw the yoke no more, are appointed to the slaughter; even so they that seek righteousness by the law, are captives, and oppressed with the yoke of bondage, that is to say, with the law; and when they have tired themselves a long time in the works of the law, with great and grievous toil, in the end this is their reward, that they are miserable and perpetual servants. And wherefore? Even of sin, death, God's wrath, and of the devil. Wherefore there is no greater or harder bondage than the bondage of the law. It is not without cause, then, that Paul calleth it the yoke of bondage. For, as we have often said before, the law doth but reveal, increase, and aggravate sin, accuse, terrify, condemn, and gender wrath, and finally it driveth poor consciences into desperation, which is the most miserable and most grievous bondage that can be (Romans iii, 3, 4, 5).

He useth, therefore, very vehement words; for he would gladly persuade them that they should not suffer this intolerable burden to be laid upon their shoulders by the false apostles, or be entangled again with their yoke of bondage. As if he should say, We stand not here upon a matter of small importance, but either of everlasting liberty, or everlasting bondage. For like as freedom from God's wrath and all evils is not temporal or carnal, but everlasting; even so the bondage of sin, death, the devil, and damnation (wherewith all they be oppressed which will be made righteous and saved by the law) is not corporeal, and such as continueth for a time, but everlasting. For such workers of the law as go about to perform and accomplish all things precisely and exactly, (for of such Paul speaketh,) can never find quietness and peace of conscience in this life. They always doubt of the good-will of God towards them; they are always in fear of death, of the wrath and judgment of

God; and after this life they shall be punished for their unbelief with everlasting damnation.

Therefore the doers of the law, and such as stand altogether upon the righteousness and works thereof, are rightly called the devil's martyrs. They take more pains, and punish themselves more in purchasing hell, (according to the proverb) than the martyrs of Christ do in obtaining heaven. For they are tormented two manner of ways: first, they miserably afflict themselves whilst they live her, by doing of many hard and great works, and all in vain; and afterwards, when they die, they reap for a recompense eternal damnation. Thus are they most miserable martyrs, both in this life and in the life to come, and their bondage is everlasting. Contrariwise, the godly have troubles in this world, but in Christ they have peace, because they believe that he hath overcome the world, (John xvi, 33). Wherefore we must stand fast in that freedom which Christ hath purchased for us by his death, and we must take good heed that we be not entangled again with the yoke of bondage: as it happeneth at this day to the fantastical spirits, who, falling away from faith and from this freedom, have procured unto themselves here a temporal bondage, and in the world to come shall be oppressed with an everlasting bondage. As for the Papists, the most part of them are become at this day plain epicures. Therefore, while they may, they use the liberty of the flesh, singing this careless song, *"Ede, bibe, lude, post mortem nulla voluptas;"* that is, "eat, drink, and make good cheer, for after this life there is no pleasure." But they are the very bond-servants of the devil, by whom they are holden captives at his will and pleasure: therefore they shall feel this everlasting bondage in hell. Hitherto, Paul's exhortation hath been vehement and earnest, but that which followeth doth far pass it.

VERSE 2. *Behold, I, Paul, say unto you, that if ye be circumcised, Christ shall profit you nothing.*

Paul here, wonderfully stirred up with zeal and fervency of spirit, thundereth against the law and circumcision: and these thunderings, proceeding of great zeal, the Holy Ghost wresteth from him, when he saith, "Behold, I, Paul," etc. I (I say) who know that I have not received the gospel by man, but by the revelation of Jesus Christ, and have commission and authority from above, to publish and to preach the same unto you, do tell you, that, if ye be circumcised, Christ shall profit you nothing at all. This is a very hard sentence, whereby Paul declareth, that to be circumcised is as much as to make Christ utterly unprofitable; not in respect of himself, but of the Galatians, who, being deceived by the subtlety of of the false apostles, believed, that, besides faith in Christ, it was needful for the faithful to be circumcised, without the which they could not obtain salvation.

This place is as it were a touchstone, whereby we may most certainly and freely judge of all doctrines, works, religions, and ceremonies of all men. Whosoever teacheth that there is any thing necessary to salvation (whether they be Papists, Turks, Jews, or sectaries) besides faith in Christ, or shall devise any work or religion, or observe any rule, tradition, or ceremony whatsoever, with this opinion, that by such things they shall obtain forgiveness of sins, righteousness, and everlasting life; they hear in this place the sentence of the Holy Ghost pronounced against them by the apostle, that Christ profiteth them nothing. Seeing Paul durst give this sentence against the law and circumcision, which were ordained of God himself, what durst he not do against the chaff and the dross of men's traditions?

Wherefore this place is a terrible thunderbolt against all the kingdom of the Pope. For all priests, monks, and hermits, that live in their cloisters (I speak of the best of them) reposed all their trust and confidence in their own works, righteousness, vows, and merits, and not in Christ, whom they most wickedly and blasphemously imagined to be an angry judge, an accuser and condemner; and therefore here they hear their judgment, that Christ profiteth them nothing. For if they can put away sins, and deserve forgiveness of sins and everlasting life, through their own righteousness and straitness of life, then to what purpose was Christ born? What profit have they by his death and blood-shedding, by his resurrection, victory over sin, death, and the devil, seeing they are able to overcome these monsters by their own strength? And what tongue can express, or what heart can conceive how horrible a thing it is to make Christ unprofitable? Therefore the apostle casteth out these words with great displeasure and indignation, "If ye be circumcised, Christ shall profit you nothing;" that is to say, no profit shall redound unto you of all his benefits, but he hath bestowed them all upon you in vain.

Hereby it appeareth sufficiently, that nothing under the sun is more hurtful than the doctrine of men's traditions and works; for they utterly abolish and overthrow at once the truth of the gospel, faith, the true worshipping of God, and Christ himself, in whom the Father hath ordained all things. In Christ are hid all the treasures of wisdom and knowledge; "in him dwelleth the fulness of the Godhead bodily," (Col. ii). Wherefore, all they that are either authors or maintainers of the doctrine of works, are oppressors of the gospel; they make the death and victory of Christ unprofitable, blemish and deface his sacraments, and utterly take away the true use thereof; and, briefly, they are blasphemers, enemies and deniers of God, and of all his promises and benefits. Whoso is not moved with these words of Paul, (which calleth the law a yoke of bondage, and saith, that they which affirm the keeping of circumcision to be necessary to salvation, make Christ unprofitable,) and cannot be driven from the law and circumcision nor yet from the confidence which he hath in his own righteousness and works, nor be stirred up to seek that liberty which is in Christ, his heart is harder than stone and iron.

This is, therefore, a most certain and clear sentence, that Christ is unprofitable, that is to say, he is born, crucified and risen again in vain to him that is circumcised, that is, which putteth his trust in circumcision. For (as I have said before) Paul speaketh not here of the work of circumcision, (which hurteth not him that hath no affiance or opinion of righteousness in it,) but of the use of the work, that is to say, of the confidence and righteousness which is annexed to the work; for we must understand Paul according to the matter whereof he entreateth, or according to the argument which he hath in hand, which is, that men be not justified by the law, by works, by circumcision, or such-like. He saith not, that works of themselves are nothing, but the confidence and righteousness of works are nothing; for that maketh Christ unprofitable. Therefore, whoso receiveth circumcision, with this opinion, that it is necessary to justification, to him Christ availeth nothing.

Let us bear this well in mind in our private temptations, when the devil accuseth and terrifieth our conscience, to drive it to desperation. For he is the father of lying, and the enemy of Christian liberty; therefore he tormenteth us every moment with false fears, that when our conscience hath lost this Christian liberty, it should feel the remorse of sin and condemnation, and always remain in anguish and terror. When that great dragon, (I say,) that old serpent the devil, (who deceiveth the whole world, and accuseth our brethren in the presence of God day and night, Apoc xii) cometh and layeth unto thy charge, that thou hast not only done no good, but hast also transgressed the law of God, say unto him, Thou troublest me with the remembrance of my sins past; thou puttest me also in mind that I have done no good. But this is nothing to me; for if either I trusted in mine own good deeds, or distrusted because I have done none, Christ should both ways profit me nothing at all.

Therefore, whether thou lay my sins before me, or my good works, I pass not; but, removing both far out of my sight, I only rest in that liberty wherein Christ hath made me free. I know him to be profitable unto me, therefore I will not make him unprofitable; which I should do, if either I should presume to purchase myself favour and everlasting life by my good deeds, or should despair of my salvation because of my sins.

Wherefore let us learn with all diligence to separate Christ far from all works, as well good as evil: from all laws, both of God and man, and from all troubled consciences; for with all these Christ hath nothing to do. He hath to do, I grant, with afflicted consciences: howbeit, not to afflict them more, but to raise them up, and in their affliction to comfort them. Therefore, if Christ appear in the likeness of an angry judge, or of a lawgiver that requireth a strait account of our life past, then let us assure ourselves that it is not Christ, but a raging fiend. For the scripture painteth out Christ to be our reconciliation, our advocate, and our comforter. Such a one he is and ever shall be: he cannot be unlike himself.

Therefore, whensoever the devil, transforming himself into the likeness of Christ, disputeth with us after this manner: This thou oughtest, being admonished by my word, to have done, and hast not done it; and this thou oughtest not to have done, and hast done it: know thou, therefore, that I will take vengeance on thee, etc. Let this nothing at all move us, but by-and-by let us thus think with ourselves: Christ speaketh not to poor, afflicted, and despairing consciences after this manner: he addeth not affliction to the afflicted; he breaketh not the bruised reed, neither quencheth he the smoking flax (Isa. xlii, 3). Indeed, to the hard-hearted he speaketh sharply; but such as are terrified and afflicted, he most lovingly and comfortably allureth unto him, saying, "Come unto me, all ye that travail and be heavy laden, and I will refresh you," (Matt. xi, 28). "I came not to call the righteous, but sinners to repentance," (Matt. ix, 13). "Be of good comfort, my son, thy sins are forgiven thee," (Matt. ix, 2). "Be not afraid, I have overcome the world," (John xvi, 33). "The Son of man came to seek out and to save that which was lost," (Luke xix, 10). We must take good heed, therefore, lest that we, being deceived with the wonderful sleights and infinite subtleties of Satan, do receive an accuser and condemner in the stead of a comforter and saviour; and so, under the vizor of a false Christ, that is to say, of the devil, we lose the true Christ, and make him unprofitable unto us. Thus much have we said as touching private and particular temptations, and how we should use ourselves therein.

EPISTLE TO THE GALATIANS

VERSE 3. *For I testify unto every man which is circumcised, that he is bound to keep the whole law.*

The first inconvenience is, indeed, very great, where Paul saith, that Christ profiteth them nothing which are circumcised, and this that followeth is nothing less, where he saith, that they which are circumcised, are bound to keep the whole law. He speaketh these words with such earnestness and vehemency of spirit, that he confirmeth them with an oath: "I testify," that is to say, I swear by the living God. But these words may be expounded two ways, negatively and affirmatively. Negatively, after this manner: I testify unto every man which is circumcised, that he is bound to keep the whole law, that is to say, that he performeth no piece of the law: yea, that in the very work of circumcision he is not circumcised, and even in the fulfilling of the law he fulfilleth it not, but transgresseth it. And this seemeth to me to be the simple and true meaning of Paul in this place. Afterwards, in the sixth chapter, he expoundeth himself, saying, "they themselves which are circumcised, keep not the law." So he saith also before, in the third chapter, "whosoever are of the works of the law, are under the curse." As if he said, Although ye be circumcised, yet are ye not righteous and free from the law: but by this deed ye are rather debtors and bond-servants of the law; and the more ye go about to satisfy the law, and to be set free from it, the more ye entangle and snare yourselves in the yoke thereof, so that it hath more power to accuse and condemn you. This is to go backward like a crab, and to wash away filth with filth.

And this which I say by occasion of Paul's words, I have learned both in myself and others. I have seen many which have painfully travailed, and upon mere conscience have done as much as was possible for them to do, in fasting, in prayer, in wearing of hair, in punishing and tormenting their bodies with sundry exercises, (whereby at length they must needs have utterly consumed them, yea, although they had been made of iron,) and all to this end that they might obtain quietness and peace of conscience: notwithstanding, the more they travailed, the more they were stricken down with fear, and especially when the hour of death approached, they were so fearful, that I have seen many murderers and other malefactors condemned to death, dying more courageously than they did, which notwithstanding had lived very holily.

Therefore it is most true, that they which do the law, do it not, for the more they go about to fulfil the law, the more they transgress it. Even so we say and judge of men's traditions.

The more a man striveth to pacify his conscience thereby, the more he troubleth and tormenteth it. When I was a monk I endeavoured as much as possible, to live after the strait rule of mine order. I was wont to shrive myself with great devotion, and to reckon up all my sins, (yet being always very contrite before:) and I returned to confession very often, and thoroughly performed the penance that was enjoined unto me; yet, for all this, my conscience could never be fully certified, but was always in doubt, and said, "This or that thou hast not done rightly; thou was not contrite and sorrowful enough; this sin thou didst omit in thy confession," etc. Therefore, the more I went about to help my weak, wavering, and afflicted conscience, by men's traditions, the more weak and doubtful, and the more afflicted I was. And thus, the more I observed men's traditions, the more I transgressed them, and in seeking after righteousness by mine order, I could never attain unto it; for it is impossible (as Paul saith) that the conscience should be pacified by the works of the law, and much more by men's traditions, without the promise and glad tidings concerning Christ.

Wherefore, they that seek to be justified and quickened by the law, are much farther off from righteousness and life, than the publicans, sinners, and harlots. For they cannot trust to their own works, seeing they be such that they cannot hope to obtain grace and forgiveness of sins thereby; for if righteousness, and works done according to the law, do not justify, how can sins justify which are committed contrary to the law? Therefore, in this point they are in far better case than the justiciaries; for they have no affiance in their own works, which greatly hindereth the true faith in Christ, if it do not utterly take it away. Contrariwise, the justiciaries, which abstain outwardly from sins, and live holily and without blame in the sight of the world, cannot be without the opinion of their own righteousness, with which the true faith in Christ cannot stand; and for this cause they be more miserable than the publicans and harlots, who offer not their good works to God in his displeasure, that for the same he may recompense them with everlasting life, (as the justiciaries do,) for they have none to offer; but desire that their sins may be pardoned for Christ's sake.

The other exposition is affirmative. He that is circumcised, is also bound to keep the whole law; for he that receiveth Moses in one point, must of necessity receive him in all. And it helpeth nothing to say, that circumcision is necessary, and not the rest of Moses' laws; for by the same reason that thou art bound to keep circumcision, thou art also bound to keep the whole law.

EPISTLE TO THE GALATIANS

Now, to be bound to keep the whole law, is nothing else but to shew in effect that Christ is not yet come. If this be true, then are we bound to keep all the Jewish ceremonies, and laws touching meats, places, and times; and Christ must be looked for as yet to come, that he may abolish the Jewish kingdom and priesthood, and set up a new kingdom throughout the whole world. But the whole scripture witnesseth, and the sequel thereof plainly declareth, that Christ is already come; that, by his death, he hath redeemed mankind; that he hath abolished the law; and that he hath fulfilled all things which all the prophets have foretold of him. Therefore, the law being clean abolished, and quite taken away, he hath given unto us grace and truth. It is not then the law, nor the works thereof, but it is faith in Jesus Christ, that maketh a man righteous.

Some would bind us, at this day, to certain of Moses' laws that like them best, as the false apostles would have done at that time. But this is in no wise to be suffered. For, if we give Moses leave to rule over us in any thing, we are bound to obey him in all things; wherefore, we will not be burthened with any law of Moses. We grant that he is to be read amongst us, and to be heard as a prophet and a witness-bearer of Christ; and moreover, that out of him we may take good examples of good laws and holy life; but we will not suffer him in any wise to have dominion over our conscience. In this case let him be dead and buried, and let no man know where his grave is, (Deut. xxxiv, 6).

The former exposition, that is to say, the negative, seemeth to me to be more apt and more spiritual; notwithstanding both are good, and both do condemn the righteousness of the law. The first is, that we are so far from obtaining righteousness by the law, that the more we go about to accomplish the law, the more we transgress the law; the second is, that he, which will perform any piece of the law, is bound to keep the whole law; and, to conclude, that Christ profiteth them nothing at all which will be justified by the law.

Hereby it appeareth that Paul meaneth nothing else, but that the law is a plain denial of Christ. Now it is a wonderful thing that Paul dare affirm that the law of Moses, which was given by God to the people of Israel, is a denial of Christ. Why, then, did God give it? Before the coming of Christ, and before his manifestation in the flesh, the law was necessary; for the law is our schoolmaster to bring us unto Christ. But, now that Christ is revealed, in that we believe in him, we are no longer under the schoolmaster. Hereof we have spoken largely enough before, in the end of the third chapter. Whoso teacheth, then, that the law is necessary to righteousness, teacheth a plain denial of Christ and of all his benefits; he maketh God a liar, yea, he maketh the law also a liar; for the law itself beareth witness of Christ, and of the promises made us concerning Christ, and hath foretold that he should be a king of grace, and not of the law.

> VERSE 4. *Ye are abolished (or separated) from Christ, whosoever are justified by the law; ye are fallen from grace.*

Here Paul expoundeth himself, and sheweth that he speaketh not simply of the law, nor of the work of circumcision, but of the confidence and opinion that men have to be justified thereby. As if he would say, I do not utterly condemn the law or circumcision, (for it is lawful for me to drink, to eat, and to keep company with the Jews, according to the law; it is lawful for me to circumcise Timothy,) but to seek to be justified by the law, as if Christ were not yet come, or, being now present, he alone were not able to justify, this is it which I condemn; for this is to be separated from Christ. Therefore, saith he, ye are abolished, that is, ye are utterly void of Christ; Christ is not in you, he worketh not in you any more: ye are not partakers of the knowledge, the spirit, the fellowship, the favour, the liberty, the life, or the doings of Christ, but ye are utterly separate from him, so that he hath no more to do with you, nor ye with him.

These words of Paul are diligently to be noted, that to seek righteousness by the law, is nothing else but to be separated from Christ, and to make him utterly unprofitable. What can be spoken more mightily against the law? What can be set up against this thunderbolt? Wherefore it is impossible that Christ and the law should dwell together in one heart; for either the law or Christ must give place. But, if thou think that Christ and the law can dwell together, then be thou sure that Christ dwelleth not in thy heart; but the devil, in the likeness of Christ, accusing and terrifying thee, and straitly exacting of thee the laws and the works thereof; for the true Christ (as I have said before) neither calleth thee to a reckoning for thy sins, nor biddeth thee to trust to thine own good works. And the true knowledge of Christ, of faith, disputeth not whether thou hast done good works to righteousness, or evil works to condemnation; but simply concludeth after this sort: If thou have done good works, thou art not therefore justified; or if thou have done evil works, thou art not therefore condemned. I neither take from good works their praise, nor commend evil works; but in the matter of justification, I say, we must look how we may hold Christ, lest, if we seek to be justified by the law, we make him unprofitable unto us. For it is Christ alone that justifieth me, both against my evil deeds, and without my good deeds. If I have this persuasion of Christ, I lay hold of the true Christ. But if I think that he exacteth the law and works of me to salvation, then he becometh unprofitable unto me, and I am utterly separated from him.

These are dreadful sentences and threatenings against the righteousness of the law, and man's own righteousness. Moreover, they are also most certain principles which confirm the article of justification. This is then the final conclusion: Either, thou must forego Christ, or the righteousness of the law. If thou retain Christ, thou art righteous before God; but if thou stick to the law, Christ availeth thee nothing; thou art bound to keep the whole law, and thou hast now sentence already pronounced against thee: "Cursed is every one that fulfilleth not all the things that are written in this law," (Deut. xxvii, 26). As we have said of the law, so we say also of men's traditions. Either the Pope, with his religious rout, must reject all those things wherein hitherto he hath put his trust, or else Christ shall be unprofitable to them. And hereby we may plainly see how pernicious and pestilent the Popish doctrine hath been; for it hath led men clean away from Christ, and made him altogether unprofitable. God complaineth in the 23d of Jeremiah, that the prophets prophesied lies and the dreams of their own heart, to the end that his people should forget his name. Therefore, like as the false prophets, leaving the right interpretation of the law, and the true doctrine concerning the seed of Abraham, in whom all the nations of the earth should be blessed, preached their own dreams, to the end that the people should forget their God; even so the Papists, having darkened and defaced the doctrine of Christ, so that they made it of none effect, taught and set forth nothing else but the doctrine of works, whereby they drew the whole world away from Christ. Whoso earnestly considereth this matter, cannot but fear and tremble.

VERSE 4. *Ye are fallen from grace.*

That is to say, ye are no longer in the kingdom of grace. For like as he that is in a ship, on which side soever he falleth into the sea, is drowned, even so he which is fallen from grace, must needs perish. He, therefore, that will be justified by the law, is fallen into the sea, and hath cast himself into danger of eternal death. Now, if they fall from grace which will be justified by the moral law, whither shall they fall, I pray you, which will be justified by their own traditions and vows? Even to the bottom of hell. No, forsooth, they fly up into heaven: for so they themselves have taught us. "Whosoever live (say they) according to the rule of St. Francis, Dominick, Benedict, or such other, the peace and mercy of God is upon them." Again, "all they that observe and keep chastity, obedience, etc., shall have everlasting life." But let these toys go to the devil, from whence they came, and hearken what Paul teacheth thee here, and what Christ teacheth, saying, "he that believeth in the Son of God, hath everlasting life: but he that believeth not in the Son, shall not see life, but the wrath of God abideth upon him," (John iii, 36). Again, "he that believeth not is judged already," (John iii, 18).

Now, like as all the doctrine of the Papists (to note this by the way) concerning men's traditions, works, vows, and merits, was most common in the world, so was it thought to be the best and most certain of all others; whereby the devil hath both set up and established his kingdom most mightily. Therefore, when we at this day do impugn and vanquish this doctrine by the power of God's word, as chaff is driven away by the wind, it is no marvel that Satan rageth so cruelly against us, raiseth up slanders and offences every where, and setteth the whole world in our tops. Then will some men say, it had been better to have held our peace; for then had none of these evils been raised up. But we ought more to esteem the favour of God, whose glory we set forth, than to care for the tyranny of the world which persecuteth us. For what is the Pope and the whole world in comparison of God? Indeed, we are weak, and bear a heavenly treasure in brittle and earthly vessels; but, although the vessels be never so brittle, yet is the treasure inestimable (2 Cor. iv, 7).

These words, "ye are fallen from grace," must not be coldly or slenderly considered: for they are weighty, and of great importance. He that falleth from grace, utterly loseth the atonement, the forgiveness of sins, the righteousness, liberty, and life, that Jesus Christ hath merited for us by his death and resurrection; and, instead thereof, he purchaseth to himself the wrath and judgment of God, sin, death, the bondage of the devil, and everlasting damnation. And this place strongly confirmeth and fortifieth our doctrine concerning faith, or the article of justification, and marvellously comforteth us against the cruel rage of the Papists, that persecute and condemn us as heretics, because we teach this article. Indeed, this place ought to fear the enemies of faith and grace, that is to say, all that seek righteous-

EPISTLE TO THE GALATIANS

ness by works, from persecuting and blaspheming the word of grace, life, and everlasting salvation. But they be so hard-hearted and obstinate, that seeing they see not, and hearing they hear not; and when they read this dreadful sentence of the apostle pronounced against them, they understand it not. Let us leave them, therefore, unto themselves; for they are blind, and leaders of the blind, (Matt. xv, 14).

VERSE 5. *For we, in spirit, wait for the hope of righteousness through faith.*

Paul here knitteth up the matter with a notable conclusion, saying, Ye will be justified by the law, by circumcision, and by works; but we see not to be justified by this means, lest Christ should be made utterly unprofitable unto us, and we become debtors to perform the whole law, and so finally fall away from grace: but we wait in spirit, through faith, for the hope of righteousness. Every word is here diligently to be noted, for they are pithy and full of power. He doth not only say, as he is wont, we are justified by faith, or in spirit by faith, but moreover, he addeth, "We wait for the hope of righteousness," including hope also, that he may comprehend the whole matter of faith.

Hope, after the manner of the scriptures, is taken two ways: namely, for the thing that is hoped for, and for the affection of him that hopeth. For the thing that is hoped for, it is taken in the first chapter to the Colossians: "For the hope's sake which is laid up for you in heaven," that is to say, the thing which ye hope for. For the affection of him that hopeth, it is taken in the eighth to the Romans: "For we are saved by hope." So hope in this place also may be taken in two ways, and so it yieldeth a double sense. The first is: We wait in spirit, through faith, for the hope of righteousness, that is to say, the righteousness hoped for, which shall be certainly revealed in such time as pleaseth the Lord to give it. The second: We wait in spirit, by faith for righteousness with hope and desire: that is to say, we are righteous; howbeit our righteousness is not yet revealed, but hangeth yet in hope. For as long as we live here, sin remaineth in our flesh; there is also a law in our flesh and members, rebelling against the law of our mind, and leading us captives unto the service of sin, (Rom. vii, 23). Now, when these affections of the flesh do rage and reign, and we on the other side do, through the spirit, wrestle against the same, then is there a place for hope. Indeed we have begun to be justified through faith, whereby also we have received the first fruits of the spirit; and the mortification of the flesh is also begun in us; but we be not yet perfectly righteous. It remaineth, then, that we be perfectly justified and this is it which we hope for. So our righteousness is not yet in actual possession, but lieth under hope.

This is a sweet and a sound consolation, whereby afflicted and troubled consciences, feeling their sin, and terrified with every fiery dart of the devil, may be marvellously comforted. For the feeling of sin, the wrath of God, death, hell, and all other terrors, is wonderful strong in the conflict of conscience; as I myself, being taught by experience, do know. Then counsel must be given to the poor afflicted, in this wise: Brother, thou desirest to have a sensible feeling of thy justification; that is, thou wouldst have such a feeling of God's favour, as thou hast of thine own sin; but that will not be. But thy righteousness ought to surmount all feeling of sin; that is to say, thy righteousness, or justification, whereupon thou holdest, standeth not upon thine own feeling, but upon the hoping that it shall be revealed when it pleaseth the Lord. Wherefore, thou must not judge according to the feeling of sin which troubleth and terrifieth thee, but according to the promise and doctrine of faith, whereby Christ is promised unto thee, who is thy perfect and everlasting righteousness. Thus the hope of the afflicted, consisting in the inward affection, is stirred up by faith, in the midst of all terrors and feeling of sin, to hope that he is righteous. Moreover, if hope be here taken for the thing which is hoped for, it is thus to be understood, and that which a man now seeth not, he hopeth in time shall be made perfect and clearly revealed.

Either sense may well stand; but the first, touching the inward desire and affection of hoping, bringeth more plentiful consolation, for my righteousness is not yet perfect, it cannot yet be felt: yet I do not despair; for faith sheweth unto me Christ, in whom I trust, and when I have laid hold of him by faith, I wrestle against the fiery darts of the devil, and I take a good heart through hope against the feeling of sin, assuring myself that I have a perfect righteousness prepared for me in heaven. So both these sayings are true, that I am made righteous already by that righteousness which is begun in me; and also I am raised up in the same hope against sin, and wait for the full consummation of perfect righteousness in heaven. These things are not rightly understood, but when they be put in practice.

What Difference there is Between Faith and Hope.

Here ariseth a question, What difference there is between faith and hope? The sophisters and schoolmen have laboured very much in this matter, but they could never shew any certainty. Yea, to us which travail in the holy scriptures with much diligence, and also with more fulness and power of spirit (be it spoken without any brag), it is hard to find any difference. For there is so great affinity between faith and hope, that the one cannot be separate from the other. Notwithstanding, there is a difference between them, which is gathered of their several offices, diversity of working, and of their ends.

First, they differ in respect of their subject, that is, of the ground wherein they rest. For faith resteth in the understanding, and hope resteth in the will; but, in very deed, they cannot be separated, the one having respect to the other, as the two cherubims of the mercy seat, which could not be divided (Exod. xxv, 20).

Secondly, they differ in respect of their office, that is, of their working. For faith telleth what is to be done; it teacheth, prescribeth, and directeth, and it is a knowledge. Hope is an exhortation which stirreth up the mind that it may be strong, bold, and courageous; that it may suffer and endure adversity, and in the midst thereof wait for better things.

Thirdly, they differ as touching their object, that is, the special matter whereunto they look. For faith hath for her object the truth, teaching us to cleave surely thereto, and looking upon the word and promise of the thing that is promised. Hope hath for her object the goodness of God, and looketh upon the thing which is promised in the word, that is, upon such matters as faith teacheth us to be hoped for.

Fourthly, they differ in order. For faith is the beginning of life before all tribulation, (Heb. xi). But hope cometh afterwards, proceeding of tribulation, (Rom. v).

Fifthly, they differ by the diversity of working. For faith is a teacher and a judge, fighting against errors and heresies, judging spirits and doctrines; but hope is, as it were, the general or captain of the field, fighting against tribulation, the cross, impatiency, heaviness of spirit, weakness, desperation, and blasphemy, and it waiteth for good things, even in the midst of all evils.

Therefore, when I am instructed by faith in the word of God, and lay hold of Christ, believing in him with my whole heart, then am I righteous by this knowledge. When I am so justified by faith, or by this knowledge, by-and-by cometh the devil, the father of wiles, and laboureth to extinguish my faith by wiles and subtleties; that is to say, by lies, errors, and heresies. Moreover, because he is a murderer, he goeth about also to oppress it by violence. Here hope wrestling, layeth hold on the thing revealed by faith, and overcometh the devil that warreth against faith; and after this victory followeth peace and joy in the Holy Ghost. So that, in very deed, faith and hope can scarcely be discerned the one from the other, and yet is there a certain difference between them. And that it may be the better perceived, I will set out the matter by a similitude.

In civil government, prudence and fortitude do differ, and yet these two virtues are so joined together, that they cannot easily be severed. Now, fortitude is a constancy of mind, which is not discouraged in adversity, but endureth valiantly, and waiteth for better things. But if fortitude be not guided by prudence, it is but temerity and rashness. On the other side, if fortitude be not joined with prudence, that prudence is but vain and unprofitable. Therefore like as, in policy, prudence is but vain without fortitude; even so, in divinity, faith without hope is nothing: for hope endureth adversity and is constant therein, and in the end overcometh all evils. And on the other side, like as fortitude without prudence is rashness, even so hope without faith is a presumption in spirit, and a tempting of God: for it hath no knowledge of Christ and of the truth which faith teacheth, and therefore it is but a blind rashness and arrogancy. Wherefore a godly man, afore all things, must have a right understanding instructed by faith, according to the which the mind may be guided in afflictions, that it may hope for those good things which faith hath revealed and taught.

To be short, faith is conceived by teaching; for thereby the mind is instructed what the truth is. Hope is conceived by exhortation; for by exhortation hope is stirred up in afflictions, which confirmeth him that is already justified by faith, that he be not overcome by adversities, but that he may be able more strongly to resist them. Notwithstanding, if the spark of faith should not give light to the will, it could not be persuaded to lay hold upon hope. We have faith, then, whereby we are taught, understand, and know the heavenly wisdom, apprehend Christ, and continue in his grace. But, as soon as we lay hold upon Christ by faith, and confess him, forthwith our enemies, the world, the flesh, and the devil, rise up against us, hating and persecuting us most cruelly, both in body and spirit. Wherefore we, thus believing and justified by faith in spirit, do wait for the hope of our righteousness: And we wait through patience; for we see and feel the flat contrary. For the world, with his prince the devil, assaileth us mightily, both within and without. Moreover, sin yet still remaineth in us, which driveth us into heaviness. Notwithstanding we give not over for all this, but raise up our mind strongly through faith, which lighteneth, teacheth, and guideth the same. And thus we abide firm and constant, and overcome all adversities through him which hath loved us, until our righteousness which we believe and wait for, be revealed. By faith therefore we began, by hope we continue, and by revelation we shall obtain the whole. In the mean time, whilst we live here, because we believe, we teach the word, and publish the knowledge of Christ unto others. Thus doing, we suffer persecution (according to this text, "I believed, and therefore did I speak; and I was sore troubled," Psalm cxvi, 10) with patience, being strengthened and encouraged through hope; whereunto the scripture exhorteth us with most sweet and comfortable promises taught and revealed unto us by faith. And thus doth hope spring up and increase in us, (Rom. xv) "That through patience and comfort of the scripture, we may have hope."

Paul therefore, not without cause, joineth patience in tribulations and hope together, in the fifth and eighth to the Romans, and in other places also, for by them hope is stirred up. But faith (as also I have shewed before) goeth before hope; for it is the beginning of life, and beginneth before all tribulation; for it learneth Christ, and apprehendeth him, without the cross. Notwithstanding, the knowledge of Christ cannot be long without the cross, without troubles and conflicts. In this case the mind must be stirred up to a fortitude of spirit, (for hope is nothing else but a spiritual fortitude, as faith is nothing else but a spiritual prudence,) which consisteth in suffering, according to this saying, "That through patience," etc. These three things, then, dwell together in the faithful: Faith, which teacheth the truth, and defendeth from errors: Hope, which endureth and overcometh all adversities, as well bodily as ghostly;: and Charity, which worketh all good things, as it followeth in the text. And so is a man entire and perfect in this life, as well within as without, until the righteousness be revealed which he waiteth for; and this shall be a perfect and an everlasting righteousness.

Moreover, this place containeth both a singular doctrine and consolation. As touching the doctrine, it sheweth that we are made righteous, not by the works, sacrifices, or ceremonies of Moses' law, much less by the works and traditions of men, but by Christ alone. Whatsoever, then, the world counteth to be good and holy without Christ, is nothing else but sin, error, and flesh. Wherefore circumcision and the observation of the law, also works, religions and vows of the monks, and of all such as trust in their own righteousness, are altogether carnal. But we (saith Paul) are far above all these things in the spirit and inward man; for we possess Christ by faith, and in the midst of our afflictions, through hope, we wait for that righteousness which we possess already by faith.

The comfort is this: that, in serious conflicts and terrors, wherein the feeling of sin, heaviness of spirit, desperation, and such-like, is very strong, (for they enter deeply into the heart and mightily assail it,) thou must not follow thine own feeling; for if thou do, thou wilt say: I feel the horrible terrors of the law and the tyranny of sin, not only rebelling against me, but also subduing and leading me captive, and I feel no comfort or righteousness at all. Therefore I am a sinner, and not righteous. If I be a sinner, then am I guity of everlasting death. But against this feeling thou must wrestle, and say: Although I feel myself utterly overwhelmed and swallowed up with sin, and my heart telleth me that God is offended and angry with me, yet in very deed it is not true, but that mine own sense and feeling so judgeth. The word of God (which in these terrors I ought to follow, and not mine own sense) teacheth a far other thing; namely, "That God is near unto them that are of a troubled heart, and saveth them that are of a humble spirit," (Psalm xxxiv, 18). Also, "He despiseth not a humble and contrite heart," (Psalm li, 17). Moreover, Paul sheweth here, that they which are justified in spirit by faith, do not yet feel the hope of righteousness, but wait still for it.

Wherefore, when the law accuseth and sin terrifieth thee, and thou feelest nothing but the wrath and judgment of God, despair not for all that, but take unto thee the armour of God, the shield of faith, the helmet of hope, and the sword of the spirit, and try how good and how valiant a warrior thou art. Lay hold of Christ by faith, who is the Lord of the law and sin, and of all things else which accompany them. Believing in him thou art justified: which thing reason and the feeling of thine own heart, when thou art tempted, do not tell thee, but the word of God. Moreover, in the midst of these conflicts and terrors, which often return and exercise thee, wait thou patiently through hope for righteousness, which thou hast now by faith, although it be yet but begun and imperfect, until it be revealed and made perfect in the kingdom of heaven.

But thou wilt say, I feel not myself to have any righteousness, or, at the least, I feel but very little. Thou must not feel, but believe that thou hast righteousness. And except thou believe that thou art righteous, thou dost great injury unto Christ, who hath cleansed thee by the washing of water through the word, (Eph. v, 26,) who also died upon the cross, condemned sin and killed death, that through him thou mightest obtain righteousness and everlasting life, (1 Cor. xv, 3). These things thou canst not deny (except thou wilt openly shew thyself to be wicked and blasphemous against God, and utterly to despise God and all his promises, Jesus Christ with all his benefits,) and so consequently thou canst not deny but that thou art righteous.

Let us learn, therefore, in great and horrible terrors, when our conscience feeleth nothing but sin, and judgeth that God is angry with us, and that Christ hath turned his face from us, not to follow the sense and feeling of our own heart, but to stick to the word of God, which saith, that God is not angry, but looketh to the afflicted, and to such as are troubled in spirit and tremble at his word, (Isa. lxvi, 2) and that Christ turneth not himself away from such as labour and are heavy laden, but refresheth and comforteth them, (Matt. vi, 28). This place, therefore, teacheth plainly, that the law and works bring unto us no righteousness or comfort at all; but this doth the Holy Ghost only in the faith of Christ, who raiseth up hope in terrors and tribulations, which endureth and overcometh all adversities. Very few there be that know how weak and feeble faith and hope are under the cross, and in the conflict. For it seemeth that they are but as smoking flax, which is ready by-and-by to be put out with a vehement wind, (Isa. xlii, 3). But the faithful, who believe in the midst of these assaults and terrors, hoping against hope, that is to say, fighting through faith in the promise, as touching Christ, against the feeling of sin and of the wrath of God, do afterwards find, by experience, that this spark of faith, being very little (as it appeareth to natural reason, for reason can scarcely feel it) is as a mighty fire, and swalloweth up all our sins and all terrors.

There is nothing more dear or precious in all the world, to the true children of God, than this doctrine. For they that understand this doctrine, do know that whereof all the world is ignorant; namely, that sin, death, and all other miseries, afflictions and calamities, as well corporeal as spiritual, do turn to the benefit and profit of the elect. Moreover, they know that God is then most near unto them, when he seemeth to be farthest off; and that he is then a most merciful and loving Saviour, when he seemeth to be most angry, to afflict, and to destroy. Also they know that they have an everlasting righteousness, which they wait for through hope, as a certain and sure possession laid up for them in heaven; even when they feel the horrible terrors of sin and death. Moreover, that they are then lords of all things, when they are most destitute of all things, according to that saying, "having nothing, and yet possessing all things." This, saith the scripture, is to conceive comfort through hope; but this cunning is not learned, without great and often temptations.

> VERSE 6. *For in Jesus Christ neither circumcision availeth any thing, neither uncircumcision, but faith which worketh by love.*

That is to say, faith which is not feigned nor hypocritical, but true and lively. This is that faith which exerciseth and requireth good works through love. It is as much as to say, he that will be a true Christian indeed, or one of Christ's kingdom, must be a true believer. Now he believeth not truly, if works of charity follow not his faith. So on both hands, as well on the right hand as on the left, he shutteth hypocrites out of Christ's kingdom. On the left hand, he shutteth out the Jews, and all such as will work their own salvation, saying, "In Christ neither circumcision," that is to say, no works, no service, no worshipping, no kind of life in the world, but faith, without any trust in works or merits, availeth before God. On the right hand, he shutteth out all slothful and idle persons, which say, if faith justify without works, then let us work nothing, but let us only believe and do what we list. Not so, ye enemies of grace, Paul saith otherwise. And although it be true, that only faith justifieth, yet he speaketh here of faith in another respect; that is to say, that, after it hath justified, it is not idle, but occupied and exercised in working through love. Paul therefore, in this place, setteth forth the whole life of a Christian man, namely, that inwardly it consisteth in faith towards God, and outwardly in charity and good works toward our neighbour. So that a man is a perfect Christian inwardly through faith before God, who hath no need of our works; and outwardly before men, whom our faith profiteth nothing, but our charity or our works. Therefore, when we have heard or understood of this form of Christian life, to wit, that it is faith and charity (as I have said) it is not yet declared what faith or what charity is; for this is another question. For as touching faith, or the inward nature, force, and use of faith, he hath spoken before, where he shewed that it is our righteousness, or rather our justification before God. Here he joineth it with charity and works, that is to say, he speaketh of the external office thereof, which is to stir us up to do good works, and to bring forth in us the fruits of charity, to the profit of our neighbor.

VERSE 7. *Ye did run well: who did let you, that ye did not obey the truth?*

These are plain words. Paul affirmeth that he teacheth them the truth, and the self-same thing that he taught them before, and that they ran well so long as they obeyed the truth, that is, they believed and lived rightly: but now they did not so, since they were misled by the false apostles. Moreover, he useth here a new kind of speech in calling the Christian life a course, or a race. For, among the Hebrews, to run or to walk signifieth as much as to live, or to be conversant. The teachers do run when they teach purely, and the hearers or learners do run when they receive the word with joy, and when the fruits of the Spirit do follow; which thing was done as long as Paul was present, as he witnessed before, in the third and fourth chapters. And here he saith, "Ye did run well," that is to say, all things went forward well and happily among you; ye lived very well, ye went on the right way to everlasting life, which the word of God promised you, etc.

These words, "Ye did run well," contain in them a singular comfort. This temptation oftentimes exerciseth the godly, that their life seemeth unto them to be rather a certain slow creeping than a running. But if they abide in sound doctrine, and walk in the spirit, let this nothing trouble them, though their doings seem to go slowly forward, or rather creep. God judgeth far otherwise; for that which seemeth unto us to be very slow and scarcely to creep, runneth swiftly in God's sight. Again, that which is to us nothing else but sorrow, mourning, and death, is before God, joy, mirth, and true happiness. Therefore Christ saith, "Blessed are ye that mourn and weep, for ye shall receive comfort," (Matt. v, 4); "ye shall laugh," etc. (Luke vi, 21). All things shall turn to the best, to them which believe in the Son of God, be it sorrow, or be it death itself. Therefore they be true runners indeed, and whatsoever they do, it runneth well and goeth happily forward, by the furtherance of God's spirit, which cannot skill of slow proceedings.

VERSE 7. *Who did let you, that you did not obey the truth?*

They are hindered in this course which fall away from faith and grace, to the law and works; as it happened to the Galatians, being misled and seduced by the false apostles, which covertly he reprehendeth with these words: "Who did let you, that you did not obey the truth?" In like manner he said before, in the third chapter, "Who hath bewitched you, that you should not obey the truth?" And here Paul sheweth, by the way, that men are so strongly bewitched with false doctrine, that they embrace lies and heresies, in the stead of the truth and spiritual doctrine. And on the other side, they say and swear that the sound doctrine, which before they loved, is erroneous; and that their error is sound doctrine, maintaining and defending the same with all their power. Even so the false apostles brought the Galatians (which ran well at the beginning) into this opinion, to believe that they erred, and went very slowly forward when Paul was their teacher. But afterwards, they being seduced by the false apostles, and falling clean away from the truth, were so strongly bewitched with their false persuasion, that they thought themselves to be in a happy state, and that they ran very well. The same happeneth at this day to such as are seduced by the sectaries and fantastical spirits. Therefore I am wont to say, that falling in doctrine cometh not of man, but of the devil, and is most perilous, to wit, even from the high heaven to the bottom of hell. For they that continue in error, are so far off from acknowledging their sin, that they maintain the same to be high righteousness. Wherefore it is impossible for them to obtain pardon.

VERSE 8. *It is not the persuasion of him that calleth you.*

This is a great consolation, and a singular doctrine, whereby Paul sheweth how the false persuasion of such as are deceived by wicked teachers, may be rooted out of their hearts. The false apostles were jolly fellows, and in outward appearance far passing Paul, both in learning and godliness. The Galatians, being deceived with this goodly shew, supposed that when they heard them, they heard Christ himself, and therefore they judged their persuasion to be of Christ. Contrariwise, Paul sheweth that this persuasion and doctrine was not of Christ, who had called them in grace, but of the devil; and by this means he won many of them from this false persuasion. Likewise we at this day revoke many from error that were seduced, when we shew that their opinions are fantastical, wicked, and full of blasphemies.

Again, this consolation pertaineth to all those that are afflicted, which, through temptation, conceive a false opinion of Christ. For the devil is a marvellous persuader, and knoweth how to amplify the least sin, yea, a very trifle, in such sort, that he which is tempted shall think it to be a most heinous and horrible crime, and worthy of eternal damnation. Here the troubled conscience must be comforted and raised up in such sort as Paul raised up the Galatians, to wit, that this cogitation or persuasion cometh not of Christ, forasmuch as it fighteth against the word of the gospel, which painteth out Christ, not as an accuser, a cruel exactor, etc., but as a meek, humble-hearted, and merciful Saviour and comforter.

But if Satan (who is a cunning workman, and will leave no way unassayed) overthrow this, and lay against thee the word and example of Christ, in this wise: True it is, that Christ is meek, gentle, and merciful, but to those which are holy and righteous: contrariwise, to the sinners he threateneth wrath and destruction, (Luke xiii). Also he pronounceth that the unbelievers are damned already, (John iii). Moreover, Christ wrought many good works; he suffered also many evils, and commandeth us to follow his example. But thy life is neither according to Christ's word, nor his example; for thou art a sinner, and there is no faith in thee: yea, thou hast done no good at all, and therefore do those sentences which set forth Christ as a severe judge, do belong to thee, and not to those comfortable sentences which shew him to be a loving and a merciful Saviour, etc. Here let him that is tempted, comfort himself after this manner:

The scripture setteth out Christ unto us two manner of ways: First, as a gift. If I take hold of him in this sort, I can want nothing. "For in Christ are hid all the treasures of wisdom and knowledge," (Col. ii, 3). He, with all that is in him, "is made unto me of God, wisdom, righteousness, sanctification, and redemption," (1 Cor. i, 30). Therefore, although I have committed both many and grievous sins, yet notwithstanding, if I believe in him, they shall all be swallowed up by his righteousness. Secondly, the scripture setteth him forth as an example to be followed. Notwithstanding, I will not suffer this Christ (I mean, as he is an example) to be set before me, but only in the time of joy and gladness, when I am out of temptation (where I can scarcely follow the thousandth part of his example), that I may have him as a mirror to behold and view how much is yet wanting in me, that I become not secure and careless. But in the time of tribulation I will not hear nor admit Christ, but as a gift, who, dying for my sins, hath bestowed upon me his righteousness, and hath done and accomplished that for me, which was wanting in my life: "For he is the end and fulfilling of the law unto righteousness to every one that believeth," (Rom. x, 4).

It is good to know these things, not only to the end that every one of us may have a sure and a certain remedy in the time of temptation, whereby we may eschew that venom of desperation, wherewith Satan thinketh to poison us: but also to the end we may be able to resist the furious sectaries and schismatics of our time. For the Anabaptists count nothing more glorious in their whole doctrine, than that they so severely urge the example of Christ and the cross; especially seeing the sentences are manifest wherein Christ commendeth the cross to his disciples. We must learn, therefore, how we may withstand this Satan, transforming himself into the likeness of an angel; which we shall do, if we make a difference between Christ set forth unto us sometimes as a gift, and sometimes as an example. The preaching of him both ways hath his convenient time, which if it be not observed, the preaching of salvation may so be turned into poison. Christ, therefore, must be set forth unto those which are already cast down and bruised through the heavy burden and weight of their sins, as a Saviour and a gift, and not as an example of a lawgiver. But to those that are secure and obstinate, he must be set forth as an example. Also the hard sentences of the scripture, and the horrible examples of the wrath of God, must be laid before them; as of the drowning of the whole world, of the destruction of Sodom and Gomorrah, and such other like, that they may repent. Let every Christian, therefore, when he is terrified and afflicted, learn to cast away the false persuasion which he hath conceived of Christ, and let him say: O cursed Satan, why dost thou now dispute with me of doing and working, seeing I am terrified and afflicted for my sins already? Nay, rather, seeing I now labour and am heavy laden, (Matt. xi, 28), I will not hearken to thee, which art an accuser and a destroyer, but to Christ, the Saviour of mankind, which saith that he came into the world to save sinners, to comfort such as are in terror, anguish, and desperation, and to preach deliverance to the captives, etc. This is the true Christ, and there is none other but he. I can seek examples of holy life in Abraham, Isaiah, John Baptist, Paul, and other saints; but they cannot forgive my sins, they cannot deliver me from the power of the devil and from death, they cannot save me and give me everlasting life. For these things belong to Christ alone, whom God the Father hath sealed, (John vi, 27,) therefore I will not hear thee, nor acknowledge thee for my teacher, O Satan, but Christ, of whom the Father hath said, "This is my beloved Son, in whom I am well pleased; hear him." Let us learn in this wise to comfort ourselves through faith in temptation, and in the persua-

EPISTLE TO THE GALATIANS 445

sion of false doctrine; else the devil will either seduce us by his ministry, or kill us with his fiery darts.

VERSE 9. *A little leaven doth leaven the whole lump.*

This whole epistle sufficiently witnesseth how Paul was grieved with the fall of the Galatians, and how often he beat into their heads (sometimes chiding and sometimes entreating them) the exceeding great and horrible enormities that should ensue upon this their fall, unless they repented. This fatherly and apostolical care and admonition of Paul moved some of them nothing at all: for many of them acknowledged Paul no more for their teacher, but preferred the false apostles far above him: of whom they thought themselves to have received the true doctrine, and not of Paul. Moreover, the false apostles, no doubt, slandered Paul among the Galatians, saying that he was an obstinate and a contentious fellow, which for a light matter would break the unity of the churches, and for no other cause but that he alone would be counted wise, and be magnified of them. Through this false accusation they made Paul very odious unto many.

Some others which had not yet utterly forsaken his doctrine, thought that there was no danger in dissenting a little from him in the doctrine of justification and faith; wherefore, when they heard that Paul made so heinous a matter of that which seemed unto them to be but light, and of small importance, they marvelled, and thus they thought with themselves: Be it so that we have swerved something from the doctrine of Paul, and that there hath been some fault in us; yet that being but a small matter, he ought to wink thereat, or at least not so vehemently to amplify it, lest by the occasion thereof the concord of the churches should be broken. Whereunto he answereth with this sentence: "A little leaven leaveneth [or maketh sour] the whole lump of dough." And this is a caveat or an admonition which Paul standeth much upon. And we also ought greatly to esteem the same at this day. For our adversaries in like manner object against us that we are contentious, obstinate, and intractable in defending our doctrine, and even in matters of no great importance. But these are the crafty fetches of the devil, whereby he goeth about utterly to overthrow our doctrine. To this we answer, therefore, with Paul, that "a little leaven soureth the whole lump."

In philosophy, a small fault in the beginning, is a great and a foul fault in the end. So in divinity, one little error overthroweth the whole doctrine; wherefore we must separate life and doctrine far asunder. The doctrine is not ours, but God's, whose ministers only we are called; therefore we may not change or diminish one tittle thereof. The life is ours: therefore, as touching that, we are ready to do, to suffer, to forgive, etc., whatsoever our adversaries shall require of us, so that faith and doctrine may remain sound and uncorrupt; of the which we say always with Paul, "a little leaven leaveneth," etc.

A small mote in the eye hurteth the eye. And our Saviour Christ saith: "The light of the body is the eye: therefore, when thine eye is single, then is thy whole body light: but if thine eye be evil, then thy body is dark." Again, "If thy body shall have no part dark, then shall all be light," (Luke xi, 34, 36). By this allegory Christ signifieth that the eye, that is to say, the doctrine, ought to be most simple, clear, and sincere, having in it no darkness, no cloud, etc. And James the apostle saith, "He that faileth in one point, is guilty of all." This place, therefore, maketh very much for us against these cavillers, which say that we break charity, to the great hurt and damage of the churches. But we protest that we desire nothing more than to be at unity with all men: so that they leave unto us the doctrine of faith, entire and uncorrupt; to the which all things ought to give place, be it charity, an apostle, or an angel from heaven.

Let us suffer them, therefore, to extol charity and concord as much as they list; but, on the other side, let us magnify the majesty of the word and faith. Charity may be neglected in time and place without any danger; but so cannot the word and faith be. Charity suffereth all things, giveth place to all men. Contrariwise, faith suffereth nothing, giveth place to no man. Charity, in giving place, in believing, in giving and forgiving, is oftentimes deceived; and yet, notwithstanding being so deceived it suffereth no loss which is to be called true loss indeed; that is to say, it loseth not Christ: therefore it is not offended, but continueth still constant in well-doing, yea even towards the unthankful and unworthy. Contrariwise, in the matter of faith and salvation, when men teach lies and errors under the colour of the truth, and seduce many, here hath charity no place: for here we lose not any benefit bestowed upon the unthankful, but we lose the word, faith, Christ, and everlasting life. Let it not move us, therefore, that they urge so much the keeping of charity and concord; for whoso loveth not God and his word, it is no matter what or how much he loveth.

Paul, therefore, by this sentence admonisheth as well teachers as hearers, to take heed that they esteem not the doctrine of faith as a light matter, wherewith they may dally at their

EPISTLE TO THE GALATIANS

pleasure. It is as a bright sun-beam coming down from heaven, which lighteneth, directeth, and guideth us. Now, like as the world, with all the wisdom and power thereof, is not able to stop or turn away the beams of the sun coming down from heaven unto the earth: even so can there be nothing added to the doctrine of faith, or taken from it; for that is an utter defacing and overthrowing of the whole.

VERSE 10. *I have trust in you through the Lord.*

As if he would say, I have taught, admonished, and reproved you enough, so that ye would hearken unto me; notwithstanding, I hope well of you in the Lord. Here riseth a question, whether Paul doth well, when he saith he hath a good hope or trust of the Galatians, seeing the holy scripture forbiddeth any trust to be put in men? Both faith and charity have their trust and belief, but after divers sorts, by reason of the diversity of their objects. Faith trusteth in God, and therefore it cannot be deceived: Charity believeth man, and therefore it is often deceived. Now, this faith that springeth of charity is so necessary to this present life, that without it life cannot continue in the world; for if one man should not believe and trust another, what life should we live upon earth? The true Christians do sooner believe and give credit through charity, than the children of this world do. For faith towards men is a fruit of the spirit, or of Christian faith in the godly. Hereupon Paul had a trust in the Galatians, yea, though they were fallen from his doctrine: but yet in the Lord. As if he should say, I have a trust in you so far forth as the Lord is in you, and ye in him, that is to say, so far forth as ye abide in the truth. From which if you fall away, seduced by the ministers of Satan, I will not trust unto you any more. Thus it is lawful for the godly to trust and believe men.

VERSE 10. *That ye will be none otherwise minded.*

To wit, concerning doctrine and faith, than I have taught you, and ye have learned of me; that is to say, I have a good hope of you, that ye will not receive any other doctrine which shall be contrary to mine.

VERSE 10. *But he that troubleth you shall bear his condemnation, whosoever he be.*

By this sentence Paul, as it were a judge sitting upon the judgment-seat, condemneth the false apostles, calling them by a very odious name, troublers of the Galatians; whom they esteemed to be very godly men, and far better teachers than

Paul. And withal he goeth about to terrify the Galatians with this horrible sentence, whereby he so boldly condemneth the false apostles, to the end that they should fly their false doctrine, as a most dangerous plague. As if he should say, What mean ye, to give ear to those pestilent fellows which teach you not, but only trouble you? The doctrine that they deliver unto you is nothing else but a trouble unto your consciences. Wherefore, how great soever they be, they shall bear their condemnation.

Now, a man may understand by these words, "whosoever he be," that the false apostles, in outward appearance, were very good and holy men; and peradventure there was amongst them some notable disciple of the apostles, of great name and authority. For it is not without cause that he useth such vehement and pithy words. He speaketh after the same manner, also, in the first chapter, saying: "If we or an angel from heaven preach unto you otherwise than we have preached unto you, let him be accursed." And it is not to be doubted, but that many were offended with this vehemency of the apostle, thinking thus with themselves: Wherefore doth Paul break charity? Why is he obstinate in so small a matter? Why doth he so rashly pronounce sentence of eternal damnation against those that are ministers as well as he? He passeth nothing of all this; but proceedeth on still, and boldly curseth and condemneth all those that pervert the doctrine of faith, be they never so highly esteemed, seem they never so holy and learned.

Wherefore (as I give often warning) we must diligently discern between doctrine and life. Doctrine is heaven, life is the earth. In life is sin, error, uncleanness, and misery, mingled with vinegar, as the proverb saith. There let charity wink, forbear, be beguiled, believe, hope, and suffer all things; there let forgiveness of sins prevail as much as may be, so that sin and error be not defended and maintained. But in doctrine, like as there is no error, so it hath no need of pardon; wherefore there is no comparison between doctrine and life. One little point of doctrine is of more value than heaven and earth; and therefore we cannot abide to have the least jot thereof to be corrupted; but we can very well wink at the offences and errors of life, for we also do daily err in life and conversation, yea, all the saints err, and this do they earnestly confess in the Lord's Prayer, and in the articles of our faith. But our doctrine, blessed be God, is pure; we have all the articles of our faith grounded upon the holy scripture: those the devil would gladly corrupt and overthrow; therefore he assaileth us so craftily with this goodly argument, that we ought not to break charity and the unity of the churches.

VERSE 11. *And brethren, if I yet preach circumcision, why do I yet suffer persecution? Then is the slander of the cross abolished.*

Paul, labouring by all means possible to call the Galatians back again, reasoneth now by his own example. I have procured to myself (saith he) the hatred and persecution of the priests and elders (Acts xiii, 50) and of my whole nation, because I take away righteousness from circumcision; which if I would attribute unto it, the Jews would not only cease to persecute me, but also would love and highly commend me. But now, because I preach the gospel of Christ and the righteousness of faith, abolishing the law and circumcision, therefore I suffer persecution. Contrariwise, the false apostles, to avoid the cross and this deadly hatred of the Jewish nation, do preach circumcision; and by this means they obtain and retain the favour of the Jews, as he saith in the sixth chapter following: "They compel you to be circumcised," etc. Moreover, they would gladly bring to pass that there should be no dissension, but peace and concord between the Gentiles and the Jews. But that is impossible to be done without the loss of the doctrine of faith, which is the doctrine of the cross, and full of offences. Wherefore, when he saith, "If I yet preach circumcision, why do I suffer persecution? Then is the slander of the cross abolished": he meaneth that it were a great absurdity and inconveniency, if the offence of the cross should cease. After the same manner he speaketh, "Christ sent me to preach the gospel, not with wisdom of words, lest the cross of Christ should be made of none effect" (1 Cor. i, 17). As if he said, I would not that the offence and cross of Christ should be abolished.

Here may some man say, the Christians, then, are madmen, to cast themselves into danger of their own accord; for what do they else by preaching and confessing the truth, but procure unto themselves the hatred and enmity of the whole world, and raise offences? This, saith Paul, doth nothing at all offend or trouble me, but maketh me more bold, and causeth me to hope well of the happy success and increase of the church, which flourisheth and groweth under the cross; for it behoveth that Christ, the head and spouse of the church, should reign in the midst of all his enemies (Psalm cx). On the contrary part, when the cross is abolished, and the rage of tyrants and heretics ceaseth on the one side, and offences on the other side, and all things are in peace, the devil keeping the entry of the house, this is a sure token that the pure doctrine of God's word is taken away.

Bernard, considering this thing, saith, that the church is then in best state, when Satan assaileth it on every side, as well by subtle sleights as by violence; and contrariwise, that it is then in worst case when it is most at ease, and he allegeth very well, and to the purpose, that sentence of Hezekiah in his song, "Behold, for felicity I had bitter grief" (Isa. xxxviii, 17) applying it to the church living in ease and quietness. Wherefore, Paul taketh it for a most certain sign that it is not the gospel, if it be preached in peace. Contrariwise, the world taketh it for a most certain sign that the gospel is heretical and seditious doctrine, because it seeth great uproars, tumults, offences and sects, and such-like, to follow the preaching thereof. Thus God sometimes sheweth himself in the similitude of the devil, and the devil likewise sheweth himself in the likeness of God: and God will be known under the similitude of the devil, and will have the devil known under the likeness of God.

The cross immediately followeth the doctrine of the word, according to that saying, "I believed and therefore have I spoken, and I was sore troubled" (Ps. cxvi). Now, the cross of Christians is persecution, with reproach and ignominy, and without any compassion, and therefore it is very offensive. First, they suffer as the vilest people in the world; and so did the prophet Isaiah foreshew even of Christ himself—"He was reputed amongst the wicked" (Isaiah liii). Moreover, murderers and thieves have their punishments qualified, and men have compassion on them. Here is no offence or slander joined with the punishment. Contrariwise, like as the world judgeth the Christians to be of all other men the most pestilent and pernicious, so doth it think that no torments are sufficient to punish them for their heinous offences. Neither is it moved with any compassion towards them, but putteth them to the most opprobrious and shameful kinds of death that can be; and it thinketh that it gaineth hereby a double commodity. For, first, it imagineth that it doth high service unto God in killing of them, (John xvi, 23). Secondly, that the common peace and tranquility is restored and established by taking away such noisome plagues. Therefore the death and cross of the faithful is full of offences. But let not this reproachful dealing (saith Paul) and the continuance of Christ's cross and offence thereof move you, but rather let it confirm you. For as long as the cross endureth, it shall go well with the gospel.

In like manner Christ also comforteth his disciples in the fifth of Matthew, "Blessed are ye (saith he) when men revile you, and persecute you, and shall falsely say all manner of evil against you, for my name's sake. Rejoice and be glad, for great is your reward in heaven; for so persecuted they the prophets which were before you." The church cannot suffer this rejoicing to be wrested from her; wherefore I would not wish to be at concord with the pope, the bishops, the princes, and the sectaries, unless they would consent unto our doctrine; for such concord were a certain token that we had lost the true doctrine. To be short, as long as the church teacheth the gospel it must suffer persecution. For the gospel setteth forth the mercy and glory of God; it discloseth the malice and sleights of the devil, painteth him out in his right colours, and plucketh from him the counterfeit visor of God's majesty, whereby he deceiveth the whole world; that is to say, it sheweth that all worshippings, religious orders invented by men, and traditions concerning single life, meats, and such other things, whereby men think to deserve forgiveness of sins and everlasting life, are wicked things and devilish doctrine. There is nothing, then, that more stirreth up the devil, than the preaching of the gospel; for that plucketh from him the dissembled visor of God, and bewrayeth him to be as he is indeed, that is to say, the devil, and not God. Wherefore it cannot be but that, as long as the gospel flourisheth, the cross and the offence thereof must needs follow it, or else truly the devil is not rightly touched, but slenderly tickled. But if he be rightly hit indeed, he resteth not, but beginneth horribly to rage, and to raise up troubles everywhere.

If Christians, then, will hold the word of life, let them not be afraid or offended, when they see that the devil is broken loose, and rageth everywhere; that all the world is in an uproar; that tyrants exercise their cruelty, and heresies spring up; but let them assure themselves that these are signs, not of terror, but of joy, as Christ himself expoundeth them, saying, "Rejoice and be glad," etc. God forbid, therefore, that the offence of the cross should be taken away; which thing should come to pass, if we should preach that which the prince of this world and his members should gladly hear, that is to say, the righteousness of works. Then should we have a gentle devil, a favourable world, a gracious Pope, and merciful princes. But, because we set forth the benefits and glory of Christ, they persecute and spoil us both of our goods and lives.

VERSE 12. *Would to God they were cut off that do disquiet you.*

Is this the part of an apostle, not only to denounce the false apostles to be troublers of the church, to condemn them, and to deliver them to Satan, but also to wish that they might be utterly rooted out and perish? And what is this else but plain cursing? Paul (as I suppose) alludeth here to circumcision. As if he would say, they compel you to cut off the foreskin of your flesh; but I would that they themselves might utterly be cut off by the root.

Here riseth a question, whether it be lawful for Christians to curse? Why not? Howbeit not always, nor for every cause; but when the matter is come to this point, that God's word must be evil spoken of, and his doctrine blasphemed, and so consequently God himself, then must we turn this sentence, and say, Blessed be God and his word, and whatsoever is without God and his word, accursed be it; yea, though it be an apostle, or an angel from heaven. So he said before, in the fifth chapter. "Although we or an angel from heaven preach otherwise unto you than that which we have preached, let him be accursed," (Gal. i, 8, 9).

Hereby it may appear how great a matter Paul made of a little leaven, which for the same durst curse the false apostles, who, in outward appearance, were men of great authority and holiness. Let not us, therefore, make little account of the leaven of doctrine; for although it be never so little, yet if it be neglected, it will be the cause that by little and little the truth and our salvation shall be lost, and God himself be denied. For when the word is corrupted, and God denied and blasphemed (which must needs follow, if the word be corrupted) there remaineth no hope of salvation. But for our parts, if we be cursed, railed upon, and slain, there is yet one that can raise us up again, and deliver us from the curse, death, and hell.

Wherefore let us learn to advance and extol the majesty and authority of God's word. For it is no small trifle, (as brain-sick heads surmise at this day); but every tittle thereof is greater than heaven and earth. Wherefore, in this respect, we have no regard of Christian charity or concord, but we sit, as it were, on the judgment-seat; that is to say, we curse and condemn all men which in the least point do deface or corrupt the majesty of God's word: "for a little leaven maketh sour the whole lump." But if they leave us God's word entire and sound, we are not only ready to keep charity and peace with them; but also we offer ourselves to be their servants, and to do for them whatsoever we are able: if not, let them perish and be cast down into hell; and not only they, but even the whole world also, so that God and his true word do remain. For as long as he remaineth, life, salvation, and the faithful shall also remain.

Paul therefore doth well, in cursing those troublers of the

Galatians, and in pronouncing sentence against them, to wit, that they are accursed, with all that they teach and do, and in wishing that they might be cut off, especially that they might be rooted out of the church of God, that is, that God should not govern nor prosper their doctrine nor their doings. And this cursing proceedeth from the Holy Ghost; as Peter also, in the eighth of Acts, curseth Simon the sorcerer, "thy money and thou perish together." And the holy scripture oftentimes useth cursing against such troublers of men's consciences, and chiefly in the Psalms, as, "Let death come upon them; let them go quick into the pit of corruption," (Ps. lv, 15). Also, "Let sinners be turned down into hell, and all they that forget God."

Hitherto Paul hath fortified the place of justification with strong and mighty arguments; moreover, to the end he might omit nothing, here and there he hath intermingled chidings, praisings, exhortations, threatenings, and such-like. In the end, he addeth also his own example, namely, that he suffereth persecution for this doctrine, thereby admonishing all the faithful, not to be offended nor dismayed when they shall see such uproars, sects and offences raised up in the time of the gospel, but rather to rejoice and be glad; for the more the world rageth against the gospel, the more the gospel prospereth and goeth happily forwards.

This consolation ought at this day to encourage us: for it is certain that the world hateth and persecuteth us for none other cause but for that we profess the truth of the gospel. It doth not accuse us for theft, murder, whoredom, and such-like; but it detesteth and abhorreth us, because we teach Christ faithfully and purely, and give not over the defence of the truth. Therefore, we may be out of all doubt, that this our doctrine is holy and of God because the world hateth it so bitterly: for otherwise there is no doctrine so wicked, so foolish, and pernicious, which the world doth not gladly admit, embrace, and defend: and moreover it reverently entertaineth, cherisheth, and flattereth the professors thereof, and doth all that may be done for them. Only the true doctrine of the gospel, life, and salvation, and the ministers thereof, it utterly abhorreth, and worketh all the spite that may be devised against them. It is an evident token, therefore, that the world is so cruelly bent against us for no other thing, but because it hateth the word. Wherefore, when our adversaries charge us, that there riseth nothing of this doctrine but wars, seditions, offences, sects, and other such infinite enormities, let us answer, Blessed be the day wherein we may see these things. But the whole world is in an uproar. And well done: for if the world were not so troubled; if the devil did not rage and stir up such broils, we should not have the pure doctrine of the gospel, which cannot be preached but these broils and turmoils must needs follow. Therefore that which ye count to be a great evil, we take to be a special happiness.

The Doctrine of Good Works.

Now follow exhortations, and precepts of life and good works. For it is the custom of the apostles, after they have taught faith and instructed men's consciences, to add precepts of good works, whereby they exhort the faithful to exercise the duties of charity towards one another. And reason itself, after a sort, teacheth and understandeth this part of doctrine; but as touching the doctrine of faith, it knoweth nothing at all. To the end, therefore, that it might appear that Christian doctrine doth not destroy good works, or fight against civil ordinances, the apostle also exhorteth us to exercise ourselves in good works, and in an honest and outward conversation, and to keep charity and concord one with another. The world cannot, therefore, justly accuse the Christians that they destroy good works, that they are troublers of the public peace, civil honesty, etc. For they teach good works and all other virtues better than all the philosophers and magistrates of the world, because they adjoin faith with their doings.

> VERSE 13. *For, brethren, ye have been called unto liberty; only use not your liberty as an occasion unto the flesh, but by love serve one another.*

As if he would say: Ye have now obtained liberty through Christ, that is to say, ye be far above all laws, as touching conscience and before God: ye be blessed and saved; Christ is your life. Therefore, although the law, sin, and death trouble and terrify you, yet can they not hurt you, nor drive you to despair; and this is your excellent and inestimable liberty. Now standeth it you in hand to take good heed that ye use not that liberty as an occasion to the flesh.

This evil is common, and the most pernicious of all others that Satan stirreth up in the doctrine of faith; namely, that in very many he turneth this liberty, wherewith Christ hath made us free, into the liberty of the flesh. Of this the apostle Jude also complaineth in his epistle—"There are crept in certain wicked men (saith he) which turn the grace of our God into wantonness," (Jude:4). For the flesh is utterly ignorant of the doctrine of grace, that is to say, it knoweth not that we are made righteous, not by works, but by faith only, and that the law hath no authority over us. Therefore, when it heareth the doctrine of faith, it abuseth and turneth it into wantonness, and by-and-by thus it gathereth: If we be without law, let us then live as we list; let us do no good, let us give nothing to the needy, and let us not suffer any evil, for there is no law to constrain us, or bind us so to do.

Wherefore there is no danger on either side, albeit the one is more tolerable than the other. If grace or faith be not preached, no man can be saved; for it is faith alone that justifieth and saveth. On the other side, if faith be preached, (as of necessity it must be,) the more part of men understand the doctrine of faith carnally, and draw the liberty of the spirit into the liberty of the flesh; this may we see in all kinds of life, as well of the high as the low. All boast themselves to be professors of the gospel, and all brag of Christian liberty; and yet, serving their own lusts, they give themselves to covetousness, pleasures, pride, envy, and such other vices. No man doth his duty faithfully, no man charitably serveth the necessity of his brother. The grief hereof maketh me sometimes so impatient, that many times I wish such swine, which tread precious pearls under their feet, were yet still remaining under the tyranny of the Pope; for it is impossible that this people of Gomorrah should be governed by the gospel of peace.

Moreover, even we which teach the word, do not know our duty with so great zeal and diligence in the light of the gospel, as we did afore in the darkness of ignorance; for the more certain we be of the freedom purchased unto us by Christ, so much the more cold and negligent we be in handling the word, in prayer, in well-doing, and in suffering adversities. And if Satan did not vex us inwardly with spiritual temptations, and outwardly with the persecutions of our adversaries, and moreover with the contempt and ingratitude of our own fellows, we should become utterly careless, negligent and untoward to all good works; and so in time we should lose the knowledge and faith of Christ, forsake the ministry of the word, and seek an easier kind of life for the flesh; which thing many of our men begin to do, for that they, travailing in the ministry of the word, cannot only not live of their labour, but also are most miserably entreated even of those whom they delivered from the servile bondage of the hope by the preaching of the gospel. These men, forsaking poor and offensive Christ, entangle themselves with the affairs of this present life, serving their own bellies, and not

Christ; but with what fruit, that shall they find by experience in time to come.

Forasmuch, then, as we know that the devil layeth wait most of all for us that hate the world, (for the rest he holdeth in captivity and slavery at his pleasure,) and laboureth, with might and main, to take from us the liberty of the spirit, or at least wise to turn the same into the liberty of the flesh; we teach and exhort our brethren with singular care and diligence, by the example of Paul, that they think not this liberty of the spirit, purchased by the death of Christ, to be given unto them, that they should make it an occasion of carnal liberty, or, (as Peter saith, 1 Peter ii, 16) should use the same as a cloak for their wickedness, but that they should serve one another through love.

To the end, therefore, that Christians should not abuse this liberty, as I have said, the apostle layeth a yoke and bondage upon their flesh, by the law of mutual love. Wherefore let the godly remember, that in conscience, before God, they be free from the curse of the law, from sin, and from death, for Christ's sake: but, as touching the body, they are servants, and must serve one another through charity, according to this commandment of Paul. Let every man, therefore, endeavour to do his duty diligently in his calling, and to help his neighbour to the uttermost of his power. This is it which Paul here requireth of us, "serve ye one another through love;" which words do not set the Christians at liberty, but shut them under bondage as touching the flesh.

Moreover, this doctrine concerning mutual love, which we must maintain and exercise one towards another, cannot be beaten into the heads of carnal men, nor sink into their hearts. The Christians do gladly receive and obey this doctrine. Others, as soon as liberty is preached, by-and-by do thus infer: If I be free, then may I do what I list; this thing is mine own, why, then, should I not sell it for as much as I may get? Moreover, seeing we obtain not salvation by our good works, why should we give any thing to the poor? Thus do they most carelessly shake off the yoke and bondage of the flesh, and turn the liberty of the spirit into wantonness and fleshly liberty. But we will tell such careless contemners, (although they believe us not, but laugh us to scorn,) that if they use their bodies and their goods after their own lust, (as indeed they do, for they neither help the poor, nor lend to the needy, but beguile their brethren in bargaining, snatching and scraping unto themselves, by hook or by crook, whatsoever they can get,) we tell them (I say) that they be not free, brag they never so much of their liberty, but have lost Christ and Christian liberty, are become bond-slaves of the devil, and are seven times worse under the name of Christian liberty, than they were before under the tyranny of the Pope. For the devil which was driven out of them, hath taken unto him seven other fiends worse than himself, and is returned unto them again: therefore, the end of these men is worse than the beginning.

As touching us, we have a commandment of God to preach the gospel, which offereth to all men liberty from the law, sin, death, and God's wrath, freely for Christ's sake, if they believe. It is not in our power to conceal or revoke this liberty now published by the gospel; for Christ hath given it unto us freely, and purchased it by his death. Neither can we constrain those swine which run headlong into all licentiousness and dissoluteness of the flesh, to help other men with their bodies or goods: therefore we do what we can, that is to say, we diligently admonish them that they ought so to do. If we nothing prevail by these admonitions, we commit the matter to God, and he will recompence these scorners with just punishment in his good time. In the meanwhile, this is our comfort: that, as touching the godly, our labour is not lost; of whom many, no doubt, by our ministry are delivered out of the bondage of the devil, and translated into the liberty of the spirit. These (which, notwithstanding, are but few) which acknowledge the glory of this liberty of the spirit, and on the other side are ready through charity to serve other men, and know themselves to be debtors to their brethren as touching the flesh, do more rejoice in us, than the innumerable multitude of those that abuse this liberty, are able to discourage us.

Paul useth here very apt and plain words, when he saith, "Brethren, ye are called into liberty." And because no man should dream that he speaketh of the liberty of the flesh, he expoundeth himself what manner of liberty he meaneth, saying, "only use not your liberty as an occasion to the flesh, but serve ye one another through love." Wherefore let every Christian know, that, as touching the conscience, Christ hath made him lord over the law, sin, and death, so that they have no power over him. Contrariwise, let him know that this outward bondage is laid upon his body, that he should serve his neighbour through love. They that understand Christian liberty otherwise, enjoy the commodities of the gospel to their own destruction, and are worse idolaters under the name of Christ, than they were before under the Pope. Now Paul goeth about to declare, out of the ten commandments, what it is to serve one another through love.

VERSE 14. *For the whole law is fulfilled in one word, which is this: Thou shalt love thy neighbour as thyself.*

Paul, after that he hath laid the foundation of Christian doctrine, is wont to build gold, silver, and precious stones upon it. Now, there is no other foundation, as he himself saith to the Corinthians, than Jesus Christ, or the righteousness of Christ, (1 Cor. iii, 11). Upon this foundation he buildeth now good works, yea, good works indeed; all which he comprehendeth in one precept, "Thou shalt love thy neighbour as thyself," as if he should say, when I say that ye must serve one another through love, I mean the same thing that the law saith in another place, "Thou shalt love thy neighbour as thyself," (Lev. xix, 18). And this is truly to interpret the scripture and God's commandments.

Now, in giving precepts of love, he covertly toucheth by the way of false teachers; against whom he setteth himself mightily; that he may defend and establish his doctrine of good works against them. As if he said, O ye Galatians, I have hitherto taught you the true and spiritual life, and now also I will teach you what be good works indeed. And this will I do, to the end ye may know that the vain and foolish works of ceremonies, which the false apostles do only urge, are far inferior to the works of charity. For such is the foolishness and madness of all wicked teachers and fantastical spirits, that not only they leave the true foundation and pure doctrine, but also, continuing always in their superstitions, they never attain to good works. Therefore (as Paul saith, 1 Cor. iii, 12, 13) they build nothing but wood, hay and stubble upon the foundation. So the false apostles, which were the most earnest defenders of works, did not teach or require the works of charity, as that Christians should love one another, that they should be ready to help their neighbours in all necessities, not only with their goods, but also with their body, that is to say, with tongue, hand, heart, and with their whole strength; but only they required that circumcision should be kept, that days, months, years and times should be observed, (Gal. iv, 10) and other good works they could teach none. Fod after they had destroyed the foundation, which is Christ, and darkened the doctrine of faith, it was impossible that there could remain any true use, exercise, or opinion of good works. Take away the tree, and the fruit must needs perish.

The apostle, therefore, diligently exhorteth the Christians to exercise themselves in good works, after that they have heard and received the pure doctrine of faith. For the remnants of sin do yet still remain, even in those that be justified; which, as they are contrary to faith, and hinder it, so do they hinder us from doing good works. Moreover, man's reason and the flesh, which in the saints themselves resisteth the spirit, and in the wicked doth mightily reign, is naturally delighted with pharisaical superstition; that is to say, it taketh more pleasure in measuring God by her own imagination, than by his word; and doth the works that she herself hath chosen, with far greater zeal than those which God hath commanded. Wherefore it is necessary that the godly preachers should as diligently teach and urge the doctrine of good works as the doctrine of faith, for Satan is a deadly enemy to both. Notwithstanding, faith must first be planted; for without faith it is impossible to understand what a good work is, or what pleaseth God.

Let no man think, therefore, that he thoroughly knoweth this commandment: "Thou shalt love thy neighbour as thyself." Indeed, it is very short and easy, as touching the words; but shew me the teachers and hearers that, in teaching, learning, and living, do exercise and accomplish it rightly. Therefore these words, "Serve ye one another through love;" and these also, "Thou shalt love thy neighbour as thyself," are full of spirit, and none of the faithful do sufficiently consider, urge, and exercise the same. And (which is wonderful) the faithful have this temptation, that if they omit never so light a matter which they ought to do, by-and-by their conscience is wounded, but they are not so troubled if they neglect the duties of charity (as daily they do), or bear not a sincere and brotherly love and affection towards their neighbour. For they do not so much regard the commandment of charity, as their own superstitions, from the which they be not altogether free during this life.

Paul therefore reprehendeth the Galatians in these words, "For the whole law is fulfilled in one word." As if he said: Ye are drowned in your superstitions and ceremonies concerning places and times, which profit neither yourselves nor others; and in the meanwhile ye neglect charity, which ye ought only to have kept. What madness is this? So saith Jerome: We wear and consume our bodies with watching, fasting, and labour; but we neglect charity, which is the only lady and mistress of works. And this may be well seen in the monks, who straitly observe their traditions concerning their ceremonies, fasting, watching, apparel, and such-like. In this case, if they omit any thing, be it ever so little, they sin deadly: but when they do not only neglect charity, but also hate one another to the death, they sin not, nor offend God at all.

Therefore, by this commandment Paul not only teacheth good

works, but also condemneth fantastical and superstitious works. He not only buildeth gold, silver, and precious stones upon the foundation, but also throweth down the wood, and burneth up the hay and stubble. God witnesseth, by examples in the Old Testament, how much he did always esteem of charity: whereunto he would have the very law itself, and the ceremonies thereof, to give place. At such time as David and they that were with him were hungry, and had not what to eat, they did eat the holy shew-bread, which by law the lay-people might not eat, but only the priests, (1 Sam. xxi, 6). Christ's disciples break the Sabbath, in plucking the ears of corn; yea, and Christ himself brake the Sabbath, (as said the Jews), in healing the sick on the Sabbath-day (Matt. xii, 1, 10). All these things shew that charity or love ought to be preferred before all laws and ceremonies, and that God requireth nothing so much at our hands as love towards our neighbour. The same thing Christ also witnesseth, when he said, "And the second is like unto this," (Matt. xxii, 39).

VERSE 14. *For all the law is fulfilled in one word.*

As if he said, Why do ye burthen yourselves with the law? Why do ye so toil and turmoil yourselves about the ceremonies of the law, about meats, days, places, and such other things; as how ye ought to eat, drink, keep your feasts, sacrifices, etc.? Leave off these follies, and hearken what I say: All the law is fully comprehended in this one saying, "Thou shalt love thy neighbour as thyself." God delighteth not in the observation of the ceremonies of the law, neither hath he any need of them. The only thing that he requireth at your hands is this, that ye believe in Christ whom he hath sent; in whom ye are made perfect, and have all things. But if unto faith, which is the most acceptable service of God, ye will also add laws, then assure yourselves that all laws are comprehended in this short commandment, "Thou shalt love thy neighbour as thyself." Endeavour yourselves to keep this commandment, which being kept, ye have fulfilled all laws.

Paul is a very good expounder of God's commandments; for he draweth all Moses into a brief sum, shewing that nothing else is contained in all his laws (which are in a manner infinite) but this short sentence: "Thou shalt love thy neighbour as thyself." Natural reason is offended with this baseness and shortness of words; for it is soon said, "believe in Christ;" and again, "love thy neighbour as thyself." Therefore it despiseth both the doctrine of faith and true good works. Notwithstanding, this base and vile word of faith (as reason taketh it), "believe in Christ," is the power of God to the faithful, whereby they overcome sin, death, the devil, etc., whereby also they attain salvation and eternal life. Thus, to serve one another through love, that is, to instruct him that goeth astray, to comfort him that is afflicted, to raise up him that is weak, to help thy neighbour by all means possible, to bear with his infirmities, to endure troubles, labours, ingratitude and contempt in the church, and in civil life and conversation to obey the magistrate, to give due honour to thy parents, to be patient at home with a froward wife and an unruly family, etc.; these (I say) are works which reason judgeth to be of no value. But, indeed, they are such works, that the whole world is not able to comprehend the excellency andd worthiness thereof, (for it doth not measure works or any other thing by the word of God, but by the judgment of wicked, blind, and foolish reasons:) yea, it knoweth not the value of any one of the least good works that can be, which are true good works indeed.

Therefore, when men dream that they know well enough the commandment of charity, they are utterly deceived. Indeed, they have it written in their heart; for they naturally judge that a man ought to do unto another, as he would another should do unto him. But it followeth not, therefore, that they understand it; for if they did, they would also peform it indeed, and would prefer love and charity before all their works. They would not so highly esteem their own superstitious toys, as to go with a heavy countenance, hanging down the head, to live unmarried, to live with bread and water, to dwell in the wilderness, to be poorly apparelled, etc. These monstrous and superstitious works, which they have devised and chosen unto themselves, God neither commanding nor approving the same, they esteem to be so holy and so excellent, that they surmount and darken charity, which is, as it were, the sun of all good works. So great and incomprehensible is the blindness of man's reason, that it is unable, not only to judge rightly of the doctrine of faith, but also of external conversation and works. Wherefore, we must fight strongly, as well against the opinions of our own heart, (to the which we are naturally more inclined in the matter of salvation than to the word of God), as also against the counterfeit visor and holy shew of our own will-works; that so we may learn to magnify the works which every man doth in his vocation, although they seem outwardly never so base and contemptible, if they have the warrant of God's word; and contrariwise, to despise those works which reason chooseth without the commandment of God, seem they never so excellent and holy.

Of this commandment I have largely entreated in another place, and therefore I will now but lightly over-run it. Indeed, this is briefly spoken, "Love thy neighbour as thyself;" but yet very aptly, and to the purpose. No man can give a more certain, a better, or a nearer example than a man's own self. Therefore, if thou wouldst know how thy neighbour ought to be loved, and wouldst have a plain example thereof, consider well how thou lovest thyself. If thou shouldst be in necessity or danger, thou wouldst be glad to have the love and friendship of all men, to be holpen with the counsel, the goods, and the strength of all men, and of all creatures. Wherefore thou hast no need of any book to instruct and to admonish thee how thou oughtest to love thy neighbour; for thou hast an excellent book of all laws, even in thy heart. Thou needest no schoolmaster in this matter; ask counsel only of thine own heart, and that shall teach thee sufficiently that thou oughtest to love thy neighbour as thyself. Moreover, love or charity is an excellent virtue, which not only maketh a man willing and ready to serve his neighbour with tongue, with hand, with money and worldly goods, but with his body, and even with his life also. And thus to do, it is not provoked by good deserts or any thing else, neither is it hindered through evil deserts or ingratitude. The mother doth, therefore, nourish and cherish her child, because she loveth it.

Now, my neighbour is every man, specially which hath need of my help, as Christ expoundeth it in the tenth chapter of Luke; who, although he hath done me some wrong, or hurt me by any manner of way, yet notwithstanding he hath not put off the nature of man, or ceased to be flesh and blood, and the creature of God most like unto myself; briefly, he ceaseth not to be my neighbour. As long, then, as the nature of man remaineth in him, so long also remaineth the commandment of love, which requireth at my hand that I should not despise mine own flesh, nor render evil for evil; but overcome evil with good, or else shall love never be as Paul describeth it (1 Cor. xiii).

Paul therefore commendeth charity to the Galatians, and to all the faithful (for they only love indeed) and exhorteth them that, through charity, one of them should serve another. As if he would say, Ye need not to burden yourselves with circumcision, and with the ceremonies of Moses' law: but, after all things, continue in the doctrine of faith which ye have received of me. Afterwards, if ye will do good works, I will in one word shew you the chiefest and greatest works, and how ye shall fulfill all laws: "Serve ye one another, through love." Ye shall not lack them to whom ye may do good, for the world is full of

EPISTLE TO THE GALATIANS

such as need the help of others. This is a perfect and a sound doctrine of faith and love; and also the shortest and the longest divinity. The shortest, as touching the words and sentences; but, as touching the use and practice, it is more large, more long, more profound, and more high than the whole world.

VERSE 15. *If ye bite and devour one another, take heed lest ye be consumed one of another.*

By these words Paul witnesseth, that if the foundation, that is to say, if faith in Christ be overthrown by wicked teachers, no peace or concord can remain in the church, either in doctrine or life; but there must needs be divers opinions and dissensions from time to time, both in doctrine and life, whereby it cometh to pass that one biteth and devoureth another; that is to say, one judgeth and condemneth another, until at length they be consumed. Hereof not only the scripture, but also the examples of all times bear witness. After that Africa was perverted by the Manichees, by-and-by followed the Donatists, who also disagreeing among themselves, were divided into three sundry sects. And how many sects have we at this day springing up one after another? One sect bringeth forth another, and one condemneth another. Thus, when the unity of the spirit is broken, it is impossible that there should be any concord either in doctrine or life, but daily new errors must needs spring up, without measure and without end.

Paul, therefore, teacheth that such occasions of discord are to be avoided, and he sheweth how they may be avoided. This, (saith he) is the way to unity and concord: Let every man do his duty in that kind of life which God hath called him unto; let him not lift up himself above others, nor find fault with any other men's works, and commend his own, but let every one serve another through love. This is a true and simple doctrine, touching good works. This do they not teach which have made shipwreck of faith, and have conceived fantastical opinions concerning faith and good works: but, disagreeing among themselves, as touching the doctrine of faith and works, they bite and devour, that is to say, they accuse and condemn one another, as Paul here saith of the Galatians: "If ye bite and devour one another, take heed lest ye be consumed one of another." As if he would say, Do not accuse and condemn one another for circumcision, for observing of holy days, or other ceremonies, but rather give yourselves to serve and help one another through charity; or else, if ye continue in biting and devouring one another, take heed that ye be not consumed, that is to say, that ye perish not utterly, yea, and that bodily, which commonly happeneth, especially to the authors of sects, as it did to Arius and others, and to certain also in our time. For he that hath laid his foundation on the sand, and buildeth hay, stubble, and suchlike, must needs fall and be consumed; for all those things are ordained for the fire. I will not say, that, after such bitings and devourings, the ruin and destruction, not of one city, but of whole countries and kingdoms are wont to follow. Now the apostle sheweth what it is to serve one another through love.

It is a hard and a dangerous matter to teach that we are made righteous by faith without works, and yet to require works withal. Here, except the ministers of Christ be faithful, and wise disposers of the mysteries of God, rightly dividing the word of truth, faith and works are by-and-by confounded. Both these doctrines, as well of faith as of works, must be diligently taught and urged; and yet so that both may remain within their bounds. Otherwise, if they teach works only, (as they do in the Pope's kingdom,) then is faith lost. If faith only be taught, then carnal men by-and-by dream that works be not needful.

The apostle began, a little before, to exhort men to do good works, and to teach that the whole law was fulfilled in one word, namely, "Thou shalt love thy neighbour as thyself." Here will some man say: Paul throughout his whole epistle taketh away righteousness from the law; for saith he, "By the works of the law shall no flesh be justified" (Gal. ii, 16). Also, "As many as are under the works of the law, are under the curse" (Gal. iii, 10). But now, when he saith that the whole law is fulfilled in one word, he seemeth to have forgotten the matter whereof he hath entreated in all this epistle, and to be of a quite contrary opinion: to wit, that they which do the works of charity, fulfil the law and be righteous. To this objection he answereth after this manner.

VERSE 16. *But I say, walk in the spirt, and ye shall not fulfil the works of the flesh.*

As if he should have said: I have forgotten my former discourse concerning faith, neither do I now revoke the same, in that I exhort you to mutual love, saying, "that the whole law is fulfilled through love;" but I am still of the same mind and opinion that I was before. To the end, therefore, that ye may rightly understand me, I add this moreover, "Walk in the spirit, and ye shall not fulfil the lusts of the flesh."

A Confutation of the Argument of the Schoolmen: Love is
the Fulfilling of the Law; Therefore the
Law Justifieth.

Although Paul speaketh here expressly and plainly enough, yet hath he little prevailed; for the schoolmen, not understanding this place of Paul, "Love is the fulfilling of the law," have gathered out of it after this manner: If love be the fulfilling of the law, it followeth then that love is righteousness; therefore, if we love, we be righteous. These profound clerks do argue from the word to the work, from doctrine or precepts, to life, after this sort: The law hath commanded love, therefore the work of love followeth out of hand. But this is a foolish consequence, to draw an argument from precepts, and to ground the conclusion upon works.

True it is that we ought to fulfil the law, and to be justified through the fulfilling thereof; but sin hindereth us. Indeed, the law prescribeth and commandeth that we should love God with all our hearts, etc., and that we should love our neighbour as ourselves: but it followeth not, this is written, therefore it is done: the law commandeth love, therefore we love. There is not one man to be found upon the whole earth, which so loveth God and his neighbour as the law requireth. But, in the life to come, where we shall be thoroughly cleansed from all vices and sins, and shall be made as pure and as clear as the sun, we shall love perfectly, and shall be righteous through perfect love. But in this life that purity is hindered by the flesh; for as long as we live, sin remaineth in the flesh; by reason whereof, the corrupt love of ourselves is so mighty, that it far surmounteth the love of God and of our neighbour. In the mean time, notwithstanding that we may be righteous in this life also, we have Christ the mercy-seat and throne of grace, and because we believe in him sin is not imputed unto us. Faith, therefore, is our righteousness in this life; but in the life to come, when we shall be thoroughly cleansed and delivered from all sins and concupiscence, we shall have no more need of faith and hope, but we shall then love perfectly.

It is a great error, therefore, to attribute justification or righteousness to love, which is nothing; or if it be any thing, yet it is not so great that it can pacify God; for love, even in the faithful, (as I have said,) is imperfect and impure. But no unclean thing shall enter into the kingdom of God, (Apoc. xxi, 27). Notwithstanding, in the meanwhile, this trust and confidence sustaineth us: that Christ, who alone committed no sin, and in whose mouth was never found any guile, doth overshadow us with his righteousness, (Isa. liii, 9; 1 Peter ii, 22). We being covered with this cloud, and shrouded under the shadow, this heaven of remission of sins and throne of grace, do begin to love and to fulfil the law; yet for this fulfilling we are not justified, nor accepted of God, whilst we live here. But, when Christ hath delivered up the kingdom to God his Father, and abolished all principality, and God shall be all in all, then shall faith and hope cease, and love shall be perfect and everlasting (1 Cor. xii). This thing the popish schoolmen understand not; and therefore, when they hear that love is the sum of the whole law, by-and-by they infer: *ergo*, the law justifieth. Or contrariwise, when they read in Paul that faith maketh a man righteous; yea, say they, faith formed and furnished with charity. But that is not the meaning of Paul, as I have largely declared before.

If we were pure from all sin, and were inflamed with perfect love both towards God and our neighbour, then should we indeed be righteous and holy through love, and God could require no more of us. This is not done in this present life, but is deferred until the life to come. Indeed we receive here the gift and first fruits of the spirit, so that we begin to love (Rom. viii, 23), howbeit very slenderly. But if we loved God truly and perfectly, as the law of God requireth, which saith (Deut. vi, 5), "Thou shalt love the Lord thy God with all thy heart, with all thy soul, and with all thy strength;" (Matt. xxii, 37) then should we be as well contented with poverty as with wealth, with pain as with pleasure, and with death as with life, yea, he that could love God truly and perfectly indeed, should not long continue in this life, but should straightway be swallowed up by this charity.

But now man's nature is so corrupt and drowned in sin, that it cannot have any right sense or cogitation of God. It loveth not God, but hateth him deadly. Wherefore, as John saith, (1 John iv, 10) "We love not God, but he loved us, and sent his Son to be a reconciliation for our sins." And as Paul saith before, in the second chapter, "Christ hath loved me, and given himself for me." And in the fourth chapter, "But when the fulness of time was come, God sent forth his Son made of a woman, and made under the law, that he might redeem them which were under the law." We, being redeemed and justified by the Son, begin to love; according to that saying of Paul in the eighth to the Romans, "That which was impossible to the law, (inasmuch as it was weak because of the flesh), God sending his own Son in the similitude of sinful flesh, and for sin, condemned sin in the flesh, that the righteousness of the law might be fulfilled in us;" that is, might begin to be fulfilled. They are mere dreams, therefore, which the sophisters and schoolmen have taught, concerning the fulfilling of the law.

Wherefore Paul sheweth by these words: "Walk in the spirit," how he would have that sentence to be understood, where he said, "Serve ye one another through love." And again, "Love is the fulfilling of the law," etc. As if he should say, When I bid you love another, this is it that I require of you, that you walk in the spirit. For I know that ye shall not fulfil the law, because sin dwelleth in you as long as ye live, therefore it is impossible that ye should fulfil the law. Notwithstanding, in the meanwhile endeavour yourselves diligently to walk in the spirit, that is, wrestle in spirit against the flesh, and follow spiritual motions, etc.

It appeareth, then, that he had not forgotten the matter of justification; for when he biddeth them to walk in the spirit, he plainly denieth that works do justify. As if he should say, When I speak of the fulfilling of the law, I mean not that ye are justified by the law; but this I mean, that there be two contrary captains in you, the spirit and the flesh. God hath stirred up in your bodies a strife and a battle; for the spirit wrestleth against the flesh, and the flesh against the spirit, (Gal. v, 17). Here I require nothing else of you, but that ye follow the spirit as your captain and guide, and that ye resist that captain the flesh; for that is all that ye are able to do. Obey the spirit, and fight against the flesh. Therefore, when I teach you to observe the law, and exhort you to love one another, think not that I go about to revoke that which I have taught concerning the doctrine of faith, and that I now attribute justification to the law or to charity; but my meaning is, that ye should walk in the spirit, and that ye should not fulfil the lusts of the flesh.

Paul useth very fit words and to the purpose. As if he would say, We come not yet to the fulfilling of the law; therefore we must walk in the spirit, and be exercised therein, that we may think, say, and do those things which are of the spirit, and resist those things which are of the flesh: therefore he addeth,

VERSE 16. *And ye shall not fulfil the lusts of the flesh.*

As if he would say, The desires or lusts of the flesh be not yet dead in us, but spring up again and fight against the spirit. The flesh of no faithful man is so good, which being offended would not bite and devour, or at the least omit somewhat of that commandment of love. Yet even at the first brunt he cannot refrain himself, but is angry with his neighbour, desireth to be revenged, and hateth him as an enemy, or at the least loveth him not so much as he should do, and as this commandment requireth; and this happeneth even to the faithful.

Therefore the apostle hath given this rule for the faithful: that they should serve one another through love; that they should bear the burthens and infirmities one of another; and that they should forgive one another. And without this bearing and forbearing, through love, it is impossible that love and concord should continue among Christians. For it cannot be, but that thou must needs often offend, and be offended. Thou seest many things in me which offend me. Here, if one bear not with another, through love, there shall be no end of dissension, discord, envy, hatred, and malice.

Wherefore Paul would have us to walk in the spirit, lest we fulfil the lusts of the flesh. As if he should say, Although ye be moved with wrath and displeasure against your brother, offending you, or doing any thing heinously against you, yet notwithstanding resist and repress these violent motions through the spirit. Bear with his weakness, and love him according to that commandment, "Thou shalt love thy neighbour as thyself." For thy brother doth not therefore cease to be thy neighbour, because he slippeth, or offendeth thee; but then hath he most need that thou shouldst exercise and shew thy charity towards him. And this commandment, "Thou shalt love thy neighbour as thyself," requireth the self-same thing; to wit, that thou shouldst not obey the flesh, which, when it is offended, hateth, biteth, and devoureth; but wrestle against it in spirit, and continue through the same in the love of thy neighbour, although thou find nothing in him worthy of love.

The schoolmen take the concupiscence of the flesh for carnal lust. Indeed it is true that even the godly, especially the younger sort, are tempted with fleshly lust. Yea, they also that be married (so corrupt and pestilent is flesh) are not without such carnal lust. Here let every one (I speak now to the godly being married, both man and wife) diligently examine himself, and no doubt many shall find this in themselves, that the beauty and conditions of another man's wife pleaseth him better than of his own, and so contrariwise, his own lawful wife he loatheth or misliketh, and loveth her which is unlawful. And this commonly is wont to happen, not in marriage only, but in all other matters. Men set light by that which they have, and are in love with that which they have not, as the poet saith: *'Nitimur in vetitum semper, cupimusque negata.'* That is,

> Of things most forbidden we always are fain:
> And things most denied we seek to obtain.

I do not deny, therefore, but that the concupiscence of the flesh comprehendeth carnal lust, but not that only. For concupiscence comprehendeth all other corrupt affections, wherewith the very faithful are infected, some more, some less: as pride, hatred, covetousness, impatiency, and such-like. Yea, Paul rehearseth afterwards among the works of the flesh, not only those gross vices, but also idolatry, heresies, and such other. It is plain, therefore, that he speaketh of the whole concupiscence of the flesh, and of the whole dominion of sin, which stirreth, even in the godly who have received the first fruits of the spirit, against the dominion of the spirit. He speaketh therefore not only of carnal lust, pride, covetousness, etc., but also of incredulity, distrust, despair, hatred and contempt of God, idolatry, heresies, and such other, when he saith, "And ye shall not fulfil the lusts of the flesh." As if he should say, I write unto you that you should love one another. This ye do not, neither can ye do it, because of the flesh, which is infected and corrupted with concupiscence, and doth not only stir up sin in you, but also is sin itself. For if ye had perfect charity, no heaviness, no adversity could be so great, which should be able to hurt or hinder that charity; for it would be spread throughout the whole body. There should be no wife, were she never so hard favoured, whom her husband would not love entirely, loathing all other women, though they were never so fair and beautiful. But this is not done, therefore it is impossible for us to be made righteous through love.

Wherefore think me not to revoke and unsay that which I have taught concerning faith; for faith and hope must continue, that by the one we may be justified, and by the other we may be raised up in adversities, and endure unto the end. Moreover, we serve one another through charity, because faith is not idle: but charity is weak and little. Therefore, when I bid you walk in the spirit, I do sufficiently declare that ye are not justified through charity.

And when I exhort you to walk in the spirit, that ye fulfil not the concupiscence of the flesh, I do not require of you that ye should utterly put off the flesh, or kill it, but that ye should bridle and subdue it. For God will have mankind to endure even to the last day; and this cannot be done without parents, which do beget and bring up children. These means continuing, it must needs be that flesh also must continue, and consequently sin, for flesh is not without sin. Therefore, in respect of the flesh we are sinners; but in respect of the spirit, we are righteous. Notwithstanding, our righteousness is much more plentiful than our sin, because the holiness and righteousness of Christ our mediator doth far exceed the sin of the whole world; and the forgiveness of sins, which we have through him, is so great, so large, and so infinite, that it easily swalloweth up all sins, so that we walk according to the spirit, etc.

The Papists dreamed that this commandment belongeth only to their clergymen, and that the apostle exhorteth them to live chastely, by subduing the flesh with watching, fasting, labour, etc., and then they should not fulfil the concupiscence of the flesh, that is to say, carnal lust. As though the whole concupiscence of the flesh were overcome, when this fleshly lust is subdued; which, notwithstanding, they were never able to suppress and keep under, with any yoke that they could lay upon the flesh. Which thing Jerome, (I say nothing of others,) who was a marvellous lover and defender of chastity, doth plainly confess. "O (saith he) how often have I thought myself to be in the midst of the vain delights and pleasures of Rome, even when I was in the wild wilderness, which, being burned up with the heat of the sun, yieldeth an ouglesome habitation to the monks!" etc. Again, "I, who for fear of hell had condemned myself to such a prison, thought myself oftentimes to be dancing among young women, when I had no other company but scorpions and wild beasts. My face was pale with fasting, but my mind was enflamed with desires in my cold body; and although my flesh was half dead already, yet the flames of fleshly lust boiled within me," etc.

If Jerome felt in himself such flames of fleshly lust, who lived in the barren wilderness with bread and water, what do our holy belly-gods, the clergymen, feel, think ye, who so stuff and stretch themselves with all kinds of dainty fare, that it is marvel their bellies burst not? Wherefore these things are written, not to hermits and monks, (as the Papists dream,) nor to sinners in the world only, but to the universal church of Christ, and to all the faithful; whom Paul exhorteth to walk in the spirit, that they fulfil not the lusts of the flesh, that is to say, not only to bridle the gross motions of the flesh, as carnal lust, wrath, impatiency, and such-like; but also the spiritual motions, as doubting, blasphemy, idolatry, contempt and hatred of God, etc.

Paul (as I have said) doth not require of the godly, that they should utterly put off or destroy the flesh, but that they should so bridle it, that it might be subject to the spirit. In the tenth to the Romans, he biddeth us cherish the flesh. For, as we may not be cruel to other men's bodies, nor vex them with unreasonable labour, even so we may not be cruel to our own bodies, (Eph. v, 29). Wherefore, according to Paul's precept, we must cherish our flesh, that it may be able to endure the labours both of the mind and of the body; but yet only for necessity's sake, and not to nourish the lusts thereof. Therefore, if the flesh begin to wax wanton, repress it and bridle it by the spirit. If it will not be, marry a wife, for it is better to marry than to burn. Thus doing, thou walkest in the spirit; that is, thou followest God's word, and doest his will.

VESRE 17. *For the flesh lusteth against the spirit, and the spirit against the flesh.*

When Paul saith that the flesh lusteth against the spirit, and the spirit against the flesh, he admonisheth us that we must feel the concupiscence of the flesh, that is to say, not only carnal lust, but also pride, wrath, heaviness, impatience, incredulity, and such-like. Notwithstanding, he would have us so feel them, that we consent not unto them, nor accomplish them; that is, that we neither think, speak, nor do those things which the flesh provoketh us unto. As, if it move us to anger, yet we should be angry in such wise (as we are taught in the fourth Psalm,) that we sin not. As if Paul would thus say: I know that the flesh will provoke you unto wrath, envy, doubting, incredulity, and such-like; but resist it by the spirit, that ye sin not. But if ye forsake the guiding of the spirit, and follow the flesh, ye shall fulfil the lusts of the flesh, and ye shall die, as Paul saith in the eighth to the Romans. So this saying of the apostle is to be understood, not of fleshly lusts only, but of the whole kingdom of sin.

VERSE 17. *And these are contrary one to the other, so that ye cannot do the same things that ye would.*

These two captains or leaders, (saith he) the flesh and the spirit, are one against another in your body, so that ye cannot do what ye would. And this place wittnesseth plainly that Paul writeth these things to the faithful, that is, to the church believing in Christ, baptized, justified, renewed, and having full forgiveness of sins. Yet notwithstanding he saith that she hath flesh rebelling against the spirit. After the same manner he speaketh of himself, in the seventh to the Romans, "I (saith he) am carnal, and sold under sin." And again, "I see another law in my members, rebelling against the law of my mind, and leading me captive unto the law of sin which is in my members." Also, "O wretched man that I am, who shall deliver me from the body of this death?" etc.

Here, not only the schoolmen, but also some of the old fathers are much troubled, seeking how they may excuse Paul. For it seemeth unto them absurd and unseemly to say, that that elect vessel of Christ should have sin. But we credit Paul's own words, wherein he plainly confesseth that he is sold under sin, that he is led captive of sin, that he hath a law in his members rebelling against him, and that in the flesh he serveth the law of sin. Here again they answer, that the apostle speaketh in the person of the wicked. But the wicked do not complain of the rebellion of their flesh, of any battle or conflict, or of the captivity and bondage of sin; for sin mightily reigneth in them. This is therefore the very complaint of Paul, and of all the faithful. Wherefore they have done very wickedly which have excused Paul and all the faithful to have no sin; for by this persuasion (which proceedeth of ignorance of the doctrine of faith) they have robbed the church of a singular consolation: they have abolished the forgiveness of sins, and made Christ of none effect.

Wherefore, when Paul saith, "I see another law in my members," etc., he denieth not that he hath flesh, and the vices of the flesh in him. It is likely, therefore, that he felt sometimes the motions of carnal lust; but yet (no doubt) these motions were well suppressed in him, by the great and grievous afflictions and temptations, both of mind and body, wherewith he was in a manner continually exercised and vexed, as his epistles do declare. Or if he at any time, being merry and strong, felt the lust of the flesh, wrath, impatiency, and such-like, yet he resisted them by the spirit, and suffered not those motions to bear rule in him. Therefore, let us in no wise suffer such comfortable places (whereby Paul describeth the battle of the flesh against the spirit, in his own body) to be corrupted with such foolish glosses. The schoolmen, the monks, and such other, never felt any spiritual temptations, and therefore they fought only for the repressing and overcoming of fleshly lust and lechery; and being proud of that victory which they never yet obtained, they thought themselves far better and more holy than married men. I will not say, that, under this holy pretence, they nourished and maintained all kinds of horrible sins, as dissension, pride, hatred, disdain, and despising of their neighbours, trust in their own righteousness, presumption, contempt of all godliness and

of the word of God, infidelity, blasphemy, and such-like. Against
these sins they never fought, nay, rather, they took them to be
no sins at all: they put righteousness in the keeping of their
foolish and wicked vows, and unrighteousness in the neglecting
and contemning of the same.

But this must be our ground and anchor-hold, that Christ is
our only and perfect righteousness. If we have nothing whereunto we may trust, yet these three things, (as Paul saith,) faith,
hope, and love, do remain. Therefore we must always believe,
and always hope; we must always take hold of Christ, as the
head and foundation of our righteousness. He that believeth
in him shall not be ashamed, (Rom. ix, 33). Moreover, we
must labour to be outwardly righteous also: that is to say, not
to consent to the flesh, which always enticeth us to some evil,
but to resist it by the spirit. We must not be overcome with
impatiency for the unthankfulness and contempt of the people,
which abuseth the Christian liberty; but through the spirit, we
must overcome this and all other temptations. Look, then, how
much we strive against the flesh by the spirit, so much are we
outwardly righteous; albeit this righteousness doth not commend
us before God.

Let no man, therefore, despair, if he feel the flesh oftentimes
to stir up new battle against the spirit, or if he cannot by-and-
by subdue the flesh, and make it obedient unto the spirit. I
also do wish myself to have a more valiant and constant heart,
which might be able, not only boldly to contemn the threatenings of tyrants, the heresies, offences and tumults which Satan
and his soldiers the enemies of the gospel stir up; but also might
by-and-by shake off the vexations and anguish of spirit, and
briefly, might not fear the sharpness of death, but receive and
embrace it as a most friendly guest. But I find another law in
my members, rebelling against the law of my mind, etc. Some
other do wrestle with inferior temptations, as poverty, reproach, impatiency, and such-like.

Let no man marvel, therefore, or be dismayed, when he feeleth in his body this battle of the flesh against the spirit; but
let him pluck up his heart, and comfort himself with these words
of Paul: "the flesh lusteth against the spirit;" also, "these are
contrary one to another, so that ye do not those things that ye
would;" for by these sentences he comforteth them that be
tempted. As if he should say, It is impossible for you to follow
the guiding of the spirit in all things, without any feeling or
hindrance of the flesh. Nay, the flesh will resist; and so resist
and hinder you, that ye cannot do those things that gladly ye
would. Here it shall be enough if ye resist the flesh, and fulfil

not the lust thereof; that is to say, if ye follow the spirit and not the flesh, which easily is overthrown by impatiency, coveteth to revenge, biteth, grudgeth, hateth God, is angry with him, despaireth, etc. Therefore, when a man feeleth this battle of the flesh, let him not be discouraged therewith, but let him resist in spirit, and say, I am a sinner, and I feel sin in me; for I have not yet put off the flesh, in which sin dwelleth so long as it liveth. But I will obey the spirit, and not the flesh: that is, I will by faith and hope lay hold upon Christ, and by his word I will raise up myself, and being so raised up, I will not fulfil the lust of the flesh.

It is very profitable for the godly to know this, and to bear it well in mind; for it wonderfully comforteth them when they are tempted. When I was a monk, I thought by-and-by that I was utterly cast away, if at any time I felt the lust of the flesh; that is to say, if I felt any evil motion, fleshly lust, wrath, hatred, or envy against any brother. I assayed many ways to help and to quiet my conscience, but it would not be: for the concupiscence and lust of my flesh did always return, so that I could not rest, but was continually vexed with these thoughts: This or that sin thou hast committed, thou art infected with envy, with impatiency, and such other sins: therefore thou art entered into this holy order in vain, and all thy good works are unprofitable. If, then, I had rightly understood these sentences of Paul, "The flesh lusteth contrary to the spirit, and the spirit contrary to the flesh, and these two are one against another, so that ye cannot do the things that ye would do;" I should not have so miserably tormented myself, but should have thought and said to myself, as now commonly I do: "Martin, thou shalt not utterly be without sin, for thou hast flesh; thou shalt therefore feel the battle thereof, according to that saying of Paul: 'The flesh resisteth the spirit.' Despair not, therefore, but resist it strongly, and fulfil not the lust thereof. Thus doing, thou art not under the law."

I remember that Staupitius was wont to say, "I have vowed unto God, above a thousand times, that I would become a better man; but I never performed that which I vowed. Hereafter I will make no such vow; for I have now learned by experience, that I am not able to perform it. Unless, therefore, God be favourable and merciful unto me for Christ's sake, and grant unto me a blessed and a happy hour, when I shall depart out of this miserable life, I shall not be able, with all my vows and all my good deeds, to stand before him." This was not only a true, but also a godly and a holy desperation; and this must all they confess, both with mouth and heart, which will be saved.

For the godly trust not to their own righteousness, but say with David, "Enter not into judgment with thy servant, for in thy sight shall none that liveth be justified" (Ps. cxliii, 2). Again: "If thou, O Lord, should straitly mark iniquities, O Lord, who shall stand?" (Ps. cxxx, 3). They look unto Christ their reconciler, who gave his life for their sins. Moreover, they know that the remnant of sin which is in their flesh, is not laid to their charge, but freely pardoned. Notwithstanding in the mean while they fight in spirit against the flesh, lest they should fulfil the lusts thereof. And although they feel the flesh to rage and rebel against the spirit, and themselves also do fall sometimes into sin through infirmity, yet are they not discouraged, nor think therefore that their state and kind of life, and the works which are done according to their calling, displease God; but they raise up themselves by faith.

The faithful, therefore, receive great consolation by this doctrine of Paul, in that they know themselves to have part of the flesh, and part of the spirit, but yet so notwithstanding that the spirit ruleth, and the flesh is subdued and kept under awe, that righteousness reigneth, and sin serveth. He that knoweth not this doctrine, and thinketh that the faithful ought to be without all fault, and yet seeth the contrary in himself, must needs at the length be swallowed up by the spirit of heaviness, and fall into desperation. But whoso knoweth this doctrine well, and useth it rightly, to him the things that are evil turn unto good (Rom. viii, 28). For when the flesh provoketh him to sin, by occasion thereof he is stirred up and forced to seek forgiveness of sins by Christ, and to embrace the righteousness of faith, which else he would not so greatly esteem, nor seek for the same with so great desire. Therefore it profiteth us very much to feel sometimes the wickedness of our nature and corruption of our flesh, that yet by this means we may be waked and stirred up to faith, and to call upon Christ. And by this occasion a Christian becometh a mighty workman and a wonderful creator, which of heaviness can make joy, of terror comfort, of sin righteousness, and of death life, when he, by this means repressing and bridling the flesh, maketh it subject to the spirit.

Wherefore let not them which feel the lust of the flesh despair of their salvation. Let them feel it, and all the force thereof, so that they consent not to it; let the passions of lust, wrath, and such other vices shake them, so that they do not overthrow them; let sin assail them, so that they do not accomplish it; yea, the more godly a man is, the more doth he feel that battle. And hereof come those lamentable complaints of the faithful in the Psalms and in the whole scripture. Of this battle, the hermits, the monks, the schoolmen, and all that seek righteousness and salvation by works, know nothing at all.

But here may some man say, that it is a dangerous matter to teach that a man is not condemned, if by-and-by he overcome not the motions and passions of the flesh which he feeleth. For when this doctrine is taught amongst the common people, it maketh them careless, negligent, and slothful. This is it which I said a little before, that if we teach faith, then carnal men neglect and reject works: if works be required, then is faith and consolation of conscience lost. Here no man can be compelled, neither can there be any certain rule prescribed; but let every man diligently try himself to what passion of the flesh he is most subject, and when he findeth that, let him not be careless, nor flatter himself; but let him watch and wrestle in spirit against it, that if he cannot altogether bridle it, yet at the least he do not fulfil the lust thereof.

This battle of the flesh against the spirit, all the children of God have had and felt; and the self-same do we also feel and prove. He that searcheth his own conscience, if he be not a hypocrite, shall well perceive that to be true in himself which Paul here saith: that the flesh lusteth against the spirit. All the faithful, therefore, do feel and confess that their flesh resisteth against the spirit, and that these two are so contrary, the one to the other in themselves, that, do what they can, they are not able to perform that which they would do. Therefore the flesh hindereth us, that we cannot keep the commandments of God, that we cannot love our neighbours as ourselves, much less can we love God with all our heart; therefore it is impossible for us to become righteous by the works of the law. Indeed there is a good will in us, and so must there be, (for it is the spirit itself which resisteth the flesh,) which would gladly do good, fulfil the law, love God and his neighbour, and such-like, but the flesh obeyeth not this good will, but resisteth it; and yet God imputeth not unto us this sin; for he is merciful to those that believe, for Christ's sake.

But it followeth not, therefore, that thou shouldst make a light matter of sin, because God doth not impute it. True it is that he doth not impute it; but to whom, and for what cause? To such as repent, and lay hold by faith upon Christ the mercy-seat, for whose sake, as all their sins are forgiven them, even so the remnants of sin, which are in them, be not imputed unto them. They make not their sin less than it is, but amplify it, and set it out as it is indeed; for they know that it cannot be put away by satisfactions, works, or righteousness, but only by the death of Christ. And yet, notwithstanding, the greatness and enormity of their sin doth not cause them to despair, but they assure themselves that the same shall not be imputed unto them, or laid unto their charge.

This I say, lest any man should think that, after faith is received, there is little account to be made of sin. Sin is truly sin, whether a man commit it before he hath received the knowledge of Christ, or after. And God always hateth sin; yea, all sin is damnable, as touching the fact itself; but in that it is not damnable to him that believeth, it cometh of Christ, who by his death hath taken away sin. But to him that believeth not in Christ, not only all his sins are damnable, but even his good works also are sin; according to that saying, "Whatsoever is not of faith is sin" (Rom. xiv, 23). Therefore the error of the schoolmen is most pernicious, which do distinguish sins according to the fact, and not according to the person. He that believeth, hath as great sin as the unbeliever; but to him that believeth, it is forgiven and not imputed: to the unbeliever it is not pardoned, but imputed. To the believer it is venial; to the unbeliever it is mortal and damnable: not for any difference of sins, or because the sin of the believer is less, and the sin of the unbeliever greater; but for the difference of the persons. For the faithful assureth himself, by faith, that his sin is forgiven him, forasmuch as Christ hath given himself for it. Therefore, although he have sin in him, and daily sinneth, yet he continueth godly; but contrariwise, the unbeliever continueth wicked. And this is the true wisdom and consolation of the godly, that although they have and commit sins, yet they know that for Christ's sake they are not imputed unto them.

This I say for the comfort of the godly. For they only feel indeed that they have and do commit sins, that is to say, they feel that they do not love God so fervently as they should do; that they do not believe him so heartily as they would, but rather they oftentimes doubt whether God have a care of them or no; they are impatient, and are angry with God in adversity. Hereof (as I have said) proceed the sorrowful complaints of the faithful in the scriptures, and especially in the Psalms, and Paul himself complaineth that he is sold under sin (Rom. vii, 14). And here he saith that the flesh resisteth and rebelleth against the spirit. But because they mortify the deeds of the flesh by the spirit (as he saith in another place, and also in the end of this chapter, "They crucify the flesh, with the desires and lusts thereof," Gal. v, 24), therefore these sins do not hurt them, nor condemn them. But if they obey the flesh, in fulfilling the lusts thereof, then do they lose faith and the Holy Ghost; and if they do not abhor their sin, and return unto Christ (who hath given power to his church, to receive and raise up those that be fallen, that so they may recover faith and the Holy Ghost), they die in their sins. Wherefore we speak not of them which dream that they have faith, and yet continue still in their sins. These men have their judgment already: they that live after the flesh shall die. Also, "The works of the flesh are manifest, which are adultery, fornication, uncleanness, wantonness, idolatry, witchcraft, hatred, debate, emulations, wrath, contentions, seditions, heresies, envy, murder, drunkenness, gluttony, and such-like, whereof I tell you before, as also I have told you, that they which do such things shall not inherit the kingdom of God."

Hereby we may see who be the very saints indeed. They be not stocks and stones (as the monks and schoolmen dream,) so that they are never moved with any thing, never feel any lust, or desires of the flesh; but as Paul saith, their flesh lusteth against the spirit, and therefore they have sin, and both can and do sin. And the thirty-second Psalm witnesseth, that the faithful do confess their unrighteousness, and pray that the wickedness of their sin may be forgiven, where it saith: "I will confess against myself my wickedness unto the Lord, and thou forgavest the punishment of my sin. Therefore shall every one that is godly make his prayer unto thee," etc. Moreover, the whole church, which indeed is holy, prayeth that her sins may be forgiven her, and it believeth the forgiveness of sins. And in Psalm cxliii, David prayeth: "O Lord, enter not into judgment with thy servant, for in thy sight shall none that liveth be justified." And in Psalm cxxx, "If thou, O Lord, shouldst straitly mark iniquities, Lord, who shall stand in thy presence? But with thee is mercy," etc. Thus do the chiefest saints and children of God speak and pray; as David, Paul, etc. All the faithful, therefore, do speak and pray the same thing, and with the same spirit. The popish sophisters read not the scriptures, or, if they read them, they have a veil before their eyes; and therefore, as they cannot judge rightly of any thing, so can they not judge rightly either of sin or of holiness.

VERSE 18. *If ye be led by the spirit, ye are not under the law.*

Paul cannot forget the doctrine of faith, but still repeateth it, and beateth it into their heads, yea, even when he treateth of good works. Here some man may object: How can it be, that we should not be under the law? And yet thou, notwithstanding, O Paul, teachest us that we have flesh, which lusteth against the spirit, and fighteth against us, tormenteth us, and bringeth us into bondage. And, indeed, we feel sin, and cannot be delivered from the feeling thereof, though we should never so fain; and what is this else but to be under the law? But, saith he, let this nothing trouble you; only do your endeavour that ye may be led by the spirit; that is to say, shew yourselves willing to follow and obey that will which resisteth the flesh, and doth not accomplish the lusts thereof (for this is, to be led and to be drawn by the spirit), then are ye not under the law. So Paul speaketh of himself (Rom. vii), "In my mind I serve the law of God:" that is to say, in spirit I am not subject to any sin; but yet in my flesh I serve the law of sin. The faithful, then, are not under the law, that is to say, in spirit; for the law cannot accuse them, nor pronounce sentence of death against them, although they feel sin, and confess themselves to be sinners. For the power and strength of the law is taken from it by Christ, "who was made under the law, that he might redeem them which were under the law" (Gal. iv, 4). Therefore the law cannot accuse that for sin in the faithful, which is sin indeed, and committed against the law.

So great, then, is the power and dominion of the spirit, that the law cannot accuse the godly, though they commit that which is sin indeed. For Christ is our righteousness, whom we apprehend by faith; he is without all sin, and therefore the law cannot accuse him. As long as we cleave fast unto him, we are led by the spirit, and are free from the law. And so the apostle, even when he teacheth good works, forgetteth not his doctrine concerning justification, but always sheweth that it is impossible for us to be justified by works. For the remnants of sin cleave fast in our flesh, and therefore, so long as our flesh liveth, it ceaseth not to lust contrary to the spirit. Notwithstanding there cometh no danger unto us thereby, because we be free from the law, so that we walk in the spirit.

And with these words, "If ye be led by the spirit, ye be not under the law," thou mayest greatly comfort thyself, and others that be grievously tempted; for it oftentimes cometh to pass, that a man is so vehemently assailed with wrath, hatred, impatiency, carnal desire, terror and anguish of spirit, or some other lust of the flesh, that he cannot shake them off, though he would never so fain. What should he do in this case? Should he despair? No, God forbid: but let him say thus with himself: thy flesh fighteth and rageth against the spirit. Let it rage as long as it listeth; only see thou that, in any case, thou consent not to it, to fulfil the lusts thereof, but walk wisely, and follow the leading of the spirit. In so doing, thou art free from the law. It accuseth and terrifieth thee, (I grant,) but altogether in vain. In this conflict, therefore, of the flesh against the spirit, there is nothing better than to have the word of God before thine eyes, and therein to seek the comfort of the spirit.

And let not him that suffereth this temptation, be dismayed, in that the devil can so aggravate sin, that during the conflict he thinketh himself to be utterly overthrown, and feeling nothing else but the wrath of God and desperation. Here in any wise let him not follow his own feeling and the judgment of reason, but let him take sure hold of this saying of Paul, "If ye be led by the spirit;" that is, to wit, if ye raise up and comfort yourselves through faith in Christ, ye be not under the law. So shall he have a strong buckler, wherewith he may beat back all the fiery darts which that wicked fiend assaileth him withal. How much soever, then, the flesh doth boil and rage, yet cannot her motions and rages hurt and condemn him; forasmuch as he, following the guiding of the spirit, doth not consent unto the flesh, nor fulfil the lusts thereof. Therefore, when the motions of the flesh do rage, the only remedy is to take to us the sword of the spirit, that is to say, the word of salvation, (which is, that God would not the death of a sinner, but that he convert and live,) and to fight against them; which if we do, let us not doubt but we shall obtain the victory, although, so long as the battle endureth, we feel the plain contrary. But set the word out of sight, and there is no counsel nor help remaining. Of this that I say, I myself have good experience. I have suffered many great passions, and the same also vehement and great; but so soon as I have laid hold of any place of scripture, and stayed myself upon it, as upon my chief anchor-hold, straightways my temptations did vanish away; which, without the word, it had been impossible for me to endure any little space, and much less to overcome them.

The sum or effect, therefore, of all that which Paul hath taught in this disputation or discourse, concerning the conflict or battle between the flesh and the spirit, is this: that the saints and the elect of God cannot perform that which the spirit desireth. For the spirit would gladly be altogether pure, but the flesh being joined unto the spirit, will not suffer that. Notwithstanding they be saved by the remission of sins, which is in Christ Jesus. Moreover, because they walk in the spirit, and are led by the spirit, they be not under the law, that is to say, the law cannot accuse of terrify them; yea, although it go about never so much so to do, yet shall it never be able to drive them to desperation.

EPISTLE TO THE GALATIANS

VERSE 19. *Moreover, the works of the flesh be manifest, which are, etc.*

This place is not unlike to this sentence of Christ, "By their fruits ye shall know them. Do men gather grapes of thorns, or figs of brambles? So every good tree bringeth forth good fruit, and an evil tree bringeh forth evil fruit," etc. (Matt. vii, 16). Paul teacheth the very same thing which Christ taught, that is to say, that works and fruits do sufficiently testify whether the trees be good or evil: whether men follow the guiding of the flesh, or of the spirit. As if he should say, lest some of you might say for himself, that he understandeth me not, now when I treat of the battle between the flesh and the spirit, I will set before your eyes first the works of the flesh, whereof many are known even to the ungodly; and then also the works of the spirit.

And this doth Paul, because there were many hypocrites amongst the Galatians (as there are also at this day among us) which outwardly pretended to be godly men, and boasted much of the spirit, and, as touching the words, they understood the true doctrine of the gospel; but they walked not occording to the spirit, but according to the flesh, and performed the works thereof. Whereby Paul manifestly convinceth them to be no such holy men indeed as they boasted themselves to be. And lest they should despise this his admonition, he pronounceth against them this dreadful sentence, that they should not be inheritors of the kingdom of heaven, to the end that being thus admonished, they might amend. Every age, even in the faithful, hath his peculiar temptations: as fleshly lusts assail a man most of all in his youth; in his middle age, ambition and vain-glory; and in his old age, covetousness. There was never yet any of the faithful whom the flesh hath not often in his lifetime provoked to impatiency, anger, vain-glory, etc. Paul, therefore, speaking here of the faithful, saith that the flesh lusteth in them against the spirit, etc., therefore they shall never be without the desires and battles of the flesh; notwithstanding, they do not hurt them. But of this matter we must thus judge, that it is one thing to be provoked of the flesh, and yet not willingly to yield to the lusts and desires thereof, but to walk after the leading of the spirit, and to resist the flesh; and another thing to assent unto the flesh, and, without all fear or remorse, to perform and fulfil the works thereof, and to continue therein, and yet notwithstanding to counterfeit holiness, and to brag of the spirit. The first he comforteth, when he saith that they be led by the spirit, and be not under the law. The other he threateneth with everlasting destruction.

Notwithstanding sometimes it happeneth that the saints also do fall, and perform the lusts of the flesh; as David fell horribly into adultery. Also he was the cause of the slaughter of many men, when he caused Urias to be slain in the forefront of the battle; and thereby also he gave occasion to the enemies to glory and triumph over the people of God, to worship their idols, and to blaspheme the God of Israel. Peter also fell most grievously and horribly, when he denied Christ. But, although these sins were great and heinous, yet were they not committed upon any contempt of God, or of a wilful and obstinate mind, but through infirmity and weakness. Again, when they were admonished, they did not obstinately continue in their sins, but repented. Such he willeth afterwards, in the sixth chapter, to be received, instructed, and restored, saying, "If a man be fallen by occasion into any sin, ye which are spiritual restore such a one with the spirit of meekness, considering thyself lest thou also be tempted." To those, therefore, which sin and fall through infirmity, pardon is not denied, so that they rise again and continue not in their sin; for of all things continuance in sin is the worst. But if they repent not, but still obstinately continue in their wickedness, and perform the desires of the flesh, it is a certain token that there is deceit in their spirit.

No man, therefore, shall be without lusts and desires, so long as he liveth in the flesh, and therefore no man shall be free from temptations. Notwithstanding, some are tempted one way and some another, according to the difference of persons. One man is assailed with more vehement and grievous motions, as with bitterness and anguish of spirit, blasphemy, distrust, and desperation; another with more gross temptations, as with fleshly lusts, wrath, envy, covetousness, and such-like. But in this case Paul requireth of us that we walk in the spirit, and resist the flesh. But whoso obeyeth the flesh, and continueth, without any fear of God or remorse of conscience, in accomplishing the desires and lusts thereof, let him know that he pertaineth not unto Christ; and, although he brag of the name of a Christian never so much, yet doth he but deceive himself; for they which are of Christ, do crucify their flesh, with the affections and lusts thereof.

WHO BE RIGHTLY CALLED SAINTS, AND BE SO INDEED?

This place (as I have also forewarned you by the way) containeth in it a singular consolation; for it teacheth us that the saints and most holy men in this world live not without concupiscence and temptations of the flesh, nor yet without sins. It warneth us, therefore, to take heed that we do not as some did, of whom Gerson writeth, which laboured to attain to such perfection, that they might be without all feeling of temptations or sins; that is to say, very stocks and stones.

The like imagination the monks and schoolmen had of their saints, as though they had been very senseless blocks and without all affections. The Virgin Mary felt great grief and sorrow of spirit when she missed her Son (Luke ii). David, in the Psalms, complaineth that he is almost swallowed up with excessive sorrow, for the greatness of his temptations and sin. Paul also complaineth that he hath battles without, and terrors within (2 Cor. vii, 5), and that in his flesh he serveth the law of sin. He saith, that he is careful for all the churches (2 Cor. xi, 28) and that God shewed great mercy towards him, in that he delivered Epaphroditus, being at the point of death, to life again, lest he should have had sorrow upon sorrow. Therefore, the saints of the Papists are like to the stoics, who imagined such wise men as in the world were never yet to be found. And by this foolish and devilish persuasion, which proceeded from the ignorance of this doctrine of Paul, the schoolmen brought both themselves and others without number into horrible desperation.

When I was a monk, I did oftentimes most heartily wish that I might once be so happy as to see the conversation and life of some saint or holy man. But in the mean time I imagined such a saint as lived in the wilderness, abstaining from meat and drink, and living only with roots of herbs and cold water; and this opinion of those monstrous saints, I had learned not only out of the books of the sophisters and schoolmen, but also out of the books of the fathers. For thus writeth Jerome, in a certain place: "As touching meats and drinks I say nothing, forasmuch as it is excess, that even such as are weak and feeble should use cold water, or eat any sodden thing," etc. But now in the light of the gospel we plainly see who they are whom Christ and his apostles call saints. Not they which live a sole and a single life, or straitly observe days, meats, apparel, and such other things, or in outward appearance do other great and monstrous works (as we read of many in the lives of the fathers): but they which being called by the sound of the gospel and baptized, do believe that they be justified and cleansed by the death of Christ. So Paul everywhere writing to Christians, calleth them holy, the children and heirs of God, etc. Whosoever, then, do believe in Christ, whether they be men or women, bond or free, are all saints: not by their own works, but by the works of God, which they receive by faith; as his word, his sacraments, the passion of Christ, his death, resurrection, victory, and the sending of the Holy Ghost. To conclude, they are saints through such a holiness as they freely receive, not through such a holiness as they themselves have gotten by their own industry, good works, and merits.

So the ministers of the word, the magistrates of commonweals, parents, children, masters, servants, etc., are true saints, if, first, and before all things, they assure themselves that Christ is their wisdom, righteousness, sanctification, and redemption: secondly, if every one do his duty in his vocation, according to the rule of God's word, and obey not the flesh, but repress the lust and desire thereof by the spirit. Now, whereas all be not of like strength to resist temptations, but many infirmities and offences are seen in the most part of men; this nothing hindereth their holiness, so that their sins proceed not of an obstinate wilfulness, but only of frailty and infirmity. For (as I have said before) the godly do feel the desires and lusts of the flesh, but they resist them, to the end that they accomplish them not. Also, if they at any time unadvisedly fall into sin, yet notwithstanding they obtain forgiveness thereof, if by faith in Christ they be raised up again; who would not that we should drive away, but seek out and bring home the straying and lost sheep, etc. Therefore, God forbid that I should straightway judge those which are weak in faith or manners, to be profane or unholy, if I see that they love and reverence the word of God, to come to the supper of the Lord, etc. For these God hath received, and counteth them righteous, through the remission of sins; to him they stand or fall, etc.

Wherefore, with great rejoicing I give thanks to God, for that he hath abundantly and above measure granted that unto me, which I so earnestly desired of him when I was a monk: for he hath given unto me the grace to see not one but many saints, yea, an infinite number of true saints; not such as the sophisters have devised, but such as Christ himself and his apostles do describe. Of the which number I assure myself to be one. For I am baptized, and I do believe that Christ my Lord, by his death, hath redeemed and delivered me from all my sins, and hath given to me eternal righteousness and holiness. And let him be holden accursed, whosoever shall not give this honour unto Christ, to believe that by his death, his word, etc., he is justified and sanctified.

Wherefore, rejecting this foolish and wicked opinion concerning the name of saints, (which, in the time of popery and ignorance, we thought to pertain only to the saints which are in heaven, and in earth to the hermits and monks, which did certain great and strange works,) let us now learn by the holy scripture, that all they which faithfully believe in Christ are saints. The world hath in great admiration the holiness of Benedict, Gregory, Bernard, Francis, and such-like, because it heareth that they have done, in outward appearance, and in the judgment of the world, certain great and excellent works. Doubtless, Hilary, Cyril, Athanasius, Ambrose, Augustine, and others, were saints also, which lived not so strait and severe a life as they did, but were conversant amongst men, and did eat common meats, drank wine, and used cleanly and comely apparel: so that in a manner there was no difference between them and other honest men, as touching the common custom, and the use of things necessary for this life, and yet were they to be preferred far above the other. These men taught the doctrine and faith of Christ sincerely and purely, without any superstition; they resisted heretics; they purged the church from innumerable errors; their company and familiarity was comfortable to many, and specially to those which were afflicted and heavy-hearted, whom they raised up and comforted by the word of God. For they did not withdraw themselves from the company of men, but they executed their offices even where most resort of people was. Contrariwise, the others not only taught many things contrary to the faith, but also were themselves the authors and first inventors of many superstitions, errors, abominable ceremonies, and wicked worshippings. Therefore, except at the hour of death they laid hold of Christ, and reposed their whole trust in his death and victory, their strait and painful life availed them nothing at all.

These things sufficiently declare who be the true saints indeed, and which is to be called a holy life. Not the life of those which lurk in caves and dens, which make their bodies lean with fasting, which wear hair, and do other like things, with this persuasion and trust that they shall have some singular reward in heaven above all other Christians; but of those which be baptized and believe in Christ, which put off the old man with his works, but not at once; for concupiscence and lust remaineth in them so long as they live: the feeling whereof doth hurt them nothing at all, if they suffer it not to reign in them, but subdue it to the spirit.

This doctrine bringeth great consolation to godly minds, that when they feel these darts of the flesh, wherewith Satan assaileth the spirit, they should not despair; as it happeneth to many in the papacy, which thought that they ought to feel no concupiscence of the flesh; whereas, notwithstanding, Jerome, Gregory, Benedict, Bernard, and others, (whom the monks set before them as a perfect example of chastity and of all Christian virtues,) could never come so far as to feel no concupiscence or lust of the flesh; yea, they felt it, and that very strongly; which thing they acknowledge and plainly confess in divers places of their books.

Therefore we rightly confess, in the articles of our belief, that we believe there is a holy church; for it is invisible, dwelling in spirit in a place that none can attain unto, and therefore her holiness cannot be seen; for God doth so hide and cover her with infirmities, with sins, with errors, with divers forms of the cross and offences, that according to the judgment of reason it is nowhere to be seen. They that are ignorant of this, when they see the infirmities and sins of those which are baptized, which have the word and believe it, are by-and-by offended, and judge them not to pertain to the church; and in the meanwhile they dream that the hermits, the monks, and such other shavelings, are the church, which honour God with their lips, and worship him in vain, because they follow not the word of God, but the doctrines and commandments of men, and teach others to do the same. And because they do certain superstitious and monstrous works, which carnal reason magnifieth and highly esteemeth, therefore they judge them only to be saints, and to be the church: and, in so doing, they change and turn this article of faith clean contrary, "I believe that there is a holy church," etc.; and in the stead of this word [I believe] they put in [I see]. These kinds of righteousness, and holiness of man's own devising, are nothing else but spiritual sorceries, wherewith the eyes and minds of men are blinded, and led from the knowledge of true holiness.

But thus teach we, that the church hath no spot nor wrinkle, but is holy, and yet through faith only in Christ Jesus. Again, that she is holy in life and conversation, by abstaining from the lusts of the flesh, and exercise of spiritual works; but yet not in such sort that she is delivered from all evil desires, or purged from all wicked opinions and errors; for the church always confesseth her sins, and prayeth that her faults may be pardoned: also, she believeth the forgiveness of sins. The saints, therefore, do sin, fall, and also err; but yet through ignorance. For they would not willingly deny Christ, forsake the gospel, etc., therefore they have remission of sins. And if through ignorance they err also in doctrine, yet is this pardoned; for in the end they acknowledge their error, and rest only upon the truth, and the grace of God offered in Christ, as Jerome, Gregory, Bernard, and others did. Let Christians, then, endeavour to avoid the works of the flesh, but the desires or lusts of the flesh they cannot avoid.

It is very profitable, therefore, for them to feel the unclean lusts of the flesh, lest they should be puffed up with some vain and wicked opinion of the righteousness of their own works, as though they were accepted before God for the same. The monks, being puffed up with this opinion of their own righteousness, thought themselves to be so holy, that they sold their righteousness and holiness to others, although they were convinced, by the testimony of their own hearts, that they were unclean. So pernicious and pestilent a poison it is for a man to trust in his own righteousness, and to think himself to be clean. But the godly, because they feel the uncleanness of their own hearts, therefore they cannot trust to their own righteousness. This feeling so maketh them to stoop, and so humbleth them, that they cannot trust to their own good works, but are constrained to fly to Christ, their mercy-seat and only succour, who hath not a corrupt and sinful, but a most pure and holy flesh, which he hath given for the life of the world, (John vi, 51.) In him they find a sound and perfect righteousness. Thus they continue in humility; not counterfeit and monkish, but true and unfeigned, because of the uncleanness which yet remaineth in their flesh; for the which, if God would straitly judge them, they should be found guilty of eternal death. But because they lift not up themselves proudly against God, but with a broken and a contrite heart, humbly acknowledging their sins, and resting wholly upon the benefit of the mediator Christ, they come forth into the presence of God, and pray that for his sake their sins may be forgiven them; God spreadeth over them an infinite heaven of grace, and doth not impute unto them their sins, for Christ's sake.

This I say, to the end that we may take heed of the pernicious errors of the Papists touching the holiness of our life, wherein our minds are so wrapped, that without great difficulty we could not wind ourselves out of them. Wherefore, do you endeavour with diligence, that ye may discern and rightly judge between true righteousness and holiness, and that which is hypocritical, then shall ye behold the kingdom of Christ with other eyes than carnal reason doth, that is, with spiritual eyes, and certainly judge those to be true saints indeed, which are baptized and believe in Christ; and afterwards, in the same faith whereby they are justified, and their sins both past and present are forgiven, do abstain from the desires of the flesh. But from these desires they are not thoroughly cleansed; for the flesh lusteth against the spirit. Notwithstanding, these unclean and rebellious lusts do still remain in them to this end, that they may be humbled, and being so humbled, they may feel the sweetness of the grace and benefit of Christ. So these remnants of unclean lusts and sins do nothing at all hinder, but greatly further the godly; for the more they feel their infirmities and sins, so much the more they fly unto Christ the throne of grace, and more heartily crave his aid and succour; to wit, that he will cover them with his righteousness, that he will increase their faith, that he will endue them with his holy spirit, by whose gracious leading and guiding they may overcome the lusts of the flesh, that they may rule and reign not over them, but may be subject unto them. Thus true Christians do continually wrestle with sin, and yet notwithstanding in wrestling they are not overcome, but obtain the victory.

This have I said, that ye may understand, not by men's dreams, but by the word of God, who be true saints indeed. We see, then, how greatly Christian doctrine helpeth to the raising up and comforting of weak consciences; which treateth not of cowls, shavings, shearings, fraternities, and such-like toys, but of high and weighty matters, as how we may overcome the flesh, sin, death, and the devil. This doctrine, as it is unknown to justiciaries, and such as trust in their own works, so it is impossible for them to instruct or bring into the right way one poor conscience wandering and going astray; or to pacify and comfort the same when it is in heaviness, terror, or desperation.

> VERSE 19. *The works of the flesh are manifest, which are adultery, fornication, uncleanness, wantonness, idolatry, witchcraft, etc.*

Paul doth not recite all the works of the flesh, but useth a certain number for a number uncertain. First, he reckoneth up the kinds of lusts, as adultery, fornication, uncleanness, wantonness, etc. Now, not only carnal lust is a work of the flesh, as the Papists dreamed, who called marriage also a work of the flesh, (so chaste and holy are these men,) whereof God himself is the author, which also they themselves reckoned among their sacraments; but he numbereth also amongst the works of the flesh (as I have said before) idolatry, witchcraft, hatred, and such other, which hereafter follow. Wherefore, this place alone doth sufficiently shew what Paul meaneth by the flesh. These words are so well known that they need no interpretation.

Idolatry

All the highest religions, the holiness and most fervent devotions of those which do reject Christ the Mediator, and worship God without his word and commandment, are nothing else but plain idolatry. As in popery it was counted a most holy and spiritual act, when the monks, being shut up in their cells, did muse and meditate of God or of his works, and when they, being inflamed with most earnest devotions, kneeled down, prayed, and were so ravished with the contemplations of heavenly things, that they wept for joy. There was no thinking of women, or of any other creature, but only of God the Creator, and of his wonderful works; and yet this most spiritual work (as reason esteemeth it) is, according to Paul, a work of the flesh, and plain idolatry. Wherefore all such religion, whereby God is worshipped without his word and commandment, is idolatry. And the more holy and spiritual it seemeth to be in outward shew, so much the more dangerous and pernicious it is. For it turneth men away from faith in Christ, and causeth them to trust in their own strength, works, and righteousness. And such is the religion of the Anabaptists at this day; albeit they daily more and more bewray themselves to be possessed with the devil, and to be seditious and bloody men.

Therefore the fasting, the wearing of hair, holy works, strait rule, and whole life of the Carthusians and Charterhouse monks, whose order, notwithstanding, is of all other the straitest and sharpest, be very works of the flesh, yea, plain idolatry. For they imagine themselves to be saints, and to be saved, not by Christ (whom they fear as a severe and cruel judge) but by observing of their rules and orders. Indeed, they think of God, of Christ, and of heavenly things, but after their own reason, and not after the word of God: to wit, that their apparel, their manner of living, and their whole conversation is holy and pleaseth Christ; whom not only they hope to pacify by this straitness of life, but also to be rewarded of him for their good deeds and righteousness. Therefore, their most spiritual thoughts (as they dream of them) are not only most fleshly, but also most wicked; for they would wipe away their sins, and obtain grace and everlasting life, by the trust and affiance they have in their own righteousness, rejecting and despising the word, faith, and Christ. All the worshippings and services of God, therefore, and all religions without Christ are idolatry and idol service. In Christ alone, the Father is well pleased; whoso heareth him, and doth that which he hath commanded, the same is beloved because of "the beloved." He commandeth us to believe his word, and to be baptized, etc., and not to devise any new worshipping or service of God.

I have said before, that the works of the flesh be manifest; as adultery, fornication, and such-like, be manifestly known to all men. But idolatry hath such a goodly shew, and is so spiritual, that it is known but to very few, that is, to the faithful, to be a work of the flesh. For the monk when he liveth chastely, fasteth, prayeth, or saith mass, is so far from thinking himself to be an idolater, or that he fulfilleth any work of the flesh, that he is assuredly persuaded that he is led and governed by the spirit; that he walketh according to the spirit; that he thinketh, speaketh, and doeth nothing else but mere spiritual things; and that he doth such service unto God as is most acceptable unto him. No man can at this day persuade the Papist that their mass is a great blasphemy against God, and idolatry, yea, and that so horrible, as never was any in the church since the apostle's time. For they are blind and obstinate, and therefore they judge so perversely of God and God's matters, thinking that idolatry to be a true service of God, and contrariwise, faith to be idolatry. But we, which believe in Christ and know his mind, are able to judge and to discern all things, and cannot truly and before God be judged of any man.

Hereby it is plain that Paul calleth flesh whatever is in man, comprehending all the three powers of the soul; that is, the will that lusteth, the will that is inclined to anger, and the understanding. The works of the will that lusteth, are adultery, fornication, uncleanness, and such-like. The works of the will inclined to wrath, are quarrellings, contentions, murder, and such other. The works of understanding or reason, are errors, false religions, superstitions, idolatry, heresies, that is to say, sects and such-like. It is very necessary for us to know these things; for this word (flesh) is so darkened in the whole kingdom of the Pope, that they have taken the work of the flesh to be nothing else but the accomplishing of fleshly lust, or the act of lechery; wherefore it was not possible for them to understand Paul. But here we may plainly see that Paul reckoneth idolatry and heresy amongst the works of the flesh, which two (as before we have said) reason esteemeth to be most high and excellent virtues, wisdom, religion, holiness, and righteousness. Paul (Col. ii) calleth it the religion of angels. But, although it seem to be never so holy and spiritual, yet it is nothing else but a work of the flesh, an abomination and idolatry against the gospel, against faith, and against the true service of God. This do the faithful see, for they have spiritual eyes; but the justiciaries judge the contrary: for a monk cannot be persuaded that his vows are works of the flesh. So the Turk believeth nothing less than that his Alcoran, his washings, and other ceremonies which he observeth, be works of the flesh.

Witchcraft

Of witchcraft I have spoken before, in the third chapter. This vice was very common in these our days, before the light and truth of the gospel was revealed. When I was a child, there were many witches and sorcerers, which bewitched both cattle and men, but specially children, and did great harm also otherwise; but now, in the light of the gospel, these things be not so commonly heard of, for the gospel thrusteth the devil out of his seat, with all his illusions. But now he bewitcheth men much more horribly, namely, with spiritual sorcery and witchcraft.

Paul reckoneth witchcraft among the works of the flesh, which notwithstanding, as all men know, is not a work of fleshly lust or lechery, but a kind of idolatry. For witchcraft covenanteth with the devil; superstition or idolatry covenanteth with God: albeit, not with the true God, but with a counterfeit god. Wherefore idolatry is, indeed, a spiritual witchcraft. For as witches do enchant cattle and men, so idolaters, that is to say, all justiciaries, or justifiers of themselves, go about to bewitch God, and to make him such a one as they do imagine. Now they imagine him to be such a one as will justify them, not of his mere grace and mercy, and through faith in Christ, but in respect of their will-worshippings, and works of their own choosing, and in recompence thereof will give them righteousness and life everlasting. But whilst they go about to bewitch God, they bewitch themselves; for if they continue in this wicked opinion which they conceive of God, they shall die in their idolatry and be damned. The works of the flesh are well known for the most part, therefore they shall not need any further declaration.

Sects

By the name of sects, Paul meaneth here, not those divisions or contentions which rise sometimes in the government of households, or of commonweals, for worldly and earthly matters; but those which rise in the church, about doctrine, faith, and works. Heresies, that is to say, sects, have always been in the church, as we have said before, in divers places. Notwithstanding the Pope is an arch-heretic, and the head of all heretics; for he hath filled the world, as it were, with a huge flood of infinite sects and errors. What concord and unity was there in so great diversity of the monks, and other religious orders? No one sort or sect of them could agree with another; for they measured their holiness by the straitness of their orders. Hereof it cometh that the Carthusian will needs be counted holier than the Franciscan, and so likewise the rest; wherefore there is no unity of spirit, nor concord of minds, but great discord in the papistical church; there is no conformity in their doctrine, faith, religion, or serving of God, but all things are clean contrary. Contrariwise, amongst the Christians, the word, faith, religion, sacraments, service, Christ, God, heart, soul, mind, and understanding, are all one and common to all; and, as touching outward conversation, the diversity of states, degrees, and conditions of life, hindereth this spiritual concord and unity nothing at all, as before I have said. And they which have this unity of the spirit, can certainly judge of all sects, which otherwise no man understandeth; as, indeed, no divine in the papacy understood that Paul in this place condemneth all the worshippings, religions, continency, honest conversation, and holy life in outward appearance, of all the Papists, sectaries, and schismatics; but they all thought that he speaketh of the gross idolatry and heresies of the Gentiles and Turks, which manifestly blaspheme the name of Christ.

Drunkenness, Gluttony

Paul doth not say that to eat and drink be works of the flesh, but to be drunken and to surfeit, which of all other vices are most common at this day. Whoso are given to this beastly dissoluteness and excess, let them know that they are not spiritual, how much soever they boast themselves so to be, but they follow the flesh, and perform the filthy works thereof. Therefore is this horrible sentence pronounced against them, that they shall not be inheritors of the kingdom of God. Paul would therefore that Christians should fly drunkenness and surfeiting, living soberly and moderately, without all excess, lest by pampering the flesh they should be provoked to wantonness; as, indeed, after surfeiting and belly-cheer, the flesh is wont to wax wanton, and to be inflamed with outrageous lust. But it is not sufficient only to restrain this outrageous wantonness and lust of the flesh, which followeth drunkenness and surfeiting, or any manner of excess; but also the flesh, when it is most sober and in his best temperance, must be subdued and repressed, lest it fulfil his lusts and desires. For it oftentimes cometh to pass, that even

EPISTLE TO THE GALATIANS

they which are most sober, are tempted most of all: as Jerome writeth of himself: "My face," saith he, "was pale with fasting, and my mind was inflamed with fleshly desires in my cold body; and although my flesh was half dead already, yet the flames of unclean lust boiled within me." Hereof I myself also had experience when I was a monk. The heat, therefore, of unclean lusts is not quenched by fasting only, but we must be aided also by the spirit, that is, by the meditation of God's word, faith, and prayer. Indeed, fasting represseth the gross assaults of fleshly lust; but the desires of the flesh are overcome by no abstinence from meats and drinks, but only by the meditation of the word of God and invocation of Christ.

VERSE 21. *And such-like.*

For it is impossible to reckon up all the works of the flesh.

VERSE 21. *Whereof I tell you, as I have also told you before, that they which do such things, shall not inherit the kingdom of God.*

This is a very hard and terrible saying, but yet very necessary against false Christians and careless hypocrites, which brag of the gospel, of faith, and of the spirit, and yet in all security they perform the works of the flesh. But chiefly the heretics, being puffed up with opinions of spiritual matters, (as they dream,) are possessed of the devil, and altogether carnal; therefore they perform and fulfil the desires of the flesh, even with all the powers of the soul. Therefore most necessary it was that so horrible and terrible a sentence should be pronounced by the apostle against such careless contemners and obstinate hypocrites, (namely, that all they which do such works of the flesh as Paul hath recited, shall not inherit the kingdom of God,) that yet some of them, being terrified by this severe sentence, may begin to fight against the works of the flesh by the spirit, that they accomplish not the same.

VERSE 22. *But the fruits of the spirit are love, joy, peace, long-suffering, sweetness, goodness, faithfulness, gentleness or meekness, temperance.*

The apostle saith not, the works of the spirit, as he said the works of the flesh, but he adorneth these Christian virtues with a more honourable name, calling them the fruits of the spirit; for they bring with them most excellent fruits and commodities; for they that have them give glory to God, and with the same do allure and provoke others to embrace the doctrine and faith of Christ.

LOVE

It had been enough to have said, "love," and no more: for love extendeth itself unto all the fruits of the spirit. And in 1 Cor. xiii, Paul attributeth to love all the fruits which are done in the spirit, when he saith, "Love is patient, courteous," etc. Notwithstanding he would set it here by itself, amongst the rest of the fruits of the spirit, and in the first place, thereby to admonish the Christians that before all things they should love one another, giving honour one to another, (Rom. xii, 10.) every man esteeming better of another than of himself, and serving one another, because they have Christ and the Holy Ghost dwelling in them, and because of the word, baptism, and other gifts of God, which Christians have.

JOY

This is the voice of the bridegroom and of the bride; that is to say, sweet cogitations of Christ, wholesome exhortations, pleasant songs or psalms, praises and thanksgivings, whereby the godly do instruct, stir up, and refresh themselves. Therefore God loveth not heaviness and doubtfulness of spirit; he hateth uncomfortable doctrine, heavy and sorrowful cogitations, and loveth cheerful hearts. For therefore hath he sent his Son, not to oppress us with heaviness and sorrow, but to cheer up our souls in him; for this cause the prophets, the apostles, and Christ himself do exhort us, yea, they command us to rejoice and be glad: (Zech. ix, 9), "Rejoice, thou daughter of Zion; be joyful, thou daughter of Jerusalem; for behold, thy king cometh to thee." And in the Psalms it is often said: "Be joyful in the Lord." Paul saith: "Rejoice in the Lord always," etc. And Christ saith: "Rejoice, because your names are written in heaven." Where this joy of the spirit is, there the heart inwardly rejoiceth through faith in Christ, with full assurance that he is our Saviour and our bishop, and outwardly it expresseth this joy with words and gestures. Also, the faithful rejoice when they see that the gospel spreadeth abroad, that many be won to the faith, and the kingdom of Christ is enlarged.

PEACE.

Both towards God and men, that Christians may be peaceable and quiet: not contentious, nor hating one another, but one bearing another's burthen, through long-suffering or perseverance, without the which, peace cannot continue, and therefore Paul putteth it next after peace.

Long-Suffering or Perseverance.

Whereby a man doth not only bear adversities, injuries, reproaches, and such-like, but also with patience waiteth for the amendment of those which have done him any wrong. When the devil cannot by force overcome those which are tempted, then seeketh he to overcome them by long continuance. For he knoweth that we be earthen vessels, which cannot long endure and hold out many knocks and violent strokes, therefore with long continuance of temptations he overcometh many. To vanquish these his continual assaults we must use long-suffering, which patiently looketh, not only for the amendment of those which do us wrong, but also for the end of those temptations which the devil raiseth up against us.

Gentleness

Which is, when a man is gentle and tractable in his conversation, and in his whole life. For such as will be true followers of the gospel, must not be sharp and bitter, but gentle, mild, courteous, and fair spoken, which should encourage others to delight in their company; which can wink at other men's faults, or, at least, expound them to the best; which will be well contented to yield and give place to others; contented to bear with those which are froward and intractable, as the very heathen said: "Thou must know the manners of thy friend, but thou must not hate them." Such a one was our Saviour Christ, as everywhere is to be seen in the gospel. It is written of Peter, that he wept so often as he remembered the sweet mildness of Christ which he used in his daily conversation. It is an excellent virtue, and most necessary in every kind of life.

Goodness.

Which is, when a man willingly helpeth others in their necessity by giving, lending, and such other means.

Faith.

When Paul here reckoneth faith amongst the fruits of the spirit, it is manifest that he speaketh not of faith which is in Christ, but of the fidelity and humanity of one man towards another. Hereupon he saith, in the thirteenth chapter of the first of the Corinthians, that charity believeth all things. Therefore he that hath this faith is not suspicious but mild, and taketh all things to the best; and although he be deceived, and findeth himself to be mocked, yet such is his patience and softness, that he letteth it pass; briefly, he is to ready to believe all men, but he trusteth not all. On the contrary, where this virtue is lacking, there men are suspicious, froward, wayward, dogged, and so neither will believe any thing, nor give place to any body; they can suffer nothing; whatsoever a man saith or doth never so well, they cavil and slander it, so that whoso serveth not their humour can never please them. Therefore it is impossible for them to keep charity, friendship, concord, and peace with men. But if these virtues be taken away, what is this life, but biting and devouring one of another? Faith, therefore, in this place is, when one man giveth credit to another in things pertaining to this present life; for what manner of life should we lead in this world, if one man should not credit the other?

Meekness.

Which is, when a man is not lightly moved or provoked to anger. There be infinite occasions in this life which provoke men to anger, but the ungodly overcome them by meekness.

Temperance, Chastity, or Continency

This is a sobriety or modesty in the whole life of man, which virtue Paul setteth against the works of the flesh. He would, therefore, that Christians should live soberly and chastely; that they should be no adulterers, no fornicators, no wantons; and if they cannot live chastely, he would have them to marry. Also, they should not be contentious or quarrellers, that they should not be given to drunkenness or surfeiting, but that they should abstain from all these things. Chastity or continency containeth all these. Jerome expoundeth it of virginity only, as though they that be married could not be chaste; or as though the apostle did write these things only to virgins. In the first and second chapter to Titus, he warneth also bishops, young women, and married folks, both man and wife, to be chaste and pure.

Verse 23. *Against such there is no law.*

Indeed there is a law, but not against such. As he saith also in another place, "The law is not given to the righteous man." For the righteous liveth in such wise that he hath no need of any law, to admonish or to constrain him; but, without constraint of the law, he willingly doth those things which the law requireth. Therefore the law cannot accuse or condemn those that believe in Christ. Indeed, the law troubleth and terrifieth our consciences; but Christ, apprehended by faith, vanquisheth it, with all his terrors and threatenings. To them, therefore, the law is utterly abolished, and hath no power to accuse them; for they do that of their own accord, which the law requireth. They have received the Holy Ghost by faith, who will not suffer them to be idle; although the flesh resist, yet do they walk after the spirit. So a Christian accomplisheth the law inwardly by faith, (for Christ is the perfection of the law unto righteousness, to all that do believe,) outwardly by works and remission of sins; but those which perform the works or desires of the flesh, the law doth accuse and condemn both civilly and spiritually.

VERSE 24. *For they that are Christ's have crucified the flesh with the affections and lusts thereof.*

This whole place, concerning works, sheweth, that the true believers are no hypocrites. Therefore, let no man deceive himself; for whosoever, saith he, pertain unto Christ, have crucified the flesh, with all the vices and lusts thereof. For the saints, inasmuch as they have not yet utterly put off the corrupt and sinful flesh, are inclined to sin, and do neither fear nor love God so perfectly as they ought to do; also, they be provoked to anger, to envy, to impatience, to unclean lusts, and such-like motions, which notwithstanding they accomplish not; for (as Paul here saith) they crucify the flesh, with all the affections and lusts thereof; which thing they do, not only when they repress the wantonness of the flesh with fasting and other exercises, but also (as Paul said before) when they walk according to the spirit; that is, when they, being admonished by the threatenings of God, whereby he sheweth that he will severely punish sin, are afraid to commit sin; also when they, being armed with the word of God, with faith, and with prayer, do not obey the lusts of the flesh.

When they resist the flesh after this manner, they nail it to the cross with the lusts and desires thereof: so that, although the flesh be yet alive, yet can it not perform that which it would do, forasmuch as it is bound both hand and foot, and fast nailed to the cross. The faithful, then, so long as they live here, do crucify the flesh, that is to say, they feel the lusts thereof, but they obey them not. For they being furnished with the armour of God, that is, with faith, hope, and the sword of the spirit, do resist the flesh, and with these spiritual nails they fasten the same unto the cross, so that it is constrained to be subject to the spirit. Afterwards, when they die, they put it off wholly: and when they shall rise again from death to life, they shall have a pure and uncorrupt flesh, without all affections and lusts.

VERSE 25. *If we live in the spirit, let us also walk in the spirit.*

The apostle reckoned before, amongst the works of the flesh, heresy and envy, and pronounced sentence against those which are envious, and which are authors of sects, that they should not inherit the kingdom of God; and now, as if he had forgotten that which he said a little before, he again reproveth those which provoke and envy one another.—Why doth he so? Was it not sufficient to have done it once? Indeed, he doth it of purpose; for he taketh occasion here to inveigh against that execrable vice of vain-glory, which was the cause of the troubles that were in all the churches of Galatia, and hath been always most pernicious and hurtful to the whole church of Christ. Therefore, in his epistle to Titus, he would not that a proud man should be ordained a bishop; for pride (as Augustine truly saith) is the mother of all heresies, or rather the headspring of all sin and confusion; which things all histories, as well holy as profane, do witness.

Now, vain-glory or arrogancy hath always been a common poison in the world, which the very heathen poets and historiographers have always vehemently reproved. There is no village wherein there is not some one or other to be found, that would be counted wiser, and be more esteemed than all the rest; but they are chiefly infected with this disease, which stand upon their reputation for learning and wisdom. In this case, no man will yield to another, according to this saying, "Ye shall not lightly find a man that will yield unto others the praise of wit and skill; for it is a goodly thing to see men point at one, and say, this is he."—But it is not so hurtful in private persons, no, nor in any kind of magistrate, as it is in them that have any charge in the church; albeit in civil government (especially if it be in great personages) it is not only a cause of troubles and ruins of commonweals, but also of the troubles and alterations of kingdoms and empires; which thing the histories both of the scripture and profane writers do witness.

But when this poison creepeth into the church, or spiritual kingdom, it cannot be expressed how hurtful it is; for there is no contention as touching learning, wit, beauty, riches, kingdoms, empires, and such-like; but as touching salvation, or damnation; eternal life, or eternal death. Therefore, Paul earnestly exhorteth the ministers of the word to fly this vice, saying: "if we live in the spirit," etc. As if he should say: If it be true that we live by the spirit, let us also proceed and walk in the spirit. For where the spirit is, it reneweth men, and worketh

EPISTLE TO THE GALATIANS

in them new motions: that is to say, whereas they were before vain-glorious, wrathful, and envious, it maketh them now humble, gentle, and patient. Such men seek not their own glory, but the glory of God; they do not provoke one another, or envy one another, but give place one to another, and in giving honour prevent one another. Contrariwise, they that be desirous of glory, and envy one another, may boast that they have the spirit and live after the spirit; but they deceive themselves: they follow the flesh and do the works thereof, and they have their judgment already, that they shall not inherit the kingdom of God.

Now, as nothing is more dangerous to the church than this execrable vice, so is there nothing more common; for when God sendeth forth labourers into his harvest, by-and-by Satan raiseth up his ministers also, who will in no wise be counted inferior to those that are rightly called. Here straightway riseth dissension. The wicked will not yield one hair's breadth to the godly; for they dream that they far pass them in wit, in learning, in godliness, in spirit, and other virtues. Much less ought the godly to yield to the wicked, lest the doctrine of faith come in danger. Moreover, such is the nature of the ministers of Satan, that they can make a goodly shew, that they are very charitable, humble, lovers of concord, and are endued with other fruits of the spirit; also, they protest that they seek nothing else but the glory of God and the salvation of men's souls; and yet are they full of vain-glory, doing all things for none other end but to get praise and estimation among men. To be short, they think that gain is godliness (1 Tim. vi, 5), and that the ministry of the word is delivered unto them that they may get fame and estimation thereby; wherefore they cannot but be authors of dissensions and sects.

Forasmuch, then, as the vain-glory of the false apostles was the cause that the churches of Galatia were troubled and forsook Paul, therefore in this chapter specially his purpose was to suppress that execrable vice; yea, this mischief gave the apostle occasion to write this whole epistle. And if he had not so done, all his travail bestowed in preaching of the gospel among the Galatians had been spent in vain. For in his absence the false apostles, which were men in outward shew of great authority, reigned in Galatia; who, besides that they would seem to seek the glory of Christ and the salvation of the Galatians, pretended also that they had been conversant with the apostles, and that they followed their footsteps, saying, that Paul had not seen Christ in the flesh, nor had been conversant with the rest of the apostles, and therefore they made no account of him, but rejected his doctrine, and boasted their own to be true and sincere. Thus they troubled the Galatians, and raised sects among them, so that they provoked and envied one another; which was a sure token that neither the teachers nor hearers lived and walked after the spirit, but followed the flesh and fulfilled the works thereof; and so, consequently, lost the true doctrine, faith, Christ, and all the gifts of the Holy Ghost, and were now become worse than the heathen.

Notwithstanding he doth not only inveigh against the false apostles, which in his time troubled the churches of Galatia, but also he foresaw in spirit, that there should be an infinite number of such, even to the world's end, which being infected with this pernicious vice, should thrust themselves into the church, boasting of the spirit and heavenly doctrine, and under this pretence should quite overthrow the true doctrine and faith. Many such have we also seen in these our days, who have thrust themselves into the kingdom of the spirit, that is to say, into the ministry of the word; and by this hypocrisy they have purchased unto themselves fame and estimation, that they were great doctors and pillars of the gospel, and such as lived in the spirit, and walked according to the same. But, because their glory consisted in men's mouths, and not in God, therefore it could not be firm and stable; but, according to Paul's prophecy, it turned to their own confusion, and their end was destruction. For "the wicked shall not stand in judgment, but shall be taken away like chaff, and scattered abroad with the wind" (Psalm i, 4).

The same judgment remaineth for all such as in preaching the gospel seek their own profit, and not the glory of Jesus Christ. For the gospel is not delivered unto us that we should thereby seek our own praise and glory, or that the people should honour and magnify us which are the ministers thereof; but to the end that the benefit and glory of Christ might be preached and published, and that the Father might be glorified in his mercy offered unto us in Christ his Son, whom he delivered for us all, and with him hath given us all things. Wherefore the gospel is a doctrine wherein we ought to seek nothing less than our own glory. It setteth forth unto us heavenly and eternal things, which are not our own, which we have neither done nor deserved; but it offereth the same unto us, I say, which are unworthy, and that through the mere goodness and grace of God. Why should we then seek praise and glory thereby? He, therefore, that seeketh his own glory in the gospel, speaketh of himself; and he that speaketh of himself is a liar, and there is unrighteousness in him. Contrariwise, he that seeketh the glory of him that sent him, is true, and there is no unrighteousness in him (John vii).

Paul therefore giveth earnest charge to all the ministers of the word, saying, "if we live in the spirit, let us walk in the spirit," that is to say, let us abide in the doctrine of truth which hath been taught unto us, in brotherly love and spiritual concord; let us preach Christ and the glory of God in simplicity of heart; and let us confess that we have received all things of him; let us not think more of ourselves than of others; let us raise up no sects. For this is not to walk rightly, but rather to range out of the way, and to set up a new and a perverse way of walking.

Hereby we may understand that God, of his special grace, maketh the teachers of the gospel subject to the cross and to all kinds of afflictions, for the salvation of themselves and of the people; for otherwise they could by no means repress and beat down this beast which is called vain-glory. For if no persecution, no cross or reproach followed the doctrine of the gospel, but only praise, reputation, and glory amongst men, then would all the professors thereof be infected and perish through the poison of vain-glory. Jerome saith, that he had seen many which could suffer great inconveniences in their body and goods, but none that could despise their own praises; for it is almost impossible for a man not to be puffed up, when he heareth any thing spoken in the praise of his own virtues. Paul, notwithstanding that he had the spirit of Christ, saith, that there was given unto him the messenger of Satan to buffet him, because he should not be exalted out of measure, through the greatness of his revelations. Therefore Augustine saith very well, "if a minister of the word be praised, he is in danger: if a brother despise or dispraise him, he is also in danger. He that heareth a preacher of the word, ought to reverence him for the word's sake; but if he be proud thereof, he is in danger. Contrariwise, if he be despised, he is out of danger; but so is not he which despised him."

Wherefore, we must honour our great benefit, that is, of the preaching of the word and receiving of the sacraments, (Rom. xiv, 16). We must also reverence one another, according to that saying, "in giving honour one to another," etc. (Rom. xii, 10). But wheresoever this is done, by-and-by the flesh is tickled with vain-glory and waxeth proud; for there is none (no, not among the godly) which would not rather be praised than dispraised, except perhaps some will be so well established in this behalf, that he will be moved neither with praises nor reproaches; as that woman said of David (2 Sam. xiv), "My lord the king is like an angel of God, which will neither be moved with blessing nor cursing." Likewise Paul saith, "by honour and dishonour, by evil report and good report," etc. (2 Cor. vi, 8). Such men as be neither puffed up with praise, nor thrown down with dispraise, but endeavour simply to set forth the benefit and glory of Christ, and to seek the salvation of souls, do walk orderly. Contrariwise, they which wax proud in hearing of their own praises, not seeking the glory of Christ but their own, also they which being moved with reproaches and slanders, do forsake the ministry of the word, walk not orderly.

Wherefore let every one see that he walk orderly, and specially such as boast of the spirit. If thou be praised, know that it is not thou that is praised, but Christ, to whom all praise is due. For in that thou teachest the word purely, and livest godly, these are not thine own gifts, but the gifts of God; therefore thou art not praised, but God in thee. When thou dost acknowledge this, thou wilt walk orderly, and not be puffed up with vain-glory, ("for what hast thou that thou hast not received?" 1 Cor. iv, 7), but wilt confess that thou hast received the same of God, and wilt not be moved with injuries, reproaches, or persecution, to forsake thy calling.

God, therefore, of his special grace at this day covereth our glory with infamy, reproach, mortal hatred, cruel persecution, railing and cursing of the whole world: also with the contempt and ingratitude even of those among whom we live, as well the common sort, as also the citizens, gentlemen, and noblemen, (whose enmity, hatred and persecution against the gospel, like as it is privy and inward, so it is more dangerous than the cruel and outrageous dealings of our open enemies,) that we should not wax proud of the gifts of God in us. This mill-stone must be hanged about our neck, that we be not infected with that pestilent poison of vain-glory. Some there be of our side, which love and reverence us for the ministry of the word; but where there is one that reverenceth us, there be on the other side a hundred that hate and persecute us. These spiteful dealings, therefore, and these persecutions of our enemies, this great contempt and ingratitude, this cruel and privy hatred of them among whom we live, are such pleasant sights, and make us so merry, that we easily forget vain-glory.

Wherefore, rejoicing in the Lord who is our glory, we remain in order. Those gifts which we have, we acknowledge to be the gifts of God, and not our own, given for the edifying of

EPISTLE TO THE GALATIANS

the body of Christ, (Eph. iv, 12) therefore we be not proud of them. For we know that more is required of them to whom much is committed, than of them which have received but little. Moreover, we know that there is no respect of persons before God, (Acts x, 34). Therefore, a poor artificer, faithfully using the gift which God hath given him, pleaseth God no less than a preacher of the word; for he serveth God in the same faith, and with the same spirit. Wherefore we ought no less to regard the meanest Christians, than they regard us. And by this means shall we continue free from the poison of vain-glory, and walk in the spirit.

Contrariwise, the fantastical spirits, which seek their own glory, the favour of men, the peace of the world, the ease of the flesh, and not the glory of Christ, nor yet the health of men's souls, (although they protest that they seek nothing else), cannot choose but discover themselves in commending their own doctrine and industry, and dispraising other men's, and all to get them a name and praise. These vain-glorious spirits do not rejoice and glory in the Lord; but then do they glory, then are they stout and hardy, when they are magnified of the people, whose hearts they win by wonderful sleights and subtleties; for in their words, gestures, and writings, they can counterfeit and dissemble all things. But when they are not praised and commended of the people, then be they the most fearful men in the world; for they hate and shun the cross of Christ and persecution. On the contrary, when they are praised and magnified, (as I said,) none are so stout, no Hector or Achilles so bold and hardy as they.

Such a sly and crafty beast, therefore, is flesh, that for no other cause it forsaketh his function, corrupteth true doctrine, and breaketh the concord of the church, than only upon this cursed vain-glory. Therefore it is not without cause that Paul so sharply inveigheth against it, both here and in other places, as before in the fourth chapter, "they are (saith he) jealous over you amiss; yea, they would exclude you from me, that ye should altogether love them:" that is to say, they would discredit me, that they themselves might be famous. They seek not Christ's glory and your salvation, but their own glory, my reproach, and your bondage.

VERSE 26. *Let us not be desirous of vain-glory.*

Which is to glory, not in God (as I have said) but in lies, in the opinion, liking and estimation of the people. Here is no right foundation of true glory, but a false foundation, and therefore impossible long to stand. He that praiseth a man as he is a man, is a liar: for there is nothing praiseworthy in him, but all things are worthy of condemnation. Therefore, as touching our person, this is our glory, that all men have sinned, and are guilty of everlasting death before God. But the case is otherwise, when our ministry is praised. Wherefore we must not only wish, but also to the utmost of our power endeavour, that men may magnify it, and have it in due reverence; for this shall turn to their salvation. Paul warneth the Romans that they offend no man, to the end (saith he) "that our commodity be not evil spoken of," (Rom. xiv, 16). And in another place "that our ministry be not reprehended," (2 Cor. vi, 3). Therefore, when our ministry is praised, we be not praised for our own person's sake, but (as the Psalm saith) we are praised of God, and in his holy name.

VERSE 26. *Provoking one another, and envying one another.*

Here he describeth the effect and fruit of vain-glory. He that teacheth any error, or is an author of any new doctrine, cannot but provoke others; and when they do not approve and receive his doctrine, by-and-by he beginneth to hate them most bitterly. We see at this day with what deadly hatred the sectaries are inflamed against us, because we will not give place to them, and approve their errors. We did not first provoke them, nor spread abroad any wicked opinion in the world; but, rebuking certain abuses in the church, and faithfully teaching the article of justification, have walked in good order. But they, forsaking this article, have taught many things contrary to the word of God. Here, because we would not lose the truth of the gospel, we have set ourselves against them, and have condemned their errors; which thing, because they could not abide, they did not only provoke us first without cause, but also do still spitefully hate us, and that upon no other occasion but only upon vain-glory; for they would gladly deface us, that they alone might rule and reign; for they imagine that it is a great glory to profess the gospel, whereas, indeed, there is no greater ignominy in the sight of the world.

CHAPTER VI.

VERSE 1. *Brethren, if a man be overtaken with any fault, ye which are spiritual restore such a one with the spirit of meekness.*

He that diligently weigheth the words of the apostle, may plainly perceive that he speaketh not of errors and offences against doctrine, but of far lesser sins, into the which a man falleth not wilfully, and of set purpose, but of infirmity; and hereof it cometh that he useth so gentle and fatherly words, not calling it error or sin, but a fault. Again, to the intent to diminish, and as it were to excuse the sin, and to remove the whole fault from man, he addeth, "If any man be overtaken," that is to say, be beguiled of the devil, or of the flesh. Yea, and this term or name of man helpeth something also to diminish and qualify the matter. As if he should say, What is so proper unto man as to fall, to be deceived, and to err? So saith Moses, in Lev. vi, 3, "They are wont to sin like men." Wherefore this is a sentence full of heavenly comfort, which once in a terrible conflict delivered me from death. Forasmuch, then, as the saints in this life do not only live in the flesh, but now and then also, through the enticement of the devil, fulfil the lusts of the flesh, that is to say, fall into impatiency, envy, wrath, error, doubting, distrust, and such-like, (for Satan always assaileth both, that is, as well the purity of doctrine, which he laboureth to take away by sects and dissensions, as also the soundness of life, which he corrupteth with daily offences;) therefore Paul teacheth how such men that are fallen should be dealt withal; namely, that they which are strong, should raise up and restore them again with the spirit of meekness.

These things it behoveth them specially to know, which are in the ministry of the word, lest, while they go about to touch all things to the quick, they forget the fatherly and motherly affection which Paul here requireth of those that have the charge of souls. And of this precept he hath set forth an example, (2 Cor. ii,) where he saith that it was sufficient that he which was excommunicate was rebuked of many, and that they ought now to forgive him and comfort him, lest he should be swallowed up with overmuch sorrow. Wherefore, I beseech you, (saith he,) use charity towards him. Therefore the pastors and ministers must indeed sharply rebuke those which are fallen, but when they see that they are sorrowful for their offences, then let them begin to raise them up again, to comfort them, and to diminish and qualify their faults as much as they can; but yet through mercy only, which they must set against sin, lest they that be fallen be swallowed up with overmuch heaviness. As the Holy Ghost is precise in maintaining and defending the doctrine of faith, so is he mild and pitiful in forbearing and qualifying men's sins, if they which have committed them be sorrowful for the same.

But as for the Pope's synagogue, like as in all other matters it hath both taught and done clean contrary to the commandment and example of Paul, even so hath it done in this thing also. The Pope, with all his bishops, have been very tyrants and butchers of men's consciences; for they have burdened them from time to time with new traditions, and for every light matter have vexed them with their excommunications; and, that they might the more easily obey their vain terrors, they annexed thereunto these sentences of Pope Gregory, "It is the part and property of good minds to be afraid of a fault where no fault is." And again, "Our censures must be feared, yea, though they be unjust and wrongful." By these sayings (which were brought into the church by the devil) they established their excommunication, and this majesty of the papacy, which is so terrible to the whole world. There is no need of such humility and goodness of minds, to be afraid of a fault where none is. O, thou Romish Satan, who gave thee this power to terrify and condemn men's consciences, that were terrified enough before, with thy unjust and wrongful sentences? Thou oughtest rather to have raised them up, to have delivered them from false fears, and to have brought them from lies and errors to the truth. This thou omittest, and according to thy title and name, to wit, the man of sin and child of perdition, thou imaginest a fault where no fault is. This is, indeed, the craft and deceit of Antichrist, whereby he hath most mightily established his excommunication and tyranny. For whosoever despised his unjust sentences was counted very obstinate and wicked; as some princes did, howbeit against their consciences; for in those times of darkness, they did not understand that the Pope's curses were vain.

Let them, therefore, to whom the charge of men's consciences is committed, learn by this commandment of Paul, how they ought to handle those that have offended. Brethren, (saith he) if any man be overtaken with sin, do not trouble him or make him more sorrowful: be not bitter unto him; do not reject or condemn him, but amend him and raise him up again; and by the spirit of lenity and mildness restore that which in his is decayed by the deceit of the devil, or by the weakness of the flesh. For the kingdom whereunto ye are called, is a kingdom not of

EPISTLE TO THE GALATIANS

terror or of heaviness, but of boldness, joy, and gladness. Therefore, if ye see any brother cast down and afflicted by occasion of sin which he hath committed, run unto him, and reaching out your hand, raise him up again, comfort him with sweet words, and embrace him with motherly arms. As for those that be hard-hearted and obstinate, which without fear continue careless in their sins, rebuke them sharply. But on the other side (as I said) they that be overtaken with any sin, and are heavy and sorrowful for their fault which they have committed, must be raised up and admonished by you that are spiritual, and that in the spirit of meekness, and not in the zeal of severe justice, as some have done, who, when they should have refreshed thirsty consciences with some sweet consolation, gave them gall and vinegar to drink, as the Jews did unto Christ hanging on the cross. Ezekiel saith of the shepherds of Israel, that they ruled the flock of God with cruelty and rigour: but a brother ought to comfort his brother that is fallen, with a loving and meek spirit. Again, let him that is fallen hear the word of him that raiseth him up, and believe it. For God would not have those that are bruised to be cast away, but to be raised up, as the Psalm saith. For God hath bestowed more upon them than we have done, that is to say, the life and blood of his own Son. Wherefore, we ought also to receive, to aid and to comfort such, with all mildness and gentleness.

VERSE 1. *Considering thyself, lest thou also be tempted.*

This is a very necessary admonition to beat down the sharp dealings of such pastors as shew no pity in raising up and restoring again them which are fallen. "There is no sin (saith Augustine) which any man hath done, but another man may do the same." We stand on a slippery ground; therefore, if we wax proud and leave off our duty, there is nothing so easy unto us as to fall. It was well said, therefore, of one in the book called *The Lives of the Fathers*, when it was told him that one of his brethren was fallen into whoredom, "He fell yesterday, (saith he) and I may fall today." Paul, therefore, addeth this earnest admonition, that the pastors should not be rigorous and unmerciful towards the offenders, or measure their own holiness by other men's sins; but that they should bear a motherly affection towards them, and think thus with themselves: This man is fallen; it may be that I also shall fall more dangerously and more shamefully than he did. And if they which be so ready to judge and condemn others, would well consider their own sin, they should find the sins of others which are fallen to be but motes, and their own sins to be great beams, (Matt. vii, 3.)

"Let him, therefore, that standeth, take heed lest he fall," (1 Cor. x, 12.) If David, which was so holy a man, full of faith and the Spirit of God, which had such notable promises of God, which also did so many and great things for the Lord, did fall so grievously, and being now stricken in years, was overthrown with youthful lusts, after so many and divers temptations, wherewith God had exercised him, why should we presume of our own constancy? And God, by such examples, doth shew unto lus, first, our own weakness, that we should not wax proud, but stand in fear; then he sheweth unto us his judgments, that he can bear nothing less than pride, either against himself, or against our brethren. Paul, therefore, saith, not without cause "considering thyself, lest thou also be tempted." They that be exercised with temptations, do know how necessary this commandment .is On the other side, they which be not tried therewith, do not understand Paul, and therefore are not touched with any pity towards them that are fallen; as was to be seen in popery, where nothing else reigned but tyranny and cruelty.

VERSE 2. *Bear ye one anothers' burdens, and so fulfil the law of Christ.*

This is a gentle commandment, to the which he joineth a great commendation. The law of Christ is the law of love. Christ, after he had redeemed us, renewed us, and made us his church, gave us no other law but the law of mutual love: "A new commandment give I to you, that ye love together," etc. (John xiii, 34.) And to love is not (as the popish sophisters dream) to wish well one to another, but one to bear another's burden, that is, to bear those things which be grievous unto thee, and which thou wouldst not willingly bear. Therefore, Christians must have strong shoulders and mighty bones, that they may bear flesh, that is, the weakness of their brethren; for Paul saith that they have burdens and troubles. Love, therefore, is mild, courteous, patient, not in receiving, but in giving; for it is constrained to wink at many things, and to bear them, (1 Cor. xiii, 4.) Faithful teachers do see in the church many errors and offences which they are compelled to bear. In the common weal, subjects are never so obedient to the laws of the magistrates as they should be. Therefore, unless the magistrate can wink and dissemble in time and place, he shall never be meet to rule the commonwealth. In household affairs there be many things done which displease the master of the house. But if we can bear and wink at our own vices and offences which we daily commit, let us also bear other men's faults, according to this saying, "bear ye one another's burdens," etc. Again, "thou shalt love thy neighbour as thyself," (Rom. xiii, 9.)

Seeing, then, there be vices in every state of life, and in all men, therefore Paul setteth forth the law of Christ unto the faithful, whereby he exhorteth them to bear one another's burdens. They which do not so, do plainly witness that they understand not one jot of the law of Christ, which is the law of love; which, as Paul saith (1 Cor. xiii,) believeth all things, hopeth all things, and beareth all the burdens of the brethren; yet always holding notwithstanding the first commandment, wherein they that offend do not transgress the law of Christ, that is to say, the law of charity; they do not hurt or offend their neighbour, but Christ and his kingdom, which he hath purchased with his own blood. This kingdom is not maintained by the law of charity, but by the word of God, by faith, and by the Holy Ghost. This commandment, then, of bearing one another's burden, belongeth not to them which deny Christ, and not only do not acknowledge their sin, but also defend it; neither doth it belong unto those which continue still in their sins, (who also do partly deny Christ;) but such must be forsaken, lest we become partakers of their evil works, (1 Tim. vi, 11.) On the contrary, they which willingly hear the word of God and believe, and yet notwithstanding against their will do fall into sin, and after they be admonished, do not only receive such admonition gladly, but also detest their sin and endeavour to amend; these, I say, are they which be overtaken with sin, and have the burdens that Paul commandeth us to bear. In this case, let us not be rigorous and merciless; but after the example of Christ, who beareth and forbeareth such, let us bear and forbear them also; for if he punish not such, (which thing, notwithstanding, he might justly do,) much less ought we so to do.

VERSE 3. *For if any man think himself to be somewhat, when indeed he is nothing, he deceiveth himself.*

Here again he reprehendeth the authors of sects, and painteth them out in their right colours, to wit, that they be hardhearted, merciless, and without compassion; such as despise the weak, and will not vouchsafe to bear their burdens, but require all things straitly and precisely, (like wayward husbands and severe schoolmasters,) whom nothing can please but what they themselves do, who also will be always thy bitter enemies, unless thou command whatsoever they say or do, and in all things frame thyself according to their appetite. Of all men, therefore, they are the proudest, and dare take upon them all things. And this is that Paul saith here, they think themselves to be somewhat; that is to say, that they have the Holy Ghost, that they understand all the mysteries of the scriptures, that they cannot err, etc.

Wherefore Paul addeth very well, that they are nothing; but that they deceive themselves with the foolish persuasions of their own wisdom and holiness. They understand nothing, therefore, either of Christ, or of the law of Christ; for if they did, they would say, Brother, thou art infected with such a vice, and I am infected with another: God hath forgiven me ten thousand talents, and I will forgive thee a hundred pence, (Matt. xviii, 24, 28.) But when they will require all things so exactly, and with such perfection, and will in no wise bear the burdens of the weak, they offend many with this their sharpness and severity, who begin to despise, hate and shun them, and seek no comfort or counsel at their hands, nor regard what or how they teach. Whereas, contrariwise, pastors ought so to behave themselves towards those over whom they have taken charge, that they might love and reverence them, not for their person, but for their office and christian virtues, which especially ought to shine in them.

Paul, therefore, in this place hath rightly pointed out such severe and merciless saints when he saith, "They think themselves to be somewhat," that is to say, being puffed up with their own foolish opinions and vain dreams, they have a marvellous persuasion of their own knowledge and holiness, and yet in very deed they are nothing, and do but deceive themselves. For it is a manifest beguiling when a man persuadeth himself that he is somewhat, when indeed he is nothing. Such men are well described in the third of the Apocalypse in these words, "Thou sayest, I am rich and increased with goods, and have need of nothing, and knowest not that thou art wretched and miserable, and poor, and blind, and naked."

> VERSE 4. *But let every man try his own work, and then he shall have rejoicing in himself only, and not in another.*

He goeth forward in painting out those proud and vain-glorious fellows; for the desire of vain-glory is an odious and cursed vice; it is the occasion of all evils, and troubleth both commonweals and consciences; and, specially, in spiritual matters it is such an evil as is incurable. And albeit that this place may be understood of the works of this life, or civil conversation, yet principally the apostle speaketh of the work of the ministry, and inveigheth against those vain-glorious heads, which with their fantastical opinions do trouble well-instructed consciences.

And this is the property of those which are infected with this poison of vain-glory, that they have no regard whether their works, that is to say, their ministry, be pure, simple, and faithful, or not; but this they only seek that they may have the praise of the people. So the false apostles, when they saw that Paul preached the gospel purely to the Galatians, and that they could not bring any better doctrine, they began to find fault at those things which he had godly and faithfully taught, and to prefer their own doctrine before the doctrine of Paul, and by this subtlety they won the favour of the Galatians, and brought Paul into hatred among them. Therefore the proud and vainglorious do join these three vices together. First, they are greedy of glory; secondly, they are marvellous witty and wily in finding fault with other men's doings and sayings, thereby to purchase the love, the well-liking, and praise of the people; and, thirdly, when they have once gotten a name, (though it be by other men's travail,) they become so stout and full of stomach, that they dare venture upon all things. Therefore they are pernicious and pestilent fellows, whom I hate even with my very heart; for they seek their own, and not that which is of Jesus Christ, etc. (Phil. ii, 21.)

Against such Paul speaketh here; as if he should say: Such vain-glorious spirits do their work, that is to say, they teach the gospel, to this end that they may win praise and estimation among men, that is, that they may be counted excellent doctors, with whom Paul and others might not be compared. And when they have gotten this estimation, then begin they to reprehend the sayings and doings of other men, and highly commend their own; and by this subtlety they bewitch the minds of the people, who, because they have itching ears, are not only delighted with new opinions, but also rejoice to see those teachers which they had afore, to be abased and defaced by these new upstarts and glorious heads, and all because they are come to a fulness and loathing of the word.

Thus it ought not to be, saith he, but let every man be faithful in his office. Let him not seek his own glory, nor depend upon the praise and commendation of the people, but let his only care be to do his work truly, that is, let him teach the gospel purely; and if his work be sincere and sound, let him assure himself that he shall lack no praise either before God or among the godly. In the mean space, if he be not commended of the unthankful world, let this nothing move him; for he knoweth that the end of his ministry is, not that he, but that Christ should be glorified thereby. Wherefore, being furnished with the armour of righteousness on the right hand and on the left, let him say, I began not to teach the gospel to the end that the world should magnify me, and therefore I will not shrink from that which I have begun, if the world hate me, slander, or persecute me. He that is such a one, teacheth the word and attendeth upon his office faithfully, without any worldly respect, that is, without regard of glory or gain, without the strength, wisdom, or authority of any man. He leaneth not to the praise of other men, for he hath it in himself.

Wherefore, he that truly and faithfully executeth his office, careth not what the world speak of him: he careth not whether the world praise or dispraise him, but he hath praise in himself, which is the testimony of his conscience, and praise or glory in God. He may therefore say with Paul, This is our rejoicing, this is our praise and glory, even the testimony of our conscience, that in simplicity and sincerity before God, and not in fleshly wisdom, but in the grace of God, we have had our conversation in the world. This glory is uncorrupt and steadfast; for it dependeth not on other men's judgments, but of our own conscience, which beareth us witness that we have taught the word purely, ministered the sacraments rightly, and have done all things well, and therefore it cannot be defaced or taken from us.

The other glory which these proud spirits do seek, is uncertain and most perilous, for that they have it not in themselves, but it consisteth in the mouth and opinion of the people; therefore can they not have the testimony of their own conscience, that they have done all things with simplicity and sincerity, for the advancing of the glory of God only, and the salvation of souls. For this is it which they seek, that they may be counted famous through the work and labour of their preaching, and be praised of men. They have therefore a glory, a trust, and a testimony, but before men, not in themselves, nor before God. The godly do not desire glory after this manner. If Paul had had his praise before men, and not in himself, he should have been compelled to despair when he saw many cities, countries, and all Asia fall from him; when he saw so many offences and slanders, and so many heresies to follow his preaching. Christ, when he was alone, that is, when he was not only sought for by the Jews to be put to death, but also was forsaken of his disciples, was not yet alone, but the Father was with him, for he had glory and rejoicing in himself, (John xvi, 32.)

So at this day, if our trust, our glory and rejoicing did depend upon the judgment and favour of men, we should die with very anguish and sorrow of heart. For so far off is it that the Papists, sectaries, and the whole world do judge us worthy of any reverence or praise, that they hate and persecute us most bitterly; yea, they would gladly overthrow our ministry, and root out our doctrine for ever. We have therefore nothing before men but reproach; but we rejoice and we glory in the Lord, and therefore we attend upon our office cheerfully and faithfully, which we know is acceptable to him. Thus doing, we care not whether our work do please or displease the devil, whether the world love us, or hate us. For we, knowing our work to be well done, and having a good conscience before God, go forward by honour and dishonour, by evil report and good report, etc. (2 Cor. vi, 8.) This, saith Paul, is to have rejoicing or glory in thyself.

And this admonition is very necessary against that execrable vice of vain-glory. The gospel is a doctrine, which both of itself, and also by the malice of the devil, bringeth with it the cross and persecution. Therefore, Paul is wont to call it the word of the cross and of offence. It hath not always steadfast and constant disciples. Many there be that to-day make profession thereof and embrace it, which to-morrow, being offended with the cross, will fall from it, and deny it. They, therefore, that teach the gospel, to the end that they may obtain the favour and praise of men, must needs perish, and their glory be turned to shame, when the people cease to reverence and magnify them. Wherefore, let all pastors and ministers of the word learn to have glory and rejoicing in themselves, and not in the mouth of other men. If there be any that praise them, as the godly are wont to do, ("by evil report and good report," saith Paul,) yet let them receive this glory but as a shadow of true glory; and let them think the substance of glory to be indeed the testimony of their own conscience. He that doth so, proveth his own work, that is, he regardeth not his own glory, but his only care is to do his office faithfully; that is to say, to teach the gospel purely, and to shew the true use of the sacraments. When he thus proveth his own work, he hath glory and rejoicing in himself, which no man can take from him; for he hath it surely planted and grounded in his own heart, and not in other men's mouths, whom Satan can very easily turn away, and can make that mouth now full of cursing, which a little before was full of blessing.

Therefore, saith Paul, if ye be desirous of vain-glory, seek it where it should be sought, not in the mouth of other men, but in your own heart; which ye then do, when ye execute your office truly and faithfully. So shall it come to pass, that besides the glory which ye have in yourselves, ye shall have praise and commendation also before men. But if ye glory in other men, and not in yourselves, that shame and confusion which ye have in yourselves, shall not be without reproach and confusion also before men. This have we seen in certain fantastical spirits in these our days, which proved not their work; that is, they did not seek only to preach the gospel purely and simply, but misused it, to gain praise among men, contrary to the second commandment. Therefore, after their inward confusion, there followed also an outward confusion and shame among men, according to that saying, "The Lord will not hold him guiltless that taketh his name in vain," (Exodus xx, 7.) And again, "They which despise me, shall be despised," (1 Sam. ii, 30.)

Contrariwise, if we seek first the glory of God, by the ministry of the word, then surely our glory will follow, according to that saying, "Him that honoureth me, I will glorify." To conclude, let every man prove his work; that is, let him do his endeavour that his ministry may be faithful; for this above all things is required in the ministers of the word, (1 Cor. iv.) As if he should say, let every man endeavour purely and faithfully to teach the word, and let him have an eye to nothing else but the glory of God, and the salvation of souls; then shall his work be faithful and sound; then shall he have glory and rejoicing in his own conscience, so that he may boldly say, this my doctrine and ministry pleaseth God. And this is, indeed, an excellent glory.

This sentence may also be well applied to those works which are done of the faithful in every state of life. As if a magistrate, a householder, a servant, a schoolmaster, a scholar, abide in his vocation, and do his duty therein faithfully, not troubling himself with those works which pertain not to his vocation, he may glory and rejoice in himself; for he may say, I have done the works of my vocation appointed unto me by God, with such faithfulness and diligence as I was able. Therefore I know that this work being done in faith and obedience to God, pleaseth God. If other speak evil of it, I pass little thereof. For there be always some which despise and slander the doctrine and life of the godly; but God hath threatened to destroy all lying lips and slanderous tongues. Therefore, whilst such men do greedily seek after vain-glory, and with lies and slanders go about to deface the godly, it happeneth to them as Paul saith, "Whose glory is their shame," (Phil. iii, 19.) And in another place, "Their foolishness shall be known to all men," (2 Tim. iii, 9.) By whom? Even by God the righteous judge, who as he will utter their false accusations and slanders, so will he reveal the righteousness of the godly like the noon-day, as it is said, Psalm xxxvii.

This clause, "in himself," (to touch this also by the way) must be so understood that God be not excluded: That is, that every man may know, in what godly state of life soever he be, that his work is a divine work; for it is a work of his vocation, having the commandment of God.

VERSE 5. *For every man shall bear his own burden.*

This is, as it were, the reason or confirmation of the former sentence, lest any man should lean to other men's judgment in praising and commending of him. As if he said: It is extreme madness for thee to seek glory in another, and not in thyself; for in the agony of death, and in the last judgment, it shall nothing profit thee that other men have praised thee; for other men shall not bear thy burden; but thou shalt stand before the judgment-seat of Christ, and shalt bear thy burden alone. There thy praisers shall nothing help thee. For when we die, these praises shall cease. And in that day, when the Lord shall judge the secrets of all hearts, the witness of thine own conscience shall stand either with thee or against thee, (Romans ii, 15.) Against thee, if thou glory in other men; with thee, if thou have it in thyself, that is to say, if thy conscience bear thee witness that thou hast done thy duty in the ministry of the word, or otherwise according to thy calling, sincerely and faithfully, having respect to the glory of God only, and the salvation of souls. And these words, "Every man shall bear his own judgment," are very vehement, and ought so to terrify us, that we should not be desirous of vain-glory.

And this, moreover, is to be noted, that we are not here in the matter of justification, where nothing availeth but mere grace and forgiveness of sins, which is received by faith alone; where all our works also, yea, even our best works, and such as are done according to God's calling, have need of forgiveness of sins; but this is another case. He treateth not here of the remission of sins, but compareth true works and hypocritical works together. These things, therefore, ought thus to be taken, that although the work or ministry of a godly pastor is not so perfect but that he have need of forgiveness of sins, yet in itself it is good and perfect, in comparison of the ministry of the vain-glorious man.

So our ministry is good and sound, because we seek thereby the glory of God, and the salvation of souls. But the ministry of the fantastical heads is not so, for they seek their own praise. Albeit, therefore, that no works can quiet the conscience before God; yet is it necessary that we should persuade ourselves that we have done our work uprightly, truly, and according to God's calling; that is, that we have not corrupted the word of God, but have taught it purely and faithfully. This testimony of conscience we have need of, that we have done our duty uprightly in our function and calling, and led our life accordingly. So far ought we then to glory, as touching our works, as we know them to be commanded of God, and that they please him; for every one in the last judgment shall bear his own burden, and therefore other men's praises shall there nothing help or profit him.

Hitherto he hath spoken against that most pestilent vice, vain-glory; for the suppresing whereof, no man is so strong, but that he hath need of continual prayer. For what man, almost even among the godly, is not delighted with his own praises? Only the Holy Ghost can preserve us, that we be not infected with this vice.

> VERSE 6. *Let him that is taught in the word, make him that teacheth him partaker of all his goods.*

Here he preacheth to the disciples or hearers of the word, commanding them to bestow all good things upon those which have taught and instructed them in the word. I have sometimes marvelled why the apostles commanded the churches so diligently to nourish their teachers. For, in popery, I saw that all men gave abundantly to the building and maintaining of goodly temples, to the increasing of the revenues and livings of those which were appointed to their idolatrous service. Hereof it came that the estimation and riches of the bishops and the rest of the clergy did so increase, that everywhere they had in possession the best and most fruitful grounds. Therefore thought I that Paul had commanded this in vain, seeing that all manner of good things were not only abundantly given to the clergy, but also they overflowed in wealth and riches. Wherefore, I thought that men ought rather to be exhorted to withhold their hands from giving, than encouraged to give any more; for I saw, that, by this excessive liberality of men, the covetousness of the clergy did increase. But now I know the cause why they had such abundance of good things heretofore, and now the pastors and ministers of the word do want.

Before time, when nothing else was taught but errors and wicked doctrine, they had such plenty of all things, that of Peter's patrimony, (which denied that he had either silver or gold) and of spiritual goods, (as they called them,) the Pope was become an emperor, the cardinals and bishops were made kings and princes of the world. But now, since the gospel hath been preached and published, the professors thereof be as rich as sometime Christ and his apostles were. We find, then, by experience, how well this commandment of nourishing and maintaining the pastors and ministers of God's word is observed, which Paul here and in other places so diligently repeateth and beateth into the heads of his hearers. There is now no city which is known to us, that nourisheth and maintaineth her pastors and preachers; but they are all entertained with these goods which were given, not unto Christ, to whom no man giveth any thing, (for when he was born he was laid in a manger instead of a bed, because there was no room for him in the inn, Luke ii, 7; afterwards, being conversant among men, he had not whereon to lay his head, Matt. viii, 20; and briefly, being spoiled of his garments and hanging nakel upon the cross between two thieves, he died most miserably, Matt. xxvii, 38,) but to the Pope, for the maintenance of his abominations, and because he, oppressing the gospel, taught the doctrines and traditions of men, and set up idolatry.

And as oft as I read the exhortations of Paul, whereby he persuadeth the churches that they should either nourish their pastors, or give somewhat to the relief of the poor saints in Jewry, I do greatly marvel and am ashamed that so great an apostle should be constrained to use so many words, for the obtaining of this benefit of the congregations. Writing to the Corinthians, he treateth of this matter in two whole chapters, (2 Cor. viii and ix.) I would be loth to defame Wittenberg, which indeed, is nothing to Corinth, as he defamed the Corinthians, in begging so carefully for the relief and succour of the poor. But this is the lot of the gospel when it is preached, that not only no man is willing to give any thing for the finding of ministers and maintaining of scholars, but men begin to spoil, to rob, and to steal, and with divers crafty means one to beguile another. To be brief, men seem suddenly to grow out of kind, and to be transformed into cruel beasts. Contrariwise, when the doctrine of devils was preached, then men were prodigal, and offered all things willingly to those that deceived them, (1 Tim. iv, 2.) The prophets do reprove the same sin in the Jews, which were loth to give any thing to the godly priests and Levites, but gave all things plentifully to the wicked.

Now, therefore, we begin to understand how necessary this commandment of Paul is, as touching the maintenance of the ministers of the church; for Satan can abide nothing less than the light of the gospel. Therefore, when he seeth that it beginneth to shine, then doth he rage, and goeth about with all main and might to quench it. And this he attempteth two manner of ways. First, by lying spirits and force of tyrants, and then by poverty and famine. But, because he could not hitherto oppress the gospel in this country (praised be God) by heretics and tyrants, therefore he attempteth to bring it to pass the other way, that is, by withdrawing the livings of the ministers of the word, to the end that they, being oppressed with poverty and necessity, should forsake the ministry, and so the miserable people, being destitute of the word of God, should become in time as savage as wild beasts. And Satan helpeth forward this horrible enormity by ungodly magistrates in the cities, and also by noblemen and gentlemen in the country, who take way the church goods, whereby the ministers of the gospel should live, and turn them to wicked uses. "These goods," saith the Prophet Micah (chap. i, 7,) "were gathered of the hire of a harlot, and therefore to a harlot's hire shall they return."

Moreover, Satan turneth men particularly also from the gospel, by overmuch fulness; for when the gospel is diligently and daily preached, many being glutted therewith, begin to loathe it, and by little and little become negligent and untoward to all godly exercises. Again, there is no man that will now bring up his children in good learning, and much less in the study of the holy scripture, but they employ them wholly to gainful arts or occupations. All these are Satan's practices, to no other end but that he may oppress the gospel in this our country without any devices of tyrants, or subtle devices of heretics.

It is not without cause, therefore, that Paul warneth the hearers of the gospel to make their pastors and teachers partakers with them in all good things. "If we (saith he to the Corinthians) have sown to you spiritual things, it is a great matter if we reap your worldly things?" (1 Cor. ix, 11.) The hearers, therefore, ought to minister carnal things to them of whom they received spiritual things. But both husbandmen, citizens and gentlemen do at this day abuse our doctrine, that under the colour thereof they may enrich themselves. Heretofore, when the Pope reigned, there was no man which paid not somewhat yearly to the priests for masses, dirges, trentals, and such trash. The begging friars had also their part. The merchandizes of Rome likewise, and daily offerings, carried away somewhat. From these, and from an infinite number of such exactions, our countrymen are now delivered by the gospel; but so far off is it that they are thankful to God for this liberty, that of prodigal givers they are now become stark thieves and robbers, and will not bestow one farthing upon the gospel or the ministers thereof, nor give any thing for the relief and succour of the poor saints; which is a certain token that they have lost both the word and faith, and that they have no spiritual goodness in them. For it is impossible that such as are godly indeed, should suffer their pastors to live in necessity and penury. But forasmuch as they laugh and rejoice when their pastors suffer any adversity, and withhold their living, or give it not with such faithfulness as they ought, it is a plain token that they are worse than the heathen.

But they shall feel, ere it be long, what calamities will follow this unthankfulness; for they shall lose both temporal and spiritual things. For this sin must needs be grievously punished; and certainly I think that the churches in Galatia, Corinth, and other places, were so troubled by the false apostles for no other cause, but for that they little regarded their true pastors and preachers. For it is good reason that he wich refuseth to give a penny to God, who offereth unto him all good things and life everlasting, should give a piece of gold to the devil, the author of all evils, and death everlasting. Whoso will not serve God in a little, and that to his own inestimable benefit, let him serve the devil in much, to his extreme and utter confusion. Now, therefore, since the light of the gospel beginneth to shine, we see what the devil is, and what the world is.

In that he saith, "in all his goods," it is not so to be taken that all men are bound to give all that they have to their ministers, but that they should maintain them liberally, and give them that whereby they may be well able to live.

VERSE 7. *Be not deceived, for God is not mocked.*

The apostle prosecuteth this place of the nourishing and maintaining of ministers so earnestly, that to his former reprehension and exhortation he addeth now also a threatening, saying, "God is not mocked." And here he toucheth to the quick the perverseness of our countrymen, which proudly despise our ministry. For they think it to be but a sport and a game; and therefore they go about (especially the gentlemen) to make their pastors subject unto them, like servants and slaves. And if we had not so godly a prince, and one that so loveth the truth, they had, ere this time, driven us out of the country. When the pastors ask their duty, or complain that they suffer penury, they cry out, "The priests be covetous; they would have plenty; no man is able to satisfy their insatiable covetousness: if they were true gospellers, they should have nothing of their own, but as poor men, ought to follow poor Christ, and to suffer all adversities," etc.

Paul horribly threateneth here such tyrants, and such mockers of God, who so carelessly and proudly do scorn the miserable preachers, and yet will seem to be gospellers, and not to be mockers of God, but to worship him very devoutly. "Be not deceived," saith he, "God is not mocked;" that is to say, he doth not suffer himself to be mocked in his ministers. For he saith, "He that despiseth you, despiseth me," (Luke x, 16.) Also he saith unto Samuel, "They have not cast thee away, but me," (1 Sam. viii, 7.) Therefore, O ye mockers, although God defer his punishment for a season, yet, when he seeth time, he will find you out, and will punish this contempt of his word and bitter hatred which ye bear against his ministers. Therefore ye deceive not God, but yourselves, and ye shall not laugh at God, but he will laugh at you, (Ps. ii.) But our proud gentlemen, citizens, and common people, are nothing at all moved with this dreadful threatening. Nevertheless they shall feel, when death approacheth, whether they have mocked themselves or us; nay rather not us, but God himself, as Paul saith here. In the meantime, because they proudly despise our admonitions with an intolerable pride, we speak these things to our comfort, to the end we may know that it is better to suffer wrong, than to do wrong; for patience is ever innocent and harmless, (Psalm xxxiv, 10.) Moreover, God will not suffer his ministers to starve for hunger, but even when the rich men suffer scarcity and hunger, he will feed them, and in the days of famine they shall have enough, (Psalm xxxvii, 19.)

VERSE 7. *For whatsoever a man soweth, that shall he reap.*

All these things tend to this purpose, that ministers should be nourished and maintained. For my part, I do not gladly interpret such sentences; for they seem to commend us, and so they do indeed. Moreover, if a man stand much in repeating such things to his hearers, it hath some shew of covetousness. Notwithstanding, men must be admonished hereof, that they may know that they ought to yield unto their pastors both reverence and a necessary living. Our Saviour Christ teacheth the same thing in the tenth of Luke. "Eating and drinking such things as they have; for the labourer is worthy of his reward." And Paul saith, in another place, "Do ye not know that they which sacrifice in the temple, live of the sacrifices; and that they which serve at the altar, are partakers of the altar? Even so hath the Lord ordained, that they which preach the gospel should live of the gospel," (1 Cor. ix, 13, 14.)

It is good that we also which are in the ministry should know these things, lest for our labour we might with evil conscience receive the stipend which is given unto us of the Pope's goods. And although such goods were heaped together by mere fraud and deceit; notwithstanding God spoiling the Egyptians, (Exod. iii, 22,) that is to say, the Papists, of their goods, turneth them here amongst us, to a good and holy use: not when noblemen and gentlemen spoil them and abuse them, but when they which set forth God's glory, and bring up youth virtuously, are maintained therewith. Let us know, then, that we may with good conscience (since God hath ordained and commanded that they which preach the gospel should live of the gospel) use those things which are given us of the church goods for the necessary sustentation of our life, to the end we may attend upon our office the better. Let no man therefore make any scruple hereof, as though it were not lawful for him to use such goods.

VERSE 8. *For he that soweth in the flesh, shall of the flesh reap corruption; but he that soweth in the spirit, shall of the spirit reap everlasting life.*

He addeth a similitude and an allegory. And this general sentence of sowing he applieth to the particular matter of nourishing and maintaining the ministers of the word, saying, "He that soweth in the spirit," that is to say, he that cherisheth the teachers of God's word, doth a spiritual work, and shall reap everlasting life. Here riseth a question, whether we deserve eternal life by good works? For so Paul seemeth to avouch in this place. As touching such sentences which speak of works and the reward of them, we have treated very largely before in the fifth chapter. And very necessary it is, after the example of Paul, to exhort the faithful to do good works, that is to say, to exercise their faith by good works; for if they follow not faith, it is a manifest token that their faith is no true faith. Therefore the apostle saith, "He that soweth in the flesh," (some understand it in his own flesh,) that is to say, he that giveth nothing to the ministers of God's word, but only feedeth and careth for himself, (which is the counsel of the flesh,) that man shall of the flesh reap corruption, not only in this present life, but also in the life to come. For the goods of the wicked shall waste away, and they themselves also at length shall shamefully perish. The apostle would fain stir up his hearers to be liberal and beneficial towards their pastors and preachers. But what a misery is it, that the perverseness and ingratitude of men should be so great, that the churches should need this admonition.

The Encratites abused this place, for the confirmation of their wicked opinion against marriage, expounding it after this manner: "He that soweth in the flesh, shall reap corruption, that is to say, he that marrieth a wife, shall be damned; *ergo*, a wife is a damnable thing, and marriage is evil, forasmuch as there is in it a sowing in the flesh. These beasts were so destitute of all judgment, that they perceived not whereabout the apostle went. I speak this to the end ye may see how easily the devil, by his ministers, can turn away the hearts of the simple from the truth. Germany shall shortly have an infinite number of such beasts, yea, and already hath very many; for, on the one side, it persecuteth and killeth the godly ministers; and on the other side it neglecteth and despiseth them, and suffereth them to live in great penury. Let us arm ourselves against these and such-like errors, and let us learn to know the true meaning of the scriptures. For Paul speaketh not here of matrimony, but of nourishing the ministers of the church, which every man, that is endued but with the common judgment of reason, may perceive. And although this nourishment is but a corporeal thing, yet notwithstanding he calleth it, a sowing in the spirit. Contrariwise, when men greedily scrape together what they can, and seek only their own gain, he calleth it a sowing in the flesh. He pronounceth those which sow in the spirit, to be blessed both in this life and the life to come; and the other which sow in the flesh, to be accursed both in this life and in the life to come.

VERSE 9. *And let us not be weary in doing good, for in due time we shall reap without weariness.*

The apostle, intending to close up his epistle, passeth from the particular to the general, and exhorteth generally to all good works. As if he should say: Let us be liberal and bountiful, not only towards the ministers of the word, but also towards all other men, and that without weariness; for it is an easy matter for a man to do good once or twice, but to continue, and not to be discouraged through the ingratitude and perverseness of those to whom he hath done good, that is very hard. Therefore he doth not only exhort us to do good, but also not to be weary in doing good; and to persuade us the more easily thereunto, he addeth, "For in due time we shall reap without weariness." As if he said: Wait and look for the perpetual harvest that is to come, and then shall no ingratitude or perverse dealing of men be able to pluck you away from well-doing; for in the harvest-time ye shall receive most plentiful increase and fruit of your seed. Thus, with most sweet words, he exhorteth the faithful to the doing of good works.

> VERSE 10. *Therefore, while we have time, let us do good unto all men, but especially to those that be of the household of faith.*

This is the knitting-up of his exhortation for the liberal maintaining and nourishing of the ministers of the word, and giving of alms to all such as have need. As if he had said, Let us do good while it is day; for when night cometh, we can no longer work, (John ix, .4) Indeed, men work many things when the light of truth is taken away, but all in vain; for they walk in darkness, and wot not whither they go, and therefore all their life, works, sufferings, and death are in vain, (John xii, 35.) And by these words he toucheth the Galatians. As if he should say, Except ye continue in the sound doctrine which ye have received of me, your working of much good, your suffering of many troubles, and such other things, profit you nothing; as he said before, in the third chapter, "Have ye suffered so many things in vain?" And by a new kind of speech he termeth those the household of faith, which are joined with us in the fellowship of faith, among whom the ministers of the word are the chiefest, and then all the rest of the faithful.

> VERSE 11. *Behold what a letter I have written unto you with mine own hand.*

He closeth up his epistle with an exhortation to the faithful, and with a sharp rebuke or invective against the false apostles—"Behold," saith he, "what a letter I have written unto you with mine own hand?" This he saith to move them, and to shew his motherly affection towards them. As if he should say: I never wrote so long an epistle with mine own hand to any other church, as I have done unto you. For as for his other epistles, as he spake, others wrote them, and afterwards he subscribed his salutation and name with his own hand, as it is to be seen in the end of his epistles. And in these words (as I suppose) he hath respect to the length of the epistle. Others take it otherwise.

VERSE 12. *As many as desire to please in the flesh, compel you to be circumcised, only because they would not suffer the persecution of the cross of Christ.*

Before he cursed the false apostles. Now, as it were, repeating the same thing again, but with other words, he accuseth them very sharply, to the end he may fear and turn away the Galatians from their doctrine, notwithstanding the great authority which they seemed to have. The teachers which ye have (saith he) are such as, first, regard not the glory of Christ, and the salvation of your souls, but only seek their own glory; secondly, they fly the cross; thirdly, they understand not those things which they teach.

These false teachers, being accused of the apostle for three such execrable enormities, were worthy to be avoided of all men. But yet all the Galatians obeyed not this warning of Paul; and Paul doth the false apostles no wrong, when he so vehemently inveigheth against them; but he justly condemneth them by his apostolic authority. In like manner, when we call the Pope Antichrist, his bishops and his shavelings, a cursed generation, we slander them not; but by God's authority we judge them to be accursed, according to that which is said in the first chapter—"If we, or an angel from heaven, preach otherwise than we have preached unto you, accursed be he:" for they hate, persecute, and overthrow the doctrine of Christ.

Your teachers (saith he) are vain heads, and, not regarding the glory of Christ and your salvation, they seek only their own glory. Again, because they are afraid of the cross, they preach circumcision, and the righteousness of the flesh, lest they should provoke the Jews to hate and persecute them. Wherefore, although ye hear them never so gladly, and never so long, yet shall ye hear but such as make their belly their God, seek their own glory, and shun the cross. And here is to be noted a certain vehemency in the world *compel*. For circumcision is nothing of itself; but to be compelled to circumcision, and when a man hath received it, to put righteousness and holiness therein: and if it be not received, to make it a sin; that is an injury unto Christ. Of this matter I have spoken largely enough heretofore.

VERSE 13. *For they themselves that are circumcised, do not keep the law; but they would have you circumcised, that they might glory in your flesh.*

Is not Paul here worthy to be called an heretic? For he saith, that not only the false apostles, but all the nation of the Jews which were circumcised, keep not the law, but rather that they which were circumcised, in fulfilling the law, fulfil it not. This is against Moses, who saith, that to be circumcised is to keep the law; and not to be circumcised is to make the covenant void, (Gen. xvii, 10, 14). And the Jews were circumcised for none other cause but to keep the law, which commandeth that every male child should be circumcised the eighth day, (Gen. xvii, 12.) Hereof we have before entreated at large, and therefore we need not now to repeat the same again. Now, these things serve to the condemning of the false apostles, that the Galatians may be feared from hearing of them. As if he should say, Behold I set before your eyes what manner of teachers you have. First, they are vain-glorious men, which seek nothing but their own profit, (Phil. ii, 21,) and care for nothing but their own belly; secondly, they fly the cross; and finally, they teach no truth or certainty, but all their sayings and doings are counterfeit and full of hypocrisy. Wherefore, although they keep the law outwardly, yet, in keeping it, they keep it not; for without the Holy Ghost the law cannot be kept. But the Holy Ghost cannot be received without Christ; and where the Holy Ghost dwelleth not, there dwelleth an unclean spirit, that is to say, despising God, and seeking his own gain and glory. Therefore, all that he doth, as touching the law, is mere hypocrisy and double sin; for an unclean heart doth not fulfil the law, but only maketh an outward shew thereof, and so is it more confirmed in his wickedness and hypocrisy.

And this sentence is diligently to be marked, that they which are circumcised keep not the law; that is to say, that they which are circumcised, are not circumcised. It may also be applied unto other works. He that worketh, prayeth, or suffereth without Christ, worketh, prayeth, and suffereth in vain; for all that is not of faith is sin, (Rom. xiv, 23.) It profiteth a man, therefore, nothing at all to be outwardly circumcised, to fast, to pray, or to do any other work, if he be within a despiser of grace, of forgiveness of sins, of faith, of Christ, etc., and be puffed up with the opinion and presumption of his own righteousness, which are horrible sins against the first table: and afterward there follow also other sins against the second table, as disobedience, whoredom, furiousness, wrath, hatred, and such other. Therefore he saith very well, that they which be circumcised, keep not the law, but only pretend that they keep it. But this counterfeiting, or rather hypocrisy, is double wickedness afore God.

What mean the false apostles, when they would have you to be circumcised? Not that ye might become righteous, although they so bear you in hand, but that they may glory in your flesh. Now, who would not detest this most pestilent vice of ambition and desire of glory, which is sought with so great peril of men's souls? There are (saith he) deceitful, shameless, and vain spirits, which serve their own belly and hate the cross. Again, (which is worst of all,) they compel you to be circumcised according to the law, that they may thereby abuse your flesh to their own glory, and in the mean season they bring your souls into danger of everlasting destruction. For what gain ye else before God, but damnation? And what else before men, but that the false apostles may glory that they are your teachers, and ye their disciples? And yet they teach you that which they themselves do not. Thus doth he sharply reprove the false apostles.

These words, "That they may glory in your flesh," are very effectual. As if he should say: They have not the word of the spirit; therefore it is impossible for you to receive the spirit by their preaching. They do but only exercise your flesh, making you fleshly justiciaries, or justifiers of yourselves. Outwardly they observe days, times, sacrifices, and such other things, according to the law, which are altogether carnal, whereby ye reap nothing else but unprofitable labour and damnation. And on the other side, this they gain thereby, that they boast that they are your teachers, and have called you back from the doctrine of Paul the heretic, unto their mother the synagogue. So at this day the Papists brag, that they call back those to the bosom of their mother the holy church, whom they deceive and seduce. Contrariwise, we glory not in your flesh, but glory as touching your spirit, because ye have received the spirit by our preaching, (Gal. iii, 2.)

VERSE 14. *But God forbid that I should glory, but in the cross of our Lord Jesus Christ.*

The apostle closeth up the matter with an indignation, and with great vehemency of spirit he casteth out these words, "But God forbid," etc. As if he should say: This carnal glory and ambition of the false apostles is so dangerous a poison, that I wish it was buried in hell, for it is the cause of the destruction of many. But let them glory in the flesh that list, and let them perish with their cursed glory; as for me, I desire no other glory, but that whereby I glory and rejoice in the cross of Christ. After the same manner speaketh he also, "We glory in our afflictions," (Rom. v.) Also in 2 Cor. xii, "I will glory in mine afflictions." Here Paul sheweth what is the glory and rejoicing of the Christians, namely, to glory and to be proud in tribulations, reproaches, infirmities, etc.

The world judgeth of the Christians, not only that they are wretched and miserable men, but also most cruelly, and yet, as it thinketh, with a true zeal hateth, persecuteth, condemneth, and killeth them, as most pernicious plagues of the spiritual and worldly kingdom, that is to say, like heretics and rebels. But because they do not suffer these things for murder, theft, and such other wickedness, but for the love of Christ, whose benefit and glory they set forth, therefore they glory in tribulation and in the cross of Christ, and are glad with the apostles that they are counted worthy to suffer rebuke, for the name of Christ, (Acts v, 41.) So must we glory at this day, when the Pope and the whole world most cruelly persecute us, condemn us, and kill us; because we suffer these things, not for our evil deeds, as thieves, murderers, etc., but for Christ's sake, our Lord and Saviour, whose gospel we truly preach.

Now, our glory is increased and confirmed principally by these two things: First, because we are certain that our doctrine is sound and perfect; secondly, because our cross and suffering is the suffering of Christ. Therefore, when the world persecuteth and killeth us, we have no cause to complain or lament, but we ought rather to rejoice and be glad. Indeed, the world judgeth us to be unhappy and accursed: But on the other side, Christ, who is greater than the world, and for whom we suffer, pronounceth us to be blessed, and willeth us to rejoice. "Blessed are ye, (saith he) when men revile you, and persecute you, and falsely say all manner of evil against you for my sake. Rejoice, and be glad," (Matt. v, 11, 12.) Our glory, then, is another manner of glory than the glory of the world is, which rejoiceth not in tribulation, reproach, persecution, and death, etc., but glorieth altogether in power, in riches, peace, honour, wisdom, and his own righteousness. But mourning and confusion is the end of this glory.

Moreover, the cross of Christ doth not signify that piece of wood which Christ did bear upon his shoulders, and to the which he was afterwards nailed; but generally it signifieth all the afflictions of the faithful, whose sufferings are Christ's sufferings, (2 Cor. i), "The sufferings of Christ abound in us." Again, "Now rejoice I in my sufferings for you, and fulfil the rest of the afflictions of Christ in my flesh, for his body's sake, which is the church," etc. (Col. i, 24.) The cross of Christ, therefore, generally signifieth all the afflictions of the church which it suffereth for Christ; which he himself witnesseth when he saith, "Saul, Saul, why persecutest thou me?" (Acts ix, 4.) Saul did no violence to Christ, but to his church. But he that toucheth it, toucheth the apple of his eye, (Zech. ii, 8.) There is a more lively feeling in the head, than in the other members of the body. And this we know by experience; for the little toe or the least part of a man's body being hurt, the head forthwith sheweth itself, by the countenance, to feel the grief thereof. So Christ our head maketh all our afflictions his own, and suffereth also when we suffer, which are his body.

It is profitable for us to know these things, lest we should be swallowed up with sorrow, or fall to despair, when we see that our adversaries do cruelly persecute, excommunicate, and kill us. But let us think with ourselves, after the example of Paul, that we must glory in the cross which we bear, not for our own sins, but for Christ's sake. If we consider only in ourselves the sufferings which we endure, they are not only grievous but intolerable; but when we may say, "Thy sufferings, O Christ, abound in us;" (2 Cor. i, 5,) or, as it is said in the 44th Psalm, "For thy sake we are killed all the day," then these sufferings are not only easy, but also sweet, according to that saying, "My burden is easy, and my yoke is sweet," (Matt. xi, 30.)

Now, it is well known that we, at this day, do suffer the hatred and persecution of our adversaries for none other cause, but for that we preach Christ faithfully and purely. If we would deny him, and approve their pernicious errors and wicked religion, they would not only cease to hate and persecute us, but would also offer us honour, riches, and many goodly things. Because, therefore, we suffer these things for Christ's sake, we may truly rejoice and glory with Paul in the cross of our Lord Jesus Christ, that is to say, not in riches, in power, in the favour of men, etc., but in afflictions, weakness, sorrow, fightings in the body, terrors in the spirit, persecutions, and all other evils, (2 Cor. vii, 5.) Wherefore, we trust it will shortly come to pass, that Christ will say the same to us that David said to Abiathar the priest, "I am the cause of all your deaths," (1 Sam. xxii, 22.) Again, "He that toucheth you, toucheth the apple of mine eye," (Zech. ii, 8.) As if he had said, He that hurteth you, hurteth me; for if ye did not preach my word and confess me, ye should not suffer these things. So saith he also, in John, "If ye were of the world, the world would love his own: But because I have chosen you out of the word, therefore the world hateth you," (John xv, 19.) But these things are treated of afore.

VERSE 14. *By whom the world is crucified to me, and I unto the world.*

This is Paul's manner of speaking: "the world is crucified to me," that is, I judge the world to be damned. "And I am crucified to the world," that is, the world again judgeth me to be damned. Thus we crucify and condemn one another. I abhor all the doctrine, righteousness, and works of the world, as the poison of the devil. The world again detesteth my doctrine and deeds, and judgeth me to be a seditious, a pernicious, a pestilent fellow, and a heretic. So at this day the world is crucified to us, and we unto the world. We curse and condemn all man's traditions concerning mass, orders, vows, will-worshippings, works, and all the abominations of the Pope and other heretics, as the dirt of the devil. They again do persecute and kill us as destroyers of religion, and troublers of the public peace.

The monks dreamed that the world was crucified to them, when they entered into their monasteries; but by this means Christ is crucified, and not the world; yea, the world is delivered from crucifying, and is the more quickened by that opinion of holiness and trust, which they had in their own righteousness that entered into religion. Most foolishly and wickedly, therefore, was this sentence of the apostle wrested to the entering into monasteries. He speaketh here of a high matter and of great importance; that is to say, that every faithful man judgeth that to be the wisdom, righteousness, and power of God, which the world condemneth as the greatest folly, wickedness, and weakness. And contrariwise, that which the world judgeth to be the highest religion and service of God, the faithful do know to be nothing else but execrable and horrible blasphemy against God. So the godly condemn the world, and again, the world condemneth the godly. But the godly have the right judgment on their side; for the spiritual man judgeth all things, (1 Cor. ii, 15.)

Wherefore the judgment of the world, touching religion and righteousness before God, is as contrary to the judgment of the godly, as God and the devil are contrary the one to the other. For as God is crucified to the devil, and the devil to God, that is to say, as God condemneth the doctrine and works of the devil, (for the Son of God aappeared, as John saith, to destroy the works of the devil, 1 John iii, 8,) and contrariwise the devil condemneth and overthroweth the word and the works of God, for he is a murderer, and the father of lies; so the world condemneth the doctrine and life of the godly, calling them most pernicious heretics and troublers of the public peace. And again, the faithful call the world the son of the devil, which rightly followeth his father's steps, that is to say, which is as great a murderer and liar as his father is. This is Paul's meaning, when he saith, "Whereby the world is crucified to me, and I unto the world." Now the world doth not only signify in the scriptures ungodly and wicked men, but the very best, the wisest, and holiest men that are of the world.

And here, by the way, he covertly toucheth the false apostles. As if he should say: I utterly hate and detest all glory which is without the cross of Christ, as a cursed thing; for the world, with all the glory thereof, is crucified to me, and I to the world. Wherefore, accursed be all they which glory in their flesh, and not in the cross of Christ. Paul therefore witnesseth by these words, that he hateth the world with a perfect hatred of the Holy Ghost; and again, the world hateth him with a perfect hatred of a wicked spirit. As if he should say, It is impossible that there should be any agreement between me and the world. What shall I then do? Shall I give place, and teach those things which please the world? No; but with a stout courage I will set myself against it, and will as well despise and crucify it, as it despiseth and crucifieth me.

To conclude, Paul here teacheth how we should fight against Satan, (which not only tormenteth our bodies with sundry afflictions, but also woundeth our hearts continually with his fiery darts, that, by this continuance, when he can no otherwise prevail, he may overthrow our faith, and bring us from the truth and from Christ,) namely, that like as we see Paul himself to have stoutly despised the world, so we also should despise the devil, the prince thereof, with all his forces, deceits, and hellish furies, and so trusting to the aid and help of Christ, should triumph against him after this manner: O Satan, the more thou hurtest and goest about to hurt me, the more proud and stout I am against thee, and laugh thee to scorn. The more thou terrifiest me, and seekest to bring me to desperation, so much the more confidence and boldness I take, and glory in the midst of thy furies and malice: not by mine own power, but by the power of my Lord and Saviour Christ, whose strength is made perfect in my weakness. Therefore, when I am weak, then am I strong, (2 Cor. xii, 9, 10.) On the contrary, when he seeth his threatenings and terrors to be feared, he rejoiceth, and then he terrifieth more and more such as are terrified already.

EPISTLE TO THE GALATIANS

VERSE 15. *For in Christ Jesus, neither circumcision availeth any thing, nor uncircumcision, but a new creature.*

This is a wonderful kind of speech which Paul here useth, when he saith, "Neither circumcision nor uncircumcision prevaileth any thing." It may seem that he should rather have said: "Either circumcision or uncircumcision availeth somewhat, seeing these are two contrary things. But now he denieth that either the one or the other do any thing avail. As if he should have said: Ye must mount up higher; for circumcision and uncircumcision are things of no such importance, that they are able to obtain righteousness before God. True it is, that they are contrary the one to the other; but this is nothing as touching Christian righteousness, which is not earthly, but heavenly; and therefore it consisteth not in corporeal things. Therefore, whether thou be circumcised or uncircumcised, it is all one thing, for in Christ Jesus neither the one nor the other availeth any thing at all.

The Jews were greatly offended when they heard that circumcision availed nothing. They easily granted that uncircumcision availed nothing; but they could not abide to hear that so much should be said of circumcision, for they fought even unto blood for the defence of the law and circumcision. The Papists also at this day do vehemently contend for the maintenance of their traditions, as touching the eating of flesh, single life, holy days, and such other; and they excommunicate and curse us, which teach that in Christ Jesus these things do nothing avail. But Paul saith that we must have another thing, which is much more excellent and precious, whereby we may attain righteousness before God. In Christ Jesus, saith he, neither circumcision nor uncircumcision, neither single life nor marriage, neither meat nor fasting, do any whit avail. Meat maketh us not acceptable before God. We are neither the better by abstaining, nor the worse by eating. All these things, yea, the whole world, with all the laws and righteousness thereof, avail nothing to justification.

Reason and the wisdom of the flesh doth not understand this, "for it perceiveth not those things that are of the spirit of God," (1 Cor. ii, 14.) Therefore it will needs have righteousness to stand in outward things. But we are taught out of the word of God, that there is nothing under the sun which availeth unto righteousness before God, but Christ only, or as Paul saith here, a new creature. Politic laws, men's traditions, ceremonies of the church, yea, and the law of Moses, are such things as are without Christ; therefore they avail not unto righteousness before God. We may use them as things both good and necessary, but in their place and time; but if we talk of the matter of justification, they avail nothing, but hurt very much.

And by these two things, circumcision and uncircumcision, Paul rejecteth all other things whatsoever, and denieth that they avail any thing in Christ Jesus, that is, in the cause of faith and salvation. For he taketh here a part for the whole, that is, by uncircumcision he understandeth all the Gentiles, by circumcision all the Jews, with all their force and all their glory. As if he said, Whatsoever the Gentiles can do, with all their wisdom, righteousness, laws, power, kingdoms, empires, it availeth nothing in Christ Jesus. Also, whatsoever the Jews are able to do, with their Moses, their law, their circumcision, their worshippings, their temple, their kingdom and priesthood, it nothing availeth. Wherefore in Christ Jesus, or in the matter of justification, we must not dispute of the laws either of the Gentiles or of the Jews, but we must simply pronounce that neither circumcision nor uncircumcision availeth any thing.

Are the laws, then, of no effect? Not so: They be good and profitable, albeit in their place and time, that is, in corporeal and civil things, which without laws cannot be guided. Moreover, we use also in the churches certain ceremonies and laws; not that the keeping of them availeth unto righteousness, but for good order, example, quietness, and concord, according to that saying, "Let all things be done comely and orderly," (1 Cor. xiv, 40.) But if laws be so set forth and urged, as though the keeping of them did justify a man, or the breaking thereof did condemn him, they ought to be taken away and to be abolished; for then Christ loseth his office and his glory, who only justifieth us, and giveth unto us the Holy Ghost. The apostle therefore by these words plainly affirmeth, that neither circumcision nor uncircumcision availeth any thing, but the new creature, etc. Now, since that neither the laws of the Gentiles, nor of the Jews avail any thing, the Pope hath done most wickedly, in that he hath constrained men to keep his laws with the opinion of righteousness.

Now, a new creature, whereby the image of God is renewed, is not made by any colour or counterfeiting of good works, (for in Christ Jesus neither circumcision availeth any thing, nor uncircumcision,) but by Christ, by whom it is created after the image of God in righteousness and true holiness. When works are done, they bring indeed a new shew and outward appearance, wherewith the world and the flesh are delighted, but not a new creature; for the heart remaineth wicked, as it was before, full of the contempt of God and infidelity. Therefore, a new creature is the work of the Holy Ghost, which cleanseth our heart by faith, (Acts xv, 9,) and worketh the fear of God, love, chastity, and other Christian virtues, and giveth power to bridle the flesh, and to reject the righteousness and wisdom of the world. Here is no colouring or new outward shew, but a thing done indeed. Here is created another sense and another judgment, that is to say, altogether spiritual, which abhorreth those things that before it greatly esteemed. The monkish life and order did so bewitch us in time past, that we thought there was no other way to salvation; but now we judge of it far otherwise. We are now ashamed of those things which we adored as most heavenly and holy, before we were regenerated into this new creature.

Wherefore the changing of garments, and other outward things is not a new creature, (as the monks dream,) but it is the renewing of the mind by the Holy Ghost; after the which followeth a change of the members and senses of the whole body. For when the heart hath conceived a new light, a new judgment, and new motions, through the gospel, it cometh to pass that the inward senses are also renewed; for the ears desire to hear the word of God, and not the traditions and dreams of men. The mouth and tongue do not vaunt of their own works, righteousness, and rules; but they set forth the mercy of God only offered to us in Christ. These changes consist not in words, but are effectual, and bring a new spirit, a new will, new senses, and new operations of the flesh, so that the eyes, ears, mouth, and tongue, do not only see, hear, and speak otherwise than they did before, but the mind also approveth, loveth and followeth another thing than it did before. For before, being blinded with popish errors and darkness, it imagined God to be a merchant, who would sell unto us his grace for our works and merits; but now, in the light of the gospel, it assureth us that we are counted righteous by faith only in Christ. Therefore it now rejecteth all will-works, and acommplisheth the works of charity and of our vocation commanded by God. It praiseth and magnifieth God; it rejoiceth and glorieth in the only trust and confidence of God's mercy through Jesus Christ. If it must suffer any trouble or affliction, it endureth the same cheerfully and gladly, although the flesh repine and grudge thereat. This Paul calleth a new creature.

VERSE 16. *And to as many walk according to this rule, peace be upon them and mercy.*

This he addeth as a conclusion. This is the only and true rule wherein we ought to walk, namely, the new creature, which is neither circumcision nor uncircumcision, but the new man created unto the image of God in righteousness and true holiness, (Eph. iv, 24,) which inwardly is righteous in the spirit, and outwardly is holy and clean in the flesh. The monks have a righteousness and holiness, but it is hypocritical and wicked, because they hope not to be justified by only faith in Christ, but by the keeping of the rule. Moreover, although outwardly they counterfeit a holiness, and refrain their eyes, hands, tongue, and other members from evil, yet they have an unclean heart, full of filthy lust, envy, wrath, lechery, idolatry, contempt and hatred of God, blasphemy against Christ, etc., for they are most spiteful and cruel enemies of the truth. Wherefore the rule and religion of the monks is most wicked, and accursed of God.

But this rule, whereof Paul speaketh in this place, is blessed; by the which we live in the faith of Christ, and are made new creatures, that is to say, righteous and holy indeed by the Holy Ghost, without any colouring or counterfeiting. To them which walk after this rule belongeth peace, that is, the favour of God, forgiveness of sins, quietness of conscience, and mercy; that is to say, help in afflictions, and pardon of the remnants of sin which remain in our flesh. Yea, although they which walk after this rule, be overtaken with any sin, yet, for that they are the children of grace and peace, mercy upholdeth them, so that their sin and fall shall not be laid to their charge.

VERSE 16. *And upon the Israel of God.*

Here he toucheth the false apostles and Jews, which gloried of their fathers, bragged that they were the people of God, that they had the law, etc. As if he said: They are the Israel of God, which, with faithful Abraham, believe the promises of God offered already in Christ, whether they be Jews or Gentiles, and not they which are begotten of Abraham, Isaac, and Jacob, after the flesh. This matter is largely handled before, in the third chapter.

VERSE 17. *For henceforth let no man put me to business.*

He concludeth his epistle with a certain indignation. As if he said: I have faithfully taught the gospel as I have received it by the revelation of Jesus Christ; whoso will not follow it, let him follow what he will, so that hereafter he trouble me no more. At a word, this is my censure, that Christ, which I have preached, is the only high-priest and saviour of the world. Therefore, either let the world walk according to this rule, of which I have spoken here and throughout all this epistle, or else let it perish for ever.

VERSE 17. *For I bear in my body the marks of the Lord Jesus.*

This is the true meaning of this place: the marks that be in my body do shew well enough whose servant I am. If I sought to please men, requiring circumcision and the keeping of the law as necessary to salvation, and rejoicing in your flesh as the false apostles do, I needed not to bear these marks in my body. But because I am the servant of Jesus Christ, and walk after a true rule, that is, I openly teach and confess that no man can obtain the favour of God, righteousness, and salvation, but by Christ alone, therefore it behoveth me to bear the badges of Christ my Lord; which be not marks of mine own procuring, but are laid upon me against my will, by the world and the devil, for none other cause but for that I preach Jesus to be Christ.

The stripes and suffering, therefore, which he did bear in his body, he calleth marks; as also the anguish and terror of spirit he calleth the fiery darts of the devil. Of these sufferings he maketh mention everywhere in his epistles, as Luke also doth in the Acts. "I think," saith he, "that God hath set forth us, the last apostles, as men appointed to death: for we are made a gazing-stock unto the world, and to the angels and to men," (1 Cor. iv, 9.) Again, "Unto this hour we both hunger and thirst, and are naked, and are buffeted, and have no certain dwelling-place, and labour working with our own hands: we are reviled, we are persecuted, we are evil-spoken of, we are made as the filth of the world, the off-scouring of all things," (1 Cor. iv, 11-13.) Also in another place, "In much patience, in afflictions, in necessities, in distresses, in stripes, in imprisonments, in tumults, in labours, by watchings, by fastings," etc. (2 Cor. vi, 4-6.) And again, "In labours more abundant, in stripes above measure, in prison more plenteously, in death oft. Of the Jews five times received I forty stripes save one. I was thrice beaten with rods, I was once stoned, I suffered thrice shipwreck, night and day have I been in the deep sea. In journeyings I was often, in perils of waters, in perils of robbers, in perils of mine own countrymen, in perils among the Gentiles, in perils in the city, in perils in the wilderness, in perils in the sea, in perils among false brethren," etc. (2 Cor. xi, 23-26.)

These be the true marks and imprinted signs, of which the apostle speaketh in this place; the which we also at this day, by the grace of God, bear in our bodies for Christ's cause. For the world persecuteth and killeth us, false brethren deadly hate us, Satan inwardly in our heart with his fiery darts terrifieth us, and for none other cause but for that we teach Christ to be our righteousness and life. These marks we choose not of any devotion, neither do we gladly suffer them; but because the world and the devil do lay them upon us for Christ's cause, we are compelled to suffer them, and we rejoice in spirit with Paul (which is always willing, glorieth, and rejoiceth,) that we bear them in our body; for they are a seal and most sure testimony of true doctrine and fatih. These things Paul spake, (as I shewed afore,) with a certain displeasure and indignation.

VERSE 18. *Brethren, the grace of our Lord Jesus Christ be with your spirit. Amen.*

This is his last farewell. He endeth the epistle with the same words wherewith he began. As if he said: I have taught you Christ purely, I have entreated you, I have chidden you, and I have let pass nothing which I thought profitable for you. I can say no more, but that I heartily pray that our Lord Jesus Christ would bless and increase my labour, and govern you with his Holy Spirit for ever.

Thus have ye the exposition of Paul's Epistle to the Galatians. The Lord Jesus Christ, our Justifier and Saviour, who gave unto me the grace and power to expound this epistle, and to you likewise to hear it, preserve and establish both you and me, (which I most heartily desire,) that we, daily growing more and more in the knowledge of his grace and faith unfeigned, may be found unblameable and without fault in the day of our redemption. To whom, with the Father and the Holy Ghost, be glory world without end. Amen.

Now unto the King eternal, immortal, invisible, the only wise God, be honour and glory, for ever and ever. Amen. (1 Timothy 1, 17.)